CONSTITUTIONAL LAW OF SCOTLAND

CONSTITUTIONAL LAW OF SCOTLAND

by

Alan Page
Professor of Public Law, University of Dundee

Published under the auspices of

SCOTTISH UNIVERSITIES LAW INSTITUTE LTD

EDINBURGH
W. GREEN
2015

W. GREEN

 THOMSON REUTERS

Published in 2015 by W. Green, 21 Alva Street,
Edinburgh EH2 4PS
Part of Thomson Reuters (Professional) UK Limited
(Registered in England & Wales, Company No.1679046. Registered Office
and address for service: 2nd Floor, 1 Mark Square, Leonard Street, London,
EC2A 4EG)

Typeset by LBJ Typesetting Ltd
Printed and bound in the Great Britain by CPI group (UK) Ltd,
Croydon, CR0 4YY

No natural forests were destroyed to make this product; only
farmed timber was used and replanted.

A CIP catalogue record for this title is available from the British Library

ISBN 978-0-414-01456-5

Thomson Reuters and the Thomson Reuters Logo
are trademarks of Thomson Reuters.

PREFACE

"There are both universal and local aspects of constitutional law. The rules may be local, but the problems are universal."[1]

"There is no right time at which to produce a book on constitutional law", Mitchell observed in the preface to *Constitutional Law,* the first edition of which was published under the auspices of the Scottish Universities Law Institute just over 50 years ago. That is certainly true of this book, much of which was written against the background of increasing constitutional uncertainty, which shows no immediate signs of diminishing despite the outcome of the independence referendum on September 18, 2014. Had Scotland voted "yes", it would have become, in time, a book about the constitutional law of an independent Scotland. Scotland having voted "no", it remains, as originally conceived, a book about the constitutional law of one of the constituent nations of the UK.

Three considerations shaped its writing from the outset. First, that it should be written from a Scottish perspective rather than the Anglo-centric perspective that inevitably dominates much UK constitutional law writing. It is about constitutional law as seen from Edinburgh rather than from London (or Cardiff or Belfast). Secondly, that it should give due weight to government as the "doing" element in the constitution; despite its importance, constitutional lawyers have been more concerned with the part played by Parliament and the courts in the constitution than the executive branch of government, an argument developed at greater length in the first chapter of Daintith and Page, *The Executive in the Constitution*.[2] The problem is an especially acute one in Scotland where we have an incomplete and outdated literature. And third, that it should reflect the "multi-level" or "multi-layered" character of the contemporary governance of Scotland.[3] It should not just be about the devolved government of Scotland, but about the whole of the governance of Scotland, including its UK and wider European dimensions.

In *A Preface to Scots Law,* Andrew Dewar Gibb wrote that it would be impossible to write a book or short essay on the constitution from a Scottish point of view "for today there is no Scottish Constitution. Whatever was written would of necessity be pure history . . . To write at length on this subject in a book of Scots Law would be something of an absurdity".[4] Devolution has changed all that. The "constitution" with which we are mainly concerned in the pages that follow is the Scottish constitution set out in the Scotland Act 1998. We are not, on the other hand, concerned with the UK constitution, save insofar as it provides the overarching framework and defines or otherwise sets the limits to Scotland's constitutional arrangements. To treat of UK as well as Scottish constitutional law would have made the book unbearably long as well as detracted from its primary focus, which is Scotland.

---

[1] JDB Mitchell, *Constitutional Law* (Edinburgh: W.Green, 1964) p.ix.
[2] Terence Daintith and Alan Page, *The Executive in the Constitution* (Oxford: OUP, 1999).
[3] Ian Bache and Matthew Flinders (eds), *Multi-level Governance* (Oxford: OUP, 2004).
[4] Andrew Dewar Gibb, *A Preface to Scots Law* (Edinburgh: W. Green, 1964) p.2.

The plan of the book is as follows:

Chapter 1 explores the foundations of Scotland's current constitutional arrangements. The story is a complicated one and requires some care in the telling. It is brought as up to date as it can be in Ch.2, which takes as its starting point the devolution settlement set out in the Scotland Act 1998. As well as the Scotland Act 1998, which established the Scottish Parliament and Scottish Government and defined the limits to their powers, the constitutional framework within which the devolved government of Scotland is carried on includes the Human Rights Act 1998, which reaches the parts of the governance of Scotland the Scotland Act does not reach. We recount the main features of the Human Rights Act in Ch.3.

From the constitutional framework, the focus shifts to the devolved government of Scotland. Chapters 4–6 examine the institutions of devolved government: the Scottish Parliament, the Scottish Government, and the Scottish courts. Chapter 7 explores the Scottish Parliament's legislative competence—Holyrood, unlike Westminster, is a parliament of limited or bounded competence—while Ch.8 examines the related question of the Scottish Government's executive competence. Chapter 9 then explains the arrangements that have been put in place for dealing with questions of vires arising out of the devolution settlement. The next three chapters complete the picture of the devolved government of Scotland: Ch.10 examines local government; Ch.11 public bodies; and Ch.12 the police. Attention is then turned to the resources of devolved government and the key questions of legislation and finance (Chs 13 and 14). The remaining chapters of this part of the book (Chs 15–18) concentrate on the various checks on devolved government—parliamentary and judicial as well as those provided by the Scottish Public Services Ombudsman and the Freedom of Information (Scotland) Act 2002.

The final two chapters of the book pick up the UK and European dimensions of the contemporary governance of Scotland. The focus in those chapters, in keeping with that of the book as a whole, is on those aspects of the government of the UK and the European Union that are of particular interest to Scotland.

A natural starting point in working out the scheme of the book was what had gone before. The first Scottish work of any length on constitutional law was Dykes and Philip's *Chapters in Constitutional Law*,[5] a reprint of four articles—on constitutional law, the cabinet, parliament and national finance—from *The Encyclopaedia of the Laws of Scotland*. What is most striking about these articles nearly a century later is how little they in fact say about Scotland. The premise on which they were based was that Scottish constitutional law was indistinguishable from that of the rest of the UK. It was only in relation to the dominions and colonies that the possibility of difference was canvassed.

Fraser's *An Outline of Constitutional Law*[6] broke new ground. Its aim was to provide an account of the subject "from the point of view of the Scottish lawyer". There were several English textbooks "but on some branches of the subject they are of little assistance to the student of Scots law; for example, the history and the present organisation of the law courts in the two countries differ widely, and there are important differences between Scots and English procedures in actions against the Crown".[7] Short and clearly written, it more than achieved its purpose.

---

[5] D Oswald Dykes and James Randall Philip, *Chapters in Constitutional Law* (Edinburgh: W.Green, 1930).

[6] Walter Ian Reid Fraser, *An Outline of Constitutional Law* (London: William Hodge & Company, 1938).

[7] Walter Ian Reid Fraser, *An Outline of Constitutional Law* (1938) preface.

Against the background of Fraser's book, Mitchell's *Constitutional Law*[8] must have come as something of a shock. SA de Smith described it as "a searching and challenging book which makes heavy demands on its readers", and its author as having "perhaps made too few concessions to the uninstructed reader".[9] Mitchell's standpoint was not that of the Scottish lawyer but of a critic of the UK constitution and of the (limited) role played by law and legal processes in the control of government:

> "Scots public law, because it absorbed the essentials of English public law, has ended up like the English system as one incapable of affording to the individual the ready and immediate redress against government which is required today."[10]

Despite the emphasis upon "Scottish institutions and rules",[11] it probably disappointed those, north as well as south of the border, who wanted to know more at a time when awareness of Scots law as a separate system of law was growing: "One would have welcomed a fuller discussion of the Scottish case law, particularly on judicial review of administrative action"[12]; "Professor Mitchell emphasises more than once that judicial control of administrative action is 'more generalised' in Scotland, but he leaves his reader hungering to know what this means in real life".[13]

Since devolution we have seen books that have attempted, with considerable success, the difficult feat of providing an account of both UK and Scottish constitutional law.[14] We have also seen the emergence, over a longer period, of separate treatments of Scottish local government law, planning law, human rights, etc. A secondary purpose of this book is to integrate those several literatures with the framework of a broader narrative of the development of Scotland's constitutional arrangements since the Union. The critical decision, however, was that this should be a book about the constitutional law of Scotland rather than of the UK or indeed of both. In treating of the one, however, we treat of the other and in so doing contribute to a fuller understanding of the UK's constitutional arrangements. One of the long standing weaknesses of UK constitutional law writing has been its neglect of the "territorial constitution".[15] It is that neglect in relation to Scotland that this book sets out to repair.

What from a different perspective has been called "subnational constitutional law" explores the discretion or space permitted the component units of federal and devolved states in the design of their constitutional arrangements, the means by which the boundaries to that space are policed, and the extent to which the component units have occupied the constitutional space permitted them.[16] A recurring theme in Scotland's case, emphasised by Mitchell, is of

---

[8] JDB Mitchell, *Constitutional Law* (Edinburgh: W.Green, 1964).
[9] Review at (1964) 27 M.L.R. 616.
[10] JDB Mitchell, "Government and Public Law in Scotland: Retrospect and Prospect"' in JA Andrews (ed), *Welsh Studies in Public Law* (Cardiff: University of Wales Press, 1970) p.80.
[11] JDB Mitchell, *Constitutional Law* (Edinburgh: W.Green, 1964) p.ix.
[12] SA de Smith, (1964) 27 M.L.R. 617.
[13] HWR Wade, (1964) 80 L.Q.R. 298.
[14] CMG Himsworth and CMO'Neill, *Scotland's Constitution: Law and Practice*, 2nd edn (Sussex: Bloomsbury Professional, 2009); Jane Munro, *Public Law*, 2nd edn (Edinburgh: W.Green, 2007).
[15] A concept more familiar to political scientists than to constitutional lawyers, but which takes as its starting point the considerable variation in governing arrangements across the different territories of the UK.
[16] Robert F Williams and G Alan Tarr, "Subnational Constitutional Space: A View from the States, Provinces, Regions, Lander and Cantons" in G Alan Tarr, Robert F Williams and Josef Marko (eds), *Federalism, Subnational Constitutions and Minority Rights* (Connecticut: Praeger, 2004) p.3.

Scots law as "separate but not necessarily distinctive". That is not to say that it should be distinctive, or more distinctive than it is, but the reminder that it is not necessarily distinctive is an important corrective to the instinctive Scottish belief in the automatic superiority of all things Scots. The problems of constitutional law are indeed universal, as Mitchell reminded us, and there is no reason to suppose that we in Scotland have devised or evolved a uniquely satisfactory way of resolving them.

I have accumulated a great many debts in the course of writing this book: to Joe Thomson, at that time academic director of the Scottish Universities Law Institute, who encouraged me to take it on and who bore with me as I began to think about what a post-devolution Scottish constitutional law text might look like—what is clear now was far from clear in the beginning; to Andrew Mylne who read every chapter in draft and made many invaluable suggestions; to Pamela Ferguson, Terence Daintith, Bob Ferguson and Janet McLean, who read and commented on individual chapters; to Paul Cackette, Andrea Howard, Richard Henderson, Sarah Hutchison, Margaret Keyse, Francesca McGrath and Sharon Nangle, who helped answer some of my questions or who drew my attention to material I might otherwise have missed; and to Fiona Clark who did an invaluable job in obtaining much of that material for me.

A near final draft of the book was completed in April 2014. Publication was then held back to allow account to be taken the result of the independence referendum and the Smith Commission process that followed. Implementation of the Smith Commission Agreement is not scheduled to take place until after the UK general election in May 2015. In the meantime, I have endeavoured to state the law as at January 31, 2015.

Cupar
January, 2015

CONTENTS

TABLE OF CASES

TABLE OF STATUTES

TABLE OF SCOTTISH STATUTES

TABLE OF STATUTORY INSTRUMENTS

TABLE OF SCOTTISH STATUTORY INSTRUMENTS

TABLE OF EUROPEAN LEGISLATION

CHAPTER 1

FOUNDATIONS

"We, gathered as the Scottish Constitutional Convention, do hereby acknowledge the sovereign right of the Scottish people to determine the form of Government best suited to their needs ... "

So began the Claim of Right adopted at the inaugural meeting of the Scottish **1–01** Constitutional Convention on March 30, 1989. The choice of title was no accident. It was in fact the third such Claim of Right, the first having been the Claim of Right 1689, which set out the terms on which the Scottish Convention of Estates offered the Crown to William and Mary after James VII (of Scotland) and II (of England) had fled to France in December 1688, and the second being the Claim of Right which the General Assembly of the Church of Scotland adopted in 1842 in protest at what it regarded as unwarranted judicial intervention in its affairs.[1] What is said to unite them is a distinctive Scottish constitutional tradition of popular sovereignty, which stands in marked contrast to the Westminster tradition of the unlimited sovereignty of parliament, which Lord Cooper famously described in *MacCormick v Lord Advocate*[2] as a "distinctively English principle which has no counterpart in Scottish constitutional law".[3]

We should be wary of accepting claims of a distinctive Scottish constitutional **1–02** tradition at face value. "All politics contains mythology, and none more so than the Scottish variety."[4] The idea that there is a Scottish tradition of popular sovereignty has been described as "one of Scotland's most enduring political myths".[5] There was a populist tradition of thought, represented most notably by George Buchanan in the late sixteenth century, which might be invoked in

---

[1] Lord Rodger of Earlsferry, *The Courts, The Church and the Constitution: Aspects of the Disruption of 1843* (Edinburgh: Edinburgh University Press, 2008).

[2] *MacCormick v Lord Advocate*, 1953 S.C. 396, 411.

[3] The most influential exponent of that view in recent times was Neil MacCormick for whom a "Scots law" interpretation of the UK constitution was one founded on a version of the doctrine of popular sovereignty: Neil MacCormick, *Questioning Sovereignty: Law, State and Nation in the European Commonwealth* (Oxford: OUP, 1999) p.55; "Is there a constitutional path to Scottish independence?' (2000) 53 Parliamentary Affairs 721, 729 ("The Scots view draws on a constitutional tradition that goes back before the Union, ultimately to the Declaration of Arbroath of 1320 ... "). TB Smith, too, was in the popular sovereignty camp: *A Short Commentary on the Law of Scotland* (Edinburgh: W.Green, 1962) p.57. ("The Scottish theory—if not always the practice—was that sovereignty resided in the community.")

[4] David McCrone, "Devolving Scotland" in Alan Balfour (ed), *Creating a Scottish Parliament* (Finlay Brown, 2005) p.7.

[5] Colin Kidd, "Sovereignty and the Scottish constitution before 1707" [2004] J.R. 225. "The notion, readily and somewhat uncritically accepted in the later 1980s by both the Scottish Constitutional Convention and the General Assembly, that Scotland enjoyed a political tradition which was markedly more 'democratic' than that of both England or post-1707 Britain is largely based on a myth": Michael Lynch and HT Dickinson, "Introduction" in HT Dickinson and Michael Lynch (eds), *The Challenge to Westminster: Sovereignty, Devolution and Independence* (East Linton: Tuckwell Press, 2000) p.3.

support of such a claim.[6] But there was also a powerful tradition of absolutist thought, which was in the ascendancy for much of the seventeenth century and to last well into the eighteenth century.[7] The revolution settlement (below) was to check some of its excesses, but there was no suggestion that sovereignty had at any point reverted to the Scottish people.[8] It seems altogether better, therefore, to view the claims to Scottish self-government that were made three centuries later in terms of simple democratic demand rather than abstract concepts and historical myths of popular sovereignty.[9]

1–03 If not with the myth of the ancient constitution where then should we begin? The Union of 1707 is the obvious place because of the influence it has exercised, and continues to exercise, on our constitutional arrangements. Before tackling the question of the Union, however, something should be said about the revolution settlement and the Claim of Right that preceded the Union.

THE REVOLUTION SETTLEMENT

1–04 The Claim of Right was adopted by the Convention of Estates on April 11, 1689.[10] Like the English Declaration of Rights on which it was based, it was intended to mark a decisive break with the past—to draw a line under claims to unlimited royal power. The Claim declared that James VII had invaded "the fundamental constitution of this Kingdom, and altered it from a legal limited monarchy to an arbitrary despotic power", as a result of which he had "forefaulted the right to the Crown, and the throne is become vacant";

> "the moment at which parliament declared James VII to have 'forfeited' the throne was the moment at which royal absolutism in Scotland ceased for good".[11]

It then set out the "undoubted rights and liberties" to which the Convention of Estates laid claim before offering the crown and royal dignity of Scotland to William and Mary on their undertaking to maintain and respect those rights and liberties.

1–05 The Claim of Right is commonly regarded as a more radical document than the English Declaration of Rights adopted two months earlier. Whereas the Claim of Right spoke of James having "forefaulted" the right to the

---

[6] On George Buchanan and the myth of the "ancient Scottish constitution", see Hugh Trevor-Roper, *The Invention of Scotland: Myth and History* (New Haven: Yale University Press, 2009). George Buchanan was the author of *De Jure Regni apud Scotos (The Right of the Kingdom of Scotland)* (1579) and *Rerum Scoticarum Historia (History of Scotland)* (1582).

[7] Brian Levack, "Law, sovereignty and the union" in Roger Mason (ed), *Scots and Britons: Scottish political thought and the union of 1603* (Cambridge: CUP, 1994) p.228; its most prominent spokesman was Sir George Mackenzie of Rosehaugh, author of *Jus Regium: Or, the Just and Solid Foundations of Monarchy in General; and more especially of the Monarchy of Scotland* (1684).

[8] John Robertson, "The Idea of Sovereignty and the Act of Union" in Dickinson and Lynch (eds), *The Challenge to Westminster: Sovereignty, Devolution and Independence* (East Linton: Tuckwell Press, 2000) p.34.

[9] Bernard Crick and David Millar, *To Make the Parliament of Scotland a Model for Democracy* (Glasgow: John Wheatley Centre, 1995) p.7.

[10] Claim of Rights Act 1689 (c.28) ix 38; for the fullest treatment, see Tim Harris, *Revolution: The Great Crisis of the British Monarchy 1685–1720* (London: Penguin, 2007) pp.391–408.

[11] Julian Goodare, "Scotland's Parliament in its British context 1603–1707" in Dickinson and Lynch (eds), *The Challenge to Westminster: Sovereignty, Devolution and Independence* (East Linton: Tuckwell Press, 2000) p.23.

Crown, the Declaration of Rights spoke "more guardedly"[12] of James having "abdicated"; "there was in Scotland no grasping at the convenient fiction of James's abdication but an implication that monarchy had been contractual".[13] The principles that the Claim of Right laid down, however, were little different from those adopted in the Declaration of Rights: no Catholic could be monarch or bear office; the prerogative could not be used to override the law ("all proclamations asserting an absolute power to cass (quash), annul and disable laws ... are contrary to law"); the consent of Parliament was necessary for the raising of supply ("the giving gifts or grants, for raising of money, without the consent of Parliament ... is contrary to law"); and parliaments should meet frequently and be able to debate freely ("for redress of all grievances, and for the amending, strengthening and preserving of the laws, Parliaments ought to be frequently called, and allowed to sit, and the freedom of speech and debate secured to the members").

What was different, as Mitchell pointed out, was the absence of any Scottish **1–06** counterpart of the seventeenth century English litigation concerning the royal prerogative from which many of these principles were derived.[14] Their adoption therefore represented a more radical break with the past than the adoption of the equivalent principles in England. The Claim of Right was not just

> "a rejection of the allegedly illegal measures pursued by Scottish monarchs; it also sought, in crucial respects, to redefine the powers of the Scottish monarchy as it had been legally reconstituted after 1660".[15]

In drawing a line under claims to unlimited royal power, the Convention was **1–07** also seeking to enhance its own position within the Scottish constitution.[16] The long list of rights and liberties set out in the Claim of Right, Dicey and Rait explained, was in effect "a demand for every power belonging to the Parliament of England", adding that:

> "If it be said that the Scottish Parliament thereby demands authority far exceeding any power which it actually possessed and exercised before the Revolution of 1689, the truth of the assertion cannot be denied."[17]

---

[12] Walter Ian Reid Fraser, *An Outline of Constitutional Law*, 2nd edn (London: William Hodge and Company, 1948) p.147.

[13] Michael Lynch, *Scotland: A New History* (London: Pimlico, 1992) p.302; on the radicalism of the Claim of Right, see Rosalind Mitchison, *Lordship to Patronage: Scotland 1603–1745* (Edinburgh: Edinburgh University Press, 1983) pp.117–119.

[14] JDB Mitchell, *Constitutional Law*, 2nd edn (W.Green, 1968) p.9, fn 17. The absence of any Scottish counterpart of that litigation is indicative of the much stronger position enjoyed by the Stuarts under the Scottish constitution, which meant that the extent of the royal prerogative was not the issue it was south of the border. The study of the Scottish constitution during the seventeenth century is "the study of the means by which the sovereign exercised his authority": Gordon Donaldson, *Edinburgh History of Scotland: James V to James VII*, Vol.3 (Edinburgh: Mercat Press, 1978) p.276. On the prerogative before the Union, see Brian Levack, *The Formation of the British State: England, Scotland, and the Union 1603–1707* (Oxford: Clarendon Press, 1987) pp.55–59.

[15] Tim Harris, *Revolution: The Great Crisis of the British Monarchy 1685–1720* (London: Penguin, 2007) p.395.

[16] Tim Harris, *Revolution: The Great Crisis of the British Monarchy 1685–1720* (London: Penguin, 2007) pp.401–402.

[17] Albert V Dicey and Robert S Rait, *Thoughts on the Union between England & Scotland* (London: Macmillan, 1920) p.63. In this mode of action, Dicey and Rait continued, the Scottish Parliament had precisely followed in the steps of the English Parliament, the authority of which "has again and again been extended, not under the form of a request for new powers, but under the

1–08 Both parliaments therefore approached union with similar expectations as to the relationship between government and parliament, and indeed it was those expectations—of an all powerful English-dominated Parliament—that lay at the root of many Scots' fears about the Union. For opponents of the Union a key issue was the security the Scots would enjoy "once the new Parliament of Great Britain, with its overwhelmingly English membership, had assumed the sovereignty previously held by the Scottish parliament".[18]

> "How could Scots be certain that the new parliament, in which the English would be hugely predominant, would not simply ignore the Treaty of Union and the protections for Scottish interests painstakingly inserted within it?"[19]

THE UNION

1–09 The Union of the Parliaments in 1707 was not an inevitable consequence of the Union of the Crowns in 1603. Indeed for a long time parliamentary union looked unlikely. When union came it was against the background of Scottish dissatisfaction with the working of the regal union:

> "A century's experience of a common sovereign, shared by two independent states but actually always resident in one of them, had not left the Scot enamoured of the system."[20]

There was also uncertainty over the succession to the separate Scottish and English crowns, Queen Anne who had succeeded to the throne after the death of William having no heirs; war with France, and the possibility that Scotland might be used to make England fight a war on two fronts; and, for Scots, the key issue of access to English markets.

1–10 The immediate spur was the succession to the crowns, the English Parliament having vested the succession to the English crown in the House of Hanover by the Act of Settlement 1701 without consulting the Scottish Parliament. The expectation was that the Scottish Parliament would follow suit, but in the Act of Security,[21] to which Royal Assent was "reluctantly given"[22] in 1704, the Scottish Parliament threatened to go their own way on the death of Queen Anne unless their dissatisfaction with the working of the regal union

---

nominal demand that an existing power which has not been fully respected should henceforth be treated as part of the known law of the land. The Scottish Parliament in short in the Claim of Rights adopted the astounding method of 'retrogressive progress' which has greatly favoured the growth, but has also disguised from many historians and constitutionalists the true nature, of the power obtained by the Parliament of England"; on the idea of "retrogressive progress", see Albert V Dicey, *An Introduction to the Study of the Law of the Constitution*, 10th edn (London: Macmillan, 1959) pp.17–19.

[18] John Robertson, "An Elusive Sovereignty: The Course of the Union Debate in Scotland 1698–1707" in John Robertson (ed), *A Union for Empire: Political Thought and the British Union of 1707* (Cambridge: Cambridge University Press, 1995) p.219.

[19] Bob Harris, "The Scots, the Westminster parliament, and the British state in the eighteenth century" in Julian Hoppit (ed), *Parliaments, Nations and Identities in Britain and Ireland, 1660–1850* (Manchester: Manchester University Press, 2003) p.124.

[20] D Oswald Dykes, *Source Book of Constitutional History from 1660* (London: Longmans, Green & Co, 1930) p.10.

[21] Act of Security 1704 (c.3) xi 136.

[22] Kilbrandon Commission, *Report of the Royal Commission on the Constitution 1969–1973* (1973) Cmnd.5460, para.68.

was addressed. The Act provided that, on the death of Anne, the Scottish Parliament should meet to nominate and declare a successor, who should not be the successor to the English crown, unless "there be such conditions of Government settled and enacted as may secure the honour and sovereignty of this Crown and Kingdom, the freedom frequency and power of Parliaments, [and] the religion, liberty and trade of the Nation from English or any foreign influence".

> "The aim of the Act was clear. The Scottish Parliament was utterly dissatisfied, as were also the people of Scotland, with the working of the mere Union of Crowns. The Act was to ensure that some arrangement as to the relation between Scotland and England satisfactory to Scotland should be arrived at, or else that Scotland should on the death of Anne become a separate and independent country, subject to a king, who should in no case be the same person as the King of England."[23]

The English Parliament's response came in the form of the Alien Act 1705, which offered the Scottish Parliament the opportunity of negotiating a treaty of union between the two countries, while at the same time holding out the threat that Scots would be treated as aliens in England and imports from Scotland banned unless Scotland accepted the Hanoverian succession.

The union was negotiated by Commissioners appointed by the Queen on behalf **1–11** of the English and Scottish Parliaments. They agreed 25 Articles of Union, which were signed and sealed at Westminster on July 22, 1706. The separate kingdoms of Scotland and England would be replaced by a new kingdom of Great Britain (art.I), with one monarch (art.II) and one parliament to be styled the Parliament of Great Britain (art.III). The political union thus created would be underpinned by an economic union with freedom of trade and navigation between the two countries, as well as equality of duties and other burdens (art. IV onwards). There was also provision for the payment of compensation to Scotland in view of the fact that a part of future customs and excise duties levied in Scotland would go to pay interest on England's national debt incurred before the Union (art.XV).

The Articles of Union were first debated in the Scottish Parliament before **1–12** being approved with minor amendments on January 16, 1707.[24] They were then approved in their amended form by the English Parliament on March 6, 1707.[25] Two other Scottish Acts forming part of the Union legislation secured the Protestant religion and the Presbyterian system of church government in Scotland and settled the manner of electing the Scottish representatives to the new Parliament of Great Britain.[26] An analogous measure to secure the Church of England was passed at Westminster.[27] The Scottish Parliament was dissolved for the last time on April 28, 1707 and the Union formally took effect on May 1, 1707.

---

[23] Albert V Dicey and Robert S Rait, *Thoughts on the Union between England & Scotland* (London: Macmillan, 1920) p.168. The Scottish Parliament had earlier opened up the prospect of an independent Scottish foreign policy, in which war involving Scotland could not be declared without the consent of the Scottish Parliament: Act anent Peace and War 1703 (c.6) xi 107.

[24] Union with England Act 1707 (c.7).

[25] Under the new calendar, 1706 under the old calendar: Union with Scotland Act 1706 (c.11).

[26] Protestant Religion and Presbyterian Church Act 1707 (c.6); Election Act 1707 (c.8).

[27] Maintenance of the Church of England Act 1706 (c.8).

The Acts of Union as fundamental law

1–13 The Union was an "incorporating" union but less than a full union. The Scots gave up their parliament, and with it the capacity to make mischief in English eyes, but not their other institutions to which they remained committed and with which the English had no wish to interfere.

> "Unlike Cromwell, English ministers had no desire to 'civilise' Scotland in 1707 or to assimilate her institutions and government to that of England. Their only desire was to remove a Scottish parliament whose recent and unwonted spirit of independence had posed a real threat to a peaceful Hanoverian succession."[28]

Written into the Union agreement in recognition of many Scots' fears about the possible effects of union were guarantees of the separate Scottish judicial system (art.XIX), the separate system of Scots law affecting private right, which was not to be altered "save for the evident utility of the subjects within Scotland" (art.XVIII), and the Scottish church and system of church government (by way of the Act for Securing the Protestant Religion annexed to the Acts).[29]

1–14 The significance of these guarantees has been much debated.[30] Never more so than at the time of the Union when the answer given was that the ultimate sanction that attached to their breach was the break-up of the Union.

> "The plain fact was, that if a majority of the new Parliament should desire to violate these articles, the only practical impediment would be the danger that outraged Scottish opinion might lead to the dissolution of the union. Since judicial review of legislation had not yet been invented, no remedy other than dissolution was conceivable."[31]

1–15 Once the Union was more securely established the orthodoxy that emerged was that they were politically rather than legally enforceable. For Dicey and Rait, the enactment of laws that were described as "unchangeable, immutable, or the like", was "not necessarily futile".

> "A sovereign Parliament ... though it cannot be logically bound to abstain from changing any given law, may, by the fact that an Act when it was

---

[28] Nicholas Phillipson, *The Scottish Whigs and the Reform of the Court of Session 1785–1830* (Edinburgh: Stair Society, 1990) p.2. "It was one of the most important effects of the union to deprive the Scots of the opportunity for independent parliamentary action, not only to settle their succession on an alternative claimant, but also, if they so wished, to withhold taxes, embroil themselves in a trade war or even embark upon a constitutional conflict with another parliament": David Hayton, "Constitutional experiments and political expediency" in Steven G Ellis and Sarah Barber (eds), *Conquest and Union: Fashioning a British State 1485–1725* (London: Longman, 1995) p.295.

[29] "Scots had previously baulked at union because they feared the erosion of the Scottish institutional order. They agreed to parliamentary union at this point only in the context of guarantees that the integrity of other key institutions would be respected": Joanna Innes, "Legislating for three kingdoms: how the Westminster parliament legislated for England, Scotland and Ireland 1707–1830" in Julian Hoppit (ed), *Parliaments, Nations and Identities in Britain and Ireland, 1660–1850* (Manchester: Manchester University Press, 2003) pp.23–24.

[30] The literature is extensive. For recent treatments, see Elizabeth Wicks, "A New Constitution for a New State? The 1707 Union of England and Scotland" (2001) 117 L.Q.R. 109; and Neil Walker, "Fundamental Law" in *Constitutional Law: Stair Memorial Encyclopaedia Reissue* (London: Butterworths/LexisNexis, 2002) paras 60–66.

[31] Jeffrey Goldsworthy, *The Sovereignty of Parliament: History and Philosophy* (Oxford: Clarendon Press, 1999) pp.169–170.

passed, had been declared to be unchangeable, receive a warning that it cannot be changed without grave danger to the Constitution of the country."[32]

For Goldsworthy they are "fundamental", but only in the traditional British sense of the term, and not in the sense of a higher law:

> "They are principles of political morality, which Parliament must take into account, as a matter of conscience and political prudence, but can legally change if there are sufficiently strong reasons for doing so."[33]

While this was not sufficient to prevent their alteration, it is nevertheless arguable that it had an inhibiting effect that contributed to the survival of distinct Scottish institutions, including the superior courts and the separate system of Scots private law, and with their survival to the maintenance of a separate sense of Scottish identity.

> "The clauses of the Treaty were periodically abrogated by parliament in the first half of the eighteenth century especially where British political security was judged to be at issue. On other occasions and matters, however, ministers proved reluctant to support measures which contravened clauses in the Treaty . . . The force of inertia in eighteenth-century government and administration, the caution with regard to threatening vested and propertied interests are well established. In the case of Scotland, the Treaty of Union gave added ideological force to this tendency, and furnished an additional layer of protection to important Scottish interests."[34]

With the rise of nationalist sentiment in the twentieth century, the notion that **1–16** the Westminster Parliament's sovereignty was unlimited when it came to the Acts of Union was challenged.[35] Seizing on Lord Cooper's dismissal of the principle in *MacCormick v Lord Advocate*,[36] "legal nationalists" argued that the Acts of Union and associated legislation formed the "basic skeletal constitution" of a new state, the parliament of which had no power to disregard the

---

[32] Albert V Dicey and Robert S Rait, *Thoughts on the Union between England & Scotland* (London: Macmillan, 1920) pp.253–254.

[33] Jeffrey Goldsworthy, The Sovereignty of Parliament: History and Philosophy (Oxford: Clarendon Press, 1999) p.172; see to similar effect, Albert V Dicey and Robert S Rait, *Thoughts on the Union between England & Scotland* (London: Macmillan, 1920) pp.253–254. Lord Rodger of Earlsferry (*The Courts, The Church and the Constitution: Aspects of the Disruption of 1843* (Edinburgh: Edinburgh University Press, 2008) pp.6–7) argued that the failure to challenge the Patronage Act 1712, one of the most disputed Acts of the Westminster Parliament, suggested "a settled view among Scottish practitioners and judges that an Act of Parliament could not be challenged on the ground that, by reason of the Act of Union, it was beyond the power of Parliament".

[34] Bob Harris, "The Scots, the Westminster parliament, and the British state in the eighteenth century" in Julian Hoppit (ed), *Parliaments, Nations and Identities in Britain and Ireland, 1660–1850* (Manchester: Manchester University Press, 2003) pp.136–137; Robertson comments that "it was almost certainly fortunate ... that the belief that the Treaty secured Presbyterian church government as a 'fundamental' was not immediately tested: when it was, by the Toleration and Patronage Acts passed by the Tory-dominated British Parliament in 1711–12, those who put their trust in it were quickly disabused": John Robertson, "An Elusive Sovereignty: The Course of the Union Debate in Scotland 1698–1707" in John Robertson (ed), *A Union for Empire: Political Thought and the British Union of 1707* (Cambridge: Cambridge University Press, 1995) p.225.

[35] TB Smith, "The Union of 1707 as Fundamental Law" [1957] P.L. 99; "Fundamental Law" in *Stair Memorial Encyclopaedia* (1987) Vol.5, paras 338–360; Neil MacCormick, "Does the United Kingdom have a Constitution? Reflections on *MacCormick v Lord Advocate*" (1978) 29 N.I.L.Q. 1; see also JDB Mitchell, *Constitutional Law*, 2nd edn (Edinburgh: W.Green, 1968) pp.69–74.

[36] *MacCormick v Lord Advocate*, 1953 S.C. 396, 411.

fundamental provisions of its constituent instrument. Were it to do so, the courts would be bound to deny effect to the legislation in the name of a higher law:

> "If I am right that the terms of Union are constituent, then Parliament can only legislate lawfully within the powers conferred upon it; and the Judiciary would be bound by their oath to pay regard to the fundamental law in preference to a mere Act of Parliament."[37]

1-17 This argument has never made much progress in the Scottish courts, although they have stopped short of rejecting it altogether. In *MacCormick v Lord Advocate*,[38] Lord President Cooper took the view that the courts could not entertain any challenge to Parliament's legislative competence with regard to matters of "public right", but reserved his opinion with regard to the Court of Session itself and to the laws "which concern private right". In *Gibson v Lord Advocate*,[39] Lord Keith rejected a challenge to the European Communities Act 1972 on the grounds that it would open fishing in Scottish coastal waters to nationals from other Member States, but reserved his opinion with regard to an Act

> "purporting to abolish the Court of Session or Church of Scotland or to substitute English law for the whole body of Scots private law".

And in *Pringle, Petitioner*,[40] one of a series of cases that arose out of the community charge or poll tax, Lord Hope rejected the petitioner's argument that he could not be required to pay the charge in Scotland before it was introduced in England, but reserved his opinion whether it would be a breach of art.IV of the Act of Union for Parliament

> "to legislate in such a way that the subjects of one part of the UK enjoyed rights, privileges and advantages in regard to the immunity from methods of taxation which were not already in force in 1707 without similar rights, privileges and advantages being communicated to those resident in the other part".

1-18 Judicial attitudes towards the sovereignty of Parliament have changed significantly over the last 30 or so years.[41] There is no mistaking, however, judicial reluctance to become involved in "unmeritorious objections to politically unpopular legislation".[42] In *Gibson v Lord Advocate*,[43] Lord Keith insisted that

> "the question whether a particular Act of the United Kingdom Parliament altering a particular aspect of Scots private law is or is not 'for the evident utility' of the subjects within Scotland is not a justiciable issue in this Court. The making of decisions upon what must essentially be a political matter is no part of the function of the Court, and it is highly undesirable that it should be. The function of the Court is to adjudicate upon the particular rights and obligations of individual persons, natural or

---

[37] TB Smith, "The Union of 1707 as Fundamental Law" [1957] P.L. 99, 114.

[38] *MacCormick v Lord Advocate*, 1953 SC 396, 412.

[39] *Gibson v Lord Advocate*, 1975 S.C. 136, 144.

[40] *Pringle, Petitioner*, 1991 S.L.T. 330, 333.

[41] *R (Jackson) v Attorney General* [2005] UKHL 56; [2006] 1 A.C. 262; especially the speeches by Lord Steyn and Lord Hope.

[42] Robert Reed, "Devolution and the Judiciary" in Jack Beatson et al (eds) *Constitutional Reform in the United Kingdom: Practice and Principles* (Oxford: Hart Publishing, 1998) p.26.

[43] *Gibson v Lord Advocate*, 1975 S.C. 136, 144.

corporate, in relation to other persons or, in certain instances, to the State. A general inquiry into the utility of specific legislative measures as regards the population generally is quite outside its competence."

While accepting that the argument that the Westminster Parliament is bound by **1–19** the Acts of Union could not be dismissed as "entirely fanciful", the courts, Lord Hope explained to the House of Lords in *Lord Gray's Motion*,[44] had always been able to find another way of disposing of the argument, making it unnecessary to resolve the question whether there had been a breach of the Acts of Union.

The Acts of Union and the Scottish Parliament

What has been claimed of Acts of the Westminster Parliament might also **1–20** be claimed of Acts of the Scottish Parliament: that they are contrary to or inconsistent with the fundamental provisions of the Union. The Scotland Act 1998 seeks to pre-empt this argument by stipulating that the Acts of Union have effect subject to the Scotland Act itself[45]; "seeks to" because if the powers of the Westminster Parliament are limited by the Acts of Union, the Westminster Parliament has no power to authorise the Scottish Parliament to do that which it itself has no power to do, namely ignore the limits on its own competence. Regardless of arguments about their status in relation to the Westminster Parliament, therefore, the intention is that the Scotland Act should take precedence over the Acts of Union. The Scotland Act has in any event deprived the "Acts of Union as fundamental law" argument of much of its significance in relation to the Scottish Parliament by providing a political means of determining what is for the "evident utility of the subjects within Scotland".

THE UNION STATE

The UK constitution is a unitary constitution. The characteristic feature of a **1–21** unitary constitution is that

> "the legislature of the whole country is the supreme law-making body in the country. It may permit other legislatures to exist and to exercise their powers, but it has the right, in law, to overrule them; they are subordinate to it".[46]

A unitary constitution, thus defined, is commonly contrasted with a federal constitution in which

> "the powers of government are divided between a government for the whole country and governments for parts of the country in such a way that each government is legally independent within its own sphere ... In particular the legislature of the whole country has limited powers, and the legislatures of the states or provinces have limited powers. Neither is subordinate to the other; both are co-ordinate".[47]

The description of a constitution as "unitary" rather than "federal", however, **1–22** tells us very little about the governing arrangements within a state:

---

44 *Lord Gray's Motion*, 2000 S.C. (HL) 46, 59.
45 Scotland Act 1998 s.37.
46 KC Wheare, *Modern Constitutions*, 2nd edn (Oxford: OUP, 1966) p.19.
47 KC Wheare, *Modern Constitutions*, 2nd edn (Oxford: OUP, 1966) p.19.

"The class of unitary Constitutions is so wide and varied, the degree and method of decentralization in practice in unitary Constitutions is so diverse, that a good deal more must be known about a Constitution described as 'unitary' before we can feel that we know what it is like."[48]

Discussing the process of state formation in Western Europe, Rokkan and Urwin draw a distinction between "union states" and "unitary states". A union state is not

"the result of straightforward dynastic conquest. Incorporation of at least parts of the territory has been achieved through personal dynastic union, for example by treaty, marriage or inheritance. Integration is less than perfect. While administrative standardization prevails over most of the territory, the consequences of personal union entail the survival in some areas of pre-union rights and institutional infrastructures which preserve some degree of regional autonomy and serve as agencies of indigenous elite recruitment".[49]

1–23 A unitary state by contrast is

"built up around one unambiguous political centre which enjoys economic dominance and pursues a more or less undeviating policy of administrative standardization. All areas of the state are treated alike and all institutions are under the control of the centre".[50]

For Rokkan and Urwin the UK is

"the prototypic union state, with an accumulation of disparate historical variations. The centre has responded with ad hoc proposals for specific problems as they arose, without any overall strategy and in this has sought to maintain a middle ground between a unitary structure and federalism".[51]

1–24 Pursuing the notion of the UK as a union state, four features of the government of Scotland after the Union stand out: separate governing arrangements that became more extensive with the expansion in the functions of government from the nineteenth century onwards; the separate Scottish legal system and with it the possibility of a "Scots law" interpretation of the UK constitution,[52] or, in less elevated terms, of conflicting decisions between the Scottish and English courts on constitutional matters, a possibility we come back to in the

[48] KC Wheare, *Modern Constitutions*, 2nd edn (Oxford: OUP, 1966) p.21. For Bulpitt, the classical approach to the analysis of territorial politics was characterised by "the neglect of unitary systems and in particular the varying structures of territorial politics which operate under that label. It is hard not to conclude that for social scientists at least the terms confederation, federation and unitary system should be pensioned off and left to the second oldest profession, the lawyers, to play with": Jim Bulpitt, *Territory and Power in the United Kingdom: An Interpretation* (Manchester: Manchester University Press, 1983) p.19.
[49] Stein Rokkan and Derek Urwin, "Introduction: Centres and Peripheries in Europe", in Stein Rokkan and Derek Urwin (eds), *The Politics of Territorial Identity: Studies in European Regionalism* (London: Sage, 1982) p.11.
[50] Stein Rokkan and Derek Urwin, "Introduction: Centres and Peripheries in Europe", in Stein Rokkan and Derek Urwin (eds), *The Politics of Territorial Identity: Studies in European Regionalism* (London: Sage, 1982) p.11.
[51] Stein Rokkan and Derek Urwin, *Economy, Territory, Identity: Politics of West European Peripheries* (London: Sage, 1983) p.187
[52] Neil MacCormick, "Is There a Constitutional Path to Scottish Independence?" (2000) 53 Parliamentary Affairs 721, 729.

final section of this chapter; separate Scottish legislation, which became more common with the expansion in the functions of government, but not, critics argued, in sufficient quantities to meet "Scottish needs"; and, allied to separate legislation, separate parliamentary arrangements, including arrangements for the oversight of the government of Scotland.[53]

Separate governing arrangements

The Acts of Union said very little about the government of Scotland after the **1–25** Union. A Secretary of State was appointed with responsibility for Scottish affairs immediately after the Union, but the office was abolished in 1746, having lain vacant between 1725 and 1742. When the Secretary of State system was reformed in 1782 responsibility was vested in the Secretary of State for the Home Department. Effective control, however, lay with an unofficial Scottish "manager" who controlled Scottish patronage and maintained relations with London. The manager system eventually came to an end in 1828, leaving the Home Secretary and the Lord Advocate, who had played a key role as the manager or manager's adviser throughout, responsible for the government of Scotland. Increasing dissatisfaction with "lawyer government", however, combined with Scottish feelings of neglect, were to lead to the appointment of a Secretary (rather than Secretary of State) for Scotland in 1885.[54] Once re-established the Secretary came to be regarded as "Scotland's Minister", while the role of the Lord Advocate reverted to its original, predominantly legal character.[55]

"Within a generation after the passage of the Secretary for Scotland Act, men had ceased to think of the Lord Advocate as primarily a political figure and had come to regard him as little more than the Government's principal legal adviser in Scotland."[56]

It was not until 1926, however, that the Secretary became a full Secretary of State,[57] and his salary was to remain below that of other Secretaries of State until 1937.

A distinct Scottish administration began to emerge during the middle years of **1–26** the nineteenth century. At first it took the form of a series of ad hoc administrative boards: the General Board of Directors of Prisons in Scotland (1840), which was later replaced by the Prisons Commission for Scotland (1877); the Board of Supervision for the Relief of the Poor in Scotland (1845), which subsequently acquired powers in relation to public health (1867); and the General Board of Commissioners in Lunacy for Scotland (1857). There was also the Board of Manufactures (1727) and its offshoot, the Board of White Herring Fisheries (1808), which became the Fishery Board for Scotland (1882).

[53] On the idea of the UK as a union state, see James Mitchell, *Strategies for Self-Government: the Campaigns for a Scottish Parliament* (Edinburgh: Polygon, 1996); see also Iain McLean and Alistair McMillan, *State of the Union* (Oxford: OUP, 2005), and Neil Walker, "Beyond the Unitary Conception of the United Kingdom Constitution?" [2000] P.L. 384. In its first report the House of Lords Constitution Committee treated the union state as one of the five basic tenets of the UK constitution: House of Lords, *Reviewing the Constitution: Terms of Reference and Method of Working* (HL 2001–2002, 11) para.21.
[54] Secretary for Scotland Act 1885; H.J. Hanham, "The Creation of the Scottish Office 1881–1887" [1965] J.R. 205.
[55] John LL J Edwards, *The Attorney General, Politics and the Public Interest* (London: Sweet and Maxwell, 1984) p.280.
[56] H.J. Hanham, "The Creation of the Scottish Office 1881–1887" [1965] J.R. 205, 244.
[57] Secretaries of State Act 1926 (c.18).

Only the Scotch Education Department (1872) was constituted as an orthodox Whitehall department; formally it was a committee of the Privy Council.

1–27 The use of boards of public officials rather than the ministerial department, which was becoming the preferred form of organisation south of the border, was partly attributable to "the difficulty of administering a country four hundred miles away from the seat of government, and the consequent difficulty of operating the ordinary type of Parliamentary Ministerial administration"[58]:

> "It seems to have been felt that the concentration of all Scottish ... administrative powers in single Ministers was undesirable when those Ministers spent at least half their time at Westminster."[59]

The board system also enabled specialists and laymen to be brought into the process of administration.

> "The intention was that administration should be directed by bodies composed partly of specialists and professional members, partly of eminent laymen representing the public."[60]

In practice, it has been claimed, "the work was carried out by professional specialists who could do as they liked".[61]

1–28 With the establishment of the Scottish Office in 1885 these boards fell under the oversight of the Secretary for Scotland. New boards, however, continued to be created—the Local Government Board for Scotland (1894), which took over the functions of the Board of Supervision; the Board of Agriculture for Scotland (1912), which incorporated the Crofters Commission (1886) and the Congested Districts Board (1897); and the Scottish Board of Health (1919), which incorporated the Local Government Board, the Scottish Insurance Commissioners (1911) and the Highlands and Islands (Medical Service) Board (1913)—and although their members were now appointed by the Secretary little in practice changed.

> "The plain truth was that with a Scottish minister in Whitehall equipped only with a small staff there was no other convenient way to administer day-to-day Scottish affairs. They had to be devolved on to subordinate bodies and the Scottish boards were the time-honoured form which subordinate bodies took in Scotland."[62]

1–29 The board system took a long time to be replaced. The McDonnell Commission, which reported in 1914, recommended that the boards' semi-independence

[58] Scottish Office, *Report of the Committee on Scottish Administration* (1937) Cmd.5563, para.15.

[59] FMG Willson, "Ministries and Boards: Some Aspects of Administrative Development Since 1832" (1955) 33 Public Administration 43, 44.

[60] Gordon Donaldson and others, "Scottish Devolution: The Historical Background" in JN Wolfe (ed), *Government and Nationalism in Scotland: An Enquiry by Members of the University of Edinburgh* (Edinburgh: Edinburgh University Press, 1969) p.8.

[61] Michael Fry, *Patronage and Principle: A Political History of Modern Scotland* (Aberdeen: Aberdeen University Press, 1987) p.71.

[62] HJ Hanham, "The Development of the Scottish Office" in JN Wolfe (ed), *Government and Nationalism in Scotland: An Enquiry by Members of the University of Edinburgh* (Edinburgh: Edinburgh University Press, 1969) p.56; according to Hanham, "the whole system still smacked strongly of the 'lawyer government' of the period before 1885, with advocates and solicitors occupying many of the key positions, often on a part-time basis".

should be ended and that they should be placed under the direct authority of the Scottish Secretary as normal departments of the civil service,[63] but it was to be 1939 before the Whitehall pattern of organisation was adopted and the boards and their successors incorporated into the Scottish Office and their functions vested in the Secretary of State. The Reorganisation of Offices (Scotland) Act 1928 abolished the boards dealing with health and agriculture, and the prison commissioners, and transferred their functions to departments under the "control and direction" of the Secretary of State. The Gilmour Committee, however, regarded the successor departments as an "anomaly":

> "It is a constitutional principle that a Department and its Minister are indistinguishable, but a Department incorporated and established by statute to carry out specified functions in the name of the Department, although acting under the control and direction of the Minister, is necessarily regarded as a separate entity. We consider that this is an anomaly which should be rectified."[64]

The Committee accordingly recommended that the three departments be abolished and their functions vested directly in the Secretary of State. Its recommendations were given effect by the Reorganisation of Offices (Scotland) Act 1939. At the same time, in a move of "immense symbolic value", the general functions of the Scottish Office in London were transferred to Edinburgh, "making Edinburgh once again a seat of government, truly a capital rather than just the headquarters of the Kirk and judiciary".[65]

After the Second World War the Scottish Office's functions steadily expanded. **1–30**

> "Some of the alterations may have been made for political reasons, others out of a desire for administrative tidiness; the river may have flowed erratically, but its main course has been clear. There has been a definite and increasing tendency to assign to a Scottish minister matters in which there is a distinctive Scottish tradition or body of law or where Scottish conditions are notably different from those in England and Wales."[66]

Among the functions transferred were electricity, roads, road passenger transport, animal health, ancient monuments, royal parks and palaces, the appointment of justices of the peace, highlands and islands development and industrial and economic planning. The Kilbrandon Commission, which reported in 1973, could see only very limited scope for transferring further functions.[67] Further functions were to follow, however, including financial assistance to industry, the arts and the environment.

> "By the end of 1998, the Secretary of State for Scotland, with six junior ministers and a Scottish Office organised in five main departments, had responsibilities extending to agriculture and fisheries, the arts, crofting,

---

[63] *Royal Commission on the Civil Service, Fourth Report* (1914) Cd.7338, paras 67–71.

[64] Scottish Office, *Report of the Committee on Scottish Administration* (1937) Cmd.5563, para.42; Fraser described the departments as "constitutional freaks", which "contravened the constitutional principle that a department and its Minister are indistinguishable": Walter Ian Reid Fraser, *An Outline of Constitutional Law*, 2nd edn (London: William Hodge and Company, 1948) p.138.

[65] Michael Fry, *Patronage and Principle: A Political History of Modern Scotland* (Aberdeen: Aberdeen University Press, 1987) pp.184–185.

[66] Sir David Milne, *The Scottish Office And Other Scottish Government Departments* (London: George Allen & Unwin, 1957) pp.20–21.

[67] Kilbrandon Commission, *Report of the Royal Commission on the Constitution 1969–1973* (1973) Cmnd.5460, para.1049.

education, the environment, the fire service, forestry, health, housing, industrial assistance, local government, police, prisons, roads, rural and urban development, social work, sport, transport, tourism, town planning, some minor departments and some public corporations operating in Scotland, and some legal matters (with other functions in connection with the Scottish legal system falling to the Lord Advocate's Department and the Crown Office, for which the Lord Advocate was responsible)."[68]

1–31 The term that came to be used to describe this system was "administrative devolution", a misleading description insofar as it suggested a greater degree of Scottish self-government than was in fact the case. What it meant was the administration of central government functions in Edinburgh rather than London.[69] As a central government department the Scottish Office had no more freedom to go its own way than any other UK government department, which is not to say that it could not adjust policies to Scottish circumstances, but on all important questions it was bound by the policy of the government of the day.

1–32 By itself this might have been of little consequence had voting behaviour in Scotland not begun to diverge from that in the rest of the UK, which it did from the 1950s on. Declining electoral popularity was to leave successive Conservative governments facing a problem of legitimacy in Scotland—the last Conservative government to win a majority of seats in Scotland was elected in 1955—which was only to intensify with the breakdown of the post-war political consensus over the role of the state. As justification for concentrating functions in the Secretary of State, the Gilmour Committee had argued that it was the Secretary of State who was ultimately accountable:

> "Yet it is clear that, however the powers of the Boards may be defined, the ultimate responsibility must constitutionally rest with the Minister."[70]

But it was a Conservative Secretary of State's lack of accountability—to the Scottish electorate rather than the House of Commons—that was to fuel demands for the "democratisation" of the Scottish Office after 1979.[71]

Scottish legislation

1–33 A third feature of the union state, consequent upon the separate administrative and legal systems, and the growth in the functions of government, was an expanding corpus of Scottish legislation, which might take the form of separate Scottish Bills or the inclusion of Scottish provisions in UK or Great Britain

---

[68] Colin R Munro, "Scottish Devolution: Accommodating a Restless Nation" in Stephen Tierney (ed), *Accommodating National Identity: New Approaches in International and Domestic Law* (Holland: Kluwer Law International, 2000) p.141.

[69] On the origins of the term, see James Mitchell, *Governing Scotland: the Invention of Administrative Devolution* (London: Palgrave Macmillan, 2003) pp.124–132, from which it is clear that what was meant was that most of the administrative work of the Scottish Office should be carried on in Edinburgh.

[70] Scottish Office, *Report of the Committee on Scottish Administration* (1937) Cmd.5563, para.18.

[71] The concentration of functions in a single minister attracted persistent criticism: "Such an office in a country containing five million inhabitants is, speaking frankly, an absurdity. For it is he, with his [junior ministerial colleagues] who alone is responsible for the work of the separate Scottish departments of Agriculture, Education, Health and so on": Andrew Dewar Gibb, *A Preface to Scots Law* (Edinburgh: W.Green, 1964) p.3. The comparison, which was not always made explicit, was with the dominions, and especially with Ireland: C de B Murray, *How Scotland is Governed* (Glasgow: Art and Educational Publishers, 1947) p.47 ("If we compare Edinburgh with Dublin, the absurdity of our position is apparent.").

Bills, but not, critics argued, in sufficient quantities to meet "Scottish needs". With the expansion in the functions of government it came to be seen as a weakness of the Union agreement that

> "while it guaranteed the future existence of the Scottish courts and the legal profession, it left the legal system with no legislature except the Westminster Parliament . . . Possibly in earlier times a legal system could survive without frequent legislative activity. But that is not the case today. While legislative policies of first importance to a determined Government will pass into law despite the inconvenience or embarrassment resulting from the political structure, on matters of secondary importance which attract opposition from Scottish circles, the probable outcome is that legislative reform is delayed".[72]

Criticism also attached to the practice of applying English provisions with the **1–34** minimum of "adaptation" to Scotland.[73] The Kilbrandon Commission recorded it as a continuing complaint that

> "there is insufficient understanding of Scots law in London, and that its peculiarities are not sufficiently catered for by United Kingdom legislation. It is said that that legislation is often applied to Scotland by the inclusion of Scottish application clauses in a Great Britain Bill when what is really needed is a separate Scottish Bill drafted in the idiom of the Scottish legal system. This method of drafting causes difficulties for Scottish lawyers and hampers the preservation and development of Scottish legal concepts. It is contended also that the existence of an 'absentee' legislature in London, remote from Scottish public opinion, results in pressure for Scots law to be changed in conformity with English law rather than on its merits".[74]

Following the recommendation of the Renton Committee,[75] the use **1–35** of adaptation clauses was abandoned, thereby increasing the legislative separation of Scottish affairs.[76]

Separate parliamentary arrangements

With the growing demand for Scottish legislation special parliamentary **1–36** arrangements were also made. The Scottish Grand Committee, a committee of the House of Commons consisting of all MPs representing Scottish constituencies, was made permanent in 1907, having first been set up in 1894, to take the committee stage of Bills relating exclusively to Scotland and to debate

---

[72] AW Bradley, "Devolution of Government in Britain—Some Scottish Aspects" in Harry Calvert (ed) *Devolution* (London: Professional Books, 1975) p.101.

[73] Lord Cooper, *The Scottish Legal Tradition* (Edinburgh: Oliver and Boyd, 1949) p.13; *Report of the Royal Commission on Scottish Affairs 1952–1954* (1954) Cmd 9212, paras 86–94; the New Towns Act 1946 (c.68), which had a single Scottish application section which ran to eight and half pages, was one of the "least attractive pieces of Scottish adaptation in modern times": Lord MacKay of Clashfern, "The Drafting of Government Bills Affecting the Law of Scotland" [1983] Stat. L.R. 68, 70.

[74] Kilbrandon Commission, *Report of the Royal Commission on the Constitution 1969–1973* (1973) Cmnd.5460, para.373.

[75] *The Preparation of Legislation* (1975) Cmnd.6053, para.12.8; Renton was a member of the Royal Commission on the Constitution.

[76] Michael Keating and Arthur Midwinter, *The Government of Scotland* (Edinburgh: Mainstream Publishing, 1983) p.78.

"Scottish matters".[77] In 1948 provision was made for the second reading debate on Scottish Bills to take place in the Committee; at the same time provision was made for it to debate Scottish estimates.[78] The resulting pressure of legislative business, with the second reading and committee stage of Scottish Bills being taken in the Committee, led to the setting up in 1957 of a Scottish standing committee in which the committee stage of Scottish Bills could be taken, with a second committee being added six years later.[79] A government's ability to make use of these arrangements, however, depended on the strength of its parliamentary support in Scotland. Where it lacked a majority in Scotland—as did Conservative governments after 1959—their use depended on opposition support, failing which it either had to rely on the normal legislative process, with the consequence that Scottish Bills had to compete for inclusion in the annual legislative programme, or else tack Scottish provisions onto UK or Great Britain Bills. The procedures by themselves did not, therefore, resolve the problem of maintaining a sufficient flow of Scottish legislation.[80]

1–37　These arrangements were later extended to include the oversight of Scottish administration. A Select Committee on Scottish Affairs was appointed on a sessional basis between 1969 and 1972 before being reconstituted as part of the new departmental select committee system in 1979. There was "a substantial feeling", the Kilbrandon Commission recorded, "that the Scottish Office should be subject to closer democratic supervision".[81] Select committee scrutiny after 1979, however, only served to underline the powerlessness of opposition MPs (the Committee was not appointed between 1987 and 1992 because of wrangling between the major political parties over its composition). The crux of the problem for the Scottish political system within the Westminster Parliament was that Scottish committees gave Scottish MPs "the right to discuss Scottish legislation and affairs, but not to overturn the wishes of the government".[82]

1–38　When we combine the weakness of parliamentary oversight with the effective absence of judicial control (below) the result was "a state within a state"[83] that was subject to little in the way of external checks, parliamentary or judicial, leaving modern ideas of "good government" dependent more on civil servants' own sense of responsibility than any ideas of external accountability.[84]

> "Broadly speaking, it comes to this: a comparatively independent Executive is called upon to do its work with tools largely of its own fashioning, and the efficiency of the result is due, not so much to any legal

---

[77] The Committee originally included a number of non-Scottish members to reflect the political balance of the House of Commons but the "added" members were removed in 1981.

[78] Scottish Home Department, *Scottish Affairs* (1948) Cmd.7308.

[79] JH Burns, "The Scottish Committees of the House of Commons, 1948–1959" (1960) 8 Political Studies 272.

[80] AW Bradley, "Devolution of Government in Britain—Some Scottish Aspects" in Harry Calvert (ed) *Devolution* (London: Professional Books, 1975) p.100; for a defence of the system as it stood at the time, see Lord MacKay of Clashfern, "The Drafting of Government Bills Affecting the Law of Scotland" [1983] Stat. L.R. 70.

[81] Kilbrandon Commission, *Report of the Royal Commission on the Constitution 1969–1973* (1973) Cmnd.5460, para.1101.

[82] James G Kellas, *The Scottish Political System*, 4th edn (Cambridge: Cambridge University Press, 1989) p.92.

[83] Michael Lynch, *Scotland: A New History* (London: Pimlico, 1992) p.442.

[84] For the distinction, see B Guy Peters, *The Politics of Bureaucracy: An Introduction to Comparative Public Administration*, 6th edn (Oxford: Routledge, 2010) p.265.

control exercised by the people, as to the traditions and calibre of the Civil Service and the sensitiveness of the administrators to manifestations of popular feeling."[85]

A UNION LAW FOR A UNION STATE?

"But it is probably settled that in questions of constitutional law English decisions are authoritative in Scotland."[86]

What, finally, of the constitutional law of the union state? As the law of the **1–39** majority jurisdiction it was English law, not surprisingly, that supplied much of the constitutional law of the Union—UK constitutional law was English constitutional law.

> "It may ... be said that the constitutional law of the United Kingdom represents in unbroken historical continuity the constitutional law of England; for upon the union of Scotland and England in 1707, the political institutions of the United Kingdom of Great Britain carried on with little or no change the practices and traditions of those of the larger kingdom."[87]

The retention of the separate Scottish judicial system, however, carried with it the possibility that the Scottish courts might take a different approach to constitutional questions from their English counterparts.[88] By and large, however, this did not happen; when specific questions arose the Scottish courts tended to follow the example of English law.[89]

There were several reasons for this, including the sheer weight of **1–40** English authority, especially when set against the relative lack of Scottish authority or writing on constitutional law; in the absence of Scottish authority it was little surprise that the Scottish courts should have taken their lead from English law, which being a far more prolific source of cases tended to address them first.[90] The principal reason, however, was that the Scottish

---

[85] John Percival Day, *Public Administration in the Highlands and Islands of Scotland* (London: University of London Press, 1918) p.37.

[86] William Murray Gloag and Robert Candlish Henderson, *Introduction to the Law of Scotland* (Edinburgh: W.Green, 1927) p.1, citing *Macgregor v Lord Advocate*, 1921 S.C. 847; the same statement appeared in the second (1933) to sixth (1956) editions; for subsequent editions, see the text accompanying fn 101 below.

[87] D Oswald Dykes, "Constitutional Law" in *Encyclopaedia of the Laws of Scotland*, 3rd edn (1927) Vol.4, para.944. TB Smith drew a distinction between UK or national constitutional law, which was heavily influenced by English law, and Scottish or domestic constitutional law, which did not reflect the same degree of English influence: *Studies Critical and Comparative* (Edinburgh: W.Green, 1962) pp.129–130.

[88] JDB Mitchell, *Constitutional Law*, 2nd edn (Edinburgh: W.Green, 1968) pp.23–24; Aileen McHarg, "Public Law in Scotland: Difference and Distinction" in Aileen McHarg and Tom Mullen (eds), *Public Law in Scotland* (Edinburgh: Avizandum, 2006) pp.17–18.

[89] The immunities and privileges of the Crown are the pre-eminent example; see JR Philip, "The Crown as Litigant in Scotland" (1928) 40 J.R. 238; JDB Mitchell, "The Royal Prerogative in Modern Scots Law" [1957] Public Law 304; and Adam Tomkins, "The Crown in Scots Law" in Aileen McHarg and Tom Mullen (eds), *Public Law in Scotland* (Edinburgh: Avizandum, 2006) p.262.

[90] "While it has been assumed as a necessary consequence of the Union of 1707 that the substantive rights of the Crown in England and Scotland have become identical, it is remarkable that Crown's immunity from delict was not canvassed judicially till 1897": JR Philip, "The Crown as Litigant in Scotland" (1928) 40 J.R. 238, 245. As to the lack of literature, "it is well know that

judiciary were in little doubt that the law should be the same: "We have had no argument as to what was the effect of the Union of the two Kingdoms in 1707," Lord Justice-Clerk Scott Dickinson said in *Macgregor v Lord Advocate*,[91]

> "but it seems to me that the legislation that then took place almost necessarily resulted in this, that the position of the Crown in such matters must be the same on both sides of the Border. Accordingly, although few questions have arisen, the English decisions have been accepted as correctly expressing the law of Scotland".[92]

1–41 A prominent theme of the literature on Scots law has been what TB Smith condemned as the "forced and ill-considered 'anglicisation' of Scottish law".[93] Far from having been imposed by the House of Lords, however, the anglicisation of Scots constitutional law was largely undertaken by the Scottish judiciary themselves.

> "What is noticeable is that these changes in public law owed little to statutory intervention or to any deliberate attempt to unify ... The process of unification . . . was carried out by the judges and, on the whole, it was not the result of pressure from the House of Lords."[94]

1–42 Regret was later expressed that unification had been taken too far.

> "There had earlier been expressed strong views on the desirability of harmonization or unification, but the process need not have been one of absorption."[95]

"There was real virtue in early and middle nineteenth-century Scots public law," Mitchell argued, which "lay in the fact that its basis was essentially

---

Lord Stair, our greatest systematic writer on law, declined writing on public or constitutional law (B 1 title 1 sect 23), an example which has been followed by our subsequent legal authorities": *King's Advocate v Lord Dunglas* 1836 15 S. 314, 324–325 (Lord Medwyn). "The classical legal literature of Scotland confined itself, on the whole, to private law": JDB Mitchell, "Government and Public Law in Scotland: Retrospect and Prospect" in JA Andrews (ed), *Welsh Studies in Public Law* (Cardiff: Cardiff University of Wales Press, 1970) p.68.

[91] *Macgregor v Lord Advocate*, 1921 S.C. 847, 851–852.

[92] "As the constitution of Scotland has been the same as that of England since 1707, there is a presumption that the same constitutional principles apply in both countries": 1921 S.C. 847, 848 (Lord Anderson).

[93] *Studies Critical and Comparative* (Edinburgh: W.Green, 1962) p.117; see especially Andrew Dewar Gibb, *Law From Over The Border: A Short Account of a Strange Jurisdiction* (Edinburgh: W.Green, 1950). Gibb's strictures were almost certainly aimed at the Scots as much as at the English: "The Union taught many of the Scottish nation to regard their own institutions as provincial, to revere and extol only the distant glories of London. People of this kind almost certainly would (in theory) prefer the justice augustly meted out by a Chancellor who had never crossed the Tweed, to the decision of the trained and expert judges of his own race": p.79

[94] JDB Mitchell, "Government and Public Law in Scotland: Retrospect and Prospect" in JA Andrews (ed), *Welsh Studies in Public Law* (Cardiff: Cardiff University of Wales Press, 1970) pp.70–71; compare CMG Himsworth, "Public Law—in Peril of Neglect?" in Hector L MacQueen (ed), *Scots Law into the 21st Century: Essays in Honour of WA Wilson* (Edinburgh: W.Green, 1996) p.225; the principal exception is the line of authority beginning with *Duncan v Findlater* (1839) Macl. & R. 911 and ending with *Virtue v Alloa Police Commissioners* (1873) 1 R. 285.

[95] JDB Mitchell, "Government and Public Law in Scotland: Retrospect and Prospect" in JA Andrews (ed), *Welsh Studies in Public Law* (Cardiff: Cardiff University of Wales Press, 1970) p.71.

functional rather than historical."[96] The uncritical acceptance of the doctrine that "the king can do no wrong" was the most commonly cited example of unification being pursued beyond its proper limits. "I know of no authority for a claim of damages against Her Majesty's Government, or any public Department of Her Majesty's Government", Lord Young said in *Smith v Lord Advocate*.[97] Its effects, as illustrated in *Macgregor v Lord Advocate*, in which the Inner House held that the Crown's immunity in tort extended to Scotland, were only reversed by the Crown Proceedings Act 1947.

Scots law was to regain a greater sense of its separate identity after the Second **1–43** World War.[98] In *Glasgow Corporation v Central Land Board*[99] the House of Lords delivered what TB Smith called a "sharp repudiation" to "the erroneous belief that in constitutional questions Scots law must conform to that of England".[100] The Scots law of Crown privilege (now public interest immunity), the House of Lords held, was different from that of England. It would be quite wrong, the Appellate Committee added, to treat Scots law as having been determined on an English appeal

> "desirable though it may be that in matters of constitutional importance the law of the two countries should not differ, yet it would be clearly improper for this House to treat the law of Scotland as finally determined upon an English appeal unless the case arose upon the interpretation of a statute common to both countries".[101]

The possibility of difference having been asserted, however, Scots law has **1–44** largely continued to follow the example of English law in constitutional matters, but with the House of Lords—and latterly the UK Supreme Court— playing a more prominent role through its Scottish members in eliminating

---

[96] JDB Mitchell, "Government and Public Law in Scotland: Retrospect and Prospect" in JA Andrews (ed), *Welsh Studies in Public Law* (Cardiff: Cardiff University of Wales Press, 1970) p.71; see also JDB Mitchell, "The Merits of Disharmony" [1956] P.L. 6.

[97] *Smith v Lord Advocate* (1897) 25 R. 112, 123; TB Smith described it as a "dubious decision": TB Smith, *A Short Commentary on the Law of Scotland* (Edinburgh: W.Green, 1962) p.49.

[98] On the "Scottish legal renaissance" of the middle years of the twentieth century, see Ian D Willock, "The Scottish Legal Heritage Revisited" in John P Grant (ed), *Independence and Devolution: The Legal Implications for Scotland* (Edinburgh: W.Green, 1976) and Lindsay Farmer, "Under the Shadow over Parliament House: The Strange Case of Legal Nationalism" in Lindsay Farmer and Scott Veitch (eds), *The State of Scots Law: Law and Government after the Devolution Settlement* (London: Butterworths, 2001).

[99] *Glasgow Corporation v Central Land Board*, 1956 S.C. (HL) 1.

[100] TB Smith, *A Short Commentary on the Law of Scotland* (Edinburgh: W.Green, 1962) p.64.

[101] *Glasgow Corporation v Central Land Board*, 1956 S.C. (HL) 1, 9–10 (Viscount Simonds). Mitchell suggested that it had taken an English lawyer, Lord Radcliffe, "to extract and reaffirm the principles of Scots law": JDB Mitchell, "Government and Public Law in Scotland: Retrospect and Prospect" in JA Andrews (ed), *Welsh Studies in Public Law* (Cardiff: Cardiff University of Wales Press, 1970) p.71, but there was no lack of awareness on the part of the Inner House that Scots law before *Duncan v Cammell Laird* [1942] A.C. 624 had been different; see especially the opinion of Lord Russell: 1955 S.C. 64, 74–78. The crucial question was whether the Scottish courts were bound by *Duncan v Cammell Laird*. The change was reflected a decade later in the 1968 edn of *Gloag and Henderson*, which now read: "Decisions of the House of Lords in English appeals cannot be taken as universally binding in questions of constitutional law in Scotland": WM Gloag and R Candlish Henderson, *Introduction to the Law of Scotland*, 7th edn (Edinburgh: W.Green, 1968) p.1, citing *Glasgow Corporation v Central Land Board*, 1956 S.C. (HL) 1; the footnote continues: "see also *MacCormick v Lord Advocate*, 1953 S.C. 396, per Lord President Cooper at 411". The editors were Alastair M Johnston and JAD Hope, later Lord Hope of Craighead.

differences between the two jurisdictions.[102] The doctrinal traffic has not been all one way. In *Conway v Rimmer*[103] the House of Lords followed the example of Scots law as it had been finally decided in *Glasgow Corporation v Central Land Board*.[104] Regardless of the direction of travel, however, the abiding concern has been that there should be no material difference between the law of the two jurisdictions. "There are many chapters of the law where for historical and other reasons it is quite proper that the law should be different in the two countries", Lord Reid said *Conway v Rimmer*[105]:

> "But here we are dealing purely with public policy—with the proper relation between the powers of the executive and the powers of the courts—and I can see no rational justification for the law on this matter being different in the two countries."[106]

---

[102] *Lord Advocate v Dumbarton District Council* [1990] 2 A.C. 580 (Crown not bound by statute save by express words or necessary implication); *Davidson v Scottish Ministers* [2005] UKHL 74; 2006 S.C. (HL) 41 (Crown Proceedings Act 1947 s.21(1) does not prevent the grant of interdict or orders for specific performance against the Crown in judicial review proceedings); *Beggs v Scottish Ministers* [2005] CSIH 25; 2005 S.C. 342 (the Scottish Ministers in the same position as UK Ministers following *M v Home Office* [1994] 1 A.C. 377); *Axa General Insurance Ltd v Lord Advocate* [2011] UKSC 46; 2012 S.C. (UKSC) 122 (no difference in the law of standing between the two jurisdictions); *Eba v Advocate General for Scotland* [2012] UKSC 29; 2012 S.C. (UKSC) 1 (errors of law reviewable in Scots law as in English law). *Dumbarton District Council* and *Davidson* were both cases in which the House of Lords took a different view from the Inner House of the Court of Session.

[103] *Conway v Rimmer* [1968] A.C. 910.

[104] *Glasgow Corporation v Central Land Board*, 1956 S.C. (HL) 1.

[105] *Conway v Rimmer* [1968] A.C. 910, 938.

[106] "While the law of England and that of Scotland may differ in many respects it is really essential, in the interests of justice to Her Majesty's subjects in both parts of the United Kingdom, that the rules relating to Crown Privilege should be the same": *Conway v Rimmer* [1968] A.C. 910, 990 (Lord Upjohn). Mitchell regarded it as "almost inconceivable that the principles of public law should vary within one Kingdom": Kilbrandon Commission, *Report of the Royal Commission on the Constitution 1969–1973* (1973) Cmnd.5460, Volume 9 of the Written Evidence, p.140.

CHAPTER 2

THE SCOTLAND ACT

INTRODUCTION

In the second edition of *Constitutional Law*, published in 1968, Mitchell **2–01** recorded "much talk of devolution which would have substantial constitutional effects, as would British adhesion to the Treaty of Rome".[1] But whereas accession to the European Communities, now the European Union, was to take place within five years it was to take another 30 years before powers were devolved to Edinburgh. In this chapter we turn our attention to the devolution settlement set out in the Scotland Act 1998 ("the Scotland Act"). We concentrate on the origins and making of the devolution settlement; the status of the Scotland Act, in particular the question of its entrenchment against unilateral amendment or repeal by the UK Parliament at Westminster; and, finally, its amendment by the Scotland Act 2012, and as agreed by the Smith Commission following the independence referendum. The details of the Act's provisions, and the proposed amendments, are dealt with in subsequent chapters.

THE ROYAL COMMISSION ON THE CONSTITUTION

The roots of the devolution settlement are traceable to the report of the Royal **2–02** Commission on the Constitution ("the Kilbrandon Commission"),[2] which was appointed in 1969 in response to the growth in electoral support for nationalist parties in Scotland and Wales—the growth of nationalist support in Scotland had been dramatically underlined by the victory of the Scottish National Party at the Hamilton by-election in November 1967. Formally, the Commission was appointed "to examine the present functions of the central legislature and government in relation to the several countries, nations and regions of the United Kingdom" and to consider "whether any changes are desirable in those functions or otherwise in present constitutional and economic relationships". In reality, its task was "to examine regional alienation and disaffection in Great Britain and to recommend for or against some form of constitutional devolution for Scotland and Wales".[3]

The Commission was in no doubt that

> "the main intention behind our appointment was that we should investigate the case for transferring or devolving responsibility for the exercise of government functions from Parliament and the central government, to

---

[1] JDB Mitchell, *Constitutional Law*, 2nd edn (Edinburgh: W.Green, 1968) p.vii.
[2] Kilbrandon Commission, *Report of the Royal Commission on the Constitution 1969–1973* (1973) Cmnd.5460.
[3] Edward McWhinney, *Constitution-making: Principles, Process, Practice* (Toronto: University of Toronto Press, 1981) p.28.

new institutions of government in the various countries and regions of the United Kingdom".[4]

2–03 The Commission took as its starting point the causes of dissatisfaction with government. Most of the complaints of substance, it concluded, arose either from the centralisation of government in London or from developments in the operation of government "which have tended to run counter to the principles of democracy".[5] The latter included what was to become a familiar catalogue of the extent of executive dominance of the House of Commons, the lack of power and influence of backbench MPs, the growth of ad hoc bodies, the lack of opportunities for popular participation in decision-making, excessive secrecy, and the undermining of civil liberties. The Commission was at pains not to exaggerate the extent of the dissatisfaction; "[w]e do not wish to give the impression that we have found evidence of seething discontent throughout the land".[6] Nevertheless, its general impression was that,

"while the people of Great Britain as a whole cannot be said to be seriously dissatisfied with their system of government, they have less attachment to it than in the past, and there are some substantial and persistent causes of discontent which may contain the seeds of more serious trouble".[7]

2–04 In Scotland and Wales, the Commission reported, dissatisfaction with government was coloured by feelings of national identity. In Scotland there was particular criticism of administrative devolution and the lack of accountability of the Secretary of State.

"The more the Secretary of State's responsibilities are widened, the more evident it appears to informed people that a great deal of specifically Scottish administration is going on in Scotland over which the Scottish people have no direct influence".[8]

There were also complaints that Scots law was not "sufficiently understood in London or catered for in United Kingdom legislation".[9] While Scottish nationalism provided no evidence that the Scottish people as a whole wished to be separated from the rest of the UK, the nature and strength of the support it had attracted over the years suggested that

"a substantial body of people in Scotland would be likely to take a favourable view of a change to a system of government which did more that the present system to recognise their separate Scottish identity".[10]

---

[4] Kilbrandon Commission, *Report of the Royal Commission on the Constitution 1969–1973* (1973) Cmnd.5460, para.13.
[5] Kilbrandon Commission, *Report of the Royal Commission on the Constitution 1969–1973* (1973) Cmnd.5460, para.269.
[6] Kilbrandon Commission, *Report of the Royal Commission on the Constitution 1969–1973* (1973) Cmnd.5460, para.324.
[7] Kilbrandon Commission, *Report of the Royal Commission on the Constitution 1969–1973* (1973) Cmnd.5460, para.1102.
[8] Kilbrandon Commission, *Report of the Royal Commission on the Constitution 1969–1973* (1973) Cmnd.5460, para.363.
[9] Kilbrandon Commission, *Report of the Royal Commission on the Constitution 1969–1973* (1973) Cmnd.5460, para.1101.
[10] Kilbrandon Commission, *Report of the Royal Commission on the Constitution 1969–1973* (1973) Cmnd.5460, para.346.

The Commission went on to suggest some general principles to be borne in **2–05** mind in considering particular proposals for reform, chief among which was the need to preserve the unity of the UK.

"The essential political and economic unity of the United Kingdom is a long-established fact, and in our opinion it ought to be preserved. It follows that Parliament must continue to represent all parts of the United Kingdom and retain overriding power."[11]

Unity, however, did not necessarily mean uniformity.

"Within the United Kingdom there is considerable diversity, based on differences of history, tradition and culture, which is already reflected in different governmental arrangements. It is a source of strength and should continue to be respected."[12]

A second general principle was the need to preserve and foster the principle of democracy—"government by the people". Elected representatives should have real control. Where day-to-day control was impracticable, there should be a chain of accountability leading back to elected representatives.[13] Proposals for constitutional reform should also respect the "strong tradition of personal liberty".[14] And any reform should be one which was likely to be found acceptable:

"Constitutional arrangements, however attractive they may appear in theory, cannot be imposed against the will of the people with any real hope of success."[15]

The Commission identified three ways in which Westminster could transfer **2–06** powers to a "region": "separatism", which would involve the transfer of complete sovereignty in all matters, in effect creating an independent state; federalism, which would involve the transfer of sovereignty in certain matters only, with sovereignty being retained in other matters, such as defence and foreign affairs; and devolution, in which sovereignty would be retained in all matters, with the exercise of selected powers being "delegated" to the regions.[16] It rejected both separatism (the necessary political will for separation did not exist; the vast majority of people simply did not want it to happen)[17] and federalism (the UK was not an appropriate place for federalism and now was not an appropriate time)[18] in favour of devolution, which would provide for

---

[11] Kilbrandon Commission, *Report of the Royal Commission on the Constitution 1969–1973* (1973) Cmnd.5460, para.417.
[12] Kilbrandon Commission, *Report of the Royal Commission on the Constitution 1969–1973* (1973) Cmnd.5460, para.417.
[13] Kilbrandon Commission, *Report of the Royal Commission on the Constitution 1969–1973* (1973) Cmnd.5460, para.418.
[14] Kilbrandon Commission, *Report of the Royal Commission on the Constitution 1969–1973* (1973) Cmnd.5460, para.418.
[15] Kilbrandon Commission, *Report of the Royal Commission on the Constitution 1969–1973* (1973) Cmnd.5460, para.419.
[16] Kilbrandon Commission, *Report of the Royal Commission on the Constitution 1969–1973* (1973) Cmnd.5460, para.423.
[17] Kilbrandon Commission, *Report of the Royal Commission on the Constitution 1969–1973* (1973) Cmnd.5460, para.497.
[18] Kilbrandon Commission, *Report of the Royal Commission on the Constitution 1969–1973* (1973) Cmnd.5460, para.539.

"the exercise of government powers at the regional level while preserving to the central authorities full sovereignty and ultimate power in all matters".[19]

Devolution, the Commission thought, could do much to reduce the dissatisfaction with government which was its starting point.

"It would counter over-centralisation, and, to a lesser extent, strengthen democracy. It would be a response to national feeling in Scotland and Wales."[20]

2–07 Devolution was thus conceived as a means of giving Scotland and Wales a greater say in the running of their own affairs while at the same time preserving the unity of the UK—and the sovereignty of the Westminster Parliament. If government in the UK was to meet the present-day needs of the people, the Commission argued in rejecting federalism, it was necessary for "the undivided sovereignty of Parliament to be maintained. We believe that only within the general ambit of one supreme elected authority is it likely that there will emerge the degree of unity, co-operation and flexibility which common sense suggests is desirable".[21]

"There is no great demand in Scotland and Wales, and practically none at all in England, for such solutions (i.e. separatism and federalism), and we are convinced that the prosperity and good government of the people of all parts of the United Kingdom will be better served if political and economic unity, including the supreme authority of Parliament, is maintained."[22]

THE SCOTLAND ACT 1978

2–08 Under pressure from the continuing growth in electoral support for the nationalist parties in Scotland and Wales, the 1974 Labour Government embarked on the politically fraught process of implementing the Royal Commission's recommendations. Its first attempt failed when the guillotine motion on a combined Scotland and Wales Bill was defeated in the House of Commons on February 22, 1977. Its second attempt was more successful, in legislative terms at least, with separate Scotland and Wales Bills enacted the following year. As a result of a backbench amendment however—the "Cunningham amendment" after the Labour MP who moved it—the Scotland Act was not to come into effect without the approval of 40 per cent of the Scottish electorate voting in a referendum; if less than 40 per cent of the electorate voted Yes, or a majority of those voting voted No, the Secretary of State was to lay before Parliament a draft Order in Council for the repeal of the Act.[23] In the referendum on March

---

[19] Kilbrandon Commission, *Report of the Royal Commission on the Constitution 1969–1973* (1973) Cmnd.5460, para.1106.

[20] Kilbrandon Commission, *Report of the Royal Commission on the Constitution 1969–1973* (1973) Cmnd.5460, para.1102.

[21] Kilbrandon Commission, *Report of the Royal Commission on the Constitution 1969–1973* (1973) Cmnd.5460, para.539.

[22] Kilbrandon Commission, *Report of the Royal Commission on the Constitution 1969–1973* (1973) Cmnd.5460, para.542.

[23] Scotland Act 1978 s.85(2).

1, 1979 there was a small majority in favour of bringing the provisions of the
Act into effect, with 52 per cent of those who voted in favour and 48 per cent
against, but the 40 per cent requirement was not met, only 30 per cent of the
electorate having voted in favour. Defeat for the Labour Government followed
on a vote of confidence in the House of Commons on 28 March 1979, after the
SNP had withdrawn their support—the first government to have been defeated
on a vote of confidence since 1924—forcing a general election, which the
Conservatives under Margaret Thatcher won.[24]

THE SCOTTISH CONSTITUTIONAL CONVENTION

Administrative devolution assumed either a government with a majority of **2–09**
seats in Scotland, and hence a claim to be as much the government of Scotland
as of the rest of the UK, a condition that no Conservative government was to
satisfy after 1959, or else a government lacking such a majority but nevertheless sensitive to differences in political opinion within the UK. With the election of a Conservative government in 1979, and the effective breakdown of the
post-war consensus over the role of the state, the latter condition also ceased to
be satisfied. Diminishing electoral support and the pursuit of policies to which
a majority of political opinion in Scotland was opposed combined to fuel
demands for a Scottish Parliament—if only as a way of preventing a recurrence of Mrs Thatcher.

A Campaign for a Scottish Assembly was formed after the 1979 referendum to **2–10**
keep alive the case for Scottish self-government. Following the 1987 general
election, which saw the Conservatives win an overall majority at Westminster
but only 10 seats in Scotland (down from 22 in 1979), it invited a group to
draw up a report on the governance of Scotland, and to make recommendations. The group's report, *A Claim of Right for Scotland*, which was published
in July 1988, was highly critical of the government of Scotland,[25] and called
for a Constitutional Convention to be set up to draw up a scheme for a Scottish
Assembly.[26]

The Scottish Constitutional Convention, in which both the Scottish Labour **2–11**
Party and the Scottish Liberal Democrats took part, but not the Conservative
Party or SNP, was set up in the following year. At its inaugural meeting on
March 30, 1989 the Convention adopted the Claim of Right acknowledging
"the sovereign right of the Scottish people to determine the form of Government
best suited to their needs". Its purpose in doing so was to "root the Convention
solidly in" the supposedly "historical and historic Scottish constitutional principle that power is limited, should be dispersed, and is derived from the
people".[27]

---

[24] The Act was repealed by the Scotland Act (Repeal) Order 1979 (SI 1979/928).

[25] "However relatively superior the English constitution may have been a hundred and fifty
years ago, it is by modern standards fundamentally flawed. It is now acceptable only so far as
Governments in general and Prime Ministers in particular exercise restraint, show sensitivity and
do not drive the constitution to its limits. It is unrealistic to expect such qualities in every case and
they have been markedly absent recently": Owen Dudley Edwards (ed), *A Claim of Right for
Scotland* (Edinburgh: Polygon, 1989) para.6.7. The report is to be distinguished from the declaration of the same name adopted at the inaugural meeting of the Scottish Constitutional Convention
a year later.

[26] Owen Dudley Edwards (ed), *A Claim of Right for Scotland* (Edinburgh: Polygon, 1989).

[27] Scottish Constitutional Convention, *Scotland's Parliament, Scotland's Right* (1995) p.10.

2-12 The Convention's first report, *Towards Scotland's Parliament*, which was published 18 months later, set out initial proposals for a Scottish Parliament, which the Convention was confident would be implemented were Labour to win the next general election.[28] The Conservatives, however, won an unprecedented fourth successive general election in 1992, marginally increasing their Scottish representation by one seat.[29] The Convention's final report, *Scotland's Parliament, Scotland's Right*, published three years later, set out a more detailed scheme, which provided the basis for the devolution settlement enacted in 1998.

THE SCOTLAND ACT 1998

2-13 New Labour came to power in May 1997 committed to devolution as the "settled will of the Scottish people", but also to a referendum on devolution and the powers of the Scottish Parliament. A White Paper was published on July 24,[30] followed by a referendum on September 11, in which substantial majorities were secured both for devolution and for the conferral of limited tax-varying powers on the Scottish Parliament.[31] The decision to seek popular approval before legislating, rather than after as happened in 1979, was taken with a view to both easing the passage of the legislation and making it difficult to reverse

> "no Parliament can bind its successors but prior popular endorsement of a devolution settlement would be a strong basis for making the settlement stick: in practice it would be difficult to reverse it without a referendum producing a contrary result. And in 1996, with four general election defeats behind Labour, there was no expectation of the huge majority that was to come. A pre-legislative popular endorsement would ease the passage of the legislation in a Westminster Parliament where the majority might have been tight".[32]

2-14 Popular endorsement having been secured, the Scotland Bill was introduced in the House of Commons on December 17, 1997. With a huge parliamentary majority, and the people having spoken, its passage was considerably smoother than that of its predecessor 20 years before.[33] The Bill was enacted with a minimum of delay, receiving Royal Assent on November 19, 1998, and the first elections to the new Scottish Parliament were held in May of the following year.

---

[28] Kenyon Wright, *The People Say Yes: The Making of Scotland's Parliament* (Edinburgh: Argyll Publishing, 1997) pp.135–136.

[29] The Conservative Government's "Taking Stock" exercise, *Scotland in the Union: A Partnership for Good* (1993) Cm.2225, was a belated attempt to demonstrate that administrative devolution could be made to work notwithstanding the Government's lack of a majority in Scotland. Under its proposals the Scottish Grand Committee was effectively reconstituted as a "Parliament within Parliament", a Scottish House of Commons, but with no real increase in its powers; see CMG Himsworth, "The Scottish Grand Committee as an Instrument of Government" (1996) 1 Edin. L.R. 79.

[30] Scottish Office, *Scotland's Parliament* (1997) Cm.3658.

[31] 74.3 per cent of those voting agreed that there should be a Scottish Parliament, 63.7 per cent that it should have tax varying powers; the turnout was 60 per cent.

[32] Derry Irvine, "A Skilful Advocate" in Wendy Alexander (ed), *Donald Dewar: Scotland's first First Minister* (Edinburgh: Mainstream Publishing, 2005) pp.125–126.

[33] Barry K Winetrobe, "Enacting Scotland's 'Written Constitution': The Scotland Act 1998" (2011) 30 Parliamentary History 85.

Rather than listing the matters devolved to the Scottish Parliament at Holyrood, **2–15** with all other matters being reserved to the UK Parliament at Westminster, which was the approach adopted by its 1978 predecessor, the Scotland Act listed the matters reserved to Westminster with all other matters being devolved to Holyrood. Defence and national security, macro-economic policy, foreign affairs, immigration, broadcasting, energy, social security and pensions, and the constitution were reserved, leaving the "majority of domestic policy" in Scotland devolved, including health, education, justice, local government, housing, planning, economic development, transport, the environment, agriculture and fisheries, sport and the arts.[34] The devolution of power, in one observer's view, was on

> "a prodigious scale. There has probably never in any country been a greater voluntary handover of power by any national government to a subnational body within its own borders".[35]

The Scotland Act, however, was not to be the last word on the Scottish Parliament's powers.

THE SCOTLAND ACT AS FUNDAMENTAL LAW

The UK constitution has traditionally not drawn a distinction between funda- **2–16** mental laws and ordinary laws.[36] In *Thoburn v Sunderland City Council*,[37] however, Laws LJ suggested that the time had come to draw a distinction between constitutional statutes and ordinary statutes, a distinction endorsed by the UK Supreme Court in the *HS2* case.[38] In the former category he included the Scotland Act and the Government of Wales Act as well as the Magna Carta, the Bill of Rights 1689, "the Act of Union",[39] the Reform Acts, and the Human Rights Act. The significance of constitutional status, as proposed by Laws LJ, is to exclude the doctrine of implied repeal; if a constitutional statute is to be amended or repealed it can only be by express words and not by implication.[40] Might we go further, however, and argue that, as a constitutional statute, the Scotland Act is entrenched against the possibility of unilateral amendment or repeal? Such was the goal of the Scottish Constitutional Convention, which was adamant that

> "the powers of Scotland's Parliament, once established, should not be altered without the consent of the Scottish Parliament representing the people of Scotland".[41]

---

[34] Commission on Scottish Devolution, *Serving Scotland Better: Scotland and the United Kingdom in the 21st Century* (June, 2009) para.2.7.

[35] Anthony King, *The British Constitution* (Oxford: OUP, 2007) p.193.

[36] Albert V Dicey, *An Introduction to the Study of the Law of the Constitution*, 10th edn (London: Macmillan, 1959) p.89.

[37] *Thoburn v Sunderland City Council* [2002] EWHC 195; [2003] Q.B. 151 [62].

[38] *R (Buckinghamshire County Council) v Secretary of State for Transport* [2014] UKSC 3; [2014] 1 W.L.R. 324 [207]–[208] (Lord Neuberger and Lord Mance); on constitutional legislation, see David Feldman, "The nature and significance of 'constitutional' legislation" (2013) 129 L.Q.R. 343.

[39] There were both Scottish and English Acts of Union.

[40] In *BH v Lord Advocate* [2012] UKSC 24 [30], Lord Hope, with whom the rest of the court agreed, held that the fundamental constitutional nature of the settlement achieved by the Scotland Act rendered it incapable of being altered otherwise than by an express enactment.

[41] Scottish Constitutional Convention, *Scotland's Parliament, Scotland's Right* (1995) p.18.

2–17 This is of course the same argument as we encountered in relation to those provisions of the Acts of Union which it is argued the UK Parliament is powerless to alter. The difficulty here as there is the doctrine of the sovereignty of Parliament, which the Labour Government insisted was not affected by its proposals:

> "The UK Parliament is and will remain sovereign in all matters: but as part of the Government's resolve to modernise the British constitution Westminster will be choosing to exercise that sovereignty by devolving legislative responsibilities to a Scottish Parliament without in any way diminishing its own powers."[42]

Under the doctrine of parliamentary sovereignty as traditionally understood no Parliament can bind its successors.[43] Were it to be able to do so it would deprive them of the legislative sovereignty which is the hallmark of the Westminster Parliament. Although Parliament had chosen to exercise its sovereignty by devolving legislative responsibilities to a Scottish Parliament, a future parliament might choose to exercise its sovereignty by altering the Scottish Parliament's responsibilities or abolishing it altogether.

2–18 Such at least was the burden of the advice given to the Scottish Constitutional Convention, which was informed that "in theory under Britain's unwritten constitution" an Act of the Westminster Parliament establishing a Scottish Parliament "can be repealed or amended without restriction".[44] A number of ways were, in fact, suggested in which the entrenchment of the Act might be attempted, or its repeal or amendment made more difficult,[45] but the Government chose not to pursue these in the legislation. There is no requirement, for example, of the Scottish Parliament's consent or of some form of special majority for its amendment or repeal. Instead the Act included an unequivocal declaration that the conferral of law-making powers on the Scottish Parliament "does not affect the power of the Parliament of the UK to make laws for Scotland",[46] a declaration the Government defended as "an essential constitutional statement of the nature of the devolved settlement".[47]

2–19 One reason why the Government may have chosen not to try and entrench the Act is because it was no part of its intention that the sovereignty of the Westminster Parliament should be affected. Another may have been because it believed that any attempt to limit its sovereignty would have been legally ineffective; no Parliament could bind its successors, no matter what was said in the legislation. Any attempt to do so would also undoubtedly have complicated the parliamentary passage of the legislation. The inclusion of s.28(7), however,

---

[42] Scottish Office, *Scotland's Parliament* (1997) Cm.3658, para.4.2.

[43] *Vauxhall Estates Ltd v Liverpool Corporation* [1932] 1 K.B. 733; *Ellen Street Estates Ltd v Minister of Health* [1934] 1 K.B. 590. In Hart's terms, sovereignty is "continuing" rather than self-embracing or self-limiting: HLA Hart, *The Concept of Law*, 2nd edn (Oxford: OUP, 1969) pp.149–150.

[44] Scottish Constitutional Convention, *Scotland's Parliament, Scotland's Right* (1995) p.18.

[45] Colin Boyd, "Parliament and Courts: Powers and Dispute Resolution" in T StJ N Bates (ed), *Devolution to Scotland: The Legal Aspects* (Edinburgh: T &T Clark, 1997).

[46] Scotland Act 1998 s.28(7).

[47] "To sum up, we are setting about a devolved settlement—nothing more, nothing less. It is not the first step on the road to some other settlement, whether that be independence or federalism. It is a self-contained settlement, based on the principles of devolution. Essential to that is the recognition that sovereignty remains with the UK Parliament. The UK Parliament retains the ability to legislate on all matters, but it devolves the power to legislate, other than on reserved matters, to the Scottish parliament": House of Lords debate, July 21, 1998, Vol 592, col.799 (Lord Sewel).

which was strictly speaking unnecessary, suggests that the Government was at least as much concerned to reassure those who feared that devolution would lead to the break-up of the Union. The Lord Chancellor, Lord Irvine of Lairg, later described it as "an unpalatable reminder to Scotland thought necessary to assuage English sentiment".[48]

The fact that the Act is not entrenched as a matter of law does not mean that it **2–20** may not be entrenched in other ways. The Scottish Constitutional Convention was confident that "[t]he popularity and contribution of the Parliament, along with its purpose and relevance, would ensure its existence more than any constitutional or legal mechanism" and that "[n]o Westminster government would be willing to pay the political price of neutralising or destroying a parliament so firmly rooted in, and supported by, the people of Scotland",[49] views echoed by the Government which believed that "the popular support for the Scottish Parliament, once established, will make sure that its future in the UK constitution will be secure".[50]

Devolution and the independence referendum have vindicated those who saw **2–21** the essential guarantee of a Scottish Parliament as lying in the support of the Scottish people. Even before the independence referendum, the Scottish Parliament's abolition without Scottish consent was inconceivable—the constitutional debate was about Scotland's future as part of the UK, not about the Scottish Parliament as part of that future. As a matter of strict law the UK Parliament may retain the power to abolish the Scottish Parliament, but for all practical purposes that power is irrelevant.

What, however, of the Scottish Parliament's powers? Even if the Parliament **2–22** itself might not be abolished, might its powers be amended by the Westminster Parliament in the normal way? The Scotland Act is entrenched in all but minor respects against Holyrood.[51] Its amendment, therefore, is essentially a matter for Westminster. When the legislation was being enacted, however, the Government said that it expected

> "a convention to be established that Westminster would not normally legislate with regard to devolved matters in Scotland without the consent of the Scottish Parliament".[52]

---

[48] Derry Irvine, "A Skilful Advocate" in Wendy Alexander (ed), *Donald Dewar: Scotland's first First Minister* (Edinburgh: Mainstream Publishing, 2005) p.128. The Scotland Bill 1978 included a similar provision but it was removed by the House of Commons (House of Commons debate, November 22, 1977, Vol.939, col.1402), prompting Bogdanor to ask whether MPs displayed a better grasp of the political realities than the government at the time: "Devolution: The Constitutional Aspects" in Jack Beatson et al (ed), *Constitutional Reform in the United Kingdom: Practice and Principles* (Oxford: Hart Publishing, 1998) p.9.

[49] Scottish Constitutional Convention, *Scotland's Parliament, Scotland's Right* (1995) p.18.

[50] Scottish Office, *Scotland's Parliament* (1997) Cm.3658, para.4.2.

[51] Scotland Act 1998 Sch.4 para.4.

[52] House of Lords debate, July 2,1998, Vol.592, col.791 (Lord Sewel); what became known as the Sewel convention is restated in the Memorandum of Understanding with the devolved administrations, which in its current form states that "the UK Government will proceed in accordance with the convention that the UK Parliament would not normally legislate with regard to devolved matters except with the agreement of the devolved legislature": Cabinet Office, *Memorandum of Understanding and Supplementary Agreements between the United Kingdom Government, the Scottish Ministers, the Welsh Ministers, and the Northern Ireland Executive Committee* (October, 2013) para.14.

The "Sewel convention", as set out in the Memorandum of Understanding between the UK Government and the devolved administrations, extends to Westminster legislation altering the Scottish Parliament's legislative competence or the executive competence of the Scottish Ministers as well as Westminster legislation in the devolved areas. Although there is nothing in law to prevent Westminster from unilaterally altering the Scottish Parliament's powers, the expectation is that any changes to its powers will be made by agreement.[53] Such indeed has proved to be the case with the amendments made to the Act so far, including those made by the Scotland Act 2012.

THE SCOTLAND ACT 2012

2–23　The formation of a minority SNP Government at Holyrood in 2007 saw the emergence of rival constitutional reform projects. The first was the SNP's *National Conversation*,[54] which was to have been followed by a referendum on independence, which it was eventually forced to drop when it became clear that it could not secure a majority for the referendum legislation in the Scottish Parliament.[55] The second was the Commission on Scottish Devolution ("the Calman Commission"), which was set up by the opposition parties in the Scottish Parliament, with the support of the UK Government

> "to review the provisions of the Scotland Act 1998 in the light of experience and to recommend any changes to the present constitutional arrangements that would enable the Scottish Parliament to serve the people of Scotland better, improve the financial accountability of the Scottish Parliament, and continue to secure the position of Scotland within the United Kingdom".

In its final report, published in June 2009, the Calman Commission recommended that the financial accountability of the Scottish Parliament should be increased through the introduction of a Scottish rate of income tax, in partial replacement of UK income tax, that intergovernmental and interparliamentary relations should be improved, and that some (minor) adjustments should be made to the boundary between reserved and devolved matters.[56]

2–24　The Scotland Bill was introduced in the Westminster Parliament in November 2010 in implementation of the Commission's recommendations.[57] The Scottish

---

[53] The Sewel convention is careful not to exclude the possibility of amendments being made other than by agreement—it states that "the UK Parliament would not *normally* legislate with regard to devolved matters except with the agreement of the devolved legislature". While it is not difficult to imagine circumstances in which Westminster might legislate on a devolved matter in the absence of Scottish Parliament consent (e.g. in an emergency, or when the Scottish Parliament is in recess), it is much harder to imagine Westminster legislating against a Scottish Parliament refusal of consent (i.e. where a legislative consent motion was defeated) given the political backlash unilateral action would be almost certain to provoke. The Scotland Act 2012 (below) provided the first real test of the Act's de facto fundamental status. What was most striking about its enactment was the unwillingness of the UK Government to proceed other than on the basis of agreement.

[54] Scottish Government, *Choosing Scotland's Future: A National Conversation* (August, 2007).

[55] Scottish Government, *Your Scotland, Your Voice* (November, 2009) set out the Scottish Government's intention to hold a referendum in November 2010. A draft Referendum Bill was published in February 2010 but not proceeded with.

[56] Commission on Scottish Devolution, *Serving Scotland Better: Scotland and the United Kingdom in the 21st Century* (June, 2009).

[57] Its introduction was accompanied by a White Paper: Scotland Office, *Strengthening Scotland's Future* (2010) Cm.7937; for the outgoing Labour Government's proposals, see Scotland Office, *Scotland's Future in the United Kingdom: Building on Ten Years of Devolution* (2009) Cm.7738.

Parliament agreed to the consideration of the Bill by Westminster in accordance with the Sewel convention in March 2011, but held over the question of its final consent until the UK Government and Parliament had had an opportunity to consider the amendments proposed by the ad hoc Scotland Bill Committee which had examined the Bill at Holyrood.[58] Had the SNP not won an outright majority at the Scottish parliamentary elections in May 2011 it is likely that the Bill would have been enacted substantially as introduced—with the Scottish Parliament's consent. The outcome of the election, however, changed the balance of power in the Scottish Parliament. An SNP Government that had been in no position to prevent an opposition majority from seeking or agreeing to amending legislation now found itself able to threaten to withhold the Scottish Parliament's consent to the legislation unless it was amended to produce "a Bill that is worthy of the name"[59]—the name of course being "Scotland".

As to what was meant by a Bill worthy of the name, the Scottish Government **2–25** identified six areas in which it wanted to see the Bill strengthened: borrowing powers; corporation tax; excise duties; the Crown Estate; digital broadcasting; and a guaranteed voice in the European Union decision-making process. The Scottish Parliament also established a new Scotland Bill Committee to consider the case for the Parliament giving its consent to the Bill. Its report, published in December 2011, took an uncompromising line:

> "On the basis of all the evidence that we have heard, the responses from the UK Government to the amendments suggested by our predecessor and by others in this new Parliamentary session, the Committee . . . is unable to recommend that the Parliament approve a Legislative Consent Motion ("LCM") unless it is amended in line with the Committee's conclusions and recommendations."[60]

In its ambition the Scottish Government largely failed, although there were **2–26** important changes to the Bill in respect of its financial powers. What was most striking about the legislation, however, was not that the Scottish Government failed to secure the changes to the devolution settlement that it wanted, but that it successfully resisted those changes to which it was opposed: included in the Bill were a number of so called "technical" amendments that would have strengthened the UK Government's hand in dealings with the Scottish Government but which were dropped from the Bill as part of the agreement between the two governments over the terms on which the Scottish Parliament's consent would be forthcoming.[61] The Scottish Parliament's consent was

---

[58] The legislative consent motion read: "That the Parliament agrees that . . . the Bill be considered by the UK Parliament; invites the UK Government and the UK Parliament to consider the amendments and proposals made in the report of the Scotland Bill Committee, and looks forward to considering any amendments made to the Bill with a view to debating them in a further legislative consent motion before the Bill is passed for Royal Assent". The Scotland Bill Committee had earlier rejected a simple yes or no to the question of consent in favour of a process of dialogue between the different levels of government: "In a complex Bill of this sort, consent is not a simple yes/no distinction. It involves a process of dialogue between the different levels of government": Scotland Bill Committee 1st Report, *Report on the Scotland Bill and relevant legislative consent memoranda* (Scottish Parliamentary Paper 608, 2011) para.221.

[59] Scottish Parliament OR May 26, 2011, col.66 (Alex Salmond).

[60] Scotland Bill Committee 1st Report, *Report on the Scotland Bill Volume 1—Conclusions and Recommendations* (Scottish Parliamentary Paper 49, 2011) para.6.

[61] These included powers to refer individual provisions of Bills rather than a whole Bill to the Supreme Court and to implement international obligations within devolved competence concurrently with Scottish Ministers. Also dropped from the Bill because of the SNP Government's

eventually secured on April 18, 2012, following which the Bill completed its parliamentary stages at Westminster before being given Royal Assent on May 1, 2012.

THE INDEPENDENCE REFERENDUM

2–27 The Scotland Bill was unfinished business after the Scottish parliamentary elections in May 2011. The new item of business was the independence referendum, which had been put to one side for the purposes of the election. The SNP having won an outright majority on a manifesto commitment to hold a referendum in the "latter half" of the next session of the Scottish Parliament, it was accepted that there would now be a referendum, the only question being whether it was within the Scottish Parliament's legislative competence to legislate for a referendum, given that the Union between the Kingdoms of Scotland and England was a reserved matter.[62] In a consultation document published in January 2012, the UK Government questioned whether as a matter of law the Scottish Parliament had the power to authorise a referendum on independence, but offered to legislate to put the matter beyond doubt in return for referendum whose outcome was "legal, fair and decisive".[63]

> "We think it is in nobody's interests ... to have referendum process subject to legal challenge with all of the delay and uncertainty that would entail, and we are optimistic that we can reach a conclusion that will be fair and legitimate to both sides of the debate and people in Scotland as a whole."[64]

2–28 The Scottish Government replied with its own consultation in which it declared its readiness to work with the UK Government to remove its doubts about the Scottish Parliament's legislative competence, and put the referendum effectively beyond legal challenge, but at the same time insisted that any alteration to the Scottish Parliament's legislative competence should be made only with the consent of both Parliaments, and without conditions:

> "The Scottish Government's electoral mandate to hold a referendum is clear. It is for the Scottish Government to propose to the Scottish Parliament the timing and terms of the referendum and the rules under which it is to be conducted. The Scottish Parliament should decide these matters."[65]

In other words, the referendum should be "made in Scotland".

The Edinburgh Agreement

2–29 An agreement was eventually reached between the two governments to promote an Order in Council under s.30 of the Scotland Act to allow a single-question referendum on Scottish independence to be held before the end of

---

opposition in principle were the re-reservation provisions in respect of insolvency and the medical professions. The agreement between the two governments was set out in an exchange of letters between the Secretary of State for Scotland and the Cabinet Secretary for Parliamentary Business and Government Strategy annexed to the legislative consent memorandum on the Scotland Bill.

[62] Scotland Act 1998 Sch.5 Pt I para.5(b).
[63] Scotland Office, *Scotland's Constitutional Future* (2012) Cm.8203.
[64] Scotland Office, *Scotland's Constitutional Future* (2012) Cm.8203, Foreword.
[65] Scottish Government, *Your Scotland, Your Referendum* (January, 2012) Summary.

2014.[66] The Order would put it "beyond doubt" that the Scottish Parliament could legislate for that referendum. It would then be for the Scottish Government to promote legislation in the Scottish Parliament for a referendum on independence (which it did in the Scottish Independence Referendum (Franchise) Act 2013 and Scottish Independence Referendum Act 2013). In the memorandum of agreement, which together with the draft s.30 Order set out the details of the agreement, the two governments looked forward to a referendum that was "legal and fair, producing a decisive and respected outcome".[67] They also affirmed their commitment

> "to continue to work together constructively in the light of the outcome, whatever it is, in the best interests of the people of Scotland and of the rest of the United Kingdom".[68]

The referendum

In the referendum held on September 18, 2014, 55.3 per cent of the electorate **2–30** voted No and 44.7 per cent Yes in answer to the question: "Should Scotland be an independent country?", a wider margin of victory for the No side than had seemed likely in the closing stages of the campaign, but not so wide as to suggest that the question of Scotland's future within the UK had been settled once and for all. The turnout was an impressive 84.6 per cent.

THE SMITH COMMISSION AGREEMENT

In the referendum negotiations, the Scottish Government sought but failed to **2–31** secure a second question on the ballot paper on enhanced powers for the Scottish Parliament, as a way of ensuring, or so its critics claimed, that it did not emerge from the process empty handed in the event of a No vote.

> "While the Scottish Government's preferred policy is independence, it recognises that there is considerable support across Scotland for increased responsibilities for the Scottish Parliament short of independence . . . The Scottish Government has consistently made it clear . . . that it is willing to include a question on further devolution in the referendum. That remains the Scottish Government's position."[69]

The UK Government, however, was adamant that only once the question of Scotland's future within the UK had been settled could there be any consideration of more powers for the Scottish Parliament. In the final days of the referendum campaign, however, with the polls suddenly narrowing, the leaders of the three main political parties at Westminster "vowed" to deliver "extensive new powers" for the Parliament "by the process and according to the timetable agreed and announced by our three parties, starting on 19 September",[70] a vow that was widely regarded, rightly or wrongly, as having sealed victory for the No campaign.

---

[66] *Agreement between the United Kingdom Government and the Scottish Government on a referendum on independence for Scotland* (October, 2012).

[67] *Agreement between the United Kingdom Government and the Scottish Government on a referendum on independence for Scotland* (October, 2012) para.30.

[68] *Agreement between the United Kingdom Government and the Scottish Government on a referendum on independence for Scotland* (October, 2012) para.30.

[69] Scottish Government, *Your Scotland, Your Referendum* (January, 2012) pp.5–6.

[70] *Daily Record*, September 16, 2014.

2–32 On the morning of September 19, once the results of the referendum had become clear, the Prime Minister announced that Lord Smith of Kelvin had agreed to oversee a set of cross-party talks with the purpose of agreeing a package of new powers to be devolved to Holyrood. By its terms of reference, which were published on September 23, the Commission was required to

> "convene cross-party talks and facilitate an inclusive engagement process across Scotland to produce, by 30 November 2014, Heads of Agreement with recommendations for further devolution of powers to the Scottish Parliament. This process will be informed by a Command Paper to be published by 31 October and will result in the publication of draft clauses by 25 January. The recommendations will deliver more financial, welfare and taxation powers, strengthening the Scottish Parliament within the United Kingdom".

Over the course of the next five weeks, the Commission in which all five political parties in the Scottish Parliament including the SNP took part, reached agreement on a package of new powers,[71] confounding those who doubted whether any form of agreement could be reached in such a short space of time (but at the same time inviting the criticism that the question of further powers had not been properly thought through).

2–33 The "Smith Commission agreement" is made up of three "pillars". Pillar 1—"providing a durable but responsive constitutional settlement for the governance of Scotland"—represents the elusive holy grail of the devolution settlement since the Scotland Act 1998. The Commission agreed that the Scottish Parliament and Scottish Government should be made permanent ("UK legislation will state that the Scottish Parliament and Scottish Government are permanent institutions"),[72] and that the Sewel convention should be "put on a statutory footing".[73] The Scottish Parliament should also have "all powers" in relation to elections to the Scottish Parliament and local government elections in Scotland (but not in relation to Westminster or European elections), together with control over its composition and functioning.[74] Acknowledging the risk that a future Scottish Government might seek to amend the legislation to suit its own ends, the Commission agreed that, rather than being amendable by ordinary process of legislation, Scottish Parliament legislation amending the franchise, the electoral system or the number of constituency and regional members for the Scottish Parliament should require to be passed by a two-thirds or super-majority of the Scottish Parliament.[75]

2–34 Pillar 2—"delivering prosperity, a healthy economy, jobs, and social justice"—tackles the question of more powers for Holyrood, particularly in the field of welfare. The Commission agreed that the state pension should remain reserved, as should universal credit, which will replace the existing income-related benefits when it is fully implemented. The Scottish Ministers, however, should

---

[71] Smith Commission, *Report of the Smith Commission for further devolution of powers to the Scottish Parliament* (November 27, 2014).

[72] Smith Commission, *Report of the Smith Commission for further devolution of powers to the Scottish Parliament* (November 27, 2014) para.21.

[73] Smith Commission, *Report of the Smith Commission for further devolution of powers to the Scottish Parliament* (November 27, 2014) para.22.

[74] Smith Commission, *Report of the Smith Commission for further devolution of powers to the Scottish Parliament* (November 27, 2014) paras 23 and 26.

[75] Smith Commission, *Report of the Smith Commission for further devolution of powers to the Scottish Parliament* (November 27, 2014) para.27.

have the power to change the frequency of universal credit payments, and the Scottish Parliament power to vary the housing costs elements, including the under-occupancy charge or so-called "bedroom tax".[76] Outside universal credit, a number of benefits should be devolved, including attendance allowance, carers allowance, disability living allowance and personal independence payment.[77] Holyrood should also have the power to create new benefits in areas of devolved responsibility.[78]

Pillar 3—"strengthening the financial responsibility of the Scottish **2–35** Parliament"—takes up the question of the Parliament's responsibility for raising the money it spends from the point at which it was left by the Scotland Act 2012. The Commission agreed that Holyrood should have the power to set the rates of UK income tax and the thresholds at which these are paid for the non-savings and non-dividend income tax of Scottish taxpayers, but not the personal allowance[79]; that the first 10 percentage points of the standard rate of VAT raised in Scotland should be assigned to the Scottish Government's budget[80]; and that air passenger duty and the aggregates levy should be devolved.[81] The Commission also agreed that the devolution of further responsibility for taxation and public spending, including elements of the welfare system, should be accompanied by an "updated fiscal framework for Scotland, consistent with the overall UK fiscal framework".[82] That framework would include a number of aspects, including continuation of the Barnett formula; borrowing powers to reflect the additional economic risks, including volatility of tax revenues, the Scottish Government would have to manage when further financial responsibilities were devolved; and enhanced independent financial scrutiny.[83]

It was also agreed that nothing in the report prevented Scotland becoming an **2–36** independent country in the future should it so choose.[84]

Draft clauses were published in accordance with the timetable laid down on **2–37** January 22, 2015.[85] These will form the basis of a Scotland Bill to be brought forward by the next UK Government following the general election in May 2015. If the clauses are enacted in their published form, the Scottish Parliament and the Scottish Government will both be "recognised as a permanent part of the United Kingdom's constitutional arrangements",[86] conferring on them the same "in all time coming" status as was conferred on the Court of Session by

---

[76] Smith Commission, *Report of the Smith Commission for further devolution of powers to the Scottish Parliament* (November 27, 2014) paras 44–45.
[77] Smith Commission, *Report of the Smith Commission for further devolution of powers to the Scottish Parliament* (November 27, 2014) para.49.
[78] Smith Commission, *Report of the Smith Commission for further devolution of powers to the Scottish Parliament* (November 27, 2014) para.54.
[79] Smith Commission, *Report of the Smith Commission for further devolution of powers to the Scottish Parliament* (November 27, 2014) paras 76–77.
[80] Smith Commission, *Report of the Smith Commission for further devolution of powers to the Scottish Parliament* (November 27, 2014) para.84.
[81] Smith Commission, *Report of the Smith Commission for further devolution of powers to the Scottish Parliament* (November 27, 2014) paras 84 and 89.
[82] Smith Commission, *Report of the Smith Commission for further devolution of powers to the Scottish Parliament* (November 27, 2014) para.94.
[83] Smith Commission, *Report of the Smith Commission for further devolution of powers to the Scottish Parliament* (November 27, 2014) para.95.
[84] Smith Commission, *Report of the Smith Commission for further devolution of powers to the Scottish Parliament* (November 27, 2014) para.18.
[85] Scotland Office, *Scotland in the United Kingdom: An enduring settlement* (2015) Cm.8890.
[86] Draft cl.1 inserting new ss.1(1A) and 44(1A) in Scotland Act 1998.

the Acts of Union three centuries before (art.XIX). It will also be recognised that the Parliament of the UK "will not normally legislate with regard to devolved matters without the consent of the Scottish Parliament".[87] The repeal of s.28(7) of the Scotland Act, which affirms the continuing power of the UK Parliament to make laws for Scotland, was not canvassed during the Smith Commission process, but implementation of the Agreement will set the seal on a federal or near federal relationship between Scotland and the rest of the UK, in which the constitutional settlement cannot be amended or legislation enacted with regard to devolved matters without the Scottish Parliament's consent.

---

[87] Draft cl.2 inserting new s.28(8) in Scotland Act 1998.

CHAPTER 3

THE HUMAN RIGHTS ACT

INTRODUCTION

The Scotland Act 1998 ("the Scotland Act") was only one of a number of **3–01** constitutional reforms enacted by the 1997 Labour Government. The other reform with major significance for Scotland, as for the rest of the UK, was the Human Rights Act 1998 ("the HRA"), which was enacted in implementation of a manifesto commitment to "bring rights home" thus enabling individuals to enforce their rights under the European Convention on Human Rights ("ECHR") in proceedings before the domestic courts rather than having to take a case to the European Court of Human Rights ("ECtHR") in Strasbourg.[1] The Scottish Constitutional Convention had expected the Scottish Parliament to make special provision for the protection of fundamental rights and freedoms within Scots law. This would be best achieved through "adoption of a Charter, advancing clear principles and specifying the rights and freedoms held to be inviolable". The Convention expected the Charter to encompass and improve on prevailing international law and convention, including the ECHR, and to be firmly based on "Scottish traditions and values".[2] In the absence of the HRA, the Scottish Parliament would have been faced with making its own provision, or else leaving the protection of human rights to the common law, as would have continued to be the case across the rest of the UK. In the event the question of fundamental rights was dealt with on a UK-wide basis.[3]

THE CONVENTION RIGHTS

Section 1 of the HRA lists the "Convention rights", i.e. the rights and freedoms **3–02** guaranteed under the Convention that have effect for the purposes of the Act.[4] They are: the right to life (art.2); freedom from torture or inhuman or degrading treatment or punishment (art.3); freedom from slavery and forced labour (art.4); the right to liberty and security of the person (art.5); the right to a fair trial (art.6); no punishment without law (art.7); the right to respect for private and family life (art.8); freedom of thought, conscience and religion (art.9);

---

[1] Home Office, *Rights Brought Home: The Human Rights Bill* (1997) Cm.3782.

[2] Scottish Constitutional Convention, *Scotland's Parliament, Scotland's Right* (1995) p.20.

[3] There is an extensive literature. The fullest Scottish treatment is to be found in Robert Reed and Jim Murdoch, *Human Rights Law in Scotland*, 3rd edn (London: Bloomsbury Professional, 2011); see also Richard Clayton and Hugh Tomlinson (eds), *The Law of Human Rights*, 2nd edn (Oxford: OUP, 2009) and Lord Lester of Herne Hill, Lord Pannick and Javan Herberg (eds), *Human Rights Law and Practice*, 3rd edn (London: LexisNexis, 2009).

[4] Strictly speaking, the Human Rights Act 1998 ("HRA") gives "further effect to" rather than "incorporates" the rights and freedoms guaranteed under the Convention. The difference between incorporating and giving further effect was summarised by the Lord Chancellor thus: "We have sought to protect the human rights of individuals against the abuse of power by the state, broadly defined, rather than to protect them against each other. That is the only practical difference between the full incorporation of the convention rights into our domestic law and the actual effect of the Bill": House of Lords debate, February 5, 1998, Vol.585, col.840.

freedom of expression (art.10); freedom of assembly and association (art.11); the right to marry and found a family (art.12); freedom from discrimination in the enjoyment of Convention rights (art.14); the right to property (art.1 of Protocol No.1); the right to education (art.2 of Protocol No.1); the right to free elections (art.3 of Protocol No.1); and the abolition of the death penalty (art.1 of Protocol No.13).[5] The principal omission is art.13 of the Convention, which guarantees the right to an effective remedy, on the argument that the HRA itself provides an effective remedy for infringements of Convention rights.

3–03   Section 2 of the HRA requires a court or tribunal determining a question which has arisen in connection with a Convention right to "take into account" any judgment, decision, declaration or advisory opinion of the ECtHR, so far as, in the opinion of the court or tribunal, it is relevant to the proceedings in which the question has arisen.[6] This duty, which applies to Scottish courts and tribunals in the same way as it applies to other UK courts and tribunals, may be contrasted with the duty imposed on the courts under the European Communities Act 1972 to determine questions of EU law "in accordance with" the principles laid down by and any relevant decisions of the European Court of Justice.[7] Although the courts are not therefore bound by decisions of the ECtHR, the House of Lords held soon after the Act came into force that, "in the absence of some special circumstances", they should nevertheless follow any "clear and constant" jurisprudence of the Strasbourg Court.[8]

> "This reflects the fact that the Convention is an international instrument, the correct interpretation of which can be authoritatively expounded only by the Strasbourg court. From this it follows that a national court subject to a duty such as that imposed by section 2 should not without strong reason dilute or weaken the effect of the Strasbourg case law."[9]

3–04   This does not mean, the Supreme Court has recently made clear, that it is bound to follow every decision of the ECtHR.

> "Not only would it be impractical to do so: it would sometimes be inappropriate, as it would destroy the ability of the court to engage in the constructive dialogue with the European court which is of value to the development of Convention law . . . Of course, we should usually follow a clear and constant line of decisions by the European court . . . But we are not actually bound to do so or (in theory, at least) to follow a decision of the Grand Chamber . . . Where, however, there is a clear and constant line of decisions whose effect is not inconsistent with some fundamental substantive or procedural aspect of our law, and whose reasoning does not appear to overlook or misunderstand some argument or point of principle, we consider that it would be wrong for this court not to follow that line."[10]

---

[5] The rights are set out in Sch.1 to the HRA.

[6] HRA 1998 s.2(1).

[7] European Communities Act 1972 s.3(1).

[8] *R (Alconbury Developments Ltd) v Secretary of State for the Environment, Transport and the Regions* [2001] UKHL 23; [2003] 2 A.C. 295 [26] (Lord Slynn); *R (Ullah) v Special Adjudicator* [2004] UKHL 26; [2004] 2 A.C. 323 [20] (Lord Bingham).

[9] *R (Ullah) v Special Adjudicator* [2004] UKHL 26; [2004] 2 A.C. 323 [20] (Lord Bingham).

[10] *Manchester City Council v Pinnock (Nos 1 and 2)* [2010] UKSC 45; [2011] 2 A.C. 104 [48] (Lord Neuberger). For criticism of the approach taken by the courts to the s.2 obligation, see Lord Irvine of Lairg, "A British Interpretation of Convention Rights" [2012] P.L. 237, and for a reply: Sir Philip Sales, "Strasbourg Jurisprudence and the Human Rights Act: A Response to Lord Irvine" [2012] P.L. 253.

Following Strasbourg is one thing, going beyond Strasbourg another. The **3–05** House of Lords also held at an early stage that the courts should not go further than, or "leap beyond", what the Strasbourg jurisprudence requires.

> "It is of course open to member states to provide for rights more generous than those guaranteed by the Convention, but such provision should not be the product of interpretation of the Convention by national courts, since the meaning of the Convention should be uniform throughout the states party to it. The duty of national courts is to keep pace with the Strasbourg jurisprudence as it evolves over time: no more, but certainly no less."[11]

The "mirror principle", as formulated by the House of Lords, has been subject **3–06** to some criticism.

> "In practice, this self-abnegating stance means that our domestic courts regard any claim which relies upon Convention rights as bound to fail unless the claimant can point to a 'clear and constant' line of Strasbourg jurisprudence which vindicates his case."[12]

In defence of the principle it is argued that, in the absence of any ECHR equivalent of the preliminary ruling procedure in EU law, it keeps open the possibility of a dialogue between the domestic courts and Strasbourg over the meaning of Convention rights. An individual who feels that the domestic court has not gone far enough in its interpretation of the Convention rights can always apply to Strasbourg. A public authority that feels that the domestic court has gone too far, on the other hand, has no right of application, thus ruling out the possibility of any dialogue between the domestic courts and Strasbourg over the correct interpretation of the Convention rights. It is better, therefore, the argument runs, for the domestic courts to err on the side of caution in interpreting Convention rights.[13]

LEGISLATION AND CONVENTION RIGHTS

The HRA gives further effect to the Convention rights in domestic law in **3–07** three main ways. First, s.3 of the Act requires all legislation, both primary and secondary, to be read and given effect in a way which is compatible with the Convention rights, "so far as it is possible to do so".[14] Secondly, the Act makes it unlawful for public authorities (including courts and tribunals) to act in a way that is incompatible with the Convention rights.[15] And thirdly, it makes the Convention rights enforceable in proceedings before the domestic courts.[16]

As to the first, the s.3 obligation of consistent interpretation applies to Scottish **3–08** courts and tribunals in the same way as it applies to other UK courts and

---

[11] *R (Ullah) v Special Adjudicator* [2004] UKHL 26; [2004] 2 A.C. 323 [20] (Lord Bingham); in *R (Al-Skeini) v Secretary of State for Defence* [2007] UKHL 26; [2008] 1 A.C. 153 [106] Lord Brown suggested that the last sentence could as well have ended: "no less, but certainly no more ... ".

[12] Lord Irvine of Lairg, "A British Interpretation of Convention Rights" [2012] P.L. 237, 249.

[13] Sir Philip Sales, "Strasbourg Jurisprudence and the Human Rights Act: A Response to Lord Irvine" [2012] P.L. 253, 262–266.

[14] HRA 1998 s.3(1).

[15] HRA 1998 s.6(1).

[16] HRA 1998 s.7(1)(a).

tribunals. It also applies to Scottish legislation, i.e. legislation made by the
Scottish Parliament or by the Scottish Ministers, in the same way as it applies
to other UK legislation.[17]

3–09   The s.3 obligation has been described as "a new and powerful tool of
interpretation".[18] Before "incorporation" the courts were prepared to take the
Convention into account in interpreting legislation but only for the purpose of
resolving legislative ambiguities.[19] Where they were faced with a statute the
meaning of which was plain, they regarded themselves as bound to give effect
to it, even though the results would be incompatible with the Convention.
Now, however, they are enjoined by s.3 to interpret legislation "so as to uphold
the Convention rights unless the legislation itself is so clearly incompatible
with the Convention that it is impossible to do so".[20]

> "Even if, construed according to the ordinary principles of interpretation,
> the meaning of the legislation admits of no doubt, section 3 may nonethe-
> less require the legislation to be given a different meaning."[21]

3–10   Although the interpretative obligation imposed by s.3 is a powerful one, it is
not without its limits; "inherent in the use of the word 'possible' in section 3(1)
is the idea that there is a Rubicon which courts may not cross".[22] Section 3 does
not require compatibility to be established at all costs; it is a "strong canon of
construction", not a "supplanting mechanism".[23] The role of the courts under
s.3 remains one of interpretation: it does not extend to law making, difficult
though it may be sometimes to distinguish between law making and
interpretation.

> "In applying section 3 courts must be ever mindful of this outer limit. The
> Human Rights Act reserves the amendment of primary legislation to
> Parliament. By this means the Act seeks to preserve parliamentary sover-
> eignty. The Act maintains the constitutional boundary. Interpretation of
> statutes is a matter for the courts; the enactment of statutes, and the
> amendment of statutes, are matters for Parliament."[24]

---

[17] The Scotland Act 1998 ("SA 1998") s.101(2) requires Scottish legislation that could be read
in such a way as to be outside competence to be read as narrowly as is required for it to be within
competence, if such a reading is possible, and to have effect accordingly. On the relationship
between s.101(2) and s.3(1) of the HRA, see *DS v HM Advocate*, 2007 S.C. (P.C.) 1 [23]–[24]
(Lord Hope): where the claim is that a provision is incompatible with Convention rights "[t]he
proper starting point is to construe the legislation as directed by s.3(1) of the Human Rights Act. If
it passes this test, so far as Convention rights are concerned it will be within competence".
[18] Lord Irvine of Lairg, "The Impact of the Human Rights Act: Parliament, the Courts and the
Executive" [2003] P.L. 319.
[19] *R v Secretary of State for the Home Department Ex p. Brind* [1991] 1 A.C. 696. The Scottish
judiciary were much slower to adopt this approach than their English counterparts, partly as a
consequence of the dismissive approach to the Convention taken by Lord Ross in *Kaur v Lord
Advocate*, 1980 S.C. 319, 328: "If the Convention does not form part of the municipal law, I do not
see why the Court should have regard to it at all"; see too *Moore v Secretary of State for Scotland*,
1985 S.L.T. 38. It was not until *T, Petitioner*, 1997 S.L.T. 724 that Scots law was brought into line
with that of the rest of the UK.
[20] Home Office, *Rights Brought Home: The Human Rights Bill* (1997) Cm.3782, para.2.7.
[21] *Ghaidan v Godin Mendoza* [2004] UKHL 30; [2004] 2 A.C. 557 [29] (Lord Nicholls).
[22] *Ghaidan v Godin Mendoza* [2004] UKHL 30; [2004] 2 A.C. 557 [49] (Lord Steyn).
[23] *R (Wooder) v Feggetter and Mental Health Act Commission* [2002] EWCA Civ 554; [2003]
Q.B. 219 [48] (Sedley LJ).
[24] *Re S (Minors) (Care Order: Implementation of Care Plan)* [2002] UKHL 10; [2002] 2 A.C.
291 [39] (Lord Nicholls); see to the same effect Lord Woolf CJ in *Poplar Housing and Regeneration
Community Association Ltd v Donoghue* [2001] EWCA Civ 595; [2002] Q.B. 48 [75], and Lord
Hope in *R v Lambert* [2001] UKHL 37; [2002] 2 A.C. 545 [79]–[81].

With this outer limit in mind, the House of Lords said that, while the actual **3–11**
language of a statute, as distinct from the concept expressed in that language,
is not necessarily determinative of its meaning, Parliament

> "cannot have intended that in the discharge of this extended interpretative
> function the courts should adopt a meaning inconsistent with a funda-
> mental feature of legislation. That would be to cross the constitutional
> boundary section 3 seeks to demarcate and preserve. Parliament has
> retained the right to enact legislation in terms which are not Convention-
> compliant. The meaning imported by application of section 3 must be
> compatible with the underlying thrust of the legislation being construed
> . . . Nor can Parliament have intended that section 3 should require courts
> to make decisions for which they are not equipped. There may be several
> ways of making a provision Convention-compliant, and the choice may
> involve issues calling for legislative deliberation".[25]

Nor does the interpretative obligation imposed by s.3 mean that the normal **3–12**
canons of statutory interpretation cease to apply. It is only where the interpretation of the legislation in the normal way yields a meaning incompatible with
the Convention rights that the s.3 obligation comes into play.[26]

Declarations of incompatibility

What happens where legislation cannot be interpreted compatibly with the **3–13**
Convention rights? The answer depends on whether the legislation is primary
or subordinate. Primary legislation in this context includes Acts of the UK
Parliament but not Acts of the Scottish Parliament,[27] it having been decided
that the Scottish Parliament should have no power to legislate incompatibly
with the Convention rights.[28] Where the legislation is primary, the higher
courts, including in Scotland the High Court of Justiciary sitting as a court of
criminal appeal, and the Court of Session, are limited to making a declaration
of incompatibility, which essentially puts the executive on notice that in the
court's opinion the legislation does not reflect the UK's obligations under the
Convention. As with devolution, the intention was that the principle of parliamentary sovereignty should not be affected.

> "To make provision . . . for the courts to set aside Acts of Parliament
> would confer on the judiciary a general power over decisions of Parliament
> which under our present constitutional arrangements they do not possess,
> and which would be likely on occasion to draw the judiciary into serious
> conflict with Parliament."[29]

There was, the White Paper continued, "no evidence to suggest that they desire
this power, nor that the public wish them to have it".[30] An Act in respect of

---

[25] *Ghaidan v Godin Mendoza* [2004] UKHL 30; [2004] 2 A.C. 55 [31]–[33] (Lord Nicholls).
Compare *Principal Reporter v K* [2010] UKSC 56; 2011 S.L.T. 271, in which the Supreme Court
read additional words into the Children (Scotland) Act 1995 to render it Convention-compliant,
with *Smith v Scott* [2007] CSIH 9; 2007 S.C. 345, in which the Registration Appeal Court declined
to "read down" s.3(1) of the Representation of the People Act 1983 so as to modify the blanket ban
on prisoner voting.
[26] *ANS v ML* [2012] UKSC 30; 2013 S.C. 20 [15]–[16] (Lord Reed).
[27] HRA 1998 s.21(1).
[28] See below, para.3–17.
[29] Home Office, *Rights Brought Home: The Human Rights Bill* (1997) Cm.3782, para.2.13.
[30] Home Office, *Rights Brought Home: The Human Rights Bill* (1997) Cm.3782, para.2.13.

which a declaration of incompatibility has been made thus remains in full force and effect until such time as it is amended to bring it into line with the Convention.[31]

3–14 Striking down subordinate legislation on the other hand normally involves no challenge to parliamentary sovereignty.

> "The courts can already strike down or set aside secondary legislation when they consider it to be outside the powers conferred by the statute under which it is made, and it is right that they should be able to do so when it is incompatible with Convention rights and could have been framed differently."[32]

Subordinate legislation which cannot be read compatibly with Convention rights accordingly falls to be struck down unless the court is satisfied that it is "inevitably incompatible", i.e. that the primary legislation under which it is made prevents removal of the incompatibility, in which case it may make a declaration of incompatibility.[33] Absent this saving, the freedom of the UK Parliament to enact or maintain incompatible legislation would be at an end.

3–15 Faced with a declaration of incompatibility, it is open to the executive to do nothing, leaving the individual with no choice but to seek a ruling from the ECtHR that the UK is in breach of its obligations under the Convention. In practice, almost all declarations of incompatibility have been remedied.[34] The exception is the blanket ban on prisoner voting,[35] which was first held to be contrary to art.3 of the First Protocol in *Hirst v UK (No.2)*.[36] A parliamentary joint committee has recommended the introduction of legislation conferring the right to vote on prisoners serving sentences of 12 months or less, but legislation to give effect to this recommendation has yet to be introduced.[37]

Remedial orders

3–16 The HRA establishes a fast track procedure for amending legislation which is declared to be incompatible with the Convention rights. Section 10 of the HRA empowers Ministers to make by order such amendments to legislation that has been declared to be incompatible, or whose incompatibility is to be inferred from a decision of the European Court in proceedings against the UK, as are considered necessary to remove the incompatibility.[38] In practice, remedial orders are rarely used. Most declarations of incompatibility have been reme-

---

[31] HRA 1998 s.4(6).

[32] Home Office, *Rights Brought Home: The Human Rights Bill* (1997) Cm.3782, para.2.15.

[33] HRA 1998 s.4(4).

[34] Ministry of Justice, *Responding to human rights judgments: Report to the Joint Committee on Human Rights on the Government response to human rights judgments 2013–2014* (2014) Cm.8962.

[35] Representation of the People Act 1983 s.3.

[36] *Hirst v UK (No.2)* (2005) 42 E.H.R.R. 849; the Grand Chamber confirmed its judgment in *Hirst* in *Scoppola v Italy (No.3)* (2012) 56 E.H.R.R. 663. The Registration Appeal Court made a declaration of incompatibility in *Smith v Scott* [2007] CSIH 9; 2007 S.C. 345. In *R (Chester) v Secretary of State for Justice* and *McGeoch v Lord President of the Council* [2013] UKSC 63; [2013] 3 W.L.R. 1076, the Supreme Court declined to make a further declaration of incompatibility.

[37] Joint Committee on the Draft Voting Eligibility (Prisoners) Bill, *Draft Voting Eligibility (Prisoners) Bill* (2013–2014, HL 103, HC 924).

[38] The power falls to be exercised by the Scottish Ministers in relation to Westminster legislation in the devolved areas: SA 1998 s.53.

died by primary legislation, with only three so far having been remedied by a s.10 order.[39]

Acts of the Scottish Parliament

Sauce for the Westminster goose under the Human Rights Act is not sauce for **3–17** the Holyrood gander. The declaration of incompatibility procedure does not apply to Acts of the Scottish Parliament, which are treated as subordinate legislation for the purposes of the Act.[40] In *Bringing Rights Home*, the Government explained that it had decided that the Scottish Parliament should have no power to legislate in a way which was incompatible with the Convention. It would, therefore, be possible to challenge such legislation in the Scottish courts on the ground that the Scottish Parliament had incorrectly applied its powers. If the challenge was successful the legislation would be held to be unlawful.[41] An Act of the Scottish Parliament that cannot be interpreted compatibly with the Convention rights accordingly falls to be struck down as outwith the legislative competence of the Scottish Parliament rather than being made the subject of a declaration of incompatibility.[42]

The Scottish Ministers have access to the remedial power under the Human **3–18** Rights Act for the purpose of amending Westminster legislation in the devolved areas which is incompatible with the Convention rights. In the Convention Rights Compliance (Scotland) Act 2001, however, they took their own remedial power, modelled on the power conferred on UK Ministers by s.107 of the Scotland Act 1998.[43] In contrast to the power conferred by the Human Rights Act, the exercise of this power is not conditional on a declaration of incompatibility or an equivalent finding by the ECtHR in proceedings against the UK. It may also be used to remedy administrative as well as legislative incompatibilities.[44]

PUBLIC AUTHORITIES AND CONVENTION RIGHTS

The second way in which the HRA gives further effect to the Convention rights **3–19** in domestic law is by requiring public authorities to act compatibly with those rights: s.6 of the Act makes it unlawful for public authorities (including courts and tribunals) to act in a way that is incompatible with the Convention rights.[45] From a Scottish perspective, the primary significance of this requirement is

---

[39] Ministry of Justice, *Responding to human rights judgments: Report to the Joint Committee on Human Rights on the Government response to human rights judgments 2013–2014* (2014) Cm.8962, Annex A.

[40] HRA 1998 s.21(1).

[41] Home Office, *Rights Brought Home: The Human Rights Bill* (1997) Cm.3782, para.2.21.

[42] Although the Human Rights Act includes a saving for "inevitably incompatible" subordinate legislation, it is not thought that an Act of the Scottish Parliament could benefit from this saving as there is nothing in the Scotland Act that would prevent the Scottish Parliament from removing any incompatibility: Iain Jamieson, "Relationship between the Scotland Act and the Human Rights Act" 2001 S.L.T. (News) 43, para.4.2.

[43] Convention Rights Compliance (Scotland) Act 2001 s.12.

[44] The power was exercised in the making of the Sexual Offences Act 2003 (Remedial) (Scotland) Order 2010 (SSI 2010/370), and Sexual Offences Act 2003 (Remedial) (Scotland) 2011 (SSI 2011/45), and the Agricultural Holdings (Scotland) Act 2003 Remedial Order 2014 (SSI 2014/98). On the HRA s.107 power, see para.9–34.

[45] HRA 1998 s.6(1); as public authorities, the courts must not act incompatibly with Convention rights when adjudicating in disputes between private individuals. The Act may therefore have an indirect effect on the obligations of individuals notwithstanding the fact that it does not bear directly on private individuals.

that it reaches the parts of the governance of Scotland the Scotland Act does not reach. Under the Scotland Act neither the Scottish Parliament nor the Scottish Government has the power to act incompatibly with Convention rights.[46] What s.6 of the HRA does is to extend the obligation to act compatibly with Convention rights to other public authorities in Scotland.

3–20 The obligation to act compatibly with Convention rights is not confined to "obvious" or "core" public authorities such as government departments, local authorities, the police and armed forces,[47] which must comply with the Convention rights across the whole range of their activities. Recognising that public functions may be carried out by private as well as public bodies, it also applies to functional or hybrid public authorities, which exercise a mixture of public and private functions— "any person certain of whose functions are functions of a public nature" in the language of the HRA[48]—but only in respect of acts done in pursuance of those functions and not acts of a private nature.[49] A private security firm would therefore be exercising public functions when running a prison but not when guarding commercial premises.

3–21 The intention behind extending the obligation to act compatibly with Convention rights to "functional" public authorities was that individuals should not be denied the protection of those rights as a result, for example, of the outsourcing of public functions by public authorities. The difficulty is that there is no universally agreed test of the public nature of a function, only a range of factors that may be taken into account, including

> "the extent to which in carrying out the relevant function the body is publicly funded, or is exercising statutory powers, or is taking the place of central government or local authorities, or is providing a public service".[50]

The difficulty was underlined in *YL v Birmingham City Council*,[51] in which the House of Lords held by a majority three to two that a private care home, providing care and accommodation under a contract with a local authority, which was under a statutory duty to arrange care and accommodation, was not performing functions of a public nature. Its decision was subsequently reversed by statute.[52] The effective scope of the obligation to comply with the Convention rights once the familiar territory of "obvious" public authorities is left behind, however, is far from clear.

Exceptions

3–22 The obligation to act compatibly with the Convention rights is not an absolute one, but subject to any limitations maintained or imposed in the exercise of the continuing sovereignty of the UK Parliament. A public authority does not act unlawfully therefore if, as the result of one or more provisions of primary legislation, it "could not have acted differently".[53] "Primary legislation" in this

---

[46] SA 1998 ss.29, 53 and 57(2).
[47] *Aston Cantlow and Wilmcote with Billesley Parochial Church Council v Wallbank* [2003] UKHL 37; [2004] 1 A.C. 546 [7] (Lord Nicholls).
[48] HRA 1998 s.6(3)(b).
[49] HRA 1998 s.6(5).
[50] *Aston Cantlow and Wilmcote with Billesley Parochial Church Council v Wallbank* [2003] UKHL 37; [2004] 1 A.C. 546 [12] (Lord Nicholls).
[51] *YL v Birmingham City Council* [2007] UKHL 27; [2008] 1 A.C. 98.
[52] Health and Social Care Act 2008 s.145(1).
[53] HRA 1998 s.6(2)(a).

context includes Acts of the UK Parliament but not Acts of the Scottish Parliament, which as we have seen are treated as a species of subordinate legislation for the purposes of the Act.[54] A public authority also does not act unlawfully if it is giving effect to or enforcing primary legislation "which cannot be read or given effect in a way which is compatible with the Convention rights".[55] As with primary legislation that requires public authorities to act in a way that is incompatible with the Convention rights, the intention is that incompatible primary legislation should continue to be given effect and enforced until such time as it is amended to bring it into line with the Convention.

An "act" for the purposes of these exceptions includes a failure to act,[56] recog-   **3–23** nising that rights can be infringed by omissions as well as by positive acts. A failure to act, however, does not include a failure to "introduce in, or lay before, Parliament a proposal for legislation; or to make any primary legislation or remedial order".[57] It is for the executive, therefore, to decide whether and on what terms to introduce remedial legislation; it cannot be compelled to do so.

ENFORCING CONVENTION RIGHTS

The final way in which the HRA gives further effect to the Convention rights,   **3–24** and the starting point for its enactment, is by making them enforceable in proceedings before the domestic courts. The Act thus enables a person who claims that a public authority has acted, or proposes to act, incompatibly with the Convention rights to bring proceedings against the authority in the appropriate court or tribunal,[58] or to rely on Convention rights "in any legal proceedings".[59] The latter enables Convention rights to be invoked in defence to criminal or civil proceedings as well as in, for example, proceedings for judicial review.

A person can rely on Convention rights, however, only if the person would be   **3–25** a victim of the act for the purposes of art.34 ECHR if proceedings in respect of the act were brought in the ECtHR.[60] This is a narrower test of standing than the test that applies for the purpose of judicial review proceedings in English law; a key difference is that the ECtHR has not been prepared to allow cases to be brought by representative bodies or pressure groups such as Greenpeace or the Child Poverty Action Group unless they themselves are victims of a breach of their Convention rights. Whether it is a narrower test than the test applied in Scots law is less clear. The Scots law on standing has recently been brought into line with English law, but whether it will prove to be as generous in practice as English law remains to be seen.[61]

---

[54] HRA 1998 s.21(1).
[55] HRA 1998 s.6(2)(b).
[56] HRA 1998 s.6(6).
[57] HRA 1998 s.6(6).
[58] HRA 1998 s.7(1)(a); see the Human Rights Act (Jurisdiction) (Scotland) Rules 2000 (SSI 2000/301).
[59] HRA 1998 s.7(1)(b).
[60] HRA 1998 s.7(1), (3), (4).
[61] *Axa General Insurance v Lord Advocate* [2011] UKSC 46; 2012 S.C. (UKSC) 122; see further para.16–19. In *Christian Institute v Lord Advocate* [2015] CSOH 7 [92]–[96], four Christian, educational and childrens' charities were held not to possess standing for the purposes of challenging the legislative competence of Pt 4 of the Children and Young People (Scotland) Act 2014.

3–26 The HRA provides that proceedings must be brought before the end of the period of one year beginning with the date on which the act complained of took place, or such longer period as the court or tribunal considers equitable having regard to all the circumstances.[62]

3–27 Where a public authority is found to have acted incompatibly with Convention rights, the court may grant such relief or remedy, or make such order, within its powers as it considers "just and appropriate".[63] Damages may be awarded, but only by a court with power to award damages, and only if the court is satisfied that damages are necessary to afford just satisfaction to the victim.[64]

3–28 The same restrictions apply where proceedings are brought under the Scotland Act 1998 rather than the HRA. A person cannot, therefore, bring proceedings on the ground that an act is incompatible with the Convention rights, or rely on the Convention rights in proceedings, unless the person would be a victim for the purposes of art.34 of the ECHR if proceedings in respect of the act were brought in the ECtHR.[65] Nor can a court or tribunal award damages in respect of an act which is incompatible with the Convention rights which it could not award if the HRA applied.[66] Under the Scotland Act as originally enacted there was no time limit within which proceedings had to be brought, in contrast to the position under the HRA, but a one year time limit was imposed following the House of Lords' decision in *Somerville v Ministers*,[67] and Scottish Government complaints that it was alone among public authorities in being denied the protection of a time limit.[68]

---

[62] HRA 1998 s.7(5).

[63] HRA 1998 s.8(1).

[64] HRA 1998 s.8(2), (3).

[65] SA 1998 s.100(1).

[66] SA 1998 s.100(3); this restriction may have been included on the mistaken assumption that damages were an automatic consequence of acting ultra vires.

[67] *Somerville v Scottish Ministers* [2007] UKHL 44; 2008 S.C. (HL) 45.

[68] SA 1998 s.100(3B), as inserted by the Convention Rights Proceedings (Amendment) (Scotland) Act 2009 s.1, and subsequently replaced by Scotland Act 2012 s.14.

CHAPTER 4

THE SCOTTISH PARLIAMENT

INTRODUCTION

" 'There shall be a Scottish Parliament.' I like that", Donald Dewar is reported **4–01** to have said of s.1 of the Scotland Act 1998. Expectations of the new Parliament after almost 300 years in which the only "Scottish" Parliament had been Westminster were high. The Scottish Constitutional Convention's "powerful hope" was that the coming of a Scottish Parliament would usher in a way of politics that was "radically different from the rituals of Westminster: more participative, more creative, less needlessly confrontational".[1] The Consultative Steering Group ("CSG"), which was set up by the Secretary of State to recommend the procedures the Parliament might be invited to adopt, was struck by the degree of consensus that existed

> "that the establishment of the Scottish Parliament offers the opportunity to put in place a new sort of democracy in Scotland, closer to the Scottish people and more in tune with Scottish needs. People in Scotland have high hopes for their Parliament, and in developing our proposals we have been keen to ensure that these hopes will be met".[2]

The CSG's recommendations, which were endorsed by the Parliament on June 9, 1999, envisaged

> "an open, accessible Parliament; a Parliament where power is shared with the people; where people are encouraged to participate in the policy making process which affects all our lives; an accountable visible Parliament; and a Parliament which promotes equal opportunities for all".[3]

There are various ways in which we might characterise the change sought by **4–02** the Scottish Constitutional Convention and others at the time. What they have in common is the idea that political power should be shared rather than concentrated in the hands of government, and that decisions should be reached by consensus rather than a majority. But whether we characterise the shift as one from a "power-hoarding" constitution to a "power-sharing" constitution,[4] or from a "majoritarian" to a "consensus" democracy,[5] we should not underestimate the challenge involved in bringing it about, or the continued attractiveness and hence likely persistence of the Westminster tradition of "winner takes

---

[1] Scottish Constitutional Convention, *Scotland's Parliament, Scotland's Right* (1995) p.9.

[2] Scottish Office, *Shaping Scotland's Parliament: Report of the Consultative Steering Group on the Scottish Parliament* (December, 1998), Foreword.

[3] Scottish Office, *Shaping Scotland's Parliament: Report of the Consultative Steering Group on the Scottish Parliament* (December, 1998), Foreword.

[4] Anthony King, *The British Constitution* (Oxford: OUP, 2007) pp.50–51.

[5] Arend Lijphart, *Patterns of Democracy: Government Forms and Performance in Thirty-Six Countries*, 2nd edn (New Haven: Yale University Press, 2012).

all". Were the Westminster tradition to simply reassert itself, however, the result would be a parliament that was closer to the people of Scotland but otherwise little real change. The CSG acknowledged that change would not be easy to achieve.

> "We have detected a great deal of cynicism about and disillusionment with the democratic process; it will require an effort both from the Parliament itself and from the people with whom it interacts to achieve the participative democracy many seek."[6]

4–03   The devolved system of government is a parliamentary system in which the government is drawn from the parliament rather than being directly elected on the separation of powers or presidential model. The primary function of parliaments in such systems, which is sometimes overlooked, is the formation of a government. Beyond the formation of a government, and sustaining it in office, the Scottish Parliament has a number of other functions: to act as a forum for the expression of Scottish opinion; to make laws for Scotland within the limits of its legislative competence; to approve the Scottish Government's proposals for taxation and expenditure; and to hold the Scottish Government to account. We examine these functions in later chapters. Here we concentrate on the Parliament as an institution—its electoral arrangements, its members and the rules governing their conduct, its administration, its committee system, and its "privileges", i.e. rights and immunities.

ELECTORAL ARRANGEMENTS

The electoral system

4–04   The Parliament is elected by a form of mixed member proportional system, known as the additional member system, which combines the election of constituency candidates with a vote for a party or, in Scotland, an independent candidate.[7] Voters have two votes each: a vote for a constituency member and a vote for a "party list" of up to 12 candidates submitted by a registered political party (or for an individual who is standing as an independent candidate within the voter's region). The party list is closed, which means that voters cannot express a preference for candidates on the list. The Parliament's 73 constituency MSPs are elected by the "first past the post" system used for elections to the House of Commons, with the 56 regional or list MSPs—seven for each of eight regions—being elected on the basis of the party's (or independent's) share of the regional vote, taking into account (in the party's case) the number of constituency seats it has won in the region. For example, if a party has already won two constituency seats in the region, its regional vote is divided by three (one plus the number of seats already won) in allocating the first regional seat. Under this system (also known as d'Hondt), the allocation of regional seats tends to compensate parties who did less well in winning constituencies than their share of the regional vote would otherwise suggest.

---

[6] Scottish Office, *Shaping Scotland's Parliament: Report of the Consultative Steering Group on the Scottish Parliament* (December, 1998) s.2 para.4.

[7] Matthew Soberg Shugart and Martin P Wattenberg, *Mixed-Member Electoral Systems: The Best of Both Worlds?* (Oxford: OUP, 2001). The Arbuthnott Commission preferred the description "mixed member system". It felt that "additional member system", which is the description used in the Scotland Act 1998 ("SA 1998") s.1(3), was "unhelpful" in that it suggested that regional members were "added on": Commission on Boundary Differences and Voting Systems, *Putting Citizens First: Boundaries, Voting and Representation in Scotland* (January, 2006) para.4.8.

The electoral system thus retains the "constituency link" as the "essential founda- **4–05** tion" of the Parliament, but at the same time is designed to secure a closer relationship between votes cast and seats won than under the first past the post system.[8] Electoral reform was the price of Liberal Democrat participation in the Scottish Constitutional Convention. For Labour, which had most to lose from the introduction of any form of proportional representation, it seemed to offer a guarantee against the possibility that the SNP might win an outright majority, and in so doing re-open the devolution "settlement", a safeguard that in the event proved illusory; after forming a minority government in 2007, the SNP won an outright majority in 2011, making inevitable a referendum on Scotland's constitutional future.

The Parliament's electoral system was examined by the Arbuthnott **4–06** Commission, which was appointed by the Secretary of State for Scotland in July 2004 following the introduction of the single transferable vote system for Scottish local government elections. The Commission was asked to examine the consequences of having four different voting systems in Scotland, and different boundaries between House of Commons and Holyrood constituencies, for voter participation, the relationship between public bodies and elected representatives, and representation of constituents by different tiers of elected members. In its report, published in 2006, the Commission recommended that the additional member system should be retained but that there should be a further review after the 2011 Scottish Parliament election, with a view to a possible move to the single transferable vote system, a recommendation subsequently endorsed by the Calman Commission.[9] In the meantime, it recommended that the closed list system used for the regional vote should be replaced by open lists to increase voter choice, a recommendation rejected by the UK Government on the grounds that it would overcomplicate the voting system.

The Arbuthnott Commission also recommended that the Scottish Parliament **4–07** and local government elections should be held on different days, a recommendation that was also rejected, with embarrassing results at the combined parliamentary and local government elections the following year when 146,097 ballot papers, or 3.47 per cent of the votes cast, were spoiled, apparently as a result of voter confusion.

Elections

The Scotland Act provides for "ordinary" general elections to take place every **4–08** four years, normally on the first Thursday in May.[10] The First Minister has no discretion, therefore, over the date of the next election, in contrast to the position at Westminster before the Fixed-term Parliaments Act 2011 when the election date was treated as a matter for the Prime Minister. Following elections in 1999, 2003, 2007 and 2011, the next election was due to take place on May 7, 2015, but the Fixed-term Parliaments Act 2011 set this as the date for the next UK parliamentary election.[11] Holding both elections on the same day was

---

[8] Scottish Office, *Scotland's Parliament* (1997) Cm.3658, para.8.1; for the features of the electoral system that limit the extent to which the list vote can compensate for the disproportionality of the constituency vote, see Nicola McEwen, "The Scottish Parliament Electoral System: Can Credibility be Restored?" in Charlie Jeffery and James Mitchell (eds), *The Scottish Parliament 1999–2009: The First Decade* (Edinburgh: Luath Press, 2009).

[9] Commission on Scottish Devolution, *Serving Scotland Better: Scotland and the United Kingdom in the 21st Century* (June, 2009) para.5.19.

[10] SA 1998 s.2(2); s.2(5) permits the presiding officer to propose a day for the holding of the poll that is not more than a month earlier or later than the first Thursday in May.

[11] Fixed-term Parliaments Act 2011 ("FTPA 2011") s.1(2).

widely regarded as undesirable, particularly by MSPs who feared their election would be overshadowed and that voters would be confused by simultaneous campaigns on different issues. The Scottish Parliament election was therefore postponed, with the Scottish Parliament's agreement, to May 5, 2016.[12] The current session of the Scottish Parliament will thus last for five years rather than the normal four years.

4–09 An extraordinary general election takes place where the Parliament either resolves that it should be dissolved or fails to nominate one of its members for appointment as First Minister.[13] A resolution dissolving the Parliament requires the support of a two-thirds majority of the Parliament, i.e. 86 MSPs.[14] The holding of an extraordinary general election has no bearing on the timing of the next ordinary general election unless it is held within six months of the date of the next ordinary general election in which case the ordinary general election is not held.[15] Were the Parliament to have been dissolved in 2009, say, and an extraordinary general election held, there would still have been a general election in 2011.

Constituencies

4–10 When the Scottish Parliament was first elected, the 73 constituencies were those used for elections to the Westminster Parliament, save that Orkney and Shetland were separate constituencies,[16] with the eight regions being those devised but never used for elections to the European Parliament.[17] As part of the devolution settlement, however, Scottish representation at Westminster was set to fall.[18] This would have meant a reduction in the number of constituency seats in the Scottish Parliament, because elections for the Scottish Parliament were based on the same constituencies as those for the House of Commons. It would also have meant a consequential reduction in the number of regional seats in order to maintain the balance between constituency and regional MSPs.[19] Following the Boundary Commission for Scotland's fifth review of Scottish constituency boundaries,[20] the number of Scottish House of Commons constituencies was reduced from 72 to 59.[21] The number of MSPs was thus set to fall from 129 to around 104. In response to a consultation on implementing the Boundary Commission's recommendations, however, it was successfully argued that reducing the number of MSPs would reduce the effectiveness of the Parliament, particularly its committee system, and that it would be unwise to destabilise the Parliament so early in its life by reducing its size. The UK Government therefore introduced legislation to remove the statutory link between the constituencies for the Scottish Parliament and those for the House of Commons, and to retain the existing regions and number of regional MSPs, thereby ensuring that the size of the Scottish Parliament remained unchanged.[22]

---

[12] FTPA 2011. s.4(2).

[13] SA 1998 s.3(1).

[14] SA 1998 s.3(1)(a).

[15] SA 1998 s.3(3),(4).

[16] SA 1998 s.1 and Sch.1.

[17] The constituencies were set out in the Parliamentary Constituencies (Scotland) Order 1995 (SI 1995/1037), the regions in the European Parliamentary Constituencies (Scotland) Order 1996 (SI 1996/1926). For the purpose of elections to the European Parliament Scotland now constitutes a single electoral region: European Parliamentary Elections Act 2002.

[18] SA 1998 s.86.

[19] SA 1998 Sch.1, para.7(3).

[20] Boundary Commission for Scotland, *Fifth Periodical Report* (2004) Cm.6427.

[21] Parliamentary Constituencies (Scotland) Order 2005 (SI 2005/250).

[22] Scottish Parliament (Constituencies) Act 2004. The Act, which also provided for the Scottish Parliament constituencies to be reviewed separately from future reviews of Scottish Westminster

The Boundary Commission for Scotland, a UK public body, is responsible for **4-11** keeping the Scottish Parliament constituency and regional boundaries under review. The constituencies, apart from Orkney and Shetland for which direct provision is made in the Scotland Act,[23] and regions are currently defined in the Scottish Parliament (Constituencies and Regions) Order 2010,[24] which implements the Boundary Commission for Scotland's First Periodic Review of Scottish Parliament Boundaries.[25] Under the Smith Commission Agreement, the Boundary Commission for Scotland will remain a UK public body, but implementation of its recommendations with regard to Scottish Parliament boundaries will become a matter for the Scottish Ministers.[26]

The Arbuthnott Commission was not persuaded that the boundaries for all **4-12** parliamentary elections in Scotland needed to be the same, but it did think there was

> "a strong case for rationalising the very wide range of boundaries that apply to elections, to the delivery of services, and to the organisation of public bodies".[27]

Rather than being based on House of Commons constituencies, it recommended that the constituency and regional boundaries for the Scottish Parliament should be based on local authority areas, with the regions revised to better reflect natural local communities and identity.[28] Implementation of the Smith Commission Agreement will enable the Scottish Parliament to act on this recommendation should it wish to do so.

Dual candidacy

The Scotland Act prohibits candidates from standing in more than one constit- **4-13** uency, but not from standing both as a constituency member for a political party and being included on the party's list for the region in which the constituency is included.[29] The possibility thereby created of securing election by party list, having stood and failed to gain election as a constituency member, proved controversial from the outset. The Arbuthnott Commission, however, rejected the introduction of a ban on this form of "dual candidacy" in the interests of maintaining electoral choice. In the Commission's view, the complaint that such dual candidacy allowed constituency "failures" into the Parliament through the back door of the regional vote, with the implication that this was somehow contrary to the wishes of the electorate, was better addressed through

---

constituencies, provides an early example of the Scottish Parliament successfully resisting a change, in this case one already provided for, to which it was opposed. For McTernan, the "umbilical link was a sign of subordination, yet at the first sustained objection the UK government backed off", demonstrating that while "formally the UK parliament retains supremacy over the Scottish Parliament, in reality it cannot force its preferences on Holyrood": *Scotland on Sunday*, November 30, 2003.

[23] SA 1998 Sch.1.

[24] Scottish Parliament (Constituencies and Regions) Order 2010 (SI 2010/2691).

[25] Boundary Commission for Scotland, *First Periodic Review of Scottish Parliament Boundaries* (May, 2010).

[26] Scotland Office, *Scotland in the United Kingdom: An enduring settlement* (2015) Cm.8990, para.1.4.10.

[27] Commission on Boundary Differences and Voting Systems, *Putting Citizens First: Boundaries, Voting and Representation in Scotland* (January, 2006) para.2.14.

[28] Commission on Boundary Differences and Voting Systems, *Putting Citizens First: Boundaries, Voting and Representation in Scotland* (January, 2006) para.3.47.

[29] SA 1998 s.5(2), (7); an independent candidate may stand both in a constituency and a region but only if the constituency is included in the region: SA 1998 s.5(8).

the replacement of closed lists by open lists rather than by preventing candidates standing as both constituency and regional members.[30]

Vacancies

4–14 Where a constituency seat falls vacant a by-election is held. This must take place within three months of the vacancy occurring, unless the by-election would be held within three months of the next general election, in which case the seat remains vacant until it is filled at that election.[31] Where a regional seat falls vacant it is filled by the next named nominee on the appropriate party's regional list. If the regional member is an independent or there are no candidates left on the relevant party's list, the seat lies vacant until the next general election.[32]

The franchise

4–15 The franchise for Scottish Parliament elections is the same as the franchise for local government elections in Scotland.[33] Under the Smith Commission Agreement, the franchise for Scottish Parliament and local government elections in Scotland will become a matter for the Scottish Parliament. In the meantime, following the precedent set by the independence referendum, the Scottish Parliament has been given the power to extend the franchise to 16 and 17 year olds in time for the 2016 Scottish Parliament elections.[34]

The conduct of elections

4–16 The conduct of Scottish Parliament elections is a reserved matter, in contrast to the conduct of local government elections, which is devolved.[35] The Gould Report, which was commissioned in the aftermath of the 2007 Scottish parliamentary and local government elections, raised the possibility of devolving responsibility for the conduct of Scottish parliamentary as well as local government elections, the division of responsibilities between London and Edinburgh having been identified as a potential contributing factor in the voter confusion at those elections.[36] Following the recommendation of the Calman Commission,[37] executive competence over some aspects of the administration of Scottish parliamentary elections was transferred to the Scottish Ministers (with the remainder continuing to be exercisable by the Secretary of State),[38] but under the Smith Commission Agreement legislative competence over the conduct of Scottish Parliament elections will be devolved to the Scottish Parliament. The Parliament will be prevented, however, from deciding that general elections to the Scottish Parliament should be held on the same day as general elections to the UK Parliament, European Parliament or local government elections in Scotland.[39]

---

[30] Commission on Boundary Differences and Voting Systems, *Putting Citizens First: Boundaries, Voting and Representation in Scotland* (January, 2006) paras 4.55–4.61; contrast Government of Wales Act 2006 s.7.

[31] SA 1998 s.9.

[32] SA 1998 s.10.

[33] SA 1998. s.11(1).

[34] The Scotland Act (Modifications of Schedules 4 and 5 and Transfer of Functions to the Scottish Ministers etc.) Order 2015 (SI 2015/692).

[35] SA 1998 Sch 5 Pt II s.B3.

[36] The Electoral Commission, *Scottish elections 2007: The independent review of the Scottish Parliamentary and local government elections 3 May 2007* (October, 2007) p.111.

[37] Commission on Scottish Devolution, *Serving Scotland Better: Scotland and the United Kingdom in the 21st Century* (June, 2009) para.5.27.

[38] SA 2012 s.1.

[39] Scotland Office, *Scotland in the United Kingdom: An enduring settlement* (2015) Cm.8990, para.1.4.4.

The size and composition of the Parliament

Under the Smith Commission Agreement, the size and composition of the **4–17** Parliament will also become a matter for the Parliament. Legislation altering the size and composition of the Parliament, however, will require to be passed by a super-majority, i.e. a two-thirds majority, of the Scottish Parliament, as will legislation altering the electoral system or the franchise.[40] Such legislation will continue therefore to be entrenched, but in a different manner and form.

MEMBERS

Disqualification

The rules governing the disqualification of members are based on those for the **4–18** House of Commons.[41] Judges, civil servants, members of the armed forces and police officers are therefore all disqualified, as are persons under 21, the mentally ill, undischarged bankrupts and convicted prisoners serving a sentence of more than one year's detention (or an indefinite sentence) in the UK or Ireland. There is also a long list of office-holders who are disqualified, including the Auditor General for Scotland, the Scottish Public Services Ombudsman, the Scottish Information Commissioner and the Commissioner for Ethical Standards in Public Life in Scotland.[42] It is open to the Parliament to disregard a disqualification incurred on certain of the grounds, but only if it considers that the ground has been removed and that it is proper to disregard the disqualification so incurred.[43] Subject to the possibility of the Parliament disregarding the disqualification, where a person is disqualified, and is returned as a member, the return is void and the seat vacant[44]; where a person is disqualified, and is a sitting member, membership ceases and the seat is vacant.[45] The Court of Session has jurisdiction to determine whether a person purporting to be a member is disqualified or has been disqualified since being returned.[46]

Under the Smith Commission Agreement, the disqualification of members will **4–19** become a matter for the Scottish Parliament, as will the circumstances in which a sitting member can be removed.[47]

There is no rule preventing members of the Westminster or European **4–20** Parliaments from standing for election to the Scottish Parliament. In 2009, however, the Committee on Standards in Public Life recommended that the practice of permitting a Westminster MP to sit simultaneously in a devolved legislature should be brought to an end.[48] In Scotland, the practice was ended

---

[40] Scotland Office, *Scotland in the United Kingdom: An enduring settlement* (2015) Cm.8990, para.1.4.12.

[41] SA 1998 s.15(1).

[42] The Scottish Parliament (Disqualification) Order 2010 (SI 2010/2476).

[43] SA 1998 s.16(3), (4).

[44] SA 1998 s.17(1).

[45] SA 1998 s.17(2).

[46] SA 1998 s.18.

[47] Scotland Office, *Scotland in the United Kingdom: An enduring settlement* (2015) Cm.8990, para.1.3.1.

[48] Committee on Standards in Public Life, *Twelfth Report: MPs' expenses and allowances. Supporting Parliament, safeguarding the taxpayer* (2009) Cm.7724, para.12.22; the recommendation was primarily directed at Northern Ireland where "double jobbing" appeared to be "unusually ingrained" in the political culture.

voluntarily.[49] Members of the House of Lords are not disqualified from membership.[50]

Standards of conduct

4–21 The Consultative Steering Group was asked, among other things, to consider how the "highest standards" might be achieved in the Parliament. It recommended the adoption of a "rigorous" code of conduct for MSPs,[51] which was drawn up by the Parliament's Standards Committee and adopted by resolution of the Parliament on February 24, 2000. The introduction to the Code, which is now in its fifth edition, states that:

> "The Scottish electorate has a high expectation of members of the Scottish Parliament and the way in which they should act in their relationships with their constituents and in the Parliament. Members must meet those expectations by ensuring that their conduct is above reproach and worthy of the trust of the electorate."[52]

It also affirms the Parliament's determination "to be at the forefront in developing best practice on standards matters".[53]

4–22 The Code comprises a mixture of key principles and ethical standards. The seven key principles, which reflect the influence of the Nolan Committee's "Seven Principles of Public Life",[54] are described as aspirational in nature. "Their intent is to guide and inspire members towards the very highest ethical ideals." They do not represent obligations, in contrast to the ethical standards, and do not therefore form the basis for the imposition of sanctions.[55] They are:

> (i)   *"Public duty."* "Members are expected to act in the interests of the Scottish people and the Scottish Parliament. Members should uphold the law and act in conformity with the rules of the Parliament."
>
> (ii) *"Duty as a representative."* "Members should be accessible to the people of the areas for which they have been elected to serve and represent their interests conscientiously."
>
> (iii) *"Selflessness."* "Members should take decisions solely in terms of the public interest. They should not act in order to gain financial or other material benefit for themselves, their family or friends."
>
> (iv) *"Integrity."* "Members have a duty not to place themselves under any financial or other obligation to any individual or organisation

---

[49] There were a number of prominent dual mandates in earlier sessions, including that of Alex Salmond.

[50] SA 1998 s.16(1). A number of peers have been MSPs at the same time: Lord (David) Steel of Aikwood, the Parliament's first presiding officer, Lord (James Douglas-Hamilton) Selkirk of Douglas, who stood down at the 2007 election, Lord (Mike) Watson of Invergowrie, who resigned as an MSP after being convicted and imprisoned for fire-raising, Lord (George) Foulkes, who stood down at the 2011 election, and Baroness (Annabel) Goldie.

[51] Scottish Office, *Shaping Scotland's Parliament: Report of the Consultative Steering Group on the Scottish Parliament* (December, 1998) s.2 para.24.

[52] Scottish Parliament, *Code of Conduct for Members of the Scottish Parliament*, 5th edn (2011) Vol.1, para.2.3.

[53] Scottish Parliament, *Code of Conduct for Members of the Scottish Parliament*, 5th edn (2011) Vol.1, para.2.9.

[54] Committee on Standards in Public Life, *Standards in Public Life* (1995) Cm.2850; the seven principles of public life, the descriptions of which were revised in 2013, are: selflessness; integrity; objectivity; accountability; openness; honesty; and leadership.

[55] Scottish Parliament, *Code of Conduct for Members of the Scottish Parliament*, 5th edn (2011) Vol.1, para.3.1.1.

that might reasonably be thought to influence them in the performance of their duties."

(v) *"Honesty."* "Members should act honestly. They must declare any
private interests (as required by the Interests of Members of the Scottish
Parliament Act 2006) relating to their public duties and take steps to
resolve any conflicts arising in a way that protects the public interest."

(vi) *"Accountability and openness."* "Members are accountable for their
decisions and actions to the Scottish people. They should consider
issues on their merits, taking account of the views of others. Members
should be as open as possible about their decisions and actions."

(vii) *"Leadership."* "Members should promote and support these principles by leadership and example, to maintain and strengthen the
public's trust and confidence in the integrity of the Parliament and
its members in conducting public business."[56]

The Code itself is made up of nine sections: members' interests (ss.1–3); paid **4–23**
advocacy (s.4); lobbying and access to MSPs (s.5); regulation of cross-party
groups (s.6); general conduct and conduct in the chamber or committee (s.7);
engagement and liaison with constituents (s.8); and enforcement (s.9).

Members' interests

The Scotland Act 1998 required the Parliament to make provision governing **4–24**
members' interests.[57] The provision made must be by or under an Act of the
Scottish Parliament.[58] The Parliament cannot therefore decide to regulate
members' interests by way of standing orders rather than legislation.[59] The
provision made must include (but need not be limited to) a register of members'
interests, which must be published and available for public inspection, the
registration and declaration of members' interests, and a ban on paid advocacy.[60] The Interests of Members of the Scottish Parliament Act 2006, which
replaced transitional arrangements made under the Scotland Act 1998,[61]
requires members to register financial interests and to declare any financial
interest they may have in a matter before taking part in proceedings relating to
that matter.[62] The types of financial interest that must be registered are those
"which might be thought to influence a member's actions, speeches or votes in
the Parliament".[63] They comprise remuneration, unremunerated directorships
or partnerships, donations to election expenses, sponsorship above a certain
amount, gifts above a certain amount, overseas visits, heritable property other
than a member's residence, and interests in shares.[64] Failure to register or
declare an interest renders a member liable to parliamentary sanctions, including

---

[56] Scottish Parliament, *Code of Conduct for Members of the Scottish Parliament*, 5th edn
(2011) Vol.1, paras 3.1.3–3.1.11.
[57] SA 1998 s.39; members include the law officers whether or not they are members of the
Parliament: s.39(8)(b).
[58] SA 1998 s.39(8)(a).
[59] *Whaley v Watson*, 2000 S.C. 340, 346.
[60] SA 1998 s.39(1), (2), (4).
[61] Scotland Act 1998 (Transitory and Transitional Provisions) (Members' Interests) Order 1999
(SI 1999/1350).
[62] Interests of Members of the Scottish Parliament Act 2006 ("IMPSA 2006") ss.3, 5, 13.
[63] Scottish Parliament, *Code of Conduct for Members of the Scottish Parliament*, 5th edn
(2011) Vol.2, para.1.1.1.
[64] The categories of registrable interest are set out in the schedule to the Act as modified by the
Interests of Members of the Scottish Parliament Act 2006 (Modification to the Schedule)
Resolution 2011 (SSI 2011/40).

exclusion from proceedings of the Parliament.[65] It is also a criminal offence, punishable on summary conviction by a fine not exceeding level 5 on the standard scale.[66] The Scotland Act 2012, however, gave the Parliament greater flexibility over the details of the members' interests regime, including power to decide that non-compliance should no longer be an automatic criminal offence.[67]

Paid advocacy

4–25   The Interests of Members of the Scottish Parliament Act 2006 also prohibits members, in consideration of any payment or benefit in kind, from advocating or initiating any cause or matter on behalf of any person or urging any other member to advocate or initiate any cause or matter on behalf of any person.[68] Payments or benefits in kind are defined as payments or benefits in kind which a member receives and which may "reasonably be considered" to result in some benefit for that member, other than a vote for the member in an election to the Parliament.[69] The prohibition does not extend to receiving legislative assistance, including assistance in connection with the preparation of a Member's Bill.[70] Breach of the ban renders a member liable to exclusion from proceedings of the Parliament.[71] It is also a criminal offence, punishable on summary conviction by a fine not exceeding level 5 on the standard scale.[72]

Lobbying and access to MSPs

4–26   The Parliament has not sought to regulate lobbying so far other than through regulating the conduct of MSPs.[73] The Code of Conduct requires members in their dealings with lobbyists to act in accordance with the relevant rules, including those laid down in the Interests of Members of the Scottish Parliament Act 2006 and the Code of Conduct, not to act in any way which could bring discredit upon the Parliament, and not to offer or accord preferential access or treatment to commercial lobbyists or their employers.[74] Following a proposal for a Member's Bill to establish a statutory register of lobbyists, the Scottish Government indicated that it would introduce legislation on lobbying within the current parliamentary session.[75]

Regulation of cross-party groups

4–27   The regulation of cross-party groups is closely related to the regulation of lobbying in that cross-party groups may serve as a thinly disguised cover for

---

[65] IMSPA 2006 ss.15–16.

[66] SA 1998 s.39(6); IMSPA 2006 s.17.

[67] SA 2012 s.7; for the background, see Commission on Scottish Devolution, *Serving Scotland Better: Scotland and the United Kingdom in the 21st Century* (June, 2009) paras 6.108–6.111. The Standards, Procedures and Public Appointments Committee has decided not recommend abolition of the existing criminal offences of failing to register or declare an interest: 2nd Report, *Members' Interests Bill* (Scottish Parliamentary Paper 681, 2015).

[68] IMSPA 2006 s.14(1).

[69] IMSPA 2006 s.14(2).

[70] IMSPA 2006 s.14(3); in *Whaley v Watson*, 2000 S.C. 340 the petitioners sought unsuccessfully to prevent the introduction of a Bill to ban hunting with dogs in alleged breach of the then ban on paid advocacy.

[71] IMSPA 2006 s.16.

[72] SA 1998 s.39(6); IMSPA 2006 s.17; the *Members' Interests Bill* (fn 67) includes provision to extend the offence of paid advocacy.

[73] The Standards Committee in Session 1 recommended the introduction of a statutory registration scheme for commercial lobbyists: 1st Report, *Report on Lobbying* (Scottish Parliamentary Paper 507, 2002).

[74] Scottish Parliament, *Code of Conduct for Members of the Scottish Parliament*, 5th edn (2011) Vol.2, paras 5.1.1–5.1.3.

[75] See Standards, Procedures and Public Appointments Committee 1st Report, *Proposal for a register of lobbying activity* (Scottish Parliamentary Paper 664, 2015).

lobbying; such groups routinely include representatives of campaign groups and interest groups. The Code confines the use of the title "Cross-Party Group in the Scottish Parliament" and access to parliamentary facilities to recognised cross-party groups.[76] In deciding whether to recognise a group, the Parliament's Standards, Procedures and Public Appointments Committee pays particular attention to the group's purpose; a group that the Committee considers is being proposed not in the public interest but, for example, to further particular commercial interests, will not be recognised.[77] The group's membership must be open to all MSPs and must include at least five MSPs, including normally at least one from each of the parties or groups represented on the Parliamentary Bureau (below).[78] The convener of the group has the primary responsibility for ensuring that it meets the requirements of the Code of Conduct.[79]

General conduct

Among other things, the Code prohibits the improper use of payments and **4–28** allowances made to members for public purposes,[80] and requires members to "treat with caution" any offer of hospitality, a gift, a favour or benefit. Members are not prohibited from accepting "reasonable hospitality" or "modest tokens of goodwill", but a member should not accept "any offer that might reasonably be thought to influence the member's judgement in carrying out Parliamentary duties".[81]

Engagement and liaison with constituents

Given the strength of the tradition of constituency representation in British **4–29** political culture, it was little surprise that tensions should have quickly emerged between some constituency MSPs and some of the regional MSPs whose regions included their constituencies, particularly where (as was commonly the case) they were drawn from different political parties. Regional MSPs were accused of cherry picking constituency business, and of targeting particular constituencies in order to increase the chances of winning them at the next election. More generally, there were persistent suggestions during the Parliament's first two sessions that regional MSPs were "second class" representatives, or not "real MSPs", and that election by party list was inferior to election by first past the post, especially where a regional MSP had stood and failed to gain election as a constituency MSP.

An attempt to address the relationship between the two groups of members was **4–30** made in Session 1. In their current, much amended, form the "Reid principles"[82]

---

[76] Scottish Parliament, *Code of Conduct for Members of the Scottish Parliament*, 5th edn (2011) Vol.2, para.6.3.5.

[77] Scottish Parliament, *Code of Conduct for Members of the Scottish Parliament*, 5th edn (2011) Vol.2, para.6.3.11.

[78] Scottish Parliament, *Code of Conduct for Members of the Scottish Parliament*, 5th edn (2011) Vol.2, para.6.4.1; the strict requirement of at least one MSP from each of the parties or groups represented on the Bureau, if not waived occasionally, would require the MSPs from the smaller parties/groups to sign up to lots of cross-party groups just to allow those groups to function.

[79] Scottish Parliament, *Code of Conduct for Members of the Scottish Parliament*, 5th edn (2011) Vol.2, para.6.5.1.

[80] Scottish Parliament, *Code of Conduct for Members of the Scottish Parliament*, 5th edn (2011) Vol.2, para.7.2.5.

[81] Scottish Parliament, *Code of Conduct for Members of the Scottish Parliament*, 5th edn (2011) Vol.2, para.7.2.6.

[82] So-called because they were drawn up by a working group under the chairmanship of George Reid, then one of the Parliament's deputy presiding officers.

concentrate on two issues: individual constituents' cases; and how members describe themselves.

4–31 As regards individual cases, the basic principle is that the wishes of constituents are paramount. Constituents are therefore free to approach any of the MSPs, constituency or regional, elected to represent them. Members for their part are expected to take on cases when approached. Where however a member is made aware that a constituent's case is already being pursued by another MSP, the member is recommended to notify that MSP, but only with the constituent's consent.[83] Members are also prohibited from dealing with a matter relating to a constituency case or constituency issue outwith their constituency or region unless by prior agreement (the "no poaching" rule).[84]

4–32 As regards members' descriptions of themselves, members "should not misrepresent the basis on which they are elected or the area they serve" (the "no misrepresentation" rule). They should describe themselves accurately so as not to confuse those with whom they deal. Regional members must not describe themselves as a "local" member for only part of the region for which they were elected, while constituency members should not describe themselves as the "sole MSP" for a particular area or constituency.[85]

4–33 The Code also insists that regional MSPs have a responsibility to all those in the region for which they were elected, and that this should be reflected in the way in which they operate within the region. They are therefore required to work in more than two constituencies within their region.[86]

4–34 There are no equivalent principles governing relations between MSPs, MPs and local councillors. The original intention had been to try to obtain a similar convention with MPs, local councillors and public bodies, but the difficulty of securing agreement across the political parties meant that this was abandoned.[87] Relations between MSPs and other elected representatives remain a source of friction and confusion with some MPs continuing to interfere in devolved matters and some MSPs routinely taking up reserved issues:

> "All the evidence I have suggests that this area remains messy. While some elected representatives do try to stay within their mandate, passing reserved or local matters to the appropriate representative—and vice versa—others do not. The usual defence is that if a constituent comes to them they cannot be seen to be doing nothing. But that is hardly in the spirit of devolution. It leads to duplication of effort and is profoundly confusing for the citizen ... I believe therefore that there is a real case for trying to establish new compacts between Holyrood, Westminster and local government on the sharing of power."[88]

---

[83] Scottish Parliament, *Code of Conduct for Members of the Scottish Parliament*, 5th edn (2011) Vol.2, paras 8.1.1–8.1.3.

[84] Scottish Parliament, *Code of Conduct for Members of the Scottish Parliament*, 5th edn (2011) Vol.2, para.8.1.4.

[85] Scottish Parliament, *Code of Conduct for Members of the Scottish Parliament*, 5th edn (2011) Vol.2, para.8.2.

[86] Scottish Parliament, *Code of Conduct for Members of the Scottish Parliament*, 5th edn (2011) Vol.2, para.8.1.5.

[87] George Reid, "The Fourth Principle", The Stevenson Lecture on Citizenship, University of Glasgow November 23, 2006.

[88] George Reid, "The Fourth Principle", The Stevenson Lecture on Citizenship, University of Glasgow November 23, 2006.

The Commissioner for Ethical Standards in Public Life in Scotland

The Commissioner for Ethical Standards in Public Life in Scotland is respon- **4–35** sible for the independent investigation of complaints about the conduct of members of the Parliament and for reporting on the outcome of investigations to the Parliament.[89] The Commissioner is appointed by the Scottish Parliamentary Corporate Body ("SPCB") with the agreement of the Parliament for a single non-renewable term of up to eight years.[90] The current Commissioner was appointed in 2014 for a term of five years. The Commissioner enjoys effective security of tenure, being removable from office only with the support of a two-thirds majority of members, i.e. 86 MSPs.[91] The Commissioner is also, by statute, not subject to the direction of any member of the Parliament, any member of the Scottish Government, or the SPCB in the performance of their functions.[92]

Certain classes of complaint are excluded from the Commissioner's jurisdic- **4–36** tion.[93] These include complaints about a member's conduct at a meeting of the Parliament, and complaints made under s.8 of the Code (engagement and liaison with constituents), both of which are referred to the presiding officer, as well as complaints about a member's use of allowances, which are referred to the SPCB. The Parliament may, however, direct the Commissioner to undertake an investigation into an excluded complaint.[94]

The Commissioner may give advice about the procedures for making a **4–37** complaint, but is prohibited from giving advice as to whether particular conduct would constitute a breach of the provisions in order to avoid the possibility of the Commissioner being called upon to investigate a matter on which advice has already been given.[95]

A detailed code governs the investigation of complaints.[96] A Memorandum of **4–38** Agreement with the Crown Office and Procurator Fiscal Service governs the steps taken in the event that a potential issue of criminality arises during an investigation.

The Commissioner reports to the Parliament's Standards, Procedures and **4–39** Public Appointments Committee on the outcome of investigations. The

---

[89] Scottish Parliamentary Commissions and Commissioners etc. Act 2010 ("SPCCA 2010") s.1; Scottish Parliamentary Standards Commissioner Act 2002 ("SPSCA 2002") s.3(1); the office was established by the Public Services Reform (Commissioner for Ethical Standards in Public Life in Scotland etc.) Order 2013 (SSI 2013/197), with the then Public Standards Commissioner for Scotland and acting Public Appointments Commissioner for Scotland as its first holder.

[90] SPCCA 2010 ss.1 and 9; under the SPSCA 2002, the Commissioner was appointed for a maximum term of five years, which term could be renewed but not more than once. The first Commissioner, who was appointed for two terms of three years, argued for a single longer term of office without the need for re-appointment in order to strengthen his perceived independence: Scottish Parliamentary Standards Commissioner, *Annual Report 2005/2006* (2006) para.46.

[91] SPCCA 2010 s.9(3), (4).

[92] SPCCA 2010 s.4; in his final annual report, the first Commissioner said: "One message I would like to pass on to my successors regards the need for vigilance to protect the independence of operation which is central to public confidence in the Commissioner's role. The Parliament laid great store by this when it chose a method of dealing with conduct complaints involving an independent investigator ... but there are at times pressures that potentially constrain that independence. Having independent legal advice is an essential component of the Commissioner's independence": Scottish Parliamentary Standards Commissioner, *Annual Report 2007/2008* (2008) para.6.

[93] SPSCA 2002 s.3(2).

[94] SPSCA 2002 s.12.

[95] SPSCA 2002 s.3(5), (6).

[96] SPSCA 2002 ss.5–8.

Commissioner expresses a view as to whether a breach has taken place, but is prohibited from expressing a view on the appropriate sanction for any breach.[97] The Committee is not bound by the Commissioner's findings of fact or conclusions, and it may direct the Commissioner to carry out further investigations.[98] In two of the 10 cases in the first eight years in which the Commissioner concluded that a breach had occurred the Standards Committee disagreed with the Commissioner's conclusion. In the first of these cases, which involved a complaint against Tricia Marwick and Kenny MacAskill, the Commissioner recorded it as "a matter of interest and concern" that the Committee and the Commissioner should judge the matter differently. "Should this happen more regularly, it would clearly be matter of serious concern."[99]

4–40 The imposition of sanctions for any breach is a matter for the Parliament acting on the Standards, Procedures and Public Appointments Committee's recommendation.[100] Sanctions include restricting a member from participating in certain proceedings of the Parliament, excluding the member from all proceedings of the Parliament, and the withdrawal of the member's rights and privileges. In the *Wendy Alexander* case, the Committee agreed by a majority with the Commissioner's conclusion that she had failed to register donations to her leadership election campaign within the appropriate timescales and recommended, again by a majority, that she be excluded from all proceedings of the Parliament for one day; the Parliament however rejected the Committee's recommendation amidst criticism that the original complaint and its subsequent treatment by the Committee had been politically driven.[101]

4–41 The Commissioner receives between 20 and 30 complaints a year. The most common type of complaint during the Parliament's first two sessions was about the level and quality of service provided by members. These complaints were subsequently transferred to the presiding officer, the then Scottish Parliamentary Standards Commissioner having questioned whether the purpose of the standards regime was not to prevent and to detect corruption and to encourage openness in making known interests which might influence political actions, rather than to police the quality and quantity of members' services to constituents.[102] Other complaints have related to the registration of financial interests, paid advocacy and consultancy, breach of privacy, and the leaking of committee reports. Having regard to the complaints received and the outcome of investigations, the current Commissioner is of the view that members "have applied high standards of conduct in carrying out their parliamentary duties".[103]

---

[97] SPSCA 2002 s.9(2).

[98] SPSCA 2002 s.10(1), (2).

[99] Scottish Parliamentary Standards Commissioner, *Annual Report 2004/2005* (2005) para.12. The second case involved a press release issued by Wendy Alexander in the course of an investigation into a complaint that she had failed to register donations to her campaign for election as leader of the Labour Group of MSPs and was secondary to the main complaint in that case: Standards, Procedures and Public Appointments Committee 7th Report, *Complaint against Wendy Alexander MSP* (Scottish Parliamentary Paper 150, 2008).

[100] Scottish Parliament Standing Orders rr.1.7, 6.4.2.

[101] Standards, Procedures and Public Appointments Committee 6th Report, *Complaint against Wendy Alexander MSP* (Scottish Parliamentary Paper 142, 2008); Scottish Parliament OR September 4, 2008 cols 10437–10460.

[102] Scottish Parliamentary Standards Commissioner, *Annual Report 2006/2007* (2007) paras 30–40.

[103] Commission for Ethical Standards in Public Life in Scotland, *Annual Report 2013/2014* (2014) p.5.

Corruption

Unlike the UK Parliament, the Scottish Parliament is a "public body" for the **4–42** purposes of the Prevention of Corruption Acts 1889–1916.[104] Members and staff of the Parliament may therefore incur criminal liability for corruptly making or accepting payments in connection with its business.

THE ADMINISTRATION OF THE PARLIAMENT

The presiding officer and deputies

Following a general election, the Parliament is required to elect a presiding **4–43** officer and two deputies from among its members.[105] The Parliament was originally required to do so at its first meeting following a general election, but this requirement was relaxed by the Scotland Act 2012, following the recommendation of the Calman Commission, so that it is now required to do so before it conducts any other proceedings, other than its members taking the oath of allegiance, and in any event within 14 days of the election.[106] In the event of a close election result this would allow the political parties enough time to conduct any negotiations necessary to form a government without having to allow one of their members to take on the non-voting role of presiding officer. The Scotland Act 2012 also empowered the Parliament to appoint additional deputies, again on the recommendation of the Calman Commission.[107]

Under the Parliament's standing orders, the presiding officer is responsible for **4–44** presiding over meetings of the Parliament, convening and chairing meetings of the Parliamentary Bureau and the Conveners Group, determining questions as to the interpretation or application of the Parliament's rules and giving rulings on such questions, and for representing the Parliament in "discussions and exchanges with any parliamentary, governmental, administrative or other body, whether within or outwith the UK".[108] George Reid, the Parliament's second presiding officer, summed up the presiding officer's role as "political facilitation, corporate direction and representation".[109] The presiding officer

> "chairs the Parliament, deciding who gets called when, and which questions and amendments are selected; chairs the Bureau, which determines the Parliament's business; chairs the Corporate Body … ; and represents the Parliament at home and abroad".[110]

A deputy presiding officer may be authorised to exercise most of the presiding officer's functions,[111] and inevitably much of the chairing of meetings of the Parliament and the representative functions is shared among the presiding officer and deputy presiding officers.

---

[104] SA 1998 s.43.
[105] SA 1998 s.19; they must not all represent the same political party: Sch.3 para.5; Scottish Parliament Standing Orders rr.3.2.7, 3.3.9, 3.3.10D.
[106] SA 1998 s.19(1A).
[107] SA 1998 s.19(1B).
[108] Scottish Parliament Standing Orders r.3.1.
[109] George Reid, "The Last Bang of the Gavel", Lecture at the University of Glasgow, March 6, 2007.
[110] George Reid, "The Last Bang of the Gavel", Lecture at the University of Glasgow, March 6, 2007.
[111] Scottish Parliament Standing Orders r.3.1.5.

4–45 The presiding officer also exercises a number of statutory functions, including: recommending to the Queen the Parliament's choice of First Minister and the designation of a member to exercise the First Minister's functions if the office is vacant or the First Minister is unable to act[112]; making written statements on the legislative competence of Bills and submitting Bills for Royal Assent[113]; recommending the date for general elections and setting the date for by-elections[114]; receiving notification of a member's resignation and of the filling of a vacancy in a regional seat[115]; and administering oaths to witnesses.[116]

4–46 Under the Parliament's standing orders, the presiding officer and deputy presiding officers are elected by secret ballot.[117] This has done much to ensure that the members elected have had the confidence of all members; a secret ballot makes it difficult for any of the political parties to "fix" the election of a favoured candidate. In the exercise of their functions, the presiding officer and deputy presiding officers are required to "act impartially, taking account of the interests of all members equally".[118] Although not formally required to do so, all presiding officers to date have resigned from their parties entirely for the duration of their office. The presiding officer exercises a casting vote in the event of a tie, but does not otherwise vote in the Parliament.[119]

The Scottish Parliamentary Corporate Body

4–47 The SPCB is responsible for ensuring that the Parliament is provided with the property, staff and services it requires.[120] It also represents the Parliament in legal proceedings.[121] As an unincorporated association, lacking legal personality, the Parliament cannot enter into contracts, own property, sue or be sued in its name. The SPCB consists of the presiding officer and at least four members of the Parliament appointed in accordance with standing orders.[122] The appointed members are elected by the Parliament to represent all MSPs and not as party representatives; the practice however has been for each of the four main parties to have a member on the SPCB. When the SPCB was first set up it was largely seen as a housekeeping body, but in reality

> "many of the issues which come before it are intensely political—taking up in the first and second Parliaments, a good 30% of the PO's time".[123]

The clerk

4–48 The Scotland Act requires there to be a Clerk of the Parliament.[124] The Clerk, who is appointed by the SPCB, is the Parliament's senior official and plays a

---

[112] SA 1998 ss.45(4), 46(4).
[113] SA 1998 ss.31(2), 32(3).
[114] SA 1998 ss.2(5), 3(1), 9(2).
[115] SA 1998 ss.10(6), 14.
[116] SA 1998 s.26; in practice, since witnesses give evidence to committees, it is committee conveners who administer the oath.
[117] Scottish Parliament Standing Orders r.11.9.
[118] Scottish Parliament Standing Orders r.3.1.2.
[119] Scottish Parliament Standing Orders r.11.5.5.
[120] SA 1998 s.21(3).
[121] SA 1998 s.40(1).
[122] SA 1998 s.21(2); originally it consisted of the presiding officer and four members of the Parliament; the possibility of additional members to reflect possible changes in the political composition of the Parliament was introduced by Scotland Act 2012 s.5.
[123] George Reid, "The Last Bang of the Gavel", Lecture at the University of Glasgow, March 6, 2007.
[124] SA 1998 s.20.

major role in its workings. As the Parliament's chief executive, the clerk has final responsibility for giving procedural advice and overseeing the administration of the Parliament as an institution. The Clerk's statutory functions include giving notice to witnesses,[125] and writing the date of Royal Assent on Acts of the Scottish Parliament.[126] In practice, the large majority of the Clerk's functions are delegated to other staff of the Parliament, of whom there around 450.

Standing orders

The Parliament's proceedings are regulated by standing orders.[127] The Scotland **4–49** Act specifies a number of matters for which provision may and in some cases must be made in the Parliament's standing orders.[128] The latter include the preservation of order, the holding of proceedings in public, the reporting and publishing of proceedings, and ensuring political balance in the composition of committees. The former include the withdrawal of members' rights and privileges. The standing orders provide a detailed set of procedural rules covering most aspects of Chamber and committee business, and are updated from time to time on the recommendation of the Parliament's Standards, Procedures and Public Appointments Committee.

The Consultative Steering Group's aim, in recommending the procedures the **4–50** Parliament might adopt, was

> "to try to capture, in the nuts and bolts of Parliamentary procedure, some of the high aspirations for a better, more responsive and truly democratic system of government that have informed the movement for constitutional change in Scotland".[129]

In submitting its proposals for debate, its hope was that the key principles on which they were based—sharing the power, accountability, access and participation and equal opportunities—would "continue to influence the life of Scotland's Parliament, not only in the letter of its Standing Orders, but in the spirit of its work".[130]

The Parliamentary Bureau

The Parliamentary Bureau is responsible for the arrangement of parliamentary **4–51** business, principally by recommending each week a business programme for the following two weeks of Chamber business, allocating time for Government and opposition debates, Chambers stages of Bills, Ministerial Statements and other business (including Members' Business). It is also responsible for proposing the establishment, remit and membership of committees and subcommittees, and for determining the competence of committees to deal with matters, and the lead committee in relation to matters falling within the competence of more than one committee.[131] The Bureau, which is chaired by the presiding officer, consists of one representative of each political party or

---

[125] SA 1998 s.24.
[126] SA 1998 s.28(4).
[127] SA 1998 s.22; *http://www.scottish.parliament.uk/parliamentarybusiness/17797.aspx* [Accessed February 12, 2015].
[128] SA 1998 Sch.3.
[129] Scottish Office, *Shaping Scotland's Parliament: Report of the Consultative Steering Group on the Scottish Parliament* (December, 1998) s.1 para.7.
[130] Scottish Office, *Shaping Scotland's Parliament: Report of the Consultative Steering Group on the Scottish Parliament* (December, 1998) s.1 para.7.
[131] Scottish Parliament Standing Orders r.5.1.

group with five or more members in the Parliament. Voting reflects party or group strength in the Parliament. In the event of a tie, the presiding officer has a casting vote. A coalition or single party government with a majority is thus certain to get its business. The Bureau meets in private, although a note of its decisions is published.

THE COMMITTEE SYSTEM

4–52 The Scottish Constitutional Convention's vision was of a Parliament that would operate through a system of powerful committees which would be able to initiate legislation as well as to scrutinise and amend government proposals, and which would have wide-ranging investigative functions.[132] *Scotland's Parliament,* the White Paper that preceded the Scotland Act 1998, described the functions of committees in identical terms, adding that this would mean that the Scottish government's legislative and policy proposals would be "appropriately scrutinised".[133] Charged with putting flesh on these bones, the CSG recommended a system of all-purpose committees that would combine the roles of select and public bill (formerly, standing) committees at Westminster, the idea being to enable members to develop expertise in particular areas and to bring an informed view to the consideration of legislation and the scrutiny of government.[134]

4–53 The Parliament's standing orders distinguish between "mandatory" committees and "subject" committees. The former are so-called because their functions are "so fundamental to the running of the Parliament that these should be required to be established".[135] There are currently seven mandatory committees: Standards, Procedures and Public Appointments; Finance; Public Audit; European and External Relations; Equal Opportunities; Public Petitions; and Delegated Powers and Law Reform.[136]

4–54 The Parliament also establishes a number of subject committees at the beginning of each session. Those established at the start of the current session were: economy, energy and tourism; education and culture; health and sport; infrastructure and capital investment; justice; local government and regeneration; and rural affairs, climate change and environment. Their remits are intended to cover, between them, the main portfolio responsibilities of the Scottish Ministers.[137]

4–55 The Parliament can also establish temporary or ad hoc committees to consider particular issues or legislative proposals, e.g. the Scotland Bill Committee and the Welfare Reform Committee in the current session were both established to consider the implications of Westminster legislation, while the Referendum (Scotland) Bill Committee (now the Devolution (Further Powers) Committee) was established to consider the legislation on which the independence

---

[132] Scottish Constitutional Convention, *Scotland's Parliament, Scotland's Right* (1995) p.26.

[133] Scottish Office, *Scotland's Parliament* (1997) Cm.3658, para.9.10.

[134] Scottish Office, *Shaping Scotland's Parliament: Report of the Consultative Steering Group on the Scottish Parliament* (December, 1998) s.2 para.13.

[135] Scottish Office, *Shaping Scotland's Parliament: Report of the Consultative Steering Group on the Scottish Parliament* (December, 1998) s.3.1 para.60.

[136] Scottish Parliament Standing Orders r.6.1.5; under the CSG's proposals the Parliamentary Bureau would have been a mandatory committee.

[137] Missing from these arrangements is any dedicated scrutiny of core constitutional and governance issues in the manner, for example, of the Public Administration Select Committee at Westminster; for criticism, see Barry K Winetrobe, "Public Accountability in Scotland" in Aileen McHarg and Tom Mullen, *Public Law in Scotland* (Edinburgh: Avizandum, 2006) pp.144–147.

referendum was based. The Parliament is also obliged to establish committees to scrutinise particular types of Bills, including Private Bills and Hybrid Bills.

The general function of a committee is to examine such matters within its **4–56** remit, or "competent matters", as it may determine appropriate, or as may be referred to it by the Parliament or another committee, and to report on them to the Parliament or another committee as appropriate.[138] As well as conducting inquiries into such competent matters as it considers appropriate, or as the Parliament or another committee requires, a committee may: scrutinise the policy and administration of the Scottish Government upon competent matters; consider proposals for legislation which relate to or affect competent matters, including proposals for primary or secondary legislation, whether before the Scottish Parliament or the UK Parliament; consider European Union legislation or international conventions or agreements or any drafts which relate to or affect competent matters; consider the need for reform of the law which relates to or affects competent matters; initiate Bills on competent matters; and consider the financial proposals and financial administration of the Scottish Government relating to or affecting competent matters.[139]

Not all committees do all of these things. Mandatory committees carry out **4–57** particular functions, directly related to their remit, which are all very different, and they do relatively little in the way of inquiry work or scrutiny of legislation. Subject committees all have essentially the same job, which involves a mixture of business referred to them (mostly scrutiny of Bills and subordinate legislation) and the inquiries or other scrutiny work they choose to undertake, with the balance between them being largely a product of how much business is formally referred to them from elsewhere in the Parliament. For some subject committees, particularly Justice, legislation dominates, while others can spend more of their time on inquiries of their own choosing. All subject committees also participate in annual budget scrutiny. Committees normally meet weekly, with meetings typically lasting for about two to three hours, with most of the time being taken up with hearing oral evidence. Most of their business is conducted in public. They occasionally meet outside Edinburgh and members also undertake visits and organise other events in connection with committee business. Committees have power to appoint reporters from among their members to consider particular topics, and may also seek approval to appoint external experts as advisers. They may also seek the approval of the Bureau and the Parliament to establish subcommittees.

The membership of committees is decided by the Parliament on a motion of **4–58** the Parliamentary Bureau. Committees, other than Private and Hybrid Bill committees, consist of between five and 15 members. In proposing members the Parliamentary Bureau is required to have regard to the balance of political parties in the Parliament and, where a member has expressed an interest in serving on a particular committee, to that member's qualifications and experience.[140] There is no rule prohibiting Ministers from being members of committees, other than the Public Audit Committee,[141] but in practice Ministers have

---

[138] Scottish Parliament Standing Orders r.6.2.1.
[139] Scottish Parliament Standing Orders r.6.2.2.
[140] Scottish Parliament Standing Orders r.6.3.4; the requirement to have regard to the balance of political parties in the Parliament derives from SA 1998 Sch.3 para.6(2); in practice the composition of committees closely matches that of the chamber. The current SNP Government thus has a majority on all of the Parliament's committees—and nine of the 14 convenerships.
[141] Scottish Parliament Standing Orders r.6.7.2.

not been member of committees. Private and Hybrid Bill committees, which are subject to additional rules on eligible MSPs, consist of between three and five members.

4-59 A Conveners Group consisting of the presiding officer and the conveners of the mandatory and subject committees is responsible for considering and making recommendations in connection with the operation of committees.[142] It was originally constituted as an informal forum where conveners could meet to discuss matters of mutual interest, and to facilitate liaison between the committees, the Parliamentary Bureau and the SPCB, before being formally constituted in 2002.

4-60 The "jewel in the crown" is the description of the Parliament's committee system commonly attributed to its first presiding officer, Sir David Steel. It is a description that is no longer used. In the first two sessions (1999–2007), lack of time together with the breadth of their remits made it difficult for some committees to cover the ground, with the demands of legislative scrutiny in particular reducing the scope for some committees to undertake their own inquiries.[143] The slackening of the legislative pace in the third session, however, when a minority government was in power, was not accompanied by any increase in scrutiny, the political focus by then having shifted to the Chamber, and Labour and Liberal Democrat MSPs being at the same time reluctant to revisit their own record by way of post-legislative scrutiny. The sometimes rapid turnover of members also meant that members did not build up the expertise anticipated. The Calman Commission encouraged all political parties to give greater recognition to the value of continuity in committee memberships by doing what they could to minimise changes in membership during a session, although the Commission recognised that some level of "churn" was probably inevitable and even desirable.[144]

4-61 The deeper concern, of which these were the most visible signs, was that not enough importance was attached to the work of committees, with the claims of government and party too often taking precedence over those of scrutiny. In its Session 3 legacy paper the Conveners Group urged the political parties in Session 4 to respect the independence of their members when working on committees, but with a single party majority government in power in the fourth session complaints of excessive partisanship have only increased, with protests by the "minority" in the run up to the independence referendum that the executive was using its majority to close down inquiries and to edit out criticisms of government policy. A "cross between a laughing stock and a downright disgrace" and "little more than ministerial fan clubs" may well be too strong but they are a mark of how far the stock of the Parliament's committee system has fallen.[145]

4-62 One question raised by the difficulty of striking a balance between legislative scrutiny and committees' own inquiry work is whether committees' functions should be split, with their legislative work being handed over to separate

---

[142] Scottish Parliament Standing Orders r.6A.2.

[143] In its Session 2 legacy paper, the Conveners Group singled out the difficulty in achieving a balance between the scrutiny of legislation and other essential scrutiny work as one of the most significant issues facing committees in that session. The Group described itself as "extremely concerned" that the scrutiny of Bills had dominated the agenda for a number of committees. "This has adversely affected the ability of some committees to undertake other work, particularly the scrutiny of the Executive through inquiries. When combined with the wide remits of a number of committees, the impact has been that large and important areas of Executive policy and administration do not receive the appropriate level of scrutiny by Parliamentary committees": Conveners Group Legacy Paper, 2nd Session (February, 2007) para.4.

[144] Commission on Scottish Devolution, *Serving Scotland Better: Scotland and the United Kingdom in the 21st Century* (June, 2009) para.6.36.

[145] Alan Cochrane, "Parliament's Toothless Watchdogs" *The Telegraph*, November 14, 2012.

legislation committees, which would leave subject committees free to concentrate on their inquiry work. In its Session 3 legacy paper, the Conveners Group considered the appropriateness of the same committees being responsible both for policy scrutiny and legislative scrutiny. It was concerned that the current system could lead to a lack of time for oversight of the delivery of government policy but believed that the benefits outweighed the disadvantages. If committee membership remained reasonably stable, members developed a shared understanding of the subject remit of the committee and were better equipped to scrutinise Bills. The Government should, however, give serious consideration to the number of Bills that could reasonably complete their stages in the final year of a session. Experience of three sessions had shown that the final year of the legislative programme resulted in committees being dominated by government legislation. This impacted on their other scrutiny functions including an inability to find time to scrutinise Members' Bills. It also led to a loss of committee time in the run up to dissolution as more Chamber time was needed to complete stage 3 proceedings. This deprived the committees of time needed to complete their work programmes.[146]

The Calman Commission acknowledged that this was not an easy issue for the **4-63** Parliament to address. It saw dual purpose committees as a pragmatic, and probably necessary, response to the practical problem of operating a committee-based parliament with only around 100 available members (once presiding officers and ministers had been excluded). Separate scrutiny and legislation committees would require either an increase in the number of committees or a reduced number of scrutiny committees, with remits wider than those of the existing subject committees, and it seemed unlikely that such alterations would enhance the overall effectiveness of the committee system.[147]

The uncomfortable truth is that procedural reform can only achieve so much. **4-64** As the Calman Commission concluded:

> "No doubt the system could be improved, but the drivers for change are likely to be less about the formal structures of the Parliament or its rules, and more about its culture and working practices, which are not easily influenced by external strictures. The committee system could work better than it does, but the motivation to achieve that can really only come from within."[148]

Power to call for witnesses and documents

The Parliament has extensive powers to call for witnesses and documents, **4-65** which may be exercised by committees as well as by the Parliament.[149] It may require persons to attend its proceedings for the purpose of giving evidence, or to produce documents in their custody or under their control "concerning any subject for which any member of the Scottish Government has general responsibility".[150] The term "general responsibility" is not defined but

---

[146] Conveners Group Legacy Paper, 3rd Session (January, 2011) paras 10–13.
[147] Commission on Scottish Devolution, *Serving Scotland Better: Scotland and the United Kingdom in the 21st Century* (June, 2009) para.6.38; the main advantage of separate legislation and subject committees at Westminster is said to be that the party whips are not interested in subject committees, raising the question whether the combination of functions at Holyrood is to the detriment of the Parliament's oversight function.
[148] Commission on Scottish Devolution, *Serving Scotland Better: Scotland and the United Kingdom in the 21st Century* (June, 2009) para.6.43.
[149] Scottish Parliament Standing Orders r.12.4.
[150] SA 1998 s.23(1).

"it is not limited to matters where functions have been conferred upon a member of the Scottish Government, whether in relation to devolved or reserved matters".[151]

The intention was that the Parliament should be able to investigate an area of policy responsibility without being confined to what in some areas might be a limited range of functions.

4–66 There are a number of restrictions on this power:

(i) A person outside Scotland cannot be required to attend unless it is in connection with the discharge by that person of functions of the Scottish Administration, or functions of a Scottish public authority or cross-border public authority, or Border river functions, which concern a subject for which a member of the Scottish Government has general responsibility.[152]

(ii) UK Ministers and civil servants cannot be required to attend in relation to the exercise of their functions unless the exercise of those functions concerns a subject for which a member of the Scottish Government has general responsibility.[153] Where, however, the exercise of their functions concerns a subject for which a member of the Scottish Government has general responsibility, they cannot be required to attend if their functions are also exercisable by the Scottish Ministers, or are exercisable only after obtaining the agreement of, or after consultation with, the Scottish Ministers, unless in the case of the latter they relate to devolved matters.[154] The intention in such cases is that the Parliament should look to the Scottish Ministers rather than UK Ministers for an explanation.

(iii) A person cannot be required to attend in connection with the discharge of the functions of a body all of whose functions relate to reserved matters.[155] *Scotland's Parliament* acknowledged that in certain reserved areas the activities of UK/Great British bodies would continue to be significant in the economic and social life of Scotland, and would therefore likely be of interest to the Parliament. The White Paper proposed, however, that the Parliament should only be able to "invite" the submissions of reports and the presentation of oral evidence before its committees from bodies operating in reserved areas in relation to their activities in or affecting Scotland.[156] Under the Smith Commission Agreement, the Parliament will be able to call for witnesses and documents from a number of UK public bodies, including the BBC, OFCOM and OFGEM.[157]

(iv) Judges and tribunal members cannot be required to attend, the latter in connection with the discharge of their functions as a tribunal member.[158]

---

[151] Scotland Act 1998, explanatory note to s.23.

[152] SA 1998 s.23(2).

[153] SA 1998 s.23(3); Cabinet Office Devolution Guidance Note 12 provides guidance to UK Ministers and civil servants on responding to invitations to attend committees of the devolved legislatures.

[154] SA 1998 s.23(4), (5).

[155] SA 1998 s.23(6); on whether the functions of a body relate to reserved matters, see s.126(3).

[156] Scottish Office, *Scotland's Parliament* (1997) Cm.3658, para.2.11.

[157] Scotland Office, *Scotland in the United Kingdom: An enduring settlement* (2015) Cm.8990, Ch.5.

[158] SA 1998 s.23(7).

(v) Witnesses are not obliged to answer questions or to produce documents which they would be entitled to refuse to answer or produce in court proceedings in Scotland.[159] The Lord Advocate may also relieve a procurator fiscal of the obligation to answer questions or produce documents concerning the operation of the system of criminal prosecution in a particular case if to do so might prejudice criminal proceedings in that case or would be otherwise contrary to the public interest.[160]

Refusal or failure without reasonable excuse to attend proceedings, answer questions, or produce documents is a criminal offence, as is the deliberate alteration, suppression, concealment or destruction of documents.[161] **4–67**

The power to compel the attendance of witnesses and the production of documents is a "weapon of last resort". Committees proceed by invitation and have not so far found it necessary to use, or publicly threaten to use, their powers of compulsion. **4–68**

RIGHTS AND IMMUNITIES

The Scottish Parliament benefits from certain statutory rights and immunities which, like parliamentary privilege at Westminster, are intended to enable it to carry out is functions effectively; "to give it a 'protected space' within which it can carry out its role robustly without fear of legal challenge."[162] **4–69**

Defamation and contempt

Freedom of speech is the most important of Westminster's traditional privileges. It is enshrined in the Bill of Rights, art.9 of which provides that "the freedom of speech and debates or proceedings in Parliament ought not to be impeached or questioned in any court or place out of Parliament"; the Scottish Claim of Right 1689 by contrast simply provided that freedom of speech and debate ought to be "secured" to the members. The Scotland Act 1998 extends two aspects of the privilege to the Parliament, its members and officers. First, the Act provides that for the purposes of the law of defamation statements made in "proceedings of the Parliament", and their publication under the authority of the Parliament, are absolutely privileged.[163] The purpose is to ensure that members are free to debate and the Parliament is free to report on matters of public interest without fear of an action for defamation being raised. The protection provided is for the purposes of the law of defamation: it does not shield members from the operation of the law in relation to other matters, e.g. the offence of incitement to racial hatred. **4–70**

Secondly, the Act disapplies the "strict liability" rule established by the Contempt of Court Act 1981 in relation to publications made in, or in reports of, proceedings of the Parliament in relation to a Bill or subordinate legislation.[164] Under the strict liability rule **4–71**

---

[159] SA 1998 s.23(9).
[160] SA 1998 s.23(10).
[161] SA 1998 s.25.
[162] Commission on Scottish Devolution, *The Future of Scottish Devolution within the Union: A First Report* (December, 2008) para.2.26.
[163] SA 1998 s.41.
[164] SA 1998 s.42.

"conduct may be treated as a contempt of court as tending to interfere with the course of justice in particular proceedings regardless of intent to do so".[165]

The purpose of disapplying the rule is to ensure that the Parliament is not prevented from legislating on any matter simply because anything said or done in the proceedings might be treated as a contempt of court under the rule, and to ensure that such proceedings can be properly reported.

4–72 As is required by the Scotland Act, the Parliament's standing orders include a requirement that members must not conduct themselves in a manner which would constitute a contempt of court (or which would constitute a criminal offence); they also include a sub judice rule limiting parliamentary discussion of cases before the courts.[166]

4–73 The expression "proceedings of the Parliament" includes proceedings of any committee or subcommittee.[167] Beyond that the expression is not defined. The intention, however, was that it should be construed in a similar way to "proceedings in Parliament" for the purpose of art.9 of the Bill of Rights.[168]

Legal proceedings

4–74 The SPCB represents the Parliament in all legal proceedings brought by or against the Parliament.[169] Other than in respect of defamation, the Scotland Act does not restrict the proceedings that may be brought against the Parliament. It does, however, restrict the remedies that may be granted in order to prevent litigation being employed as a tactic to disrupt parliamentary business, e.g. by preventing the Parliament from considering a Bill. In proceedings against the Parliament, therefore, the court cannot grant a coercive order, which would require the Parliament to do something or to refrain from doing something, but may instead make a declarator, which would leave it to the Parliament to decide how it should react.[170]

4–75 The same protection is extended to MSPs, the presiding officer and deputy presiding officers, the SPCB and staff of the Parliament, if the effect of making an order would be to give relief against the Parliament "which could not have been given in proceedings against the Parliament".[171] In *Whaley v Watson*,[172] the Lord President stressed that

> "the immunity thus granted to members of the Parliament is not granted in order to afford protection to the members themselves but simply to buttress the immunity of the Parliament from orders of that kind".

---

[165] Contempt of Court Act 1981 s.1.

[166] Scottish Parliament Standing Orders rr.7.3.2 and 7.5; SA 1998 Sch.3 para.1(1); applied Scottish Parliament OR May 15, 2002 cols 8855–8856.

[167] SA 1998 s.126(1).

[168] House of Lords debate July 28, 1998, Vol.592, cols 1447–1448; for extensive discussion of the concept, see the First Report of the Joint Committee on Parliamentary Privilege (1998–1999, HL 43, HC 214) pp.97–129.

[169] SA 1998 s.40(1).

[170] SA 1998 s.40(3).

[171] SA 1998 s.40(4).

[172] *Whaley v Watson*, 2000 S.C. 340, 349.

CHAPTER 5

THE SCOTTISH GOVERNMENT

INTRODUCTION

"There shall be a Scottish Government … "[1] As well as the Scottish Parliament, **5–01** the Scotland Act 1998 established a Scottish Government, which is drawn from the Parliament on the Westminster model and responsible to it for the devolved government of Scotland. The Scottish Government was originally called the Scottish Executive, in a vain attempt to distinguish it from the UK Government, but the term never achieved any degree of popular recognition or understanding. When Henry McLeish became First Minister after the death of Donald Dewar in 2000 it was suggested that the Scottish Executive call itself the "Scottish Government", but the suggestion was dropped in the face of opposition from London. On its election in 2007, however, the SNP Government renamed the Scottish Executive the Scottish Government, and the change was subsequently given formal legal effect by the Scotland Act 2012.[2]

MINISTERS

The Scottish Government consists of the First Minister, other Scottish Ministers **5–02** appointed by the First Minister, the Lord Advocate and the Solicitor-General for Scotland.[3] Collectively they are referred to as "the Scottish Ministers".[4] The Scotland Act 1998 ("the Scotland Act") also makes provision for the appointment of junior Scottish Ministers, who are office-holders in the Scottish Administration, which is the expression the Scotland Act uses for the whole of the devolved central government of Scotland,[5] but not members of the Scottish Government. In the course of a general inflation of titles, Ministers have become Cabinet Secretaries and junior Ministers have become Ministers, having previously been deputy Ministers.[6] The Scotland Act prohibits members of the Scottish Government, including junior Scottish Ministers, from holding office in the UK Government[7]; a person cannot therefore be a minister in both the UK Government and Scottish Government at the same time.

The First Minister

The Scotland Act requires the Parliament to nominate one of its members for **5–03** appointment as First Minister within 28 days of a general election, failing

---

[1] Scotland Act 1998 ("SA 1998") s. 44(1).
[2] Scotland Act 2012 ("SA 2012") s.12.
[3] SA 1998 s.44(1).
[4] SA 1998 s.44(2).
[5] SA 1998 s.126(6)–(8).
[6] While the SA 2012 recognised the rebranding of the Scottish Executive as the Scottish Government, it is perhaps noteworthy that did not recognise the new ministerial titles of Cabinet Secretary and Minister. It remains to be seen whether these titles will be adopted by any non-SNP government.
[7] SA 1998 s.44(3).

which an extraordinary general election must be held.[8] The length of time negotiations between potential partners to a coalition can last is thus strictly limited. Once nominated the First Minister nominate is appointed by the Queen on the recommendation of the presiding officer.[9] The decision, however, is that of the Parliament rather than the Queen, in contrast to the appointment of the Prime Minister where in exceptional circumstances there may be a need for the exercise of choice by the Queen.[10]

5–04   A First Minister may lose office as a result of defeat at a general election (Jack McConnell). Between elections a vacancy in the office of First Minister may arise as a result of the resignation (Henry McLeish, Alex Salmond) or death (Donald Dewar) of the incumbent[11]; a vacancy may also arise should the incumbent cease to be an MSP.[12] Resignation may be voluntary or enforced, the latter as a result of the Parliament passing a motion of no confidence in the Scottish Government.[13] A voluntary resignation need not lead to an extraordinary general election unless it is impossible for the governing coalition or party to unite behind a successor. A forced resignation, on the other hand, would almost certainly lead to an election unless the majority forcing the resignation was sufficiently cohesive to form an alternative government. Where the office is vacant or the First Minister is unable to act, the presiding officer may designate a member to exercise the First Minister's functions,[14] as happened on the death of Donald Dewar and the resignation of Henry McLeish.

5–05   The office of First Minister is held "at Her Majesty's pleasure".[15] In theory, therefore, the First Minister could be dismissed by the Queen. Given, however, that the Parliament has in its power to force the resignation of a government by passing a motion of no confidence in it, it is very hard to envisage circumstances in which the Queen acting would be justified in dismissing a First Minister who continued to enjoy the confidence of the Parliament.[16]

The Deputy First Minister

5–06   In the first two coalition governments the leader of the junior party in the coalition was appointed Deputy First Minister, an office for which no provision is made in the Scotland Act but to which real power attached, with ministerial appointments, for example, being made only after consultation with the Deputy First Minister.[17] The First Minister and Deputy First Minister were also said to meet regularly to discuss the delivery of the government's programme and to take stock of particularly significant or sensitive policy issues.[18] The tradition of appointing a Deputy First Minister has been continued under both SNP

---

[8] SA 1998 ss.46(2)(a), 3(1)(b).

[9] SA 1998 ss.45(1), 46(4).

[10] Rodney Brazier, "The Scottish government" [1998] P.L. 216.

[11] SA 1998 s.46(2)(b), (c).

[12] SA 1998 s.46(2)(d).

[13] SA 1998 s.45(2); the prospect of a motion of no confidence may of course lead to a "voluntary" resignation.

[14] SA 1998 s.45(4).

[15] SA 1998 ss.45(1), 47(3)(a).

[16] Rodney Brazier, "The Scottish government" [1998] P.L. 216, 219.

[17] Scottish Executive, *Partnership for Scotland* (May, 1999) and *Scottish Ministerial Code* (August, 1999) para.4.1; and, to like effect, *Partnership for a Better Scotland* (May, 2003) and *Scottish Ministerial Code* (August, 2003) para.4.1.

[18] Executive Secretariat, *The Scottish Executive: A Guide to Collective Decision Making* (August, 1999) para.2.7; Scottish Executive, *Guide to Collective Decision Making* (August, 2003) para 2.7.

administrations with Nicola Sturgeon appointed Deputy First Minister in 2007, followed by John Swinney when she became First Minister in 2014.

Ministers

Once appointed the First Minister appoints the other members of the Scottish **5–07** Government (with the exception of the law officers who are appointed by the Queen on the recommendation of the First Minister made with the agreement of the Parliament). Formally, Ministers, or Cabinet Secretaries as they are currently known, are appointed by the First Minister from among the members of the Parliament with the approval of the Queen and the agreement of the Parliament.[19] The agreement of the Parliament, which has no equivalent at Westminster, is sought to the appointment of members to be Ministers as a group rather than individually but it is open to the Parliament to withhold its agreement to the appointment of a member or members by amending the motion of approval.[20] In contrast to their appointment, Ministers' removal from office is at the sole discretion of the First Minister.[21] Like the First Minister they hold office at Her Majesty's pleasure, and must resign if the Parliament passes a vote of no confidence in the Scottish Government.[22]

There are no statutory restrictions on the number of Ministers who may be **5–08** appointed. Currently there are nine Ministers, an increase of four from the first SNP Government: the Deputy First Minister and Cabinet Secretary for Finance, Constitution and Economy; the Cabinet Secretary for Infrastructure, Investment and Cities; the Cabinet Secretary for Fair Work, Skills and Training; the Cabinet Secretary for Education and Lifelong Learning; the Cabinet Secretary for Health, Wellbeing and Sport; the Cabinet Secretary for Social Justice, Communities and Pensioners' Rights; the Cabinet Secretary for Justice; the Cabinet Secretary for Rural Affairs, Food and Environment; and the Cabinet Secretary for Culture, Europe and External Affairs.

The allocation of ministerial portfolios

The structure and allocation of ministerial portfolios is a matter for the First **5–09** Minister.[23] In the first two coalition governments it was a matter for discussion and agreement between the First Minister and Deputy First Minister.[24] Statutory functions conferred on the Scottish Ministers by that name may be exercised by any of them.[25] There is no need therefore to formally transfer functions between them following a reallocation of responsibilities.

Junior Ministers

The First Minister also appoints junior Scottish Ministers, currently known as **5–10** Ministers, and before that as deputy Ministers, from among members of the Parliament "to assist the Scottish Ministers in the exercise of their functions".[26] The statutory language is apparently intended to reflect the *Carltona* doctrine, by which civil servants are able to act for Ministers, so that junior Scottish

---

[19] SA 1998 s.47(1), (2).
[20] Scottish Parliament Standing Orders r.4.6.3.
[21] SA 1998 s.47(3)(b).
[22] SA 1998 s.47(3)(a), (c).
[23] Scottish Government, *Scottish Ministerial Code* (2011) para.4.4.
[24] Scottish Executive, *Scottish Ministerial Code* (August, 1999) para.4.2; *Scottish Ministerial Code* (August, 2003) para.4.2.
[25] SA 1998 s.52(3).
[26] SA 1998 s.49(1).

Ministers are able to act for the Scottish Ministers.[27] In contrast to Ministers, i.e. those ministers now called Cabinet Secretaries, junior Scottish Ministers are not members of the Scottish Government.

5–11 The provisions governing the appointment and removal from office of junior Scottish Ministers mirror those for Ministers. They are appointed by the First Minister with the approval of the Queen and the agreement of the Parliament,[28] and they may be removed from office at the sole discretion of the First Minister. (Under the first two coalition governments they were appointed following consultation with the Deputy First Minister.[29]) In common with members of the Scottish Government, junior Scottish Ministers hold office at Her Majesty's pleasure, and must resign if the Parliament passes a vote of no confidence in the Scottish Government.[30]

5–12 The Cabinet Secretaries for Finance, Constitution and Economy, Education and Lifelong Learning, Health, Wellbeing and Sport, and Social Justice, Communities and Pensioner's Rights are each supported by two Ministers; the Cabinet Secretaries for Infrastructure, Investment and Cities, Fair Work, Skills and Training, Justice, Rural Affairs, Food and Environment and Culture, Europe and External Affairs each by one Minister.

Parliamentary liaison officers

5–13 Parliamentary liaison officers, formerly known as ministerial parliamentary aides, may also be appointed to support Cabinet Secretaries in the discharge of their parliamentary duties.[31] Parliamentary liaison officers are not members of the Scottish Government and, in contrast to junior Scottish Ministers, are not bound by the principle of collective responsibility (below). Currently, there are 10 parliamentary liaison officers.

Defects in appointments

5–14 The Scotland Act provides that the validity of acts of members of the Scottish Government, or junior Scottish Ministers, is not affected by any defect in the parliamentary proceedings relating to their appointment.[32]

> "It would therefore not be possible to challenge the acts of a Minister on the basis, for example, that his or her nomination or appointment was not made in accordance with the Act."[33]

Remuneration

5–15 The remuneration (salaries, allowances and pension arrangements) of members of the Scottish Government, including for this purpose junior Scottish Ministers, is a matter for the Parliament.[34] The Scotland Act requires information about

---

[27] Scotland Act 1998, explanatory note to s.49; *Carltona Ltd v Commissioners of Works* [1943] 2 All E.R. 560.
[28] SA 1998 s.49(1), (3).
[29] Scottish Executive, *Scottish Ministerial Code* (August, 1999) para.4.1; *Scottish Ministerial Code* (August, 2003) para.4.1.
[30] SA 1998 ss.49(4), 47(3)(c).
[31] Scottish Government, *Scottish Ministerial Code* (2011) paras 4.8–4.13.
[32] SA 1998 s.50.
[33] Scotland Act 1998, explanatory note to s.50.
[34] SA 1998 s.81. The Scottish Parliament Salaries Scheme was made by resolution of the Parliament on March 21, 2002 (Scottish Parliamentary Paper 554, 2002).

the sums paid to members of the Scottish Government to be published for each financial year.[35] The First Minister's salary (from April 1, 2014) is £143,680, a Minister's salary £102,775, and a junior Minister's salary £86,300.

Oaths

Members of the Scottish Government are required to take the official oath in **5–16** the form provided by the Promissory Oaths Act 1868, and to take the oath of allegiance if they have not already taken it as MSPs.[36] The official oath is the same oath as is sworn by Ministers of the Crown:

> "I do swear that I will well and truly serve her Majesty Queen Elizabeth in the Office of ... so help me God."

The oath of allegiance is the same as is used in the Westminster Parliament:

> "I do swear that I will be faithful and bear true allegiance to Her Majesty Queen Elizabeth, her heirs and successors, according to law. So help me God'."

Junior Scottish Ministers must take the oath of allegiance if they have not already taken it as MSPs.[37] A member of the Scottish Government who has not taken an oath cannot be paid a salary or any other form of remuneration.[38]

THE LAW OFFICERS

As well as the First Minister and Ministers, the Scottish Government includes **5–17** the two Scottish law officers, the Lord Advocate and the Solicitor General for Scotland. While Ministers must be appointed from among members of the Parliament, the law officers need not be so appointed, acknowledging that lawyers of sufficient standing may not be found among MSPs. Traditionally they were recruited from the Faculty of Advocates—indeed the argument was that they could only be recruited from the Faculty of Advocates[39]—but under devolution the pool from which they may be recruited has been widened to include the Crown Office and the solicitor branch of the profession. Unlike Ministers, who are appointed by the First Minister with the approval of the Queen and the agreement of the Parliament, and who may be freely removed from office by the First Minister, the law officers are appointed directly by the Queen, and may only be removed by the Queen, acting in both cases on a recommendation from the First Minister made with the agreement of the Parliament.[40] Thus, they enjoy a greater degree of security of tenure than Ministers, a reflection of the importance attached to the continued exercise of their prosecution functions free from political or other forms of influence.

The Lord Advocate has two main roles within the devolved government of **5–18** Scotland: as head of the systems of criminal prosecution and investigation of

---

[35] SA 1998 s.83.

[36] SA 1998 s.84(4), (6); but could a member be appointed a Minister without having first taken the oath as an MSP? An affirmation can be made in place of the oath: Oaths Act 1978 s.5.

[37] SA 1998 s.84(5), (6), the comment in fn 36 also applies.

[38] SA 1998 s.83(2).

[39] J Ll J Edwards, *The Attorney General, Politics and the Public Interest* (London: Sweet & Maxwell, 1984) pp.282–283.

[40] SA 1998 s.48(1).

deaths in Scotland, i.e. the chief prosecutor; and as the Scottish Government's principal or chief legal adviser. The Lord Advocate also represents the Scottish Government in civil proceedings, and the public interest in a range of statutory and common law civil functions. The Solicitor General is the Lord Advocate's deputy, and may discharge any of the Lord Advocate's functions where the office of Lord Advocate is vacant, the Lord Advocate is unable to act owing to absence or illness, or where the Lord Advocate authorises the Solicitor General to act in any particular case.[41]

5–19 The Scottish Parliament has no power to remove the Lord Advocate as head of the systems of criminal prosecution and investigation of deaths in Scotland.[42] The incumbent may change but the role cannot. This limitation was conceived as one of the guarantees of the independence of criminal prosecutions after devolution. The effectiveness of the guarantee depends of course on the independence of the Lord Advocate, to which end the Scotland Act insists that decisions taken by the Lord Advocate as head of the systems of criminal prosecution and investigation of deaths in Scotland must "continue to be taken by him independently of any other person", thereby giving the force of law to the long standing convention governing the exercise of the Lord Advocate's prosecution functions.[43] The Scotland Act also excludes the exercise of the Lord Advocate's "retained functions", in effect the Lord Advocate's functions as head of the systems of criminal prosecution and investigation of deaths, and any other functions conferred on the Lord Advocate by name, from the collective legal responsibility of members of the Scottish Government.[44] The Lord Advocate and the Lord Advocate alone, therefore, is legally responsible for the exercise of those functions.

5–20 In common with other members of the Scottish Government, the law officers must resign if the Parliament passes a vote of no confidence in the Government.[45] The Act, however, makes provision for the Lord Advocate to remain in office until replaced by the incoming administration, but only for the purpose of exercising the Lord Advocate's retained functions, thus securing continuity in criminal proceedings during a possible change in government.[46]

5–21 The law officers' other main responsibility is for the provision of legal advice to the Scottish Ministers on "all matters relating to the law of Scotland".[47] The Scottish Ministerial Code states that the law officers

> "are concerned to ensure that the Government acts lawfully at all times. Accordingly, the general principle is that they must be consulted in good time before the Government is committed to significant decisions involving legal considerations".[48]

The Code offers the following examples of the kind of situation in which advice should be sought:

---

[41] Law Officers Act 1944 s.2.
[42] SA 1998 s.29(2)(e).
[43] SA 1998 s 48(5); the Lord Advocate's duty to act independently of any other person "is ... distilled ... from the Westminster convention which existed prior to devolution": Elish Angiolini, "Legislation, Litigation and Prosecution: the Role of a Scottish Law Officer" [2003] J.R. 219, 231.
[44] SA 1998 s.52(5)(b), (6).
[45] SA 1998 s.48(2).
[46] SA 1998 ss.48(3), 52(6).
[47] Scottish Government, *Scottish Ministerial Code* (2011) para.2.30.
[48] Scottish Government, *Scottish Ministerial Code* (2011) para.2.31.

(i) The legal consequences of action by the Government might have important repercussions.

(ii) A legal adviser in the Scottish Government has doubts about the legality or constitutional propriety of proposed legislation or executive action.

(iii) Ministers, or their officials, wish to have the advice of the law officers on questions involving legal considerations.

(iv) There is a particular legal difficulty that may raise sensitive policy issues.[49]

The law officers' advice is normally sought through the Scottish Government **5–22** Legal Directorate ("SGLD"), which is the primary source of legal advice for the Scottish Government. The law officers are "operationally responsible" for SGLD, a term that was deliberately chosen for its vagueness, but which means essentially that they are responsible for the general provision of legal advice to the Scottish Government but not for the advice provided by SGLD in individual cases, leaving the law officers free to provide their own advice should this be necessary.[50]

The law officers' close relationship with SGLD is one manifestation of the **5–23** much more central role they play in the Scottish Government than their predecessors played in relation to the former Scottish Office. Their more significant role is a reflection of two factors in particular—over and above the fact that they are physically present in Scotland and can therefore devote much more time to "Scottish", i.e. devolved business, than could their predecessors.

The first is the much higher profile of law and legal issues in the devolved **5–24** Scotland. As Elish Angiolini, who was Lord Advocate between 2006 and 2011, explained, the effect of the "overarching constitutional framework" within which the Scottish Parliament and the Scottish Government must operate is

"to raise the profile of law much higher than at Westminster. The combination of European law and human rights law and the reserved matters in Sch.5 makes the legal issue—the issue of competence—much more of an immediate concern to the Scottish Ministers and administrators than is the case south of the Border".[51]

The second factor is the collective legal as opposed to political responsibility **5–25** of the Scottish Government (below), which is said to give the law officers a close interest in the legality of the actings of their ministerial colleagues— hence the Ministerial Code's description of them as being concerned to ensure that the Government acts lawfully at all times—while simultaneously reducing their colleagues' scope to go their own way, since they cannot argue that whether or not to do so is a matter for them and them alone; in contrast to UK Ministers their colleagues cannot simply take a departmental decision "to run

---

[49] Scottish Government, *Scottish Ministerial Code* (2011) para.2.32; see also *Guide to Collective Decision Making* (2008) para.4.16 and Annex B.

[50] Elish Angiolini, "Legislation, Litigation and Prosecution: the Role of a Scottish Law Officer" [2003] J.R. 219, 223; the *Scottish Ministerial Code* (2011) para.2.30 now describes the law officers as having "ministerial responsibility" for the provision of legal advice, which seems to come to the same thing.

[51] Elish Angiolini, "Legislation, Litigation and Prosecution: the Role of a Scottish Law Officer" [2003] J.R. 219, 223.

the risks signalled by the law officers".[52] The Lord Advocate and Solicitor General are

> "whether they like it or not, members of the Scottish Executive. They are Scottish Ministers. They are responsible along with their fellow Ministers for the policies and decisions of the Scottish Executive and, since their contribution to that policy making process is legal, it is their duty to make sure that those policies are within the law".[53]

5–26 Devolution and the increased legalisation of decision-making has thus led to a highly centralised and coordinated system of legal advice, one in which the scope for individual elements of the devolved administration to form their own view of the law is much less than traditionally has been the case in Whitehall.[54]

5–27 The Scottish Government has retained the UK government practice of not disclosing the fact or content of law officers' advice without their authority. The Scottish Ministerial Code insists that the fact that legal advice has or has not been given to the Scottish Government by the law officers and the content of any advice given by them or anyone else must not be revealed outwith the Scottish Government without the law officers' prior consent.[55] Law officers' advice, like other ministerial communications, is exempt information under the Freedom of Information (Scotland) Act 2002.[56] In October 2012, the Deputy First Minister "confirmed", with the Lord Advocate's agreement, that the Government had sought the law officers' advice on an independent Scotland's position within the European Union. She also revealed that the Government had not sought the law officers' advice before, contrary to the impression created by the First Minister.[57]

5–28 Notwithstanding the Scotland Act's insistence on the Lord Advocate's independence in criminal prosecutions, there is a view that devolution has substantially undermined the independence of the Lord Advocate, compared with the traditions of the office, by bringing the Lord Advocate much more closely into the Scottish Government. Whether for that reason or not, devolution has seen a deliberate distancing of the Lord Advocate from the political process. The first Lord Advocate, Lord Hardie, who was Lord Advocate between 1997 and 2000, was a full voting member of the Cabinet (below). His successor, Colin Boyd, who was Lord Advocate between 2000 and 2006, attended meetings but was not formally a member of the Cabinet. In 2007, however, the incoming SNP Government decided that the Lord Advocate would not be a member of the Cabinet, and should not normally attend meetings, in order to ensure that the law officers were seen to be "independent of politics". The then Lord Advocate, Elish Angiolini, was also the first Lord Advocate to remain in post

---

[52] Terence Daintith and Alan Page, *The Executive in the Constitution: Structure, Autonomy and Internal Control* (Oxford: OUP, 1999) p.312.

[53] Elish Angiolini, "The Lord Advocate in the 21st Century", KPMG Annual Law Lecture (February, 2007).

[54] Terence Daintith and Alan Page, *The Executive in the Constitution: Structure, Autonomy and Internal Control* (Oxford: OUP, 1999) Ch.10.

[55] Scottish Government, *Scottish Ministerial Code* (2011) para.2.35; *Guide to Collective Decision Making* (2008) para.4.30. The only exception to this rule is that it is acknowledged publicly that the law officers have advised on the legislative competence of Government Bills introduced in the Parliament.

[56] Freedom of Information (Scotland) Act 2002 s.29(1).

[57] Scottish Parliament OR October 23, 2012, cols 12406–12409.

following a change in government.[58] The more remote the Lord Advocate is from the deliberations of government, however, the more difficult it is to envisage the Lord Advocate as a meaningful check on the legality of the actings of ministerial colleagues (above).

Where the law officers are not MSPs, they may participate in proceedings of **5–29** the Parliament but they may not vote.[59] (The extent of their participation is governed by standing orders, as is the extent to which they are governed by the rules applying to members, but they are automatically bound by the rules on members' interests and paid advocacy.[60]) They can therefore be questioned by MSPs about the exercise of their functions, but they may decline to provide documents or answer questions about particular criminal cases if they consider that to do so might prejudice proceedings in a case or would otherwise be contrary to the public interest.[61] The Lord Advocate may extend the same protection to a procurator fiscal where documents or answers to questions might prejudice criminal proceedings in a case or would otherwise be contrary to the public interest.[62]

The decision whether or not to prosecute has always been liable to attract **5–30** parliamentary interest.[63] The most important consequence of devolution for the law officers has been increased parliamentary scrutiny, especially of prosecution decisions. From time to time it is suggested that responsibility for criminal prosecutions should be transferred to an "independent" prosecutor, but it is open to question whether MSPs would be willing to accept the loss of direct personal responsibility such a transfer would entail.[64]

THE SCOTTISH MINISTERIAL CODE

The Scottish Ministerial Code was first issued in August 1999. By convention, **5–31** the Code is revised at the commencement of each new Parliamentary term. Like the UK Ministerial Code on which it is based, the Scottish Ministerial Code is made up of a mixture of principles of ministerial conduct and more detailed guidance on procedures. The Code, which states that it should be read against the background of the

> "overarching duty on Ministers to comply with the law, including international law and treaty obligations, and to uphold the administration of justice and to protect the integrity of public life"

---

[58] It remains to be seen whether a future government will revert to the earlier tradition of appointing a political sympathiser to the office.

[59] SA 1998 s.27(1).

[60] SA 1998 s.39(8); Interests of Members of the Scottish Parliament Act 2006 s.19.

[61] SA 1998 s.27(3).

[62] SA 1998 s.23(10).

[63] Before devolution, see the Glasgow rape case, discussed by J Ll J Edwards, *The Attorney General, Politics and the Public Interest* (London: Sweet & Maxwell, 1984) pp.306–309, and the Thurso boy case, *Report of the Tribunal appointed to inquire into the Allegation of Assault on John Waters* (1959) Cmnd.718; see also J Ll J Edwards, *The Law Officers of the Crown* (London: Sweet & Maxwell, 1964) p.188, fn 37.

[64] Devolution coincided with a "crisis" in the Crown Office; see *Report of an Inquiry into Crown Decision-Making in the Case of the Murder of Surjit Singh Chhokar* (Scottish Parliamentary Paper 425, 2001). Although parliamentary scrutiny was "uncomfortable", it is said to have been used to good advantage.

emphasises that "Scottish Ministers are expected to behave in a way that upholds the 'highest standards of propriety'".[65] In particular, they are expected to observe the Seven Principles of Public Life set out in the first report of the Nolan Committee on Standards in Public Life,[66] together with the following principles of ministerial conduct:

(i)   the principle of collective ministerial responsibility (below);

(ii)   a duty to the Parliament "to account, and be held to account, for the policies, decisions and actions taken within their field of responsibility";

(iii)   a duty "to give accurate and truthful information to the Parliament". It is of "paramount importance" the Code insists, that Ministers "give accurate and truthful information to the Parliament, correcting any inadvertent error at the earliest opportunity". Ministers who "knowingly mislead" the Parliament, it warns, will be expected to offer their resignation to the First Minister;

(iv)   a duty to be as "open as possible" with the Parliament and the public, reflecting the aspirations set out in the Report of the Consultative Steering Group on the Scottish Parliament.[67] They should refuse to provide information only in accordance with the Freedom of Information (Scotland) Act 2002 and other relevant statutes;

(v)   a duty to require civil servants who give evidence before committees on their behalf and under their direction to be "as helpful as possible in providing accurate, truthful and full information in accordance with the duties and responsibilities of civil servants as set out in the Civil Service Code";

(vi)   a duty to ensure that "no conflict arises, or appears to arise, between their public duties and their private interests";

(vii)   a duty not to accept "any gift or hospitality which might, or might reasonably appear to, compromise their judgement or place them under an improper obligation";

(viii) a duty to keep separate their roles as Minister and as constituency or regional list member;

(ix)   a duty not to use public resources for party political purposes; and

(x)   a duty to uphold the political impartiality of the Civil Service and not ask civil servants to act in any way which would conflict with the Civil Service Code.[68]

5–32 The Code also provides that:

> "In all their dealings with the Parliament, Ministers should seek to uphold and promote the key principles which guided the work of the Consultative Steering Group on the Scottish Parliament."[69]

5–33 The Code offers guidance to Ministers on how they should act and arrange their affairs in order to uphold these standards. It lists the principles which may apply in particular situations, drawing on past precedent, but emphasises that it

---

[65] Scottish Government, *Scottish Ministerial Code* (2011) paras 1.1–1.2.

[66] Committee on Standards in Public Life, *Standards in Public Life* (1995) Cm.2850; the seven principles, the descriptions of which were revised in 2013, are: selflessness; integrity; objectivity; accountability; openness; honesty; and leadership.

[67] Scottish Office, *Shaping Scotland's Parliament: Report of the Consultative Steering Group on the Scottish Parliament* (December, 1998).

[68] Scottish Government, *Scottish Ministerial Code* (2011) para.1.2.

[69] Scottish Government, *Scottish Ministerial Code* (2011) para.3.1; the key principles are set out at para.3.2.

is not a rulebook.[70] Ministers are personally responsible for deciding how to act and conduct themselves in the light of the Code and for justifying their actions to the Parliament and the public, but the First Minister is the ultimate judge of the standards of behaviour expected of a Minister and the appropriate consequences of a breach of those standards. "Ministers can only remain in office for so long as they retain [her] confidence."[71]

The 2008 revision of the Code saw the introduction of a panel of independent **5–34** advisers from whom the First Minister may seek advice on any action required in respect of ministerial conduct.[72] Six complaints have been referred to the panel, five of which were dismissed, and the sixth the panel declined to consider.[73] Following the most recent complaint—about whether the former First Minister had misled the public over whether the Scottish Government had sought the law officers' advice about an independent Scotland's continuing membership of the EU—it was suggested that the Code should be split with questions of propriety becoming a matter for the Parliament rather than the First Minister.[74] The standards would therefore be laid down and approved by the Parliament, rather than being based on resolutions of the Westminster Parliament, which have never been approved by Holyrood. The advisers would also be appointed by the Parliament rather than the First Minister as at present, with references to them being made by the Parliament's Standards, Procedures and Public Appointments Committee. There is also the question of the application of the standards to the First Minister, who under the current arrangements refers complaints about her conduct to her own advisers, an arrangement hardly calculated to foster public confidence in the process.

THE CABINET

The Scotland Act made no provision for a Scottish Cabinet. The fact of a **5–35** Cabinet, and the Ministers who are members of it, are matters for the First Minister. Like the UK Cabinet, on which it is modelled, the Scottish Cabinet "reconciles Ministers individual responsibilities with their collective responsibility ... and is the ultimate arbiter of all policy on devolved matters".[75] It currently consists of the First Minister and the nine Cabinet Secretaries. The Minister for Parliamentary Business attends meetings but is not a member of

---

[70] Scottish Government, *Scottish Ministerial Code* (2011) para.1.3.

[71] Scottish Government, *Scottish Ministerial Code* (2011) para.1.5.

[72] Scottish Government, *Scottish Ministerial Code* (2011) para.1.6. The first two advisers were Lord Steel of Aikwood and George Reid, both former presiding officers. They were replaced in August 2011 by Lord Fraser of Carmyllie and Dame Elish Angiolini, both former Lord Advocates. Sir David Bell, who was appointed in October 2012, conducted the inquiry into the complaint by Catherine Stihler MEP (see fn 73). James Hamilton, a former Irish Director of Public Prosecutions, was appointed in February 2013.

[73] See the Reports of the Scottish Ministerial Code Inquiry into a complaint from Tavish Scott MSP regarding exchanges at First Minister's Questions (March, 2009), into a complaint from Iain Gray MSP about First Minister's Answers on Open Prison Absconds (August, 2009), into a complaint from Jim Sheridan MP about the role of the First Minister in the award of a knighthood to Brian Souter (November, 2011), into a complaint by Paul Martin MSP about the use of Bute House, the First Minister's official residence (June, 2012), and into a complaint by Catherine Stihler MEP about comments the First Minister had made in an interview with Andrew Neil on the BBC about the legal advice the Scottish Government had received concerning an independent Scotland's continuing membership of the EU (January, 2013). The original panel expressed concern that complaints of alleged misconduct should not become a kind of "long-stop" to points of order to the presiding officer.

[74] Jim Gallagher, "Time to crack the Scottish Ministerial Code" *The Scotsman* January 12, 2013.

[75] Scottish Government, *Guide to Collective Decision Making* (2008) para 4.1.

the Cabinet. The Lord Advocate attends meetings where the Cabinet requires the Lord Advocate's advice on a particular issue or the Lord Advocate's retained functions are on the agenda. The Lord Advocate also retains the right to address Cabinet where he considers it appropriate.[76] The Cabinet meets weekly when the Parliament is in session—usually on a Tuesday afternoon—and by arrangement at other times.

5–36 The principle of collective responsibility (below) is central to the operation of the Cabinet system. The principle requires Ministers to abide by government decisions, and to defend them as necessary, from which it follows that

> "every effort must normally be made to ensure that every Minister with an interest in an issue has a chance to have his or her say—in an appropriate forum or manner—before a decision is taken".[77]

The machinery of cabinet government, however, is not just about presenting a united front and keeping Ministers on board by ensuring that they have the opportunity to make their views known before decisions are made; it is also about the effective coordination of policy. As at the UK level, the Cabinet serves as the main instrument of policy coordination in the devolved Scotland.

Cabinet business

5–37 There are no hard and fast rules about what decisions must be approved by Cabinet and what may be settled by individual Ministers. Essentially, Cabinet business is business which has the potential to engage the collective responsibility of the Scottish Government. The Scottish Ministerial Code defines it as consisting, in the main, of questions which "significantly engage the collective responsibility of the Government, either because they raise major issues of policy or because they are of critical importance to the public".[78]

> "The Cabinet should normally be invited to consider all matters which significantly engage the collective responsibility of the Government including, as a general rule, any proposal which involves a change in the Government's agreed objectives or priorities, a change in the general allocation of public expenditure, primary legislation ... or the making of a statement to the Parliament on a significant or sensitive policy issue."[79]

"Matters wholly within the responsibility of a single Minister which do not significantly engage collective responsibility" on the other hand,

> "need not be brought to the Cabinet unless the Cabinet Secretary or Secretaries concerned wish to have the advice of colleagues in a full meeting of the Cabinet. It is not possible to give a precise definition of the matters which should be referred to the Cabinet for decision. As a general rule, however, Cabinet members should put before their colleagues the sorts of issues on which they themselves would wish to be consulted."[80]

---

[76] Scottish Government, *Guide to Collective Decision Making* (2008) para 4.2.
[77] Scottish Government, *Guide to Collective Decision Making* (2008) para 1.2.
[78] Scottish Government, *Scottish Ministerial Code* (2011) para.2.10.
[79] Scottish Government, *Guide to Collective Decision Making* (2008) para.4.7.
[80] Scottish Government, *Scottish Ministerial Code* (2011) para.2.11.

Other mechanisms

Much of the business which requires a ministerial decision is dealt with below **5–38** the level of the Cabinet.

> "This helps to relieve the pressure on the Cabinet by enabling business to be settled at a lower level; or, failing that, by helping to clarify the issues and define the points of disagreement before an issue goes to the Cabinet. It also supports the principle of collective responsibility by ensuring that, even though an important issue may not be determined by the Cabinet itself, the decision will be fully considered by those Ministers with a direct portfolio interest in it and that the final judgment will be sufficiently authoritative to ensure that the Government as a whole can reasonably expected to accept responsibility for it."[81]

There is a range of mechanisms by which this may be done, including minutes to Ministers, Ministerial meetings and Cabinet subcommittees.[82] The principal Cabinet subcommittee is the Cabinet Subcommittee on Scottish Government Resilience ("CSC-SGoR"), which meets three or four times a year to review the Scottish Government's arrangements for dealing with civil contingencies; it may also be convened in response to specific events. There are also Cabinet Subcommittees on Legislation ("CSCL"), which is responsible for the Scottish Government's legislative programme, and on Climate Change ("CSC-CC").

A Cabinet Secretariat works on behalf of all Ministers and all directorates in the **5–39** Government to "co-ordinate and facilitate collective decision-making".[83] Its role includes providing advice on the handling of issues and on the preparation and circulation of papers for consideration by Cabinet Secretaries in Cabinet and to Cabinet Secretaries and other Ministers in other fora, and collating and distributing papers for Cabinet meetings, briefing the First Minister for Cabinet, recording Cabinet conclusions and following up decisions.

COLLECTIVE RESPONSIBILITY

The Scottish Ministerial Code requires Ministers to observe the principle of **5–40** collective responsibility as defined in s.2 of the Code. The principle is the conventional, i.e. political, as opposed to legal, expression of the unity of the executive branch of government. As defined in s.2 of the Code, the principle has two aspects. The first is an obligation on Ministers to maintain a united front once decisions have been reached (the "unanimity rule").

> "This means that all decisions reached by the Scottish Ministers, individually or collectively, are binding on all members of the Government. Ministers are therefore required to abide by them and defend them as necessary."[84]

The second is an obligation to maintain the privacy of opinions expressed and advice offered within the Government (the "confidentiality rule").

---

[81] Scottish Government, *Guide to Collective Decision Making* (2008) para.3.1.
[82] Scottish Government, *Guide to Collective Decision Making* (2008) para.3.4.
[83] Scottish Government, *Guide to Collective Decision Making* (2008) para.5.1.
[84] Scottish Government, *Scottish Ministerial Code* (2011) para.2.1.

"Collective responsibility requires that Ministers should be able to express their views frankly in the expectation that they can argue freely in private while maintaining a united front once decisions have been reached. This in turn requires that the privacy of opinions expressed and advice offered within the Government should be maintained."[85]

The third aspect of the principle at the UK level of government—the obligation on a government to resign if it loses the confidence of Parliament (the "confidence rule")—is a matter of statute at the devolved level rather than constitutional convention.[86]

5–41 How far does the principle of collective responsibility extend? The principle applies to Ministers and junior Scottish Ministers (Cabinet Secretaries and Ministers) alike despite the latter not being members of the Scottish Government or the Cabinet. The only exceptions to the principle are decisions taken by the Lord Advocate as head of the systems of criminal prosecution and investigation of deaths in Scotland, in which capacity the Lord Advocate acts independently of other Ministers, and decisions taken by the First Minister in the exercise of functions conferred on the First Minister alone.[87] It also does not apply to parliamentary liaison officers.

5–42 Collective responsibility assumes a new significance in a coalition government. The difficulty is that Ministers drawn from one party may be called upon to defend decisions made by Ministers drawn from another. The Labour and Liberal Democrat partners accordingly felt it important to set out their own understanding of the doctrine in the partnership agreements that underpinned the 1999–2007 coalition governments. In the event the principle was defined in terms little different from the conventional understanding. Collective responsibility was accepted by the partners to mean that:

(i) all the business of the Executive, including decisions, announcements, expenditure plans, proposed legislation and appointments, engages the collective responsibility of the Executive as a whole and must be handled with an appropriate degree of consultation and discussion so as to ensure the support of all Ministers;

(ii) ministers have the opportunity to express their views frankly as decisions are reached;

(iii) opinions expressed and advice offered within the Executive remain private;

(iv) decisions of the Executive are binding on and supported by all Ministers; and

(v) mechanisms for sharing information and resolving disputes are followed.[88]

The partners also undertook to "agree and publish formal documents setting out the principles of collective decision-making and the procedures to be followed to promote the good conduct of business".[89]

[85] Scottish Government, *Scottish Ministerial Code* (2011) para.2.1.
[86] SA 1998 ss.45(2), 47(3)(c), 48(2).
[87] Scottish Government, *Scottish Ministerial Code* (2011) para.2.8; SA 1998 s.52(5).
[88] Scottish Executive, *Partnership for Scotland* (May, 1999); *A Partnership for a Better Scotland* (May, 2003).
[89] Executive Secretariat, *The Scottish Executive: A Guide to Collective Decision Making,* which was based on the equivalent UK guidance, was first published in August 1999; see now the Scottish Government, *A Guide to Collective Decision Making* (2008).

The Scottish Ministerial Code was initially silent on what a Minister should do in **5–43** the event that the Minister is unable to uphold the principle of collective responsibility. In 2008, however, the Code was revised to make clear that where a Minister

> "feels that he or she cannot support a decision reached collectively by the Scottish Government and wishes publicly to dispute that decision, the Minister in question should consider whether it is appropriate to resign from his or her Ministerial role".[90]

In March 2001 the Deputy Parliament Minister, Tavish Scott, resigned because he was unable to support Executive policy on fisheries; in December 2006 the Communities Minister, Malcolm Chisholm, resigned after he had voted against the Labour Party's policy on the replacement of Trident. A Minister who signals his disagreement or otherwise fails to uphold the principle but who tries to hang onto office risks being sacked by the First Minister. The Code emphasises that a Minister can only remain in post "for so long as he or she retains the confidence of the First Minister".[91] Whether a Minister is dismissed, however, depends very much on the political circumstances. In September 2002, the First Minister was criticised for not taking action against a Minister, Mike Watson, who had publicly opposed government policy on the provision of hospital services in Glasgow.[92] The Code was subsequently revised to make it clear that where a portfolio Minister takes a decision that might be unpopular in the constituency or region represented by another Minister, that Minister

> "must be prepared to defend that decision, even if, individually, he or she might have argued against it in private, or, in the case of a constituency issue, might have made representations as a constituency or regional MSP".[93]

THE STRUCTURE OF GOVERNMENT

The first two devolved administrations retained the departmental structure **5–44** inherited from the Scottish Office essentially unchanged.[94] The Scottish Executive, as it then was, was in many respects the Scottish Office "with the name changed".[95]

> "One of the consequences of coalition government was to strengthen the desire of individual Cabinet Ministers to maximise their degree of autonomy and, consequently, that of their Department. There was unhappiness when a Cabinet Minister with a relatively small portfolio did not have their own Department devoted exclusively to that portfolio and, by extension, their own exclusive Head of Department."[96]

---

[90] Scottish Government, *Scottish Ministerial Code* (2011) para.2.9.
[91] Scottish Government, *Scottish Ministerial Code* (2011) para.2.9.
[92] Barry K Winetrobe, "Collective responsibility in devolved Scotland" [2003] P.L. 24.
[93] Scottish Government, *Scottish Ministerial Code* (2011) para.2.6.
[94] There were five departments: agriculture; environment and fisheries; development; education and industry; health; and home affairs.
[95] Richard Parry and Amy Jones, "The Transition from the Scottish Office to the Scottish Executive" (2000) 15 Public Policy and Administration 53, 64.
[96] Sir John Elvidge, *Northern Exposure: Lessons from the first twelve years of devolved government in Scotland* (London: Institute for Government, 2011) pp.31–32.

5–45 The 2007 SNP Government embarked upon a radical departure in the organisation of government. The Scottish model of government is based on the idea of government as a single organisation, rather than a federation of organisations,

> "working towards a single defined government purpose based on outcomes, and establishing a partnership based on that purpose with the rest of the public sector which is capable of being joined by other parts of civil society".[97]

The Scottish Government's purpose and strategic objectives are set out in the National Performance Framework (below). Departments were abolished, leaving the divisions of which they were made up, which were renamed directorates, as self-standing policy areas (schools, criminal justice, transport and so on).

> "By making the Directorate or Executive Agency the centrepiece of our new structures, we make it easier for people to see the Scottish Government as a single, coherent unit rather than a group of departments with separate identities. Each of us works for the Executive, in a Directorate or Agency, the title of which should 'say what it does on the tin'."[98]

Heads of department were replaced by directors general, one for each of five strategic objectives (below), with line management responsibility for a family of directorates clustered around the strategic objective for which they are responsible. Together with the Permanent Secretary to the Scottish Government, they form a strategic board, the role of which is to support Ministers collectively, to support Cabinet, and to focus on that rather than on a one-to-one relationship between members of the board and individual Cabinet Secretaries.

The National Performance Framework

5–46 The Scottish Government's purpose and strategic objectives are set out in the National Performance Framework, which was launched in November 2007 as part of the SNP Government's commitment to a more strategic approach to government with a single overarching purpose and a greater focus on outcomes. The Framework, which was revised in December 2011, defines the Scottish Government's purpose as being

> "to focus government and public services on creating a more successful country, with opportunities for all of Scotland to flourish, through increasing sustainable economic growth".[99]

Its purpose is underpinned by five strategic objectives, which describe "the kind of Scotland we want to live in" and to which all policies and resources are intended to be aligned: to make Scotland wealthier and fairer, healthier, safer and stronger, smarter and greener. The strategic objectives are in turn supported by 16 national outcomes, which describe in more detail what the Government wants to achieve, e.g. "we live in a Scotland that is the most attractive place for doing business in Europe", and which are intended to "help to sharpen the

---

[97] Sir John Elvidge, *Northern Exposure: Lessons from the first twelve years of devolved government in Scotland* (London: Institute for Government, 2011) p.4.
[98] Staff Message from Permanent Secretary: "Changes in Our Structures", May 16, 2007.
[99] For discussion, see Carnegie UK Trust, *More than GDP: Measuring What Matters* (May, 2011).

focus of government, enable our priorities to be clearly understood and provide a clear structure for delivery". There are also seven high-level purpose targets, e.g. to close the gap with the top five Organisation for Economic Co-Operation and Development ("OECD") economies by 2017, and 50 national indicators, e.g. an increase in the number of businesses or a reduction in the number of alcohol-related hospital admissions, which are intended to show progress towards the purpose and national outcomes.[100]

As well as giving strategic direction to central government, the National **5–47** Performance Framework is intended to provide the basis for a partnership between central government and the rest of the public sector.

Executive agencies

Besides directorates, which are the basic building blocks of the revised struc- **5–48** ture, the Scottish Government includes a number of executive agencies, which are responsible for carrying out discrete areas of work within a policy and resources framework set by Ministers. There are currently seven executive agencies: the Accountant in Bankruptcy; Disclosure Scotland; Education Scotland; the Scottish Prison Service; the Scottish Public Pension Agency; the Student Awards Agency for Scotland; and Transport Scotland. In common with directorates, agencies are purely administrative arrangements within the Scottish Government; they have no separate legal existence or functions of their own. What distinguishes agencies from directorates is said to be a "stronger focus on the operational management and direct delivery of public services", directorates in common with departments before them being concerned primarily with "the provision of policy advice to Ministers and providing funding to other public bodies in pursuit of policy objectives".[101] The abolition of the departmental structure in 2007 was followed by the case-by-case consideration of executive agencies as a result of which some were absorbed into the core of government. Those that remained were required to align their performance measurement arrangements with the National Performance Framework.[102]

Non-ministerial departments

Non-ministerial departments are part of the Scottish Administration but not of **5–49** the Scottish Government, the former being the umbrella term used by the Scotland Act for the whole of the devolved central government of Scotland, including a number of non-ministerial or "associated" departments that never formed part of the pre-devolution Scottish Office.[103] Like the non-departmental public body (below), the non-ministerial department provides a means of distancing the exercise of functions from Ministers. Instead of being vested in the Scottish Ministers, functions are vested in an office holder, who may be an individual or a board, and who is in turn responsible for the exercise of those functions to the Scottish Parliament rather than to the Scottish Ministers. There are currently seven non-ministerial departments: National Records of Scotland, which was formed by the merger of the General Register Office for

---

[100] *Scotland Performs*, an online reporting system launched in June 2008, is intended to provide a public and transparent way of reporting progress towards the purpose targets and national outcomes.

[101] Auditor General for Scotland, *How government works in Scotland* (November, 2002) para.1.3.

[102] Sir John Elvidge, *Northern Exposure: Lessons from the first twelve years of devolved government in Scotland* (London: Institute for Government, 2011) p.35.

[103] The term is defined in SA 1998 s.126(6)–(8).

88 *Constitutional Law of Scotland*

Scotland (the department of the Registrar General for Scotland) and National Archives of Scotland (the department of the Keeper of the Records of Scotland); the Office of the Scottish Charity Regulator ("OSCR"), which was established by the Charities and Trustee Investment (Scotland) Act 2005[104]; Registers of Scotland (the department of the Keeper of the Registers); the Scottish Courts and Tribunals Service, a former executive agency which was reconstituted as a non-ministerial department by the Judiciary and Courts (Scotland) Act 2008; the Scottish Housing Regulator, another former executive agency which was reconstituted as a non-ministerial department by the Housing (Scotland) Act 2010; Revenue Scotland, which is responsible for the collection and management of devolved taxes under the Revenue Scotland and Tax Powers Act 2014; and Food Standards Scotland, which was established by the Food (Scotland) Act 2015.

THE CIVIL SERVICE

5–50 The staff of the Scottish Administration are members of the "civil service of the State", i.e. the UK civil service, rather than a separate Scottish civil service.[105] The maintenance of a unified civil service was conceived as one of the "checks and balances of the devolution settlement, designed to prevent any drift towards conflict and isolation".[106] The Scottish Government, however, has delegated responsibility for the recruitment and management of its own staff within the overall framework laid down by the Constitutional Reform and Governance Act 2010.[107] That framework includes the principle of selection on merit on the basis of fair and open competition, and the "core" civil service values of integrity, honesty, objectivity and impartiality. A separate Scottish version of the Civil Service Code governs the conduct of civil servants who serve the Scottish Government.[108] The Constitutional Reform and Governance Act 2010 provides that the Code must require civil servants who serve the Scottish Government "to carry out their duties for the assistance of the administration as it is duly constituted for the time being, whatever its political complexion".[109] The Code duly makes it clear that the loyalties of staff lie to the Scottish Ministers: "As a civil servant you are accountable to Scottish Ministers, who in turn are accountable to the Scottish Parliament".[110] The Act also provides that the Code must require civil servants to carry out their duties with integrity and honesty, and with objectivity and impartiality.[111]

Ministers and civil servants

5–51 The Scottish Ministerial Code provides as a general principle that:

"Ministers must uphold the political impartiality of the Civil Service, and not ask civil servants to act in any way which would conflict with the

---

[104] OSCR seems to have been set up as a non-ministerial department rather than a non-departmental public body because Scottish Government policy at the time was that non-departmental public bodies should be brought "closer into the fold".
[105] SA 1998 s.51(2).
[106] Richard Parry, *The Home Civil Service after Devolution*, Devolution Policy Papers (2004).
[107] SA 1998 s.51(4); delegation is by the Minister for the Civil Service, i.e. the Prime Minister, to the First Minister.
[108] Scottish Government, *Civil Service Code* (December, 2010).
[109] Constitutional Reform and Governance Act 2010 ("CRGA 2010") s.7(2).
[110] Scottish Government, *Civil Service Code* (December, 2010) para.2.
[111] CRGA 2010 s.7(4).

Civil Service Code and the requirements of the Constitutional Reform and Civil Governance Act 2010."[112]

Ministers have a duty to

"give fair consideration and due weight to informed and impartial advice from civil servants, as well as to other considerations and advice, in reaching policy decisions; ensure that influence over appointments is not abused for partisan purposes; and observe the obligations of a good employer with regard to the terms and conditions of those who serve them".[113]

They should also not ask civil servants to

"engage in activities likely to call into question their political impartiality, or to give rise to the criticism that people paid from public funds are being used for party political purposes".[114]

The independence referendum raised concerns about the politicisation of the **5–52** civil service, on both sides of the debate.[115] Whether the Scottish civil service's "neutrality', in the sense of its ability to identify with successive governments of quite different political complexions, has been irretrievably compromised, will depend ultimately on whether its members are capable of commanding the confidence of a future Scottish Government of a different political complexion.[116] In the meantime, what has emerged, despite the initial emphasis on the maintenance of a unified civil service as part of the "glue" of the Union state, is a separate Scottish civil service in all but name.

Special advisers

The Constitutional Reform and Governance Act 2010 makes provision with **5–53** regard to the appointment of special advisers to assist the Scottish Ministers.[117] As well as providing assistance to Ministers in the development of government policy and its presentation, the appointment of special advisers is said to "reinforce the political impartiality of the permanent Civil Service by providing a separate channel for political advice and assistance available to Ministers".[118] Special advisers are appointed by the First Minister personally and their appointment must end with the end of the First Minister's term of office.[119] The First Minister is responsible for deciding on the distribution of all special adviser posts within the Scottish Government, whether in support of individual Ministers or as a collective resource. Responsibility for the management and conduct of special advisers, including discipline, also rests with the First

---

[112] Scottish Government, *Scottish Ministerial Code* (2011) para.6.1.
[113] Scottish Government, *Scottish Ministerial Code* (2011) para.6.2.
[114] Scottish Government, *Scottish Ministerial Code* (2011) para.6.3.
[115] Public Administration Select Committee, *Lessons for Civil Service impartiality from the Scottish Independence referendum* (HC 2014–2015, III).
[116] Terence Daintith and Alan Page, *The Executive in the Constitution: Structure, Autonomy and Internal Control* (Oxford: OUP, 1999) pp.59–60.
[117] CRGA 2010 s.15.
[118] Scottish Government, *Scottish Ministerial Code* (2011) para.4.14; on the importance of the role of special advisers in coalition and minority governments, see Sir John Elvidge, *Northern Exposure: Lessons from the first twelve years of devolved government in Scotland* (London: Institute for Government, 2011) pp.25–27.
[119] CRGA 2010 s.15(1).

Minister.[120] The First Minister is required to lay an annual report containing information about the number and cost of special advisers before the Scottish Parliament.[121] In 2012–2013 the Scottish Government employed 13 special advisers, at a cost of £925,105.

---

[120] Scottish Government, *Scottish Ministerial Code* (2011) paras 4.15–4.17. Their appointment and terms and conditions of service, which must include conditions approved by the Prime Minister as Minister for the Civil Service, is governed by the Cabinet Office's Model Contract for Special Advisers; there is also a Code of Conduct for Special Advisers.
[121] CRGA 2010 s.16; the Public Services Reform (Scotland) Act 2010 s.33 imposes essentially the same obligation.

CHAPTER 6

THE SCOTTISH COURTS

"The Scottish judiciary stands at the very heart of the Scots body politic. It is the most important organ of government to have survived in unbroken continuity since the earliest days of the early modern Scottish state."[1]

INTRODUCTION

The Scottish constitution as set out in the Scotland Act 1998 ("the Scotland **6–01** Act") differs from the UK constitution in a number of respects. It is a codified constitution, a work of "conscious art" rather the result of "natural growth".[2] It has the status of a "higher" law, the Scottish Parliament having no power to amend the Scotland Act save in minor respects.[3] (Under the Smith Commission Agreement, the Parliament will assume control over its size and composition, the electoral system and the franchise, but amending legislation will require a two-thirds majority of the Parliament.) And it is judicially enforceable: should the Scottish Parliament exceed the bounds of its legislative competence, the courts have the power to set aside its legislation as unlawful, a power they do not possess in relation to Acts of the UK Parliament, being confined to making a declaration of incompatibility with Convention rights or, in the case of incompatibility with EU law, to denying effect to the offending legislation. Devolution thus placed the courts—particularly the Court of Session and the High Court of Justiciary—in a position which was "novel and potentially uncomfortable" in relation to the other branches of devolved government.[4] In this chapter we concentrate on the main features of the judicial branch of devolved government in Scotland, before turning in Chs 9 and 16 to the role of the courts in the devolved constitution.

THE COURTS

The Scotland Act devolved responsibility for the courts and the administration **6–02** of justice to the Scottish Parliament. Devolution is subject, however, to the "continued existence" as reserved matters of the High Court of Justiciary as a criminal court of first instance and of appeal and of the Court of Session as a civil court of first instance and of appeal,[5] maintaining in a new form the guarantee of their continued existence first provided by the Acts of Union.

---

[1] Scott Crichton Styles, "The Scottish Judiciary" in Aileen McHarg and Tom Mullen (eds), *Public Law in Scotland* (Edinburgh: Avizandum, 2006) p.174.
[2] Leslie Wolf-Phillips, *Comparative Constitutions* (London: Macmillan, 1972) p.32.
[3] Scotland Act 1998 ("SA 1998") Sch.4 para.4.
[4] Robert Reed, "Devolution and the Judiciary" in Jack Beatson et al (eds), *Constitutional Reform in the United Kingdom: Practice and Principles* (Oxford: Hart Publishing, 1998) p.28.
[5] SA 1998 Sch.5 Pt I para.1(d), (e).

The Court of Session

6–03 The Court of Session is Scotland's highest civil court. The Court, which was founded in 1532, sits in Edinburgh and has jurisdiction throughout Scotland. It is divided into the Inner House and the Outer House, with the Outer House hearing cases at first instance, and the Inner House dealing mainly with appeals. The Inner House consists of two divisions, the First Division comprising the Lord President (the most senior judge) and five senior judges, and the Second Division comprising the Lord Justice Clerk (the second most senior judge) and five other senior judges.[6] Both divisions are of equal authority. It is common for an Extra Division to sit, due to pressure of business. The Court consists of a maximum of 34 judges.[7] It also relies on retired and temporary judges with the latter being drawn from the ranks of members of the bar and serving or retired sheriffs.[8] An appeal lies to the UK Supreme Court, formerly the House of Lords, from any final judgment of the Inner House of the Court of Session.[9] The appeal, which was established shortly after the Union,[10] traditionally lay as of right, in contrast to appeals from other parts of the UK, but under the Courts Reform (Scotland) Act 2014 it will lie only with permission of the Inner House or, if permission is refused, the Supreme Court.[11]

The High Court of Justiciary

6–04 The High Court of Justiciary is Scotland's highest criminal court. It sits as a trial court in cities and larger towns throughout Scotland and as an appeal court in Edinburgh. The Court, which was first established in 1672, was reconstituted by the Criminal Procedure (Scotland) Act 1887, which provided that its membership should be the same as that of the Court of Session.[12] An appeal lies from the High Court sitting as a trial court to the High Court sitting as a court of criminal appeal. Before devolution the High Court sitting as an appeal court was the final court of appeal, the House of Lords' jurisdiction in Scottish criminal cases having never gained the same acceptance as its jurisdiction in civil cases,[13] but devolution saw the introduction of a right of appeal from the High Court for the first time. The appeal, which at first lay to the Judicial Committee of the Privy Council, now lies to the UK Supreme Court, to which the Judicial Committee's devolution issues jurisdiction was transferred by the Constitutional Reform Act 2005.[14]

---

[6] Court of Session Act 1988 ("CSA 1988") s.2(2), as amended by the Number of Inner House Judges (Variation) Orders 2007 (SSI 2007/258) and 2010 (SSI 2010/449). Promotion to the Inner House from the Outer House used to be by seniority alone but is now through selection by the Lord President and the Lord Justice Clerk with the consent of the Scottish Ministers: CSA 1988 s.2(6).

[7] CSA 1998 s.1(1), as amended by the Maximum Number of Judges (Scotland) Order 2004 (SSI 2004/499).

[8] Provision for the appointment of retired judges and temporary judges was made by the Law Reform (Miscellaneous Provisions) (Scotland) Act 1985 s.22, and 1990 s.35(3); for the background to these provisions, see *Kearney v HM Advocate* [2006] UKPC D1; 2006 S.C. (P.C.) 1 [24]–[32] (Lord Hope).

[9] CSA 1988 s.40; see Neil Walker, *Final Appellate Jurisdiction in the Scottish Legal System* (Edinburgh: Scottish Government, 2010).

[10] *Greenshields v Edinburgh Magistrates* (1710–1711) Robert 12, HL; see further Ch.19.

[11] CSA 1988 s.40, as substituted by Courts Reform (Scotland) Act 2014 ("CR(S)A 2014") s.117.

[12] Criminal Procedure (Scotland) Act 1887 s.44; see now Criminal Procedure (Scotland) Act 1995 s.1(2).

[13] The House of Lords eventually declined jurisdiction in *MacIntosh v Lord Advocate* (1876) 3 R. (HL) 34; see further para.19–43.

[14] See Ch.9.

The sheriff court

The sheriff court is Scotland's principal local court with an extensive jurisdic- **6–05** tion in both civil and criminal matters. Scotland is divided into six sheriffdoms, each presided over by a sheriff principal. The six sheriffdoms are in turn divided into 49 sheriff court districts, each with a court presided over by one or more sheriffs.[15] Retired sheriffs principal and sheriffs may also be appointed as a temporary measure to facilitate the disposal of sheriff court business.[16]

The Sheriff Courts (Scotland) Act 1971 made sheriffs principal responsible for **6–06** securing the "speedy and efficient" disposal of business in the sheriff courts of their sheriffdoms.[17] This obligation, which in its current form requires them to secure the "efficient" disposal of sheriff court business,[18] must now be read subject to the overriding responsibility of the Lord President of the Court of Session under the Judiciary and Courts (Scotland) Act 2008 for maintaining arrangements for securing the efficient disposal of business in the Scottish courts, to which end he may give sheriff principals directions of an "adminis- trative character", i.e. directions which do not bear on the outcome of a partic- ular case, with which sheriffs principal must comply.[19] Sheriffs principal have, in turn, power to give binding administrative directions to sheriffs and to staff of the Scottish Courts and Tribunals Service ("SCTS").[20] The Lord President may also take over the functions of a sheriff principal where he considers that they are being exercised in a way which is prejudicial to the efficient disposal of business in, or the efficient organisation or administration of, the sheriff courts of the sheriffdom, or is otherwise against the interests of the public.[21]

Under the Courts Reform (Scotland) Act 2014, which implements many of the **6–07** recommendations of the Scottish Civil Courts Review chaired by Lord Gill,[22] the sheriff court's jurisdiction will be increased, and a new judicial tier created within the sheriff court, presided over by summary sheriffs, to deal with low level civil and summary criminal business.

The sheriff appeal court

The Courts Reform (Scotland) Act 2014 also establishes a new sheriff appeal **6–08** court made up of sheriffs principal and other appeal sheriffs to deal with civil appeals from sheriff courts and summary criminal appeals from sheriff and justice of the peace courts.[23] At present, an appeal in civil proceedings lies from the sheriff to the Inner House of the Court of Session, either directly or via the sheriff principal, and in summary criminal proceedings to the High Court of Justiciary sitting as a court of criminal appeal. In future, an appeal in civil proceedings will lie to the sheriff appeal court and from there to the Inner House of the Court of Session with permission of the sheriff appeal court or, if permission is refused, the Inner House[24]; and in summary criminal proceedings

---

[15] The sheriff court district or districts in which a person appointed to hold the office of sheriff or summary sheriff is to sit is designated by the Lord President: CR(S)A 2014 s.33.

[16] CR(S)A 2014 s.12.

[17] Sheriff Courts (Scotland) Act 1971 ("SC(S)A 1971") s.15.

[18] CR(S)A 2014 s.27(1).

[19] Judiciary and Courts (Scotland) Act 2008 ("JC(S)A 2008") s.2(3).

[20] CR(S)A 2014 s.27(4).

[21] CR(S)A 2014 s.29.

[22] Scottish Civil Courts Review, *Report of the Scottish Civil Courts Review* (2009).

[23] CR(S)A 2014 s.46.

[24] CR(S)A 2014 ss.110, 113.

to the sheriff appeal court and from there on a point of law to the High Court
of Justiciary sitting as a court of criminal appeal, but only with permission of
the High Court.[25]

Justice of the peace courts

6–09 Justice of the peace courts are local courts dealing with minor criminal matters.
They were established under the Criminal Proceedings etc. (Reform) (Scotland)
Act 2007 in place of district courts run by local authorities. They are presided
over by lay justices of the peace, who sit with a legally qualified clerk; in
Glasgow, there are also legally qualified stipendiary magistrates, who are to be
appointed summary sheriffs under the Courts Reform (Scotland) Act 2014.[26]
Sheriffs principal are responsible for securing the efficient disposal of business
in justice of the peace courts in their sheriffdoms, to which end they may give
binding administrative directions to justices of the peace, stipendiary magistrates and staff of the SCTS.[27]

Tribunals

6–10 Tribunals are specialist judicial bodies that decide disputes in particular areas
of law. Their growth is mainly a consequence of the expansion in the functions
of government that saw the settlement of many disputes arising out of the exercise of those functions entrusted to administrative tribunals rather than the
"ordinary" courts.[28] The majority of the tribunals that sit in Scotland are GB
tribunals that deal with reserved matters.[29] There are also a small number of
"Scottish" tribunals that deal only with devolved matters. The devolved tribunals, many of which are local in character, include: the Additional Support
Needs Tribunals for Scotland; Education Appeal Committees; the Mental
Health Tribunal for Scotland; the Private Rented Housing and Homeowner
Housing Committees; the Traffic Commissioner for Scotland; and Valuation
Appeal Committees.[30]

6–11 The creation of a unified UK tribunals system under the Tribunal, Courts and
Enforcement Act 2007 highlighted the complex and fragmented nature of
the devolved tribunal system in Scotland and the lack of some of the safeguards of tribunal independence that had been put in place for GB and
UK tribunals, e.g. with regard to the appointment of tribunal members and
chairs. Following publication by the Scottish Committee of the Administrative
Justice and Tribunals Council of a blueprint for "an independent, coherent and

---

[25] CR(S)A 2014 ss.118, 119, inserting a new s.194ZB in the Criminal Procedure (Scotland) Act
1995.

[26] CRS(A) 2014 s.128.

[27] Criminal Proceedings etc. (Reform) (Scotland) Act 2007 s.61 as substituted by JC(S)A 2008
s.58.

[28] For the argument that administrative tribunals in the UK are best understood as a species of
court, see Peter Cane, *Administrative Tribunals and Adjudication* (Oxford: Hart Publishing, 2009)
pp.69–72.

[29] The Administrative Justice Steering Group preferred the term GB rather than UK tribunals as
most non-devolved tribunals operate only in England, Scotland and Wales: Scottish Consumer
Council, *Options for the Future Administration and Supervision of Tribunals in Scotland*
(September, 2008) p.8, fn 4.

[30] Administrative Justice and Tribunals Council, *Options for Tribunal Reform in Scotland*
(June, 2010), Annex 4. For statistics on the number of cases dealt with by tribunals operating in
Scotland, see the Scottish Committee of the Administrative Justice and Tribunals Council's Annual
Report 2010/2011, Annex D. As we would expect, the number of cases dealt with by reserved
tribunals far exceeds the number dealt with by devolved tribunals.

user-friendly tribunal system in Scotland",[31] the Tribunals (Scotland) Act 2014 creates the framework for an integrated Scottish tribunal system, based on the UK model of a First-tier Tribunal and an Upper Tribunal, under the overall leadership of the Lord President but with day-to-day management delegated to a President of the Scottish Tribunals. The intention is that all devolved tribunals, including the Scottish tax tribunals established by the Revenue Scotland and Tax Powers Act 2014, should be transferred into the new system by 2016.

Under the Smith Commission Agreement, it is proposed that all powers over **6–12** the management and operation of reserved tribunals, other than the Special Immigration Appeals Commission, the Proscribed Organisations Appeals Commission, the Pathogens Access Commission and the Investigatory Powers Tribunal, should be devolved to the Scottish Parliament. The laws they administer, however, will remain reserved.[32] What might have seemed an overly elaborate structure for the relatively small number of devolved tribunals will therefore come into its own once reserved tribunals are devolved.

THE PRINCIPLE OF JUDICIAL INDEPENDENCE

"Judicial independence is a constitutional guarantee that is common to all legal **6–13** systems based on the rule of law."[33] The principle that the judiciary must be independent of the executive has been described as a "fundamental principle of our constitutional law".[34] In Scotland, the principle traces its origins to the Claim of Right 1689, which asserted that

> "the sending letters to the Courts of Justice ordaining the Judges to stop or desist from determining Causes, or ordaining them how to proceed in Causes depending before them, and the changing the nature of the Judges' gifts *ad vitam aut culpam* into Commissions *durante bene placito* are contrary to law".[35]

Two reasons are commonly advanced in support of the principle.[36] The first is **6–14** that independence is "a condition of impartiality and therefore also of fair trials".[37] The effectiveness of the courts as conflict-solving agencies depends on a number of factors, one of the most important of which is the extent to which people have confidence in judicial impartiality,

---

[31] Administrative Justice and Tribunals Council, *Tribunal Reform in Scotland: A Vision for the Future* (February, 2011).

[32] Scotland Office, *Scotland in the United Kingdom: An enduring settlement* (2015) Cm.8990, paras 6.3.1–6.3.7.

[33] Gernot Sydow, "Independence of the judiciary in Germany" in Katja S Ziegler, Denis Baranger and Anthony W Bradley (eds), *Constitutionalism and the Role of Parliaments* (Oxford: Hart Publishing, 2007) p.226.

[34] Lord Hope, "Judicial Independence" 2002 S.L.T. (News) 105.

[35] *Ad vitam aut culpam* means for life or until fault or blame is established, *durante bene placito* that the office holder holds office only during the appointing authority's pleasure.

[36] Torstein Eckhoff, "Impartiality, Separation of Powers and Judicial Independence" (1965) 9 *Scandinavian Studies in Law* 1; see also Lord Cullen, "The Judge and the Public" 1999 S.L.T. (News) 261.

[37] Torstein Eckhoff, "Impartiality, Separation of Powers and Judicial Independence" (1965) 9 *Scandinavian Studies in Law* 1, 11. "Judicial independence serves one very specific purpose. Its purpose is to preserve the judge's impartiality, whatever the case is with which he or she has to deal and whatever the circumstances": Lord Hope, "Judicial Independence" 2002 S.L.T. (News) 105, 106.

"it is not sufficient, and perhaps even not necessary, that judges shall be impartial in any objective sense. What counts is the extent to which people have *confidence* in judicial impartiality. In particular it is important that the public can feel assured that a judge is influenced neither by his personal interest in the outcome of the case nor by positive or negative attitudes towards a party in the case or towards a group or category of people to which a party belongs".[38]

A key purpose of the principle therefore is to foster public confidence in the impartiality of judicial decision-making.[39]

6–15 The second reason, which applies to all checks on government and not just to the judiciary, is that it "makes for a separation of powers which enables the courts to check the activities of the other branches of the government".[40] The rule of law "presupposes courts which are sufficiently independent of the other branches of government to serve as a check on their activities".[41] The fact that the courts are independent of the other branches of government does not of course guarantee they will serve as a check on their activities; the principle also

"presupposes judges who possess what Alexander Hamilton in *The Federalist* (No.78) called an 'independent spirit'. They must be willing to take a critical attitude to legislative and administrative practices and to vindicate the legal ideals even if this causes conflicts".[42]

6–16 Judicial independence thus has both an individual and an institutional dimension. The former includes what is commonly referred to as the judge's

"adjudicative independence. It is the complete autonomy which the judge must have when he or she is called on to render a decision in a specific case. There must be no interference with this freedom of conscience, and ideally it should function without fear or apprehension".[43]

The latter recognises that

"the courts are not charged solely with the adjudication of individual cases. That is of course one role. It is also the context for a second, different and equally important role, namely as protector of the Constitution and the fundamental values embodied in it—rule of law,

---

[38] Torstein Eckhoff, "Impartiality, Separation of Powers and Judicial Independence" (1965) 9 *Scandinavian Studies in Law* 1, 12, original emphasis.

[39] "Impartiality is not the same as independence, although the two are closely linked. Impartiality is the tribunal's approach to deciding the cases before it. Independence is the structural or institutional framework which secures this impartiality, not only in the minds of the tribunal members but also in the perception of the public": *Gillies v Secretary of State for Work and Pensions* [2006] UKHL 2; 2006 S.C. (HL) 71 [38] (Lady Hale).

[40] Torstein Eckhoff, "Impartiality, Separation of Powers and Judicial Independence" (1965) 9 *Scandinavian Studies in Law* 1, 11.

[41] Torstein Eckhoff, "Impartiality, Separation of Powers and Judicial Independence" (1965) 9 *Scandinavian Studies in Law* 1, 23.

[42] Torstein Eckhoff, "Impartiality, Separation of Powers and Judicial Independence" (1965) 9 *Scandinavian Studies in Law* 1, 23.

[43] Canadian Judicial Council, *Alternative Models of Court Administration* (September, 2006) p.36.

fundamental justice, equality, preservation of the democratic process, to name perhaps the most important. In other words, judicial independence is essential for fair and just dispute-resolution in individual cases. It is also the lifeblood of constitutionalism in democratic societies".[44]

The Judiciary and Courts (Scotland) Act 2008 provides a statutory guarantee **6–17** of the "continued independence" of the judiciary in Scotland, modelled on s.3 of the Constitutional Reform Act 2005.[45] It places a duty on the First Minister, the Lord Advocate, the Scottish Ministers, MSPs and other persons responsible for matters relating to the judiciary or the administration of justice in Scotland to "uphold the continued independence of the judiciary".[46] In particular, the First Minister, the Lord Advocate and the Scottish Ministers must not seek to influence particular judicial decisions through any special access to the judiciary, and must have regard to the need for the judiciary to have the support necessary to enable them to carry out their functions.[47]

The value of such a guarantee has been questioned.[48] It would have looked **6–18** decidedly odd, however, had Scotland not followed the example of the rest of the UK and introduced such a guarantee at a time when, as Lord Reed observed in evidence to the Scottish Parliament's Justice Committee, "a relatively new set of institutions—the Parliament and the Executive—are, for the first time, trying to define in legislation the boundaries and relationships between the different institutions of Government in Scotland".[49] Its inclusion in the Act is a "powerful and obvious reminder to those in the executive branch of government, as well as elsewhere, of the constitutional significance of judicial independence".[50]

---

[44] *Beauregard v Canada* [1986] 2 S.C.R. 56 [2] (Dickson CJ).

[45] The guarantee was first introduced in Northern Ireland: Justice (Northern Ireland) Act 2002 s.1 as substituted by the Constitutional Reform Act 2005 s.4.

[46] JC(S)A 2008 s.1(1); the position of the guarantee in the Act reflects the "fundamental importance" of the principle: Scottish Executive, *Proposals for a Judiciary (Scotland) Bill* (February, 2007) para.2.4.

[47] JC(S)A 2008 s.1(2); the Tribunals (Scotland) Act 2014 s.3 extends the guarantee to tribunals.

[48] See, e.g. John McCluskey, "Unnecessary and Misconceived: Some Reflections on the Judiciary and Courts (Scotland) Bill" (2008) 12 Edin. L.R. 288. Stevens observed of the equivalent guarantee in s.3 of the Constitutional Reform Act 2005 that "[w]ithout unpacking the concept of the independence of the judiciary, the statute would be largely meaningless": Robert Stevens, "Reform in haste and repent at leisure: Iolanthe, the Lord High Executioner and Brave New World" (2004) 24 Legal Studies 1, 25.

[49] Scottish Parliament OR Justice Committee March 11, 2008, col.584. Lord Reed had earlier stressed the importance of legal guarantees of judicial independence in *Starrs v Ruxton*, 2000 J.C. 208, 250: "The effect given to the European Convention by the Scotland Act and the Human Rights Act ... represents, to my mind, a very important shift in thinking about the constitution. It is fundamental to that shift that human rights are no longer dependent solely on conventions, by which I mean values, customs and practices of the constitution which are not legally enforceable. Although the Convention protects rights which reflect democratic values and underpin democratic institutions, the Convention guarantees the protection of those rights through legal processes, rather than political processes. It is for that reason that art.6 guarantees access to independent courts. It would be inconsistent with the whole approach of the Convention if the independence of those courts itself rested upon convention rather than law."

[50] Scottish Executive, *Proposals for a Judiciary (Scotland) Bill* (February, 2007) para.2.4.

JUDICIAL APPOINTMENTS

6–19 Before devolution, the Secretary of State for Scotland was responsible for the appointment of Court of Session judges, other than the Lord President and the Lord Justice Clerk, who were appointed on the recommendation of the Prime Minister. In making recommendations to the Queen for appointments, the Secretary of State acted by convention on the recommendation of the Lord Advocate. "In practice, the Secretary of State accepted the Lord Advocate's recommendations, often with little or no substantive discussion."[51] Sheriffs principal and sheriffs were also appointed by the Secretary of State, again after consultation with the Lord Advocate.

6–20 The Scotland Act 1998 transferred the Secretary of State's role in judicial appointments to the First Minister but retained the Prime Minister's role in the most senior appointments. Recommendations to the Queen for appointment as Lord President or Lord Justice Clerk continue to be made by the Prime Minister, but the Act provides that the Prime Minister must not recommend anyone who has not been nominated by the First Minister.[52] While the Prime Minister is unable, therefore, to recommend anyone not nominated by the First Minister, it would be open to the Prime Minister to refuse to recommend the First Minister's nominee, thus forcing the First Minister to come up with an alternative nominee. The First Minister is required to consult the Lord President and the Lord Justice Clerk before making a nomination.[53] Other Court of Session judges, sheriffs principal, sheriffs and summary sheriffs are appointed by the Queen on the recommendation of the First Minister, who must consult the Lord President before making a recommendation.[54]

The Judicial Appointments Board for Scotland

6–21 The judicial appointments system as it stood at the time of devolution had long been the subject of criticism.[55] Two criticisms in particular stood out. The first was of the part played by the Lord Advocate in judicial appointments.

> "For selection to be in the hands of a politician—albeit a distinguished legal politician—is bad enough; for it to be in the hands of that distinguished legal politician in whose name (or in the name of whose local representatives) virtually all criminal prosecutions are brought and conducted before our courts is quite simply unacceptable in a modern society, and renders us an object of ridicule in the eyes of lawyers from countries with a less medieval and more transparent appointments system."[56]

That the Lord Advocate might recommend his own name for appointment— as did Lord Hardie within less than a year of devolution—served only to

---

[51] Scottish Executive, *Judicial Appointments: An Inclusive Approach* (April, 2000) para.2.2. "Because the Secretary of State does not normally have personal knowledge of suitable nominees, he relies on the Lord Advocate, who submits names to him for his consideration": Lord Fraser of Tullybelton, "The Judiciary", *Stair Memorial Encyclopaedia* (1987) Vol.5, para.629.

[52] SA 1998 s.95(1), (2).

[53] SA 1998 s.95(3).

[54] SA 1998 s.95(4); CR(S)A 2014 s.5.

[55] CM Campbell, "Judicial Selection and Impartiality" (1973) J.R. 254.

[56] Robert Black, "The Scottish Parliament and the Scottish Judiciary" 1998 S.L.T. (News) 322; see also Scottish Executive, *Judicial Appointments: An Inclusive Approach* (April, 2000) para.2.2, paras 2.9–2.10.

underline how out of step the judicial appointments system was with the standards regarded as axiomatic in other parts of the public service.[57]

The other criticism was of the system's lack of openness and transparency, **6–22** which inevitably bred suspicion of bias in appointments. However well the appointment system might work in practice, the Scottish Executive acknowledged in a consultation paper on judicial appointments published in April 2000, it was not sufficiently transparent.[58]

The Scotland Act 1998 anticipated that additional statutory requirements might **6–23** be laid down with regard to judicial appointments,[59] a provision apparently included for the express purpose of

> "enabling and requiring the First Minister to take into account the recommendations of a Judicial Appointments Board set up by or under an Act of the Scottish Parliament".[60]

A Judicial Appointments Board for Scotland was set up in 2002, initially on a non-statutory basis in the interests of making "early improvements",[61] before being given statutory backing by the Judiciary and Courts (Scotland) Act 2008.[62] It is made up of 10 members: three judicial members appointed by the Lord President; two legal members appointed by the Scottish Ministers; and five lay members also appointed by the Scottish Ministers, one of whom they must appoint as the chairing member.[63] It is responsible for recommending to "members of the Scottish Government" individuals for appointment to judicial offices within its remit, and for providing advice to members of the Scottish

---

[57] Edwards described it as "a well-established tradition, however embarrassing in its application, that the Lord Advocate recommended himself or his colleague if the urge to change roles from Law Officer to the Bench is made manifest": John Ll J Edwards, *The Attorney General, Politics and the Public Interest* (London: Sweet & Maxwell, 1984) p.284. In defence of the tradition it was said that it had the effect of "infusing an element of experience not shared generally by the practising advocate": Lord Wylie, "The Law Officers of the Crown", *Stair Memorial Encyclopaedia* (1987) Vol.5, para.538. The extent of the shift in attitudes was underlined by Lord Rodger: "Holding office as Lord Advocate and taking part in debates in Parliament was once the accepted route to high judicial office in Scotland. We have now reached the position where it actually risks becoming a disqualification from taking a full part in the work of the court": Lord Roger, *The Courts, the Church and the Constitution: Aspects of the Disruption of 1843* (Edinburgh: Edinburgh University Press, 2010) p.70, a reference to *Davidson v Scottish Ministers (No.2)* [2004] UKHL 34; 2005 1 S.C. (HL) 7, in which the House of Lords held that, because of Lord Hardie's prior involvement as Lord Advocate, the decision of the Extra Division must be set aside on grounds of apparent bias. The tradition whereby appointments to the higher judicial offices of Lord President and Lord Justice Clerk went to the Lord Advocate or a former Lord Advocate went into decline somewhat earlier. Before Lord Emslie's appointment in 1972, every Lord President in over 250 years had been or was Lord Advocate, but since Lord Emslie, only one other Lord President (Lord Rodger, 1996–2001) has previously served as Lord Advocate.

[58] Scottish Executive, *Judicial Appointments: An Inclusive Approach* (April, 2000) para.2.15.

[59] SA 1998 s.95(5).

[60] Scottish Executive, *Judicial Appointments: An Inclusive Approach* (April, 2000) Annex A, para.14.

[61] Scottish Executive, *Judicial Appointments: An Inclusive Approach* (April, 2000) para.4.6.

[62] JC(S)A 2008 s.9(1).

[63] JC(S)A 2008 Sch.1. "The insistence on 'non-political' lay members was seen to be important in Scotland, which has a relatively recent history of political appointments to judicial and legal posts, and seems to have been a significant factor in achieving recognition that the Board is completely independent": Select Committee on the Lord Chancellor's Department, *Judicial Appointments: lessons from the Scottish experience* (HC 2002–2003, 902) para.25.

Government in connection with such appointments.[64] In addition to Court of Session judges, the offices within the Board's remit include those of temporary judge (except where the individual to be appointed holds or has held certain judicial offices), sheriff principal, sheriff, summary sheriff, and part-time sheriff and summary sheriff.[65] In carrying out its functions, the Board is not subject to the direction or control of any member of the Scottish Government or any other person.[66] The Scottish Ministers and the Lord President may however issue guidance to the Board as to the procedures to be followed by it in carrying out its functions to which the Board "must have regard".[67] The Board is required to publish an annual report that must be sent to the Scottish Ministers and laid before the Scottish Parliament.[68]

6–24 The Scotland Act stipulates that the selection of individuals for recommendation for appointment must be "solely on merit" and that the Board must be satisfied that an individual is of "good character".[69] Merit is not defined in the Act but the Explanatory Notes say that it encompasses an applicant's

> "abilities and competencies in respect of the criteria for the particular judicial office. It is wider than professional knowledge and would extend to attributes such as strong interpersonal skills".

The lay members may not take part in the assessment of candidates' legal knowledge, skills and competence.[70] In carrying out its functions, the Board is also required to have regard to the need to encourage diversity in the range of individuals available for selection for recommendation for appointment,[71] but the need to encourage diversity is subject to the requirements that individuals be selected solely on merit and that they be of good character.[72]

---

[64] JC(S)A 2008 s.9(2); according to the explanatory notes to the Act, the expression "members of the Scottish Government" acknowledges that some judicial appointment functions are exercised by the First Minister alone; it also takes account of the fact that functions conferred on the Scottish Ministers collectively may be exercised by any of them. It thus allows for recommendations to the First Minister and to individual Scottish Ministers, e.g. the Cabinet Secretary for Justice.

[65] JC(S)A 2008 s.10; it will also include tribunal appointments: Tribunals (Scotland) Act 2014 Sch.9 para.12.

[66] JC(S)A 2008 s.9(3).

[67] JC(S)A 2008 s.15.

[68] JC(S)A 2008 s.18.

[69] JC(S)A 2008 s.12.

[70] JC(S)A 2008 s.13.

[71] JC(S)A 2008 s.14(1).

[72] JC(S)A 2008 s.14(2). The pool from which judges may be drawn has traditionally been extremely limited. The Acts of Union (art.XIX) confined eligibility for appointment to the Court of Session bench to advocates of five years' standing and Writers to the Signet of 10 years' standing who had passed an examination in civil law before the Faculty of Advocates two years before appointment to the bench. No Writer to the Signet was ever appointed. In 1990 eligibility was extended to sheriffs principal and sheriffs who had served as such for five years, and to solicitors who had rights of audience in both the Court of Session and the High Court for a continuous period of five years: Law Reform (Miscellaneous Provisions) (Scotland) Act 1990 s.35 and Sch.4 paras 1 and 2. In 2008 it was further extended to solicitors who had rights of audience in either the Court of Session or High Court: JC(S)A 2008 s.21. Eligibility for appointment to the shrieval bench is confined to advocates or solicitors of at least 10 years' standing: CR(S)A 2014 s.14. For critical comment, see Scott Crichton Styles, "The Scottish Judiciary" in Aileen McHarg and Tom Mullen (eds), *Public Law in Scotland* (Edinburgh: Avizandum, 2006) pp.183–185. As Walker points out, the argument "is as much about the culture of democracy—about public confidence in the representativeness of the judiciary—as it is about any supposedly objective relationship between social background and patterns of decision-making": Neil Walker, *Final Appellate Jurisdiction in the Scottish Legal System* (Edinburgh: Scottish Government, 2010) p.51.

An individual cannot be appointed, or nominated or recommended for **6–25** appointment, unless they have first been recommended for appointment by the Board.[73] The relevant Minister may decline to accept a recommendation for appointment, in which case the Board must reconsider its recommendation, but the Minister must give reasons for not accepting the recommendation.[74] Having reconsidered its recommendation, the Board must make a further recommendation, which may be of the same individual.[75] "Ministers are expected to adhere to the Board's advice in its recommendations, unless there is compelling reason to the contrary."[76] Ministers have, in fact, accepted all the Board's recommendations for appointments since it was first established, in one case after reconsideration.[77] In form the Board is advisory: in practice the power of appointment is exercised by it.

The offices of Lord President and Lord Justice Clerk do not fall within the **6–26** Board's remit. Recommendations to the First Minister for nomination to the Prime Minister for appointment as Lord President or Lord Justice Clerk are made not by the Board but by an ad hoc panel established for the purpose, chaired by the Board's chairing member, another lay member of the Board and two judges.[78] The same criteria apply to the selection of individuals to be recommended as suitable for appointment to the offices of Lord President and Lord Justice Clerk as apply to the selection of individuals to be recommended for appointment to the judicial offices within the Board's remit: the individual must be selected solely on merit and the panel must be satisfied that he or she is of good character.[79] In deciding whom to nominate, however, the First Minister is required only to have regard to the panel's recommendation.[80]

There is no provision for parliamentary scrutiny or oversight of judicial **6–27** appointments. The Scottish Executive did not consider approval by the legislature or investigation by a committee of the legislature "necessary or desirable in the Scottish context. Such requirements introduce an unnecessary political dimension into the appointment process". Hearings could also prove an additional disincentive to anyone who was unwilling to have it known publicly that he or she wished to be considered for appointment.[81] The rejection of any form of parliamentary involvement in appointments means however that one opportunity for what has been termed "constructive engagement" between politicians and judges has been passed over.[82] It may also leave the judiciary more

---

[73] JC(S)A 2008 s.11(1).

[74] JC(S)A 2008 s.11(3).

[75] JC(S)A 2008 s.11(5); according to the explanatory notes to the Act, these provisions are merely intended to enable the Minister to seek clarification or further information in respect of the Board's recommendations

[76] Scottish Executive, *Strengthening Judicial Independence in a Modern Scotland: A consultation on the unification, appointment, removal and management of Scotland's Judiciary* (February, 2006) para.1.5.

[77] Judicial Appointments Board for Scotland, *Annual Report 2009–2010*, p.9.

[78] JC(S)A 2008 s.19(2), Sch.2.

[79] JC(S)A 2008 s.20.

[80] JC(S)A 2008 s.19(5).

[81] Scottish Executive, *Judicial Appointments: An Inclusive Approach* (April, 2000) para.4.8. Although the establishment of the Judicial Appointments Board has addressed one of the principal criticisms of the system, by taking appointments out of the hands of the Lord Advocate, the gains in openness and transparency have been limited, in part because of the requirements of applicant confidentiality.

[82] Judiciary of England and Wales, *The Lord Chief Justice's Review of the Administration of Justice in the Courts* (March, 2008) para.4.15.

vulnerable to attack, from politicians who feel they have had no say in their appointment.[83]

Justices of the peace

6–28   Justices of the peace are appointed by the Scottish Ministers on the recommendation of the justice of the peace advisory committee for the local sheriffdom, which must act in accordance with procedures approved by the Judicial Appointments Board.[84]

SECURITY OF TENURE

6–29   Security of tenure has traditionally been regarded as the most important safeguard of judicial independence in that it ensures that judges cannot be dismissed or threatened with dismissal because their decisions do not find favour with government. In Scotland, as we have seen, its importance has been recognised since at least the Claim of Right 1689, which insisted that judicial appointments should be made *ad vitam aut culpam*—for life or until fault is established. In *Mackay and Esslemont v Lord Advocate*[85] it was held to be inconsistent with the nature of a judicial office at common law that its tenure should be precarious or of any less security than tenure *ad vitam aut culpam*. A condition that had been inserted in the commissions of members of the Scottish Land Court requiring them to retire on reaching the age of 65 was accordingly ultra vires and illegal.[86] Court of Session judges and sheriffs no longer hold office for life but subject to a statutory retirement age, which was initially set at 75 before being reduced to 70 by the Judicial Pensions and Retirement Act 1993.

Temporary judges

6–30   In *Starrs v Ruxton*[87] the High Court of Justiciary held that temporary sheriffs appointed under s.11 of the Sheriff Courts (Scotland) Act 1971 were not "an independent and impartial tribunal" within the meaning of art.6(1) ECHR; this because appointments were subject to annual renewal and could be recalled at any time. The subsequent Bail, Judicial Appointments etc. (Scotland) Act 2000 abolished the office of temporary sheriff and replaced it with that of part-time sheriff; part-time sheriffs are appointed for five years and have security of tenure during the term of their appointment.[88] Subsequent challenges to the use of temporary judges in the Court of Session and the High Court of Justiciary

---

[83]   Robert Stevens, "Reform in haste and repent at leisure: Iolanthe, the Lord High Executioner and Brave New World" (2004) 24 Legal Studies 1, 27. Robert Reed, now Lord Reed, did not rule out parliamentary approval of appointments, but thought it would be unfortunate if the Parliament were to divide on party lines or to institute the type of investigation into candidates familiar in Senate confirmation hearings in the United States. What was essential was that the judiciary continue to be appointed in a way which preserved their political neutrality and did not deter candidates of appropriate calibre: Robert Reed, "Devolution and the Judiciary" in Jack Beatson et al (eds), *Constitutional Reform in the United Kingdom: Practice and Principles* (Oxford: Hart Publishing, 1998) pp.29–30.
[84]   Justices of the Peace (Scotland) Order 2007 (SSI 2007/210) art.3(3).
[85]   *Mackay and Esslemont v Lord Advocate*, 1937 S.C. 860.
[86]   The effect of the decision was reversed by the Scottish Land Court Act 1938, which introduced a compulsory retirement age of 65 for members of the Court (other than the chairman, whose tenure was the same as that of a Court of Session judge).
[87]   *Starrs v Ruxton*, 2000 J.C. 208.
[88]   CR(S)A 2014 s.8; the maximum number of part-time sheriffs who may be appointed is 80: Maximum Number of Part-Time Sheriffs (Scotland) Order 2006 (SSI 2006/257).

were unsuccessful,[89] but the Judiciary and Courts (Scotland) Act 2008 strengthened the tenure of temporary judges in line with that of part-time sheriffs.[90]

The removal of judges

Court of Session judges hold office subject to good behaviour, but it was not **6–31** until the Scotland Act that a procedure was put in place for their removal.[91] Under the Bill as originally introduced a judge would have been removable by the Queen on the recommendation of the First Minister made with the support of a two thirds majority of the Scottish Parliament, but this proposal attracted widespread criticism on the grounds that it afforded the judiciary insufficient guarantees of their independence at a time when they had taken on "new and potentially controversial responsibilities".[92] A widely quoted example at the time was a judicial decision that an Act of the Scottish Parliament authorising a referendum on independence was beyond the Parliament's legislative competence.[93]

The procedure now set out in the Scotland Act was introduced in response to **6–32** that criticism. Under it a Court of Session judge may be removed by the Queen on the recommendation of the First Minister made with the approval of the Parliament.[94] Before making a motion recommending the removal of a judge, however, the First Minister must first have received a written report from a specially constituted tribunal concluding that the judge is unfit for office by reason of "inability, neglect of duty or misbehaviour"[95] and giving reasons for that conclusion; if the judge in question is Lord President or Lord Justice Clerk, the First Minister must also have consulted the Prime Minister.[96]

The Scotland Act required provision for a tribunal to investigate and report on **6–33** a judge's fitness for office to be made by or under an Act of the Scottish Parliament. The Act of the Scottish Parliament must include provision for a tribunal to be constituted by the First Minister when requested by the Lord President to do so as well as in such other circumstances as the First Minister thinks fit, for the tribunal to be chaired by a member of the Judicial Committee of the Privy Council and to consist of at least three persons, and for the tribunal's report to be laid before the Scottish Parliament.[97]

---

[89] *Clancy v Caird*, 2000 S.C. 441; *Kearney v HM Advocate* [2006] UKPC D1; 2006 S.C. (PC) 1.

[90] JC(S)A 2008 s.22.

[91] In the absence of express provision, one view was that the English procedure—involving resolutions of both Houses of Parliament—would be followed: see e.g. *M'Creadie v Thomson*, 1907 S.C. 1176, 1182 (Lord Justice Clerk Macdonald). Another view was that an Act of Parliament would be required: Lord Fraser of Tullybelton, "The Judiciary", *Stair Memorial Encyclopaedia* (1987) Vol.5. para.664. See also JR Philip, "The Judicial Immunity of the Lords of Session" (1927) 39 J.R. 1. The practical effect of the uncertainty was to make Court of Session judges de facto irremovable.

[92] Robert Reed, "Devolution and the Judiciary" in Jack Beatson et al (eds), *Constitutional Reform in the United Kingdom: Practice and Principles* (Oxford: Hart Publishing, 1998) p.29.

[93] House of Lords debate November 2, 1998, Vol.594, col.60 (Lord Mackay of Drumadoon).

[94] SA 1998 s.95(6), (7).

[95] In *Stewart v Secretary of State for Scotland*, 1998 S.C. (HL) 81, the House of Lords held that "inability" was not confined to physical or mental infirmity but extended to defects of character or quirks of behaviour that did not amount to mental illness but which meant that an individual was wholly unfitted to perform judicial functions.

[96] SA 1998 s.95(10); for the parliamentary debates relating to these provisions, see CMG Himsworth, "Securing the tenure of Scottish judges: a somewhat academic exercise?" [1999] P.L. 14.

[97] SA 1998 s.95(8), (9).

6–34 The Judiciary and Courts (Scotland) Act 2008, which replaced temporary arrangements made under the Scotland Act,[98] made provision for a tribunal consisting of four members, two judicial members (including at least one member of the Judicial Committee of the Privy Council and one judge or former judge of the Court of Session), an advocate or solicitor of at least ten years standing, and a lay member (who must not have been a judge or an advocate or solicitor). The member who chairs the tribunal, who must be a member of the Judicial Committee of the Privy Council, has a casting vote.[99] The Act also made provision for the removal of temporary judges.[100]

Sheriffs

6–35 The Judiciary and Courts (Scotland) Act 2008 brought the procedure for the removal of sheriffs into line with that for the removal of Court of Session judges.[101] A sheriff principal, sheriff, summary sheriff, or part-time sheriff or summary sheriff may be removed from office by the First Minister, by order subject to annulment by the Scottish Parliament, but only after a tribunal with the same composition as that for Court of Session judges, save that the second judicial member must be a sheriff principal or sheriff, has established unfitness for office by reason of inability, neglect of duty or misbehaviour.

Justices of the peace

6–36 A justice of the peace may be removed from office by order of a tribunal appointed by the Lord President, consisting of a sheriff principal, a member of the legal profession and another person, following an investigation carried out at the instance of the sheriff principal for the sheriffdom for which the justice was appointed.[102]

Conduct and discipline

6–37 In the consultation paper that preceded the Judiciary and Courts (Scotland) Act 2008 the Scottish Executive argued that arrangements for dealing efficiently and effectively with judicial conduct falling short of unfitness were as important to maintaining public confidence in the legal system as arrangements for removing judges when circumstances required.[103] Questions of judicial misconduct falling short of grounds for removal from office had traditionally been treated as a matter for the judges themselves, but under the Judiciary and Courts (Scotland) Act 2008 the Lord President is now formally responsible for making and maintaining appropriate arrangements for the investigation and determination of matters concerning the conduct of judicial office holders and the review of such determinations.[104] Where an investigation has been carried out into the conduct

[98] Scotland Act 1998 (Transitory and Transitional Provisions) (Removal of Judges) Order 1999 (SI 1999/1017).

[99] JC(S)A 2008 s.35(11).

[100] JC(S)A 2008 s.39.

[101] JC(S)A 2008 s.40; two sheriffs were removed from office under the previous procedure: by the Sheriff (Removal from Office) Orders 1977 (SI 1977 (unnumbered)), and 1992 (SI 1992/1677).

[102] Criminal Proceedings etc. (Reform) (Scotland) Act 2007 s.71.

[103] Scottish Executive, *Strengthening Judicial Independence in a Modern Scotland: A consultation on the unification, appointment, removal and management of Scotland's Judiciary* (February, 2006) para.8.3.

[104] JC(S)A 2008 ss.2(2)(e), 28; Complaints about the Judiciary (Scotland) Rules 2013; James Harrison, "Judging the Judges: The New Scheme of Judicial Conduct and Discipline in Scotland" (2010) 13 Edin. L.R. 427. The Lord President also has power under s.34 of the Act to suspend a judge if he considers it necessary for the purpose of maintaining public confidence in the judiciary.

of a judge, and the person carrying out the investigation has recommended disciplinary action, the Lord President may give the judge formal advice, a formal warning or a reprimand; the matter may also be dealt with informally.[105] Of the 309 complaints concluded in the first three years of the new complaints procedure, 18 resulted in investigations, nine of which were the subject of reports to the Lord President, two of which were upheld with no formal action being taken.[106] The Act also made provision for the appointment of a judicial complaints reviewer to review whether complaints investigations have been carried out in accordance with the rules; the reviewer's role is confined to the procedures followed and does not extend to the merits of complaints.[107]

The Scottish Executive anticipated that the required standards would be deter- **6–38** mined by the judiciary and set down in a code of conduct or judicial ethics under the authority of the Lord President or, perhaps, the Judicial Council.[108] A *Statement of Principles of Judicial Ethics for the Scottish Judiciary* was subsequently drawn up, after consultation, by the Judicial Council for Scotland.[109] The *Statement*, which is based on the *Bangalore Principles of Judicial Conduct*[110] and the *Guide to Judicial Conduct* issued by the Judges' Council of England and Wales,[111] addresses judicial independence, impartiality, integrity, propriety, equality and competence and diligence. It gives guidance,

> "in the light of which judges will make their own decisions. It does not provide an answer to every ethical question with which a judge may be confronted nor does prescribe a code of conduct".[112]

A standing committee on judicial conduct is responsible for keeping the *Statement* under review.

OTHER SAFEGUARDS OF JUDICIAL INDEPENDENCE

Immunity from suit

Immunity from suit constitutes a second important safeguard of judicial inde- **6–39** pendence in addition to security of tenure. Judges enjoy immunity from actions for damages in respect of words spoken while exercising their judicial functions "unless it can be demonstrated ... that the words used had no connection with the case in hand".[113] Judges of the Court of Session and the High Court of

---

[105] JC(S)A 2008 s.29.

[106] Judicial Office for Scotland, *Complaints about the Judiciary (Scotland) Rules 2011 and 2013*.

[107] JC(S)A 2008 s.30; for criticism of the narrowness of the reviewer's statutory role, see the outgoing first Judicial Complaint Reviewer's *Third Annual Report 2013/2014*.

[108] Scottish Executive, *Proposals for a Judiciary (Scotland) Bill* (February, 2007) para.8.11.

[109] Judicial Office for Scotland, *Statement of Principles of Judicial Ethics for the Scottish Judiciary* (Revised May, 2013).

[110] The Bangalore Principles were promulgated by the Round Table Meeting of Chief Justices held at the Hague in November 2002; they are based on the Draft Code of Judicial Conduct adopted by the Judicial Group on Strengthening Judicial Integrity, meeting at Bangalore in 2001.

[111] Judiciary of England and Wales, *Guide to Judicial Conduct* (March, 2013).

[112] Judicial Office for Scotland, *Statement of Principles of Judicial Ethics for the Scottish Judiciary* (Revised May, 2013), Foreword; "it must be emphasised that it is not intended to be prescriptive, like the contents of a statute; rather it is in the nature of guidance and should be seen as such": para.1.4.

[113] *Primrose v Waterston* (1902) 4 F. 783, 793 (Lord Moncrieff); on whether the immunity in respect of words spoken need be so far-reaching, see DL Carey Miller, "Defamation by a Judge? Fixing the Limits" [1980] J.R. 88.

Justiciary,[114] and it is thought sheriffs principal and sheriffs,[115] are also immune from actions of damages for acts done or sentences imposed when acting in their judicial capacity, "otherwise no man but a beggar, or a fool, would be a judge".[116] The immunity enjoyed by justices of the peace is in theory more limited but in practice hardly less extensive.[117]

Salaries

6–40 The determination of judicial salaries is a reserved matter, i.e. a matter for the determination of the UK Government rather than the Scottish Government.[118] Salaries are determined by the Secretary of State on the recommendation of the Senior Salaries Review Body.[119] They are also charged on the Scottish Consolidated Fund, which means that their payment does not require annual parliamentary approval.[120]

Political criticism

6–41 One of the benefits of the fact that judicial salaries do not require annual parliamentary approval was sometimes said to be that it avoided the risk that the conduct of judges might be subject to political criticism in the same way as the conduct of Ministers.[121] That risk is no longer avoided with the same certainty it once was. At Westminster the long-standing convention that Ministers should exercise restraint in their criticism of the judiciary and judicial decisions has been largely abandoned in recent years as the boundaries between political and judicial decision-making have become less clear cut.[122] Nor was there much evidence of restraint in the responses of the First Minister and the Cabinet Secretary for Justice to the UK Supreme Court's decisions in *Cadder*[123] (in which the court held that suspects in custody were entitled to legal advice before being interviewed) and *Fraser*[124] (in which the appellant's conviction for murder was quashed on grounds of non-disclosure of evidence) with the First Minister accusing the Supreme Court of "routinely interfering" in Scottish criminal appeals and the Justice Secretary threatening to withhold funding from the Supreme Court ("he who pays the piper, as they say, calls the tune").[125] There was a widespread feeling, however, that the First Minister and Justice Secretary had overstepped the boundaries of acceptable criticism, with the Dean of the Faculty of Advocates and the President of the Law Society of Scotland intervening to remind the First Minister and the Justice Secretary of their obligation under the Judiciary and Courts (Scotland) Act to uphold the independence of the judiciary, including justices of the UK Supreme Court, and to invite them to

---

[114] *McCreadie v Thomson*, 1907 S.C. 1176.

[115] *Harvey v Dyce* (1876) 4 R. 265; *Russell v Dickson*, 1997 S.C. 269.

[116] Stair, *The Institutions of the Law of Scotland*, Vol.IV.1.5.

[117] Criminal Procedure (Scotland) Act 1995 s.170(1).

[118] SA 1998 Sch.5 Pt II s.L1.

[119] See most recently, Review Body on Senior Salaries, *Thirty-Sixth Report on Senior Salaries* (2014) Cm.8822.

[120] SA 1998 s.119(3), Sch.4 para.5(a).

[121] Walter Ian Reid Fraser, *An Outline of Constitutional Law*, 2nd edn (Glasgow: William Hodge & Co, 1948) pp.78–79.

[122] Andrew Le Sueur, "The Judicial Review Debate: From Partnership to Friction" (1996) 31 Government and Opposition 8.

[123] *Cadder v HM Advocate* [2010] UKSC 43; 2011 S.C. (UKSC) 13.

[124] *Fraser v HM Advocate* [2011] UKSC 24; 2011 S.L.T. 515.

[125] *Scotland on Sunday*, June 5, 2011; see also Richard Cornes, "A Constitutional Disaster in the Making. The Communications Challenge Facing the United Kingdom's Supreme Court" [2013] P.L. 266, 284–286.

"carefully reflect on the consequences of what are perceived to be repeated and now highly personal attacks on respected members of the legal profession".[126]

In a different category was the statement made by the Lord Advocate to the **6-42** Parliament following the collapse of the *World's End* murder trial in 2007, which the Lord President interpreted as critical of the trial judge. In a letter to the Lord Advocate, the Lord President wrote:

"The independence of the judiciary depends, in my view, not only on the freedom of individual judges from prior interference with decisions they have to take but a preparedness by the Lord Advocate and others to recognise, in all public pronouncements, that final decisions made by judges ... reflect the law as it stands and must be respected as such. If such respect is not afforded, the independence of the judiciary as the final arbiter of legal issues is put at risk. An open challenge to the correctness of the final decision does not afford the requisite respect. Rather, it tends to undermine for the future the confidence which judges, faced with difficult decisions in controversial cases, can reasonably expect to have that their decisions will not be openly criticised by other organs of government."[127]

The Lord President's view that the Lord Advocate should refrain from criti- **6-43** cising judicial decisions, even while accounting to the Parliament, was not shared by the Lord Advocate. In her reply she wrote:

"My independence does not and can not make my decisions immune from comment or criticism. In a democracy such as ours, where public institutions are subject to greater scrutiny and accountability, the Lord Advocate must be able to explain her position in public where that is necessary. Law Officers and prosecutors are from time to time criticised and we must be free to respond publicly to that criticism in appropriate circumstances."[128]

The point was underlined by the First Minister in response to a parliamentary **6-44** question:

"We live in an age of parliamentary accountability. In days gone by, law officers in Scotland were seldom subjected to direct parliamentary accountability. It is to the benefit and credit of our system that we now have such accountability. The Lord Advocate was absolutely right to come to Parliament and give her view on the collapse of the *World's End* case. Given the public interest and concern in the case, no member of Parliament and very few people in Scotland would expect anything less. Inevitably, in giving that statement and answering questions, the Lord Advocate put forward the point of view of the Crown, or the prosecution service, as was done in open court. I do not agree that that should be taken as a direct criticism of a trial judge. It was a law officer responding to public concern and subjecting herself to parliamentary scrutiny."[129]

---

[126] Joint Statement, June 16, 2011.
[127] Letter from Lord Hamilton, the Lord Justice General, to Elish Angiolini, the Lord Advocate, September 26, 2007.
[128] Letter to the Lord Justice General, September 27, 2007.
[129] Scottish Parliament OR, September 27, 2007, col.2227.

In short, the obligation to account, in the Lord Advocate and First Minister's view, took precedence over the convention.

6–45 There is no rule in the Scottish Parliament forbidding attacks of a personal nature on judges.[130] The presiding officer does, however, have a more or less unfettered power to maintain order, including by setting and enforcing standards about what is considered unparliamentary language, which could well include a ban on personal attacks on judges.[131] MSPs are also bound by the Judiciary and Courts (Scotland) Act 2008 to uphold the independence of the judiciary,[132] which obligation might be readily construed as providing statutory backing for parliamentary restraint in the criticism of judges.

UNIFYING THE JUDICIARY

6–46 It was to be expected that devolution would generate a certain amount of tension between the new and the old institutions of devolved governance, between the Parliament and the Executive on the one hand and the courts on the other. That tension came to a head over Scottish Executive proposals to unify the separate branches of the judiciary under the leadership of the Lord President of the Court of Session. A review of the Scottish Court Service, the executive agency responsible for the provision of administrative support to the courts, had identified the lack of a modern approach to management and accountability within the judiciary as a fundamental weakness of the existing arrangements.[133] One of the difficulties the Scottish Court Service faced, the review argued, was that the judiciary was composed of individuals

> "with no management structure which the SCS can consult, or relate to, in any formal way or which can speak on behalf of its members".[134]

In its response to the review, the Scottish Executive proposed the creation of a unified judiciary as an essential preliminary to the more active involvement of the judges in improving the administration of justice, or, in the contemporary idiom, the "modernisation" of the judicial system.[135]

---

[130] For Westminster, see Sir Malcolm Jack (ed), *Erskine May's Treatise on the Law, Privileges Proceedings and Usage of Parliament*, 24th edn (London: LexisNexis, 2011) pp.396 and 443–444.

[131] As is required by the Scotland Act, the Parliament's standing orders include a requirement that members must not conduct themselves in a manner which would constitute a criminal offence or contempt of court: Scottish Parliament Standing Orders r.7.3.2; as to contempt of court, see Gerald H Gordon, *The Criminal Law of Scotland*, edited by Michael GA Christie, 3rd edn (Edinburgh: W.Green, 2001) Vol.2, Ch.50.

[132] JC(S)A 2008 s.1; see para.6–17.

[133] Scottish Executive Justice Department, *Agency Review of the Scottish Court Service* (January, 2006), and see earlier Scottish Executive, *Judicial Appointments: An Inclusive Approach* (April, 2000) Ch.6.

[134] Scottish Executive Justice Department, *Agency Review of the Scottish Court Service* (January, 2006) para.7.3. "This absence of a corporate structure for the judiciary is arguably inappropriate in modern public administration, disadvantages individual members of the judiciary, and can delay progress in delivering effective justice ... It is time to extend the greater openness pioneered by the creation of the Judicial Appointments Board to embrace the creation of a structured judiciary which can talk on behalf of its members to the SCS, the Justice Department, Ministers, the Scottish Parliament and, indeed, a much wider audience": para.7.8.

[135] Scottish Executive, *Strengthening Judicial Independence in a Modern Scotland: A consultation on the unification, appointment, removal and management of Scotland's judiciary* (February, 2006).

The Scottish Executive's proposals met with a generally hostile reaction from **6–47** the judiciary, prompted no doubt partly by the references to "managing" the judges in the consultation paper.[136] The Court of Session judges' response made it clear that their acceptance and support for a unified judiciary was conditional upon the unified judiciary having

> "strategic control of the Scottish Court Service so that the service is answerable to the Lord President ... we consider that the way to strengthen judicial independence, which is the aim of the consultation paper, is to link the unification of the judiciary, which may assist the more efficient use of public resources, with the introduction of a court service under judicial control".[137]

Stripped of constitutional principle, the argument was that the Lord President should not assume overall responsibility for the efficient disposal of business in the courts without having control over administrative support for the courts.[138]

Further discussions followed, the results of which were given effect in the **6–48** Judiciary and Courts Scotland Act 2008. As well as providing a statutory guarantee of the "continued independence" of the judiciary in Scotland, the 2008 Act made the Lord President the head of the Scottish judiciary with overall responsibility for making and maintaining arrangements for the efficient disposal of the business in the courts and new statutory responsibilities in relation to judicial conduct, training, welfare and deployment,[139] and reconstituted the Scottish Court Service as a non-ministerial department under the direction and control of the judiciary rather than of Ministers.[140] The Act also put the Judicial Appointments Board for Scotland, which had been set up in 2002, on a statutory basis, and standardised the procedure for the removal of judges (above).

The Scottish Courts and Tribunals Service ("SCTS")

The SCTS is a body corporate and the holder of an office in the Scottish **6–49** Administration.[141] The SCTS, which is chaired by the Lord President, consists of 13 members: seven judicial members, including the Lord President and the Lord Justice Clerk, and six non-judicial members, including the chief executive. The members other than the Lord Justice Clerk and the chief executive are appointed by the Lord President. The Scottish Ministers may change the number of members in each category of membership with the consent of the Lord President, but not if the effect would be to deprive the judicial members of their majority.[142]

---

[136] David Edward described it as a weakness of the consultation paper that it did not distinguish sufficiently between "managing" the judicial system as a whole and "managing" judges as individuals or collectively. "The essence of judicial independence is that the judge is not 'managed', directly or indirectly, in the performance of his/her judicial function": David Edward, *Response to the Consultation Paper*, para.1.5.

[137] Response by the Judges' Council on behalf of the Judges of the Court of Session Response A para.4; a revised version of the response (Appendix B), which was submitted on behalf of a number of the judges, expressed an "alternative but consistent view".

[138] Scottish Executive, *Proposals for a Judiciary (Scotland) Bill* (February, 2007) para.12.2.

[139] JC(S)A 2008 s.2.

[140] JC(S)A 2008 Pt 4.

[141] JC(S)A 2008 s.60(1), Sch.3 para.1; the Scottish Court Service was renamed the Scottish Courts and Tribunals Service by the CR(S)A 2014 s.130.

[142] JC(S)A 2008 Sch.3 para.2; the order making power conferred by the Public Services Reform (Scotland) Act 2010 s.14, cannot be used to amend the SCS's constitution as set out in JC(S)A 2008 Sch.3.

6–50 Although the SCTS is no longer under ministerial control, the Scottish Ministers are not cut out of the picture altogether. The SCTS is required to prepare and submit to the Scottish Ministers for their approval a corporate plan describing how it proposes to carry out its functions, which must be laid before the Scottish Parliament and published once it has been approved.[143] It must also "have regard to" any guidance issued by the Scottish Ministers in carrying out its functions.[144] And it is open to the Scottish Ministers to resume the functions of the SCTS if they consider that the SCTS is failing to carry out its functions to such an extent that there is a significant risk to the efficient and effective functioning of the Scottish courts, or is carrying them out in such a way that there is such a risk.[145]

6–51 The SCTS is under a duty to publish an annual report that must be laid before the Parliament.[146] The Scottish Ministers may also request additional information from the SCTS.[147] The Parliament, as we have seen, does not have the power to compel the attendance of judges as witnesses,[148] but the Lord President made it clear in evidence to the Parliament's Justice Committee that he would be willing to attend to answer questions about the performance of the SCTS,[149] an undertaking that, in the opinion of the Cabinet Secretary for Justice, would be "morally binding" on future Lord Presidents.[150] The framework document that governs the relationship between the SCTS and the Scottish Ministers confirms that the Lord President will consider invitations received from the Parliament relating to judicial members of the SCTS, and, in consultation with other judicial members of the SCTS and the relevant Committee of the Parliament, decide whether it is appropriate for a judicial member to attend, consistent with their responsibilities within the SCTS. At the same time it emphasises that members would not expect to be asked questions about matters that did not relate directly to their role within the SCTS, and that judicial members in particular "would not answer questions about the exercise of their judicial functions, for which they are constitutionally not accountable to the Scottish Parliament".[151]

REPRESENTING THE VIEWS OF THE JUDICIARY

6–52 As head of the Scottish judiciary, the Lord President is responsible for representing the views of the judiciary to the Scottish Parliament and the Scottish Ministers.[152] He also has the power to lay written representations before the Parliament on matters that appear to him to be "matters of importance relating to the Scottish judiciary or the administration of justice".[153] Taken together with his power to lay written representations before the UK Parliament under

---

[143] JC(S)A 2008 s.66.
[144] JC(S)A 2008 s.69.
[145] JC(S)A 2008 s.70.
[146] JC(S)A 2008 s.67.
[147] JC(S)A 2008 s.68.
[148] SA 1998 s.23(7).
[149] Scottish Parliament OR Justice Committee, March 11, 2008, col.570.
[150] Letter from the Cabinet Secretary for Justice to Bill Aitken MSP, Convener of the Justice Committee, September 17, 2008.
[151] Scottish Court Service, *Scottish Court Service Framework Document: Agreement between the Scottish Ministers and the Scottish Court Service* (October, 2013) paras 4.3–4.4.
[152] JC(S)A 2008 s.2(2)(b).
[153] JC(S)A 2008 s.2(2)(c).

the Constitutional Reform Act 2005,[154] these responsibilities in the view of the then Lord President, Lord Hamilton, would

> "allow the concerns of the whole judicial family in Scotland to be channelled through a single point from which they can authoritatively—with the weight of the whole judiciary behind them—be passed to other arms of government. The prospect of the judiciary realising its full potential as the third arm of government is thereby improved".[155]

The Lord President is assisted in his responsibility for representing the views **6–53** of the judiciary by the Judicial Council for Scotland, which was established on a non-statutory basis in January 2007, with a membership drawn from all categories of judicial office holder in Scotland, for the purpose of providing information and advice to the Lord President and the judiciary of Scotland on matters relevant to the administration of justice in Scotland.[156] In contrast to the Judges' Council for England and Wales, the Judicial Council for Scotland disavows a public role. As an internal advisory body it does not, for example, respond to consultations in its own name or comment publicly on issues affecting the judiciary. The range of matters affecting the judiciary and the judicial system on which the Council has assisted in the development of policies include the Judiciary and Courts (Scotland) Bill, the Scottish Sentencing Council, tribunal reform and the development of the Statement of Principles of Judicial Ethics. The Council is supported by the Judicial Office for Scotland, a separate part of the Scottish Court Service created to provide support to the Lord President in his role as head of the Scottish judiciary.

---

[154] CRA 2005 s.5(1); the power to lay written representations before the UK Parliament does not extend to matters within the legislative competence of the Scottish Parliament unless they are matters to which a Bill for an Act of Parliament relates, i.e. devolved matters on which Westminster is proposing to legislate: CRA 2005 s.5(2).

[155] Address on the opening of the legal year September 18, 2009; by "realising its full potential as the third arm of government" presumably was meant playing a full part in improving the administration of justice.

[156] In *Strengthening Judicial Independence in a Modern Scotland* (February, 2006), the Scottish Executive had proposed the creation of a statutory judges' council, chaired by the Lord President, as a means of allowing the collective development and consistent implementation of policies on issues affecting the judiciary and the operation of the courts. The Lord President, however, saw no need for a statutory council.

CHAPTER 7

LEGISLATIVE COMPETENCE

"Wherever legislative power is distributed between two or more legislatures, or where a single legislature has limited powers, problems of classification arise."[1]

INTRODUCTION

The Scottish Parliament has the power to make laws, "to be known as Acts of **7–01** the Scottish Parliament".[2] Acts of the Scottish Parliament are the devolved Scottish equivalent of Acts of the UK Parliament at Westminster. They have the same force of law. In *Axa General Insurance Ltd v Lord Advocate*,[3] Lord Hope said of the Scottish Parliament that it

> "takes its place under our constitutional arrangements as a self-standing democratically elected legislature. Its democratic mandate to make laws for the people of Scotland is beyond question. Acts that the Scottish Parliament enacts which are within its legislative competence enjoy, in that respect, the highest legal authority".

Where Holyrood differs from Westminster is in being a parliament of limited legislative competence. The Parliament's power to make laws is subject to s.29 of the Scotland Act 1998 ("the Scotland Act"), which provides that an Act of the Scottish Parliament "is not law so far as any provision of the Act is outside the legislative competence of the Parliament".[4] In this chapter we concentrate on the limits to the Parliament's legislative competence and the principles and rules that apply in determining whether a provision of an Act of the Scottish Parliament is outwith its legislative competence.[5]

LIMITS

The limits on the Parliament's legislative competence are set out in s.29(2) of **7–02** the Scotland Act, which provides that a provision of an Act of the Scottish Parliament is outside the Parliament's legislative competence

> "so far as any of the following paragraphs apply—
>
> (a) it would form part of the law of a country or territory other than Scotland, or confer or remove functions exercisable otherwise than in or as regards Scotland;

---

[1] Harry Calvert, *Constitutional Law in Northern Ireland: A Study in Regional Government* (Northern Ireland: Stevens & Sons, 1968) p.175.
[2] Scotland Act 1998 ("SA 1998") s.28(1).
[3] *Axa General Insurance Ltd v Lord Advocate* [2011] UKSC 46; [2012] 1 A.C. 868 [46].
[4] SA 1998 s.29(1).
[5] The statutory presumption of competence in SA 1998 s.101(2) is discussed at paras 16–23—16–26.

(b) it relates to reserved matters;

(c) it is in breach of the restrictions in Schedule 4;

(d) it is incompatible with any of the Convention rights or with EU law; or

(e) it would remove the Lord Advocate from his position as head of the systems of criminal prosecution and investigation of deaths in Scotland."

TERRITORIAL LIMITS

7–03 The Parliament's power is a power to make laws for Scotland. "Scotland" includes so much of the internal waters and territorial sea of the UK as are adjacent to Scotland.[6] The Parliament cannot therefore legislate as a matter of English law, for example, but it is not prevented from legislating with extraterritorial effect so long as it does so only as a matter of Scots law.[7] It has, for example, legislated to make war crimes committed by UK nationals or residents outwith the UK a criminal offence.[8] Because the Parliament can only legislate as a matter of Scots law, it may require Westminster's assistance to make any changes to the law in other parts of the UK or in the reserved areas that are needed in order to give full effect to its legislation, for which purpose s.104 of the Scotland Act confers powers on UK Ministers to make such changes in consequence of an Act of the Scottish Parliament as are considered "necessary or expedient".[9]

7–04 A provision of an Act of the Scottish Parliament is also outside the Parliament's legislative competence so far as it would "confer or remove functions exercisable otherwise than in or as regards Scotland".[10] What is meant by a function exercisable "as regards Scotland" is not defined, but it is "clear that there has to be some connection or nexus with Scotland".[11] Power has also been taken to specify by Order in Council functions that are to be treated as being or as not being exercisable in or as regards Scotland.[12]

RESERVED MATTERS

7–05 "The most extensive and complicated restriction of the Parliament's legislative competence is that of the reservation of specified matters."[13] As was noted in

---

[6] SA 1998 s.26(1); see also the Scottish Waters Adjacent Boundaries Order 1999 (SI 1999/1126), made under s.126(2) of the SA 1998.

[7] SA 1998, explanatory note to s.29(2). The explanatory notes were only published in 2004, some six years after the enactment of the Act. In *Imperial Tobacco v Lord Advocate* [2012] UKSC 61; 2013 S.C. (UKSC) 153 [33], Lord Hope said it would be "wrong to pay any regard to Explanatory Notes, as they do not form any part of the contextual scene of the statute. They are no doubt useful as they provide guidance, but unlike the Notes on Clauses they have no more weight than any other post-enactment commentary as to the meaning of the statute".

[8] International Criminal Court (Scotland) Act 2001 s.1(2).

[9] This "topping up" power has been extensively used; for judicial discussion of the power, and the shorthand description, see *Martin v Most* [2010] UKSC 10; 2010 S.C. (UKSC) 40 [78]–[90] (Lord Rodger).

[10] SA 1998 s.29(2)(a).

[11] SA 1998, explanatory note to s.29(2).

[12] SA 1998 s.30(3); see the Scotland Act 1998 (Functions Exercisable in or as Regards Scotland) Order 1999 (SI 1999/1748), and Scotland Act 1998 (Functions Exercisable in or as Regards Scotland) Order 2004 (SI 2004/3324).

[13] Daniel Greenberg (ed), *Craies on Legislation*, 10th edn (London: Sweet & Maxwell, 2012) para.4.2.5.

Ch.2, the method adopted in the Scotland Act to define the matters over which the Parliament is intended to have legislative competence is to list the matters reserved to the UK Parliament, with everything else being devolved to the Scottish Parliament; unless the Scotland Act specifically reserves a matter to Westminster, it is devolved to the Holyrood. The Scotland Act 1978, by contrast, listed the matters devolved to the Scottish Assembly with everything else being reserved to Westminster, leading to widespread criticism of the Act for its "complexity and difficulty of comprehension".[14] The Labour Government's assessment 20 years later was that it would have required "frequent updating and might have given rise to regular legal arguments about whether particular matters were or were not devolved".[15] In the interests of "maximum clarity and stability", therefore, it was decided to list the matters reserved in the Scotland Act rather than the matters devolved.[16]

Whether the aim of maximum clarity and stability was achieved is debatable. **7–06** The clarity of the devolution settlement depends not just on whether the reserved or devolved matters are listed in the legislation, but also on exactly where the line between reserved and devolved matters is drawn, and therefore how complex and fine-grained a boundary it defines. Rather than whole topics such as health or defence falling entirely on one side or the other, the line picks its way carefully between closely related topics, separating some to one side and some to another by reference to subtle and complex distinctions. Animal welfare, for example, is devolved but not scientific procedures on live animals.[17] The result is a settlement in which considerable amounts of lawyerly time and effort are spent on trying to decide whether Scottish Parliament Bills and ASPs are or are not on the "right" side of the line, with some subject areas remaining grey areas even now because of the (otherwise very welcome) lack of case law to provide the clarity that was intended but in many ways not delivered in the framing of the Scotland Act.

As for stability, what was probably meant was avoiding the need for frequent **7–07** updating rather than securing a settlement that commanded support across the political spectrum, but if the latter was the aim it was not achieved either.

Despite its weaknesses in practice, one of the undoubted advantages of the **7–08** retained powers or reserved powers model on which the devolution settlement is based is that it signals a progressive approach to devolution, in which devolution becomes the natural default option and areas of uncertainty are liable to be resolved in the Parliament's favour. It is this that has enabled the Parliament, for example, to legislate without challenge on climate change (in the Climate Change (Scotland) Act 2009), simply because it is not mentioned in the Scotland Act, whereas on the 1978 Act approach any such "new" subject matter would have been regarded as reserved (because not explicitly devolved). One consequence of this is that, over time, there is likely to be a general trend towards devolved competence growing; it is also in tune with the concept of

---

[14] "One fears that only lawyers and Civil Servants, but by no means all of them, will be able to work out or give reliable advice on the full meaning of the affirmations as qualified by the negations. Beyond doubt, this complexity and difficulty of comprehension is a defect of the Act. It infringes the principle of intelligibility of law, a principle most to be prized in constitutional enactments": Neil MacCormick, "Constitutional Points" in Donald I Mackay (ed), *Scotland: the Framework for Change* (Edinburgh: Paul Harris Publishing, 1979) p.53.

[15] Scottish Office, *Scotland's Parliament* (1997) Cm.3658, para.4.3.

[16] Scottish Office, *Scotland's Parliament* (1997) Cm.3658, para.4.3.

[17] SA 1998 Sch.5 Pt II s.B7.

subsidiarity (which puts the onus on those seeking to exercise powers from the centre to demonstrate why this is necessary).

SCHEDULE 5

7–09 The reserved matters are set out in Sch.5 to the Act, which sets out some "general reservations" (Pt I) and then a long list of "specific reservations" (Pt II).

7–10 Part I of the Schedule sets out something of a mixed bag of six general reservations: the constitution, including the Crown, the Union, and the continued existence of the High Court of Justiciary and the Court of Session as courts of first instance and of appeal; the registration and funding of political parties; foreign affairs, including the conduct of relations with the European Union; the civil service, with an exception for court staff; defence, with exceptions for some aspects of civil defence and sea fishing enforcement; and treason.

7–11 The specific reservations in Pt II are set out under 11 broad "heads", which are subdivided into 69 sections. Most of the heads correspond to a UK Government department, which accounts for the sometimes rather eclectic list of sections under a head, e.g. Head B—Home Affairs. (The titles of the heads and sections are signposts—they do not form part of the definition of reserved matters.[18] But it is proper to have regard to them if help is needed as to the meaning of any of the reservations.[19]) In some sections the reserved policy area or "subject" is defined in general terms, e.g. A1 (fiscal, economic and monetary policy) or B6 (immigration and nationality). In other sections it is defined by reference to the subject matter of a particular enactment or enactments, e.g. B2 (data protection) or B4 (firearms). References to the subject matter of an enactment are to be read as references to the enactment as it had effect on the "principal appointed day", i.e. July 1, 1999.[20] It does not matter if the enactment is amended or even repealed after that date, the reservation remains the same. In some sections both approaches are employed, e.g. B3 (elections) or C5 (import and export control). Several of the reservations are subject to exceptions, which allow Holyrood to legislate within the scope of the exception and which, like the reservations, are sometimes defined in general terms ("though it stands to reason that greater detail is used than in the reservations themselves"),[21] e.g. C2 (insolvency) or C3 (competition), sometimes by reference to the subject matter of particular enactments, e.g. C4 (intellectual property) or D1 (electricity), and sometimes by a combination of both, e.g. D2 (oil and gas) or E3 (marine transport). Some sections include interpretation provisions, e.g. L2 (equal opportunities) or F1 (social security schemes), and two include illustrations (F1 (social security schemes) and F4 (war pensions)).

Adjusting the boundary

7–12 Section 30 of the Scotland Act makes provision for the adjustment of the boundary between reserved and devolved matters by Order in Council, subject to the approval of both Parliaments.[22] There are no restrictions on the use that

---

[18] SA 1998, explanatory note to Sch.5 Pt II.
[19] *Imperial Tobacco v Lord Advocate* [2012] UKSC 61; 2013 S.C. (UKSC) 153 [17] (Lord Hope).
[20] SA 1998 Sch.5 Pt III para.5.
[21] Cabinet Office, Devolution Guidance Note 14, *Use of Scotland Act Section 30(2) Orders* para.4.
[22] SA 1998 s.30(2).

may be made of this power; the adjustments that may be made are simply those that are considered necessary or expedient. In this sense, as the SNP's National Conversation White Paper pointed out, the Act set up

> "a system of 'unlimited' devolution, in which any reserved matters could be devolved to the Scottish Parliament, using the mechanisms already in the Act. No further primary legislation would be required at Westminster or Holyrood".[23]

But while the power is unlimited in the sense that it allows *anything* further to be devolved (or indeed reserved), it was clearly not designed to enable *everything* to be devolved; and there is no realistic prospect of it ever being so used (or used, for example, to devolve wholesale defence or foreign affairs). If the relationship between Scotland and the rest of the UK is to be radically altered it would need to be done on a different basis.

The Calman Commission thought it a weakness of the devolution settlement **7–13** that there was no "reverse Sewel" mechanism whereby the Westminster Parliament could consent to Scottish Parliament legislation in reserved areas. The only way in which competence could be devolved was by amending Sch.5 so that a matter was no longer reserved. The Commission regarded the response of the two governments to the House of Lords' decision in *Somerville v Scottish Ministers*[24] as having set a "helpful precedent".[25] That response saw Sch.4 to the Scotland Act modified to allow the Scottish Parliament to impose the same one-year time limit on actions against the Scottish Ministers under the Scotland Act as apply to such actions under the Human Rights Act 1998 ("the HRA"),[26] on the understanding that the new time limit would subsequently be enshrined in Westminster legislation and the modification of Sch.4 reversed so as to restore the boundary between reserved and devolved matters to its former place, both of which were done by the Scotland Act 2012.[27] The Calman Commission's recommendation for a new order-making power was not implemented, but s.9 of the Scotland Act 2012 provides that a provision of an Act of the Scottish Parliament does not cease to have effect because the boundary has been changed since it was enacted, making the temporary devolution of legislative competence a simpler and more practical proposition than the cumbersome procedure followed after *Somerville*.

One important consequence of the s.30 power is to reduce the need for flexi- **7–14** bility in the interpretation of the Act; if "adjustments" are required they can be made expressly rather than in the guise of interpretation. The power, however, is not intended to replace the role of the courts in the interpretation of the Act. Cabinet Office guidance states that it should not routinely be used only for the purposes of clarification—that should generally be left to the courts. At the same time, the guidance recognises that exceptions will inevitably arise from time to time, e.g. it might be appropriate for a reservation or exception to be clarified if the Scottish Government intends inviting the Scottish Parliament to

---

[23] Scottish Government, *Choosing Scotland's Future: A National Conversation* (August, 2007) para.1.10.
[24] *Somerville v Scottish Ministers* [2007] UKHL 44; 2008 S.C. (HL) 45.
[25] Commission on Scottish Devolution, *Serving Scotland Better: Scotland and the United Kingdom in the 21st Century* (June, 2009) para.4.179.
[26] Scotland Act 1998 (Modification of Schedule 4) Order 2009 (SI 2009/1380).
[27] SA 2012 s.14.

legislate in an area *and* both governments "see the risks and consequences of a successful legal challenge as being significant in the wider context".[28]

7–15 The s.30 power has not been extensively used. Only 12 orders have been made, eight of these during the Parliament's first two sessions (1999–2007).[29] The most significant is the Scotland Act 1998 (Modification of Schedule 5) Order 2013,[30] empowering the Parliament to legislate for a referendum on the independence of Scotland from the rest of the UK, subject to certain requirements being met, one of which was that the referendum be held before the end of 2014. Other adjustments have enabled the Parliament to legislate with regard to the insolvency of social landlords,[31] the promotion and construction of railways,[32] fire safety on construction sites[33] and the provision of financial assistance for the purposes of meeting immediate short-term needs or facilitating community care.[34] Others have been about "clarifying" the scope of reserved matters, making it clear when the Parliament cannot legislate as well as when it can, and the terms in which it can legislate (see e.g. Scotland Act 1998 (Modifications of Schedules 4 and 5) Order 1999 art.5 (freedom of information)[35]); and updating legislative references (e.g. Scotland Act 1998 (Modification of Schedule 5) Order 2004 art.2 picking up a missing consequential[36]).

SCHEDULE 4 RESTRICTIONS

7–16 Schedule 4 to the Scotland Act prevents the Parliament from modifying certain enactments. Regardless of whether or not the subject matter of those enactments is reserved, the Parliament has no power to modify them. It also prevents the Parliament from modifying "the law on reserved matters". "Modify" includes, but is not confined to, amend or repeal.[37]

Protected enactments

7–17 Under the Act as originally drafted, the Scotland Act was the only Act protected from modification, but the list of enactments "entrenched" against modification grew during the passage of the legislation. The enactments entrenched by Sch.4 include:

---

[28] Cabinet Office, Devolution Guidance Note 14, *Use of Scotland Act Section 30(2) Orders*, para.6(ii).

[29] The Scotland Act 1998 (Modifications of Schedules 4 and 5) Order 1999 (SI 1999/1749); the Scotland Act 1998 (Modifications of Schedule 5) Order 2000 (SI 2000/3252); the Scotland Act 1998 (Modifications of Schedule 5) Order 2001 (SI 2001/1456); the Scotland Act 1998 (Modifications of Schedule 5) Order 2002 (SI 2002/1629); the Scotland Act 1998 (Modifications of Schedule 5) Order 2004 (SI 2004/3329); the Scotland Act 1998 (Modifications of Schedule 5) Order 2005 (SI 2005/865) and the Scotland Act 1998 (Modifications of Schedule 5) (No.2) Order 2005 (SI 2005/866); the Scotland Act 1998 (Modifications of Schedule 5) Order 2006 (SI 2006/609); the Scotland Act 1998 (Modifications of Schedule 5) Order 2013 (SI 2013/242) and the Scotland Act 1998 (Modifications of Schedule 5) (No.2) Order 2013 (SI 2013/192); the Scotland Act 1998 (Modifications of Schedule 5) Order 2014 (SI 2014/1559); and the Scotland Act (Modifications of Schedules 4 and 5 and Transfer of Functions to the Scottish Ministers etc.) Order 2015 (SI 2015/692).

[30] Scotland Act 1998 (Modification of Schedule 5) Order 2013 (SI 2013/242).

[31] Scotland Act 1998 (Modification of Schedule 5) Order 2001 (SI 2001/1456).

[32] Scotland Act 1998 (Modification of Schedule 5) Order 2002 (SI 2002/1629).

[33] Scotland Act 1998 (Modification of Schedule 5) Order 2005 (SI 2005/865).

[34] Scotland Act 1998 (Modification of Schedule 5) (No.2) Order 2013 (SI 2013/192).

[35] Scotland Act 1998 (Modification of Schedules 4 and 5) Order 1999 (SI 1999/1749).

[36] Scotland Act 1998 (Modification of Schedule 5) Order 2004 (SI 2004/3329).

[37] SA 1998 s.126(1).

(i) Articles 4 and 6 of the Acts of Union so far as they relate to freedom of trade.[38] The Union is a reserved matter by virtue of para.1 of Sch.5. However, the Acts of Union also contain provisions which relate to freedom of trade. In the absence of this provision it might be argued that it was open to the Parliament to modify those provisions within the context of the continuation of Union. In *Imperial Tobacco v Lord Advocate*,[39] the Inner House held that ss.1 and 9 of the Tobacco and Primary Medical Services (Scotland) Act 2010, which created offences involving the display of tobacco products at point of sale and the use of vending machines to sell tobacco products, did not "purport to any extent to supersede, amend or otherwise modify article 6 of the Acts of Union".[40] The argument was not pursued before the UK Supreme Court. In *Scotch Whisky Association v Lord Advocate*,[41] the Lord Ordinary rejected as "ill-founded" an argument to the effect that the introduction of minimum unit pricing for alcohol in Scotland would be contrary to the Acts of Union. This aspect of the decision was not challenged before the Inner House.[42]

(ii) The Private Legislation Procedure (Scotland) Act 1936, which governs the making of Scottish private legislation at Westminster.[43]

(iii) The key provisions of the European Communities Act 1972 which give effect to EU law in the UK.[44] The Parliament cannot therefore alter the effect given to EU law in Scotland.

(iv) The HRA, which gives effect to the Convention rights in domestic law.[45] The Parliament cannot therefore alter the effect given to the Convention rights in Scotland.

(v) The Scotland Act itself and enactments modified by it.[46] The ban on the Act's modification is not a complete one, but in its key respects, too, the Act is beyond the Parliament's reach. Implementation of the Smith Commission Agreement will see this restriction relaxed to allow the Scottish Parliament a greater role in setting its own internal arrangements and those of the Scottish Government.[47]

"the law on reserved matters"

The Scotland Act also prevents the Parliament from modifying the "law on **7–18** reserved matters".[48] The Act defines "the law on reserved matters" as enactments and rules of law whose subject matter is reserved by Sch.5.[49] In other

---

[38] SA 1998 Sch.4 para.1(2)(a).

[39] *Imperial Tobacco v Lord Advocate* [2012] CSIH 9; 2012 S.L.T. 749.

[40] *Imperial Tobacco v Lord Advocate* [2012] CSIH 9; 2012 S.L.T. 749 [157] (Lord Reed); see also [216] (Lord Brodie).

[41] *Scotch Whisky Association v Lord Advocate* [2013] CSOH 70; 2013 S.L.T. 776 [25] (Lord Doherty).

[42] *Scotch Whisky Association v Lord Advocate* [2014] CSIH 38 [1]; the case has been referred to the European Court of Justice.

[43] SA 1998 Sch.4 para.1(2)(b); the 1936 Act procedure does not apply where the powers sought are wholly within the competence of the Scottish Parliament: Private Legislation Procedure (Scotland) Act 1936 s.1(5), inserted by SA 1998 Sch.8 para.5. Scottish private legislation at Westminster has become a rarity as result, with only two Acts confirming provisional orders since devolution.

[44] SA 1998 Sch.4 para.1(2)(c).

[45] SA 1998 Sch.4 para.1(2)(f).

[46] SA 1998 Sch.4 paras 4 and 5.

[47] Scotland Office, *Scotland in the United Kingdom: An enduring settlement* (2015) Cm.8990, paras 1.3.1–1.3.2.

[48] SA 1998 Sch.4 para.2(1).

[49] SA 1998 Sch.4 para.2(2).

words, the law the Parliament cannot modify is the law *about* reserved matters rather than law that *applies* or may apply *to* reserved matters. So Sch.4 does not prevent the Parliament modifying, e.g. planning law, which is devolved but which may apply to reserved matters such as coal mining or electricity generation.[50] As we shall see, the Parliament is not prevented from legislating merely because a provision would affect reserved matters; some effect on reserved matters is permitted so long as the provision's purpose is devolved, i.e. it does not relate to reserved matters. The effect of this restriction, however, is that the Parliament cannot modify the law on reserved matters regardless of the purpose for which it is legislating.

7–19 This restriction is subject to two exceptions. First, it does not apply to modifications of rules of Scots private or criminal law unless the rule in question is "special to a reserved matter", i.e. results in its "distinct and separate treatment",[51] or the subject matter of the rule is one of a specified list (the list includes interest on sums due in respect of taxes and excise duties and refunds of such taxes or duties, and the obligations of the trustees or managers of occupational and personal pension schemes).[52] The purpose of this exception is

> "to ensure that the Scottish parliament can legislate on the general rules of Scots private law and criminal law across the board and without fragmenting the general principles which distinguish Scots law as a separate system of law".[53]

If the rule in question is not special to a reserved matter, i.e. it applies to both reserved and non-reserved matters, it may be modified but only if the purpose of the modification is to make the law in question apply consistently to reserved and devolved matters (below).[54] Scots private law and criminal law are defined in s.126(4) and (5) of the Act.

7–20 The second exception allows the Parliament to make modifications to the law on reserved matters, which are "incidental to, or consequential on", provision which does not "relate to" reserved matters, i.e. which is for devolved purposes, on condition that they do not have a greater effect on reserved matters than is necessary to give effect to the purpose of the provision.[55] The fact that incidental or consequential modifications could be made by an Act of the UK Parliament, or by order under s.104 of the Scotland Act, does not make them unnecessary.[56] "Clearly it is sensible to allow the Scottish parliament to complete its legislative task."[57]

7–21 The question whether a provision is "incidental to, or consequential on" another provision was considered in the *Welsh Byelaws* case.[58] The answer depended, Lord Hope said, on the significance of the provision when seen "in the context of the Act as a whole". If the provision has

---

[50] House of Lords debate July 21, 1998, Vol.592, col.821(Lord Sewel).

[51] House of Lords debate July 21, 1998, Vol.592, col.821(Lord Sewel).

[52] SA 1998 Sch.4 para.2(3), as amended by the Scotland Act 1998 (Modifications of Schedule 4) Order 2000 (SI 2000/1831).

[53] House of Lords debate, July 21, 1998, Vol.592, col.821 (Lord Sewel).

[54] SA 1998 s.29(4).

[55] SA 1998 Sch.4 para.3(1).

[56] SA 1998 Sch.4 para.3(2).

[57] House of Lords debate, July 21, 1998, Vol.592, col.822 (Lord Sewel).

[58] *Local Government Byelaws (Wales) Bill 2012—Reference by the Attorney General for England and Wales* [2012] UKSC 53; [2013] 1 A.C. 792.

"an end and purpose of its own, that will be one thing. It will be outside competence. If its purpose or effect is merely subsidiary to something else in the Act, and its consequence when it is put into effect can be seen to be minor or unimportant in the context of the Act as a whole, that will be another. It can then be regarded as merely incidental to, or consequential on, the purpose that the Bill seeks to achieve".[59]

In *Martin v Most*,[60] Lord Rodger described the exception of incidental and consequential modifications as

"intended to cover the kinds of minor modifications which are obviously necessary to give effect to a piece of devolved legislation, but which raise no separate issue of principle".

There are also a number of general exceptions to the restrictions in Sch.4, which **7–22** ensure for example that the Parliament is not prevented from restating the law or repealing spent enactments, or changing various titles, including the titles of courts and judges, or unduly limited in legislating about its own subordinate legislation procedure. There is also provision for the transfer of some but not all ministerial functions under protected enactments to the Scottish Ministers.[61]

Schedule 4, like Sch.5, may be modified by Order in Council subject to the **7–23** approval of both parliaments.[62]

CONVENTION RIGHTS AND EU LAW

The Kilbrandon Commission saw no need to include in the devolution **7–24** legislation

"statutory provisions designed to secure the preservation of basic human rights of a kind which in some overseas countries are enshrined in Bills of Rights ... If there were to be any infringement of or failure to protect essential human rights through actions of the assemblies, Parliament could use its paramount powers to provide the remedy".[63]

The Scotland Act 1978, accordingly, made no provision for the protection of individual rights and freedoms. Rights protection, by contrast, is an integral part of the 1998 settlement. New Labour's manifesto commitment to "bring rights home" raised the question whether the Scottish Parliament should be given the same latitude to legislate incompatibly with the Convention rights as the UK Parliament. As we have seen, it was decided that it should not.[64] A

---

[59] *Local Government Byelaws (Wales) Bill 2012—Reference by the Attorney General for England and Wales* [2012] UKSC 53; [2013] 1 A.C. 792, [83].

[60] *Martin v Most* [2010] UKSC 10; [2010] S.C. (UKSC) 40, [128].

[61] SA 1998 Sch.4 paras 7, 9, 11 and 13.

[62] SA 1998 s.30(2); as to the use made of the power, see the Scotland Act 1998 (Modifications of Schedules 4 and 5) Order 1999 (SI 1999/1749), the Scotland Act 1998 (Modification of Schedule 4) Order 2000 (SI 2000/1831), the Scotland Act 1998 (Modification of Schedule 4) Order 2009 (SI 2009/1380), and the Scotland Act (Modifications of Schedules 4 and 5 and Transfer of Functions to the Scottish Ministers etc.) Order 2015 (SI 2015/692).

[63] *Report of the Royal Commission on the Constitution 1969–1973* (1973) Cmnd.5460, para.1328; for critical comment, see Terence Daintith, "The Kilbrandon Report: Some Comments" in Harry Calvert (ed), *Devolution* (London: Professional Books, 1975) pp.31–33.

[64] Home Office, *Rights Brought Home: The Human Rights Bill* (1997) Cm.3782, para.2.21.

provision of an Act of the Scottish Parliament which cannot be interpreted compatibly with the Convention rights accordingly falls to be struck down as outwith the Parliament's legislative competence rather than being made the subject of a declaration of incompatibility under the HRA. The expression "the Convention rights" has the same meaning as in the Human Rights Act.[65] Most challenges to the legislative competence of Acts of the Scottish Parliament so far have been on Convention rights rather than reserved matters grounds.[66]

7–25 The Parliament also has no power to legislate incompatibly with EU law.[67] "EU law" here refers to

> "all those rights, powers, liabilities, obligations and restrictions from time to time created or arising by or under the EU Treaties, and all those remedies and procedures from time to time created or arising by or under the EU Treaties".[68]

Were the Parliament not to be bound by EU law there would be no guarantee that the UK as a Member State of the European Union would be able to fulfil its obligations under the Treaties, which include an obligation to ensure that EU law is given effect throughout its territory.[69] In contrast to an Act of the UK Parliament, an Act of the Scottish Parliament that cannot be interpreted compatibly with EU law falls to struck down as outwith the legislative competence of the Scottish Parliament rather than being denied effect or "disapplied".[70]

The test of validity

7–26 A provision will be outside the Parliament's legislative competence if it is "incompatible" with any of the Convention rights or EU law. This is a different test of validity from the test that applies where the provision is challenged on the grounds that it relates to a reserved matter. Whether a provision relates to a reserved matter is to be determined having regard to its purpose and effect (below). On the face of it, the purpose and effect of a provision, other than its legal effect, have no bearing on its compatibility (with the Convention rights or EU law). It is either compatible or it is not. As in the *Scotch Whisky Association* case, however, the determination of the compatibility of a provision may require an inquiry into its purpose and effect.[71]

THE ROLE OF THE LORD ADVOCATE

7–27 Finally, a provision of an Act of the Scottish Parliament is outside the Parliament's legislative competence so far as "it would remove the Lord Advocate from his position as head of the systems of criminal prosecution and

---

[65] SA 1998 s.126(1).
[66] See para.16–27.
[67] SA 1998 s.29(2)(d).
[68] SA 1998 s.126(9).
[69] *Commission v Belgium* Case 77/69; [1970] ECR 237. The same imperative was not felt in relation to the UK's international obligations. However, that was to change with the (unsuccessful) attempt to take the power to implement international obligations in relation to matters within devolved competence in the Scotland Act 2012.
[70] European Communities Act 1972 s.2(4); *R v Secretary of State for Transport, Ex p. Factortame (No.2)* [1991] 1 A.C. 603.
[71] *Scotch Whisky Association v Lord Advocate* [2014] CSIH 38, currently under reference to the European Court of Justice (minimum pricing of alcohol; a measure of equivalent effect to a quantitative restriction on imports; whether justified on grounds of public health).

investigation of deaths in Scotland".[72] As we have seen, this limitation was conceived as one of the guarantees of the independence of criminal prosecutions after devolution. The effectiveness of the guarantee depends of course on the independence of the Lord Advocate, to which end the Scotland Act insists that decisions taken by the Lord Advocate as head of the systems of criminal prosecution and investigation of deaths in Scotland must continue to be taken independently of any other person.[73]

CHARACTERISING LEGISLATION: GENERAL PRINCIPLES

As a constitutional statute, the question arises whether the Scotland Act should **7–28** be interpreted according to the normal rules of statutory interpretation or differently. The question is of particular relevance to the question of whether a provision of an Act of the Scottish Parliament is outside the Parliament's legislative competence. In *Imperial Tobacco Ltd v Lord Advocate*,[74] Lord Hope, with whom the other justices agreed, laid down three principles that should be followed when undertaking the exercise of determining whether a provision of an Act of the Scottish Parliament is outside competence:

"First, the question of competence must be determined in each case according to the particular rules that have been set out in section 29 of and Schedules 4 and 5 to the 1998 Act. It is not for the courts to say whether legislation on any particular issue is better made by the Scottish Parliament or by the Parliament of the UK at Westminster . . . How that issue is to be dealt with has been addressed and determined by the UK Parliament . . . The statutory language was informed by principles that were applied to resolve questions that had arisen in federal systems, where the powers of various legislatures tend to overlap . . . But the intention was that it was to the 1998 Act itself, not to decisions as to how the problem was handled in other jurisdictions, that one should look for guidance. So it is to the rules that the 1998 Act lays down that the court must address its attention, bearing in mind that a provision may have a devolved purpose and yet be outside competence because it contravenes one of the rules . . .

Second, those rules must be interpreted in the same way as any other rules that are found in a UK statute. The system that those rules laid down must, of course, be taken to have been intended to create a system for the exercise of legislative power by the Scottish Parliament that was coherent, stable and workable. This is a factor that it is proper to have in mind. But it is not a principle of construction that is peculiar to the 1998 Act. It is a factor that is common to any other statute that has been enacted by the legislature, whether at Westminster or at Holyrood. The best way of ensuring that a coherent, stable and workable outcome is achieved is to adopt an approach to the meaning of a statute that is constant and predictable. This will be achieved if the legislation is construed according to the ordinary meaning of the words used.

Third, the description of the Act as a constitutional statute cannot be taken, in itself, to be a guide to its interpretation. The statute must be interpreted like any other statute. But the purpose of the Act has informed the statutory language. Its concern must be taken to have been that the

---

[72] SA 1998 s.29(2)(e).
[73] SA 1998 s.48(5).
[74] *Imperial Tobacco v Lord Advocate* [2012] UKSC 61; 2013 S.C. (UKSC) 153 [12]–[15].

Scottish Parliament should be able to legislate effectively about matters that were intended to be devolved to it, while ensuring that there were adequate safeguards for those matters that were intended to be reserved. That purpose provides the context for any discussion about legislative competence. So it is proper to have regard to the purpose if help is needed as to what the words actually mean. The fact that section 29 provides a mechanism for determining whether a provision of an Act of the Scottish Parliament is outside, rather than inside, competence does not create a presumption in favour of competence. But it helps to show that one of the purposes of the 1998 Act was to enable the Parliament to make such laws within the powers given to it by section 28 as it thought fit. It was intended, within carefully defined limits, to be a generous settlement of legislative authority."

7–29   It is therefore the rules laid down by the Scotland Act to which the courts must give effect in determining whether a provision of an Act of the Scottish Parliament is outside the Parliament's legislative competence. "As to what they mean," Lord Hope said in *Martin v Most*,[75] "the Scotland Act provides its own dictionary."

SECTION 29(3) AND THE PURPOSE TEST

7–30   A provision of an Act of the Scottish Parliament is outside the Parliament's legislative competence so far as it relates to reserved matters.[76] The question immediately arises of what is meant by "relates to". Is it enough that the provision affects a reserved matter or must it instead be "directed to" the reserved matter? The answer provided by s.29(3) of the Act is that the question is to be determined "by reference to the purpose of the provision, having regard (among other things) to its effect in all the circumstances". Explaining the background to s.29(3) at the Bill's committee stage in the House of Lords, Lord Sewel said that it was one of several technical amendments designed to ensure that the Scottish Parliament was not "hamstrung from the start by a literal interpretation of the test of its legislative competence".[77] The original intention, Lord Sewel explained, had been to rely on the "respection doctrine", which the courts had developed in determining whether a provision was "in respect of" a particular matter in cases arising under Commonwealth constitutions and the Government of Ireland Act 1920".[78] The classic statement of the respection doctrine was by Lord Atkin in *Gallagher v Lynn*[79]:

"It is well established that you are to look at the 'true nature and character of the legislation' ... the 'pith and substance of the legislation'. If, on the view of the statute as a whole, you find the substance of the legislation is within the express powers, then it is not invalidated if incidentally it affects matters which are outside the authorised field."

7–31   Were the courts not to apply the respection doctrine and to hold instead that a provision related to a devolved matter merely because it "affected" it, the result

---

[75] *Martin v Most* [2010] UKSC 10; 2010 S.C. (UKSC) 40 [15].
[76] SA 1998 s.29(2)(b).
[77] House of Lords debate, July 21, 1998, Vol.592, col.822.
[78] The history of the doctrine was briefly reviewed by Lord Hope in *Martin v Most* [2010] UKSC 10; 2010 S.C. (UKSC) 40 [11]–[13].
[79] *Gallagher v Lynn* [1937] A.C. 863, 870.

would be to "severely fetter the Scottish Parliament's ability to legislate about subjects which are, in terms of the White Paper, to be devolved".[80] The example Lord Sewel gave was legislation on pollution control, which was intended to be devolved, but which the courts might hold to be outside the Parliament's competence because it affected the reserved matter of coal mining. In order to avoid any doubt therefore as to whether the courts would apply the doctrine, it was restated in statutory form as the purpose test in s.29(3) of the Scotland Act.

The courts are therefore required to determine whether a provision relates to a **7–32** reserved matter by reference to "the purpose of the provision". If its purpose is a permitted one, i.e. it does not relate to reserved matters, it is no objection to the provision that it may affect matters outside the Parliament's legislative competence.[81]

In the event, the courts have construed "relates to" as meaning something more **7–33** than "affects".

> "In ordinary English, 'relates to' does not mean the same as 'affects'; and, although it is a wide expression, it cannot be intended to be given such a wide construction as to invalidate all legislation affecting matters listed in Sch.5, however slight, indirect or remote the effect may be."[82]

The purpose of a provision

The difficulty is that a provision may often be said to have several purposes or, **7–34** in the language of the Act, to relate to several matters, some of which may be devolved but others reserved. Does a Bill to ban smoking in public places relate to health (devolved) or health and safety at work (reserved)? Do restrictions on the display of tobacco products relate to health (devolved) or to the regulation of the sale of goods to consumers (reserved)? "Much of the grist of constitutional adjudication derives from the fact that any given law will often exhibit more than one salient feature."[83] What s.29(3) enjoins the courts to do in cases of this kind, however, is to determine "the" purpose of the provision "or, in other words, what the provision is about, what is its 'true nature', its 'pith and substance'".[84] If it is about a devolved matter then it will be within the Parliament's legislative competence, no matter that it may affect reserved matters. Conversely, if it is about a reserved matter it will be outside the Parliament's competence, no matter that it may affect devolved matters.

The purpose of the provision is sometimes treated as synonymous with its **7–35** "pith and substance". The pith and substance approach to characterisation is likewise sometimes another way of saying the purposive approach.[85] It may be preferable, however, to treat the purpose of a provision as part of a wider

---

[80] House of Lords debate, July 21, 1998, Vol.592, col.819 (Lord Sewel).

[81] "Once the pith and substance of the law has been held to be within the powers of the enacting legislative body, it is no objection that the law may have some effect on matters outside the powers of the enacting legislative body": Peter W Hogg, *Constitutional Law of Canada*, 5th edn (Toronto: Thomson Carswell, 2007) para.36.7(a).

[82] *Imperial Tobacco v Lord Advocate* [2012] CSIH 9; 2012 S.C. 297 [120] (Lord Reed); in the same case in the Supreme Court, Lord Hope said that the phrase indicates something more than a "loose or consequential connection": [2012]UKSC 61; 2013 S.C. (UKSC) 153 [16].

[83] Christopher D Gilbert, *Australian and Canadian Federalism 1867–1984: A Study of Judicial Techniques* (Melbourne: Melbourne University Press, 1986) pp.7–8.

[84] SA 1998, explanatory note to s.29.

[85] See e.g. Peter W Hogg, *Constitutional Law of Canada*, 5th edn (Toronto: Thomson Carswell, 2007) para.15.5(d), fn 47.

inquiry into the pith and substance or "true nature and character" of the provision.[86] One conclusion to be drawn from the case law arising from Canada, Australia and Northern Ireland, Lord Reed said in *Imperial Tobacco*,[87] was that "pith and substance" was not synonymous with "purpose"

> "rather, the purpose of the legislation has been regarded in some jurisdictions (but not all) as one of the factors to be taken into account in determining its 'pith and substance' or its true nature and character".

7–36 In *Imperial Tobacco*,[88] Lord Reed reserved his position on whether the Scotland Act compelled the attribution of one purpose and one purpose only to a provision,

> "although section 29(3) refers to 'the purpose of the provision', in the singular, in real life legislation may be enacted in order to achieve a number of objectives. In such a situation, it may be unrealistic to regard a provision as relating only to a single matter; and it is possible that, in such a situation, one of the matters to which it relates may be reserved, and another may not be . . . Unlike the position in Canada, where legislation must be characterised as relating to only one, predominant, matter in order to avoid a conflict between the two lists, it may be arguable that the court is not driven by the logic of the Scotland Act to follow that approach".

7–37 "In such a situation," Lord Hope said in the Supreme Court,[89] "the fact that one of its purposes relates to a reserved matter will mean that the provision is outside competence, unless its purpose can be regarded as consequential and thus of no real significance when regard is had to what the provision overall seeks to achieve."

The effect of a provision

7–38 The purpose of a provision is to be determined having regard to "its effect in all the circumstances". A criticism of the pith and substance doctrine as it had been applied under the Government of Ireland Act was that it provided an opportunity for "subjective evaluation" when what was required was an inquiry into the "respection or aim of the legislation".[90] In determining this pith and substance of the legislation the courts had not looked beyond the legislation itself. What the courts are being urged to do in s.29(3), through the requirement to determine the purpose of the provision having regard to "its effect in all the circumstances", is to range as widely as is necessary in order to arrive at a proper understanding of its purpose.

7–39 The effect of a provision is not confined to its legal effect:

---

[86] Other synonyms for pith and substance include the "matter" of the law or the "subject matter" of the law, the "true meaning" of the law, the "leading feature" of the law, and the "true nature and character" of the law. "The general idea of these and similar formulations is that it is necessary to identify the dominant or most important characteristic of the challenged law": Peter W Hogg, *Constitutional Law of Canada*, 5th edn (Toronto: Thomson Carswell, 2007) para.15.5(a).

[87] *Imperial Tobacco v Lord Advocate* [2012] CSIH 9; 2012 S.C. 297 [105].

[88] *Imperial Tobacco v Lord Advocate* [2012] CSIH 9; 2012 S.C. 297 [123].

[89] *Imperial Tobacco v Lord Advocate* [2012] UKSC 61; 2013 S.C. (UKSC) 153 [43].

[90] Harry Calvert, *Constitutional Law in Northern Ireland: A Study in Regional Government* (Northern Ireland: Stevens & Sons, 1968) pp.195–196.

"The process of characterisation is not a technical, formalistic exercise, confined to the strict legal operation of the impugned law . . . The Court will look beyond the direct legal effects to inquire into the social or economic purposes which the statute was enacted to achieve."[91]

It will do so in particular "if there is reason to believe that the direct legal effects of the statute are directed to the indirect achievement of other purposes".[92] "In such a case", Lord Maugham said in *Attorney-General for Alberta v Attorney-General for Canada*,[93]

"the Court must take into account any public general knowledge of which the Court would take judicial notice, and may in a proper case require to be informed by evidence as to what the effect of the legislation will be".

The effect of a provision includes its effect on reserved matters. As we have 7–40 seen, it is no objection to a provision that it may affect reserved matters. The effect on reserved matters may even be a significant one without the validity of the provision being called into question. There must come a point, however, at which the effect on reserved matters is so great as to call into question whether the provision's purpose is indeed a devolved one.

"among other things"

In determining the purpose of a provision, the court is required to have regard 7–41 to its effect "among other things". The courts in the past varied in their willingness to go beyond the words used in a statute in ascertaining the intention of the legislature, but it is now

"beyond doubt that they will go to any sensible length to discern and give effect to the underlying policy intention of legislation, and that in construing a statute they will use all kinds of material available to them as tools to discover that intention".[94]

The "other things" to which regard may be had include the "mischief" the legislation was designed to cure.

"One of the circumstances to which it is proper to have regard in determining the purpose of a provision is the situation before the provision was enacted, which it was designed to address. Reports to and papers issued by the Scottish Ministers prior to the introduction of the Bill, the policy memorandum that accompanied it and statements by Ministers during the proceedings in the Scottish Parliament may all be taken into account in this assessment."[95]

One of the striking features of the way in which the courts have dealt with chal- 7–42 lenges to the validity of legislation under the Act, on Convention rights as well

---

[91] Peter W Hogg, *Constitutional Law of Canada*, 5th edn (Toronto: Thomson Carswell, 2007) para.15.5(d).
[92] Peter W Hogg, *Constitutional Law of Canada*, 5th edn (Toronto: Thomson Carswell, 2007) para.15.5(e).
[93] *Attorney-General for Alberta v Attorney-General for Canada* [1939] A.C. 117, 130.
[94] Daniel Greenberg (ed), *Craies on Legislation*, 10th edn (London: Sweet & Maxwell, 2012) para.18.1.3.
[95] *Martin v Most* [2010] UKSC 10; 2010 S.C. (UKSC) 40 [25] (Lord Hope).

as reserved matters grounds, has been their preparedness to resort to extrinsic aids to construction in order to arrive at a proper understanding of the pith and substance or true nature and character of the provision under scrutiny.[96]

Section 29(4) and Scots Law

7–43 The purpose test is qualified in its application to provisions that modify Scots private law, or Scots criminal law, as it applies to reserved matters. The application of the purpose test may result in the conclusion that such a provision does not relate to reserved matters even though it substantially affects them (above). Section 29(4), however, provides that such a provision is to be treated as relating to reserved matters, and hence as invalid, unless its purpose is "to make the law in question apply consistently to reserved matters and otherwise", i.e. to both reserved and devolved matters.[97] On one view the purpose of this provision is to ensure that Parliament is not prevented from legislating for Scots law by reason of the fact that its legislation affects reserved matters:

> "In effect, the 'unless' clause in section 29(4) allows the Scottish Parliament to make a general reform of Scottish private or criminal law, even though it modifies the law which applies to reserved matters."[98]

But given that such legislation would not necessarily relate to reserved matters, it may also have been designed to prevent the Parliament from legislating for reserved matters under the guise of legislating for Scots law. The measure of the genuineness of the Parliament's purpose in legislating for Scots law is, therefore, whether the modifications apply consistently to reserved and devolved matters. It is only where reserved and devolved matters are treated in the same way that the Parliament can legislate for Scots law.[99]

Scots law and the law on reserved matters

7–44 As we have seen, the Parliament has no power to modify the law on reserved matters. What, however, if reserved matters are governed by Scots law—the law on reserved matters is Scots law? Is the Parliament prevented from modifying it? The Act's answer is that the Parliament may modify it so long as the provision is not special or unique to a reserved matter (or one of a specified list). If it is special to a reserved matter it may be modified only by Westminster.[100] It may also be modified, as we have seen, if the modification is incidental to, or consequential on, a provision of an Act of the Scottish Parliament that is within devolved competence.[101]

7–45 The question whether a rule of Scots criminal law was "special to a reserved matter" arose in *Martin v Most*.[102] The Supreme Court held unanimously that

---

[96] *Martin v Most* [2010] UKSC 10; 2010 S.C. (UKSC) 40 [25] (Lord Hope), [75] Lord Rodger, [162] Lord Kerr; *Imperial Tobacco v Lord Advocate* [2012] CSIH 9; 2012 S.C. 297 [125], Lord Reed; [2012] UKSC 61, 2013 S.C. (UKSC) 153 [17] Lord Hope.

[97] SA 1998, explanatory note to s.29(4).

[98] *Martin v Most* [2010] UKSC 10; 2010 S.C. (UKSC) 40 [118] (Lord Rodger).

[99] "Paragraph 29(4)'s default position is restrictive: the modification is to be treated as relating to reserved matters 'unless the purpose of the provision is to make the law in question apply consistently to reserved matters and otherwise'.": *Martin v Most* [2010] UKSC 10; 2010 S.C. (UKSC) 40 [49] (Lord Walker).

[100] SA 1998 Sch.4 para.2.

[101] SA 1998 Sch.4 para.3; see para.7–27.

[102] *Martin v Most* [2010] UKSC 10; 2010 S.C. (UKSC) 40.

s.45 of the Criminal Proceedings etc. (Reform) (Scotland) Act 2007, which increased the summary sentencing powers of the sheriff, did not relate to the reserved matter of road traffic law. Its purpose, Lord Hope said, was to contribute to the reform of the summary criminal justice system by reducing pressure on the higher courts.[103] The Supreme Court justices disagreed, however, on whether s.45 fell foul of the prohibition on modifying a rule of Scots criminal law that was special to the reserved matter of road traffic law, holding by a majority of three to two that it did not.

While the outcome of the case was clear, the decision was less than illumi- **7–46** nating about the meaning of the phrase "special to a reserved matter". There being unanimity that the provision's purpose was a permitted one, the majority clearly felt that the Parliament should be left to get on with it, without feeling the need to discuss what the phrase meant:

> "Given that the Scottish Parliament is plainly intended to regulate the Scottish legal system I am disinclined to find a construction of Schedule 4 which would require the Scottish Parliament, when modifying that system, to invoke Westminster's help to do no more than dot the i's and cross the t's of the necessary consequences."[104]

"In case of doubt," Lord Hope said, "a generous application of para.2(3) which favours competence is to be preferred, as opposed to one which applies it narrowly."[105] It was left to Lord Rodger, in the minority, to offer the fullest discussion:

> "In my view, a statutory rule of law is 'special to a reserved matter' if it has been specially, specifically, enacted to apply to the reserved matter in question—as opposed to being a general rule of Scots private or criminal law which applies to, inter alia, a reserved matter . . . If interpreted in this way, para 2(3) means that para 2(1) prevents the Scottish Parliament from modifying any enactment which must be taken to reflect the conscious choice of Parliament to make special provision for the particular circumstances, rather than to rely on some general provision of Scottish private or criminal law. Whether or not to modify such an enactment involves questions of policy which must be left for the UK government and Parliament which are responsible for the matter."[106]

Whereas his interpretation placed a "comprehensible limit" on what the **7–47** Scottish Parliament could do,[107] the reasoning of the majority in his view was difficult to fathom:

> "Until now, judges, lawyers and law students have had to try to work out what Parliament meant by a rule of Scots criminal law that is 'special to a reserved matter'. That is, on any view, a difficult enough problem. Now, however, they must also try and work out what the Supreme Court means by these words. It is a new and intriguing mystery."[108]

---

[103] *Martin v Most* [2010] UKSC 10; 2010 S.C. (UKSC) 40 [31].
[104] *Martin v Most* [2010] UKSC 10; 2010 S.C. (UKSC) 40 [66] (Lord Brown).
[105] *Martin v Most* [2010] UKSC 10; 2010 S.C. (UKSC) 40 [38].
[106] *Martin v Most* [2010] UKSC 10; 2010 S.C. (UKSC) 40 [139].
[107] *Martin v Most* [2010] UKSC 10; 2010 S.C. (UKSC) 40 [139].
[108] *Martin v Most* [2010] UKSC 10; 2010 S.C. (UKSC) 40 [149].

7–48 It may be going too far, however, to suggest that penalties for offences, as opposed to the offences for which they are imposed, reflect the conscious choice of the UK Parliament to make special provision for the circumstances, bearing in mind the absence of any general provision of Scots criminal law with regard to penalties on which it might otherwise have relied. Examples of provisions of Scots private law and criminal law that, it was suggested during the parliamentary debates on the Bill, were special to reserved matters include: s.90 of the Copyright, Design and Patents Act 1988, which governs the assignation of copyright; the rule that gaming contracts are unenforceable as *sponsiones ludicrae*; and the Proceeds of Crime (Scotland) Act 1995, which makes provision for the confiscation of the proceeds of drug trafficking.[109] The matter remains to be decided.

EVERYTHING IS DEVOLVED UNLESS RESERVED

7–49 Finally, it is important to recall the basic premise on which the Scotland Act is based, which is that everything is devolved unless it is specifically reserved:

> "As the purpose of Part II of Schedule 5 is to define the limits of the legislative competence of the Scottish Parliament, anything that does not fall within the matters listed there must be taken to be within competence. These considerations cannot be used to override the clear meaning of the words used in the Schedule. But they are part of the overall context."[110]

7–50 Because a broad interpretation of the reserved matters would have the effect of narrowing the Parliament's legislative competence, a narrow approach is sometimes urged to their interpretation. What is being sought in the interpretation of Sch.5, however, is not an artificially narrow or for that matter broad interpretation of reserved matters but rather a determination of the intended coverage of the reservations.[111] Applying Lord Hope's second principle, this will be most likely to be achieved if the legislation is construed according to the ordinary meaning of the words used.[112]

CHECKS ON LEGISLATIVE COMPETENCE

7–51 The Act provides two checks on legislative competence: s.31 (scrutiny of Bills before introduction) and s.33 (scrutiny of Bills by the Supreme Court). There is also the possibility of a challenge to the vires of legislation once it is enacted (ss.98–103 and Sch.6).

Scrutiny of Bills before introduction

7–52 A person in charge of a Bill must, on or before introducing it, "state that in his view the provisions of the Bill would be within the legislative competence of the Parliament".[113] This requirement used to apply only to members of the Scottish Government (introducing Government Bills). It was extended to all persons (i.e. MSPs introducing Members' Bills, conveners introducing

---

[109] House of Lords debate, July 21, 1998, Vol.592, col.821(Lord Sewel).
[110] *Imperial Tobacco v Lord Advocate* [2012] UKSC 61; 2013 S.C. (UKSC) 153 [29] (Lord Hope).
[111] Cabinet Office, Devolution Guidance Note 14, *Use of Scotland Act Section 30(2) Orders* para.4.
[112] *Imperial Tobacco v Lord Advocate* [2012] UKSC 61; 2013 S.C. (UKSC) 153 [14].
[113] SA 1998 s.31(1).

Committee Bills and promoters introducing Private Bills) by the Scotland Act 2012, on the recommendation of the Calman Commission.[114] The presiding officer must also decide "whether or not in his view the provisions of the Bill would be within the legislative competence of the Parliament and state his or her decision".[115] In both cases this has always been done by a formulaic one sentence statement ("In my view, the provisions of the [. . .] Bill would be within the legislative competence of the Scottish Parliament"), but if the presiding officer is of the view that the Bill would be outside the Parliament's legislative competence, the Parliament's standing orders require reasons to be given. The Calman Commission recommended that a general indication of the legislative competence issues considered should be included in the Bill's explanatory notes.[116]

Scrutiny of Bills by the Supreme Court

Any one of the three principal law officers (the Advocate General, the Lord Advocate or the Attorney General) may refer a question of legislative competence to the Supreme Court.[117] This power may only be exercised within four weeks of the passing of the Bill by the Parliament. The Bill cannot be submitted for Royal Assent within that period unless all three law officers have notified the presiding officer that they do not intend to make a reference. **7–53**

If a reference is made to the Supreme Court and if the Supreme Court refers a question to the European Court of Justice, then (before either reference is decided or disposed of) the Parliament can resolve to reconsider the Bill. The Parliament may also reconsider the Bill if the Supreme Court decides it is ultra vires (or if the Secretary of State blocks it under s.35 of the Scotland Act). Reconsideration is a further amending stage in the Parliament, during which the challenged provision may be amended or removed. There is then a further four week period during which the law officers can check its vires again and, if need be, challenge it again (and the Secretary of State can do likewise). **7–54**

Post-enactment challenge

There is also the possibility of a challenge to the vires of the legislation once it is enacted. **7–55**

These checks are explored in Ch.9 (judicial proceedings), Ch.12 (law making), and Ch.16 (judicial review). **7–56**

---

[114] SA 2102 s.6; Commission on Scottish Devolution, *Serving Scotland Better: Scotland and the United Kingdom in the 21st Century* (June, 2009) para.6.92.

[115] SA 1998 s.31(2).

[116] Commission on Scottish Devolution, *Serving Scotland Better: Scotland and the United Kingdom in the 21st Century* (June, 2009) para.6.92. This was initially supported by the (Session 3) Standards, Procedures and Public Appointments Committee: 5th Report, *The recommendations of the Commission on Scottish Devolution regarding Scottish Parliament procedures* (Scottish Parliamentary Paper 490, 2010) paras 105–109; but when the Session 4 Committee looked at it again, post-Scotland Act 2012, it rejected the idea on the recommendation of the Scottish Government: 5th Report, *Scotland Act 2012 Standing Order rule changes—Legislative Competence Statements* (Scottish Parliamentary Paper 190, 2012) paras 5–8.

[117] SA 1998 s.33.

CHAPTER 8

EXECUTIVE COMPETENCE

INTRODUCTION

When a minority SNP Government took office in May 2007 it was widely **8–01**
assumed that it would struggle to govern given that there could be no certainty
that it would be able to get its legislation. The ability to get its legislation
does matter to a Scottish Government. In particular it needs legislative sanction for its spending plans in the form of the annual Budget Act. What the
widely held assumption overlooked, however, was how much of the business
of government a minority government would be able to carry out on the basis
of existing powers, which in the Scottish case had traditionally been widely
drawn because of the Scottish Office's difficulty in gaining access to legislative time at Westminster in competition with other Whitehall departments:

> "We explained that a very substantial proportion of the business of
> government is carried out on the basis of executive power, often within
> boundaries set by existing legislation; and that the necessity to obtain the
> explicit consent of Parliament to the actions of Ministers was not a signif-
> icant factor in the conduct of such government business. This is a charac-
> teristic shared with the UK Government but is more marked in Scotland
> because the shortage of Parliamentary time for Scottish legislation pre-
> devolution led to the development of an approach to legislation which
> built in considerable flexibility, in order to reduce the need to re-legislate
> as circumstances changed or policy evolved."[1]

In this chapter we concentrate on the Scottish Government's "functions", i.e. **8–02**
powers and duties[2]—their derivation, whether they are exercisable solely by
the Scottish Ministers, or by UK Ministers concurrently with their Scottish
counterparts, the statutory provisions governing their exercise, and the limits to
which their exercise is subject, including the question of the Crown's immunity
from statute. We also note the powers of intervention retained by UK Ministers.

GENERAL TRANSFER OF FUNCTIONS

The Scottish Ministers, like their UK counterparts, exercise a mixture of statu- **8–03**
tory and common law functions. Their functions derived initially from the
Scotland Act 1998 ("the Scotland Act"), s.53 of which transferred existing
ministerial functions to the Scottish Ministers "so far as they are exercisable
within devolved competence".[3] The functions transferred included the statutory

---

[1] Sir John Elvidge, *Northern Exposure: Lessons from the first twelve years of devolved government in Scotland* (London: Institute for Government, 2011) p.23.
[2] The Scotland Act 1998 ("SA 1998") s.126(1), provides that "functions" includes powers and
duties, and "confer", in relation to functions, includes "impose".
[3] SA 1998 s.53(1); as well as making provision for the transfer of existing ministerial functions
to the Scottish Ministers, the Act (s.106) made provision for the modification of functions by

functions conferred on UK Ministers by "pre-commencement enactments" which, broadly speaking, are enactments passed or made before devolution.[4] (After devolution some enactments were deemed to be pre-commencement enactments thus enabling the transfer of functions conferred by those enactments to the Scottish Ministers, but this practice has now ceased.[5]) They also included UK Ministers' "prerogative and other executive functions",[6] together with any other functions conferred on UK Ministers by prerogative instruments such as Orders in Council.[7] They did not, on the other hand, include the Lord Advocate's retained functions, i.e. the functions exercised by the Lord Advocate as a Minister of the Crown immediately before devolution, which the Lord Advocate continued to exercise as a member of the Scottish Government after devolution, but which did not therefore become part of the general pool of functions exercisable by the Scottish Ministers.[8] The transfer of UK Ministers' non-statutory functions is not confined to those functions UK Ministers were recognised as possessing at the time of devolution. The Scottish Ministers would therefore be able to claim the benefit of any subsequent judicial decisions as to the extent of the prerogative powers in the Crown's hands.[9]

8-04 Ministerial functions were transferred under s.53 "so far as they are exercisable within devolved competence".[10] Section 54 of the Scotland Act defines the concept of "devolved competence" by reference to the legislative competence of the Scottish Parliament. Whether a function is exercisable within devolved competence depends essentially on whether it could be conferred by Act of the Scottish Parliament.

> "In general, a function is exercisable within devolved competence if it could be conferred by an Act of the Scottish Parliament. The intention [was] to align the executive competence of the Scottish Ministers closely with the legislative competence of the Parliament."[11]

The functions transferred under s.53 do not therefore include functions that would not be within the Scottish Parliament's legislative competence, e.g.

---

subordinate legislation, e.g. to make them exercisable separately in or as regards Scotland, for the purpose of enabling or otherwise facilitating their transfer to the Scottish Ministers: see the Scotland Act (Modification of Functions) Order 1999 (SI 1999/1756); Scotland Act (Modification of Functions) Order 2000 (SI 2000/1458); Scotland Act (Modification of Functions) Order 2004 (SI 2004/2980); and Scotland Act (Modification of Functions) Order 2014 (SI 2014/2753).

[4] SA 1998 s.53(2)(c) and (3).

[5] Constitution Committee, *Devolution: Its Effect on the Practice of Legislation at Westminster* (House of Lords 2003–2004, 192) App.1, para.28. ("It appears that the 'pre-commencement enactment' device used 'retrospectively', though certainly still technically available, has now fallen out of favour with the draftsmen, perhaps because of its increasing artificiality as time passes.")

[6] As agents of the Crown, UK Ministers may exercise any of the powers that the Crown has power to exercise except so far as they are precluded from doing so by statute—the so called "Ram doctrine": Terence Daintith and Alan Page, *The Executive in the Constitution: Structure, Autonomy and Internal Control* (Oxford: OUP, 1999) pp.33–34.

[7] SA 1998 s.53(2)(a) and (b); "prerogative instruments" are defined in s.126(1) of the Act.

[8] SA 1998 ss.53(2), 52(6).

[9] In *R v Home Secretary, Ex p. Northumbria Police Authority* [1989] Q.B. 26, for example, the Home Office successfully asserted a prerogative power to keep the peace within the realm in the exercise of which it could supply baton rounds to a police force without the need for the local police authority's consent.

[10] SA 1998 s.53(1).

[11] SA 1998, explanatory note to s.54; closely but not exactly because the Act envisages that the Scottish Ministers may exercise functions in areas reserved to Westminster.

because they relate to reserved matters or because they would be incompatible with the Convention rights or EU law.[12]

The significance of transfer

As a general rule, functions which were transferred to the Scottish Ministers by **8–05** virtue of s.53 of the Scotland Act ceased to be exercisable by UK Ministers in or as regards Scotland; they are now exercisable by the Scottish Ministers instead of Ministers of the Crown.[13]

> "While the UK *Parliament* retains competence to legislate in areas of activity that are not reserved by the Scotland Act, UK *Ministers*— Ministers of the Crown—have no general competence to take executive action in areas of activity which have not been reserved. The Scotland Act not only prevents Ministers in the Scottish Executive from purporting to act in areas which are reserved, it also prevents Ministers of the Crown from acting in areas in which ministerial responsibility has been transferred to Scottish Ministers."[14]

There is no "executive equivalent of the continuing (supreme) power of the Westminster Parliament to legislate for Scotland on all matters, whether reserved or devolved".[15]

Where the exercise of transferred functions was subject to a requirement of **8–06** consultation or agreement with other UK Ministers, the Scotland Act removed such requirements as no longer appropriate.[16]

The transfer of UK Ministers' statutory and common law powers so far as they **8–07** were exercisable within devolved competence was accompanied by the revision of the administrative arrangements governing the exercise of various non-statutory advisory functions to take account of devolution.[17]

CONFERRED FUNCTIONS

To the functions transferred by the Scotland Act have since been added func- **8–08** tions conferred by the UK as well as by the Scottish Parliament. Westminster legislation has proved a more prolific source of functions for the Scottish Ministers than may have been anticipated at the time of devolution. One explanation for the frequency of "Sewel motions" by which Holyrood consents to Westminster legislation in the devolved areas, including legislation conferring powers on the Scottish Ministers, is that they provide a quicker and less cumbersome means of getting powers into the hands of Scottish Ministers than executive devolution orders under s.63 of the Scotland Act (below). Much

---

[12] This is the source of the so called "mangle effect" observed by Lord Reed in *Starrs v Ruxton*, 2000 J.C. 208, 251–252.

[13] SA 1998 s.53(1).

[14] Colin Boyd, "Ministers and the Law" [2006] J.R. 179, 182, original emphasis.

[15] Chris Himsworth, "The Domesticated Executive of Scotland" in Paul Craig and Adam Tomkins (eds), *The Executive and Public Law: Power and Accountability in Comparative Perspective* (Oxford: OUP, 2006) p.199.

[16] SA 1998 s.55(1); s.55(2) made an exception for Treasury consent to the designation of enterprise zones—because of the tax privileges conferred by enterprise zone status.

[17] See House of Commons debate June 30,1999, Vol.334, cols 215–216 W—advice by the First Minister instead of a Minister of the Crown to Her Majesty in respect of the exercise of her functions in relation, principally, to the making of appointments and the use of the royal prerogative.

Scottish Parliament legislation is also taken up with conferring functions on the Scottish Ministers and other authorities.

EXECUTIVE DEVOLUTION ORDERS

8–09 The devolved administration of laws on reserved matters was always envisaged as part of the devolution settlement. The Scottish Parliament would have no power to make laws in relation to those matters, but any functions relating to those matters, including any powers to make subordinate legislation, would be exercisable in or as regards Scotland by the Scottish Ministers. The Scotland Act accordingly made provision for the transfer of functions in relation to reserved matters, i.e. matters in respect of which primary legislation remains a matter for the Westminster Parliament, to the Scottish Ministers by Order in Council subject to the approval of both Parliaments.[18] The idea was that this would "allow detailed administrative arrangements to meet distinctive Scottish circumstances within a coherent and consistent UK legislative framework";[19] legislative devolution would continue therefore to be supplemented by the system of administrative devolution that obtained before the Scotland Act.

8–10 The s.63 power was used extensively after devolution to adjust the executive functions of the Scottish Ministers in the light of the devolution settlement, i.e. where the boundary between reserved and devolved matters had been drawn. Some 16 executive devolution orders were made between 1999 and 2008, with the most significant being those made immediately after devolution when many of the Secretary of State for Scotland's responsibilities in relation to reserved matters were transferred to the Scottish Ministers.[20] More recently, as new legislation has been framed in relation to reserved matters at Westminster, executive devolution orders have largely been replaced by a combination of UK primary legislation, conferring power on the Scottish Ministers as well as their UK counterparts, and legislative consent motions signifying the Scottish

---

[18] SA 1998 s.63; the functions that may be transferred are not confined to functions which relate to reserved matters but extend to any functions exercisable by UK Ministers in or as regards Scotland. The breadth of the provision avoids any possible argument about whether an executive devolution order is ultra vires, e.g. because the functions transferred are not reserved.

[19] Scottish Office, *Scotland's Parliament* (1997) Cm.3658, para.2.7.

[20] Scotland Act 1998 (Transfer of Functions to the Scottish Ministers etc.) Order 1999 (SI 1999/1750); followed by Scotland Act 1998 (Transfer of Functions to the Scottish Ministers etc.) (No.2) Order 1999 (SI 1999/3321); Scotland Act 1998 (Transfer of Functions to the Scottish Ministers etc.) Order 2000 (SI 2000/1563); Scotland Act 1998 (Transfer of Functions to the Scottish Ministers etc.) (No.2) Order (SI 2000/3253); Scotland Act 1998 (Transfer of Functions to the Scottish Ministers etc.) Order 2001 (SI 2001/954); Scotland Act 1998 (Transfer of Functions to the Scottish Ministers etc.) (No.2) Order (SI 2001/3504); Scotland Act 1998 (Transfer of Functions to the Scottish Ministers etc.) Order 2002 (SI 2002/1630); Scotland Act 1998 (Transfer of Functions to the Scottish Ministers etc.) Order 2003 (SI 2003/415); Scotland Act 1998 (Transfer of Functions to the Scottish Ministers etc.) (No.2) Order 2003 (SI 2003/2617); Scotland Act 1998 (Transfer of Functions to the Scottish Ministers etc.) Order 2004 (SI 2004/2030); Scotland Act 1998 (Transfer of Functions to the Scottish Ministers etc.) Order 2005 (SI 2005/849); Scotland Act 1998 (Transfer of Functions to the Scottish Ministers etc.) Order 2006 (SI 2006/304); Scotland Act 1998 (Transfer of Functions to the Scottish Ministers etc.) Order (No.2) 2006 (SI 2006/1040); Scotland Act 1998 (Transfer of Functions to the Scottish Ministers etc.) (No.3) Order 2006 (SI 2006/3258); Scotland Act 1998 (Transfer of Functions to the Scottish Ministers etc.) Order 2007 (SI 2007/2915) and Scotland Act 1998 (Transfer of Functions to the Scottish Ministers etc.) Order 2008 (SI 2008/1776).

Parliament's consent to the powers conferred. The s.63 power, however, remains available, and is occasionally used.[21]

Where functions are transferred by means of a s.63 devolution order, or **8–11** conferred by UK Act of Parliament, it may be on the basis:

(i) that they are exercisable by the Scottish Ministers instead of UK Ministers;
(ii) that they are exercisable concurrently with UK Ministers, i.e. by UK Ministers as well as by the Scottish Ministers; or
(iii) that they remain with UK Ministers, but are exercisable only with the agreement of, or after consultation with, the Scottish Ministers.[22]

Where functions are devolved on the basis that they are exercisable by the Scottish Ministers, or by the Scottish Ministers concurrently with UK Ministers, the order may provide that they are exercisable only with the agreement of, or after consultation with, UK Ministers.[23]

Where a s.63 order devolves a function to the Scottish Ministers, or provides that **8–12** it is exercisable concurrently with UK Ministers, an existing requirement that it be exercised with the agreement of, or after consultation with, other UK Ministers ceases to apply unless the order expressly provides otherwise.[24] Requirements of consultation with other persons, on the other hand, continue to apply.

The Scotland Act also made provision for the "reverse transfer" of functions **8–13** from the Scottish Ministers to UK Ministers by Order in Council subject to the approval of both Parliaments.[25] This power has not so far been exercised.

SHARED FUNCTIONS

As we have seen, the significance of the general transfer of functions under **8–14** s.53 of the Scotland Act was that the functions transferred ceased to be exercisable in or as regards Scotland by UK Ministers; they became exercisable instead by the Scottish Ministers rather than their UK counterparts. The Act, however, made provision for the shared or concurrent exercise of functions, i.e. their exercise in or as regards Scotland by UK as well as Scottish Ministers,[26] under various enactments thereby enabling the UK Government to continue, for example, to implement UN Security Council resolutions, to fund scientific research and related matters, to provide financial assistance to industry and to promote and fund road safety measures in Scotland as well as the rest of the UK.[27] The power conferred by the European Communities Act 1972 s.2(2), to

---

[21] Scotland Act 1998 (Transfer of Functions to the Scottish Ministers etc.) Order 2014 (SI 2014/2198) and the Scotland Act (Modifications of Schedules 4 and 5 and Transfer of Functions to the Scottish Ministers etc.) Order 2015 (SI 2015/692).

[22] SA 1998 s.63(1).

[23] SA 1998 s.63(3).

[24] SA 1998 s.63(2).

[25] SA 1998 s.108.

[26] "Where a function is vested in two Ministers concurrently, either may perform it, acting alone, on any occasion": Daniel Greenberg (ed), *Craies on Legislation*, 10th edn (London: Sweet & Maxwell, 2012) para.3.12.6, confirmed in *Local Government Byelaws (Wales) Bill 2012: Reference by the Attorney General for England and Wales* [2012] UKSC 53; [2013] 1 A.C. 792 [36]–[41] (Lord Neuberger).

[27] SA 1998 s.56 and the Scotland Act 1998 (Concurrent Functions) Order 1999 (SI 1999/1592).

implement EU obligations by subordinate legislation also continues to be exercisable in or as regards Scotland by UK Ministers concurrently with their Scottish counterparts.[28] This gives the Scottish Ministers the option of relying on GB or UK legislation where they judge it appropriate. It also means that the UK Government, whose responsibility for complying with EU law is not affected by devolution, can intervene to give effect to EU obligations in the devolved areas should the Scottish Ministers for whatever reason fail to do so. The UK Government sought the same power in relation to the implementation of international obligations in the Scotland Act 2012, but that was dropped as part of the agreement between the two governments over the terms of the Scottish Parliament's consent to the Bill.

JOINT FUNCTIONS

8–15 Shared or concurrent functions are exercisable separately by the Scottish Ministers and UK Ministers. They are to be distinguished from joint functions, i.e. functions in respect of which Scottish Ministers and UK Ministers may only act in agreement and together; if there is no agreement they cannot act. "Where a function is vested in two Ministers jointly, each exercise requires the involvement of both Ministers, acting together."[29] The Scotland Act, for example, makes provision for the joint establishment of bodies with cross-border responsibilities.[30]

AGENCY ARRANGEMENTS

8–16 UK Ministers may make arrangements for the Scottish Ministers to exercise specified functions on their behalf and vice versa.[31] Such arrangements do not affect responsibility for the exercise of specified functions.[32] Instead of being transferred the functions are exercised by one government on behalf of the other. The functions specified may not include those of making, confirming or approving subordinate legislation.[33] Some 17 Orders in Council have been made in the exercise of this power, most involving the exercise of functions by the Scottish Ministers on behalf of UK Ministers.[34] The Scotland Act 2012 amended the Scotland Act 1998 to provide that the collection and management of devolved taxes is a specified function of the Scottish Ministers.[35] It would thus have been open to the Scottish Ministers to contract out the collection and management of devolved taxes; in the event they chose to set up their own tax authority in the form of Revenue Scotland.

---

[28] SA 1998 s.57(1), and see below Ch.20.
[29] Daniel Greenberg (ed), *Craies on Legislation*, 10th edn (London: Sweet & Maxwell, 2012) para.3.12.6.
[30] SA 1998 s.56(4).
[31] SA 1998 s.93(1).
[32] SA 1998 s.93(2).
[33] SA 1998 s.93(3).
[34] See e.g. the Scotland Act 1998 (Agency Arrangements) (Specification) Order 2008 (SI 2008/1035) (administration of animal health and welfare licensing and inspection regimes) or the Scotland Act 1998 (Agency Arrangements) (Specification) (No.2) Order 2008 (SI 2008/1788) (electronic monitoring of offenders); for an example of the exercise of functions by UK Ministers on behalf of the Scottish Ministers, see the Scotland Act (Agency Arrangements) (Specification) Order 2011 (SI 2011/ 2439), which allowed the UK government to purchase a stockpile of flu vaccines on behalf of Scottish Ministers ahead of the winter flu season.
[35] SA 1998 s.80B(3).

EXERCISE OF FUNCTIONS

The Scotland Act provides for statutory functions to be conferred on the Scottish **8–17** Ministers "by that name".[36] The Scottish Ministers' statutory functions do not have to be exercised collectively, however, but may be exercised by any member of the Scottish Government.[37] The parallel with functions conferred by UK Acts of Parliament on the Secretary of State is clear: in law the office of Secretary of State is treated as one and indivisible with the result that functions conferred on the Secretary of State, other than a named Secretary of State, may be exercised by any Secretary of State.[38] Although statutory functions may be exercised individually rather than collectively, the Scotland Act expressly provides that acts of individual members of the Scottish Government are binding on all of them.[39] The Scottish Government cannot therefore disavow legal responsibility for the acts and omissions of its individual members. The principle that functions conferred on the Scottish Ministers may be exercised by any member of the Scottish Government does not extend to functions conferred on the First Minister alone and the Lord Advocate's retained functions, which on normal administrative law principles must be exercised by them alone and no-one else. Nor are their acts attributable to the Scottish Government as a whole.[40] They and they alone therefore are "solely legally responsible for how they exercise, or fail to exercise, their respective functions".[41]

LIMITS

As a Parliament of limited competence the Scottish Parliament cannot empower **8–18** the Scottish Ministers to do anything that it has no power to do itself. It cannot therefore empower the Scottish Ministers to act otherwise than in or as regards Scotland, in relation to the reserved matters listed in Sch.5, in breach of the restrictions in Sch.4, incompatibly with the Convention rights or EU law, or to remove the Lord Advocate as head of the systems of criminal prosecution and investigation of deaths in Scotland.[42] The same limits apply to the functions transferred to the Scottish Ministers by s.53 of the Scotland Act, which were transferred only "so far as they are exercisable within devolved competence" (above).

The limits on the Scottish Parliament's legislative competence on the other **8–19** hand do not apply to functions conferred upon the Scottish Ministers by UK Acts of Parliament or executive devolution orders (save in the case of the former to the extent that the Act provides that it is to be treated as a pre-commencement Act, in which case the functions are transferred only so far as they are exercisable within devolved competence). Section 57(2) of the Scotland Act, however, expressly provides that a member of the Scottish Government "has no power to make any subordinate legislation, or to do any other act, so far as the legislation or act is incompatible with any of the Convention rights or EU law". The Scottish Ministers thus have no power to act incompatibly with the

---

[36] SA 1998 s.52(1).
[37] SA 1998 s.52(3).
[38] For the treatment in law of the office of Secretary of State, see Terence Daintith and Alan Page, *The Executive in the Constitution: Structure, Autonomy and Internal Control* (Oxford: OUP, 1999) pp.32–33.
[39] SA 1998 s.52(4).
[40] SA 1998 s.52(5).
[41] SA 1998, explanatory note to s.52.
[42] SA 1998 s.29(2).

Convention rights or EU law regardless of the derivation of the functions they are exercising. It would, of course, be open to the UK Parliament to empower the Scottish Ministers to disregard these limits, but given the Scotland Act's constitutional status it would need to do so by express words rather than by implication.[43]

8–20 In *R v HM Advocate* the view was expressed that an "act" for the purposes of s.57(2) of the Scotland Act did not include a failure to act.[44] The Convention Rights Proceedings (Amendment) (Scotland) Act 2009, which imposed the same one-year time limit on proceedings against the Scottish Ministers or a member of the Scottish Government under the Scotland Act as applies to such proceedings under the Human Rights Act 1998 ("HRA"), however, made clear that an "act" for the purpose of such proceedings includes a failure to act (including a failure to make legislation).[45]

8–21 Under the Scotland Act, as originally enacted, s.57(2) applied to the Lord Advocate in exactly the same way as it applied to other members of the Scottish Government. Following the controversy over the Supreme Court's jurisdiction in Scottish criminal cases, however, acts of the Lord Advocate in prosecuting offences or as head of the systems of criminal prosecution and investigation of deaths in Scotland were removed from the scope of the section, and separate arrangements made for the purpose of determining the compatibility of Scottish criminal law and procedure with the Convention rights.[46] Although s.57(2) no longer applies to such acts, the Lord Advocate remains bound by s.6(1) of the HRA to refrain from acting incompatibly with the Convention rights. Section 57(2) also continues to apply to the Lord Advocate's other functions.

IMMUNITY FROM STATUTE

8–22 The English law presumption that the Crown is not bound by statute save by express words or necessary implication was not recognised in Scots law before the Union. After the Union the same presumption came to be applied in Scots law as in English law.[47] That presumption was reversed, and the pre-Union position restored, in relation to Scottish legislation, i.e. Acts of the Scottish Parliament and Scottish statutory instruments, by the Interpretation and Legislative Reform (Scotland) Act 2010, s.20 of which provides that:

> "An Act of the Scottish Parliament or a Scottish instrument binds the Crown except in so far as the Act or instrument provides otherwise."

The Crown, including the Scottish Government, is therefore bound in the same way as anyone else unless the legislation expressly provides otherwise.[48] The

---

[43] *BH v Lord Advocate* [2012] UKSC 24 [30] (Lord Hope).

[44] *R v HM Advocate*, 2003 S.C. (P.C.) 21, [47] (Lord Hope), [125] (Lord Rodger).

[45] See now Scotland Act 2012 ("SA 2102") s.14, inserting new subss.(3A)–(3E) in the SA 1998, s.100, in place of subss.(3A)–(3E) inserted by the Convention Rights Proceedings (Amendment) (Scotland) Act 2009.

[46] SA 2012 ss.35–36; as originally enacted, s.57(3) of the Scotland Act extended the same protection to the Lord Advocate as is extended to other public authorities by s.6(2) of the Human Rights Act 1998, thereby enabling incompatible Westminster legislation to be given effect and enforced in Scotland in the same way as in the rest of the UK.

[47] *Lord Advocate v Dumbarton District Council* [1990] 2 A.C. 580.

[48] See e.g. Property Factors (Scotland) Act 2011 s.32; Forth Crossing Act 2011 s.78; Land and Buildings Transaction Tax (Scotland) Act 2013 s.69.

position in relation to UK legislation, i.e. Acts of the UK Parliament and instruments made under them, remains unchanged: the Crown continues to be bound only by express words or necessary implication.

POWERS OF INTERVENTION

Inherent in the concept of devolution was the idea that the UK Government **8–23** would retain powers of intervention that could be used to override the actions of a devolved administration notwithstanding the fact that the latter was acting within the limits of its powers. As well as the power to legislate, if necessary against the wishes of a devolved assembly, the Kilbrandon Commission envisaged that UK Ministers would retain a power of veto over legislation passed by an assembly:

> "However unlikely this may be, circumstances could arise in which a veto would have to be considered, whether to ensure compliance with international obligations, or to safeguard some other essential British interest, or to prevent adoption of policies considered to be inconsistent with the maintenance of the essential political and economic unity of the UK. We regard this power of veto, like the retention of Parliament's paramount power to legislate, as an essential feature of a non-federal constitution."[49]

Under the Scotland Act, UK Ministers retain three more narrowly defined **8–24** powers of intervention, as well as the power in theory at least to legislate in the devolved areas without the Scottish Parliament's consent. Two of the powers of intervention are specific to the issue of securing compliance with the UK's international obligations. The first is a power to direct a member of the Scottish Government to refrain from taking action which would be incompatible with the UK's international obligations,[50] the second a power to direct a member of the Scottish Government to take action the member is capable of taking which is required for the purpose of giving effect to such obligations.[51] The actions a member of the Scottish Government may be directed to take or to refrain from taking include making subordinate legislation.[52] A member may also be directed to introduce a Bill in the Parliament—although there is, of course, no requirement on the Parliament to pass it.[53] It was, presumably, the unworkability of this power that led the UK Government to seek power in the Scotland Act 2012 to implement the UK's international obligations in the devolved areas concurrently with the Scottish Ministers (above).

The third and final power is a power to revoke subordinate legislation made by **8–25** a member of the Scottish Government, or that a member of the Scottish Government has power to revoke, which is incompatible with the UK's international obligations or the interests of defence or national security, or which makes modifications of the law as it applies to reserved matters that have an adverse effect on the operation of the law as it applies to reserved matters.[54]

---

[49] *Report of the Royal Commission on the Constitution 1969–1973* (1973) Cmnd.5460, para.765.
[50] SA 1998 s.58(1).
[51] SA 1998 s.58(2).
[52] SA 1998 s.58(3).
[53] SA 1998 s.58(3).
[54] SA 1998 s.58(4); for the equivalent power in relation to Acts of the Scottish Parliament, see SA 1998 s.35(1).

8–26   The Memorandum of Understanding, which governs relations between the UK Government and the devolved administrations, states:

> "Although the UK Government is prepared to use these powers if necessary, it sees them very much as a matter of last resort. The UK Government and the administration concerned will therefore aim to resolve any difficulties through discussion so as to avoid any action or omission by the devolved administration having an adverse impact on non-devolved matters. If formal intervention should become necessary, the UK Government will whenever practicable inform the devolved administration of its intentions in sufficient time to enable that administration to make any representations it wishes, or to take any remedial action."[55]

The powers are exercisable by order subject to negative resolution procedure.[56] Reasons must be given for making an order, which would facilitate judicial review of the exercise of the power.[57]

---

[55] Cabinet Office, *Memorandum of Understanding and Supplementary Agreements between the UK Government, the Scottish Ministers, the Welsh Ministers and the Northern Ireland Executive Committee* (October, 2013) para.27.

[56] SA 1998 s.58(5).

[57] SA 1998 s.58(5).

CHAPTER 9

JUDICIAL PROCEEDINGS

INTRODUCTION

The Scotland Act 1998 ("the Scotland Act") made special provision for dealing **9–01** with "devolution issues", or questions of vires, arising out of the devolution settlement, including questions of vires of Acts of the Scottish Parliament.[1] The intention was to provide a (relatively) quick and authoritative means of deciding such questions, thereby avoiding the risk of uncertainty and conflicting decisions that would arise were they left to be decided in the normal course of litigation. Under the Scotland Act as originally enacted devolution issues fell to be determined ultimately by the Judicial Committee of the Privy Council, following the model of the Scotland Act 1978,[2] but the Judicial Committee's devolution issues jurisdiction was subsequently transferred to the new UK Supreme Court by the Constitutional Reform Act 2005.[3]

The choice of the Judicial Committee rather than the House of Lords as the **9–02** final court of reference and appeal was shaped by a number of considerations. The Judicial Committee had long experience of division of powers or demarcation disputes that, allied to its power to issue advisory opinions, was thought to make it especially suited to the task of the pre-enactment scrutiny of Scottish Parliament Bills. The House of Lords had no jurisdiction over Scottish criminal matters; there was accordingly thought to be less risk of offending Scottish sensitivities than if an appeal were to lie to the House of Lords.[4] And the Judicial Committee also avoided the problem of one parliament being seen to adjudicate on the legislation of another

> "many will misunderstand it if legislation which has been passed by an Assembly which the UK Parliament has authorised to legislate is subject to review in the one Chamber which, whatever its qualities, has no elected element at all".[5]

The Supreme Court, which inherited the Judicial Committee's devolution **9–03** issues jurisdiction, was not open to the same objection as the House of Lords in this last respect, since it was not part of the Westminster Parliament, but by the time it started work in October 2009 some elements of Scottish political

---

[1] Scotland Act 1998 ("SA 1998") s.98 and Sch.6; similar provision was made in the Government of Wales Act 1998 (Sch.8) and the Northern Ireland Act 1998 (Sch.10).
[2] Scotland Act 1978 s.65 Sch.12.
[3] Constitutional Reform Act 2005 s.40(4)(b), Sch.9.
[4] Speaking in the second reading debate on the Scotland Bill 1978, Lord Scarman saw no reason why the House of Lords in its judicial capacity should be considered inappropriate "except possibly the rogue elephant in our constitutional picture, the rogue elephant which Scotsmen, I think, treat as a pet elephant; namely, that there is no right of appeal in criminal matters from the Court of Justiciary to the House of Lords": House of Lords debate, March 14, 1978, Vol.389, col.1229.
[5] House of Lords debate, April 18, 1978, Vol.390, col.1112 (Lord Scarman).

and judicial opinion had been offended, leading to the creation of a separate compatibility issues jurisdiction by the Scotland Act 2012.

DEVOLUTION ISSUES

Definition

9–04 Devolution issues are defined in Sch.6 to the Scotland Act.

> "In this Schedule 'devolution issue' means—
>
> (a) a question whether an Act of the Scottish Parliament or any provision of an Act of the Scottish Parliament is within the legislative competence of the Parliament,
> (b) a question whether any function (being a function which any person has purported, or is proposing, to exercise) is a function of the Scottish Ministers, the First Minister or the Lord Advocate,
> (c) a question whether the purported or proposed exercise of a function by a member of the Scottish Government is, or would be, within devolved competence,
> (d) a question whether a purported or proposed exercise of a function by a member of the Scottish Government is, or would be, incompatible with any of the Convention rights or with EU law,
> (e) a question whether a failure to act by a member of the Scottish Government is incompatible with any of the Convention rights or with EU law,
> (f) any other question about whether a function is exercisable within devolved competence or in or as regards Scotland and any other question arising by virtue of this Act about reserved matters."[6]

9–05 As the catch-all "any other question" indicates, the definition of devolution issues was intended to capture all possible questions of vires arising out of the devolution settlement.

9–06 As amended by the Scotland Act 2012, the definition of devolution issues no longer includes questions of compatibility with the Convention rights or with EU law arising in the course of criminal proceedings:

> "But a question arising in criminal proceedings in Scotland that would, apart from this paragraph, be a devolution issue is not a devolution issue if (however formulated) it relates to the compatibility with any of the Convention rights or with EU law of—
>
> (a) an Act of the Scottish Parliament or any provision of an Act of the Scottish Parliament,
> (b) a function,
> (c) the purported or proposed exercise of a function,
> (d) a failure to act."[7]

9–07 These questions fall to be resolved in accordance with the new compatibility issues procedure introduced by the Scotland Act rather than the devolution issues procedure. Other devolution issues arising in criminal proceedings, however, e.g. whether an Act of the Scottish Parliament or acts of the Scottish

---

[6] SA 1998 Sch.6 para.1.
[7] Scotland Act 2012 ("SA 2012") s.36(4).

Ministers are outside competence because they relate to a reserved matter, continue to fall to be determined in accordance with the devolution issues procedure.

Schedule 6 also provides that a devolution issue should not be taken to arise **9–08** merely because a party argues that there is such a question if the court or tribunal considers the argument frivolous or vexatious.[8]

Procedure

The devolution issues procedure established by the Scotland Act has three **9–09** main features.

Reference to a higher court

First, it is open to a lower court to refer a devolution issue to a higher court **9–10** rather than decide the issue itself. Where the issue arises in proceedings before a court below the level of the Inner House of the Court of Session or a court consisting of two or more judges of the High Court of Justiciary, i.e. the High Court sitting as a court of criminal appeal, the court may either decide the issue itself or refer it to the Inner House or to the High Court as the case may be.[9] Where the issue arises in proceedings before a tribunal, the tribunal may refer the issue to the Inner House unless there is no appeal from its decision in which case it must refer the issue to the Inner House.[10]

Where the issue arises in proceedings before the Inner House or the High Court **9–11** sitting as a court of appeal, the court may likewise decide the issue itself or refer it to the Supreme Court.[11] But where the issue has been referred to the Inner House or the High Court by a lower court or tribunal, the court must decide the issue itself rather than simply pass it on to the Supreme Court.[12]

The law officers

Second, provision is made for the involvement of the Advocate General and **9–12** the Lord Advocate in recognition of the executive interest in questions of vires arising out of the devolution settlement. They thus have the power to institute proceedings for the determination of devolution issues; their determination is therefore not solely dependent on the vagaries of litigation.[13] They must be notified of devolution issues arising in the course of litigation, thus enabling them to take part in proceedings should they wish to do so.[14] They may require a court or tribunal to refer a devolution issue that has arisen in proceedings to which they are a party to the Supreme Court.[15] (As a less provocative

---

[8] SA 1998 Sch.6 para.2; this provision was described by Robert Reed, now Lord Reed, as "a welcome aspect of the procedure in the light of the Scottish courts' experience of the use made of the Act of Union to raise unmeritorious objections to unpopular legislation": Robert Reed, "Devolution and the Judiciary" in Jack Beatson et al (eds), *Constitutional Reform in the UK: Practice and Principles* (Oxford: Hart Publishing, 1998) p.26.

[9] SA 1998 Sch.6 paras 7, 9.

[10] SA 1998 Sch.6 para.8.

[11] SA 1998 Sch.6 paras 10, 11.

[12] SA 1998 Sch.6 paras 10, 11.

[13] SA 1998 Sch.6 para.4.

[14] SA 1998 Sch.6, paras 5, 6.

[15] SA 1998 Sch.6 para.33; a number of cases have arisen as a result of references: *Clark v Kelly* [2003] UKPC D1; 2003 S.C. (P.C.) 77; *Spiers v Ruddy*, 2009 S.C. (P.C.) 1 (to resolve the conflict between *R v HM Advocate*, 2003 S.C. (P.C.) 21 and *Attorney General's Reference (No.2 of 2001)* [2004] 2 A.C. 72; *HM Advocate v Murtagh*, 2010 S.C. (P.C.) 39; and the so called "sons of *Cadder*"

alternative, the Advocate General may refer a devolution issue that has arisen in criminal proceedings before a lower court to which he is a party to the High Court for their opinion.[16]) And they may refer a devolution issue that is not the subject of proceedings directly to the Supreme Court.[17] Where the issue relates to the proposed exercise of a function by a member of the Scottish Government, no member of the Scottish Government may exercise the function in the manner proposed until the reference is decided or otherwise disposed of.[18] By referring an issue to the Supreme Court the law officers can therefore interdict a member of the Scottish Government from exercising a function.

The Supreme Court

9–13 Finally, as already mentioned, devolution issues fall to be determined ultimately by the Supreme Court. Such issues may reach the Supreme Court by the following routes:

> (a) on a reference from the Inner House or the High Court sitting as a court of appeal[19];
> (b) on appeal from the Inner House or the High Court sitting as a court of appeal.[20] An appeal against the determination of a devolution issue by the High Court (or by the Inner House against which there would otherwise be no appeal) lies only with leave of the High Court (or Inner House) or, failing such leave, with special leave of the Supreme Court[21];
> (c) on a reference from the law officers.[22]

9–14 The Supreme Court's assumption of the Judicial Committee's devolution issues jurisdiction restored a single apex to the UK court system, and in so doing put an end to the possibility of conflicting decisions between two "final" courts of appeal.[23]

COMPATIBILITY ISSUES

Background

9–15 The right of appeal to the Judicial Committee of Privy Council in criminal matters quickly became controversial despite being confined to devolution issues and questions preliminary or ancillary to their determination.[24] In a

---

cases: *Ambrose v Harris* [2011] UKSC 43; 2011 S.L.T. 1005; *HM Advocate v P* [2011] UKSC 44; 2011 S.L.T. 1097; *McGowan v B* [2011] UKSC 54; 2012 S.L.T. 37; and *Jude v HM Advocate* [2011] UKSC 55; 2012 S.L.T. 75.
    [16] Criminal Procedure (Scotland) Act ("CP(S)A 1995") s.288A(2), inserted by SA 2012 s.34(7).
    [17] SA 1998 Sch.6 para.34.
    [18] SA 1998 Sch.6 para.35.
    [19] SA 1998 Sch.6 paras 10, 11.
    [20] SA 1998 Sch.6 paras 12, 13.
    [21] SA 1998 Sch.6 para.13; a refusal by the High Court to receive a devolution minute does not deprive the Supreme Court of its jurisdiction to determine the issue on appeal: *McDonald v HM Advocate*, 2010 S.C. (P.C.) 1; *Fraser v HM Advocate* [2011] UKSC 24; 2011 S.L.T. 515. So, too, a refusal of leave in respect of a devolution issue raised in an application for leave to appeal: *Cadder v HM Advocate* [2010] UKSC 43; 2011 S.C. (UKSC) 13.
    [22] SA 1998 Sch.12 paras 33, 34.
    [23] As happened in *R v HM Advocate*, 2003 S.C. (P.C.) 21 and *Attorney General's Reference (No.2 of 2001)* [2004] 2 A.C. 72. The difference was finally resolved in *Spiers v Ruddy*, 2009 S.C. (P.C.) 39.
    [24] A point stressed by Lord Hope in *Robertson v Higson* [2006] UKPC D2; 2006 S.C. (P.C.) 22 [5]–[6]; *McInnes v HM Advocate* [2010] UKSC 7; 2010 S.C. (UKSC) 28 [5]; and *Fraser v HM Advocate* [2011] UKSC 24; 2011 S.L.T. 515 [11].

submission to the Calman Commission, the Court of Session judiciary outlined the difficulties to which, it was said, the devolution issues procedure had given rise for the Scottish criminal justice system:

> "While the Human Rights Act 1998 may have been expected to raise a number of human rights issues, the facility provided by section 57(2) of the Scotland Act, to challenge by way of devolution minute virtually any act of a prosecutor has led to a plethora of disputed issues, with consequential delays to the holding of trials and to the hearing and completion of appeals against conviction. The jurisdiction of the Judicial Committee, while by no means the only factor, has arguably created, or at least substantially contributed to, delay in the handling of criminal business."[25]

The frequency with which devolution issues arose in criminal cases was a **9–16** consequence of two principal factors: the inclusion of the Lord Advocate among the members of the Scottish Government whose "acts" could give rise to a devolution issue, and in particular the Lord Advocate's subjection to s.57(2) of the Scotland Act, which provides that a member of the Scottish Government has

> "no power to make any subordinate legislation, or to do any other act, so far as the legislation or act is incompatible with any of the Convention rights or with EU law";

and, secondly, the broad definition of "acts" of the Lord Advocate favoured by the Judicial Committee, led by its Scottish members, with the result that any act of the Lord Advocate in prosecuting offences was potentially the subject of challenge.[26]

The Calman Commission concluded that the question of the Supreme Court's **9–17** jurisdiction in matters of Scottish criminal law and procedure was beyond its remit.[27] Following the 2010 UK general election, however, and the furore that erupted that autumn over the Supreme Court's decision in *Cadder v HM Advocate*,[28] the Advocate General set up an expert group under the chairmanship of Sir David Edward to examine whether, and if so under what conditions, the Supreme Court should have jurisdiction to consider matters relating to the conduct of criminal proceedings in Scotland.

---

[25] *Submission by the Judiciary in the Court of Session* (October, 2008) para.13; for an earlier statement of the difficulties, see Lord Bonomy's review of the High Court of Justiciary: *Improving Practice—the 2002 Review of the Practices and Procedures of the High Court of Justiciary* (2002) para.17.14. ("In the absence of compelling reasons for treating these issues as devolution issues, there can be no justification for the delay and disruption that is caused to certain cases. I am unable to identify any justification for treating these cases exceptionally, given that these issues can be dealt with under the Human Rights Act without any special procedure and without a further appeal to the Judicial Committee of the Privy Council ... Schedule 6 of the Scotland Act should be amended to make it clear that acts or failures to act by the Lord Advocate as prosecutor ... are excluded from the definition of a devolution issue. The Scottish Executive should urge the UK Parliament to make that amendment.")

[26] *Brown v Stott*, 2001 S.C. (P.C.) 43. Doubts were earlier expressed in *Montgomery v HM Advocate*, 2001 S.C. (P.C.) 1. The Lord Advocate sought unsuccessfully to re-open the issue in *R v HM Advocate*, 2003 S.C. (P.C.) 1.

[27] Commission on Scottish Devolution, *Serving Scotland Better: Scotland and the United Kingdom in the 21st Century* (2009) para.5.37.

[28] *Cadder v HM Advocate* [2010] UKSC 43; 2011 S.C. (UKSC) 13.

9–18 In their report, published in November 2010, the expert group concluded that
the Supreme Court's jurisdiction should be maintained

> "both for reasons of constitutional propriety and, more importantly, to
> ensure that fundamental rights enshrined in international obligations are
> secured in a consistent manner for all those who claim their protection in
> the United Kingdom".[29]

The expert group recommended, however, that the Supreme Court's jurisdiction should be put on a self-standing basis, which made it clear that its sole
purpose was to ensure compliance with the UK's international obligations
with particular reference to Convention rights and EU law.[30] Describing the
inclusion of the Lord Advocate's retained functions, i.e. the Lord Advocate's
prosecution functions, within the statutory framework as "constitutionally
inept",[31] the group also recommended that acts of the Lord Advocate in prosecuting offences or as head of the systems of criminal prosecution and investigation of deaths in Scotland should be excluded from the scope of s.57(2) of
the Scotland Act.[32]

9–19 In January 2011 the Advocate General announced that implementation of the
expert group's recommendations would represent a "positive and sensible"
reform in the light of the experience of devolution issues over the previous
decade. The Scotland Bill then before the UK Parliament would therefore be
amended to remove acts of the Lord Advocate in prosecuting offences or as
head of the systems of criminal prosecution and investigations of deaths in
Scotland that were incompatible with Convention rights or EU law from the
scope of s.57(2) of the Scotland Act. More controversially, but in line with the
recommendations of the expert group, the existing devolution issues procedure
would be replaced by a statutory right of appeal from the High Court, sitting as
a criminal appeal court, to the Supreme Court in cases where it was alleged that
the Lord Advocate had acted incompatibly with Convention rights or EU law,
which right of appeal would continue be exercisable with leave from either the
High Court or the Supreme Court itself.

9–20 The proposed new right of appeal was opposed by the SNP Government at
Holyrood, which sought a complete end to the Supreme Court's jurisdiction in
Scottish criminal cases. As a minority government, however, it was not in a
position to prevent the majority in the Scottish Parliament from agreeing to the
proposed changes under the Sewel convention. This was to change when it
won an outright majority at the Scottish parliamentary elections in May 2011.
Following the election, and renewed controversy over the Supreme Court's
jurisdiction following its decision in *Fraser v HM Advocate*,[33] it set up its own

---

[29] Expert Group appointed by the Advocate General, *Section 57(2) and Schedule 6 of the
Scotland Act 1998 and the role of the Lord Advocate* (2010) para.4.15.

[30] Expert Group appointed by the Advocate General, *Section 57(2) and Schedule 6 of the
Scotland Act 1998 and the role of the Lord Advocate* (2010) para.4.27.

[31] Expert Group appointed by the Advocate General, *Section 57(2) and Schedule 6 of the
Scotland Act 1998 and the role of the Lord Advocate* (2010) para.4.22; for a rejoinder, see Iain
Jamieson, "Scottish Criminal Appeals and the Supreme Court: Quis Custodiet Ipsos Custodes?"
(2012) 16 Edin. L.R. 80.

[32] Expert Group appointed by the Advocate General, *Section 57(2) and Schedule 6 of the
Scotland Act 1998 and the role of the Lord Advocate* (2010) para.5.4.

[33] *Fraser v HM Advocate* [2011] UKSC 24; 2011 S.L.T. 515; the decision prompted an extraordinary attack on the two most senior members of the Scottish judiciary by the Cabinet Secretary
for Justice and the First Minister: see para.6–41.

review group under the chairmanship of Lord McCluskey in June 2011 with the following terms of reference

> "to consider and assess the mechanisms created under the Scotland Act 1998 and the Human Rights Act 1998, and developed since then, for applying Human Rights law to criminal cases in Scotland, including particularly the regulation, subject matter and scope of appeals from the High Court of Justiciary to the Supreme Court of the United Kingdom; to consider the criticisms of and various suggested amendments to those mechanisms in light of current assessments, including responsibility for their operation; and advise on the ways in which they might best be altered, if appropriate by legislation, or otherwise, to ensure Scotland's unique system of Criminal Law and Procedure is fully protected, within the context of the accepted need for that system to comply with the Human Rights Act".

If the SNP Government's hope had been that the review group would recom- **9–21** mend that the Supreme Court's jurisdiction in criminal cases should be ended that hope was to be disappointed:

> "For those who do not wish to be part of the UK State, arguments about the retention of the Supreme Court as a matter of constitutional integrity will carry no weight. Nevertheless while Scotland remains in the United Kingdom it is clear, in our judgment, that . . . the prevailing constitutional position makes it unrealistic to suggest that the Supreme Court should not have a continued jurisdiction to determine what might conveniently be called demarcation questions."[34]

The review group accordingly agreed with the expert group that there should be a continuing role for the Supreme Court in criminal appeals raising devolution issues. Where it disagreed was over the proposition that the Supreme Court should continue to be able to grant special leave to appeal where leave to appeal had been refused by the High Court; in its view it should not be possible to appeal unless the High Court certified that the case raised a point of law of general public importance. It also recommended that the Supreme Court should be confined to answering the point of law raised, leaving disposal of the case to the High Court.[35]

The review group's recommendations were endorsed by the Scottish **9–22** Government, and by the Court of Session judiciary.[36] In the ensuing negotiations between the two governments over the Scotland Bill, the UK Government drew the line at certification (which would have left an appeal to the Supreme Court at the discretion of the High Court), but agreed that the Supreme Court

---

[34] The Review Group, *First Report of Review Group, Examination of the Relationship between the High Court of Justiciary and the Supreme Court in Criminal Cases* (June, 2011) paras 34–35. The hope was not entirely fanciful given Lord McCluskey's publicly stated views on the European Convention on Human Rights, which were the subject of *Hoekstra v HM Advocate (No.2)*, 2000 J.C. 391; 2000 S.L.T. 605. The perception of bias, however, is clearly not the same bar to participation in the political process as it is in the judicial process, even in the guise of "independent" expert.

[35] The Review Group, *Final Report of Review Group, Examination of the Relationship between the High Court of Justiciary and the Supreme Court in Criminal Cases* (September, 2011) Executive Summary, paras 7–8.

[36] In a submission to the Scottish Parliament's Scotland Bill Committee (October 25, 2011), the Lord President wrote that the judiciary found much to commend in the report, particularly on the point of certification.

should be a court of reference rather than appeal. "Agreement" over the question of certification was eventually secured by an undertaking to review the new arrangements, including the question of certification, after three years (below).

Procedure

9–23 The compatibility issues procedure differs from the devolution issues procedure mainly in its treatment of the Advocate General and the Supreme Court.

Reference to a higher court

9–24 The reference procedure is retained. Where a compatibility issue arises in criminal proceedings before a court other than the High Court sitting as an appeal court, the court may, instead of determining the issue, refer it to the High Court.[37] Where the issue arises in criminal proceedings before the High Court sitting as an appeal court, otherwise than on a reference from the law officers, the High Court may, instead of determining the issue, refer it to the Supreme Court.[38] Where the issue is referred to the High Court by a lower court, the High Court continues to be unable simply to pass it on to the Supreme Court.

The law officers

9–25 There is no requirement of notification to the Advocate General. The Advocate General may however take part in criminal proceedings so far as they relate to a compatibility issue.[39] A "compatibility issue" is defined for the purposes of the Advocate General's right to take part in proceedings as a question (arising in criminal proceedings) as to:

(a) whether a public authority has acted (or proposes to act) in a way which is made unlawful by s.6(1) of the Human Rights Act 1998, or in a way which is incompatible with EU law; or
(b) whether an Act of the Scottish Parliament or any provision of an Act of the Scottish Parliament is incompatible with any of the Convention rights or with EU law.[40]

9–26 The Lord Advocate or the Advocate General, if a party to criminal proceedings before a lower court, may require the court to refer a compatibility issue to the High Court.[41] Where the Lord Advocate or Advocate General requires a lower court to refer an issue to the High Court, the High Court has the option of determining the issue itself or referring it to the Supreme Court.[42]

9–27 As a less disruptive alternative to requiring a lower court to refer a compatibility issue to the High Court, the Advocate General may await the conclusion of the trial proceedings before referring the issue to the High Court.[43]

---

[37] CP(S)A 1995 s.288ZB(1), as inserted by SA 2012 s.35.
[38] CP(S)A 1995 s.288ZB(4), as inserted by SA 2012 s.35.
[39] CP(S)A 1995 s.288ZA(1), as inserted by SA 2012 s.34(3).
[40] CP(S)A 1995 s.288ZA(2), as inserted by SA 2012 s.34(3).
[41] CP(S)A 1995 s.288ZB(2), as inserted by SA 2012 s.35.
[42] CP(S)A 1995 s.288ZB(3), as inserted by SA 2012 s.35.
[43] CP(S)A 1995 s.288A(2A), as inserted by SA 2012 s.34(7).

The Lord Advocate or the Advocate General, if a party to proceedings before **9–28** the High Court sitting as an appeal court, may require the High Court to refer a compatibility issue that has arisen in the proceedings, otherwise than on a reference, to the Supreme Court.[44]

The Supreme Court

An appeal for the purpose of determining any compatibility issue lies from the **9–29** High Court to the Supreme Court.[45] The Supreme Court's powers on appeal, however, are exercisable only for the purpose of determining the compatibility issue; it may reformulate the issue but again only for the purpose of determining the issue.[46] Once it has determined the issue it must remit the proceedings to the High Court.[47] The same restrictions apply to the Supreme Court's powers on a reference.[48] An appeal lies only with the permission of the High Court or, failing that permission, with the permission of the Supreme Court (unless it is an appeal by the Lord Advocate or the Advocate General against a determination by the High Court of a compatibility issue on a reference).[49] There are strict time limits governing appeals. An application for permission to appeal must be made to the High Court within 28 days of the determination of the appeal or such longer period as the High Court considers equitable.[50] If the High Court refuses permission, an application to the Supreme Court must be made within 28 days of the refusal of permission or such longer period as the Supreme Court considers equitable.[51] (The same time limits apply to appeals on devolution issues (as opposed to compatibility issues) in criminal proceedings.[52])

Post-legislative review

The Scotland Act requires the Secretary of State to arrange a review of the new **9–30** arrangements.[53] The review must be carried out as soon as practicable three years after the new arrangements came into force (on April 22, 2013), but it may take place earlier if the Secretary of State considers it appropriate.[54] The review, which will be chaired by the Lord President, must consider in particular whether an appeal to the Supreme Court should lie only with the High Court's certificate that the compatibility issue raises a point of law of general public importance.[55] Following the review, the Secretary of State may, after consulting the Scottish Ministers, amend the provision made, or make further provision, by order subject to affirmative resolution procedure.[56] An order requires the approval of both Houses of Parliament, but not of the Scottish Parliament.[57]

---

44 CP(S)A 1995 s.288ZB(5), as inserted by SA 2012 s.35.
45 CP(S)A 1995 s.288AA(1), as inserted by SA 2012 s.36(6).
46 CP(S)A 1995 s.288AA(2), as inserted by SA 2012 s.36(6).
47 CP(S)A 1995 s.288AA(3), as inserted by SA 2012 s.36(6).
48 CP(S)A 1995 s.288ZB(6)–(8), as inserted by SA 2012 s.35.
49 CP(S)A 1995 s.288AA(5)–(6), as inserted by SA 2012 s.36(5).
50 CP(S)A 1995 s.288AA(7), as inserted by SA 2012 s.36(6).
51 CP(S)A 1995 s.288AA(8), as inserted by SA 2012 s.36(6).
52 SA 1998 Sch.6 paras 13A and 13, as inserted by SA 2012 s.37.
53 SA 2012 s.38(1).
54 SA 2012 s.38(2).
55 SA 2012 s.38(3).
56 SA 2012 s.38(4)–(8).
57 SA 2012 s.34(9).

PROSPECTIVE OVERRULING

9–31 A finding that a provision of an Act of the Scottish Parliament is beyond its competence, or that subordinate legislation is beyond the powers of the Scottish Ministers, could cause considerable disruption and uncertainty, e.g. where the legislation has been widely relied upon, possibly for a number of years. The courts were therefore given the power to make an order removing or limiting the retrospective effect of a finding of invalidity, or suspending its effect in order to allow the defect to be corrected.[58] In deciding whether to make an order, the court is required to "have regard to the extent to which persons who are not parties to the proceedings would otherwise be adversely affected".[59] Notice must also be given to the Lord Advocate and, where the decision relates to a devolution or compatibility issue, to the Advocate General, who may take part in the proceedings so far as they relate to the making of the order.[60] This power was originally confined to Acts of the Scottish Parliament and subordinate legislation made by the Scottish Ministers, but it was extended to any other purported exercise of a function by a member of the Scottish Government outside devolved competence by the Scotland Act 2012.[61]

9–32 In *Salvesen v Riddell*,[62] the Supreme Court made an order suspending the effect of its decision (that s.72(10) of the Agricultural Holdings (Scotland) Act 2003 was incompatible with art.1 of the First Protocol (the right to property)) for 12 months to allow the Parliament, guided by the Scottish Ministers, to take appropriate remedial action. Delivering the judgment of the Court, Lord Hope, with whom the other justices agreed, said:

> "Decisions as to how the incompatibility is to be corrected, for the past as well as for the future, must be left to the Parliament guided by the Scottish Ministers. Both sides of the industry will need to be consulted, after the necessary research has been carried out and proposals for dealing with the situation that respects the parties' Convention rights have been formulated. That process will take time, and the court should do what it can to enable it to be conducted in as fair and constructive a manner as possible."[63]

9–33 In *Cameron v Cottam*,[64] the only other case in which a provision of an Act of the Scottish Parliament has been struck down, the High Court agreed, in the interests of "clarity and legal certainty", to limit the retroactive effect of its decision (that s.58 of the Criminal Justice and Licensing (Scotland) Act 2010 was incompatible with art.5 ECHR (the right to liberty)) to "live" cases, i.e. cases that had not yet been concluded (as had the Supreme Court in *Cadder*,[65] relying on its inherent power to limit the retrospective effect of its decisions).

---

[58] SA 1998 s.102(1), as amended by SA 2012 s.15.

[59] SA 1998 s.102(3).

[60] SA 1998 s.102(4)–(7). In *Cameron v Cottam* [2012] HCJAC 31; 2013 J.C. 21 [5] the Advocate General's stance was described as one of "benevolent neutrality" (Lord Eassie).

[61] SA 21012 s.15; where the decision is a decision of the Supreme Court on a compatibility issue, the power is exercisable by the High Court of Justiciary instead of by the Supreme Court: SA 1998 s.102(5A), inserted by SA 2012 s.36(3).

[62] *Salvesen v Riddell* [2013] UKSC 22.

[63] *Salvesen v Riddell* [2013] UKSC 22 [57]; the incompatibility was corrected by the Agricultural Holdings (Scotland) Act 2003 Remedial Order 2014 (SSI 2014/98).

[64] *Cameron v Cottam* [2012] HCJAC 31; 2013 J.C. 21.

[65] *Cadder v HM Advocate* [2010] UKSC 43; 2011 S.C. (UKSC) 13.

REMEDIAL ORDERS

The UK Government also has the power to make by order such provision as it **9–34** considers "necessary or expedient" in consequence of an Act of the Scottish Parliament, or any provision of an Act of the Scottish Parliament, that is not, or may not be, within the legislative competence of the Parliament, or any purported exercise by a member of the Scottish Government of their functions that is, or may not be, an exercise or a "proper exercise" of those functions.[66] The exercise of this power is not conditional on a judicial finding of ultra vires. It could be used, therefore, to remedy a defect, or suspected defect, before judicial proceedings had been started. This power has been used only once: to repeal a provision in the Regulation of Care (Scotland) Act 2001 which was discovered to relate to a reserved matter during the four week period after its passing. Instead of referring it to the Judicial Committee of the Privy Council, which would have served no useful purpose because there was no dispute for the court to settle, it was agreed by the two governments that it should be repealed as soon as the Act had received Royal Assent.[67]

Where the defect or suspected defect is incompatibility with the Convention **9–35** rights, it would open to the Scottish Ministers to remedy the incompatibility using the power conferred by s.12 of the Convention Rights (Compliance) (Scotland) Act 2001.

---

[66] SA 1998 s.107.
[67] Which was done by the Scotland Act 1998 (Regulation of Care (Scotland) Act 2001) Order 2001 (SI 2001/2478).

CHAPTER 10

LOCAL GOVERNMENT

INTRODUCTION

The Scottish Government delivers very little policy at its own hand. It relies **10–01**
instead on a variety of "delivery agencies"—a mixture of local authorities,
health boards, other public bodies, private contractors and voluntary organisations. Local authorities stand out among these agencies by reason of their
multi-purpose character; the services for which they are currently responsible
include: education; social services; roads; planning; environmental health;
waste collection; and leisure and recreation. They also stand out by reason of
the fact that they are elected, a feature they share in common with the Scottish
Parliament. A local authority, the Royal Commission on Local Government in
Scotland said in 1969

> "unites the character of a popular assembly with that of a government,
> and this gives (or should give) local accountability a particularly keen
> edge".[1]

The Scottish Constitutional Convention regarded it as vital that the relation- **10–02**
ship between the Parliament and local authorities be "positive, co-operative
and stable".[2] It expected the Scottish Parliament to investigate new ways of
"co-operative working" between the two levels of government. Relations
between local and central government, it argued, had "too often fallen victim
to confrontational Government policies aimed at systematically removing
powers from elected representatives".[3] The creation of Scotland's Parliament
would mark

> "a distinct change of approach, by placing a culture of co-operation and
> stability at the heart of the relationship between the Parliament and local
> authorities".[4]

The Constitutional Convention also wanted the devolution legislation to **10–03**
include a provision committing the Parliament to securing and maintaining a
"strong and effective system of local government", and to embody the principle of subsidiarity "so as to guarantee the important role of local government
in service delivery".[5] No such provision was included in the Scotland Act 1998
("the Scotland Act"). In the White Paper that preceded the Act, the Labour
Government confined itself to saying that it did not expect the Scottish
Parliament and its Executive "to accumulate a range of new functions at the

---

[1] The Wheatley Report, *Report of the Royal Commission on Local Government in Scotland
1966–1969* (1969) Cmnd.4150, para.118.
[2] Scottish Constitutional Convention, *Scotland's Parliament, Scotland's Right* (1995) p.16.
[3] Scottish Constitutional Convention, *Scotland's Parliament, Scotland's Right* (1995) p.16.
[4] Scottish Constitutional Convention, *Scotland's Parliament, Scotland's Right* (1995) p.16.
[5] Scottish Constitutional Convention, *Scotland's Parliament, Scotland's Right* (1995) p.17.

centre which would be more appropriately and efficiently delivered by other bodies within Scotland", adding that it believed that "the principle that decisions should be made as close as possible to the citizen holds good within Scotland as it does within the United Kingdom".[6]

HISTORICAL BACKGROUND

10–04 Local government has a long history in Scotland—the first royal burghs were established in the twelfth century—but it was in the nineteenth century that the foundations of the modern system were laid.[7] The century saw a rapid increase in the number of authorities with locally defined responsibilities and, allied to that increase, the gradual extension of the elective principle. Town councils, responsible for the financial and administrative business of burghs, were first elected in 1833.[8] In 1889 elected county councils were established in place of the Commissioners of Supply (committees of landowners) which had been the principal local authority in the countryside since the seventeenth century.[9] School boards, popularly elected every three years, were established in 1872.[10] And in 1894 elected parish councils took over poor relief and local rating from the parochial boards established by the Poor Law (Scotland) Act 1845.[11] Although these were all elected bodies, the local government franchise remained confined to owners and occupiers of heritable property until it was eventually brought into line with the parliamentary franchise by the Representation of the People Act 1945.[12]

10–05 The twentieth century saw successive rationalisations of the system, culminating in the current structure of 32 unitary or all-purpose authorities, including three islands councils, which was put in place by the Local Government etc. (Scotland) Act 1994. The first rationalising measure was the Local Government (Scotland) Act 1929, which drastically reduced the number of authorities (from 1,340 to 425), while at the same time widening the area over which many services were administered.

> "Ingeniously drawn up, the Act [was] open to the objection that its abolition of the small and intimate, if 'amateurish', parish councils, on top of the disappearance of the school boards in 1918, deprived the elector, and in particular the country dweller, of any chance of familiarity with the persons placed in authority over him: central direction counted for more and more, local initiative for less and less."[13]

10–06 By the 1960s the need for further structural reform was widely acknowledged

---

[6] Scottish Office, *Scotland's Parliament* (1997) Cm.3658, para.6.4.

[7] The history of local government in Scotland is inextricably bound up with the history of the "police" in the original Scottish sense of "improvement". For an instructive account of the latter, see John Prest, *Liberty and Locality: Parliament, Permissive Legislation and Ratepayers' Democracies in the Nineteenth Century* (Oxford: OUP, 1990).

[8] Royal Burghs (Scotland) Act 1833; Parliamentary Burghs (Scotland) Act 1833.

[9] Local Government (Scotland) Act 1889.

[10] Education (Scotland) Act 1872.

[11] Local Government (Scotland) Act 1894.

[12] Representation of the People Act 1945 s.1.

[13] George S Pryde, *Scotland from 1603 to the Present Day* (Edinburgh: Thomas Nelson, 1962) p.285.

"the evolution of local government in Scotland has now reached a stage where boundaries are becoming increasingly artificial and where areas of many individual authorities are too small".[14]

Following the recommendations of the Royal Commission on Local Government in Scotland, the Local Government (Scotland) Act 1973 replaced the multi-tier system then in operation outside the cities with a two-tier system. The essential idea on which the new system was based was that services should be provided by authorities of an appropriate size, for which purpose Scotland was divided into nine regions, 53 districts, and three "all-purpose" or "most-purpose" island authorities. Regions were responsible for the provision of large scale services, i.e. those services that required substantial resources or were more effectively discharged over a large area, including education, town and country planning, social services, highways, transport, water and sewerage, police and fire services; districts for more local services, including local planning, minor roads, museums, building control, public health, but also housing; while the three island authorities were responsible for all local government services with the exception of police and fire services.

The final rationalisation measure was the Local Government etc. (Scotland) **10–07** Act 1994, which replaced the two-tier system established by the Local Government (Scotland) Act 1973 with a single tier of unitary or all-purpose authorities. As justification for replacing the two-tier system, the Conservative Government argued, in a brief consultation paper, that the system was not readily understood, and that there was considerable confusion in the public mind about which tier was responsible for what, which led inevitably to "a clouding of accountability".[15] It was also "clear that old allegiances, particularly to some of the old counties and county towns, live[d] on", and that some of the regions were seen as "too large and too remote" from the local communities they served, even where there were operational advantages. In more practical terms, the two-tier system inevitably resulted in "a measure of duplication and waste"; there were also delays and frictions between the two tiers.[16]

The replacement of the two-tier system was politically controversial, and the **10–08** rather cursory nature of the case put forward for reform attracted criticism, especially when compared with the lengthy public deliberations that had preceded the introduction of the two-tier system. That is not to say there were no criticisms of the two-tier system. The Stodart Committee, which was set up to review the working relationship among authorities, felt "duty bound" to report any major criticisms emerging from the evidence, which challenged the two-tier structure itself.

"Thus we must take note . . . of the substantial body of opinion—not least among some local authorities—which maintains the belief that only the creation of all- or at least most-purpose authorities throughout the country will produce a wholly satisfactory system of local government."[17]

---

[14] Scottish Office, *The Modernisation of Local Government in Scotland* (1963) Cmnd.2067, para.15.

[15] Scottish Office, *The Structure of Local Government in Scotland: A Consultation Paper* (June, 1991) para.9.

[16] Scottish Office, *The Structure of Local Government in Scotland: A Consultation Paper* (June, 1999); see too Scottish Office, *The Structure of Local Government in Scotland: Shaping the New Councils* (October, 1992).

[17] *Report of the Committee of Inquiry into Local Government in Scotland* (1981) Cmnd.8115, para.15; the Committee went on to say that provided the obstacles involved in such a change could

10–09 Rationalisation of structure was accompanied by the "loss" of functions to a combination of central government, public bodies and the private sector.[18] The result by the time of devolution was a system in which local government—and with it local elected representatives—had come to play a less significant part in the provision of services, with its place being taken by a combination of a surrogate upper tier of national public bodies (e.g. Scottish Water), local spending bodies (e.g. registered social landlords and further education colleges), and private contractors and voluntary organisations.

THE MCINTOSH COMMISSION

10–10 The Scottish Constitutional Convention, as we have seen, regarded the relationship between central and local government as a key element of the devolution settlement. The Labour Government responded to the Convention's recommendations by announcing the establishment an independent committee to study how to build the most effective relations between the Scottish Parliament and Scottish Executive and a strong and effective local government.[19] The McIntosh Commission on Local Government and the Scottish Parliament was appointed by the Secretary of State for Scotland in January 1998, following publication of *Scotland's Parliament,* to consider

> "how to build the most effective relations between local government and the Scottish Parliament and the Scottish Executive", and "how councils can best make themselves responsive and democratically accountable to the communities they serve".

10–11 The Commission's proposals, published 18 months later, were based on

> "the cardinal principle that, in view of the common democratic basis of Parliament and local government, *relations between local government and the Parliament should be conducted on the basis of mutual respect and parity of esteem*".[20]

This was very much in the spirit of the Scottish Constitutional Convention. Where the Commission went beyond the Convention was in suggesting that mutual respect and parity of esteem were by no means guaranteed. Parity of esteem, the Commission argued, would require nothing less than a "programme for the renewal of local government", encompassing proportional representation for local government elections, and a review by each council of its management of business and working practices, under the guiding principles of "accountability and accessibility".[21]

> "We do not think that the parliament can reasonably be expected to treat with local government on any basis of equality unless local government

---

be overcome, "a network of single-tier authorities would undoubtedly have considerable attractions and would avoid most of the difficulties ... inherent in a two-tier arrangement": para.17.

[18] For a sceptical view of the idea of a loss of functions, see Jim Bulpitt, *Territory and power in the UK: An interpretation* (Manchester: Manchester University Press, 1983) pp.22–24.

[19] Scottish Office, *Scotland's Parliament* (1997) Cm.3658, para.6.4.

[20] Commission on Local Government and the Scottish Parliament, *Moving Forward: Local Government and the Scottish Parliament* (June, 1999) para.20, original emphasis.

[21] Commission on Local Government and the Scottish Parliament, *Moving Forward: Local Government and the Scottish Parliament* (June, 1999) paras 89 and 94.

as a whole embraces the kind of renewal process which we are advocating."[22]

Were local government not to embrace that process and effectively renew itself, the Commission warned, it would find itself "progressively stripped of functions and influence".[23]

The electoral system

One focus of renewal has been the electoral system. Elections originally took **10–12** place in accordance with the first past the post system used for Westminster elections, but following the recommendations of the McIntosh Commission, which was convinced that a move to proportional representation was an essential step towards the goal of enhancing local democracy,[24] the Local Governance (Scotland) Act 2004 abolished first past the post elections in favour of the single transferable vote ("STV") system of proportional representation with council areas divided into multi-member wards for the purpose.[25] Under this system, candidates must reach a fixed share of the vote or quota in order to be elected. Voters number the candidates in order of choice. The first choice votes are then counted and any candidate who reaches the quota elected. Their surplus votes are then transferred (according to a weighted formula) to the second choice on those voters' ballot papers. If not enough candidates have then reached the quota, the candidate with the fewest first choices is eliminated and their votes transferred to the next choice on their ballot papers, with the process being repeated until all the seats have been filled. The change in the voting system has resulted in a reduction in the number of councils in which there is a single party majority administration. After the 2007 elections, 26 authorities were controlled by either a coalition or minority administration, compared with 11 following the 2003 elections. After the 2012 elections, coalition or minority political control remains the norm, with coalition or minority administrations in 23 of the 32 local authorities.

The timing of elections

The McIntosh Commission recommended that local government elections be **10–13** held on the same four year cycle as elections to the Scottish Parliament—under the Local Government etc. (Scotland) Act 1994 elections were held every three years. It also recommended that elections not be held at the same time as the parliamentary elections,

---

[22] Commission on Local Government and the Scottish Parliament, *Moving Forward: Local Government and the Scottish Parliament* (June, 1999) para.175.

[23] Commission on Local Government and the Scottish Parliament, *Moving Forward: Local Government and the Scottish Parliament* (June, 1999) paras 22–28.

[24] Commission on Local Government and the Scottish Parliament, *Moving Forward: Local Government and the Scottish Parliament* (June, 1999) para.88.

[25] The Renewing Local Democracy Working Group, which was appointed following the report of the McIntosh Commission, recommended the adoption of the STV system of election from multi-member wards: *The Report of the Renewing Democracy Working Group* (June, 2000). The 2003 coalition agreement, *A Partnership for a Better Scotland*, included a commitment to introduce, by the time of the 2007 elections, the STV system of election, with multi-member wards of three or four members depending on local circumstances.

"although that might produce a higher turnout, it does also mean that the local elections would tend always to be held under the shadow, as it were, of the parliamentary election and that national issues will dominate local elections even more than they tend to do whenever those elections are held".

The result would be "to weaken the democratic mandate of local government".[26] The Scottish Executive accepted the Commission's recommendation that elections be held every four years, but preferred to hold elections at the same time as elections to the Scottish Parliament in the interests of increasing voter turnout, which historically had always been low.[27] The Scottish Local Government (Elections) Act 2002 accordingly put local authority elections on the same four year cycle as the parliamentary elections, but provided for them to be held in the same year as elections to the Parliament.

10–14 The policy of combining parliamentary and local government elections was to be effectively undone by the widespread voter confusion that marked the May 2007 elections. The Gould Report into the debacle recommended that the elections be split

" ... we are convinced that combined elections are not only a disservice to the local councils and candidates but also to the electorate as well. In essence, the local government elections are not simply about ensuring a reasonable number of voters show up at the polls on polling day. More important is that they engage with the campaign in a meaningful manner and make a knowledgeable decision on their ballot paper. Therefore, we recommend separating the Scottish parliamentary and local government elections, preferably by a period of about two years".[28]

10–15 The elections were subsequently decoupled by the Scottish Local Government Elections Act 2009, which provided for local government elections in 2012, 2017 and then every fourth year after that. But instead of taking place halfway through the Scottish Parliament's term, as was originally proposed, elections will now take place a year after the Scottish Parliament election, as a result of the postponement of the next election to 2016, unless the local government election timetable is altered in the interim. The separation of the elections has been accompanied by a marked fall in voter turnout for local elections—from an average turnout of 54 per cent in the three combined elections between 1999 and 2007 to 39 per cent in 2012.

---

[26] Commission on Local Government and the Scottish Parliament, *Moving Forward: Local Government and the Scottish Parliament* (June, 1999) para.7. The Arbuthnott Commission also recommended that Scottish Parliament and local government elections not be held on the same day. Holding the elections on different days, the Commission argued, would "reduce the complexity of voting, potentially reduce voter confusion and help keep the number of invalid votes to a minimum"; it would also "enhance the transparency of the electoral process, especially allowing attention to be focused on local issues": Commission on Boundary Differences and Voting Systems, *Putting Citizens First: Boundaries, Voting and Representation in Scotland* (January, 2006) para.4.91.

[27] The average turnout for Scottish local government elections between 1974 and 1995 was 46 per cent: The Electoral Commission, *Scottish Elections 2007: The independent review of the Scottish Parliamentary and local government elections 3 May 2007* (October, 2007) p.35.

[28] The Electoral Commission, *Scottish Elections 2007: The independent review of the Scottish Parliamentary and local government elections 3 May 2007* (October, 2007) p.115.

Standards of conduct

Following the Third Report of the Committee on Standards in Public **10–16** Life,[29] which was critical of the lack of clarity of standards of conduct in local government across the UK, the Scottish Office consulted on proposals to establish a Scottish Standards Commission and a code of conduct for local government.[30] The proposed code of conduct constituted unfinished business at the time of devolution. The proposals, which were subsequently extended to include public bodies, were given effect by the Ethical Standards in Public Life etc. (Scotland) Act 2000, which required the Scottish Ministers to issue a code of conduct for councillors and a model code of conduct for members of the devolved public bodies listed in Sch.3 to the Act.[31] Devolved public bodies were required to adopt their own individual versions of the model code.[32]

The Councillors' Code of Conduct

The Councillors' Code of Conduct was prepared by the Convention of Scottish **10–17** Local Authorities ("COSLA"), the representative body of Scottish local authorities, at the invitation of Scottish Ministers and approved by the Scottish Parliament in March 2002. The Code, which is now in its third edition, is based on nine "key principles" which are similar in tone and content to the key principles which govern the conduct of MSPs.[33] The principal difference reflects the fact that councillors are much more likely to be involved in decision-making than MSPs who, unless they are Ministers, have no involvement in or responsibility for decision-making. Councillors are therefore under a duty to make decisions solely on merit when carrying out public business including making appointments, awarding contracts or recommending individuals for rewards and benefits. They are also under a duty to "respect all other councillors and all council employees and the role they play, treating them with courtesy at all times". The remaining sections of the Code provide "additional information on how the key principles should be interpreted and applied in practice".[34] As well as general conduct, they address the registration and declaration of interests, lobbying and access to councillors, and taking decisions on "quasi-judicial or regulatory applications", including dealing with planning applications. The last of these addresses the need to ensure a fair and proper hearing and the avoidance of any impression of bias in dealing with applications.

Registration of interests

The registration of interests is governed by the Ethical Standards in Public Life **10–18** etc. (Scotland) Act 2000 (Register of Interests) Regulations 2003.[35] There are

---

[29] Committee on Standards in Public Life, *Standards of Conduct in Local Government in England, Scotland and Wales* (1997) Cm.3702.

[30] Scottish Office, *A New Ethical Framework for Local Government in Scotland* (April, 1998).

[31] Ethical Standards in Public Life etc. (Scotland) Act 2000 ("ESPL(S)A 2000") ss.1–2.

[32] ESPL(S)A 2000 s.3.

[33] See para.4–22.

[34] Standards Commission Scotland, *The Councillors' Code of Conduct*, 3rd edn (2010) para.1.6.

[35] Ethical Standards in Public Life etc. (Scotland) Act 2000 (Register of Interests) Regulations 2003 (SSI 2003/135), as amended by the Ethical Standards in Public Life etc. (Scotland) Act 2000 (Register of Interests) Amendment Regulations 2003 (SSI 2003/203), Ethical Standards in Public Life etc (Scotland) Act 2000 (Register of Interests) Amendment Regulations 2010 (SSI 2010 2010/392), and Ethical Standards in Public Life etc. (Scotland) Act 2000 (Register of Interests) Regulations 2014 (SSI 2014/50).

eight categories of registrable interests: remuneration; directorships held in related undertakings; contracts; assistance towards election expenses; ownership or any other right or interest in houses, land and buildings; interests in shares and securities above certain limits; gifts and hospitality received; and non-financial interests "which members of the public might reasonably think could influence your actions, speeches or votes in the Council".[36] Councils (and devolved public bodies) are required to set up, maintain and make available for public inspection a register of councillors' (or members') interests.[37]

The Standards Commission for Scotland

10–19 The Standards Commission for Scotland is responsible for the promotion and enforcement of the codes of conduct for councillors and members of devolved public bodies. The members of the Commission, which is supported by the Scottish Parliamentary Corporate Body, are appointed by the Scottish Ministers.[38] The Commission adjudicates on complaints of misconduct against councillors and members of public bodies and has the power to impose sanctions on a councillor or member found to be in breach of the relevant code. The Commissioner for Ethical Standards in Public Life in Scotland is responsible for the independent investigation of complaints of breaches of the codes against councillors and members of public bodies.[39] The Commissioner is required to comply with any directions given by the Commission in carrying out their functions, but the Commission has no power to direct the Commissioner as to how any particular investigation is to be carried out.[40] Where the Commissioner is of the view that a councillor or member is in breach of the relevant code, the councillor or member concerned must first be given an opportunity to make representations before a report is made to the Commission.[41] On receipt of a report, the Commission may direct the Commissioner to carry out further investigations, hold a hearing, or take no action.[42] Where the members of the Commission appointed to hold a hearing find that a councillor or member has contravened the relevant code, they may censure, suspend (for a maximum period of one year) or disqualify the councillor or member concerned.[43] An appeal lies from the Commission to the sheriff principal and from the sheriff principal to the Court of Session.[44]

10–20 In 2013–2014 the Commissioner received 331 complaints, a 62 per cent increase on the previous year, most of which were against councillors rather than members of public bodies. In five of the 146 cases investigated during the year a breach was found and reported to the Commission.[45] The most significant categories of complaints related to failure to declare an interest, "disrespect" of councillors, officials and employees, misconduct in dealing with individual applications and breach of the key principles. Having regard to the outcomes of the investigations, including the limited number of breaches of the

---

[36] Standards Commission Scotland, *The Councillors' Code of Conduct*, 3rd edn (2010) para.4.22.
[37] ESPL(S)A 2000 s.7(1).
[38] ESPL(S)A 2000 s.8(3).
[39] Scottish Parliamentary Commissions and Commissioners etc. Act 2010 ("SPCCA 2010") s.1; ESPL(S)A 2000 s.9; the office was established by the Public Services Reform (Commissioner for Ethical Standards in Public Life in Scotland etc.) Order 2013 (SSI 2013/197).
[40] ESPL(S)A 2000 s.10(2).
[41] ESPL(S)A 2000 s.14(2).
[42] ESPL(S)A 2000 s.16.
[43] ESPL(S)A 2000 s.19.
[44] ESPL(S)A 2000 s.22.
[45] Commissioner for Ethical Standards in Public Life in Scotland, *Annual Report 2013/2014* (2014).

Code and the minimal number of cases relating to members of devolved public bodies, the Commissioner considers that councillors and public body members

> "have generally applied high standards of conduct in undertaking their official responsibilities ... Nevertheless, there are no grounds for complacency, and it is clear from the increased volume of complaints that local authorities in particular must continue, actively and as a priority, to promote high ethical standards as part of their arrangements for corporate governance".[46]

MANAGEMENT OF BUSINESS

The McIntosh Commission also sought changes in the way in which councils **10–21** conducted their business. The local government tradition is one of decision-making by committee: functions are vested in the council as a whole, rather than in a separate executive as in central government, and the council may exercise these functions itself or delegate them to a committee or to an officer but not to an individual councillor.[47] The Widdicombe Committee summarised the strengths of the committee model of administration as adaptability, openness and participation, the latter in the sense of maximising councillor participation in the decision-making process, while at the same time acknowledging that decision-making by committee was open to criticism on grounds of lack of political realism, accountability and efficiency.[48] These criticisms were taken up by the McIntosh Commission which reported complaints that "decisions take far too long to emerge: nothing can happen until it has been through a committee and the committee report has been through the council"; that "council and committee meetings are a charade: the business comes pre-packaged, usually from a party group, and the meeting is either a pure formality, finished in minutes, or taken up with political jousting"; and that "the process generates an unmanageable volume of paperwork and takes an inordinate amount of councillors' time"; being a councillor had become a full time job, limiting the pool from which potential councillors could be drawn.[49]

The Commission accordingly sought a clearer separation between functions in **10–22** local government, with a clearly identified political executive subject to scrutiny by the non-executive members of the council. Councils were not required to adopt a particular model, in contrast to England and Wales, but instead to review their arrangements with the assistance of a Leadership Advisory Panel.

> "A prime aim of these reviews should be to set on a formal, open and accountable footing the political leadership within the council, in whatever form is most appropriate to the circumstances of the individual council, so that policy proposals and matters for decision by the council are subject to open debate; and that the council may effectively scrutinise the actions of the leadership and hold it to account for its performance."[50]

---

[46] Commissioner for Ethical Standards in Public Life in Scotland, *Annual Report 2013/2014* (2014) pp.4–5.
[47] Local Government (Scotland) Act 1973 ("LG(S)A 1973") s.56.
[48] Department of the Environment, *The Conduct of Local Authority Business: Report of the Committee of Inquiry into the Conduct of Local Authority Business* (1986) Cmnd.9797, paras 5.6–5.9 and 5.11–5.13.
[49] Commission on Local Government and the Scottish Parliament, *Moving Forward: Local Government and the Scottish Parliament* (June, 1999) Consultation Paper 2, para.76.
[50] Commission on Local Government and the Scottish Parliament, *Moving Forward: Local Government and the Scottish Parliament* (June, 1999) para.13.

The separation of functions recommended by the Commission has not commended itself to all councils: 12 of the 32 councils are reported to operate under an "executive" or "cabinet" model in which the ruling administration takes decisions that are monitored and challenged by scrutiny committees, typically chaired by a councillor who is not a member of the ruling administration; four under hybrid arrangements that combine elements of the traditional and cabinet models; with the remaining 16 continuing to operate under the traditional model.[51]

FUNCTIONS

The power to advance well-being

10-23 Local authorities have long sought relief from the strictness of the ultra vires doctrine in its application to them through a "power of general competence", i.e. a power to do anything for the benefit of their areas which is not expressly prohibited or otherwise provided for in statute. The Scottish Constitutional Convention argued strongly in favour of such a power, invoking the European Charter of Local Self-Government in its support.[52] The McIntosh Commission was sympathetic: as well as enabling councils to take any action on behalf of their communities that was not specifically prohibited or restricted by other legislation, a power of general competence would be a way of expressing in statute

> "the fundamental, but unspoken and unwritten purpose of a council ... namely to be the voice of its people and to promote their interests".[53]

It should also help facilitate the process of community planning (below), by increasing the freedom of councils to take part in joint action in partnership with other agencies.

10-24 The Local Government in Scotland Act 2003, which was the first major local government enactment passed by the Scottish Parliament, empowers a local authority to do anything which it considers likely to promote or improve the well-being of its area, persons in that area, or both of these.[54] The power is a broad one: it includes power to incur expenditure, give financial assistance to any person, enter into arrangements or agreements with any person, co-operate with, or facilitate or co-ordinate the activities of, any person, exercise on behalf of any person any functions of that person, and provide staff, goods, materials, facilities, services or property to any person.[55] Scottish Executive guidance, to which local authorities must have regard before exercising the power, suggests a number of ways in which it may be used: to promote sustainable development, to tackle climate change, to improve mental, social and physical health,

---

[51] Accounts Commission, *Responding to challenges and change: An overview of local government in Scotland 2013* (March, 2013) para.87.

[52] Scottish Constitutional Convention, *Scotland's Parliament, Scotland's Right* (1995) p.17; art.4(2) of the European Charter provides: "Local authorities shall, within the limits of the law, have full discretion to exercise their initiative with regard to any matter which is not excluded from their competence nor assigned to any other authority".

[53] Commission on Local Government and the Scottish Parliament, *Moving Forward: Local Government and the Scottish Parliament* (June, 1999) para.51.

[54] Local Government in Scotland Act 2003 ("LGSA 2003") s.20, which replaced the power to incur expenditure in the interests of its area or inhabitants conferred by the LG(S)A 1973 s.83.

[55] LGSA 2003 s.20(2).

to tackle poverty and deprivation, to promote financial inclusion in disadvantaged communities, to reduce inequalities and promote equalities, to promote local culture and heritage, to protect, enhance and promote biodiversity, and, to improve community safety.[56]

The power is subject to a number of restrictions. It does not enable a local **10–25** authority to do anything that is expressly prohibited, prevented, restricted or limited by other legislation.[57] It must not be exercised in a way that unreasonably duplicates the statutory functions of another body or person.[58] And it does not enable a local authority to impose charges in respect of anything done by it in pursuance of certain functions, including education in schools, the provision of a public library service, the registration of elections, the conduct of elections, and any other functions prescribed by the Scottish Ministers.[59]

There are also safeguards against the abuse of the power. Where it appears to **10–26** the Scottish Ministers that a local authority has "significantly exceeded" its power to advance well-being, they may, after serving a preliminary notice on the authority informing it of the apparent excess of power and giving it an opportunity to respond, direct the authority to take specified action to remedy or prevent the recurrence of the excess of power.[60]

Community planning

Local government exists, the Royal Commission on Local Government in **10–27** Scotland argued

> "to provide local *government*. This means that services are in a real sense locally controlled. There must be an element of choice exercisable locally. More than that, it is implicit that local authorities should in some degree provide a means for the self-expression of local communities".[61]

The McIntosh Commission acknowledged that what it described as the "representational" function of local government remained to a degree unrealised. There was scope, the Commission argued, for local authorities "not merely to plan and deliver services under their own authority but to take the lead in drawing together the plans and activities of the whole range of public bodies, as well as the business community and the voluntary sector within their areas, with the aim of addressing the needs of the community".[62]

> "The council is not the only service provider in its area, but is uniquely placed to take an overview of the needs of its citizens: this role of community planning or community leadership, is one which all councils should develop."[63]

---

[56] LGSA 2003 s.21; Scottish Executive, *The Local Government in Scotland Act 2003—Power to Advance Well-Being Guidance* (April, 2004).

[57] LGSA 2003 s.22(1), (2).

[58] LGSA 2003 s.22(4).

[59] LGSA 2003 s.22(9).

[60] LGSA 2003 ss.26–27.

[61] The Wheatley Report, *Report of the Royal Commission on Local Government in Scotland 1966–1969* (1969) Cmnd.4150, para.114, original emphasis.

[62] Commission on Local Government and the Scottish Parliament, *Moving Forward: Local Government and the Scottish Parliament* (June, 1999) para.16.

[63] Commission on Local Government and the Scottish Parliament, *Moving Forward: Local Government and the Scottish Parliament* (June, 1999) para.26.

10–28 The Commission's recommendation was implemented by the Local Government in Scotland Act 2003 ("the 2003 Act"), which imposed a duty on local authorities to initiate, maintain and facilitate "a community planning process", defined as

> "a process by which the public services provided in the area of the local authority are provided and the planning of that provision takes place after consultation among all the public bodies (including the local authority) responsible for providing those services, and with such community bodies and other bodies or persons as is appropriate; and after and by way of such co-operation among those bodies and persons as is appropriate".[64]

Local authorities, health boards, the chief constable of the Police Service of Scotland, the Scottish Fire and Rescue Service, Scottish Enterprise, Highlands and Islands Enterprise, and regional transport partnerships all have a duty to participate in community planning.[65] The 2003 Act also requires the Scottish Ministers to promote and encourage community planning.[66]

10–29 Local authorities have established non-statutory community planning partnerships ("CPPs") to lead and manage community planning in their areas. Initial experience of their effectiveness was mixed; a report prepared by Audit Scotland found that, in order to help community planning achieve the potential envisaged in the legislation, the Scottish Government and partner organisations needed to agree priorities for community planning.[67] The subsequent introduction of single outcome agreements (below), which are focused on outcomes for local areas, was said to have helped to give partnership working "renewed momentum",[68] while at the same time highlighting some of the difficulties involved. These included the differences in the accountability arrangements of the community planning partners, with some partners accountable to Ministers and others to local elected members, which was said to limit the extent to which CPPs could hold partners to account for their contribution to delivering agreed outcomes or be held to account themselves for delivery of single outcome agreements.

10–30 In a Statement of Ambition published shortly before the 2012 local government elections, the Scottish Government and COSLA placed effective community planning arrangements at the core of the public service reform agenda set out by the Christie Commission on the Future Delivery of Public Services:

> "Effective community planning arrangements will be at the core of public service reform. They will drive the pace of service integration, increase the focus on prevention and secure continuous improvement in public service delivery, in order to achieve better outcomes for communities."[69]

---

[64] LGSA 2003 s.15(1); the National Health Service Reform (Scotland) Act 2004 s.2 required health boards to establish community health partnerships, which are in the course of being replaced by integrated health and social care arrangements under the Public Bodies (Joint Working) (Scotland) Act 2014.

[65] LGSA 2003 s.16(1).

[66] LGSA 2003 s.16(8).

[67] Audit Scotland, *Community Planning: An Initial Review* (June, 2006).

[68] Audit Scotland, *Making an impact: an overview of the audits of Best Value and Community Planning 2004–2009* (October, 2009) para.30.

[69] Scottish Government, *Review of Community Planning and Single Outcome Agreements: Statement of Ambition* (March, 2012); *Commission on the Future Delivery of Public Services* (June, 2011).

Community planning partnerships have some way to go if this ambition is to **10–31** be realised. The most recent assessment found that, 10 years after community planning had been put on a statutory basis, CPPs were not able to show that they had had a significant impact in delivering improved outcomes across Scotland,[70] a view shared by the Parliament's Local Government and Regeneration Committee.[71] Among the barriers preventing community planning acting as a "key driver" of public service reform were

> "complex and differing accountability arrangements for partners and tensions between a focus on local areas, that is at the core of community planning, and national policy and performance priorities with their much broader focus".[72]

Under the Community Empowerment (Scotland) Bill, currently before the **10–32** Parliament, CPPs will be put on a statutory basis, their core duties in the planning and delivery of outcomes more clearly defined and, following the recommendation of the Christie Commission, all community planning partners will be under a duty to support CPPs in fulfilling their core duties. In COSLA's view the proposed statutory duty on other public sector partners to participate in community planning will bring about a "paradigm shift" in community planning. The Local Government and Regeneration Committee Committee is less convinced:

> "We do not believe that a proposed statutory duty will be enough in itself to ensure that all public bodies participate effectively in community planning, and deliver the public services communities want to see."[73]

The Scottish Ministers may take enforcement action against a local authority **10–33** that fails to comply with its duties in relation to community planning, either on the recommendation of the Accounts Commission, which is responsible for the external audit of local authorities, including their performance of their duties in relation to community planning (below), or on their own initiative if they believe that enforcement is justified to protect the public from "substantial harm".[74] After serving a preliminary notice on the authority informing it of its apparent failure and giving it an opportunity to respond, they may direct the authority to take specified action to remedy or prevent the recurrence of its failure to comply.[75] The problems faced by community planning, however, are clearly not reducible to a failure on the part of local authorities to comply with their statutory duties.

FINANCE

For the Royal Commission on Local Government in Scotland, popular election **10–34** and power to raise finance went hand in hand. In a comment which foreshadowed a criticism that was to be later levelled at the Scottish Parliament it said:

---

[70] Audit Scotland, *Improving community planning in Scotland* (March, 2013) para.9; see also Audit Scotland, *Community planning: Turning ambition into action* (November, 2014).

[71] Local Government and Regeneration Committee 9th Report, *Public Services Reform in Scotland: Strand 3—Developing New Ways of Delivering Services* (Scottish Parliamentary Paper 370, 2013) paras 7 and 132.

[72] Audit Scotland, *Improving community planning in Scotland* (March, 2013) para.32.

[73] Local Government and Regeneration Committee 9th Report, *Public Services Reform in Scotland: Strand 3—Developing New Ways of Delivering Services* (Scottish Parliamentary Paper 370, 2013) para.38.

[74] LGSA 2003 s.23(1), (2).

[75] LGSA 2003 ss.23–24.

"If an authority has one without the other, it is not truly accountable . . . authorities which depend wholly or mainly for finance not on the electorate whom they purport to represent, but on requisitioning from another source, or on Exchequer funds, are not in a healthy condition."[76]

But if financial dependence is the mark of an unhealthy condition, it is one which local authorities in Scotland have been in for most of their history, with few if any authorities able to fund the services for which they are responsible from their own resources. Local authorities have the power to raise local taxes in the form of the council tax, a power which has been effectively "frozen" since 2007, but the proceeds of the council tax account for only 20 per cent or so of local authority expenditure, with the remainder being met from the Scottish Government in the form of a mixture of general and specific grants and non-domestic rate income.[77]

10–35 Successive governments have for different reasons left the system of local government finance unchanged. The McIntosh Commission recommended an inquiry into local government finance but its recommendation was not accepted by the first Scottish Executive. Its successor commissioned a review of local government finance, as part of the coalition agreement, which recommended the replacement of the council tax by a local property tax, but the review was more notable for its categorical rejection of the Royal Commission's argument that local tax-raising powers were an essential element of local accountability:

> "To us, the principal distinction between local *government* and local *administration* does not turn solely on the extent or otherwise of tax-raising powers. Accountability depends on how well the services delivered by the local authority meet the community needs and the power that authority has to prioritise and shape local services, as well as to deliver them."[78]

It was a clear indication of a shifting agenda in which tax-raising powers were not seen as an answer to the problems faced by local government. The first SNP Government subsequently consulted on proposals for a "local" income tax, set nationally, which would almost certainly have provoked a legal challenge on the grounds that it was outwith the Scottish Parliament's legislative competence, but it was forced to drop the proposals in the absence of sufficient parliamentary support.[79] The current SNP Government has now proposed an independent commission to examine alternatives to the council tax system.

AUDIT

10–36 Audit provides one of the principal external checks on local government. The Accounts Commission for Scotland, which consists of between six and 12 members appointed by the Scottish Ministers, is responsible for financial and value for money audit in local government.[80] Following devolution, responsi-

---

[76] The Wheatley Report, *Report of the Royal Commission on Local Government in Scotland 1966–1969* (1969) Cmnd.4150, para.633.
[77] The council tax is levied under the Local Government Finance Act 1992 s.70(1).
[78] Local Government Finance Review Committee, *A Fairer Way: Report of the Local Government Finance Review Committee* (2006) s.6, para.23, original emphasis.
[79] Scottish Government, *A Fairer Local Tax for Scotland* (March, 2008).
[80] LG(S)A 1973 s.97.

bility for the audit of health authorities was transferred from the Accounts Commission to the Auditor General for Scotland (below), but the Accounts Commission retained control of local authority audit in recognition of "the autonomy of local government as a separate democratically accountable tier of government".[81]

The Controller of Audit, who is appointed by the Accounts Commission after **10–37** consultation with, and subject to the approval of, the Scottish Ministers,[82] is responsible for reporting matters arising from local authority audits to the Commission. The Controller of Audit may, and if so required by the Commission must, make reports to the Commission with respect to the accounts of local authorities, any matters arising from the accounts or the audit of those accounts that the Controller considers should be considered by a local authority or brought to the attention of the public, and the performance by a local authority of their duties relating to best value (below) and community planning.[83]

On a report being made to it by the Controller of Audit, the Commission may **10–38** direct the Controller to carry out further investigations, hold a hearing, state its findings, or take no action.[84] The Commission may state its findings with or without a public hearing. For the Commission, public hearings are "an important part of the governance and accountability framework of local government in Scotland". "Other than through elections, there is no other mechanism for councils to be publicly held to account in this way."[85]

A local authority is required to consider the Commission's findings at a meeting **10–39** of the full council held with three months of receiving them; where the findings contain recommendations, the local authority is required to decide whether to accept them and what action, if any, to take in response to them, and to notify the Commission accordingly. At least seven days' public notice must be given of the meeting and a summary of the council's decision approved by the Commission must be published in a local newspaper.[86] Where the Commission is not satisfied by a council's response to its findings, or has doubts about its ability to deliver improvement, it can ask for a follow-up audit report.

The Controller also has power to make a special report to the Accounts **10–40** Commission where in the Controller's opinion there has been illegal expenditure or a failure to account for money; where there has been a loss because of negligence, misconduct or because of the body's failure to carry out a duty; or where there has been a mistake in the accounts which the authority is not putting right.[87] On receipt of a special report, the Commission may direct the Controller to carry out further investigations, hold a hearing, state a case on any question of law arising on the special report for the opinion of the Court of Session, or take no action.[88] The Commission must hold a hearing if requested to do so by the local authority, or any officer or member named or referred to in the report in connection with an item of account being contrary to law, or

[81] Scottish Office, *Principles of the Scottish Parliament's Financial Procedures: Final Report of the Financial Issues Advisory Group* (1999) para.6.41.
[82] LG(S)A 1973 s.97(4).
[83] LG(S)A 1973 s.102(1).
[84] LGSA 2003 s.3; reports are made under LG(S)A 1973 s.102(1).
[85] Audit Scotland, *Making an impact: an overview of the audits of Best Value and Community Planning 2004–2009* (October, 2009) paras 8 and 12.
[86] LGSA 2003 s.5.
[87] LG(S)A 1973 s.102(3).
[88] LG(S)A 1973 s.103B(1).

whose failure, negligence or misconduct is a subject of the report.[89] It must also state a case if directed to do so by the Court of Session.[90]

10–41 Where the members of the Commission appointed to hold a hearing find that there has been illegality or financial loss due to negligence or misconduct, they may impose sanctions ranging from censure to disqualification from office.[91] An appeal lies to the sheriff principal against the imposition of sanctions, other than seemingly disqualification, and from the sheriff principal to the Court of Session.[92]

10–42 The local authority is also required to consider the Commission's findings.[93]

National performance audits

10–43 As well as securing the audit of local authority accounts and following up issues of concern, the Accounts Commission carries out or promotes comparative and other studies designed to enable it to make recommendations for the securing by local authorities of best value (below); improving economy, efficiency and effectiveness in the provision of services by local authorities; and improving the financial and other management of local authorities.[94]

BEST VALUE

10–44 The Local Government in Scotland Act 2003 requires local authorities to "make arrangements which secure best value", which the Act defines as "continuous improvement in the performance of the authority's functions".[95] In securing best value, an authority is required to maintain an "appropriate balance" between the quality of its performance of its functions and the cost of that performance (including the cost to persons of any service provided on a wholly or partly rechargeable basis).[96] In maintaining the balance between quality and cost, an authority is required to have regard to the efficiency, effectiveness and economy of its actions and the need to comply with the requirements of equal opportunities legislation.[97] It is also required to discharge its duties in a way which contributes to the achievement of sustainable development.[98] The statutory requirements are supplemented by guidance issued by the Scottish Ministers to which local authorities are required to have regard.[99]

10–45 In auditing a local authority's accounts, auditors are required to satisfy themselves that the authority has made proper arrangements for securing best value

---

[89] LG(S)A 1973 s.103B(2).

[90] LG(S)A 1973 s.103B(3); see, e.g. *Commission for Local Authority Accounts in Scotland v Stirling District Council*, 1984 S.L.T. 442; *Commission for Local Authority Accounts in Scotland v City of Edinburgh District Council*, 1988 S.L.T. 767; *Commission for Local Authority Accounts in Scotland v Grampian Regional Council*, 1994 S.L.T. 1120.

[91] LG(S)A 1973 s.103F.

[92] LG(S)A 1973 s.103J.

[93] LG(S)A 1973 s.103D.

[94] LG(S)A 1973 s.97A.

[95] LGSA 2003 s.1(2); the duty to secure best value replaced the compulsory competitive tendering regime introduced by the Local Government, Planning and Land Act 1980 and extended by the Local Government Act 1988 and the Local Government Act 1992.

[96] LGSA 2003 s.1(3).

[97] LGSA 2003 s.1(4).

[98] LGSA 2003 s.1(5).

[99] Scottish Executive, *The Local Government in Scotland Act 2003 Best Value Guidance* (2004), issued under LGSA 2003 s.2(1)(a).

(and is complying with its community planning duties).[100] The Controller of Audit may make a report to the Accounts Commission with respect to the performance by a local authority of their duties in relation to best value and community planning, which may be followed up by the Commission in the manner already described; two public hearings were held during the first phase of Best Value ("BV") audits: into West Dunbartonshire Council and Aberdeen City Council. The Scottish Ministers also have the power to take enforcement action against a local authority on their own initiative, as well as on the recommendation of the Accounts Commission, if they believe that enforcement is justified in order to protect the public from "substantial harm".[101] After serving a preliminary notice on the authority informing it of its apparent failure to comply with its duty to secure best value and giving it an opportunity to respond, they may direct the authority to take specified action to remedy or prevent the recurrence of its failure.[102]

PUBLIC PERFORMANCE REPORTING

The duty on local authorities to make arrangements which secure best value is **10–46** complemented by a duty to make arrangements for the reporting to the public of the outcome of the performance of their functions.[103]

> "A local authority which secures Best Value will be able to demonstrate accountability [through] the use of public performance reporting, so that stakeholders are told what quality of service is being delivered and what they can expect in the future."[104]

> "Public services are provided on behalf of the public and in their interests: they are not just 'customers'. This means that in addition to the legitimacy authorities derive from the democratic process, they must be ready to be held to account for their performance on an ongoing basis."[105]

The Accounts Commission, which is responsible for issuing an annual direc- **10–47** tion to local authorities prescribing the information about their performance they must publish,[106] has encouraged the local government "community" to develop its own performance information.

> "We want to be able to use our statutory role to underpin performance reporting designed by councils themselves, rather than impose an additional regime."[107]

It is sufficiently encouraged by the progress that has been made to rely mainly on the Local Government Benchmarking Framework, while reserving the right to reintroduce specific statutory performance indicators should progress not be maintained.[108]

---

[100] LG(S)A 1973 s.99(1)(c).
[101] LGSA 2003 s.23(1), (2).
[102] LGSA 2003 ss.23–24.
[103] LGSA 2003 s.13.
[104] Scottish Executive, *The Local Government in Scotland Act 2003 Best Value Guidance* (2004) Ch.10.
[105] Scottish Executive, *The Local Government in Scotland Act 2003 Best Value Guidance: Measures to Support Public Performance Reporting* (January, 2005) Pt 3.
[106] Local Government Act 1992 s.1; see the Local Government Act 1992 Statutory Performance Indicators Direction 2014 (December, 2014).
[107] Local Government Act 1992 Statutory Performance Indicators Direction 2011, Introduction.
[108] Local Government Act 1992 Statutory Performance Indicators Direction 2013, Introduction.

CENTRAL-LOCAL RELATIONS

10–48 As we have seen, the Scottish Constitutional Convention expected the Scottish Parliament to investigate new ways of co-operative working between the two levels of government. The McIntosh Commission recommended that the Parliament and the 32 local authorities commit themselves to a covenant setting out the basis of their working relationship, with a standing joint conference providing a place where parliamentarians and local government representatives may hold a dialogue "on the basis of equality".[109] It also recommended that a formal working agreement should be established between local government and the Scottish Ministers.[110] The proposed covenant between the Parliament and local government did not materialise but the notion of a partnership has proved an enduring feature of central-local relations since devolution. The first Labour-Liberal Democrat Executive entered into a Partnership Framework with the Convention of Scottish Local Authorities in 2001, while the first SNP Government sought a partnership with local government through the combination of an overarching concordat with local government and single outcome agreements with individual local authorities.

The concordat

10–49 The concordat between the Scottish Government and COSLA, entered into in November 2007, set out the terms of what was described as "a new relationship between the Scottish Government and local government based on mutual respect and partnership"—the cardinal principle laid down by the McIntosh Commission. The concordat involved a package of measures, which on the Scottish Government side included the total amount of funding to be made available to local authorities over the next three years, a substantial reduction in the number of ring-fenced funding streams, and a commitment not to pursue structural reform of local government.[111] On the local government side it included the development of single outcome agreements for each local authority area, supported by streamlined external scrutiny and effective performance management, and an agreement to deliver on a specified set of commitments from within the funding provided, together with provision for joint oversight and monitoring of the partnership, and a new performance reporting system, Scotland Performs, to provide "regular, timely and transparent" reporting on progress against the national outcomes set out in the National Performance Framework, in addition to local reporting on progress against related local outcomes. The partners also agreed that they would do what was required to ensure delivery of key government policies and programmes, including freezing council tax rates.

Single outcome agreements

10–50 The concordat anticipated that each local authority would aim to reach a single outcome agreement with the Scottish Government based on the national outcomes set out in the National Performance Framework and, under a common

---

[109] Commission on Local Government and the Scottish Parliament, *Moving Forward: Local Government and the Scottish Parliament* (June, 1999) para.34.

[110] Commission on Local Government and the Scottish Parliament, *Moving Forward: Local Government and the Scottish Parliament* (June, 1999) para.45.

[111] The power conferred by s.14 of the Public Services Reform (Scotland) Act 2010 does not therefore extend to local government; while functions may be transferred or delegated to local authorities (s.14(5)), the power may not be used to remove functions from local authorities or to make any structural change in relation to local government.

framework, local outcomes to take account of local priorities.[112] The single outcome agreement would cover all local government services in each local authority area as well as a significant range of the responsibilities of community planning partnerships where local authorities had a significant part to play. First phase single outcome agreements with local authorities were concluded in 2008, with the second phase of agreements—which ran for three years from 2009–2010—being extended to community planning partnerships (above). Following the local government elections in May 2012, preparations began on a third phase of agreements, which were agreed with the Scottish Government in June 2013.

As agreed between community planning partnerships and the Scottish **10–51** Government, single outcome agreements constitute a "shared, explicit and binding 'plan for place' ".[113] They are not legally binding but the community planning partners are expected to take shared responsibility for the effectiveness of the CPP, including for the development and delivery of the new single outcome agreements ("SOAs") and the provision of the resources required to do this.[114] Under the Community Empowerment (Scotland) Bill, as mentioned, all community planning partners will be under a duty to support CPPs in fulfilling their core duties. How these duties will be enforced is unclear but in the meantime elected members will

> "hold councils to account for their contribution to CPPs, including for the development and delivery of new SOAs, just as the Scottish Government will hold Health Boards and other public bodies to account for their contribution to CPPs and for the development and delivery of new SOAs".[115]

The Scottish Government has started to use existing performance management and accountability arrangements to monitor the contribution of public bodies to community planning, but it is "not yet consistently holding central government bodies or the NHS to account for their performance within CPPs".[116]

THE FUTURE

The Scottish local government tradition is said to be based on pragmatism not **10–52** ideology.

> "While a belief in the virtues of local government has undoubtedly been a part of Scottish political culture, there has also been an equal emphasis

---

[112] On the National Performance Framework, see para.5–47.

[113] Scottish Government and COSLA, *Single Outcome Agreements. Guidance to Community Planning Partnerships* (December, 2012) p.1.

[114] Scottish Government and COSLA, *Single Outcome Agreements. Guidance to Community Planning Partnerships* (December, 2012) p.10. It was regarded as a "significant indication of more mature relationships, arising from shared learning and experience," that references to "nationally agreed arrangements for attributing and addressing the causes of non-delivery of local outcomes" and a "pre-agreed process ... for resolving disputes and for securing arbitration between the Scottish government, the council and community planning partners" were not seen as "helpful or necessary" in the second edition of the guidance on single outcome agreements: *Interim Report from Local Government on the 1st Phase Single Outcome Agreements in 2008–2009* (April, 2009) para.26.

[115] Scottish Government and COSLA, *Single Outcome Agreements. Guidance to Community Planning Partnerships* (December, 2012) pp.10–11.

[116] Audit Scotland, *Improving community planning in Scotland* (March, 2013) para.33.

on the efficient performance of functions. Where the structure of authorities stands in the way of efficiency, Scots have been ready change it, and there does not seem to be the almost mystical belief in local democracy which has dominated English thought."[117]

Partnership working and structural reform are not alternatives. No Scottish government is likely to want to proceed other than on the basis of the partnership with local government, but whether partnership working supplemented by mandatory cooperation will prove sufficient to achieve the Scottish Government's purpose remains to be seen.

10–53 Allied to the question of structure is the question of democracy—the Scottish local government tradition notwithstanding. In his foreword to the Smith Commission Agreement, Lord Smith recorded "a strong desire to see the principle of devolution extended further, with the transfer of powers from Holyrood to local communities". Acknowledging that this was an issue that would require "significant further thought and discussion", he welcomed

> "the enthusiasm of all parties for greater empowerment of our communities. The Scottish Government should work with the Parliament, civic Scotland and local authorities to set out ways in which local areas can benefit from the powers of the Scottish Parliament".[118]

Whether this recommendation will be acted upon, and if so in what form, also remains to be seen. In the meantime, we may note that local government and local communities are by no means synonymous. Empowering local communities, if that is indeed the objective, would require a radical restructuring of local government in Scotland.[119]

---

[117] James G Kellas, *The Scottish Political System*, 4th edn (Cambridge: Cambridge University Press, 1989) pp.163–165.

[118] The Smith Commission, *Report of the Smith Commission for further devolution of powers to the Scottish Parliament* (November 27, 2014) Foreword.

[119] COSLA's Commission on Strengthening Local Democracy, which saw the current scale and functions of elected local governments in Scotland as limiting the possibility of participative local democracy, has recommended a fundamental review of the structure, boundaries, functions and democratic arrangements for all local governance in Scotland: *Effective Democracy: Connecting with Communities* (2014); see also Local Government and Regeneration Committee 8th Report, *Flexibility and Autonomy in Local Government* (Scottish Parliamentary Paper 573, 2014).

CHAPTER 11

PUBLIC BODIES

Introduction

For the Scottish Constitutional Convention the purpose of electing a Scottish **11–01** Parliament was to give the people of Scotland a representative say over the way in which their affairs were run. The need for this "fundamental democratic principle" had gained "added force in recent years because of the steady transfer of important areas of government from elected representatives to unelected and unrepresentative appointed bodies".[1] The Convention expected the Parliament to "attach a high priority to reversing this anti-democratic trend". Accordingly, the Parliament should, in its view, have power to examine the role of quangos operating in Scotland, and to bring their activities under democratic control where it considered this necessary. It should also have powers to ensure that where such bodies remained they would be subject to greater accountability and accessibility.[2] The 1997 Labour Government agreed that the extent to which "Scotland's vital public services are now run by unelected bodies" was a matter of concern, but cautioned that some functions of government were best delivered by public bodies established for the purpose, provided that democratic accountability was ultimately retained by Ministers.[3] The Scottish Executive would therefore have responsibility for all Scottish public bodies whose functions and services were devolved and would be accountable to the Scottish Parliament for them.[4]

Public bodies were, accordingly, divided into two principal groups for the **11–02** purposes of devolution: those whose functions related to devolved matters and were exercisable only in or as regards Scotland, which became part of the devolved machinery of government; and those whose functions related to reserved matters, which remained part of the UK machinery. Some of the latter, including the Bank of England, the BBC, and what is now the Commission for Equality and Human Rights, were expressly reserved, thus putting them beyond the legislative competence of the Scottish Parliament.[5] This left a third, inter-mediate group of authorities with "mixed" functions, i.e. functions relating to both reserved and devolved matters, or functions relating to devolved matters but exercisable on a UK or GB-wide rather than Scotland-only basis, some of which were also reserved as "cross border public authorities" on the assump-tion that the Scottish Parliament would

---

[1] Scottish Constitutional Convention, *Scotland's Parliament, Scotland's Right* (1995) p.17.
[2] Scottish Constitutional Convention, *Scotland's Parliament, Scotland's Right* (1995) p.17.
[3] Scottish Office, *Scotland's Parliament* (1997) Cm.3658, para.6.7.
[4] Scottish Office, *Scotland's Parliament* (1997) Cm.3658, para.6.8.
[5] Scotland Act 1998 ("SA 1998") Sch.5 Pt III para.3.

"want to continue most such UK or GB arrangements in the light of the advantages of sharing knowledge and expertise on a UK or GB wide basis and of the greater efficiency in the use of resources".[6]

It is open to the Scottish Parliament, however, to make alternative arrangements for the exercise of functions relating to devolved matters, e.g. by setting up a separate body to exercise those functions.

THE PUBLIC BODIES LANDSCAPE

11–03   A striking feature of the public bodies landscape in Scotland, as in the UK as a whole, is its complexity. The Scottish Government's national public bodies directory lists no fewer than nine categories of public body—executive agencies, non-ministerial departments, non-departmental public bodies ("NDPBs") (which are subdivided into executive NDPBs, advisory NDPBs and tribunals), public corporations, health bodies, and parliamentary commissioners and ombudsmen—as well as a miscellaneous group of "other significant national bodies" that do not fall into any of the other categories. Not included in the list are what the Committee on Standards in Public Life termed "local spending bodies", i.e. " 'not for profit' bodies that are neither fully elected nor appointed by Ministers, but which provide public services, often at local level, that are largely or wholly publicly funded".[7]

11–04   *Executive agencies.* The inclusion of executive agencies might be thought surprising given that they are an integral part of the Scottish Government. Their inclusion, however, reflects the fact that they have, in theory at least, a greater degree of operational autonomy than the directorates that form the "core" of the Scottish Government.

11–05   *Non-ministerial departments.* The inclusion of non-ministerial departments, which as we have seen are part of the Scottish Administration but not of the Scottish Government, is more readily understandable given that more recent additions such as Office of the Scottish Charity Regulator could equally well have been established as non-departmental public bodies.

11–06   *Executive NDPBs.* Executive NDPBs carry out administrative, commercial, executive or regulatory functions which are considered to be better delivered at arm's length from Ministers. They are normally established by statute, but they may be established by royal charter or under the Companies Acts; they employ their own staff—who are not civil servants—and manage their own budgets; and they are accountable to a board whose members are normally appointed by Ministers.[8] There are currently some 34 executive NDPBs, including the Scottish Environment Protection Agency, Scottish Natural Heritage and Scottish Enterprise.

---

[6] Scottish Office, *Scotland's Parliament* (1997) Cm.3658, para.2.10; Scotland Act 1998 (Cross-Border Public Authorities) (Specification) Order 1999 (SI 1999/1319).

[7] Second Report of the Committee on Standards in Public Life, *Local Public Spending Bodies* (1996) Cm.3270, para 3; they comprise further education colleges, higher education institutions, and registered social landlords, mainly housing associations.

[8] Scottish Government, *Guide to Public Bodies in Scotland* (December, 2011) para.7.

Advisory NDPBs. Advisory NDPBs provide independent expert advice to **11–07** Ministers and others or input to the policy-making process. They are normally established by Ministers on a non-statutory basis; they do not normally employ staff (administrative support is usually provided by the Scottish Government); and they are not normally responsible for expenditure other than remuneration for board members. They are accountable to a board whose members are normally appointed by Ministers.[9] There are currently six advisory bodies, including the Scottish Law Commission, which was established by the Law Commissions Act 1965, and the Judicial Appointments Board for Scotland, which was placed on a statutory footing by the Judiciary and Courts (Scotland) Act 2008.

Tribunals. Although their functions are essentially judicial, tribunals are sepa- **11–08** rate from the formal court system. As we have seen, the Tribunals (Scotland) Act 2014 establishes a new two-tier structure for Scottish tribunals into which existing tribunal jurisdictions will be transferred. There are currently six tribunals listed in the public bodies directory, including the Additional Support Needs Tribunals for Scotland, the Lands Tribunal for Scotland and the Mental Health Tribunal for Scotland.

Public corporations. Public corporations operate commercially and recover **11–09** most of their costs from fees charged to customers. They employ their own staff, who are not civil servants, and manage their own budgets. They are accountable to a board whose members are appointed by Ministers.[10] There are currently six public corporations, including David MacBrayne Ltd and Scottish Water.

Health bodies. Health bodies for the most part provide healthcare services or **11–10** management, technical or advisory services within the National Health Service. There are currently some 23 NHS bodies, including the 14 regional or area health boards. The Mental Welfare Commission for Scotland is also included in this category.

Parliamentary commissioners and ombudsmen. Parliamentary commissioners **11–11** and ombudsmen have a variety of advocacy, investigative and complaints handling functions. Their staff are employed by the Scottish Parliamentary Corporate Body ("SPCB"), which is also responsible for their funding and sponsorship, and they report directly to the Scottish Parliament. There are currently six commissioners (including two commissions) and ombudsmen: the Commissioner for Ethical Standards in Public Life; the Commissioner for Children and Young People in Scotland; the Scottish Human Rights Commission; the Scottish Information Commissioner; the Scottish Public Services Ombudsman; and the Standards Commission for Scotland.

Other significant national bodies. Other significant national bodies have a **11–12** direct relationship with either the Scottish Government or the Parliament but do not fall within any of the other categories of public body. There are currently 20 other significant national bodies, including Audit Scotland, Justice of the Peace Advisory Committees and the Scottish Police Authority.

---

[9] Scottish Government, *Guide to Public Bodies in Scotland* (December, 2011) para.7.
[10] Scottish Government, *Guide to Public Bodies in Scotland* (December, 2011) para.9.

RATIONALES

11–13 A number of potentially overlapping rationales may be offered for entrusting functions to bodies at one or more removes from direct ministerial control. One is that it serves to insulate the carrying out of functions from the political process in the knowledge that public confidence is likely to be impaired if those functions are not seen to be carried out independently of Ministers; the range of functions which it is thought should be insulated from the political process for this reason has steadily increased over the years, but they include functions such as dispute settlement, inspection and regulation, and the distribution of public funding. Another rationale is that it provides a means of involving external skills and expertise in the business of government. And a third, widely employed in relation to the former nationalised industries, is that the traditional ministerial department, accountable to Parliament for everything it does, is an unsuitable instrument for participation in economic activity: "its organisation [is] too inflexible and its personnel too cautious to achieve the requisite degree of initiative and efficiency".[11]

SIMPLIFYING THE LANDSCAPE

11–14 The first Scottish Executive undertook a review of Scottish public bodies against the background of the "new, more democratic political context and thus the requirement for bodies to be more accountable".[12] Devolution had brought the network of arm's length advisory and executive bodies into much sharper focus and had given "added weight to concerns about their contemporary role, their value and, in particular, about their accountability".[13] The review was carried out with a view to:

(a) securing a set of principles underpinning the organisation and delivery of devolved central government services in the new Scotland;

(b) testing all public bodies against those principles, and abolishing those whose existence was not justified by reference to them; and

(c) ensuring that those that remained operated effectively and were appropriately accountable to Ministers and Parliament and had legitimacy in the eyes of the public.[14]

11–15 In terms of underpinning principles, the review took as its starting point the proposition that Ministers must be, and must be seen to be, directly accountable to the Scottish Parliament for the overall policy and strategic framework within which all devolved functions are carried out. As regards the execution of functions, however, absent a "very strong argument" for Ministers remaining "directly accountable" to Parliament, the presumption should be against functions being carried out within the Scottish Executive (either within the "core" or by an executive agency).[15] In other words, the presumption should be in favour of functions being carried out at one or more removes from Ministers. The review, it was claimed, had demonstrated that in many circumstances arm's length public bodies, operating within "a new framework of accountability",

[11] FMG Willson, "Ministries and Boards: Some Aspects of Administrative Development since 1832" (1955) 33 Public Administration 43, 55.

[12] Scottish Executive, *Review of Public Bodies: Discussion Paper* (January, 2001) para.7.

[13] Scottish Executive, *Public Bodies: Proposals for Change* (June, 2001) paras 2 and 5.

[14] Scottish Executive, *Public Bodies: Proposals for Change* (June, 2001) para.6.

[15] Scottish Executive, *Public Bodies: Proposals for Change* (June, 2001) para.13.

were better placed than any other type of organisation, including the Scottish Executive itself, to carry out functions on behalf of Ministers.[16]

Following the review, the Scottish Executive announced the abolition of 52 of **11–16** the 180 or so existing bodies and the "ongoing fundamental review" of a further 61 with a presumption in favour of abolition.[17] The emphasis on numbers was misleading.

> "A few minor bodies were abolished and others amalgamated into a smaller number of larger bodies but there was certainly no centripetal dynamic in favour of taking functions back into departments of the Scottish Executive."[18]

The Executive also announced proposals for the reform of the remainder, aimed at making them more open, accountable and effective, and ensuring that they worked, where appropriate, to the Executive's agenda (below).[19]

"Rationalising and improving Scotland's complex landscape of national public **11–17** bodies" was also a key element of the first SNP Government's public services reform programme.[20] In October 2007, it announced its intention to reduce the number of devolved, national public organisations by 25 per cent by April 2011, against a baseline list of 199 public bodies. The Public Services Reform (Scotland) Act 2010, which was enacted in implementation of the programme, made extensive changes to the public bodies landscape. As well as establishing new bodies (for arts and culture, social care and social work scrutiny and health care scrutiny), and abolishing and merging others, the power was taken to make further changes by order,[21] a power which it argued was required in order to avoid the situation where "necessary" changes were delayed, or did not proceed at all, because a suitable legislative opportunity was not available. This power is subject to a sunset clause and will expire on August 1, 2015 unless it is extended.[22] So far the principal use made of it has been to reconstitute the General Teaching Council for Scotland as a professional body, rather than an advisory NDPB, and to merge the offices of Public Standards Commissioner for Scotland and Public Appointments Commissioner for Scotland to form the office of Commissioner for Ethical Standards in Public Life in Scotland.[23]

The SNP Government's simplification programme, like the earlier review, saw **11–18** a headline reduction in the number of national public bodies—from 199 in October 2007 to 144 in July 2011 when the programme came to an end—but

---

[16] Scottish Executive, *Public Bodies: Proposals for Change* (June, 2001) para.10.

[17] Scottish Parliament OR June 21, 2001 col.1832; five bodies were abolished by the Public Appointments and Public Bodies etc. (Scotland) Act 2003 ("PAPB(S)A 2003") s.4.

[18] Matthew Flinders, *Delegated Governance and the British State: Walking Without Order* (Oxford: OUP, 2008) p.272; for a detailed account, see Matthew Denton and Matthew Flinders, "Democracy, devolution and delegated governance in Scotland" (2006) 16 Regional and Federal Studies 70.

[19] Scottish Executive, *Public Bodies: Proposals for Change* (June, 2001).

[20] Scottish Government, *First Minister's Statement on More Effective Government: Supporting Information* (January, 2008) para.2.

[21] Public Services Reform (Scotland) Act 2010 ("PSR(S)A 2010") s.14.

[22] PSR(S)A 2010 s.134(3), (4).

[23] Public Services Reform (General Teaching Council for Scotland) Order 2011 (SSI 2011/215); Public Services Reform (Commissioner for Ethical Standards in Public Life in Scotland) Order 2013 (SSI 2013/197); see also the Public Services Reform (Functions of the Common Services Agency for the Scottish Health Service) Order 2013 (SSI 2013/220).

no real change in the scope of delegated governance. A smaller number of bodies, with in some cases broader responsibilities, continues to exercise essentially the same range of functions as before. Nor has the number of different types of public body been reduced. The Crerar Review, which identified the complexity of organisational structures as a constraint on developing and delivering an appropriate scrutiny regime across public services, recommended that all external scrutiny organisations should have one status with clearly defined lines of accountability to the Parliament and to Ministers, but this recommendation was not pursued.[24] Devolution has not therefore led to a reduction in either the scope or the organisational complexity of delegated governance in Scotland.

PUBLIC APPOINTMENTS

11–19   Members of the governing boards of public bodies are commonly appointed by Ministers.[25] Public appointments have traditionally been treated as being in the gift of Ministers, giving rise to widespread suspicions of political bias or cronyism in appointments, which had begun to be tackled before devolution. The devolution White Paper said that the Scottish Executive would be required to put arrangements in place to ensure that appointments to Scottish public bodies were subject to independent scrutiny and conformed to the ("GB") Commissioner for Public Appointments' Code of Practice for Ministerial Appointments to Public Bodies.[26] Devolved appointments continued to be subject to the GB regime until a separate Scottish regime was put in place by the Public Appointments and Public Bodies etc. (Scotland) Act 2003 ("the 2003 Act").

11–20   The 2003 Act established a Commissioner for Public Appointments in Scotland.[27] The Commissioner, whose functions were transferred to the Commissioner for Ethical Standards in Public Life in Scotland in 2013,[28] is responsible for the preparation and publication of a code of practice in respect of the making by the Scottish Ministers of appointments or recommendations for appointment to the offices and bodies ("specified authorities") listed in Sch.2 to the Act[29]; for keeping the code of practice under review; and for

---

[24] Crerar Review, *The Report of the Independent Review of Regulation, Audit, Inspection and Complaints Handling of Public Services in Scotland* (September, 2007) para.8.25. The Accountability and Governance Action Group, which was set up to devise practical ways of implementing the Review's recommendations, saw operational independence being secured through a "set of key governance principles rather than primarily through the status of a scrutiny body": *Report to Ministers* (December, 2008) para.50. For a simpler UK taxonomy in which organisational form is more closely related to function, see Tom Gash with Sir Ian Magee et al, *Read Before Burning: Arm's length government for a new administration* (Institute for Government, 2010), and Public Administration Select Committee, *Who's accountable? Relationships between Government and arm's-length bodies* (HC 2013–2014, 110).

[25] Provision for elected members is made under the National Parks (Scotland) Act 2000 and the Crofting Reform (Scotland) Act 2010. Provision was also made under the Health Boards (Membership and Elections) (Scotland) Act 2009 but the idea was abandoned after pilot schemes saw very low turnouts at elections.

[26] Scottish Office, *Scotland's Parliament* (1997) Cm.3658, para.6.8; the GB Code was put in place following the First Report of the Committee on Standards in Public Life, *Standards in Public Life* (1995) Cm.2850.

[27] PAPB(S)A 2003 s.1.

[28] Public Services Reform (Commissioner for Ethical Standards in Public Life in Scotland) Order 2013 (SSI 2013/197); for the Commissioner's appointment and security of tenure, see Ch.4.

[29] PAPB(S)A 2003 s.2(1); Sch.2 has been extensively amended.

promoting compliance with the code (to which end the Commissioner may issue guidance to the Scottish Ministers).[30] The Act requires the Commissioner's functions to be exercised with a view to ensuring that appointments and recommendations for appointment are made fairly and openly, and, so far as reasonably practicable, all categories of person are afforded an opportunity to be considered for appointment and recommendation for appointment to the specified authorities.[31]

The Code of Practice for Ministerial Appointments to Public Bodies in **11–21** Scotland, which was first issued in 2006 and has since been revised twice, is based on three overarching principles:

  (i) *Merit.* All public appointments must be made on merit. Only persons judged best able to meet the requirements of the post will be appointed.
 (ii) *Integrity.* The appointments process must be open, fair and impartial. The integrity of the process must earn the trust and have the confidence of the public.
(iii) *Diversity and equality.* Public appointments must be advertised publicly in a way that will attract a strong and diverse field of suitable candidates. The process itself must provide equality of opportunity.

The Code also provides that the public appointments process should be **11–22** "outcome focused" and "applicant focused" and that the Commissioner's scrutiny responsibilities should be undertaken on the basis of "independence and impartiality, efficiency and effectiveness and reasonableness and proportionality".[32]

The Code is supported by a handbook of guidance that is intended to facilitate **11–23** implementation and understanding of the Code.

The 2003 Act requires the Commissioner to examine the methods and prac- **11–24** tices employed by the Scottish Ministers in making appointments and recommendations for appointment to ensure they comply with the Code.[33] The Commissioner is also charged with investigating complaints arising from the making of any appointment or recommendation for appointment.[34] Where it appears to the Commissioner that the Code has not been complied with "in a material regard", the Scottish Ministers must be informed, thereby affording them the opportunity to remedy the breach. If after having been informed of the breach the Scottish Ministers fail to comply with the Code, or seem unlikely to comply with the Code, the Commissioner must then report the case to the Scottish Parliament; if the appointment or recommendation has not been made, the Commissioner may direct the Scottish Ministers to delay making the appointment or recommendation until the Parliament has considered the case.[35] The first Commissioner laid seven reports of material non-compliance before

---

[30] PAPB(S)A 2003 s.2(3), (6).
[31] PAPB(S)A 2003 s.2(9).
[32] Commissioner for Ethical Standards in Public Life in Scotland, *Code of Practice for Ministerial Appointments to Public Bodies in Scotland* (October, 2013). The original Code was based on seven principles: ministerial responsibility; merit; equality; probity and respect; independent scrutiny; openness and transparency; and proportionality.
[33] PAPB(S)A 2003 s.2(5).
[34] PAPB(S)A 2003 s.2(5).
[35] PAPB(S)A 2003 s.2(7), (8).

the Parliament, five about appointments to individual public bodies, and two about succession planning and reappointments.[36]

11-25	In contrast to Westminster, there has been little interest in either giving the Parliament, or the Parliament assuming, a role in public appointments in Scotland. The Scottish Executive's consultation on the public appointments system[37] was said to have revealed very little support for pre-appointment parliamentary involvement, e.g. by way of confirmation hearings, and not much more for post-appointment parliamentary involvement.

> "The main message seemed to be that existing Parliamentary powers of scrutiny, supplemented with an annual debate on the Executive's Annual Report on Public Appointments, would provide ample opportunity for MSPs to monitor appointments."[38]

STANDARDS OF CONDUCT

11-26	The Ethical Standards in Public Life etc. (Scotland) Act 2000 required the Scottish Ministers to issue a model code of conduct for members of devolved public bodies as well as a code of conduct for councillors.[39] The public bodies listed in Sch.3 to the 2000 Act were required to submit their own version of the code to Ministers for their approval.[40] The members' model code is based on the same principles as the councillors' code (duty, selflessness, integrity, objectivity, accountability and stewardship, openness, honesty, leadership and respect). In addition to the principles, the code addresses general conduct, the registration and declaration of interests, and lobbying and access to members.[41] In contrast to councillors, who generate around 200 complaints a year, there are only a handful of complaints against members of public bodies each year.

THE SCOTTISH MINISTERS AND PUBLIC BODIES

11-27	The 2007 SNP Government, like its coalition predecessors, sought to redefine the relationship between the Scottish Government and public bodies. A key theme of the projected new relationship, which was launched under the banner "greater trust within a firm national framework", was delivery of the National Performance Framework using the "outcome based approach".[42] Public bodies were required to align their activities with the Scottish Government's purpose and the national outcomes set out in the National

---

[36] The Office of the Commissioner for Public Appointments in Scotland, *Annual Report 2007/2008*, p.24; *Annual Report 2010/2011*, p.24. The Commissioner was of the opinion that the failure to follow Code-compliant practices with regard to succession planning and re-appointment was "endemic" within the Scottish Government: Commission for Ethical Standards in Public Life in Scotland, *Annual Report 2011/2012*, p.35.

[37] Scottish Executive, *Appointments to Public Bodies: Modernising the System* (February, 2000). There is no annual report or debate.

[38] Scottish Executive, *Public Bodies: Proposals for Change* (June, 2001) para.25.

[39] ESPL(S)A 2000 s.2; for the Councillors' Code of Conduct, see para.10–17.

[40] ESPL(S)A 2000 s.3; s.32 establishes a parallel regime for members of specified Scottish public authorities.

[41] Scottish Government, *Model Code of Conduct for Members of Devolved Public Bodies* (February, 2014).

[42] Scottish Government, *First Minister's Statement on More Effective Government: Supporting Information* (January, 2008) para.17.

Performance Framework.[43] Some public bodies were also required, as we have seen, to engage with community planning partners in the delivery of single outcome agreements.[44]

Framework documents

The relationship between the Scottish Ministers and individual public bodies is **11–28** defined in a non-statutory framework document and, where relevant, the legislation or other instrument establishing the body concerned. The framework document should contain clear descriptions of key roles and responsibilities, including those of Ministers.[45] Under the model framework document contained in the Scottish Public Finance Manual, the Scottish Ministers, who are ultimately accountable to the Scottish Parliament for the activities of public bodies and their use of resources, are responsible for setting the strategic direction and the framework of accountability and governance for public bodies, but not for day to day operational matters; they also determine, subject to the requirements of governing legislation, the objectives public bodies are expected to deliver and the funding that is available to them.[46] Framework documents should be kept under review and formally reviewed at least once every three years or more frequently if required.[47]

Corporate plans

Corporate plans, normally covering a three year period, explain how public **11–29** bodies will deliver agreed objectives as well as providing the basis for monitoring and assessing their performance against agreed objectives and targets. The corporate plan, which requires ministerial approval, should therefore provide the body and Minister with: an agreed view on the long term direction of the body; a clear analysis of the environment in which the body operates, including the legislative framework, the strategic policy framework set by Ministers and the long term direction of the organisation; the contribution the body is making towards the National Performance Framework and a "meaningful number" of national outcomes; clear aims and objectives for the plan period alongside agreed targets and indicators against which performance will be measured, including the evidence that will show the body's contribution towards relevant national outcomes; a description of how the body is collaborating with government and other partners in pursuit of shared outcomes; an account of how resources and expenditure are linked to the delivery of outcomes; and details of planned efficiencies describing how the body proposes to achieve better value for money.[48]

---

[43] Scottish Government, *Outcome Based Approach: "Working" Guidance for Scottish Public Bodies* (September, 2008); *Outcome Based Approach: "Working" Guidance for Scottish Public Bodies Supplementary Note* (February, 2009); Public Bodies: Scottish Government Statement of Corporate Expectations (July, 2012).

[44] See para.10–28.

[45] NDPB Sponsorship Guidance Note 2, *Accountability: Key Roles and Responsibilities* (December, 2011) para.1.

[46] NDPB Sponsorship Guidance Note 2, *Accountability: Key Role and Responsibilities* (December, 2011) para.6; *Scottish Public Finance Manual*, Section on Accountability, Annex 3: Model Framework Document for Executive NDPBs.

[47] NDPB Sponsorship Guidance Note 2, *Accountability: Key Roles and Responsibilities* (December, 2011) para.3.

[48] NDPB Sponsorship Guidance Note 3, *Planning and Monitoring* (December, 2011) para.5.

Statutory powers

11–30 Where a public body is established by statute, Ministers retain certain powers of control in relation to the body. The extent of the powers retained will vary depending on the degree of independence the body is intended to possess in the exercise of its functions, but the retention of a significant number of powers calls into question the rationale for creating a public body in the first place. Besides power to appoint (and dismiss) the chair and other members of the governing board, the powers retained may include a requirement that the body exercise particular functions subject to guidance from Ministers, and/or in accordance with plans approved by Ministers; general or specific ministerial powers of direction; a requirement that the exercise of certain financial powers—e.g. borrowing, or capital expenditure—be subject to ministerial approval or consent; staff numbers, terms and conditions of service, and pension arrangements to be subject to ministerial approval; and powers to require the production of information which Ministers need in order to answer satisfactorily for the body's affairs.[49]

11–31 If we take the Scottish Police Authority as a recent example, Scottish Ministers have power to appoint and remove the chair and other members[50]; to make grants to the Scottish Police Authority subject to any conditions they may specify[51]; to determine the Scottish Police Authority's strategic priorities[52]; to approve the Scottish Police Authority's strategic police plan[53]; to give the Scottish Police Authority directions of a general or specific nature[54]; to approve the appointment of the chief constable[55]; to approve the location of the Scottish Police Authority's principal office premises[56]; to determine the form of the Scottish Police Authority's statement of accounts and the information it must contain[57]; and to require reports, statistics or other information from the Scottish Police Authority.[58]

11–32 All public bodies face the risk of unwarranted ministerial intervention in their affairs, in Scotland no less so than elsewhere in the UK. Although Ministers in theory are not responsible for operational matters, the approach to ministerial accountability that has evolved since devolution, according to Sir John Elvidge, a former Permanent Secretary to the Scottish Government

> "has tended to treat Ministers as accountable even for matters which are formally delegated to Non-Departmental Public Bodies or, within central government itself, to Executive Agencies. This is most striking in relation to the operational decisions and performance of Health Boards but it extends to the actions of many other bodies".[59]

---

[49] Cabinet Office, *Public Bodies: A Guide for Departments* (January, 2007) Ch.3, para.5.2, which is consistent with practice at the devolved level of government.

[50] Police and Fire Reform (Scotland) Act 2012 ("PFR(S)A 2012) Sch.1 paras 2 and 5.

[51] PFR(S)A 2012 s.88.

[52] PFR(S)A 2012 s.33.

[53] PFR(S)A 2012 s.34.

[54] PFR(S)A 2012 s.5.

[55] PFR(S)A 2012 s.7.

[56] PFR(S)A 2012 Sch.1 para.13.

[57] PFR(S)A 2012 s.40(2).

[58] PFR(S)A 2012 s.84.

[59] Sir John Elvidge, "Governance and the Institutional Framework" in Andrew Goudie (ed), *Scotland's Future: The Economics of Constitutional Change* (Dundee: Dundee University Press, 2013) pp.280–281.

Unless this approach to accountability is to be "robustly resisted", Elvidge warns, it creates "a driver towards centralisation",[60] to the possible detriment of the purposes for which public bodies were established. It also creates the risk of a blurring of responsibility and accountability, with public bodies being held responsible for matters they do not in fact control, and Ministers escaping a responsibility that is rightfully theirs.

ACCOUNTABILITY

Parliamentary accountability

Devolution has not meant an end to criticism of the lack of accountability of **11–33** Scottish public bodies; ministerial accountability continues to be treated as the hallmark of democratic accountability.[61] But just as devolution has meant that central government is exposed to much greater parliamentary scrutiny than in the past so too it has meant that delegated governance is exposed to greater scrutiny than before. The Parliament, through its committees, may invite chairs and chief executives of public bodies to attend and ask questions of them. Questions may also be asked of Ministers, including questions about the exercise or non-exercise of their powers in relation to them. Rather than refusing to answer questions on the basis that this is a matter for the public body, Ministers have sought to satisfy members by reporting information and action on the issue raised.[62] Public bodies' annual reports and accounts are also laid before the Parliament.

The Session 1 Procedures Committee considered it vital that the Parliament **11–34** develop a high profile, well-resourced and systematic approach to the scrutiny of arm's-length bodies. Without such an approach accountability and power sharing were unlikely to prove adequate. The Committee recommended that its successors consult on and produce a framework for the scrutiny of delegated governance.[63] No attempt has been made to do this, underlining the Parliament's lack of any equivalent of the Public Administration Select Committee at Westminster whose remit would include examining matters such as the relationship between the Scottish Government and public bodies or initiatives such as the National Performance Framework.[64] The Parliament's scrutiny resources are such however that it cannot realistically pursue much more than a "fire alarm" rather than "police patrol" model of oversight,[65] a weakness highlighted by the discussion of the parliamentary scrutiny of policing.[66]

---

[60] Sir John Elvidge, "Governance and the Institutional Framework" in Andrew Goudie (ed), *Scotland's Future: The Economics of Constitutional Change* (Dundee: Dundee University Press, 2013) p.281.

[61] See e.g. Geoff Mawdsley and Alison Payne, *Democratic Power* (Reform Scotland, 2010)— public bodies are not accountable in the same way as the core executive: therefore they are not accountable.

[62] Richard Parry, "Quangos, Agencies and the Scottish Parliament" in Charlie Jeffery and James Mitchell (eds), *The Scottish Parliament 1999–2009* (Edinburgh: Luath Press, 2009) p.135.

[63] Procedures Committee 3rd Report, *The Founding Principles of the Scottish Parliament: the application of Access and Participation, Equal Opportunities, Accountability and Power Sharing in the work of the Parliament* (Scottish Parliamentary Paper 818, 2003) p.557.

[64] Barry K Winetrobe, "Public Accountability in Scotland" in Aileen McHarg and Tom Mullen (eds), *Public Law in Scotland* (Edinburgh: Avizandum, 2006) pp.144–147; see also Richard Parry, "Quangos, Agencies and the Scottish Parliament" in Charlie Jeffery and James Mitchell (eds), *The Scottish Parliament 1999–2009* (Edinburgh: Luath Press, 2009) p.138.

[65] For the two models of oversight, see Matthew Flinders, *Delegated Governance and the British State: Walking Without Order* (Oxford: OUP, 2008) p.184.

[66] See para.12–19.

11–35 One category of public body whose relationship with the Parliament might be recast are scrutiny bodies such as the Accounts Commission or Healthcare Improvement Scotland engaged in the audit, inspection and regulation of public services. The Crerar Review proposed a revised model of accountability for such bodies in which independence from Ministers was balanced by responsibility to the Parliament. There was, the Review argued, an opportunity to strengthen democratic scrutiny through further refinement of the Parliament's role in the scrutiny process and for Parliament to be more proactive in seeking assurance that public services were well-managed, safe and fit for purpose and that public money was being used properly. This would involve placing a strong and appropriate duty on scrutiny bodies to give an account for their activities and use of resources to the Parliament, which would in turn require adapting the existing governance and reporting arrangements for scrutiny bodies.[67]

11–36 The Accountability and Governance Action Group, one of five action groups set up by Ministers to devise practical ways of implementing the Review's recommendations, was sceptical. While endorsing a "strong role" for the Parliament, the Group concluded that the Parliament's powers, "if co-ordinated and used more consistently, were already entirely adequate to hold scrutiny bodies to account". It added that scrutiny bodies represented in the group would welcome a more active and co-ordinated role for the Parliament in relation to their work.[68] Notwithstanding the Group's scepticism, there is no reason why different categories of public body should not have different relationships with the Parliament. As it is, however, the Parliament's relationship with public bodies continues to be mediated by Ministers.

Other forms of accountability

11–37 Public bodies are sometimes said to operate in a world of "multiple accountabilities", which in the devolved context has been defined as meaning that they have

> "a duty to continuously improve and strengthen their links to stakeholders, users, customers and the general public, as well as to be accountable to Ministers and Parliament".[69]

In *Public Bodies: Proposals for Change*, the first Scottish Executive announced its intention to require boards to become "even more open, accountable and effective" by making them consult users and the public, partner organisations and local authorities more imaginatively, and by requiring them to make information about their activities available more widely.[70] Public bodies are thus expected to have decision making processes that are open, transparent and

---

[67] Crerar Review, *The Report of the Independent Review of Regulation, Audit, Inspection and Complaints Handling of Public Services in Scotland* (September, 2007) para.5.10.

[68] Crerar Review, *The Report of the Independent Review of Regulation, Audit, Inspection and Complaints Handling of Public Services in Scotland* (September, 2007) para.4.

[69] Scottish Executive, *Public Bodies: Proposals for Change* (June, 2001) para.14; for a more recent statement of the same point, see *Scottish Government and Scotland's NDPBs: Accountability and Governance* (December, 2011) para.8.

[70] Scottish Executive, *Public Bodies: Proposals for Change* (June, 2001) paras 27–28; many of the proposals traced their origins to the 1997 Labour Government's White Paper, *Quangos: Opening the Doors* (1998), which set out "proposals to make the operation of bodies more open, to make the appointments system more transparent, and to enhance the accountability of bodies through increased public consultation, open meetings, and strengthened links with local government".

informed by the needs of stakeholders, customers and employees.[71] They are also required to have in place an effective and accessible complaints handling system which is consistent with guidance from the Scottish Public Services Ombudsman.[72]

For the most part "downward accountability" through open meetings, consul- **11–38** tation and the like has been pursued as a matter of encouragement rather than legal obligation. Under the Public Services Reform (Scotland) Act 2010, however, "listed scrutiny authorities" are required to make arrangements which secure and demonstrate continuous improvement in user focus in the exercise of their scrutiny functions[73]; "scheduled scrutiny authorities" are also required to co-operate with each other, and where appropriate, the Scottish Ministers, with a view to improving the exercise of their scrutiny functions in relation to local authorities, social services and health services, having regard to efficiency, effectiveness and economy.[74]

---

[71] NDPB Sponsorship Guidance Note 4, *Effective Boards* (December, 2011) para.16.
[72] NDPB Sponsorship Guidance Note 4, *Effective Boards* (December, 2011) para.22.
[73] PSR(S)A 2010 s.112.
[74] PSR(S)A 2010 s.114; note also the reporting duties imposed on listed public bodies by ss.31–32.

CHAPTER 12

THE POLICE

"One service, police, must be mentioned specifically, since constitutionally it has anomalous features."[1]

INTRODUCTION

Policing was a local government function in origin, but as the Royal **12–01** Commission on Local Government in Scotland observed in 1969 it was not a local government function like any other.[2] For one thing, a police authority was not strictly speaking responsible for the policing of its area; its job was essentially that of maintaining and equipping an efficient police force and ensuring its proper administration.[3] For another, the relationship between central and local government was different from that in other branches of local authority work; the central government was "concerned with and accountable for the police service to quite an exceptional degree".[4] But its most unusual feature, to which the Royal Commission made only passing reference, was the degree of independence or autonomy accorded to the third element of the tripartite framework within which policing was carried on—the chief constable of the force—an independence justified in the interests of insulating the force from improper local pressures, but the uncertain limits to which meant that the business of policing was subject to few external checks.[5]

The Royal Commission thought that there was real value in continuing to treat **12–02** the police as a local service, but that should the needs of policing cease to match the pattern of local government the advantages claimed for associating the police with local government would be much weakened.[6] The association between the police and local government was to be weakened, but not as a result of the changing needs of policing. With local government reorganisation in 1975, policing became a regional responsibility, but when the regions were

---

[1] JDB Mitchell, *Constitutional Law*, 2nd edn (Edinburgh: W.Green, 1968) p.247.

[2] The Wheatley Report, *Report of the Royal Commission on Local Government in Scotland* (1969) Cmnd.4150, para.477; on the origins of Scottish policing, see David G Barrie, *Police in the Age of Improvement: Police development and the civil tradition in Scotland, 1775–1865* (Oxford: Willan Publishing, 2008), and Kit Carson and Hilary Idzikowska, "The Social Production of Scottish Policing, 1795–1900" in Douglas Hay and Francis Snyder (eds), *Policing and Prosecution in Britain 1750–1850* (Oxford: OUP, 1989).

[3] The Wheatley Report, *Report of the Royal Commission on Local Government in Scotland* (1969) Cmnd.4150, para.477.

[4] The Wheatley Report, *Report of the Royal Commission on Local Government in Scotland* (1969) Cmnd.4150, para.482.

[5] The Wheatley Report, *Report of the Royal Commission on Local Government in Scotland* (1969) Cmnd.4150, para.482; on the doctrine of constabulary independence, or the "duty of operational independence" as it is now described in Scotland, see Neil Walker, *Policing in a Changing Constitutional Order* (London: Sweet & Maxwell, 2000) pp.44–53.

[6] The Wheatley Report, *Report of the Royal Commission on Local Government in Scotland* (1969) Cmnd.4150, para.483.

dismantled 20 years later the Conservative government saw no overriding need to change the regional structure of policing, given the scope for the introduction of joint arrangements. The result was to leave Strathclyde Police, Scotland's largest police force, subject to the nominal oversight of a joint police board made up of representatives of no fewer than 12 local authorities.[7] At the same time the role of central government continued to expand, most notably as a result of the Police and Magistrates' Courts Act 1994.[8] The tripartite system of police governance and accountability, however, was left unchanged.

12–03 With devolution most policing functions were devolved, the principal exception being those relating to national security.[9] Devolution, however, did not signal an immediate end to the culture of "pragmatism and minimalism" that had characterised the Scottish Office's approach to policing.[10] A review of the organisation of policing commissioned by the Scottish Ministers immediately after devolution recommended that the number of forces remain unchanged but that the range of common police services be extended.[11] The latter, including the Scottish Drug Enforcement Agency, were put on a statutory basis by the Police, Public Order and Criminal Justice (Scotland) Act 2006. Financial retrenchment was to provide the spur to further restructuring, and with it a reshaping of police governance and accountability. In a consultation paper published in February 2011 the Scottish Government argued that gaps in governance and accountability together with the complexity of collaboration and partnership working and increasing financial pressures meant that the status quo was no longer sustainable.[12] Most policing was local and community based but local authorities had no direct say in the policing of their area, while at the national level there was no "consistent form of accountability for national policing functions".[13]

---

[7] The Royal Commission thought it essential that the link with local government be direct; the fundamental objection in its eyes to joint arrangements was that police boards were "not directly responsible to anybody": the Wheatley Report, *Report of the Royal Commission on Local Government in Scotland* (1969) Cmnd.4150, paras 484 and 629. In the event, the persistent complaint was not that joint police boards were not directly responsible but that they exercised little real oversight over the service: see, e.g. Audit Scotland, *Best Value in police authorities and police forces in Scotland: Overview report* (November, 2012).

[8] Neil Walker, "Police and Government in Scotland: A Constitutional Landmark" 1995 S.L.T. (News) 199.

[9] Scotland Act 1998 ("SA 1998") Sch.5 Pt II s.B8.

[10] Neil Walker, *Policing in a Changing Constitutional Order* (London: Sweet & Maxwell, 2000) p.167; an independent review of policing commissioned in 2008 suggested that less attention was given to policing after devolution than before—because most policing matters had been dealt with by the Home Office: HMICS, *Independent review of policing in Scotland: A report for the Cabinet Secretary for Justice* (January, 2009) App.A.

[11] Scottish Executive, *Supporting Police, Protecting Communities: Proposals for Legislation* (February, 2005) para.2.1.

[12] Scottish Government, *A Consultation on the Future of Policing in Scotland* (February, 2011) para.61; in 2008, the Parliament's Justice Committee had recommended that the Scottish Government initiate an independent review of the role and responsibilities of the police in Scotland: 4th Report, *Report on Inquiry into the Effective Use of Police Resources* (Scottish Parliamentary Paper 50, 2008) para.364. The subsequent independent review of policing argued that there was a need for greater clarity over governance and accountability and that the time was right for the Scottish Government "to provide that clarity as well as to re-balance the tripartite arrangement so that both police authorities/boards and Government itself can play more active parts in maintaining and improving policing in Scotland": HMICS, *Independent review of policing in Scotland: A report for the Cabinet Secretary for Justice* (January, 2009) App.A.

[13] Scottish Government, *A Consultation on the Future of Policing in Scotland* (February, 2011) paras 42–43.

"It is our view that, whatever the future structure of Scotland's police forces, there needs to be clearer responsibility and accountability at the national level for national policing issues and capability."[14]

The consultation paper identified three options for reform: enhanced collaboration between the existing eight forces[15]; a rationalised regional model with three or four forces; and a single national force. In September 2011, the Scottish Government announced that it would bring forward legislation to create a single police service—the Police Service of Scotland.

THE POLICE AND FIRE REFORM (SCOTLAND) ACT 2012

The Police and Fire Reform (Scotland) Act 2012 ("the 2012 Act") established the **12–04** framework for a single police service (and single fire and rescue service). One of the key issues raised by reform was the relationship between the Scottish Ministers and the new service, given the accepted need for policing to be free and to be seen to be free from political interference. The 2012 Act's solution was to structure the relationship between the Scottish Ministers and the Police Service along conventional public body lines, with a Scottish Police Authority ("SPA") serving as a buffer between the Scottish Ministers and the Police Service. The Scottish Ministers are, therefore, responsible for the strategic direction and funding of the Service, the SPA for governing the Police Service and holding the chief constable to account, and the chief constable for leading and managing the Police Service.

The 2012 Act also lays down a set of policing principles to which the Scottish **12–05** Ministers, the SPA and the chief constable are obliged to have regard in carrying out their responsibilities. The policing principles define the main purpose of policing as being "to improve the safety and well-being of persons, localities and communities in Scotland"; they also enjoin the Police Service, working in collaboration with others where appropriate, to endeavour to achieve that purpose by policing in a way which "is accessible to, and engaged with, local communities", and "promotes measures to prevent crime, harm and disorder".[16] While the 2012 Act includes safeguards of the "operational independence" of policing (below), the independence of policing is not among the principles to which the Scottish Ministers and the SPA must have regard in carrying out their responsibilities.

THE SCOTTISH POLICE AUTHORITY

The SPA's purpose within the general scheme of the 2012 Act is to ensure **12–06** a "clear separation" between the Scottish Ministers and the Police Service of Scotland.[17] The Act defines the Authority's main functions as being: to

---

[14] Scottish Government, *A Consultation on the Future of Policing in Scotland* (February, 2011) para.49.

[15] The consultation paper was pessimistic about the prospects for collaboration. "There is insufficient evidence to conclude that collaboration on its own will deliver the necessary capability and capacity to the timetable needed to keep pace with budget reductions and to maintain frontline services": Scottish Government, *A Consultation on the Future of Policing in Scotland* (February, 2011) para.35. The pessimism of the consultation paper may be contrasted with the Scottish Government's optimism about the prospects for collaboration elsewhere in the public sector.

[16] Police and Fire Reform (Scotland) Act 2012 ("PFR(S)A 2012") s.32.

[17] Scottish Government, *Keeping Scotland Safe and Strong: A Consultation on Reforming Police and Fire And Rescue Services in Scotland* (September, 2011) para.3.1.

maintain the Police Service; to promote the statutory "policing principles"; to promote and support continuous improvement in the policing of Scotland; to keep under review the policing of Scotland; and to hold the chief constable to account for the policing of Scotland.[18] The Authority consists of a chair and between 10 and 14 other members appointed by the Scottish Ministers from persons they consider to have the skills and expertise relevant to the functions of the Authority.[19] The 2012 Act provides that the Authority must try to carry out its functions in a way that is "proportionate, accountable and transparent and which is consistent with any principle of good governance which appears to it to constitute best practice".[20]

The Scottish Ministers and the Scottish Police Authority

12–07   The relationship between the Scottish Ministers and the SPA is defined in the Act and a non-statutory framework document.[21] In addition to determining the SPA's budget through the annual budgetary process, the Scottish Ministers have power under the 2012 Act to determine the SPA's strategic priorities and to approve its strategic police plan. They also retain a power of direction over the SPA.

Strategic police priorities

12–08   The Act empowers the Scottish Ministers to determine the SPA's strategic priorities, which may relate to the policing of Scotland or to the carrying out of the SPA's functions.[22] The Scottish Ministers must have regard to the policing principles when determining the SPA's strategic priorities.[23] The SPA's strategic priorities must be published and a copy laid before the Scottish Parliament.[24]

Strategic police plan

12–09   The Act requires the SPA to prepare a strategic police plan for the approval of the Scottish Ministers. The plan must: set out the main objectives for the SPA and for the policing of Scotland; explain the reasons for selecting each main objective; describe what the SPA considers should be done by it or by the Police Service in order to achieve the main objectives; where reasonably practicable, identify outcomes by reference to which the achievement of the main objectives may be measured; and include any other information connected with the SPA's functions, or policing, that the SPA considers appropriate.[25] The 2012 Act prescribes in some detail the procedure to be followed by the SPA in the preparation of a plan: it must make arrangements for obtaining the views of "persons whom it considers likely to have an interest in policing"; it must involve the chief constable in the preparation of a plan, who must provide it with such assistance as it may reasonably require; and it must send a copy of the draft plan for comment to each local authority, the inspectors of constabulary and such other persons as it considers likely to have an interest in

---

[18] PFR(S)A 2012 s.2(1).

[19] PFR(S)A 2012 Sch.1 para.2.

[20] PFR(S)A 2012 s.2(3).

[21] Scottish Government, *The Scottish Police Authority Governance and Accountability Framework Document* (January, 2014).

[22] PFR(S)A 2012 s.33(1), (2).

[23] PFR(S)A 2012 s.33(4).

[24] PFR(S)A 2012 s.33(5), (6); the SPA's four strategic priorities are directed to: making communities safer and reducing harm, strengthening Scotland's reputation as a successful and safe country, providing an efficient, effective service, and making communities stronger and improving wellbeing by increasing public confidence and reducing fear of crime.

[25] PFR(S)A 2012 s.34(2).

the plan.[26] The 2012 Act expressly provides that the SPA must have regard to the policing principles in the preparation of the plan; it must also have regard to, and ensure that the plan is not inconsistent with, its strategic priorities.[27] The Act leaves open the question of what happens in the event that the Scottish Ministers do not approve the plan, but the SPA is required to use its "best endeavours to secure their approval of the plan (with or without modifications)".[28] Where a plan is approved it must be published and laid before the Scottish Parliament.[29] The SPA must review an approved plan at least once every three years, and either prepare a replacement plan or notify the Scottish Ministers that there is no need to replace the existing plan.[30]

Directions

The Scottish Ministers also have the power to give the SPA general or specific **12–10** directions, with which the SPA must comply.[31] Their power of direction does not extend to "a specific operation being or to be carried out by the Police Service", or "the way in which the Police Service is carrying out (or is to carry out) a specific operation".[32] The power of direction was one of the more controversial features of the legislation. The Scottish Government rejected the argument that there was no need for it, but anticipated it being used only "as a last resort, including when necessary to give effect to the will of Parliament".[33] Where directions are given, they must be published and laid before the Scottish Parliament.[34]

THE CHIEF CONSTABLE

The chief constable "is responsible, and must account to the SPA, for the **12–11** policing of Scotland".[35] This general responsibility embraces a number of particular responsibilities, which include: the "direction and control" of the police service[36]; the "day to day administration" of the service, including the allocation and deployment of resources received from the SPA[37]; and seeking to secure continuous improvement in the policing of Scotland (in which regard the chief constable is under a duty to make arrangements that secure best value for the police service).[38] The chief constable and other senior officers of the Police Service are appointed by the SPA, the chief constable with the approval of Scottish Ministers, the deputy and assistant chief constables after consultation with the chief constable.[39]

---

[26] PFR(S)A 2012 s.34(3)–(5).
[27] PFR(S)A 2012 s.36.
[28] PFR(S)A 2012 s.34(6).
[29] PFR(S)A 2012 s.34(7); the SPA's strategic police plan was laid before the Parliament in March 2013.
[30] PFR(S)A 2012 s.34(8).
[31] PFR(S)A 2012 s.5(1); the Scottish Ministers also have the power to give the SPA directions following an adverse report from Her Majesty's Inspectorate of Constabulary for Scotland: PFR(S)A 2012 s.81
[32] PFR(S)A 2012 s.5(2).
[33] Scottish Government, *Keeping Scotland Safe and Strong: A Consultation on Reforming Police and Fire And Rescue Services in Scotland* (September, 2011) para.3.10.
[34] PFR(S)A 2012 s.5(3).
[35] PFR(S)A 2012 s.17(1).
[36] PFR(S)A 2012 ss.17(2)(a) and 21.
[37] PFR(S)A 2012 s.17(2)(b).
[38] PFR(S)A 2012 ss.17(2)(e) and 37(2).
[39] PFR(S)A 2012 s.7.

Annual police plan

12–12   The 2012 Act provides that the chief constable must seek to ensure that the policing of Scotland is done with due regard to the policing principles, and in accordance with the strategic police priorities, the most recently approved strategic police plan, and the "relevant annual police plan".[40] The annual plan, which is prepared by the chief constable, sets out the proposed arrangements for the policing of Scotland during the year in question, describes how those arrangements are expected to contribute towards the achievement of the main objectives for the policing of Scotland set out in the strategic police plan, and includes any other information connected with policing which the chief constable considers appropriate.[41] In the preparation of the plan, the chief constable must have regard to the policing principles and the strategic police priorities, and ensure that the plan is not inconsistent with the strategic police priorities and the most recently approved strategic police plan.[42] The plan is scrutinised by the SPA but does not require its approval; the chief constable is required only to send a copy of a draft plan to the SPA and to have regard to any comments received from the SPA within a specified period.[43] The plan must be published and laid before the Scottish Parliament.[44]

The Scottish Police Authority and the chief constable

12–13   The chief constable does not stand in the same relationship to the SPA as the chief executive of a public body stands to its governing board. Although the chief constable is accountable to the SPA for the policing of Scotland, the SPA has no power to give the chief constable directions, only a power to make recommendations and issue guidance on the policing of Scotland, which must not be inconsistent with the strategic police priorities, the most recently approved strategic police plan, and any guidance or instructions issued to the chief constable by the Lord Advocate or a procurator fiscal in relation to the investigation or reporting of offences.[45] Nor does the SPA have the power to dismiss the chief constable if the policing of Scotland is not to its liking, only a power to call on the chief constable to resign or, where appropriate, retire from office in the interests of the efficiency or effectiveness of the Police Service, which power is exercisable only after consulting the Scottish Ministers.[46] The chief constable thus enjoys a degree of security of tenure that, like the absence of a power of direction, may be seen as an important safeguard of the "continued independence" of policing. The 2012 Act stops short, however, of the express guarantee of independence found for example in relation to the judiciary, perhaps for fear that it would complicate the relationship between the SPA and the chief constable, which even before the new arrangements came into force seemed difficult enough without the added complication of a statutory guarantee of independence.[47]

---

[40] PFR(S)A 2012 s.17(4).
[41] PFR(S)A 2012 s.35(2).
[42] PFR(S)A 2012 s.36.
[43] PFR(S)A 2012 s.35(3).
[44] PFR(S)A 2012 s.35(4).
[45] PFR(S)A 2012 s.17(5), (6).
[46] PFR(S)A 2012 s.14; the SPA is also the disciplinary authority for senior officers under the Police Service of Scotland (Senior Officers) (Conduct) Scotland Regulations 2013 (SSI 2013/62).
[47] Audit Scotland, *Police reform: Progress update 2013* (November, 2013).

Instructions from judges and prosecutors

The chief constable remains under the same duty as his predecessors to comply **12–14** with "lawful" instructions from the "appropriate prosecutor" in relation to the investigation of offences, and from the Lord Advocate with regard to the reporting of offences for consideration of the question of prosecution.[48] The Lord Justice General and the sheriff principal for the place where police operations are to be carried out, also have the power to issue instructions to the chief constable.[49] The sheriff principal's power of direction is the sole remaining vestige of a responsibility once shared by the sheriff, justices and magistrates for the maintenance of public order.[50] It is not clear why it was extended to the Lord Justice General, but it may be that it was thought anomalous for a sheriff principal but not the Lord Justice General to have such a power in relation to what is now a national rather than a local service. Given the absence of a clear continuing rationale, however, it might have been better to abolish the power altogether.

LOCAL POLICING

As well as the opportunity to improve accountability at a national level, **12–15** restructuring was seen as providing the opportunity to "devolve greater responsibility at the local level with improvements in local engagement and accountability".[51] Local authorities were to be given a direct say in the policing of their areas, something they had lost in all but two cases (Dumfries and Galloway, and Fife) as a result of local government reorganisation in 1995. The chief constable, who must ensure that there are adequate arrangements in place for the policing of each local authority area,[52] must therefore, after consulting the local authority, designate a local commander for each local authority area, who must in turn involve the local authority in the setting of priorities and objectives for the policing of its area.[53] The principal means of involving local authorities in the setting of priorities and objectives is through local police plans, which local commanders were required to prepare and submit to local authorities for their approval following approval of the first strategic police plan.[54] A local plan must set out the main priorities and objectives for the policing of a local authority's area; explain the reasons for selecting each of those priorities and objectives; set out the proposed arrangements for the policing of a local authority's area (and how those arrangements are expected to achieve the main priorities and objectives); where reasonably practicable, identify outcomes by reference to which the achievement of those priorities and objectives may be measured; describe how those priorities, objectives and arrangements are expected to contribute to the delivery of any other relevant local outcomes that are identified by community planning; and

---

[48] PFR(S)A 2012 s.17(3); the Lord Advocate's instructions are issued under the Criminal Procedure (Scotland) Act 1995 s.12.

[49] PFR(S)A 2012 s.17(3).

[50] James Mill, *The Scottish Police: An Outline of their Powers and Duties* (Edinburgh: W.Green, 1944) pp.30–33; see e.g. *Beaton v Ivory* 1887 14 R. 1057. See also *Dumfries County Council v Phyn*, 1895 22 R. 538 at 550 (Lord President Robertson).

[51] Scottish Government, *A Consultation on the Future of Policing in Scotland* (February, 2011) para.9.

[52] PFR(S)A 2012 s.44(1).

[53] PFR(S)A 2012 ss.44(2) and 45(1); the same commander may be designated for more than one local authority area: s.44(3); there are some 14 local policing divisions led by local commanders and supported by 73 area commanders.

[54] PFR(S)A 2012 s.47(1).

include any other information connected with the policing of a local authority's area that the local commander considers relevant.[55] In the preparation of a plan, the local commander must have regard to the most recently approved strategic police plan.[56] A local authority may also specify policing measures it wishes the commander to include in a plan.[57] As with the strategic police plan, the Act leaves open the question of what happens in the event that a local authority does not approve a plan, e.g. because it does not include measures it wishes to see included. Approved local policing plans must be published, and reviewed at a minimum of three yearly intervals.[58] Local policing plans have been drawn up for each of the 353 multi-member ward areas as well as the 32 local authority areas.

12–16 The local commander also participates in community planning on behalf of the chief constable with a view to ensuring that local policing priorities reflect the wider locally agreed priorities for the area.[59]

ACCOUNTABILITY

12–17 The accountability of policing attracted more attention in the course of the scrutiny of the legislation than the insulation of the service from improper political pressures. At the national level the chain of accountability runs from the chief constable through the SPA to the Scottish Ministers. The SPA's main functions, as we have seen, include holding the chief constable to account for the policing of Scotland, while the chief constable is under a statutory obligation to account to the SPA for the policing of Scotland.[60] The chief constable must therefore provide the SPA with an annual report of his assessment of the Police Service's performance in the policing of Scotland.[61] The SPA may also require information from the chief constable relating to the Police Service, police functions or the state of crime.[62] If the chief constable considers that complying with the requirement would or might prejudice the carrying out of any operation by the Police Service or the prosecution of offenders, he may refer the requirement to the Scottish Ministers, in which case the requirement has effect only if confirmed by them.[63] Whether the SPA will prove any more effective than the former joint police boards in holding the chief constable to account remains to be seen; the early signs, however, have not been encouraging (below).

12–18 The SPA, for its part, is accountable to the Scottish Ministers for its performance in carrying out its functions, including its performance in holding the chief constable to account. It is required to prepare an annual report setting out an assessment of its performance in carrying out its functions, an assessment of the Police Service's performance in the policing of Scotland, and such other information relating to its functions, or to policing, as it considers appropriate.[64] It is also under an obligation to provide the Scottish Ministers

---

[55] PFR(S)A 2012 s.47(2).
[56] PFR(S)A 2012 s.47(3).
[57] PFR(S)A 2012 s.45(3).
[58] PFR(S)A 2012 s.47(4), (5).
[59] PFR(S)A 2012 s.46.
[60] PFR(S)A 2012 ss.2(2)(e) and 17(1).
[61] PFR(S)A 2012 s.39(4).
[62] PFR(S)A 2012 s.84(3).
[63] PFR(S)A 2012 s.84(4), (5).
[64] PFR(S)A 2012 s.39(1)–(3).

with such reports, statistics or other information relating to the SPA or the Police Service as they may reasonably require.[65] Its annual report must be published, provided to the Scottish Ministers, and laid before the Scottish Parliament.[66]

The SPA and chief constable are also accountable to the Scottish Parliament. **12–19** The SPA's annual report is laid before the Scottish Parliament, as are its strategic priorities, the strategic policing plan and annual plans, and any directions, recommendations and guidance. There is no requirement of parliamentary approval of the strategic priorities laid down by Ministers or of the SPA's strategic policing plan but it would be open to the Parliament's Justice Committee to take evidence from the Cabinet Secretary, the SPA and the chief constable as well as local councils and community representatives.[67] During the parliamentary proceedings on the Bill, concerns were expressed about the likely sufficiency of parliamentary scrutiny and amendments put forward for a Scottish Policing Commission, made up of MSPs, that would be responsible for keeping the arrangements for policing under review. These were withdrawn on the understanding that further talks would take place to find ways of improving accountability through "more pro-active parliamentary scrutiny". The Parliament has set up a subcommittee of the Justice Committee to oversee the operation of the 2012 Act as it relates to policing, but this is an ad hoc solution for Session 4 only and not a permanent arrangement.

At the local level the expectation is that local authorities will monitor and scru- **12–20** tinise performance against local policing plans. The 2012 Act provides that a local authority may monitor and provide feedback to the local commander on the policing of its area—though why it should have been felt necessary to empower it to do so is not obvious.[68] An authority may therefore require reports from the local commander on the carrying out of police functions in its area (including by reference to any local policing plan in force for the area), statistical information on complaints made about the Police Service in, or the policing of, its area, and other information about the policing of its area. If, however, the local commander considers that complying with the requirement would or might prejudice the carrying out of any operation by the Police Service or the prosecution of offenders, the commander may refer the requirement to the chief constable, in which case it has effect only if confirmed by the chief constable.[69] The local authority has no power to remove the local commander, but there would be nothing to prevent it from making the reasons for its dissatisfaction known.

The 2012 Act left open the means by which local authorities would become **12–21** involved in the preparation of local plans and the scrutiny of performance against those plans, e.g. by setting up a dedicated police committee. Acknowledging the widespread criticisms of the performance of joint police authorities before restructuring, the Government made it clear that it expected the chair or convenor of the local mechanism to provide effective leadership of the relationship between the council and the police and to ensure other services

---

[65] PFR(S)A 2012 s.84(1).
[66] PFR(S)A 2012 s.39(6).
[67] Scottish Government, *Keeping Scotland Safe and Strong: A Consultation on Reforming Police and Fire And Rescue Services in Scotland* (September, 2011) para.3.26.
[68] PFR(S)A 2012 s.45(2), (4).
[69] PFR(S)A 2012 s.45(5)–(7).

worked effectively with the police to secure delivery of local outcomes.[70] The first anniversary of the new force saw complaints that local authorities were not doing enough to hold local police commanders to account; to which local authorities replied that with the machinery of joint police boards having been dismantled they no longer had the infrastructure or the resources with which to play a meaningful role in the scrutiny of local policing.

ASSESSMENT

12–22 Although there had been no lack of criticism of the "anomalous features" of policing beforehand—the uncertain limits to the "operational independence" enjoyed by chief constables coupled with the lack of effective oversight—it is difficult to avoid the conclusion that it was the rationalisation of the existing structure in the interests of cost saving rather than considerations of governance and accountability that was uppermost in the framing of Act.[71] Aside from the substitution of the SPA for local authorities, and its unusually heavy reliance on the language of management, the Act did little more than recreate the previous tripartite framework, with perhaps predictable results. The most serious conflict to have arisen so far has been over the deployment of armed officers, criticism of which was at first dismissed on the grounds that it was an operational matter for the chief constable, before the policy was eventually revised in the face of widespread political opposition, including from local authorities.[72] Controversy has also arisen over the industrial scale use of stop and search in the major cities and suggestions of a move away from local variations of the style of policing towards the top-down imposition of a single "Strathclyde model" across Scotland. Clearly, there is much to be done if the new arrangements are to represent an improvement in terms of the governance and accountability of Scottish policing as well as efficiency and effectiveness.

POLICE COMPLAINTS

12–23 It was not until 2006 that provision was made for the independent review of the handling of complaints against the police in Scotland—some 30 years after such provision was first made for England and Wales by the Police Act 1976.[73] The

---

[70] Scottish Government, *Keeping Scotland Safe and Strong: A Consultation on Reforming Police and Fire And Rescue Services in Scotland* (September, 2011) para.3.21.

[71] An Audit Scotland report found that, while much had been achieved before the new service was launched, the move to a single police service had been hampered by poor information, conflicting interpretations of the Act (over what the SPA's responsibility for "maintaining" the police service involved), and difficult relationships between the Scottish Government, the SPA and Police Scotland: *Police reform: Progress update 2013* (November, 2013). In an unprecedented move for a parliamentary audit committee, the Parliament's Public Audit Committee divided along party lines over its response to Audit Scotland's report: Public Audit Committee 3rd Report, *Report on Police Reform* (Scottish Parliamentary Paper 496, 2014).

[72] HM Inspectorate of Constabulary in Scotland, *Review of Standing Firearms Authority for Armed Response Vehicle Crews within Police Scotland* (October, 2014).

[73] The Police (Scotland) Bill 1976 made provision for a Police Complaints Panel for Scotland but it was withdrawn in the face of opposition from the police. Under the Police and Magistrates' Court Act 1994 s.61, a complainant could ask Her Majesty's Inspectorate of Constabulary for Scotland to examine the manner in which a complaint had been dealt with. In *Ruddy v Chief Constable of Strathclyde Police and the Lord Advocate* [2013] CSIH 73, an Extra Division of the Inner House held that the absence of an independent element meant that the arrangements were not ECHR compliant.

Police, Public Order and Criminal Justice (Scotland) Act 2006 established a Police Complaints Commissioner for Scotland with power to review the handling of non-criminal complaints against the police; criminal complaints continued to be referred to the Crown Office and Procurator Fiscal Service after a preliminary investigation as before. The Police and Fire Reform (Scotland) Act 2012 renamed the Commissioner the Police Investigations and Review Commissioner, and extended the Commissioner's functions to include the investigation of criminal allegations and other "serious incidents" involving the police, which previously would have been investigated by officers from another force, the former where directed to do so by the appropriate prosecutor, the latter where requested to do so by the SPA or chief constable.[74] The Commissioner was also given the power to investigate other police matters at the Commissioner's own initiative where an investigation is considered to be in the public interest.[75] In 2013–2014 the Commissioner carried out 39 investigations, 18 at the direction of the Crown Office, as a result of which 34 recommendations were made to Police Scotland and three to the SPA. The Commissioner also carried out 592 complaint handling reviews, as a result of which 242 recommendations were made, a number of which were directed to improving systems and processes within police bodies, rather than individual complaint issues.[76]

---

[74] PFR(S)A 2012 ss.61–62.
[75] PFR(S)A 2012 s.62.
[76] Police Investigations and Review Commissioner, *Establish, Engage, Evidence: PIRC Annual Report 2013–2014* (2014).

CHAPTER 13

LEGISLATION

INTRODUCTION

The Scottish Parliament was not meant to be the "Scottish Westminster", a **13–01** "legislative sausage machine" churning out laws on the Westminster model.[1] It was meant to be different. What being "not like Westminster"[2] might mean for law-making was not widely discussed before devolution, but one possibility was a legislative process in which the Parliament played a more significant role than traditionally had been the case at Westminster—in Polsby's terms, a "transformative" rather than an "arena" legislature with a greater degree of independence from the executive than Westminster.[3] Such at least seems to have been the goal of some commentators at the time of devolution. Crick and Millar thus looked forward to a system in which the executive "need not and should not have such total domination over the legislative process as has evolved at Westminster".[4] What has emerged, however, is a process in which Westminster assumptions about the exercise of legislative power continue to hold sway, and which is therefore much closer to the Westminster model than the Constitutional Convention and others envisaged. Coalition governments with comfortable working majorities in the Parliament's first two sessions partly account for this—possession of a parliamentary majority was treated as bringing with it the right to pursue a legislative programme[5]—but a minority government in the third session did not result in any change in the pattern established in those years. Lacking an overall majority, the SNP Government legislated less but—as was observed at the time—there was

---

[1] Scottish Parliament OR September 5, 2001, col.2211 (David McLetchie).

[2] The phrase is Winetrobe's: Barry K Winetrobe, *Realising the Vision: A Parliament with a Purpose* (London: Constitution Unit, 2001) p.12.

[3] Polsby's analysis locates legislatures on a spectrum of legislative power, ranging from "transformative" legislatures at one end to "arena" legislatures at the other. Transformative legislatures "possess the independent capacity, frequently exercised, to mould and transform proposals from whatever source into laws". Arena legislatures by contrast, "serve as formalised settings for the interplay of significant political forces in the life of the political system". "Britain is customarily, and understandably, identified as the home of an arena like legislature": Nelson W Polsby, "Legislatures" in Fred I Greenstein and Nelson W Polsby (eds), *Handbook of Political Science*, Vol.5, *Government Institutions and Processes* (Reading, Mass: Addison Wesley, 1975) pp.277–278 and 281.

[4] Bernard Crick and David Millar, *To Make the Parliament of Scotland a Model for Democracy* (Glasgow: John Wheatley Centre, 1995) p.5.

[5] In evidence to the Procedures Committee in Session 1, the Minister for Parliament insisted that " ... the Executive's first and foremost duty is to deliver the programme for government on which it was elected. That has involved, and will continue to involve, an ambitious and substantial legislative programme": Procedures Committee 3rd Report, *The Founding Principles of the Scottish Parliament: the application of Access and Participation, Equal Opportunities, Accountability and Power Sharing in the work of the Parliament* (Scottish Parliamentary Paper 818, 2003) para.52.

"no rush by the opposition parties to fill the legislative void. They remain[ed] comfortable with the Westminster model of law-making and an opportunity for a greater share of the spoils come the next election".[6]

THE LEGISLATIVE INITIATIVE

13–02 Public Bills may be introduced by the Scottish Government, by individual MSPs or by committees, the latter in a departure from the Westminster pattern. As was anticipated by the Consultative Steering Group, which was set up by the Secretary of State to recommend the procedures the Parliament might be invited to adopt, most of the legislation passed by the Parliament has been initiated by the Scottish Government, with Government Bills accounting for 50 of the 62 Bills passed in Session 1; 53 of the 66 in Session 2; 41 of the 53 in Session 3; and 32 of the 36 passed in the first three years of Session 4.[7] In its report on the application of the Parliament's founding principles in the first session, the Parliament's Procedures Committee defended the "substantial volume of Executive inspired law" as not necessarily at odds with the principle of power sharing, but envisaged the proportion of non-Executive Bills increasing, and thought it vital that this process be encouraged by the allocation of sufficient resources, including the allocation of committee and plenary time.[8]

CABINET SUBCOMMITTEE ON LEGISLATION

13–03 The Scottish Executive started out with no machinery for planning or managing a legislative programme.[9] The gap was filled over the course of the first session:

> "Procedurally, within the Executive, a growing realisation of the amount of legislation it was promoting, of the extent to which legislation could be used to obtain political and practical results and of its centrality to governmental and parliamentary business, has brought about increasingly sophisticated internal procedures for the planning, monitoring and progress-chasing of the Executive's legislative programme and of the individual Bills in it."[10]

13–04 At the heart of the current government's legislative machinery is a cabinet subcommittee on legislation made up of the Deputy First Minister and Cabinet Secretary for Finance, Constitution and Economy, the Minister for

---

[6] James Johnston, "The Legislative Process: The Parliament in Practice" in Charlie Jeffery and James Mitchell (eds), *The Scottish Parliament 1999–2009: The First Decade* (Edinburgh: Luath Press, 2009) p.35.

[7] Scottish Office, *Shaping Scotland's Parliament: Report of the Consultative Steering Group of the Scottish Parliament* (December, 1998) s.3.5.5; these figures do not include government "hand-out" Bills, i.e. Members' Bills that are Government Bills in all but name. The Mortgage Rights (Scotland) Act 2001 was a classic "hand-out" Bill.

[8] Procedures Committee 3rd Report, *The Founding Principles of the Scottish Parliament: the application of Access and Participation, Equal Opportunities, Accountability and Power Sharing in the work of the Parliament* (Scottish Parliamentary Paper 818, 2003) paras 49 and 713–714.

[9] For the UK machinery, see Terence Daintith and Alan Page, *The Executive in the Constitution: Structure, Autonomy and Internal Control* (Oxford: OUP, 1999) pp.241–246.

[10] John McCluskie, "New approaches to UK legislative drafting: the view from Scotland" (2004) Stat. L.R. 136, 139–140.

Parliamentary Business and the Lord Advocate. Before the subcommittee was set up in early 2002 regular reports on the progress of the legislative programme were made to the Cabinet by the Minister for Parliament, as he was then styled, but the legislative programme came to be regarded as sufficiently important to warrant its own machinery. The committee's current terms of reference are to:

- monitor the management of the Government's current legislative programme and submit regular progress reports to the Cabinet;
- keep under regular review the Government's priorities for future legislation and recommend future legislative programmes to the Cabinet;
- consider proposals for significant changes in the policy content of Bills following approval by the Cabinet of that policy content;
- consider proposals for Members' Bills, Committee Bills, and Private Bills and make a recommendation on the position to be taken by the Government on each proposal;
- approve proposals for the Parliament to be invited to give consent, by means of a legislative consent motion, to the inclusion in UK Bills of legislation relating to devolved matters; and keep the operation of the Sewel Convention which governs Westminster legislation in the devolved areas under review;
- consider other matters relating to the management of the Government's legislative programme, monitor the position of the Government's programme of subordinate legislation; and
- monitor the transposition of EU obligations and infraction cases.

Where the committee considers proposed changes to the policy content of a **13–05** Bill or the subject matter of a proposed non-Government Bill or legislative consent motion to be of such significance or sensitivity as to require Cabinet consideration (or where it is unable to agree on a course of action), the matter is referred to the Cabinet for decision together with the committee's recommendation (where appropriate). In other cases the committee takes a final decision on behalf of the Cabinet.

THE LEGISLATIVE PROGRAMME

The Westminster tradition is one of single-party government. Until the election **13–06** of a majority SNP Government in 2011, the Holyrood tradition looked set to be one of coalition or minority government; ironically, the election of a majority government at Holyrood followed the formation of the first coalition government at Westminster since the Second World War. Coalition government requires agreement between the coalition partners over the legislative programme. In the first two sessions the core of the programme was worked out in negotiation between the coalition partners as part of the process of putting the coalition together. The resulting agreement, which in legislative terms became much more detailed with the growth in importance of legislation to the coalition,[11] formed the basis of a more detailed rolling legislative programme, which was regularly reviewed and updated throughout the life of

---

[11] Compare *Making it Work Together: A Programme for Government* (September, 1999) with *A Partnership for a Better Scotland* (May, 2003); for an insight into the background to the agreements, and in particular their increasing degree of specificity, see Sir John Elvidge *Northern Exposure: Lessons from the first twelve years of devolved government in Scotland* (London: Institute for Government, 2012).

the coalition. As a single party government, the 2007 SNP Government was not constrained by the wishes of a coalition partner in framing its legislative programme, but as a minority government it had no choice but to engage in "majority building" if it was to have any prospect of realising its legislative ambitions or of giving effect to its spending plans.[12] Only with an outright majority in 2011 did the SNP escape the need for some form of agreement or understanding with other parties over its legislative plans.

An annual programme

13–07	The Holyrood session is (normally) a four year session: there is no annual cut-off as there is at Westminster. The idea was that a four year session would allow more time for proper scrutiny; there would be no question either of important Bills being lost at the end of the annual cycle.[13] The Consultative Steering Group anticipated that in the absence of an annual cut-off the Executive would announce a legislative programme for the four-year session, which it would be free to revise in response to changing circumstances, and that it would inform the Parliament annually of its planned timetable for bringing forward legislation.[14] Following Westminster (with its tradition of an annual Queen's Speech), however, the practice has been to announce a legislative programme once a year—in Holyrood's case, by means of a statement by the First Minister, normally in September.[15]

13–08	For some observers the pursuit of an annual legislative programme suggests a desire to obtain legislation as quickly as possible rather than realise the potential benefits of a devolved legislative process in terms of increased participation, more effective scrutiny, and, ultimately, "better" legislation. In evidence to the Procedures Committee in Session 1, the presiding officer argued that the Parliament had failed to adapt fully to the concept of a four-year legislative term:

> "In general the Parliament, in particular the Executive, still works to an annual cycle, aiming to complete the bulk of the legislative work by each summer recess. This leads to unnecessary pressure on the Parliamentary timetable at that time. It has also led to complaints from civil society about insufficient consultation time in between the different stages of Bills."[16]

13–09	The absence of legislative "sudden death" as practised at Westminster, however, does not mean that legislation does not generate its own pressures for delivery—from politicians who may be impatient for results and hence critical of what may seem an unnecessarily complex and time-consuming process. An annual programme is thus seen as a useful discipline, providing an opportunity to take stock of what has been achieved in the year just ended and what is

---

[12] James Mitchell, "The narcissism of small differences: Scotland and Westminster" (2010) 63 *Parliamentary Affairs* 113.

[13] Scottish Office, *Shaping Scotland's Parliament: Report of the Consultative Steering Group on the Scottish Parliament* (December, 1998) s.3.5.22.

[14] Scottish Office, *Shaping Scotland's Parliament: Report of the Consultative Steering Group on the Scottish Parliament* (December, 1998) ss.3.4.2 and 3.5.23.

[15] See most recently, *One Scotland: The Government's Programme for Scotland 2014–2015* (November, 2014); the statement was postponed because of the First Minister's decision to stand down following the outcome of the referendum.

[16] Procedures Committee 3rd Report, *The Founding Principles of the Scottish Parliament: the application of Access and Participation, Equal Opportunities, Accountability and Power Sharing in the work of the Parliament* (Scottish Parliamentary Paper 818, 2003) para.333.

planned for the next year. During the first two sessions the Scottish Executive was prepared to use the flexibility afforded by the lack of annual cut-off where difficulties were encountered, but adamant that this flexibility must not be abused by taking longer than expected over the preparation and enactment of legislation.

THE PRE-PARLIAMENTARY STAGES OF THE LEGISLATIVE PROCESS

Policy formation and consultation

The Consultative Steering Group's proposals were based on a concern that **13–10** individuals and organisations found it difficult to inform and influence the policy making process

> "in the case of legislation it was felt that the opportunity to influence legislation was limited after it had been introduced; and that the consultation process leading up to the introduction was ineffective, in part because the detailed content of the legislation was often not known until a Bill was introduced to Parliament".[17]

What was sought was a more participative approach to policy-making with a clearly defined policy development stage that would allow individuals and groups to influence the policy making process at a much earlier stage.[18] "Consultation in the form of inviting comments on specific legislative proposals", the Consultative Steering Group insisted

> "would not meet our aspiration for a participative policy development process ... What is desired is an earlier involvement of relevant bodies from the outset—identifying issues which need to be addressed, contributing to the policy-making process and the preparation of legislation".[19]

The Scottish Executive, however, continued to consult on legislative proposals in much the same way as the Scottish Office had done before devolution.[20]

Under the Consultative Steering Group's proposals, consultation would be **13–11** undertaken by the Executive, with the process being overseen by the relevant subject committee of the Parliament. Committees themselves would not engage in consultation, although they might do so if they considered government consultation inadequate. They would also be involved in deciding who should be consulted and kept informed of progress.[21] Rather than confining themselves to checking the sufficiency of government consultation, however, committees have preferred to conduct their own consultation, leading to complaints from the Executive in the first two sessions that they were being

---

[17] Scottish Office, *Shaping Scotland's Parliament: Report of the Consultative Steering Group on the Scottish Parliament* (December, 1998) s.2, para.18.

[18] Scottish Office, *Shaping Scotland's Parliament: Report of the Consultative Steering Group on the Scottish Parliament* (December, 1998) s.3.5.3.

[19] Scottish Office, *Shaping Scotland's Parliament: Report of the Consultative Steering Group on the Scottish Parliament* (December, 1998) s.3.5.4.

[20] For the Scottish Government's approach to consultation, see *Consultation Good Practice Guidance* (May, 2008). The Scottish Executive originally set itself a target of two rounds of consultation on each Bill. The policy memoranda that accompany Bills should show the extent of consultation, but the distinction between an extended but single consultation process and separate rounds is seldom clear cut.

[21] Scottish Office, *Shaping Scotland's Parliament: Report of the Consultative Steering Group on the Scottish Parliament* (December, 1998) ss.3.5.5–3.5.6.

"standoffish" and a "bit precious", in not responding to consultations, and from affected interests of consultation overload.[22]

13–12   Committees have normally waited until a Bill has been formally introduced before carrying out their own consultation. They have not become involved in pre-legislative scrutiny of Bills published in draft of the kind that has become more common at Westminster in recent years. The Procedures Committee, in Session 2, acknowledged that pre-legislative scrutiny as practised at Westminster "can offer a real opportunity to make a constructive contribution to the shape of the eventual legislation", but felt that this must inevitably be at the risk of compromising a committee's independence, or the perception of it, at later stages.

> "It is difficult for a committee that sees itself as a partner in the law-making process also to be seen as a detached and critical scrutineer."[23]

In the committee's view, committees should be free to embark on pre-legislative scrutiny "where they wish to and have the time—but neither should it be expected as a normal part of the legislative process".[24] There is of course no certainty that a government would welcome attempts by committees to become involved at an earlier stage, but it may be that by not becoming involved in pre-legislative scrutiny committees are passing up the opportunity to shape legislation before it assumes its final form.[25]

Drafting

13–13   The Parliamentary Council Office (formerly the Office of the Scottish Parliamentary Counsel) is responsible for the drafting of Government Bills introduced in the Scottish Parliament; it also drafts Scottish provisions for inclusion in UK Government Bills at Westminster. Since devolution the complement of the Office has more than doubled. As in Whitehall, the task of drafter is conceived as being to ensure draft legislation is prepared on time, and that it is effective, both in the sense of being capable of withstanding parliamentary scrutiny—"bills are made to pass as razors are made to sell"[26]—and in the sense of being capable of withstanding scrutiny by the courts.

> "The principal concern in drafting a Bill is to achieve the intended legal effect. Normally this involves making provision that is as clear, certain and unambiguous as possible, leaving minimal scope for the courts to determine what legal effect the provision has ... Considerations other

---

[22] Procedures Committee 3rd Report, *The Founding Principles of the Scottish Parliament: the application of Access and Participation, Equal Opportunities, Accountability and Power Sharing in the work of the Parliament* (Scottish Parliamentary Paper 818, 2003) para.977; interviews with officials.

[23] Procedures Committee 7th Report, *Timescales and Stages of Bills* (Scottish Parliamentary Paper 228, 2004) paras 105 and 107.

[24] Procedures Committee 7th Report, *Timescales and Stages of Bills* (Scottish Parliamentary Paper 228, 2004) para.107; the Committee took the same non-prescriptive approach to the question of the publication of Bills in draft, arguing (para.111) that it was for the Scottish Executive to decide, according to the particular circumstances, where publication in draft could make a useful contribution to consultation and policy development.

[25] On Westminster, see Jennifer Smookler, "Making a difference? The effectiveness of pre-legislative scrutiny" (2006) 59 Parliamentary Affairs 522.

[26] For the origins of the phrase, see George Engle, "Bills are made to pass as razors are made to sell: practical constraints in the preparation of legislation" (1983) 4 Stat. L.R. 7.

than achieving the intended legal effect, including comprehensibility and accessibility of language, are necessarily secondary."[27]

Secondary but not unimportant: the Office's main aim is **13–14**

"to draft Government Bills to be introduced in the Scottish Parliament in a way which ensures that the resultant Acts of the Scottish Parliament deliver Ministers' policy effectively in language that is easy to understand".

The Office is also committed to drafting legislation in plain language. "The aim is to produce clear, precise and accessible law."[28] At an early stage it was decided that the Office did not have primary responsibility for ensuring that Bills were within the Parliament's legislative competence (below).

It is for the Scottish Parliament, at least in principle, to determine how its legis- **13–15** lation is expressed[29]; in practice, Scottish Bills are very similar in terms of layout, structure and the conventions of legislative drafting to Westminster Bills. This is primarily because Acts of the Scottish Parliament are conceived as fitting into a single UK statute book, with no room for differences in, for example, statutory interpretation. The view taken at the outset was that

"however profound and far-reaching the constitutional and governmental changes to be brought about by devolution, there would be no benefit in bringing about any departure or exception from the homogeneity and continuity of British statutes . . . Our devolved legislation should . . . slip easily into the warp and weft of pre-devolution Scottish legislation and of GB and UK legislation whether pre- or post-devolution. In particular, it should be drafted so as to be consistent with those parts of *post*-devolution Westminster legislation which, by reason either of being on non-devolved topics or being enacted by Westminster in pursuance of its continuing legislative sovereignty, applies to Scotland".[30]

For the drafter, the homogeneity of the statute book is one of the main virtues **13–16** of legislation in the UK, making it easy, for example, to apply the provisions of an earlier Act for the purposes of a later one, and facilitating the substantial textual amendment of earlier Acts by later ones.[31]

The Interpretation and Legislative Reform (Scotland) Act 2010 makes provi- **13–17** sion for the interpretation of Acts of the Scottish Parliament that receive Royal Assent, and Scottish statutory instruments that are made, on or after the Act came into force on June 4, 2010, replacing the "temporary" provision made under the Scotland Act 1998 at the time of devolution.[32]

---

[27] Scottish Parliament, *Guidance on Public Bills*, 3rd edn (Directorate of Clerking and Reporting, 2007) Annex B.
[28] Following a reference to the Scottish Law Commission, the Office of the Scottish Parliamentary Counsel prepared a booklet on plain language drafting: *Plain Language and Legislation* (February, 2006).
[29] Scottish Parliament, *Guidance on Public Bills*, 3rd edn (Directorate of Clerking and Reporting, 2007) Annex B.
[30] John McCluskie, "New approaches to UK legislative drafting: the view from Scotland" (2004) Stat. L.R. 136, 137–138.
[31] John McCluskie, "New approaches to UK legislative drafting: the view from Scotland" (2004) Stat. L.R. 136, 143.
[32] Scotland Act (Transitory and Transitional Provisions) (Publication and Interpretation etc. of Acts of the Scottish Parliament) Order 1999 (SI 1999/1379); the Order continues to apply to Acts

Scrutiny of legislative competence

13–18 As the Scottish Government's chief legal adviser it falls to the Lord Advocate to clear Government Bills for introduction. A Government Bill cannot be introduced without a ministerial statement that it is within the legislative competence of the Parliament,[33] and a Minister cannot make a statement on legislative competence without the law officers' clearance.

13–19 The Lord Advocate's role is not confined to narrow questions of vires. What began as a concern with legislative competence broadened early on into a more general concern with the proper management of the legislative programme, i.e. with ensuring that Bills were ready on time and of an appropriate quality. A Bill management meeting is mandatory before a Bill can be formally announced or introduced to Parliament. The purpose of the meeting, which usually takes place after drafting instructions have been submitted to the Parliamentary Counsel Office, is to allow the law officers and the Minister for Parliamentary Business to assess a Bill's readiness in discussion with the lead Minister. The meeting also provides early notice of any questions of legislative competence that may arise.

13–20 A Bill must also be accompanied by a statement from the presiding officer stating whether or not (in the presiding officer's view) its provisions are within legislative competence.[34] In order to obtain this statement a copy of the draft Bill, together with a note of the Government's view on its legislative competence, is sent to the Solicitor to the Scottish Parliament at least three weeks before the date set for its formal introduction. During this three week period the Office of the Solicitor prepares advice to the presiding officer on the Bill's legislative competence. This process has been criticised for failing to provide "the independent check on the legislative competence of Bills intended by the Scotland Act".[35] The Calman Commission acknowledged that it was not a "particularly transparent process", but defended it on the grounds that it "appears to be effective in identifying and resolving potential problems".[36]

THE PARLIAMENTARY STAGES

13–21 The Scotland Act 1998 provides that the Parliament's standing orders must include provision for general debate on a Bill with an opportunity for members to vote on its general principles; the consideration of, and an opportunity for members to vote on, the details of a Bill; and a final stage at which a Bill can be passed or rejected.[37] There must also be an opportunity for the reconsideration of a Bill which is referred to the Supreme Court by the law officers or blocked by the Secretary State after it has been passed (below). The Act provides that the validity of an Act of the Scottish Parliament "is not affected

---

of the Scottish Parliament and Scottish statutory instruments which received Royal Assent or were made before the 2010 Act came into force: Interpretation and Legislative Reform (Scotland) Act 2010 ("ILR(S)A 2010") s.55(2).

[33] Scotland Act 1998 ("SA 1998") s.31(1); there is not, of course, the option of making a statement of non-compliance, as is permitted by s.19 of the Human Rights Act 1998.

[34] SA 1998 s.31(2).

[35] Iain Jamieson, "Held in Check" (2007) 52(6) J.L.S.S. 48–50.

[36] Commission on Scottish Devolution, *Serving Scotland Better: Scotland and the United Kingdom in the 21st Century* (2009) para.6.89.

[37] SA 1998 s.36(1); under s.36(3) different provision may be made for certain categories of Bills, e.g. Private Bills.

by any invalidity in the proceedings of the Parliament leading to its enactment".[38] An Act cannot therefore be challenged on the grounds that the Parliament has failed to follow its own procedures.

The parliamentary stages of the legislative process begin with the formal intro-   **13–22**
duction of a Bill. A Bill as introduced must be accompanied by a number of documents which must be printed and published with the Bill. In the case of Government Bills these comprise:

(i)   a statement from the appropriate Minister that the Bill is within the Parliament's legislative competence[39];

(ii)   a statement from the presiding officer as to whether the Bill would be within the Parliament's legislative competence.[40] A "negative" statement does not prevent a Bill from being introduced or even passed—though it would provide a good reason for MSPs to be reluctant to proceed with it. A "positive" statement, on the other hand, should not be regarded "as precluding the Parliament, or any committee, from critically examining a Bill on grounds of legislative competence during its passage".[41] On the three occasions on which the presiding officer has made negative statements, all involving Members' Bills, the Parliament accepted the lead committee's recommendation that the Bill's general principles not be agreed to[42];

(iii) a financial memorandum estimating the administrative, compliance and other costs to which the Bill would give rise, and distinguishing separately such costs as would fall upon the Scottish Administration, local authorities, and other bodies, individuals and businesses[43];

(iv)   explanatory notes summarising objectively the provisions of the Bill, to the extent that they require explanation or comment, and giving other information necessary or expedient to explain its effect[44];

(v)   a policy memorandum setting out the Bill's policy objectives, whether alternative ways of meeting those objectives were considered and, if so, why the approach taken in the Bill was adopted; the consultation, if any, which was undertaken on those objectives and the ways of meeting them or on the detail of the Bill and a summary of the outcome of that consultation; and an assessment of the effects, if any, of the Bill on equal opportunities, human rights, island communities, local government, sustainable development and any other matter which the Scottish Ministers consider relevant[45]; and

---

[38] SA 1998 s.28(5).

[39] SA 1998 s.31(1), Scottish Parliament Standing Orders r.9.3.1A; following the recommendation of the Calman Commission (Commission on Scottish Devolution, *Serving Scotland Better: Scotland and the United Kingdom in the 21st Century* (2009) para.6.92), the Scotland Act 2012 s.6, extended the requirement of a statement on legislative competence to any person introducing a Bill in the Parliament.

[40] SA 1998 s.31(2), Scottish Parliament Standing Orders r.9.3.1.

[41] Scottish Parliament, *Guidance on Public Bills*, 3rd edn (Directorate of Clerking and Reporting, 2007) para.2.14.

[42] The three Bills were the Provision of Rail Passenger Services Bill (Scotland) 2006, the Civil Appeals (Scotland) Bill 2006, and the Criminal Sentencing (Equity Fines) (Scotland) Bill 2010; for discussion, see Chris Himsworth, "Presiding Officer Statements on the Competence of Bills", 2007 11 Edin. L.R. 397.

[43] Scottish Parliament Standing Orders r.9.3.2.

[44] Scottish Parliament Standing Orders r.9.3.2A.

[45] Scottish Parliament Standing Orders r.9.3.3(c). A Member's Bill must also be accompanied by a policy memorandum; a Committee Bill may be but need not be: Scottish Parliament Standing Orders r.9.3.3A.

(vi) a Bill that contains any provision charging expenditure on the Scottish Consolidated Fund must also be accompanied a report from the Auditor General for Scotland on whether the charge is appropriate.[46]

Once a Bill has been published, together with its accompanying documents, it embarks upon its parliamentary stages.

13–23 The Stage 1 debate and vote on the general principles of the Bill takes place in the Chamber. Before the debate takes place, however, the Bill is referred to the relevant subject committee, which considers and reports on the principles of the Bill to inform the debate and vote in the plenary session; the Parliament's subject committees, as we have noted, combine the roles of select and public bill (formerly standing) committees at Westminster, the idea being to enable members

> "to develop an expertise in particular areas and to bring an informed view to the consideration of legislation and scrutiny of the Executive".[47]

The Stage 1 inquiry is regarded as "crucial to the effectiveness of the Parliament's whole legislative process" in that, as well as taking place in public, it allows affected interests, including those who may not have been consulted prior to introduction, direct access to the legislature and with it an opportunity to

> "contribute to the formulation of a considered view both of the policy intention and of how it has been given detailed expression in legislation".[48]

13–24 Secondary committees sometimes share with the lead committee the task of scrutinising a Bill on policy grounds. The Subordinate Legislation Committee also scrutinises any proposals to delegate powers, and the Finance Committee the financial memorandum, as part of the Stage 1 scrutiny of a Bill.

13–25 The Stage 2 consideration of the details of the Bill, assuming it has been agreed to at Stage 1, usually takes place in the relevant subject committee. The Bill is subjected to line-by-line scrutiny and amendments are considered and decided upon. While all MSPs may lodge and move amendments, it is only the committee members who vote on amendments. Given the small size of committees, and the fact that (by convention) Ministers are not members of them, committees and backbenchers thus find themselves empowered over Ministers in a significant departure from the Westminster tradition. It is also significant that all admissible amendments are called at Stage 2; there is no selection at this stage, as there is at Stage 3.

13–26 At Stage 3 the Bill comes back to the Chamber. There is a further opportunity to amend the Bill, followed by a debate on whether to pass the Bill or reject it. It is open to the Parliament to refer a Bill back to committee for further Stage

---

[46] Scottish Parliament Standing Orders r.9.3.4. A charge on the Scottish Consolidated Fund is expenditure for which no further parliamentary authorisation is required; by agreeing to expenditure being charged on the Fund the Parliament is therefore giving up its right to scrutinise the expenditure as part of the annual budget process: see further para.14–18.

[47] Scottish Office, *Shaping Scotland's Parliament: Report of the Consultative Steering Group on the Scottish Parliament* (December 1998) s.2, para.13.

[48] Procedures Committee 7th Report, *Timescales and Stages of Bills* (Scottish Parliamentary Paper 228, 2004) para.112.

2 consideration. The debate to pass the Bill may also be adjourned, immediately after the Stage 3 amendments have been dealt with, to allow a limited category of further amendments to be lodged. The first of these options has never been used, and the second only once, but they offer a degree of flexibility to the process.

Amendments may be made at both Stage 2 and Stage 3. The assumption at the **13–27** outset was that the relative lack of amending stages, compared with Westminster, would mean that Bills would need to be as near to the finished article as possible before their introduction:

> "The paucity of amendable stages, compounded by the disinclination to pursue substantial amendment at Stage 2, is a strong factor which drives us to ensure that everything which is to be done in a Bill is included in it before introduction. The facility, which we enjoyed at Westminster, of adding substantial new material to Bills in Committee or at Report stages, including those stages in the second House, is noticeably diminished."[49]

But whatever inhibitions may have been felt at the outset about introducing significant amendments seem to have been quickly shrugged off, leading to complaints that entirely new provisions are sometimes introduced late in the process, shortly before the legislation is passed, thereby bypassing detailed scrutiny in committee (below).

Particular types of Bills

Government programme Bills are only one among several different types of **13–28** Bills for which procedural provision is made in the Parliament's standing orders.

Members' Bills

The Member's Bill procedure was used with some success, outwardly at least, **13–29** in the Parliament's first session to challenge government policy, as well as for the more familiar purpose of effecting desirable but essentially minor changes in the law.[50] Faced with potentially competing demands for Executive and Members' Bills, the Parliament adopted new requirements for the introduction of Members' Bills early in the second session, which included raising the "threshold" for introducing Bills, i.e. the number of other members who have indicated support for a proposal, from 11 to 18, and the introduction of a requirement of cross-party support, the latter in line with the Procedures Committee's view that the main purpose of the Member's Bill procedure was to provide a channel for legislative ideas with "broad general appeal".[51] Following their adoption, the number of Members' Bills passed fell

---

[49] John McCluskie, "New approaches to UK legislative drafting: the view from Scotland" (2004) Stat. L.R. 136, 140–141.

[50] The most prominent example of the former was Tommy Sheridan's Abolition of Poinding and Warrant Sales Act 2001, which reached the statute book despite significant Executive misgivings. The Act, however, was repealed in its entirety, and its effect arguably largely undone, by the Executive's "remedial" Debt Arrangement and Attachment Act (Scotland) Act 2002.

[51] Procedures Committee 6th Report, *A New Procedure for Members' Bills* (Scottish Parliamentary Paper 193, 2004). As well as a higher threshold and a requirement of cross-party support, the Committee recommended that there should be a minimum of 12 weeks' consultation on proposals for Bills, that there should be a limit on the number of proposals for Bills that members may promote at any time, and that the Scottish Executive should be able to block members' legislation where either it or the UK Government were planning equivalent legislation.

sharply—from eight in Session 1 to three in the Session 2—but this was more likely attributable to a greatly reduced willingness by the Parliament to pass such Bills than to the changes in the procedure relating to their introduction. Seven Members' Bills were passed in Session 3, and one in the first three years of the current Session.[52]

13–30 Once introduced, Members' Bills are subject to the same procedure as Government Bills, save that, at Stage 1, it is open to a lead committee that is not persuaded of the case for a Member's Bill, its legislative competence, or its drafting, to recommend to the Parliament that its general principles be not agreed to, thus relieving the committee of the need to undertake a full Stage 1 inquiry.[53]

Committee Bills

13–31 The Constitutional Convention's vision was of a Parliament that would operate through a system of powerful committees which would be able to initiate legislation as well as scrutinise and amend government proposals.[54] Committee Bills have not featured prominently in the legislative output of the Parliament, with only three Bills enacted in Session 1, one in the Session 2 and two in Session 3 (there have been none so far in Session 4). Rather than a means whereby committees may take the legislative initiative on matter of public policy, as the Constitutional Convention envisaged, they have become a useful means of handling necessary legislation on matters of parliamentary "house-keeping" (e.g. members' interests, creating a Standards Commissioner, members' pensions) where it is considered inappropriate for either the Scottish Government or any one political party to be seen to take the initiative. Only one Committee Bill—the Protection from Abuse (Scotland) Act 2001—has dealt with a matter of public policy that could equally well have been the subject of a Government or Member's Bill.

13–32 A committee that wishes to introduce a Bill must first draw up a proposal (in the form of a committee report); if the Parliament endorses the proposal following a Chamber debate, the convener obtains the right to introduce a Bill to give effect to the proposal. Once introduced, Committee Bills are subject to the same procedure as Government Bills, save that a Bill is not referred to a lead committee at Stage 1 for a report on its general principles, the committee's original proposal report (and the inquiry that preceded it) serving an equivalent purpose. Committee Bills pose particular problems for effective parliamentary scrutiny in a single chamber parliament given that they reflect a measure of cross-party consensus. In an attempt to address this issue, the Parliament's standing orders prevent a member taking an active part in committee consideration of a Committee Bill at Stage 1 or Stage 2 if they were a member of the committee that proposed the Bill[55]; this has the effect of requiring a Committee Bill to be referred at Stage 2 either to an entirely separate committee or (more

---

[52] The "success" of members' legislation is not easily measured. Members' Bills that do not reach the statute book may pave the way for later, successful legislation, e.g. the ban on smoking in public places introduced by the Smoking, Health and Social Care (Scotland) Act 2005. Conversely, a Member's Bill may be passed but not ultimately succeed, as in the case of the Abolition of Poinding and Warrant Sales Act 2001, fn.50 above.

[53] Scottish Parliament Standing Orders r.9.14.18(b).

[54] Scottish Constitutional Convention, *Scotland's Parliament, Scotland's Right* (1995) p.26.

[55] Scottish Parliament Standing Orders r.9.13A.

likely, in view of committee remits) to an ad hoc committee created for the purpose with no commonality of membership.

Budget Bills

Most Scottish Government expenditure requires annual parliamentary authori- **13–33** sation in the form of a Budget Act.[56] Where authorisation has not been secured by the start of the financial year expenditure may continue, but only for the purposes and within the limits laid down by the previous Budget Act.[57] The Budget Bill procedure is discussed in Ch.14.[58]

Consolidation Bills, Codification Bills, Statute Law Repeal Bills and Statute Law Revision Bills

The Scotland Act 1998 provided that the Parliament might adopt different **13–34** procedures for the consideration of Bills that restated the law and Bills that repealed spent enactments.[59] Consolidation involves bringing together earlier enactments on an area of law "with a view to making the legislation easier to find and more user-friendly while at the same time tidying up the statute book".[60] A Consolidation Bill may make minor amendments to the law (including amendments to give effect to Scottish Law Commission recommendations) as well as simply restate it, but it may not contain substantial new revisions, nor make substantial changes to the existing law.[61] The Parliament has passed one Consolidation Bill: the Salmon and Freshwater Fisheries (Consolidation) (Scotland) Act 2003. A Codification Bill, on the other hand, restates existing statute and common law, rather than just statute, whether or not with amendments to give effect to Law Commission recommendations. There have been no examples of Codification Bills, although there have been examples of provisions in Bills that have codified elements of the law. Statute Law Repeals and Statute Law Revision Bills are also intended to tidy up the statute book, mainly by repealing spent enactments or enactments no longer in force.

> "In the case of a Statute Law Revision Bill, this involves re-enacting those provisions in particular statutes that still have application while repealing the remainder of them."[62]

Again there have been no examples of either type of Bill.[63]

---

[56] Public Finance and Accountability (Scotland) Act 2000 ("PFA(S)A 2000") s.1. The principle does not extend to expenditure charged directly on the Scottish Consolidated Fund.

[57] PFA(S)A 2000 s.2.

[58] See para.14–23.

[59] SA 1998 s.36(3); Scottish Parliament Standing Orders rr.9.18–9.20.

[60] Scottish Law Commission, *Annual Report 2011*, p.27.

[61] Scottish Parliament, *Guidance on Public Bills*, 3rd edn (Directorate of Clerking and Reporting, 2007) para.3.36. In the Bill that become the Interpretation and Legislative Reform (Scotland) Act 2011, the Scottish Government sought the power, exercisable by order, to make pre-consolidation modifications to enactments in order to facilitate their consolidation or codification, which power would have superseded the existing provision for amendments to give effect to Law Commission recommendations, but concerns about the width of the power being sought led to it being dropped from the Bill.

[62] Scottish Parliament, *Guidance on Public Bills*, 3rd edn (Directorate of Clerking and Reporting, 2007) para.3.43.

[63] The Scottish Law Commission undertakes work on statute law repeals, defined as the repeal of "obsolete or otherwise unnecessary legislation", jointly with the Law Commission for England and Wales. The Scottish Parliament passed legislative consent motions (below) agreeing to the inclusion of the Scottish repeals in the Statute Law (Repeals) Act 2008 and 2013.

Scottish Law Commission Bills

13-35 Scottish Law Commission Bills are a new addition to the types of Bills for which a different procedure has been adopted. The purpose of the procedure is to provide more parliamentary time to consider and implement certain Commission proposals for legislation.[64] Instead of being considered by the relevant subject committee at Stages 1 and 2, they are considered by the Subordinate Legislation Committee, which has been renamed the Delegated Powers and Law Reform Committee in recognition of the change in its role.

Emergency Bills

13-36 The Scotland Act also provided that the Parliament might expedite proceedings in relation to particular Bills.[65] An Emergency Bill is a Government Bill that the Parliament agrees

> "needs to be enacted more rapidly than the normal timetable allows, for example to amend the law in response to a recent court judgement which has exposed a loophole or problem of interpretation in an existing enactment".[66]

Once a Bill has been classed as an Emergency Bill, the rules allow all three stages to be taken in a single day, and, in particular, remove the need for a Stage 1 committee inquiry. The first Bill passed by the Parliament was an Emergency Bill: the Mental Health (Public Safety and Appeals) (Scotland) Act 1999. There have been a further six Emergency Bills, the most recent being the Criminal Procedure (Legal Assistance, Detention and Appeals) (Scotland) Act 2010, which introduced a right of access to legal advice before and during police questioning, following the Supreme Court's decision in *Cadder v HM Advocate*.[67] An emergency procedure carries with it the risk that it may be used to stifle or curtail debate on a Bill, as arguably happened with the Convention Rights Proceedings (Amendment) (Scotland) Act 2009, which imposed a one year limit on the bringing of claims for breach of Convention rights against the Scottish Ministers.[68] In June 2011 the Parliament agreed that the Offensive Behaviour at Football and Threatening Communications (Scotland) Bill should be treated as an Emergency Bill, which would have allowed it to be enacted in time for the start of the new football season, but following protests it was agreed that for the purposes of Stages 2 and 3 it should no longer be so treated.

Private Bills

13-37 A Private Bill is a Bill introduced for the purpose of obtaining particular powers or benefits for its promoter that are "in excess of or in conflict with the general law".[69] Private Bill procedure differs from Public Bill procedure in a number of respects, including the provision of an opportunity for persons

---

[64] Standards, Procedures and Public Appointments Committee 2nd Report, *Implementing Scottish Law Commission reports* (Scottish Parliamentary Paper 307, 2013).

[65] SA 1998 s.36(2).

[66] Scottish Parliament, *Guidance on Public Bills*, 3rd edn (Directorate of Clerking and Reporting, 2007) para.3.45.

[67] *Cadder v HM Advocate* [2010] UKSC 43; 2011 S.C. (UKSC) 13.

[68] For discussion, see Aidan O Neill, "Human Rights and People and Society" in Elaine E Sutherland et al, *Law Making and the Scottish Parliament: The Early Years* (Edinburgh: Edinburgh University Press, 2011); see also Constitution Committee, *Fast-track Legislation: Constitutional Implications and Safeguards* (HL 2008–2009, 116).

[69] Scottish Parliament Standing Orders r.9A 1.1.

whose interests are adversely affected to lodge objections and for any objections to be considered by a specially constituted Private Bill Committee, which is also responsible for the general scrutiny of the Bill. The Parliament passed 11 Private Bills in its first two sessions, most involving the grant of approval for the construction of railways and tramlines. Following the Transport and Works (Scotland) Act 2007, which enables approval for such projects to be obtained by ministerial order rather than by private legislation, Private Bills have become less common.[70] Two such Bills were enacted in the Session 3, and three in the first three years of Session 4.

Hybrid Bills

The Parliament has also adopted a Hybrid Bill procedure, combining elements **13–38** of both Public Bill and Private Bill procedure, for Government Bills which

> "adversely affect ... a particular interest of a person or a body in a manner different to the private interests of other individuals or bodies of the same category or class".[71]

The Forth Crossing Act 2011 is the only Hybrid Bill to have been enacted to date.

REFERENCE TO THE SUPREME COURT

Once a Bill has been passed there is a four week holding period before the **13–39** presiding officer submits it for Royal Assent during which any of the three principal law officers (the Advocate General, the Lord Advocate and the Attorney General) may refer the question whether the Bill or any provision of the Bill would be within the Parliament's legislative competence to the Supreme Court.[72] The Office of the Solicitor to the Advocate General ("OSAG") examines Bills before they are first introduced, as well as formally once they have completed their parliamentary stages, with a view to ensuring that the UK Government has

> "early warning of issues of competence of Bills of the Scottish Parliament or actings of the Scottish Executive, and can engage in constructive dialogue with the Scottish Executive to address them".[73]

The threat of a reference was apparently sufficient to resolve such differences of opinion as arose during the first two sessions (1999–2007). Faced with the likelihood of a six month delay to a Bill, and the consequent disruption to its legislative programme that a reference would have entailed, it seems that the Scottish Executive preferred to remove offending sections or redraft the legislation rather than invite the UK Government to test its arguments in court. In the Bill that became the Scotland Act 2012, the UK Government sought the power to refer individual provisions of a Bill as well as a whole Bill to the

---

[70] For a full account of the background to that Act, and the Parliament's Private Bill procedure, see CMG Himsworth and CM O'Neill, *Scotland's Constitution: Law and Practice*, 2nd edn (London: Bloomsbury Professional, 2009) para.8.27.

[71] Scottish Parliament Standing Orders r.9C.1; see also Standards, Procedures and Public Appointments Committee 7th Report, *Hybrid Bills* (Scottish Parliamentary Paper 299, 2009).

[72] SA 1998 s.33.

[73] House of Commons debate, January 25, 2002, Vol.378, col.1126W.

Supreme Court, suggesting that the threat had lost some of its potency, but the provision was dropped as part of the agreement between the two governments over the terms on which the Scottish Parliament's consent to the Scotland Bill would be forthcoming.

THE SECRETARY OF STATE'S "VETO" POWER

13–40 The UK Government also retains a limited power to prevent a Bill passed by the Parliament from becoming law, the rationale for which was discussed in Ch.8 (powers of intervention). The Secretary of State may, by order subject to negative resolution procedure, prohibit the presiding officer from submitting a Bill for Royal Assent which contains provisions that "would be incompatible with any international obligations or the interests of defence or national security", or which make modifications of the law as it applies to reserved matters "which would have an adverse effect on the operation of the law as it applies to reserved matters".[74] This power is exercisable within four weeks of a reference to the Supreme Court being decided as well as within the initial four week holding period.[75] The UK's international obligations, the interests of defence or national security, and the operation of the law as it applies to reserved matters thus take precedence over the narrower question of vires. Like the law officers' power to refer a Bill to the Supreme Court, and the equivalent powers of intervention in relation to executive action, the power to prevent a Bill from becoming law is seen "very much as a matter of last resort".[76] Should disputes arise the expectation is that these will be resolved bilaterally, or through the good offices of the Secretary of State, with the possibility of resort to the Joint Ministerial Committee in the event that these prove unsuccessful.[77]

RECONSIDERATION STAGE

13–41 The Scotland Act provides that there must be an opportunity for the reconsideration of a Bill that has been referred to the Supreme Court or blocked by the Secretary State after it has been passed.[78] Where a Bill is referred to the Supreme Court, the Parliament cannot reconsider it before the Supreme Court has reached a decision—if the Supreme Court decides that the Bill is within the competence of the Parliament there is no need to reconsider the Bill unless, of course, the Secretary of State subsequently blocks it—or has referred a question arising from it to the European Court of Justice; in the latter case there is provision for the reference to be withdrawn to avoid the additional delay arising from the reference to the European Court.[79] The purpose of the reconsideration stage is to allow the provisions that have been challenged to be

---

[74] SA 1998 s.35(1); s.58 confers analogous powers of intervention in relation to executive action

[75] SA 1998 s.35(3).

[76] Cabinet Office, *Memorandum of Understanding and Supplementary Agreements between the United Kingdom Government, the Scottish Ministers, the Welsh Ministers and the Northern Ireland Executive Committee* (October, 2013) para.27.

[77] Cabinet Office, *Memorandum of Understanding and Supplementary Agreements between the United Kingdom Government, the Scottish Ministers, the Welsh Ministers and the Northern Ireland Executive Committee* (October, 2013) para.26; on the Joint Ministerial Committee, see para.19–19.

[78] SA 1998 s.36(4).

[79] SA 1998 s.36(4).

amended so that the basis of the challenge is removed.[80] A Bill approved after reconsideration may be challenged by the law officers or the Secretary of State in exactly the same way as after it was first passed; there is no limit to the number of times a Bill may be approved or subsequently challenged.

ROYAL ASSENT

Once a Bill has been passed by the Parliament, or approved after reconsidera- **13–42** tion, and the four week holding period has expired, the presiding officer submits it for Royal Assent. A Bill may be submitted for Royal Assent before the four week period has expired if the law officers and the Secretary of State waive their right of challenge.[81] Once a Bill receives Royal Assent it becomes an Act of the Scottish Parliament.[82]

EFFECTIVENESS OF SCRUTINY

For the Constitutional Convention it was important that as a single-chamber **13–43** legislature the Parliament's procedures "provide for the rigorous scrutiny of proposed legislation".[83] Almost from the outset, however, concerns were expressed about the effectiveness of parliamentary scrutiny. The Parliament, it was said

"does not yet have quite the same degree of legislative curiosity as at Westminster ... [It] tends to concentrate in its debates, even in Committee, on the policy and political dimensions of the Bills which it is scrutinising and tends to leave to one side questions about, for example, the particular application to particular cases of the provisions of its Bills".[84]

The implication was that the Parliament might yet develop that "curiosity". **13–44** Other observers were less sanguine. For Lord Hope:

"The committee system, which was designed to provide an opportunity for careful, informed study of all the relevant detail, is not working as it should. Responsibility for both initial scrutiny of a Bill at Stage 1 and detailed scrutiny at Stage 2 rests with the same committee. At both stages this process tends to become the focus for political debate and point-scoring. Elected committee members lack the independence of mind and the opportunity for detachment and genuine self-criticism that is essential to effective scrutiny."[85]

In the Parliament's defence the argument was that the parliamentary stages had **13–45** been too rushed to allow for effective scrutiny. The Procedures Committee, in its examination of the application of the founding principles in Session 1 found

---

[80] Scottish Parliament, *Guidance on Public Bills*, 3rd edn (Directorate of Clerking and Reporting, 2007) para.2.66.

[81] SA 1998 ss.33(3), 35(4).

[82] SA 1998 s.28(2).

[83] Scottish Constitutional Convention, *Scotland's Parliament, Scotland's Right* (1995) p.24.

[84] John McCluskie, "New approaches to UK legislative drafting: the view from Scotland" (2004) Stat. L.R. 136, 141.

[85] Lord Hope, "What a second chamber can do for legislative scrutiny" (2004) 25 Stat. L.R. 3, 8.

"clear evidence that the committee system in the Scottish Parliament is under severe pressure of work, and that the quality of output is threatened by the deadlines to which committees are working".[86]

If the devolution settlement was to operate as the Parliament intended when it adopted the founding principles, it continued, the Executive had to ensure that "committees are not so burdened that the quality of legislation, or other tasks that are central to committee work, is put at risk".[87] In its reply, the Executive conceded there had been pressures to complete Bill stages for Public Bills "more quickly than may have been ideal in some cases", before affirming its willingness

"to discuss timetabling issues with the parliamentary authorities having regard to the concerns raised and the need to ensure the timely passage of legislation".

Privately, it suggested that if the Parliament wanted to spend more time on legislation the answer might be for it to work harder; increased scrutiny, in other words, should not be at the expense of the Executive's legislative agenda.[88]

13–46 The Procedures Committee returned to the question of the speed of the process in Session 2 with a series of recommendations designed to enable

"the quality and robustness of the Parliament's legislative output to be enhanced without threatening the legitimate expectation on the part of the Executive (and others) that they will be able to deliver legislative solutions within a reasonable timescale".[89]

The goal of improved scrutiny, however, has proved an elusive one. The Calman Commission reported continued concerns about the robustness of the Parliament's procedures for scrutinising legislation:

"In particular, we have heard concerns that, despite the focus early on in the process on consultation, and on an evidence-based approach, the later amending stages are often rushed giving outside interests insufficient opportunity to make representations. A related concern is that new provisions are sometimes introduced late in the process, shortly before the legislation is passed, thereby bypassing detailed scrutiny in committee."[90]

---

[86] Procedures Committee 3rd Report, *The Founding Principles of the Scottish Parliament: the application of Access and Participation, Equal Opportunities, Accountability and Power Sharing in the work of the Parliament* (Scottish Parliamentary Paper 818, 2003) para.101.

[87] Procedures Committee 3rd Report, *The Founding Principles of the Scottish Parliament: the application of Access and Participation, Equal Opportunities, Accountability and Power Sharing in the work of the Parliament* (Scottish Parliamentary Paper 818, 2003) para.1018.

[88] Comments by the First Minister to this effect were reported in *The Scotsman* June 26, 2003.

[89] Procedures Committee 7th Report, *Timescales and Stages of Bills* (Scottish Parliamentary Paper 228, 2004) para.170.

[90] Commission on Scottish Devolution, *Serving Scotland Better: Scotland and the United Kingdom in the 21st Century* (2009) para.6.44.

The Commission rejected the idea of introducing a second chamber or **13–47** unelected element to provide detached and expert scrutiny of legislation,[91] but raised the possibility that there might be scope for making the Parliament's procedures more robust and effective, for example by separating the second main amending stage from the decision to pass a Bill, or by prohibiting amendments that raise new issues at a late stage.[92] In its final report it recommended that the legislative procedure should become a four-stage procedure, with Stage 3 becoming limited to a second main amending stage, taken in the Chamber, while the final debate on whether to pass the Bill would become a new Stage 4, which would routinely be taken on a later day.[93] The Standards, Procedures and Public Appointments Committee, in its initial response, considered that there was sufficient flexibility within the current rules for a Bill to be subject to a four stage process if required.[94] In its legacy paper, however, it recommended that consideration be given to a review of the legislative process as a whole, which its successor has now embarked on.[95]

WESTMINSTER LEGISLATION IN THE DEVOLVED AREAS

At the time of devolution it was widely assumed that Westminster would cease **13–48** to legislate in the devolved areas. In his statement on the Executive's first legislative programme, the First Minister spoke of there being

> "exceptional and limited circumstances in which it is sensible and proper that the Westminster Parliament legislates in devolved areas of responsibility . . . [But] day in day out, it is here that the law of the land will be shaped and laid down".[96]

Westminster legislation in the devolved areas, however, has proved to be a more common occurrence than may have been anticipated at the time of devolution. Since devolution there have been more than 140 "Sewel" or "legislative consent" motions signifying the consent of the Parliament to Westminster legislation in the devolved areas (or altering its legislative competence or the executive competence of the Scottish Ministers).[97]

Westminster legislation in the devolved areas may commend itself for a number **13–49** of reasons. It allows policies to be implemented on a UK or GB wide basis; it also means that there is no need to disentangle the devolved from the reserved

---

[91] As to which, see Lord Hope, "What a second chamber can do for legislative scrutiny" (2004) 25 Stat. L.R. 3, 12–14.

[92] Calman Commission, *The Future of Scottish Devolution within the Union: A First Report* (2008) para.8.15.

[93] Commission on Scottish Devolution, *Serving Scotland Better: Scotland and the United Kingdom in the 21st Century* (2009) para.6.64.

[94] Standards, Procedures and Public Appointments Committee 5th Report, *The recommendations of the Commission on Scottish Devolution regarding Scottish Parliament procedures* (Scottish Parliamentary Paper 490, 2010) paras 87–95.

[95] Standards, Procedures and Public Appointments Committee 4th Report, *Legacy Paper* (Scottish Parliamentary Paper 637, 2011) paras 18–19.

[96] Scottish Parliament OR June 16, 1999, col.403 (Donald Dewar).

[97] As well as Westminster legislation in the devolved areas, the Parliament's consent is sought for Westminster legislation altering its legislative competence or the executive competence of the Scottish Ministers. In the latter respects the Sewel convention mirrors the requirement for the Parliament's consent to changes in its legislative competence or the executive competence of the Scottish Ministers where these are made by subordinate legislation under ss.30(2) or 63 of the Scotland Act 1998.

aspects of a proposal—on which the Scottish Parliament would be unable to legislate. It enables the more effective judge-proofing of legislation through the doctrine of parliamentary sovereignty. And it has the major advantage from the point of view of the Scottish Government of enabling policies which it supports, or to which it is not opposed, to be given legislative effect at little or no cost to itself in terms of scarce legislative resources, leaving it free to concentrate on its own legislative priorities.

13–50 Advantageous though it may be, reliance on Westminster's concurrent legislative competence carries with it the obvious risk of abuse, of the Scottish Parliament being denied the opportunity to consider the details of legislation that is properly its concern. The practice initially proved controversial, partly for this reason. Defenders of the practice argued that for the most part Westminster legislation on devolved matters made only minor changes to the law. But while this was true of much Westminster legislation in the devolved areas, some of it, for example on gender recognition and same-sex registered partnerships, was on precisely the sorts of subjects that the Scottish Parliament might have been expected to legislate after devolution.[98]

13–51 The Parliament was slow to adapt its procedures to Westminster legislation in the devolved areas. The expectation from the outset was that Westminster "would not normally legislate with regard to devolved matters in Scotland without the consent of the Scottish Parliament",[99] but the procedures for obtaining the Parliament's consent provided little assurance that Westminster was legislating on devolved matters only where it was "sensible and proper" to do so. Moreover, there were few real constraints on Ministers once approval was given. The challenge for the Parliament was to treat Westminster legislation in the devolved areas with the same seriousness as it treated the other forms of legislation for which it was responsible. That challenge was eventually tackled during the second session when, following a comprehensive review by the Procedures Committee,[100] the Parliament put its procedures on a formal basis.

13–52 The Parliament's "legislative consent" procedure applies to Bills under consideration in the UK Parliament that make provision applying to Scotland for any purpose within the legislative competence of the Parliament or that alter that legislative competence or the executive competence of the Scottish Ministers.[101] Consent is sought by means of a legislative consent motion, which must be preceded by a legislative consent memorandum, lodged by the Scottish Government, summarising what the Bill does and its policy objectives, specifying the extent to which it makes provision for any purpose within the legislative competence of the Scottish Parliament, or alters that competence or the executive competence of the Scottish Ministers, and either including a draft legislative consent motion or explaining why it does not intend to seek the Parliament's consent to the relevant provision. Where it does not intend to seek the Parliament's consent it is open to any MSP to seek the Parliament's consent

---

[98] On the early experience, see Alan Page and Andrea Batey, "Scotland's Other Parliament: Westminster Legislation about Devolved Matters in Scotland since Devolution" [2002] P.L. 501.

[99] See para.2–22.

[100] Procedures Committee 7th Report, *The Sewel Convention* (Scottish Parliamentary Paper 428, 2005).

[101] Scottish Parliament Standing Orders r.9B.1.1.

in its place.[102] The memorandum is then considered by the relevant subject committee, which reports to the Parliament with its recommendations. If the motion is agreed to, the Parliament's consent is conveyed to the UK Parliament; if its consent is withheld, the expectation is that the UK Government will amend the Bill accordingly or withdraw it entirely. In December 2011 the Parliament withheld its consent, in part, to the Welfare Reform Bill, an essentially symbolic gesture since the Parliament had no alternative but to enact its own legislation to protect access to "passported benefits" in Scotland, which it subsequently did in the Welfare Reform (Further Provision) (Scotland) Act 2012. If the Westminster Bill is amended during its passage so as to take it beyond the scope of the consent already conferred, then a further process of seeking and securing consent by an additional legislative consent motion is required.

By embedding the main elements of scrutiny within the Parliament's formal **13–53** procedures, the Procedures Committee sought to ensure that the Parliament had the information it needed at a sufficiently early stage to enable it to carry out the task of scrutiny effectively. It also sought

> "to secure a degree of consensus about the general need for procedures of this sort and a shared understanding of how and when they should be used, and at the same time lay to rest some of the persistent misunderstandings that have arisen".[103]

In this ambition the Committee was successful. In a letter to the presiding officer in November 2007, following the Queen's Speech at Westminster, the Minister for Parliamentary Business confirmed that the SNP Government was committed to considering proposals for legislative consent motions on a case by case basis, and that it believed that the Sewel convention would remain a "key part of the current constitutional arrangements as long as the United Kingdom Parliament retains its current powers".

SUBORDINATE LEGISLATION

The number of Scottish statutory instruments far exceeds that of Acts of the **13–54** Scottish Parliament with more than 5,000 Scottish statutory instruments having been made since devolution compared with 220 or so Acts of the Scottish Parliament. Following the recommendations of the Consultative Steering Group,[104] the Parliament's arrangements for the scrutiny of subordinate legislation, and proposals for delegated law making powers, were modelled on those at Westminster, with the Parliament's Delegated Powers and Law Reform Committee (formerly the Subordinate Legislation Committee) combining the functions of the Joint Committee on Statutory Instruments and the House of Lords Delegated Powers and Regulatory Reform Committee. The Committee's primary concern is with technical scrutiny, i.e. the legality and drafting of instruments, not their political merits. It is empowered to draw the attention of the Parliament to an instrument on any of a number of technical and legal

---

[102] This covers the situation where a minority government is opposed to legislation by Westminster, but a majority of MSPs are or may be in favour.

[103] Procedures Committee 7th Report, *The Sewel Convention* (Scottish Parliamentary Paper 428, 2005) paras 5–6.

[104] Scottish Office, *Shaping Scotland's Parliament: Report of the Consultative Steering Group on the Scottish Parliament* (December, 1998) s.3.5 paras 27–33.

policy grounds that do not impinge on the substance of an instrument or the policy behind it. Among the grounds on which attention may be drawn to an instrument are that its drafting appears to be defective, that its form or meaning could be clearer, that there appears to be a doubt about whether it is intra vires, that it raises a devolution issue, that it appears to make some unusual or unexpected use of the powers conferred by the parent Act, that it is made under an Act excluding the instrument from challenge in the courts, or that it purports to have retrospective effect despite the absence of express provision in the parent Act.[105]

13–55 The Delegated Powers and Law Reform Committee is also responsible for maintaining the "correct balance" between primary and secondary legislation, through scrutiny of the delegated powers memorandum, which must be lodged immediately after a Bill that contains proposals for delegated law making powers is introduced.[106]

13–56 While all subordinate legislation is considered by the Delegated Powers and Law Reform Committee, the extent to which they are subject to other scrutiny in the Parliament depends, as at Westminster, largely on the provision made in the parent Act. The Interpretation and Legislative Reform (Scotland) Act 2010 ("the 2010 Act"), which was enacted following an extensive inquiry by the Subordinate Legislation Committee (below), reduced the procedures to which instruments may be subject under Acts of the Scottish Parliament to three: the affirmative procedure under which instruments require the Parliament's express approval, the negative procedure under which the Parliament retains a right of veto only, and the so-called "no procedure" or "no procedure other than laying" under which instruments are brought to the Parliament's attention through publication in the business bulletin, and subject to technical scrutiny by the Delegated Powers and Law Reform Committee, but are not subject to any other form of procedure. The intention was that future Acts of Scottish Parliament would provide for Scottish statutory instruments made under them to be subject to one of those three procedures, but this does not preclude the Parliament from demanding that instruments be subject to a heightened level of scrutiny, e.g. by way of super affirmative procedure (where the Parliament has an initial opportunity to comment on a draft before a final version is laid for approval in the normal way).[107] The 2010 Act also includes provision for the procedures to which instruments are subject to be changed.[108]

13–57 The policy as opposed to technical scrutiny of instruments takes place in subject committees (rather than ad hoc delegated legislation committees as at Westminster). Where an instrument is subject to the negative procedure, any member may, not later than 40 days after the instrument is laid, lodge a motion proposing that the lead committee recommend annulment of the instrument. If the lead committee agrees to recommend annulment, the Parliamentary Bureau must lodge a motion for annulment for debate in the Parliament, the debate on which is

---

[105] Scottish Parliament Standing Orders r.10.3; the Committee produces a very full annual report of its work; see most recently, Delegated Powers and Law Reform Committee 58th Report, *Report on Instruments considered in 2013–2014* (Scottish Parliamentary Paper 599, 2014).

[106] Scottish Parliament Standing Orders r.9.4A; Delegated Powers and Law Reform Committee 58th Report, *Report on Instruments considered in 2013–2014* (Scottish Parliamentary Paper 599, 2014) paras 236–258.

[107] See, e.g. National Parks (Scotland) Act 2000 s.6; Convention Rights Compliance (Scotland) Act 2001 ss.12, 13; Further and Higher Education (Scotland) Act 2005 ss.9(13), (14); Public Services Reform (Scotland) Act 2010 s.25.

[108] ILR(S)A 2010 s.34.

restricted to three minutes by the member proposing the motion and three minutes by the Minister in response.[109] The 2007 SNP minority government saw, not surprisingly, the first examples of successful motions to annul instruments.[110]

Where an instrument is subject to affirmative procedure, the lead committee **13–58** considers, on a motion from the Minister, whether to recommend approval of the instrument. If the committee agrees to recommend approval, the Parliamentary Bureau must lodge a motion for approval of the instrument, the debate on which is restricted in the same way as the debate on negative instruments.[111] If the committee does not recommend approval, it remains open to the Government to "appeal" directly to the Parliament by lodging a motion for approval of the instrument.[112]

The inquiry into the regulatory framework

The Subordinate Legislation Committee undertook an extensive inquiry into **13–59** subordinate legislation during Session 2 as a preliminary to instructing a Bill to replace the Statutory Instruments Act 1946 in its application to Scottish statutory instruments.[113] The Committee began by looking at the "regulatory framework", i.e. the framework governing the making of subordinate legislation, an unfortunate choice of phrase because of the risk, which to some extent materialised, of confusing subordinate legislation with regulation and, in particular, the imposition of burdens on business—the Committee's purpose might have been more aptly defined as being to examine the extent to which subordinate law making in the devolved Scotland conformed to "best practice" in subordinate law-making rather than best practice in regulation.[114]

In the second phase of its inquiry, the Committee turned its attention to the **13–60** parliamentary scrutiny of subordinate legislation. Had the Parliament been given the opportunity to devise a system and procedures for the scrutiny of subordinate legislation at the outset, the Committee suggested, it would not have chosen the system currently in operation, which the Committee and others found "unwieldy and complex".[115] It was of the view that

---

[109] Scottish Parliament Standing Orders r.10.4.

[110] Following the Justice Committee's recommendation, the Parliament agreed that nothing further be done under the Home Detention Curfew Licence (Prescribed Standard Conditions) (Scotland) Order 2008 (SSI 2008/36). The instrument was subsequently relaid and the motion for its annulment defeated. After motions recommending their annulment were supported by the Transport, Infrastructure and Climate Change Committee, the Government revoked the Mobility and Access Committee for Scotland Revocation Regulations 2008 (SSI 2008/187), and the Public Transport Users' Committee for Scotland Amendment Order 2008 (SSI 2008/186): Subordinate Legislation Committee 37th Report, *Report of Scottish Statutory Instruments laid in 2008* (Scottish Parliamentary Paper 316, 2009) paras 33–34.

[111] Scottish Parliament Standing Orders r.10.6.

[112] As happened with the Home Detention Curfew Licence (Amendment of Specified Days) (Scotland) Order 2008, which the Parliament approved after it was rejected by the Justice Committee: Scottish Parliament OR, March 12, 2008, col.6841.

[113] The Scotland Act 1999 (Transitory and Transitional Provisions (Statutory Instruments) Order 1999 (SI 1999/1096) applied the Statutory Instruments Act 1946 with modifications to the making of Scottish statutory instruments pending the making by the Parliament of its own arrangements.

[114] Subordinate Legislation Committee 31st Report, *Inquiry into the Regulatory Framework in Scotland* (Scottish Parliamentary Paper 397, 2005).

[115] Subordinate Legislation Committee 14th Report, *Report on the Inquiry into the Regulatory Framework in Scotland* (Scottish Parliamentary Paper 751, 2007) para.25.

"a new Parliament, with new and innovative ways of working, should devise a simplified system that is fit for purpose and is open to full and transparent scrutiny within realistic timescales".[116]

It accordingly recommended the replacement of the existing multiplicity of procedures with a new streamlined "Scottish statutory instrument procedure" under which Scottish statutory instruments, with certain exceptions, would be laid in draft before the Parliament, which would be able to disapprove an instrument within 40 days. Under the new procedure the Executive would be relieved of the need to obtain approval of instruments subject to affirmative resolution procedure—it would be enough that they had not been disapproved. The Committee recommended, however, that the Parliament be given advance notice of the Executive's programme of subordinate legislation, which would allow lead committees to concentrate their efforts on those instruments thought to merit the closest scrutiny. The Parliament itself would not be given the power to amend instruments, but the Executive would be able to amend a draft within the 40-day period in response to criticism made by the Subordinate Legislation Committee.

13–61 The Committee returned to the issue in Session 3, with an entirely new membership, its predecessor's recommendations having failed to gain the support of the outgoing Scottish Executive or its successor. It acknowledged the attractions of an entire overhaul of the system, but cautioned that the Parliament needed to be certain that any wholesale change in procedures would deliver benefits sufficient to outweigh any perceived drawbacks. There were, in its view, a number of difficulties with the proposed procedure, which led it to conclude that "the most workable outcome for both the Parliament and the Scottish Government would be to improve procedures within the existing framework".[117] Subject to some improvements, the current arrangements and procedures for scrutinising subordinate legislation should therefore be retained. Its recommendations were implemented by the Interpretation of Legislative Reform (Scotland) Act 2010, which, as well as rationalising the procedures to which instruments may be subject, makes provision for the numbering, printing and publication of Scottish statutory instruments, and of Acts of the Scottish Parliament, in place of the "temporary" provision made under the Scotland Act at the time of devolution.[118]

---

[116] Subordinate Legislation Committee 14th Report, *Report on the Inquiry into the Regulatory Framework in Scotland* (Scottish Parliamentary Paper 751, 2007) para.26.

[117] Subordinate Legislation Committee 12th Report, *Inquiry into the Regulatory Framework in Scotland* (Scottish Parliamentary Paper 74, 2008) para.18.

[118] Scotland Act 1998 (Transitory and Transitional Provisions (Statutory Instruments) Order 1999 (SI 1999/1096).

CHAPTER 14

FINANCE

INTRODUCTION

The power of the purse is no less important to the Parliament's position in the **14–01** devolved constitution than the power to make laws. Under the devolution settlement the power to tax was mainly reserved, save that the Parliament was given the power to vary the basic rate of income tax by up to three pence in the pound.[1] The power to spend, on the other hand, was devolved in line with the devolution of legislative and executive competence. The Scotland Act 1998 ("the Scotland Act") required the Scottish Parliament to establish effective arrangements for the scrutiny and audit of the Scottish Executive's expenditure, but left it to the Parliament to work out the details of those arrangements.[2] A Financial Issues Advisory Group ("FIAG") was set up to assist the Consultative Steering Group in developing the financial procedures the Parliament might be invited to adopt.[3] Its recommendations were accepted by the Scottish Executive and given legislative effect by the Public Finance and Accountability (Scotland) Act 2000, which was the first Bill passed by the Parliament after the emergency Mental Health (Public Safety and Appeals) (Scotland) Act 1999.

REVENUE

The block grant

Under the devolution settlement the Scottish Executive was to be mainly **14–02** financed by a grant paid by the Secretary of State for Scotland, from funds voted by the UK Parliament, to the Scottish Parliament. The choice of Treasury block grant rather than taxes as the principal means of financing the Scottish Executive reflected a number of considerations: the availability of an already existing mechanism for determining the Scottish Office's share of UK public expenditure in the shape of the population-based "Barnett formula"; Treasury opposition to the devolution of tax raising powers[4]; and, last but by no means least, a concern on the part of Scots to ensure that Scotland continued to receive its "fair share" of UK public expenditure. For the Scottish Constitutional Convention it was essential that Scotland continue to be "guaranteed her fair

---

[1] Scotland Act 1998 ("SA 1998") s.73; local taxes to fund local authority expenditure were also excepted from the reserved matter of fiscal, economic and monetary policy: SA 1998 Sch.5 Pt II s.A1.

[2] SA 1998 s.70(1); Scottish Office, *Scotland's Parliament* (1997) Cm.3658, para.7.27.

[3] Scottish Office, *Principles of the Scottish Parliament's Financial Procedures: Final Report of the Financial Issues Advisory Group* (1999). The Consultative Steering Group ("CSG") endorsed FIAG's recommendations, a summary of which is provided in Annex I of the CSG's Report, *Shaping Scotland's Parliament* (November, 1998).

[4] As to which, see Richard Rose, *Understanding the United Kingdom: The Territorial Dimension in Government* (London: Longman, 1982) p.201.

share of UK resources, as of right",[5] a concern acknowledged in the devolution White Paper, which said that the arrangements for financing the Scottish Parliament would, among other things, ensure that Scotland continued to benefit from its "appropriate share of UK public expenditure".[6]

14–03 As regards the method by which the block grant (or "assigned budget") would be determined, the White Paper said that it would be "objective, transparent and widely accepted".[7] The method is set out, not in the Scotland Act, but in a Treasury *Statement of Funding Policy*,[8] which Rawlings rightly describes as "one of the most important constitutional documents in the reinvention of the union state".[9] The arrangements set out in the statement (the terms of which have been agreed, in line with the principle of "mutual respect", between the Chief Secretary to the Treasury and the Secretaries of State for Scotland, Wales and Northern Ireland, following consultation with the Scottish Government, the Welsh Assembly Government and the Northern Ireland Executive) are said to represent, in many cases, "the continuation of long-standing conventions that have guided funding for Scotland, Wales and Northern Ireland".[10] The principle on which they are based is that changes in the budgetary provision of the devolved administrations funded by UK tax revenues or by borrowing will generally be linked to changes in planned spending on comparable public services by departments of UK Government, with this linkage generally being achieved by the population-based "Barnett Formula".[11] If, therefore, the UK Government increases health spending, the Scottish Government gets a population-based share (the "Barnett consequential") as extra funding; conversely, if the UK Government cuts health spending, the Scottish Government gets less. The advantage of this method of determining the devolved administrations' share of public expenditure is said to be that it that it largely removes the need to negotiate directly the allocation between Treasury Ministers, Secretaries of State and Ministers of the devolved administrations.[12] The purely conventional basis of the arrangements means, however, that the devolved administrations lack any guarantees of their funding.[13]

14–04 Aside from the method by which it is calculated, and its actual amount, the most important feature of the block grant from the point of view of the Scottish Government is that it is unconditional, i.e. it comes without strings attached. Subject to the requirement of annual parliamentary authorisation (below), and its statutory obligations, the Scottish Government is free to determine its own

---

[5] Scottish Constitutional Convention, *Scotland's Parliament, Scotland's Right* (1995) p.27.

[6] Scottish Office, *Scotland's Parliament* (1997) Cm.3658, para.7.2.

[7] Scottish Office, *Scotland's Parliament* (1997) Cm.3658, para.7.2.

[8] HM Treasury, *Funding the Scottish Parliament, National Assembly of Wales, and Northern Ireland Assembly: Statement of Funding Policy*, 6th edn (October, 2010).

[9] Richard Rawlings, *Delineating Wales: Constitutional, Legal and Administrative Aspects of National Devolution* (Cardiff: University of Wales Press, 2003) p.73.

[10] HM Treasury, *Funding the Scottish Parliament, National Assembly of Wales, and Northern Ireland Assembly: Statement of Funding Policy*, 6th edn (October, 2010) para.2.3.

[11] HM Treasury, *Funding the Scottish Parliament, National Assembly of Wales, and Northern Ireland Assembly: Statement of Funding Policy*, 6th edn (October, 2010) para.3.2, and House of Commons debate December 9, 1997, Vol.302, cols 510–513W.

[12] HM Treasury, *Funding the Scottish Parliament, National Assembly of Wales, and Northern Ireland Assembly: Statement of Funding Policy*, 6th edn (October, 2010) para 3.2.

[13] The Independent Expert Group, which advised the Calman Commission, saw it as a weakness of the arrangements that they were not enshrined in statute with the result that changes did not require parliamentary approval or the agreement of the devolved administrations: Independent Expert Group, *First Evidence from the Independent Expert Group to the Commission on Scottish Devolution* (November, 2008) para.1.7.8.

spending priorities.[14] If, therefore, in the example given, the UK Government allocates more to health spending, the Scottish Government gets the Barnett consequential as extra funding, but is free to spend it not on health but on other priorities. Conversely, if the UK Government cuts health spending, the Scottish Government gets less but can choose to apply the cuts elsewhere and protect health.

The Scotland Act 2012

The Scottish Constitutional Convention did not ignore the question of the **14–05** Parliament's financial accountability: it regarded the proposed tax varying power as "vital" if the Parliament was to be "properly accountable".[15] The Parliament's financial accountability, however, has been the subject of increasing attention since devolution, which may be said to have begun with Sir David Steel's Donald Dewar Memorial lecture in 2003 in which he argued that

> "no self-respecting parliament should expect to exist permanently on 100% handouts determined by another parliament, nor should it be responsible for massive public expenditure without any responsibility for raising revenue in a manner accountable to its electorate".[16]

Or, as Mitchell pithily summed it up, the pleasure of spending ought not to be divided from the odium of collecting.[17]

The Calman Commission was accordingly asked to recommend any changes **14–06** to the present constitutional arrangements that would, among other things, "improve the financial accountability of the Scottish Parliament". The Commission recommended that the Parliament should be responsible for raising more of its revenue, with part of its budget being found from devolved taxation under its control rather than from grant from the UK Parliament.[18] It recommended that the existing tax varying power should be replaced by a new Scottish rate of income tax, in partial replacement of UK income tax, and that certain other taxes (stamp duty land tax, the aggregates levy, landfill tax and air passenger duty) should be devolved. The Parliament should also be empowered to introduce further new devolved taxes with the agreement of the UK Parliament. The Commission was confident that its recommendations, once implemented, would make it clear that the Scottish Parliament was not "wholly dependent on grant from another Parliament" and was now responsible for raising "a significant proportion of its revenue", estimated at 35 per cent, "in a manner accountable to the electorate".[19]

The Calman Commission's recommendations were given effect (with some **14–07** modifications) by the Scotland Act 2012 ("the 2012 Act") in what the accompanying White Paper described as "the largest transfer of fiscal power from London since the creation of the United Kingdom",[20] a somewhat exaggerated

---

[14] Scottish Office, *Scotland's Parliament* (1997) Cm.3658, para.7.2.

[15] Scottish Constitutional Convention, *Scotland's Parliament, Scotland's Right* (1995) p.27.

[16] Lord Steel of Aikwood, Donald Dewar Memorial Lecture (Edinburgh International Book Festival) 2003.

[17] JDB Mitchell, *Constitutional Law*, 2nd edn (Edinburgh: W.Green, 1968) p.241.

[18] Commission on Scottish Devolution, *Serving Scotland Better: Scotland and the United Kingdom in the 21st Century* (2009) para.3.206.

[19] Commission on Scottish Devolution, *Serving Scotland Better: Scotland and the United Kingdom in the 21st Century* (2009) para.3.208.

[20] HM Government, *Strengthening Scotland's Future* (2010) Cm.7973, p.11.

claim given that the only previous transfer had been under the Government of Ireland Act 1920, and that was almost entirely eaten up by exceptions.[21] The 2012 Act, which inserts a new Pt 4A in the Scotland Act 1998, alters the Scottish Parliament's financial arrangements in three respects. It replaces the Scottish variable rate with a Scottish rate of income tax in partial replacement of UK income tax. It devolves stamp duty land tax and landfill tax, with provision for the devolution of other taxes with the agreement of the UK Parliament. And it increases the Scottish Ministers' borrowing powers.

Scottish rate of income tax

14–08 When the relevant provisions come into force in April 2016, the basic rate, higher rate and additional rate of income tax on the non-savings income of Scottish taxpayers will be reduced by 10 per cent, and the block grant to Scotland reduced accordingly.[22] It will then be for the Scottish Parliament to set a Scottish rate of income tax, in anticipation of the reduction, which will apply equally to all these rates.[23] The Calman Commission regarded it as a weakness of the tax varying power that if the Parliament did nothing its budget was unaffected.[24] Under the new regime the Parliament will have no choice but to set a rate even if it is only to make up the reduction in its budget; if it wishes to spend more (or less) it will need to set the rate accordingly. Like the tax varying power which it replaces, the power to set the Scottish rate will be exercisable by resolution of the Parliament, which under the Parliament's standing orders will only be able to be moved by a member of the Scottish Government.[25]

14–09 The tax varying power, which the Scottish rate of income tax replaces, was never exercised before it was repealed by the 2012 Act. Before its repeal the power had been allowed to lapse as a result of the first SNP Government's decision not to keep the record of Scottish taxpayers up to date. Its failure to inform the Parliament of its decision, which rendered the power unusable by a future administration, was the subject of extensive criticism.[26]

Devolved taxes

14–10 The Scotland Act 2012 devolves stamp duty land tax and landfill tax.[27] It also makes provision for the addition of new devolved taxes, and the modification of existing devolved taxes, by order made with the agreement of both Parliaments.[28] The boundary between reserved and devolved taxes may thus be

---

[21] Government of Ireland Act 1920 s.21(1); for comment, see Harry Calvert, *Constitutional Law in Northern Ireland: A Study in Regional Government* (London: Stevens & Sons, 1968) p.243.

[22] Scotland Act 2012 ("SA 2012") s.26.

[23] SA 1998 s.80C.

[24] Commission on Scottish Devolution, *Serving Scotland Better: Scotland and the United Kingdom in the 21st Century* (2009) para.3.172.

[25] SA 1998 s.80C(1), (8).

[26] Finance Committee 3rd Report, *The Scottish Variable Rate of Income Tax* (Scottish Parliamentary Paper 596, 2011).

[27] SA 2012 ss.28 and 30; UK stamp duty land tax is replaced with effect from April 2015 by a Scottish land and buildings transaction tax under the Land and Buildings Transactions Tax (Scotland) Act 2013, the first Act passed by the Parliament allowing the Scottish Government to set and collect a proportion of its own revenue.

[28] SA 1998 s.80B(1); tax-raising powers are devolved by creating an exception in favour of "devolved taxes" to the reserved matter of fiscal, economic and monetary policy. The Calman Commission did not anticipate the power to devolve "new" taxes being used to a great extent, but thought it should be available: Commission on Scottish Devolution, *Serving Scotland Better: Scotland and the United Kingdom in the 21st Century* (2009) para.3.171.

adjusted, and devolved taxes modified, without the need for UK primary legislation.

Borrowing

Under the devolution settlement the Scottish Ministers had no power to borrow money other than up to £500 million from the Secretary of State for the limited purposes of meeting a temporary shortfall or providing a working balance in the Scottish Consolidated Fund—the fund into which the block grant and the Scottish Government's other receipts are paid.[29] The 2012 Act extends the purposes for which the Scottish Ministers may borrow from the Secretary of State to include meeting the differences between forecast and outturn receipts from devolved taxes or from income tax charged by virtue of a Scottish rate resolution; they may also borrow with the Treasury's consent for the purpose of meeting capital expenditure.[30] Borrowing is fixed at £2.7bn, divided between £2.2bn for capital expenditure and £500m for current expenditure,[31] which limits may be varied by order, but not below the initial limits for capital and current expenditure.[32] **14–11**

Annual reports

The Secretary of State and the Scottish Ministers are required to make annual reports on the implementation and operation of the new financial arrangements, which reports must be laid before the Scottish Parliament and both Houses of Parliament.[33] **14–12**

Revenue Scotland

Revenue Scotland, a Scottish non-ministerial department established by the Revenue Scotland and Tax Powers Act 2014, is responsible for the collection and management of devolved taxes. The Scottish rate of income tax will continue to be collected by Her Majesty's Revenue and Customs. **14–13**

The Smith Commission Agreement

The Smith Commission Agreement recommended that Scottish Parliament should be given control over the rates and bands of UK income tax, but not the personal allowance; that the first 10 percentage points of the standard rate of VAT raised in Scotland should be assigned to the Scottish Government's budget; and that air passenger duty and the aggregates levy should be devolved as had been recommended by the Calman Commission. The Agreement also recommended that, as part of an updated fiscal framework for Scotland, consistent with the overall UK fiscal framework, the Scottish Government's borrowing powers should be increased **14–14**

> "to reflect the additional economic risks, including volatility of tax revenues, that the Scottish Government will have to manage when further financial responsibilities are devolved".[34]

---

[29] SA 1998 s.66.

[30] SA 1998 s.66(1), (1A).

[31] SA 1998 ss.67(2) and 67A(1).

[32] SA 1998 ss.67(3A), 67A(3).

[33] SA 2012 s.33.

[34] Smith Commission, *Report of the Smith Commission for further devolution of powers to the Scottish Parliament* (November 17, 2014) para.94(5).

PARLIAMENTARY AUTHORISATION OF EXPENDITURE

The need for parliamentary authorisation

14–15 The Scottish Government cannot spend money without the Scottish Parliament's approval. "That fundamental principle is at the heart of the relationship between the Parliament and the Executive."[35] The Public Finance and Accountability (Scotland) Act 2000 provides that the "use of resources" by the Scottish Administration and bodies or office holders whose expenditure is payable out of the Scottish Consolidated Fund

> "for any purpose in any financial year must be authorised for that year by Budget Act and must not exceed any amount so authorised in relation to that purpose".[36]

As at Westminster, the need for parliamentary approval of the broad purposes of expenditure, and of the amounts to be applied to such purposes, constitutes one of the fundamental supports of the central position of the Parliament within the devolved constitution.[37]

The financial initiative

14–16 As at Westminster, the government possesses the exclusive initiative in relation to finance. A Budget Bill seeking authorisation for expenditure may therefore only be introduced by a member of the Scottish Government[38]; amendments to a Budget Bill may also only be moved by a member of the Scottish Government (or a junior Scottish Minister).[39] A Bill that charges expenditure on the Scottish Consolidated Fund, or that gives rise to significant expenditure payable out of the Fund, also cannot be proceeded with after Stage 1, unless the Parliament has agreed to the expenditure by a financial resolution, which may be moved only by a member of the Scottish Government or a junior Scottish Minister.[40] There is no scope, therefore, for the Parliament to impose expenditure on the Scottish Government to which the latter is opposed.[41]

Budget Act authorisation is not enough

14–17 Parliamentary authorisation in the form of the annual Budget Act is a necessary but not a sufficient condition of propriety in devolved public expenditure. Statutory approval is also required for the activity giving rise to the expenditure. The Scottish Public Finance Manual acknowledges that Ministers may possess common law powers to undertake certain activities entailing expenditure, but insists that it would only be proper for them to use these powers in conjunction with the spending authority in a Budget Act where the expenditure

---

[35] Scottish Parliament OR September 30, 1999 col.971 (Donald Dewar).

[36] Public Finance and Accountability (Scotland) Act 2000 ("PFA(S)A 2000") s.1(1); the terminology reflects the move to "resource budgeting", i.e. to planning and controlling public expenditure in resource rather than cash terms.

[37] Terence Daintith and Alan Page, *The Executive in the Constitution: Autonomy, Structure and Internal Control* (Oxford: OUP, 1999) pp.104–105.

[38] Scottish Parliament Standing Orders r.9.16.2.

[39] Scottish Parliament Standing Orders r.9.16.6.

[40] Scottish Parliament Standing Orders r.9.12; where a Bill as introduced does not require a financial resolution an amendment at Stage 2 that would trigger the need for one cannot be voted on without a financial resolution first being agreed.

[41] On the executive's monopoly of the financial initiative as a defence against the extravagance of the legislature, see Gordon Reid, *The Politics of Financial Control: The Role of the House of Commons* (London: Hutchinson & Co, 1966) pp.35–45.

is below £1 million a year, or the expenditure is of a "one-off" nature, or the use of common law powers is temporary pending the seeking of statutory powers.[42]

Charges on the Scottish Consolidated Fund

The requirement of annual parliamentary authorisation for expenditure does not **14–18** extend to expenditure such as judges' salaries which is "charged on the [Scottish Consolidated] Fund by any enactment".[43] By agreeing to expenditure being charged on the Scottish Consolidated Fund, the Parliament waives its right to scrutinise the expenditure as part of the annual budget process (below). A Bill charging expenditure on the Scottish Consolidated Fund must therefore be accompanied by a report from the Auditor General for Scotland on the appropriateness of the charge, i.e. on whether it is appropriate for the Parliament to relinquish its right to approve the expenditure as part of the annual budget process.[44]

The budget process

FIAG sought a budget process that was less executive-dominated and subject **14–19** to greater parliamentary scrutiny than the process at Westminster

> "the Scottish Parliament should play a larger and more meaningful role in the scrutiny and approval of spending decisions than is currently the case at Westminster".[45]

It recommended the adoption of a three stage annual budget process, with the first stage being devoted to a discussion of strategic priorities for the following financial year, the second stage to consideration of a preliminary draft budget, and the third to obtaining formal parliamentary approval for a detailed budget drawn up in accordance with the priorities indicated by the Parliament at the first two stages. Parliamentary approval should be by means of primary legislation, but standing orders should enable financial legislation to be passed more quickly than was normally the case, by, for example, limiting the opportunities for non-Executive amendments. This would have the advantage of giving more opportunities for parliamentary scrutiny than would be the case if secondary legislation was used, without at the same time making the process impractical.[46] The Parliament should aim to complete this (largely formal) part of the process some weeks before the start of the new financial year.[47]

The budget process as revised

Following a review by the Parliament's Finance Committee,[48] the original **14–20** three stage process, as recommended by FIAG, has become essentially a two stage process, with the first of the original three stages now taking place only

[42] Scottish Government, *Scottish Public Finance Manual*, section on Expenditure without Statutory Authority.
[43] SA 1998 s.65(1)(a).
[44] Scottish Parliament Standing Orders r.9.3.4; no Bill so far introduced has required an Auditor General's report.
[45] Scottish Office, *Principles of the Scottish Parliament's Financial Procedures: Final Report of the Financial Issues Advisory Group* (1999) para.3.8.
[46] Scottish Office, *Principles of the Scottish Parliament's Financial Procedures: Final Report of the Financial Issues Advisory Group* (1999) para.3.50.
[47] Scottish Office, *Principles of the Scottish Parliament's Financial Procedures: Final Report of the Financial Issues Advisory Group* (1999) para.3.28.
[48] Finance Committee 5th Report, *Report on the Review of the Budgetary Process* (Scottish Parliamentary Paper 315, 2009).

once during the parliamentary session. The three stages have also been renamed, with Stage 1 becoming the Budget Strategy Phase, Stage 2 the Draft Budget Scrutiny Phase and Stage 3 the Budget Bill Phase. In addition to the Parliament's standing orders, important aspects of the process are governed by a written agreement between the Parliament's Finance Committee, which has overall responsibility for scrutinising public expenditure and the budget, and the Scottish Government.[49]

Budget strategy phase

14–21 Stage 1 of the original budget process was intended to allow the Parliament to express its views on future spending plans and priorities. It was meant to take place on an annual basis, but in 2005 it was agreed that, because major changes to the Scottish budget were unlikely to take place in non-UK spending review years, it should only take place in a year in which there was a UK spending review (in the event it did not take place in 2007, the year of the next UK spending review, because of the Scottish Parliament elections that year). In its report on the review of the budget process, the Finance Committee recommended that a "strategic scrutiny phase" should be undertaken at least once in each session of the Parliament, but that the timing and objectives of this phase should remain flexible.[50] A budget scrutiny phase was carried out in 2013 as part of the Finance Committee's draft budget scrutiny 2014–2015.

Draft budget scrutiny phase

14–22 The Draft Budget Scrutiny phase (formerly Stage 2 of the budget process), which is now the first of the two stages of the normal annual budget process, takes place between September and December each year, and is devoted to a detailed examination of the Scottish Government's draft budget for the coming financial year. Under its agreement with the Finance Committee, the Scottish Government undertakes to publish a draft budget by September 20 at the latest. The draft budget is examined by the Parliament's subject committees (and the equal opportunities committee), which report to the Finance Committee. A report to the Parliament is then prepared by the Finance Committee, which may include alternative spending proposals but which cannot increase the total expenditure proposed by the Government. The experience of conveners is that the timetable for budget scrutiny leaves insufficient time for committees to undertake this work in the level of detail it merits.[51] The Finance Committee's report is debated by the Parliament before the Christmas recess. Committees and individual members may seek to propose amendments to the Scottish Government's expenditure proposals by tabling amendments to the Finance Committee motion on which the report is debated. Under the agreement between the Finance Committee and the Scottish Government, however, amendments may not seek to increase the total expenditure proposed; amendments proposing an increase in one area must therefore recommend how the increase should be paid for.[52]

---

[49] Scottish Parliament, *Written Agreement between the Finance Committee and the Scottish Government on the Budget Process in Session 4 of the Scottish Parliament*; the Finance Committee also has written agreements with the Scottish Parliamentary Corporate Body and (through the Scottish Commission for Public Audit) with Audit Scotland, whose budgets are determined separately from the Scottish Government's.

[50] Finance Committee 5th Report, *Report on the Review of the Budgetary Process* (Scottish Parliamentary Paper 315, 2009) para.44.

[51] Conveners Group Legacy Paper—Session 3, para.24.

[52] Scottish Parliament, *Written Agreement between the Finance Committee and the Scottish Government on the Budget Process in Session 4 of the Scottish Parliament*, paras 10–15.

The Budget Bill phase

The Budget Bill phase (formerly Stage 3 of the budget process) constitutes the **14–23** second and final stage of the normal annual budget process. Under the agreement between the Finance Committee and the Scottish Government, the Scottish Ministers undertake to introduce a Budget Bill by January 20 each year.[53] The Bill goes through the same three stages as other Public Bills, but the opportunities for debate and amendment are more limited, the justification for their limitation being that the proposals have already been subject to scrutiny and that parliamentary authorisation needs to be secured before the start of the new financial year. The Stage 1 debate on the Bill's general principles takes place without the need for a Stage 1 report.[54] Amendments (at Stages 2 and 3) may be moved only by a member of the Scottish Government or a junior Scottish Minister.[55] And Stage 3 must be completed within 30 days of the Bill's introduction; if it is not completed within 30 days the Bill falls.[56] The failure of a Bill is not a bar to its re-introduction.[57] The minority SNP Government was defeated on the Budget Bill in January 2009 but succeeded in securing a revised Bill under the Emergency Bill procedure within a week of the defeat.

Emergency arrangements

FIAG regarded it as vital that the Parliament retain the right to accept or reject **14–24** the Scottish Executive's detailed spending proposals in their entirety.

> "[Rejection] should be seen as an option of last resort ... but it gives the Parliament the leverage to ensure the Executive does not flout its rules to an unacceptable degree."[58]

It was nevertheless anxious to avoid any suggestion of a budget crisis in the event that the Executive's expenditure proposals were not approved before the start of a financial year. Where, therefore, authorisation has not been secured by the start of the year, expenditure may continue but only for the purposes and within the limits laid down by the previous Budget Act.[59]

Budget revisions

The annual Budget Act makes provision for in-year adjustments to budget allo- **14–25** cations by order subject to the affirmative procedure.[60] Within portfolio budgets, as set out in the Budget Act, the Scottish Government retains the freedom to move funds between "budget sections" in response to changes in need, subject to informing the Parliament of transfers on a regular basis. It has undertaken not to move funds from one budget section to another in such a way as to increase the total budget for that section by more than 15 per cent, or £70

---

[53] Scottish Parliament, *Written Agreement between the Finance Committee and the Scottish Government on the Budget Process in Session 4 of the Scottish Parliament*, para.18.
[54] Scottish Parliament Standing Orders r.9.16.3.
[55] Scottish Parliament Standing Orders r.9.16.6.
[56] Scottish Parliament Standing Orders r.9.16.5.
[57] Scottish Parliament Standing Orders r.9.16.8.
[58] Scottish Office, *Principles of the Scottish Parliament's Financial Procedures: Final Report of the Financial Issues Advisory Group* (1999) para.3.19.
[59] PFA(S)A 2000 s.2 (resources); Budget (Scotland) Act 2014 ("B(S)A 2014") s.6 (cash/ payments out of the Scottish Consolidated Fund).
[60] see, e.g. B(S)A 2014 s.7 and the Budget (Scotland) Act 2014 Amendment Order 2014 (SSI 2014/363).

million at 2011 values, whichever is the lesser, without seeking the specific approval of the Parliament through the Budget revision procedure.[61]

Contingency payments

14–26 The Public Finance and Accountability (Scotland) Act 2000 recognises that there may be circumstances in which the Scottish Ministers need to undertake expenditure without Budget Act authorisation. They may, therefore, authorise the use of resources up to a maximum of 0.5 per cent of the total budget in any financial year where they consider that their use is necessarily required in the public interest, and it is not reasonably practicable, for reasons of urgency, for their use to be authorised by a Budget Act.[62] The annual Budget Act places a separate cash limit on this power, which is currently set at £50 million.[63] Where the Scottish Ministers invoke this power, they must, as soon as possible, lay before the Parliament a report setting out the circumstances of the authorisation and why they considered it necessary[64]; unless the circumstances are such that extreme urgency makes it impossible, the Scottish Ministers have undertaken to lay a report before the Parliament at least 14 days before undertaking any expenditure.[65]

Effectiveness of scrutiny

14–27 Although the Parliament's procedures compare favourably with those at Westminster, FIAG's aim of a budget process that is less executive-dominated and subject to greater parliamentary scrutiny has not been achieved. According to a former Permanent Secretary to the Scottish Government, while the Parliament's committee system has delivered some important benefits, "the effective scrutiny of the draft annual Budgets presented by successive governments, and the exercise of the scope to present alternative proposals, could not be judged to be among them",[66] a view shared by the first Auditor General for Scotland, for whom parliamentary scrutiny had not been as "robust and effective" as FIAG envisaged, with examination of the budget continuing to be, "for the most part, short term and incremental".[67]

14–28 Implementation of the Smith Commission Agreement, and with it the devolution of additional financial powers, raises the question of whether the Parliament would be better supported in its "challenge function" by a more specialised and expert body, along the lines of the UK Office of Budget Responsibility established by the Budget Responsibility and National Audit

---

[61] *Agreement on in Year Changes to Expenditure Allocations*, appended to the *Written Agreement between the Finance Committee and the Scottish Government on the Budget Process in Session 4 of the Scottish Parliament*, paras 4–7.

[62] PFA(S)A 2000 s.3.

[63] B(S)A 2014 s.5.

[64] PFA(S)A 2000 s.3(5); B(S)A 2014 s.5(6).

[65] *Agreement on in Year Changes to Expenditure Allocations*, appended to the *Written Agreement between the Finance Committee and the Scottish Government on the Budget Process in Session 4 of the Scottish Parliament*, paras 8–9.

[66] Sir John Elvidge, "Governance and the Institutional Framework' in Andrew Goudie (ed), *Scotland's Future: The Economics of Constitutional Change* (Dundee: Dundee University Press, 2013) p.279; see also the same author's *Northern Exposure: Lessons from the first twelve years of devolved government in Scotland* (London: Institute of Government, 2012) pp.28–30.

[67] Robert W Black, *Unlocking the Potential in Scotland's Public Services: From Good to Great by 2020* (Hume Occasional Paper No.96, December 2012) pp.30–31. In its Session 3 legacy paper, the Finance Committee emphasised the need to take a longer term and more strategic approach to financial scrutiny that was not limited to the annual budget process: 7th Report, *Session 3 Legacy Paper* (Scottish Parliamentary Paper 651, 2011).

Act 2011, "than by the present reliance on the Parliament own staff and, indirectly and unsystematically, Audit Scotland".[68] The Smith Commission agreed that, as part of an updated fiscal framework for Scotland, consistent with the overall UK fiscal framework, the Scottish Parliament should

> "seek to expand and strengthen the independent scrutiny of Scotland's public finances in recognition of the additional variability and uncertainty that further tax and spending devolution will introduce into the budgeting process".[69]

Following a recommendation from the Parliament's Finance Committee,[70] the Scottish Government established a non-statutory Scottish Fiscal Commission in June 2014, but in the White Paper that accompanied publication of draft clauses to implement the Smith Commission Agreement, the UK Government made it clear that a "sustainable and effective fiscal framework" would require "enhanced" independent scrutiny.

> "Given the increased importance of effective scrutiny as more responsibilities are transferred to the Scottish Parliament, independence, transparency and resources will be particular areas for further progress."[71]

FINANCIAL CONTROL AND ACCOUNTABILITY

The Scottish Consolidated Fund

The Scottish Consolidated Fund, into which the block grant and sums received **14–29** by office-holders in the Scottish Administration are paid, and from which the expenditure of the Scottish Administration is met, is central to the control of public expenditure in the devolved Scotland.[72] Payments from the fund are strictly controlled. The Scotland Act provides that a sum may only be paid out of the fund if:

(a) it has been charged on the fund by any enactment;
(b) it is payable out of the fund without further approval by virtue of the Scotland Act; or
(c) it is paid out "in accordance with rules made by or under an Act of the Scottish Parliament" for or in connection with the purposes of meeting expenditure of the Scottish Administration, or meeting expenditure payable out of the fund under any enactment.[73]

The Public Finance and Accountability (Scotland) Act 2000 provides that **14–30** payment in the last of these categories must be authorised by the annual Budget Act.[74] Payments from the fund thus require parliamentary authorisation, either

---

[68] Sir John Elvidge, "Governance and the Institutional Framework" in Andrew Goudie (ed), *Scotland's Future: The Economics of Constitutional Change* (Dundee: Dundee University Press, 2013) p.279.
[69] Smith Commission, *Report of the Smith Commission for further devolution of powers to the Scottish Parliament* (November 17, 2014) para.95(7).
[70] Finance Committee 1st Report, *Report on Proposals for a Scottish Fiscal Commission* (Scottish Parliamentary Paper 466, 2014).
[71] Scotland Office, *Scotland in the United Kingdom: An enduring settlement* (2015) Cm.8990, para.2.4.34.
[72] The Scottish Consolidated Fund was established by SA 1998 s.64.
[73] SA 1998 s.65(1), (2).
[74] PFA(S)A 2000 s.4(3).

in the form of permanent legislation charging expenditure on the fund, which legislation includes the Scotland Act, or else in the form of the annual Budget Act.

14–31 Access to the Scottish Consolidated Fund is controlled by the Auditor General for Scotland (below) whose written authority is required for payments from the fund. Under the Public Finance and Accountability (Scotland) Act 2000, sums cannot be paid out of the fund except in accordance with a credit granted on the fund by the Auditor General.[75] Credits are granted at the request of the Scottish Ministers, but a credit must not be granted if, in the Auditor General's opinion, the proposed payment would not comply with the requirements of the Scotland Act governing payments from the fund.[76]

Accountable officers

14–32 The Scotland Act provides that sums paid out of the Scottish Consolidated Fund must not be applied for any purpose other than that for which they were charged or paid out.[77] The Act also required provision to be made by or under Act of the Scottish Parliament for the designation of members of staff of the Scottish Administration to be answerable to the Parliament for the expenditure and receipts of each part of the Scottish Administration.[78] FIAG recommended that the Parliament introduce a system of "accountable officers", modelled on the accounting officer system at Westminster, who would be answerable to the Parliament for the actions of the Scottish Administration.[79] The Public Finance and Accountability (Scotland) Act 2000 accordingly designates the most senior member of staff of the Scottish Administration, i.e. the Permanent Secretary to the Scottish Government, as the principal accountable officer for the Scottish Administration.[80] The principal accountable officer in turn designates accountable officers for individual parts of the Scottish Administration, as well as for other public bodies, i.e. bodies and office holders outwith the Scottish Administration whose accounts are subject by statute to audit by, or under the control of, the Auditor General for Scotland.[81]

14–33 The Permanent Secretary's responsibilities as principal accountable officer are set out in the Public Finance and Accountability (Scotland) Act 2000. As the principal accountable officer for the Scottish Administration, the Permanent Secretary is answerable to the Parliament for the exercise of the following functions: signing the accounts of the expenditure and receipts of the Scottish Administration or any part of it, so far as it is not the function of any designated accountable officer to do so; signing the account of the Scottish Consolidated Fund; ensuring the propriety and regularity of the finances of the Scottish Administration; ensuring that the resources of the Scottish Administration are used economically, efficiently and effectively; designating

---

75 PFA(S)A 2000 s.5(1).

[75] PFA(S)A 2000 s.5(1).

[76] PFA(S)A 2000 s.5(3).

[77] SA 1998 s.65(3).

[78] SA 1998 s.70(1)(e).

[79] On the accounting officer system, see Terence Daintith and Alan Page, *The Executive in the Constitution: Autonomy, Structure and Internal Control* (Oxford: OUP, 1999) pp.126–129; FIAG preferred the description "accountable" rather than "accounting" as more accurately reflecting the role such individuals would have in being accountable to the Parliament for the actions of the Scottish Administration: Scottish Office, *Principles of the Scottish Parliament's Financial Procedures: Final Report of the Financial Issues Advisory Group* (1999) para.5.3.

[80] PFA(S)A 2000 s.14(1).

[81] PFA(S)A 2000 s.15(1), (3); ss.16 and 18 make separate provision for the appointment of accountable officers for the SPCB and Audit Scotland.

accountable officers, and determining their functions; and ensuring the performance of those functions by accountable officers for parts of the Scottish Administration.[82]

Accountable officers, for their part, are answerable to the Parliament for the **14–34** exercise of their functions as determined by the Permanent Secretary.[83] Their responsibilities are set out in separate memoranda from the Permanent Secretary to accountable officers for parts of the Scottish Administration and to accountable officers for other public bodies.[84] As determined by the Permanent Secretary, the functions for which they are answerable to the Parliament range from ensuring that effective management systems, including financial monitoring and control systems, are in place, to ensuring that managers at all levels have a clear view of their objectives, and the means to assess and measure outputs, outcomes and performance in relation to those objectives.[85] The essence of their role, however, is a *personal* responsibility for the propriety and regularity of the public finances for the part of the Scottish Administration or body for which they are answerable, and ensuring that its resources are used economically, efficiently and effectively.[86]

"Regularity" involves compliance with relevant legislation (including the **14–35** annual Budget Act) and guidance issued by the Scottish Ministers, in particular the Scottish Public Finance Manual and, in the case of public bodies, the framework document defining the key roles and responsibilities which underpin the relationship between the body and the Scottish Government. "Propriety" involves "respecting the Parliament's intentions and conventions and adhering to values and behaviours appropriate to the public sector".[87] Economy, efficiency and effectiveness in the use of resources is defined as "value for money within a framework of Best Value".[88] Accountable officers for parts of the Scottish Administration also have a particular responsibility for ensuring compliance with parliamentary requirements in the control of expenditure, including the fundamental requirement that funds should be applied only to the extent and for the purposes authorised by the Parliament in the annual Budget Act.[89]

---

[82] PFA(S)A 2000 s.14(3).

[83] PFA(S)A 2000 s.15(6).

[84] Scottish Public Finance Manual, *Memorandum to Accountable Officers for Parts of the Scottish Administration*, Section on Accountability, Annex 2; Scottish Public Finance Manual, *Memorandum to Accountable Officers for other Public Bodies*, Section on Accountability, Annex 3.

[85] Scottish Public Finance Manual, *Memorandum to Accountable Officers for Parts of the Scottish Administration*, Section on Accountability, para.5; Scottish Public Finance Manual, *Memorandum to Accountable Officers for other Public Bodies*, Section on Accountability, para.3.

[86] Scottish Public Finance Manual, *Memorandum to Accountable Officers for Parts of the Scottish Administration*, Section on Accountability, para.4.1; Scottish Public Finance Manual, *Memorandum to Accountable Officers for other Public Bodies*, Section on Accountability, para.2.1, original emphasis.

[87] Scottish Public Finance Manual, *Memorandum to Accountable Officers for Parts of the Scottish Administration*, Section on Accountability, para.7.1; Scottish Public Finance Manual, *Memorandum to Accountable Officers for other Public Bodies*, Section on Accountability, para.4.1.

[88] Scottish Public Finance Manual, *Memorandum to Accountable Officers for Parts of the Scottish Administration*, Section on Accountability, para.8.2; Scottish Public Finance Manual, *Memorandum to Accountable Officers for other Public Bodies*, Section on Accountability, para.5.2.

[89] Scottish Public Finance Manual, *Memorandum to Accountable Officers for Parts of the Scottish Administration*, Section on Accountability, para.7.2.

14-36 Particular importance attaches to accountable officers' role in ensuring that appropriate advice is tendered to Ministers and public bodies on all matters of financial propriety and regularity and on the economic, efficient and effective use of resources. Where an accountable officer for part of the Scottish Administration is instructed to take action that the officer considers inconsistent with the proper performance of an accountable officer's functions, including those of ensuring the propriety and regularity of finances and that resources are used economically, efficiently and effectively, the accountable officer is under a statutory duty to obtain written instructions from, as the case may be, the Scottish Ministers, the Lord Advocate (as head of the Crown Office and Procurator Fiscal Service) or the body or office holder in question.[90] Cabinet procedures for dealing with requests for such authority require any written authorities from Ministers to be assessed separately by the Deputy First Minister and Cabinet Secretary for Finance, Constitution and Economy, and cleared by the First Minister.[91] A Minister cannot therefore choose to go it alone in disregarding official advice. By the same token, the decision to disregard official advice, assuming it is confirmed by the Permanent Secretary,[92] is one that must be taken by the most senior Ministers in the administration in the knowledge that the Auditor General and the Public Audit Committee must be informed.[93]

ACCOUNTS AND AUDIT

The Auditor General for Scotland

14-37 The principal external, as opposed to internal, check on regularity and propriety and value for money is provided by the machinery of public audit. The Auditor General for Scotland, who is appointed by the Queen on the nomination of the Parliament for a single non-renewable term of eight years,[94] is responsible for auditing the accounts of the Scottish Ministers, the Lord Advocate and other persons to whom sums are paid out of the Scottish Consolidated Fund, and for initiating examinations into the economy, efficiency and effectiveness with which certain bodies and office holders have used their resources in discharging their functions. The Auditor General, who may be removed from office only with the support of a two-thirds majority of MSPs,[95] enjoys effective security of tenure, as well as being, by statute, not subject to the direction or control of

---

[90] PFA(S)A 2000 s.15(8); s.14(4) imposes a parallel duty on the principal accountable officer. The requirement to obtain written authority on value for money grounds applies only to the implementation of policy, policy itself being treated as a matter for Ministers: Scottish Public Finance Manual, *Memorandum to Accountable Officers for Parts of the Scottish Administration*, Section on Accountability, para.8.3. For the responsibility of accountable officers for public bodies, see Scottish Public Finance Manual, *Memorandum to Accountable Officers for Parts of the Scottish Administration*, Section on Accountability, paras 5.1–5.4.

[91] Scottish Public Finance Manual, *Memorandum to Accountable Officers for Parts of the Scottish Administration*, Section on Accountability, para.8.1.

[92] The relationship between the Permanent Secretary as principal accountable officer and accountable officers is addressed at Scottish Public Finance Manual, *Memorandum to Accountable Officers for Parts of the Scottish Administration*, Section on Accountability, para.3.

[93] Written ministerial authority was obtained in respect of the relocation of the headquarters of Scottish Natural Heritage from Edinburgh to Inverness in 2006: Audit Committee 1st Report, *Relocation of Scottish Executive departments, agencies and NDPBs* (Scottish Parliamentary Paper 758, 2007).

[94] SA 1998 s.69(1); PFA(S)A 2000 s.13(4A), (5A); the Public Finance and Accountability (Scotland) Act originally provided that the Auditor General held office until the age of 65 or until such later date as the Parliament might by resolution determine; the age limit was removed by the Employment Equality (Age) (Consequential Amendments) Regulations 2007 (SI 2007/825) reg.4.

[95] SA 1998 s.69(2).

any member of the Scottish Government or of the Parliament.[96] Appointment for a single term means also that the Auditor General cannot be influenced by the prospect of not being reappointed.

Audit Scotland

The Auditor General is assisted by Audit Scotland, which provides audit services to the Accounts Commission as well as to the Auditor General. Audit Scotland consists of the Auditor General, the Chairman of the Accounts Commission and three other members appointed by the Scottish Commission for Public Audit.[97] It was formed by the merger of the Accounts Commission for Scotland and National Audit Office (Scotland). Being subject to the directions of both the Auditor General and the Accounts Commission,[98] Audit Scotland has the appearance of something of a compromise, but one dictated by the importance attached to preserving "the autonomy of local government as a separate democratically accountable tier of government".[99] The Scottish Commission for Public Audit, which consists of the convenor of the Parliament's Public Audit Committee and four other MSPs, also examines Audit Scotland's budget proposals and arranges for the audit of its accounts.[100]

14–38

Audit of accounts

The Scottish Ministers, the Lord Advocate and every other person to whom sums are paid out of the Scottish Consolidated Fund in a financial year must prepare accounts of their expenditure and receipts for that year, which must be sent to the Auditor General for auditing.[101] The Scottish Ministers must also prepare an account of payments into and out of the fund, which likewise must be sent to the Auditor General for auditing.[102] Accounts may be audited by the Auditor General or by a suitably qualified person on the Auditor General's behalf.[103] Like the Auditor General, persons auditing expenditure on the Auditor General's behalf are not subject to the direction or control of any member of the Scottish Government or of the Parliament in the exercise of their functions.[104]

14–39

Although the basic principles of financial audit are common to both the public and private sectors, the "special accountabilities" that attach to the conduct of public business, and the use of public money, mean that public sector audits are planned and undertaken from a wider perspective than audits in the private sector. As well as the accounts, auditors also review and report on the arrangements made by audited bodies to ensure the proper conduct of their affairs with respect to regularity, propriety, the management of performance and the use of resources in accordance with the principles of Best Value and value for money.[105]

14–40

---

[96] SA 1998 s.69(4).

[97] PFA(S)A 2000 s.10(2).

[98] PFA(S)A 2000 s.10(4).

[99] Scottish Office, *Principles of the Scottish Parliament's Financial Procedures: Final Report of the Financial Issues Advisory Group* (1999) para.6.41; the Scottish Commission for Public Audit saw merit in delivering the existing functions within a simplified audit structure: 1st Report, *Review of the corporate governance of Audit Scotland* (Scottish Parliamentary Paper 160, 2008) paras 85–86, but the Public Services Reform (Scotland) Act 2010 left the structure unchanged.

[100] PFA(S)A 2000 ss.12, 25.

[101] PFA(S)A 2000 s.19(1), (7).

[102] PFA(S)A 2000 s.19(2), (7).

[103] PFA(S)A 2000 s.21(3).

[104] SA 1998 s.70(5).

[105] Auditor General for Scotland, *How government works in Scotland* (November, 2002) para.8.2; Audit Scotland, *Code of Audit Practice* (May, 2011) paras 10–11.

14–41 The auditor's report must set out the auditor's findings on a number of matters, including whether sums paid out of the Scottish Consolidated Fund have been applied for the purpose for which they were charged or paid out.[106] Where accounts have been audited on the Auditor General's behalf, they are sent together with the auditor's report to the Auditor General, who may prepare a section 22 report on the accounts, drawing attention to any issues raised in the course of the audit. The Auditor General must then send the accounts, the auditor's report and the section 22 report, if any, to the Scottish Ministers in sufficient time to enable them to lay these documents before the Parliament and to publish them within nine months of the end of the financial year to which they relate.[107] Reports sent to the Scottish Ministers enjoy absolute privilege in the law of defamation.[108]

3E examinations

14–42 The Auditor General may also initiate examinations into the economy, efficiency and effectiveness with which certain public bodies and office-holders have used their resources in discharging their functions.[109] (These 3E examinations are also commonly referred to as section 23 examinations/reports, value for money ("vfm") examinations/reports and performance audits/reports.) Three categories of bodies and office-holders may be subject to 3E examinations: bodies and office-holders whose accounts are audited by the Auditor General (above); bodies or office-holders, or classes of bodies or office-holders, specified by ministerial order; and bodies and office-holders not falling into either of these two categories but which agree to such an examination, e.g. as a condition of the receipt of public funding.[110]

14–43 The Scottish Ministers may only specify a body or office-holder if they reasonably believe that it received more than a quarter of its income, or more than £500,000, from public funds in a financial year, or, in the case of a class of body or office holder, if they reasonably believe that at least half of those in the class received more than a quarter of their income from public funds in a financial year.[111] David MacBrayne Ltd, Highlands and Islands Airports Ltd and the Scottish Futures Trust Ltd, among others, have been specified.[112]

14–44 3E examinations are carried out at the discretion of the Auditor General: "It is for the Auditor General personally to initiate an examination ... and to decide who is to carry out the examination".[113] The Auditor General must, however, take into account any proposals made by the Parliament in determining whether to carry out an examination.[114] The Parliament's Public Audit Committee is consulted each year on the Auditor General's work programme and it has used the opportunity to explore other possible topics with the Auditor General.[115] The examiner carrying out the examination is not entitled to question the merits of the policy objectives of the body or office-holder in question, on the basis that these are primarily a matter for Ministers, but the accuracy and

---

[106] PFA(S)A 2000 s.22(1).
[107] PFA(S)A 2000 s.22(3)–(5).
[108] PFA(S)A 2000 s.23A.
[109] PFA(S)A 2000 s.23(1).
[110] PFA(S)A 2000 s.23(2).
[111] PFA(S)A 2000 s.23(3).
[112] The Public Finance and Accountability (Scotland) Act 2000 (Economy, efficiency and effectiveness examinations) (Specified bodies etc.) Order 2010 (SSI 2010/389).
[113] PFA(S)A 2000 s.23(8).
[114] PFA(S)A 2000 s.23(6).
[115] Public Audit Committee 6th Report, *Legacy Paper Session 3* (Scottish Parliamentary Paper 620, 2011) para.15.

completeness of information on the basis of which policy decisions are reached, the means by which objectives are pursued, the implementation arrangements and controls, the costs incurred and the results achieved are all treated as legitimate subjects for examinations.[116] The examiner must report the results to the Auditor General, who may, but is not obliged to, report the results to the Parliament and publish them.[117] The results of examinations reported to the Parliament also enjoy absolute privilege in the law of defamation.[118]

Access to documents and information

Auditors and examiners have statutory rights of access to any documents in the **14–45** possession or under the control of bodies or office holders they may reasonably require when carrying out audits or 3E examinations; they may also require such information, explanation and assistance as they reasonably think necessary from any person holding, or accountable for, such documents.[119] They also have rights of access to and explanations of documents held by bodies in receipt of public funding from bodies audited or examined by the Auditor General, and by contractors, including subcontractors, for the provision of goods or services to bodies audited or examined by the Auditor General.[120]

The public audit committee

FIAG thought it essential that the Parliament have a powerful audit committee, **14–46** independent of the Scottish Executive, modelled on the Public Accounts Committee of the House of Commons.[121] The Public Audit Committee, the convener of which must not belong to the governing political party or parties,[122] considers and reports on accounts laid before the Parliament, reports laid before or made to the Parliament by the Auditor General, and other documents laid before the Parliament, or referred to it by the Parliamentary Bureau or by the Auditor General, concerning financial control, accounting and auditing in relation to public expenditure.[123] The bulk of its work consists of consideration of reports from the Auditor General. The Committee, which is briefed by the Auditor General, may respond to a report in a number of ways, including by simply noting it, by seeking clarification from the appropriate accountable officer, or by agreeing to conduct an inquiry, which usually results in the publication of its own report. In deciding whether to conduct an inquiry, the Committee has regard to the added value its published report might bring. In Session 3 the Committee published 19 reports, 14 of which arose from section 23 reports on economy, efficiency and effectiveness, and five from section 22 reports on the audit of the accounts of individual public bodies.[124]

---

[116] PFA(S)A 2000 s.23(9), Scottish Public Finance Manual, Section on Auditor General for Scotland, Annex 2: 3E Examinations, para.2.

[117] PFA(S)A 2000 s.23(10), (11).

[118] PFA(S)A 2000 s.23A.

[119] PFA(S)A 2000 s.24(1), (3).

[120] PFA(S)A 2000 s.24(2), (4), and the Public Finance and Accountability (Scotland) Act 2000 (Access to Documents and Information) (Relevant Persons) Order 2003 (SSI 2003/530).

[121] Scottish Office, *Principles of the Scottish Parliament's Financial Procedures: Final Report of the Financial Issues Advisory Group* (1999) para.3.8.

[122] Scottish Parliament Standing Orders r.6.7.2.

[123] Scottish Parliament Standing Orders r.6.7.1; the Committee's title was changed following the Standards, Procedures and Public Appointments Committee 8th Report, *Audit Committee— Title and Remit* (Scottish Parliamentary Paper 151, 2008).

[124] Public Audit Committee 6th Report, *Legacy Paper Session 3* (Scottish Parliamentary Paper 620, 2011) para.8; in Session 1 the Committee concentrated on section 23 reports, but in Session 2 it sought to strike a balance between addressing strategic issues and carrying out effective scrutiny of individual public bodies by extending its inquiry work to include section 22 reports: Audit Committee 3rd Report, *Legacy Paper Session 2* (Scottish Parliamentary Paper 796, 2007) para.12.

The Scottish Government has undertaken to respond to Committee reports within two months of publication.[125] Responses should make clear whether or not the Government agrees with or accepts, in part or in full, the Committee's conclusions and recommendations. Accountable officers are responsible for implementing recommendations that are accepted, and the Committee monitors, once or twice a session, their progress in doing so (by reference to a sample of recommendations). There have been calls for the Committee's powers to be extended to enable it to carry out inquiries without a report from the Auditor General, and to pursue local authority-related expenditure—which is a matter for the Accounts Commission.[126]

[125] Scottish Parliament, *Protocol between the Scottish Parliament and the Scottish Government in relation to the handling of Committee business* (October, 2009) para.41.
[126] Scottish Parliament OR March 3, 2011 cols 33800–33801 and 33812–33813.

CHAPTER 15

PARLIAMENTARY SCRUTINY

"The priority for Parliament is holding the Scottish Government to account. However there are numerous demands on the time of MSPs."[1]

INTRODUCTION

The Scottish Constitutional Convention expected the Parliament to provide **15–01** through its practices and procedures "a form of government in whose accountability, accessibility, openness and responsiveness the people of Scotland will have confidence and pride".[2] Accountability was not conceived solely in terms of parliamentary (or judicial) accountability,[3] but the Parliament was expected to play a prominent part in holding the Scottish Executive to account. The Consultative Steering Group ("CSG"), which believed that much of the work of the Parliament would be devoted to scrutiny, was thus "careful" to develop procedures designed to ensure that the Scottish Executive was "fully accountable" to the Scottish Parliament for its actions.[4] Recommending the CSG principles to the Parliament, Henry McLeish, the former chair of the CSG, claimed that the Scottish Executive would be "much more accountable to the Parliament in Scotland than the Government is to the Parliament in Westminster".[5] But although the Parliament's procedures compare favourably with those at Westminster in providing a range of mechanisms that individual MSPs and opposition parties can use to hold the Scottish Government to account, it is doubtful whether it is "much more accountable" to Holyrood than the UK Government is to Westminster.

MINISTERIAL ACCOUNTABILITY

The link between the Scottish Government and the Parliament is formed by **15–02** Ministers who are drawn from the Parliament (with the possible exception of

---

[1] Standards, Procedures and Public Appointments Committee 2nd Report, *Reform of Parliamentary business inquiry Phase 1 Report: Remodelling the Parliamentary Week* (Scottish Parliamentary Paper 57, 2011) para.15.

[2] Scottish Constitutional Convention, *Scotland's Parliament, Scotland's Right* (1995) p.24.

[3] Winetrobe suggests that what was sought was "some sort of uniquely Scottish synthesis of traditional representative democracy and a more direct or participatory democracy born out of supposed Scottish constitutional notions of the "sovereignty of the people": Barry K Winetrobe, "Public Accountability in Scotland" in Aileen McHarg and Tom Mullen, *Public Law in Scotland* (Edinburgh: Avizandum, 2006) p.136.

[4] Scottish Office, *Shaping Scotland's Parliament: Report of the Consultative Steering Group on the Scottish Parliament* (December, 1998) section 2, para.25 and section 3.4, para 1; accountability was one of the key principles on which the CSG's proposals were based: "the Scottish Executive should be accountable to the Scottish Parliament, and the Parliament and Executive should be accountable to the people of Scotland".

[5] Scottish Parliament OR June 9, 1999 col.367.

the law officers), appointed with the agreement of the Parliament,[6] and accountable to the Parliament on the Westminster model. The Scottish Ministerial Code defines the accountability of Ministers in essentially the same terms as the UK Ministerial Code, the terms themselves following closely resolutions on ministerial accountability adopted by the House of Commons and the House of Lords in the dying days of the 1992 Parliament.[7] Like their UK counterparts, the Scottish Ministers are under a duty to the Parliament "to account, and be held to account, for the policies, decisions and actions taken within their field of responsibility".[8]

15–03 The Scottish Ministerial Code imposes two related duties on Ministers. The first is a duty to give "accurate and truthful information" to the Parliament. It is of "paramount importance", the Code insists, that Ministers give "accurate and truthful information to the Parliament, correcting any inadvertent error at the earliest opportunity". "Ministers who knowingly mislead the Parliament", it warns, "will be expected to offer their resignation to the First Minister".[9]

15–04 The second is a duty to be "as open as possible" with the Parliament and the public, reflecting the aspirations set out in the CSG's report.[10] Ministers should refuse to provide information only in accordance with the Freedom of Information (Scotland) Act 2002 and other relevant statutes.[11] They should also require civil servants who give evidence before committees on their behalf and under their direction to be as helpful as possible in providing accurate, truthful and full information in accordance with the duties and responsibilities of civil servants as set out in the Civil Service Code.[12]

15–05 The Scottish Ministerial Code also provides that:

> "In all their dealings with the Parliament, Ministers should seek to uphold and promote the key principles which guided the work of the Consultative Steering Group on the Scottish Parliament."

The key principles endorsed by CSG were: sharing the power, accountability, access and participation and equal opportunities.[13]

---

[6] Scotland Act 1998 ("SA 1998") s.47(2).

[7] House of Commons debate March 19, 1997, Vol.291, cols 1046–1047; House of Lords debate March 20, 1997, vol.597, cols 1055–62.

[8] Scottish Government, *Scottish Ministerial Code* (2011) para.1.2(b). The duty under the UK Ministerial Code is a duty to account, and be held to account, for the policies, decisions and actions "of their department and agencies", the difference in language reflecting the abolition of Scottish Government departments in 2007.

[9] Scottish Government, *Scottish Ministerial Code* (2011) para.1.2(c). Apologies, more or less sincere, for misleading the Parliament have become not uncommon in recent years: see, for example, Scottish Parliament OR November 24, 2010 cols 30725–30766 (failure to inform the Parliament that the tax-varying power had been allowed to lapse); and Scottish Parliament OR November 15, 2012 cols 13591–13593 and November 20, 2012 cols 13605–13610 (college funding). Several of the complaints to the panel of independent advisers have also involved the duty to give accurate and truthful information: see para.5–34.

[10] The CSG sought an "open, accessible and, above all, participative Parliament, which will take a proactive approach to engaging with the Scottish people—in particular those groups traditionally excluded from the democratic process": Scottish Office, *Shaping Scotland's Parliament: Report of the Consultative Steering Group on the Scottish Parliament* (December, 1998) s.2, para.4.

[11] Scottish Government, *Scottish Ministerial Code* (2011) para.1.2(d).

[12] Scottish Government, *Scottish Ministerial Code* (2011) para.1.2(e).

[13] Scottish Government, *Scottish Ministerial Code* (2011) paras 3.1–3.2.

Discussion of the doctrine of ministerial responsibility tends to concentrate on **15–06** the consequences of administrative or other failure for Ministers, rather than the day-to-day business of giving an account and being held to account which is the doctrine's principal concern. When matters go wrong, there is a clear expectation that Ministers will take appropriate remedial action, at least so far as it is in their power to do so. There is no expectation, on the other hand, that they will resign, which is not to say that they will not come under pressure to do so, or that there will not be occasions when resignation is the only fitting outcome. As is the case with the Scottish Government as a whole, the Parliament has it in its power to force the removal of an individual Minister through a motion of no confidence. A Minister in whom a motion of no confidence is passed is not under a legal obligation to resign, in contrast to the Scottish Government,[14] but a Minister in whom a motion of no confidence was passed would doubtless resign—or be removed by the First Minister.

So long as the Scottish Government retains command of a majority in the **15–07** Parliament, the outcome of a motion of no confidence ought not to be in doubt.[15] Where the Government lacks a majority, as was the case in Session 3, the position is potentially different. Stewart Stevenson's resignation in December 2010 over the handling of the traffic chaos caused by extreme winter weather was prompted by the realisation that he could not survive a motion of no confidence. His resignation, however, was very much the exception. On other occasions in Session 3, the First Minister was able to use the threat of his own resignation, which would have prompted an extraordinary general election, to prevent the opposition parties from seeking to remove a Minister through a motion of no confidence. When, therefore, it emerged in November 2010 that the tax-varying power had been allowed to lapse without the Parliament being informed, the Parliament confined itself to passing a motion criticising Ministers for "misleading" the Parliament over its continued availability, and condemning its abandonment without the Parliament's approval as an "abuse of power", rather than a motion of no confidence in the responsible Minister.[16]

Stewart Stevenson's is the only resignation so far to have arisen as a result of **15–08** administrative failure. Other ministerial resignations have been as a result of disagreements over policy or, in one case, personal indiscretion.[17]

QUESTIONS

Over and above the opportunities provided by the Scottish Government's need **15–09** for parliamentary approval of its legislative and spending proposals, there are

---

[14] SA 1998, ss.45(2), 47(3)(c), 49(4)(c).

[15] There have been three formal motions of no confidence in individual ministers, all unsuccessful: Sam Galbraith over the Scottish Qualifications Authority, Scottish Parliament OR December 13, 2000, cols 841–864; Sarah Boyack over transport policy, Scottish Parliament OR February 15, 2001, cols 1279–1305; and Alex Neil over mental health service provision in Lanarkshire, Scottish Parliament OR May 21, 2014, cols 31285–31299; and two de facto motions of no confidence that were also unsuccessful: Malcolm Chisholm over hospital reorganisation and closures, Scottish Parliament OR September 30, 2004, cols 10743–10796; and Kenny MacAskill over police reform: Scottish Parliament OR October 8, 2014, cols 32–58.

[16] Scottish Parliament OR November 24, 2010, cols 30725–30766.

[17] Tavish Scott resigned in March 2001 over the Executive's fisheries policy, and Malcolm Chisholm in December 2006 over the replacement of Trident; Richard Simpson resigned in November 2002 after making disparaging comments about striking fire fighters.

three principal mechanisms by which the Parliament holds the Government to account: questions, debates, and committee inquiries.

15–10   "Any member may put a question to the Scottish Government for answer in the Parliament."[18] The right of members to ask questions of the Scottish Government is regarded as an essential part of the process by which the Parliament holds the Government to account. The Parliament's standing orders, which govern the admissibility of questions, provide that questions must, among other things, "relate to a matter for which the First Minister, the Scottish Ministers or the Scottish Law Officers have 'general responsibility'".[19] Questions on reserved matters are therefore not admissible, but where a decision or policy on a reserved matter has a clear impact on a matter for which the Scottish Government has responsibility, the Scottish Government can be asked what representations it has made to the UK Government regarding the decision or policy on the reserved matter.[20]

15–11   In advance of the independence referendum, there were many questions asking what would be the position in an independent Scotland in relation to various reserved matters, e.g. defence or social security. Because the Scottish Government was elected on a manifesto that included holding a referendum on independence, its view was that it was entitled to use civil service resources to pursue all aspects of the wider independence agenda, including by answering such questions. As a devolved administration, however, it was not clear on what basis anything other than making arrangements for the referendum itself, a matter which was devolved, could be said to fall within the Scottish Government's "general responsibilities".

"Inspired" questions

15–12   "Inspired" or "planted" questions are questions initiated by the Scottish Government (although lodged by backbench MSPs rather than by Ministers) to bring matters to the attention of the Parliament, e.g. a new policy initiative or the outcome of a consultation exercise. A common criticism of such questions is that they provide a means of avoiding scrutiny through the questioning or debate that follows a ministerial statement in the chamber.[21] There is no satisfactory way, however, of distinguishing the use of inspired questions for the purpose of bringing matters to the attention of the Parliament from their use as a means of avoiding answering awkward or embarrassing questions. The same inspired question can both bring information to the attention of the Parliament, and avoid some of the scrutiny that would accompany the use of another procedural mechanism. Nor is it always clear at the time a parliamentary question is lodged what appetite there may be for debate; the Scottish Government could therefore opt for the inspired question route in good faith but still find itself criticised for trying to avoid scrutiny.

Question time

15–13   Question time has become an increasingly prominent feature of the Parliament's proceedings. Questions were originally taken only on Thursdays but are now taken on each day the Parliament is sitting: topical questions for up to 15 minutes normally on Tuesdays, portfolio questions for up to 40 minutes

---

[18] Scottish Parliament Standing Orders r.13.3.1.
[19] Scottish Parliament Standing Orders r.13.3.3.
[20] Scottish Parliament, *Guidance on Parliamentary Questions*, 2nd edn (March, 2014) s.5.
[21] See e.g. Scottish Parliament OR December 4, 2012 cols 14284–14285.

normally on Wednesdays, and First Minister's questions ("FMQs") for up to 30 minutes and general questions (which must not concern the Ministerial portfolio or portfolios taken at portfolio questions that week) for up to 20 minutes normally on Thursdays. Emergency questions may also be asked, but only nine have been put in the Chamber in 14 years.[22]

Topical questions were introduced in Session 4 as part of a more general effort **15–14** to secure a greater degree of topicality and relevance in the Parliament's proceedings, by enabling backbenchers to question the Government at short notice on matters with national implications or national significance. The deadline for submitting questions was also relaxed and the time allocated to questions increased (from an hour to 1 hour 15 minutes, excluding FMQs) as part of the same effort to improve the Parliament's responsiveness.[23]

First Minister's questions and topical questions are selected for answer by the **15–15** Presiding Officer from questions submitted by members. Portfolio and general questions are asked by members selected by ballot. Supplementary questions may be asked. Oral questions not reached or asked receive a written answer. Upwards of 1,000 oral questions are answered in the course of a parliamentary year; in 2013–2014, 215 questions were answered at First Minister's question time, and 1,007 questions at general and portfolio question time, with 76 topical questions also being answered.

Written questions

There is no limit on the number of written questions members may ask but **15–16** members are expected to exercise restraint in their use of written questions.[24] Written questions should normally be answered within 10 "counting days", i.e. days on which the Parliament is open for business and excluding public holidays,[25] but it is open to the Scottish Government to issue a "holding answer", saying that it will reply to the member as soon as possible. Answers to written questions are published in a separate written answers report. After showing little change for many years the number of written questions fell sharply in 2013–2014: from 6,630 questions lodged for answer the previous year to 5,044 questions.

The Scottish Government has issued guidance on drafting answers to parlia- **15–17** mentary questions, which is intended to ensure that MSPs receive "prompt, accurate, and helpful responses to PQs, whilst avoiding disproportionate burden on the Government".[26] The guidance provides that every question should be approached with a view to giving the relevant information "consistent with the Code of Practice on Access to Scottish Executive Information"— disregarding the fact that the Code of Practice was superseded by the Freedom

---

[22] Scottish Parliament Fact sheet, *Emergency Questions* (October, 2013); there is a slot for questions at First Minister's Questions that is traditionally used for urgent constituency matters.

[23] For a generally favourable assessment, see Standards Procedures and Public Appointments Committee 1st Report, *Review of Parliamentary Reform* (Scottish Parliamentary Paper 451, 2014) paras 8–20.

[24] Scottish Government, *Guidance for SG Staff on Scottish Parliamentary Questions* (2013) s.11.

[25] Scottish Parliament Standing Orders r.13.5.2.

[26] Scottish Government, *Guidance for SG Staff on Scottish Parliamentary Questions* (2013); the guidance is modelled on UK guidance, now much cut down, which was first issued in the wake of the arms to Iraq scandal.

of Information (Scotland) Act in 2005. The more important point, however, is that it is for Ministers to decide how questions should be answered:

> "It is a civil servant's responsibility to help Ministers to fulfil their obligations but ultimately it is the Minister's right and responsibility to decide how to do so."[27]

Accordingly, where there is

> "a particularly fine balance between the aim of openness and the need for non-disclosure and where the draft answer gives precedence to the later—this should be explicitly drawn to the Minister's attention. Similarly, when the draft answer provides information of a sort which is not normally disclosed, this should be drawn to the Minister's attention".[28]

15–18 The quality and relevance of answers to parliamentary questions is a recurring issue at Westminster,[29] but not one that has arisen formally at least at Holyrood.

DEBATES

15–19 Debates provide the other principal means of holding the Scottish Government to account in the Chamber.

> "General debates offer the Executive an opportunity to present its policies and decisions, and non-Executive parties with opportunities to scrutinise Executive actions and policies, and to present their own policy proposals."[30]

Under the Parliament's standing orders a certain amount of time is earmarked for opposition and committee business, with the remainder of the time being treated as de facto at the disposal of the Government. In the current session 16 "half sitting days" in each parliamentary year are devoted to business chosen by political parties not represented in the Scottish Government (and any group formed under r.5.2.2),[31] with the business of committees being given priority over Government business on a further 12 half sitting days.[32] This leaves 40 or so half sitting days or "debate slots" that are at the disposal of the Scottish Government, over and above the 30 or so that are taken up with legislation and ministerial statements.[33] The Government thus enjoys a substantial

---

[27] Scottish Government, *Guidance for SG Staff on Scottish Parliamentary Questions* (2013) p.10.

[28] Scottish Government, *Guidance for SG Staff on Scottish Parliamentary Questions* (2013) p.10.

[29] See most recently, Procedure Committee, *Written Parliamentary questions: monitoring report* (HC 2013–2014, 1046).

[30] Procedures Committee 3rd Report, *The Founding Principles of the Scottish Parliament: the application of Access and Participation, Equal Opportunities, Accountability and Power Sharing in the work of the Parliament* (Scottish Parliamentary Paper 818, 2003) para.486.

[31] Scottish Parliament Standing Orders r.5.6.1(b).

[32] Scottish Parliament Standing Orders r.5.6.1(a).

[33] A debate slot does not equal half a sitting day. It is in fact the amount of time left from a half day (i.e. a meeting of the Parliament, usually beginning after lunch—the committee slot in the morning being the other "half" of that sitting day) once certain procedurally required items (Time for Reflection, oral questions, Decision Time, Members' Business) and certain other items scheduled for that day (e.g. ministerial statements) have been discounted. A debate slot can, therefore, shrink in some cases to only about 90 minutes—while still being counted (if it is an opposition or committee debate) as one of the mandatory "half days".

advantage over the opposition parties when it comes to the use of debating time in the Chamber.

There is also a period of up to 45 minutes set aside each day for members' **15–20** business.[34] Members may use this opportunity to raise particular constituency or regional matters or to draw attention to causes in which they are interested. There have been suggestions, supported by the Standards, Procedures and Public Appointments Committee, that the "constituency link" for members' business be dropped in order to help combat the perception that chamber business is "pre-programmed down party political lines", but the Parliamentary Bureau has resisted these on the grounds that the CSG's objective was to "allow members to raise non-controversial, constituency related issues".[35] There is no reason, however, why the Parliament should continue to be limited by the CSG's conception of members' business.

Debates in the normal course of events are a weak instrument of parliamentary **15–21** control. Debates in the Scottish Parliament are no exception. So long as the Scottish Government retains command of a majority their outcome is not in question. There has also been persistent criticism of their relevance and quality. The Session 2 Procedures Committee agreed with concerns that Chamber time was too often used for debates on "relatively anodyne subjects".

> "There is a perception that, apart from their own spokespersons, the parties often struggle to find members willing to speak in these debates, and Chamber attendance tends to be limited mainly to those on the speakers' list. We believe all political parties should reflect on how to address these issues."[36]

The criticism is one that the Parliament has yet to overcome.

COMMITTEE INQUIRIES

As a committee-based Parliament it is to the Parliament's committees that we **15–22** might look to make the biggest difference in holding the Scottish Government to account, but as we saw in Ch.4, the Parliament's committees have fallen some considerable way short of initial expectations when it comes to the business of holding government to account.

Official information and accountability

Under s.23 of the Scotland Act 1998, committees have the power to require **15–23** any person, including Ministers and officials, to appear before them or to produce documents concerning "any subject for which a member of the

---

[34] Scottish Parliament Standing Orders r.5.6.1(c).

[35] Standards, Procedures and Public Appointments Committee 2nd Report, *Reform of Parliamentary Business Inquiry Phase 1 Report: Remodelling the Parliamentary Week* (Scottish Parliamentary Paper 57, 2011) paras 86–91; Standards, Procedures and Public Appointments Committee 2nd Report, *Parliamentary Reform—Standing Order Rule Changes* (Scottish Parliamentary Paper 138, 2012) Annexe A; Scottish Office, *Shaping Scotland's Parliament: Report of the Consultative Steering Group on the Scottish Parliament* (December, 1998) s.3.3, para.7.

[36] Procedures Committee 11th Report, *Review of Parliamentary Time* (Scottish Parliamentary Paper 699, 2006) para.87.

Scottish Government has general responsibility".[37] A critical question which arose at an early stage was whether committees would be prepared to use this power to compel the disclosure of information against the wishes of the Scottish Executive. Following an inquiry in which a committee was denied copies of advice given by officials to Ministers, a Scottish Executive motion on official information and accountability set out the principles which in its view should "inform and underpin" the relationship between the Parliament and the Executive.[38]

15–24 In the first of three principles, which the motion commended to the Parliament's committees as guidelines to be followed in their dealings with the Executive, the Executive affirmed its commitment to being as open as possible in its dealings with the Parliament and its committees

> "consistent with its policy of openness, the Executive should always seek to make as much information as possible publicly available as a matter of course and should respond positively to requests for information from the Parliament and its Committees".

In the second principle, the Executive reiterated the traditional orthodoxy of ministerial accountability—"officials are accountable to Ministers and Ministers are in turn accountable to the Parliament"—from which it followed that "while officials can provide Committees with factual information, Committees should look to Ministers to account for the policy decisions they have taken".

15–25 The crucial principle, however, was the final one in which the Executive underlined the importance it attached to maintaining the confidentiality of exchanges between Ministers and officials

> "where, exceptionally, Committees find it necessary to scrutinise exchanges between officials and Ministers on policy issues, arrangements should be made to ensure that the confidentiality of these exchanges is respected".

The hope was that an arrangement whereby committees were given sight of that advice without it being made public would make it unnecessary for committees to have recourse to their formal powers.

> "If we can develop a responsible and mature relationship between the Executive and the Parliament, characterised by mutual respect and trust, I believe that the Parliament should not find it necessary to exercise its formal powers under section 23."[39]

That belief has yet to be confounded.

The "MacOsmotherly rules"

15–26 The Executive's motion on official information and accountability was followed three months later by guidance for officials called upon to give

---

[37] SA 1998 s.23(8); Scottish Parliament Standing Orders r.12.4.1.
[38] Scottish Parliament OR November 1, 2000 cols 1197–1245; Education, Culture and Sport Committee 11th Report, *Exam Results Inquiry* (Scottish Parliamentary Paper 234, 2000) para.11. For critical comment, see Barry K Winetrobe, "Public Accountability in Scotland" in Aileen McHarg and Tom Mullen, *Public Law in Scotland* (Edinburgh: Avizandum, 2006) pp.143–144.
[39] Scottish Parliament OR November 1, 2000 col.1204 (Henry McLeish).

evidence before committees, which is sometimes referred to as the "MacOsmotherly rules" after the UK Osmotherly rules on which it is based.[40] The guidance emphasises, in line with the traditional understandings of the doctrine of ministerial accountability, that officials who give evidence to committees do so "on behalf of their Ministers, under their directions and with their approval".

> "Officials are accountable to Ministers and are subject to their instruction; but they are not directly accountable to the Parliament. This does not mean, of course, that officials may not be called upon to give a full account of Executive policies, or indeed of their own actions or recollections of particular events. But their purpose in doing so is to contribute to the central process of Ministerial accountability, not to offer personal views or judgements on matters of political controversy ... "[41]

Within the overall limits of their constitutional position, officials are enjoined **15–27** to be "as helpful as possible" in providing information relevant to committee inquiries.

> "Officials should comply with the Code of Practice on Access to Scottish Executive Information and its accompanying guidance. Officials should be as forthcoming as they can in providing information under the terms of the Code, whether in writing or in oral evidence, relevant to a Committee's field of inquiry. Any withholding of information should be limited to reservations that are necessary in the public interest, which should be decided in accordance with the law and the exemptions as set out in the Code."[42]

The injunction to be as helpful as possible does not mean that there are no **15–28** limits to how helpful the Scottish Government is prepared to be, with the summoning of named officials as well as access to official advice both clearly identified as "red lines" beyond which it will not go.[43] The more recent protocol between the Scottish Parliament and the Scottish Government in relation to the handling of committee business also strikes a rather less helpful note:

> "When conveners and clerks request written information or oral evidence Scottish Ministers will consider whether such requests are within the limits of what they can divulge ... "[44]

---

[40] Scottish Executive, *Evidence and Responses to Committees of the Scottish Parliament* (February, 2001). The UK guidance was revised in 2005, and again 2014, but the Scottish guidance has not been revised since it was first issued, suggesting that its relationship with the Parliament is not an issue for the Scottish Government.

[41] Scottish Executive, *Evidence and Responses to Committees of the Scottish Parliament* (February, 2001) paras 3.1–3.2.

[42] Scottish Executive, *Evidence and Responses to Committees of the Scottish Parliament* (February, 2001) para.4.1; the current version of the UK guidance provides that in giving evidence to committees, "officials should care to ensure no information is withheld which would not be exempted if a parallel request were made to the Department under the Freedom of Information Act": Cabinet Office, *Giving Evidence to Select Committee: Guidance for Civil Servants* (October, 2014) para.1.

[43] Scottish Executive, *Evidence and Responses to Committees of the Scottish Parliament* (February, 2001) paras 3.11 and 4.11; see also the *Protocol between the Scottish Parliament and the Scottish Government in relation to the handling of Committee business* (October, 2009) paras 19 and 21.

[44] *Protocol between the Scottish Parliament and the Scottish Government in relation to the handling of Committee business* (October, 2009) para.18.

At Westminster, the Osmotherly rules on which the Scottish Executive guidance is based have long been controversial with calls by the liaison committee for a review of the relationship between government and select committees with the aim of producing joint guidelines for departments and select committees, which "recognise ministerial accountability, the proper role of the Civil Service and the legitimate wish of Parliament for more effective accountability".[45] What is most striking about a Parliament that was meant to be "different" is that essentially the same rules seem to have been accepted without demur.

Recommendations

15–29   The committees' power is a power to make recommendations; they cannot require the Scottish Government to take action on or accept their recommendations.[46] Under a protocol with the Parliament, the Government is expected to respond to recommendations in reports within two months of publication.[47] In its Session 3 legacy paper, the Conveners Group urged committees to ensure that their recommendations were followed up.[48] The pressure of business means, however, that this seldom happens.

PROSPECTS

15–30   With a single party majority government, with its uncomfortable echoes of Lord Hailsham's "elective dictatorship",[49] in power in Session 4, the weakness of the Parliament in relation to the Scottish Government is apparent as never before, with protests by the minority in the run up to the independence referendum that the Government was using its majority to close down inquiries or to edit out criticisms of government policy.[50] In contrast to Westminster, however, there have been few signs of willingness to acknowledge much less address the underlying tension between sustaining the Scottish Government in power and holding it to account—to ensure that the Parliament gets its scrutiny as well as the Government its business.[51]

15–31   Faced with an avalanche of criticism at the end of Session 3,[52] the Parliament embarked on what the Standards, Procedures and Public Appointments

---

[45] Liaison Committee, *Select committee effectiveness, resources and powers* (HC 2012–2013, 697) para.115.

[46] Scottish Parliament, *Guidance on Committees* para.5.78.

[47] *Protocol between the Scottish Parliament and the Scottish Government in relation to the handling of Committee business* (October, 2009).

[48] Convenors Group Legacy Paper—Session 3 (2011) para.21.

[49] Lord Hailsham, *The Dilemma of Democracy: Diagnosis and Prescription* (London: Collins, 1978) 125.

[50] See e.g. Public Audit Committee, 3rd Report, *Police Reform* (Scottish Parliamentary Paper 496, 2014); Finance Committee 5th Report, *Appointments to the Scottish Fiscal Commission* (Scottish Parliamentary Paper 558, 2014); European and External Relations Committee, 2nd Report, *Report on the Scottish Government's proposals for an independent Scotland: membership of the European Union* (Scottish Parliamentary Paper, 2014).

[51] Reform Committee, *Rebuilding the House* (HC 2008–2009, 1117) para.20: "The key principle that guides our recommendations is that Government should get its business, the House should get its scrutiny and the public should get listened to. Everything within this report can be measured against that simple proposition".

[52] See e.g. "Lord Foulkes attacks 'pathetic' Scottish Parliament" *Telegraph*, September 21, 2010, Jackson Carlaw, "It's time to realise the potential of the Scottish Parliament" (October, 2010), Jack McConnell, "Why the 'pedestrian' Scottish Parliament needs overhauling" *Telegraph*, November 24, 2010, "Holyrood's 'three wise men' back parliament overhaul" *Telegraph* November 24, 2010, "Veteran MSP in call for-shake-up of Parliament" *Herald* May 23, 2011, Bruce Crawford, "All parties needed to help change Holyrood" *Scotland on Sunday*, June 12, 2011.

Committee billed as a "thorough MOT" of its performance.[53] In a letter to all MSPs in July 2011, the presiding officer wrote:

> "I am pleased to report that the conveners enthusiastically endorsed a reform agenda that should enable parliamentary committees to increase their agility, responsiveness and focus."[54]

So far, however, the Conveners Group's programme for change seems to have been more about securing favourable media coverage for the work of committees than improving their effectiveness in holding the Scottish Government to account. If the reputation of committees is to be enhanced it will only be by doing the job they are supposed to do, and doing it well.

The Scottish Parliament was not just about "the sovereign right of the Scottish people to determine the form of Government best suited to their needs". It was also about the subjection of the government of Scotland to democratic scrutiny and control. The more extensive the Parliament's powers the more serious the lack of robust parliamentary scrutiny of those powers will become. Lord Smith saw the Parliament's increased powers as demanding improvements in parliamentary scrutiny, and he recommended that the presiding officer continue to build on her work on parliamentary reform by undertaking an "inclusive review" that would produce recommendations to run alongside the transfer of additional powers.[55] The Standards, Procedures and Public Appointments Committee has now embarked on an inquiry at the presiding officer's request into the election of committee conveners.[56]   **15–32**

---

[53] Standards, Procedures and Public Appointments Committee 2nd Report, *Reform of Parliamentary business inquiry Phase 1 Report: Remodelling the Parliamentary Week* (Scottish Parliamentary Paper 57, 2011) para.6.

[54] Letter from the Presiding Officer to all members, July 8, 2011.

[55] Smith Commission, *Report of the Smith Commission for further devolution of powers to the Scottish Parliament* (November 27, 2014) Foreword.

[56] In its Session 3 legacy paper, the Conveners Group noted the growth of "assertive" parliamentary committees over the last 30 years at Westminster, including the position whereby committee members and chairs were elected by the House, effectively removing control of the process from the party whips, and recommended that the Standards, Procedures and Public Appointments Committee consider introducing a system of election of committee members and conveners: Convenors Group Legacy Paper—Session 3 (2011) paras 7–9.

CHAPTER 16

JUDICIAL REVIEW

"What has been described is the formal structure of the courts, together with the rules which establish the independence of courts and judges. The operation of the courts, and thus their true constitutional significance, cannot be so easily described, and yet that is perhaps one of the most important subjects in constitutional law today."[1]

INTRODUCTION

It is a fundamental principle of the UK constitution that the courts do not have **16–01** the power to set aside Acts of Parliament. "In the courts there may be argument as to the correct interpretation of an enactment: there must be none as to whether it should be on the Statute Book at all."[2] The same principle does not apply to Acts of the Scottish Parliament, which the courts have the power to strike down on the grounds that they infringe the limits on the Scottish Parliament's legislative competence. Without this power the only checks on the new Parliament's potential for "arbitrary and oppressive action"[3] would have been political—in the form of UK ministerial intervention—which would have been a recipe for intergovernmental conflict as well as affording individuals no guarantee of effective redress. In the White Paper that preceded the Scotland Act 1978, the UK Government left open the question whether Acts of the Scottish Assembly should be open to review on grounds of vires, but in a supplementary statement the following year it announced that it had decided that there should be a right of access to the courts.[4] Had judicial review been excluded—and had the courts acquiesced in the exclusion of their jurisdiction—it would have meant, as was pointed out in the debates on the Scotland Bill, that there would have been no effective protection against abuse of the Assembly's law making powers.[5]

---

[1] JDB Mitchell, *Constitutional Law*, 2nd edn (Edinburgh: W.Green, 1968) p.264.

[2] *British Railways Board v Pickin* [1974] A.C. 765, 789 (Lord Morris of Borth–y-Gest).

[3] Terence Daintith, "The Kilbrandon Report: Some Comments", in Harry Calvert (ed), *Devolution* (Oxford: Professional Books, 1975) p.31.

[4] *Our Changing Democracy: Devolution to Scotland and Wales* (1975) Cmnd.6348, paras 62–65; *Devolution to Scotland and Wales: Supplementary Statement* (1976) Cmnd.6585, para.14; see also Constitution Unit, *Scotland's Parliament: Fundamentals for a New Scotland Act* (1996) paras 126–133.

[5] "We should be setting up a subordinate Assembly with powers to pass Assembly Acts. Its powers will be limited on paper, but, unless there is some provision for judicial or other review, there is no means by which the citizen who feels his rights infringed by ultra vires Acts of the Assembly can do anything about it: he is powerless. The only remedy he can possibly have is to take the matter to court": House of Lords debate, March 14, 1978, vol.389, col.1430 (Lord Fraser of Tullybelton).

16–02 The power to set aside Acts of the Scottish Parliament nevertheless raised the prospect of conflict between the Parliament and the courts. "To make provision for the courts to set aside Acts of [the UK] Parliament", the White Paper that accompanied the Human Rights Act said

> "would be likely on occasions to draw the judiciary into serious conflict with Parliament. There is no evidence to suggest that they desire this power, nor that the public would wish them to have it".[6]

There was no reason to suppose either that setting aside Acts of the Scottish Parliament would be any less likely to lead to conflict, or that the Scottish judiciary were any more desirous of the power. How the courts would approach the exercise of this new constitutional review jurisdiction was therefore one of the more intriguing questions raised by the devolution settlement.[7]

THE COURT OF SESSION'S SUPERVISORY JURISDICTION

16–03 The Court of Session has long exercised a jurisdiction to control the legality of administrative action, a jurisdiction which it is said to have inherited from the Scottish Privy Council after the latter's abolition in 1708.[8]

> "Under the cognisance of the privy council in Scotland came many injuries, which, by the abolition of that court, are left without any peculiar remedy; and the court of session have with reluctance been obliged to listen to complaints of various kinds, that belonged properly to the privy council while it had a being. A new branch of jurisdiction has thus sprung up in the court of session which daily increasing by new matter will probably in time produce a general maxim, That it is the province of this court, to redress all wrongs for which no other remedy is provided. We are, however, as yet far from being ripe for adopting this maxim. The utility of it is indeed perceived, but perceived too obscurely to have any steady influence on the practice of the court; and for that reason their proceedings in such matters are far from being uniform."[9]

16–04 During the nineteenth century the Court of Session exercised a broad supervisory jurisdiction over the administrative apparatus of what was still essentially a local state.

> "Wherever any inferior tribunal or any administrative body has exceeded the powers conferred upon it by statute to the prejudice of the subject, the jurisdiction of the Court to set aside such excess of power as incompetent and illegal is not open to dispute."[10]

---

[6] Home Office, *Rights Brought Home: The Human Rights Bill* (1997) Cm.3782, para.2.13.

[7] Alan Page, "Constitutionalism, Judicial Review and the 'Evident Utility of the Subjects Within Scotland'" in Lindsay Farmer and Scott Veitch (eds), *The State of Scots Law: Law and Government after the Devolution Settlement* (London: Butterworths, 2001).

[8] The Scottish Privy Council was abolished by the Union with Scotland (Amendment) Act 1707 ("an Act for rendering the Union of the Two Kingdoms more intire and complete").

[9] Kames, *Historical Law Tracts*, 4th edn (Edinburgh: Bell & Bradfute and Creech, 1792) pp.228–229; see also *West v Secretary of State for Scotland*, 1992 S.C. 385, 393–394 (Lord Hope). A more recent view traces its origins to the earliest days of the College of Justice: *Eba v Advocate General for Scotland* [2010] CSIH 78; 2011 S.C. 70 [34] (Lord President Hamilton).

[10] *Moss Empires v Assessor for Glasgow*, 1917 S.C. (H.L.) 1, 6 (Lord Kinnear); for examples, see Lord Clyde and Denis J Edwards, *Judicial Review* (Edinburgh: W.Green, 2000) paras 2.25–2.29.

With the twentieth century expansion in the functions of government, however, the Court's jurisdiction declined to such an extent that by the 1970s it was essentially moribund.[11] The principal factors in its decline were the growth in alternative, statutory forms of redress, coupled with the evolution of what appeared to be an effective system of parliamentary control. Faced with claims that these were matters for which Ministers were responsible to Parliament, the Scottish judiciary, in common with their English counterparts, effectively wrote themselves out of the script.[12]

Clyde and Edwards question whether judicial reluctance to intervene was as **16–05** true of Scotland as of England:

"It is not evident that the reluctance to interfere which overcame the English Courts during the middle years of the twentieth century was significantly echoed in Scotland. The relatively smaller number of cases in the smaller jurisdiction may make it less easy to identify a trend, but if there was less reluctance in Scotland that may reflect a more robust attitude in the Scottish Courts."[13]

Mitchell, however, saw it as equally true of Scotland: **16–06**

"It is as impossible for one part of a political union to stand apart from the general constitutional pattern of thought of that union, as it is for part of an economic union to isolate its own economy. Thus patterns of thought, dependent on the doctrine of ministerial responsibility or of the place of Parliament ... had as great an effect in Scotland as in England on the evolution of patterns of judicial reticence which resulted."[14]

THE INTRODUCTION OF THE APPLICATION FOR JUDICIAL REVIEW PROCEDURE

Scots law was to take longer than English law to emerge from what has been **16–07** called the "great depression" in administrative law.[15] After rejecting a recommendation from the Law Commission, made with the support of the Scottish Law Commission, for a wide-ranging inquiry into administrative law,[16] the 1966 Labour Government asked both Commissions to review the existing remedies for the judicial control of administrative acts and omissions with a view to evolving "a simpler and more effective procedure". In its report

---

[11] Lord Fraser of Tullybelton, "The Judiciary", *Stair Memorial Encyclopaedia* (1987) Vol.5, para.669.

[12] JDB Mitchell, "The Causes and Effects of the Absence of a System of Public Law in the UK" [1965] P.L. 95.

[13] Lord Clyde and Denis J Edwards, *Judicial Review* (Edinburgh: W.Green, 2000) para.2.36, citing *Magistrates of Ayr v Lord Advocate*, 1950 S.C. 102 and *Barrs v British Wool Marketing Board*, 1957 S.C. 72.

[14] "Government and Public Law in Scotland: Retrospect and Prospect" in JA Andrews (ed), *Welsh Studies in Public Law* (Cardiff: University of Wales Press, 1970) p.72. "The consequences of the inadequacy of the system", he added, "have perhaps been more strongly felt in Scotland because of the remoteness of Parliament".

[15] HWR Wade and CF Forsyth, *Administrative Law*, 10th edn (Oxford: OUP, 2009) p.14; a Scottish Law Commission memorandum published in 1971 commented that "the volume of case law in this field between 1960 and 1970 does not afford evidence of an increase in judicial scrutiny of governmental matters like that experienced in England during the same period": *Remedies in Administrative Law* (Scottish Law Commission No.14, 1971) para.4.4.

[16] Law Commission, *Administrative Law* (Law Commission No.20, 1969).

published in 1976, *Remedies in Administrative Law*,[17] the Law Commission recommended the introduction of a single procedure—the application for judicial review—in which any one or more of the principal common law remedies, including damages, could be sought. Its recommendation was accepted and implemented in 1977 by a series of amendments to Order 53 of the Rules of the Senior Courts,[18] the main elements of which were later re-enacted with modifications by s.31 of the Senior Courts Act 1981.

16–08 The Scottish Law Commission's inquiry, by contrast, gradually petered out. A memorandum, *Remedies in Administrative Law*,[19] was circulated in 1971 in which comments were invited on a number of issues, including in particular whether Scots law would benefit from the introduction of a flexible petition for review of official acts and omissions along the lines suggested by the Law Commission:

> "In view of the Scottish reliance on 'ordinary' remedies, a question of principle presents itself even more strongly in regard to Scotland than England—have these general remedies proved effective in the public law sector in the past, and are they effective in this sector today? It may be that the advantages of the Scottish system are more apparent (as a matter of law) than real (as a matter of day-to-day social utility). Merely because Scots law is free of many of the irksome procedural difficulties which are such a marked feature of English administrative law, it does not necessarily follow that Scots law would not benefit from the introduction of a flexible petition for review of official acts and omissions ... even though the particular advantages of such a remedy would be different as between England and Scotland."[20]

Consultations were completed in 1973, but the inquiry was then put to one side before being finally abandoned in 1976 with devolution seemingly imminent and research being conducted on the administrative jurisdiction of the sheriff court.[21]

16–09 Matters might conceivably have remained there had it not been for the confusion and uncertainty revealed by attempts to challenge local authority decisions under the Housing (Homeless Persons) Act 1977 in the sheriff court rather than the Court of Session. The uncertainty was eventually resolved in *Brown v Hamilton District Council*,[22] in which the House of Lords held that the Court of Session's supervisory jurisdiction was not shared with the sheriff court,

> "the reason why the Sheriff Court is not competent to review the decisions of administrative bodies is not merely a matter of procedure, but springs from a fundamental lack of jurisdiction in this field".[23]

[17] Law Commission, *Remedies in Administrative Law* (Law Commission No.73, 1976).
[18] Rules of the Supreme Court (Amendment No.3) 1977 (SI 1977/1955); the "Supreme Court" was the term used to describe the higher courts in England and Wales until it was changed by the Constitutional Reform Act 2005.
[19] *Remedies in Administrative Law* (Scottish Law Commission No.14, 1971).
[20] *Remedies in Administrative Law* (Scottish Law Commission No.14, 1971) para.4.3.
[21] Scottish Law Commission, *Eleventh Annual Report 1975–1976* (Scottish Law Commission No.43, 1977) para.50.
[22] *Brown v Hamilton District Council*, 1983 S.C. (H.L.) 1.
[23] *Brown v Hamilton District Council*, 1983 S.C. (H.L.) 1, 45 (Lord Fraser of Tullybelton).

In the course of his speech in *Brown*, however, Lord Fraser suggested that there might be advantages in developing or reviving special procedure in Scotland, comparable to the English application for judicial review procedure, for obtaining judicial review of decisions by public bodies.[24]

The Lord President subsequently established a working party, after discussion **16–10** with the Lord Advocate,

> "to devise and recommend for consideration a simple form of procedure, capable of being operated with reasonable expedition, for bringing before the court, for such relief as is appropriate, complaints by aggrieved persons (1) against acts or decisions of inferior courts, tribunals, public bodies, authorities, or officers, in respect of which no right of appeal is available alleging that the acts or decisions are ultra vires, or that they have been done or taken without compliance with particularly statutory procedural requirements; and (2) of failure of any body or person to perform a statutory duty, which it or he could be compelled to perform in terms of section 91 of the Court of Session Act 1868".

In place of the existing procedure, which they described as "ill-suited to the **16–11** urgent determination of the validity or invalidity of an act or decision of a public body", the working party recommended the introduction of a new and more streamlined procedure, similar but not identical to the application for judicial review introduced in England and Wales six years earlier.[25] The working party's recommendation was accepted and implemented with effect from April 30, 1985, when Rule of Court 260B, which governed the new procedure, came into force.[26]

Since the introduction of the new procedure, the Court of Session's supervi- **16–12** sory jurisdiction has undergone a modest revival, assisted in its latter stages by devolution and the "incorporation" of the European Convention of Human Rights ("ECHR"). The most prolific source of petitions is immigration, which accounted for 80 per cent of all petitions in 2011–2012 and 76 per cent in 2012–2013.[27] The other major source of petitions in recent years has been prisons, following the decision in *Napier v The Scottish Ministers*,[28] which reached a peak of 107 in 2009–2010, since when the number has dropped dramatically (10 in 2012–2013). The only other source of petitions to reach double figures in recent years is planning (11 in 2011–2012).

---

[24] *Brown v Hamilton District Council*, 1983 S.C. (H.L.) 1, 49, a suggestion he repeated in *Stevenson v Midlothian District Council*, 1983 S.C. (H.L.) 50, 59.

[25] Judicial Review of Administrative Acts, *Report to the Rt Hon Lord Emslie, Lord President of the Court of Session, by the Working Party on Procedure for Judicial Review of Administrative Action* (1984).

[26] Act of Sederunt (Rules of Court Amendment No.2) (Judicial Review) 1985 (SI 1985/500). The rules on judicial review are now contained in Ch.58 of the Rules of the Court of Session: Act of Sederunt (Rules of the Court of Session) 1994 (SI 1994/1443).

[27] The actual figures were 195 out of a total of 243 petitions in 2011/2012 and 224 out of 293 in 2012/2013.

[28] *Napier v The Scottish Ministers* [2005] CSIH 16; 2005 1 S.C. 307.

JUDICIAL REVIEW OF ADMINISTRATIVE ACTION

16–13 Judicial review is mainly about administrative action. Its principal features in that context may be summarised as follows.[29]

Legality not merits

16–14 Judicial review lies to control the legality of administrative action, not its merits, which are treated as a matter for the initial decision-maker subject to any right of appeal that may have been provided.

> "Judicial review is available, not to provide machinery for an appeal, but to ensure that the decision-maker does not exceed or abuse his powers or fail to perform the duty which has been delegated or entrusted to him. It is not competent for the court to review the act or decision on its merits, nor may it substitute its own opinion for that of the person or body to whom the matter has been delegated or entrusted."[30]

Changing judicial attitudes towards the control of government mean, however, that the dividing line between legality and merits is not necessarily drawn where it was drawn in the past.[31]

The grounds of review

16–15 There is no difference of substance between the grounds of review in Scots law and English law.[32] Until recently it was thought that the Court of Session lacked the power to correct errors of law made by a decision-maker within its jurisdiction,[33] but in *Eba v Advocate General for Scotland*[34] the Supreme Court held that this view of the law was incompatible with the House of Lords' decision in *Anisminic v Foreign Compensation Commission*[35] and should therefore no longer be followed.

> "Once again it must be stressed that there is, in principle, no difference between the law of England and Scots law as to the substantive grounds on which a decision by a tribunal which acts within its jurisdiction may be open to review."[36]

16–16 Various classifications of the grounds of review are possible, with Lord Diplock's threefold classification of illegality, irrationality and procedural

---

[29] For a full treatment, see Lord Clyde and Denis J Edwards, *Judicial Review* (Edinburgh: W.Green, 2000), AW Bradley and CMG Himsworth, "Administrative Law", *Stair Memorial Encyclopaedia Reissue* (2000), and Supperstone et al (eds), *Judicial Review*, 5th edn (London: Butterworths, 2014) Ch.22.

[30] *West v Secretary of State for Scotland*, 1992 S.C. 385, 413 (Lord Hope); *Moss Empires v Assessor for Glasgow*, 1917 S.C. (H.L.) 1, 11 (Lord Shaw).

[31] "Any judicial statements on matters of public law if made before 1950 are likely to be a misleading guide to what the law is today": *R v Inland Revenue Commissioners, Ex p. National Federation of the Self-Employed and Small Businesses Ltd* [1982] A.C. 617, 640 (Lord Diplock).

[32] *Brown v Hamilton District Council*, 1983 S.C. (H.L.) 1, 42 (Lord Fraser of Tullybelton); *West v Secretary of State for Scotland*, 1992 S.C. 385, 413 (Lord Hope).

[33] *Watt v Lord Advocate*, 1979 S.C. 102, 131 (Lord Emslie).

[34] *Eba v Advocate General for Scotland* [2011] UKSC 29; 2012 S.C. (UKSC) 1.

[35] *Anisminic v Foreign Compensation Commission* [1969] 2 A.C. 147.

[36] *Eba v Advocate General for Scotland* [2011] UKSC 29; 2012 S.C. (UKSC) 1 [34] (Lord Hope).

impropriety having quickly found favour in Scotland.[37] "Illegality" means that

> "the decision-maker must understand correctly the law that regulates his decision-making power and give effect to it. Whether he has or not is par excellence a justiciable question to be decided, in the event of dispute, by those persons, the judges, by whom the judicial power of the state is exercisable".[38]

"Irrationality", or "Wednesbury unreasonableness" after *Associated Provincial Picture Houses Ltd v Wednesbury Corporation,*[39]

> "applies to a decision which is so outrageous in its defiance of logic or of accepted moral standards that no sensible person who had applied his mind to the question could have arrived at it. Whether a decision falls within this category is a question that judges by their training and experience should be well equipped to answer, or else there is something badly wrong with our judicial system".[40]

Irrationality has nevertheless always been regarded as the most problematic ground of review—because it comes closest to the courts taking a view on the merits of decisions, which they have been at pains to stress is no part of their function (above). "Procedural impropriety", finally, embraces the common law requirements of natural justice and fairness as well as any statutory requirements that may have been imposed. The courts have also left open the possibility of further grounds being added as a result of judicial decisions.

> "The categories of what may amount to an excess or abuse of jurisdiction are not closed, and they are capable of being adapted in accordance with the development of administrative law."[41]

Standing

Scots law has also differed from English law until recently in taking a more **16–17** restrictive approach to the question of standing, on the basis of Lord Dunedin's dictum in *D&J Nicol v Dundee Harbour Trustees*[42] that for a person to have title to sue

> "he must be a party ... to some legal relation which gives him some right which the person against whom he raises the action either infringes or denies".

In *Axa General Insurance Ltd v Lord Advocate,*[43] however, the Supreme Court held that the traditional test of title and interest to sue should be replaced by a test based on the sufficiency of the applicant's interest in the subject matter of

---

[37] *Council of Civil Service Unions v Minister for the Civil Service* [1985] A.C. 374, 410.
[38] *Council of Civil Service Unions v Minister for the Civil Service* [1985] A.C. 374, 410 (Lord Diplock).
[39] *Associated Provincial Picture Houses Ltd v Wednesbury Corporation* [1948] 1 K.B. 223.
[40] *Council of Civil Service Unions v Minister for the Civil Service* [1985] A.C. 374, 410 (Lord Diplock).
[41] *West v Secretary of State for Scotland,* 1992 S.C. 385, 413 (Lord Hope); *Council of Civil Service Unions v Minister for the Civil Service* [1985] A.C. 374, 410 (Lord Diplock).
[42] *D&J Nicol v Dundee Harbour Trustees,* 1915 S.C. (H.L.) 7, 12.
[43] *Axa General Insurance Ltd v Lord Advocate* [2011] UKSC 46; 2012 S.C. (UKSC) 122.

the application, thereby bringing Scots law into line with the larger jurisdiction. In *Walton v Scottish Ministers*,[44] Lord Reed explained that the Supreme Court's decision in *Axa* had been intended

> "to put an end to an unduly restrictive approach to standing which had too often obstructed the proper administration of justice: an approach which presupposed that the only function of the court's supervisory jurisdiction was to redress individual grievances, and ignored its constitutional function of maintaining the rule of law".[45]

One factor in the failure to relax the requirements sooner was the assumption that change would require legislation, an assumption rejected by Lord Reed in *Axa* who argued that that courts were responsible for ensuring the supervisory jurisdiction's "continuing development, on an incremental basis, so as to meet the needs of the time".[46]

Time limits and permission

16–18 Scots law also differs from English law in that there is currently no time limit within which applications must be brought, but following the recommendations of the Scottish Civil Courts Review, a three month time limit is being introduced, as is a requirement of permission for the application to proceed.[47] The Review also recommended the statutory relaxation of the rules relating to title and interest to sue, but that recommendation was overtaken by the Supreme Court's decision in *Axa* (above).

16–19 Since its recent revival, the Scots law of judicial review has thus moved steadily closer to English law, with most of the remaining differences in the course of being dismantled. Where it continues to differ is in being somewhat broader in its scope that the English application for judicial review procedure in that it also applies to private bodies such as golf clubs and the like.[48] In its application to government, however, there are no real differences between the two jurisdictions.

A remedy of last resort

16–20 Finally, we may note that judicial review is a remedy of last resort. An applicant will, therefore, normally be expected to have exhausted any statutory remedies before seeking to invoke the Court of Session's supervisory jurisdiction.[49] One factor that helped mask the extent of the supervisory jurisdiction's decline in the course of the twentieth century was the growth in statutory forms

---

[44] *Walton v Scottish Ministers* [2012] UKSC 44 [90].

[45] For criticism of the law as it stood before *Axa General Insurance Ltd v Lord Advocate* [2011] UKSC 46; 2012 S.C. (UKSC) 122, see Lord Hope of Craighead, "Mike Tyson Comes to Glasgow—A Question of Standing" [2001] P.L. 294, and Tom Mullen, "Standing to Seek Judicial Review" in Aileen McHarg and Tom Mullen (eds), *Public Law in Scotland* (Edinburgh: Avizandum, 2006).

[46] *Axa General Insurance Ltd v Lord Advocate* [2011] UKSC 46; 2012 S.C. (UKSC) 122, [171].

[47] Courts Reform (Scotland) Act 2014 s.89, inserting new ss.27A and 27B in Court of Session Act 1988; applications will be considered by a single judge who must be satisfied that an applicant can demonstrate a "sufficient interest" in the subject matter of the application and that the application has a real prospect of success. If permission is refused, applicants will have seven days within which to request a review of the decision at an oral hearing.

[48] *West v Secretary of State for Scotland*, 1992 S.C. 385; for the Court of Session's "golf clubs" jurisdiction, see e.g. *Smith v Nairn Golf Club*, 2007 S.L.T. 909.

[49] *O'Neill v Scottish Joint Negotiating Committee for Teaching Staff*, 1987 S.C. 90; *McCue v Glasgow City Council* [2014] CSOH 124; 2014 S.L.T. 891.

of redress. It was only where these were absent, as was the case under the Housing (Homeless Persons) Act 1977, that the full extent of its decline became apparent.

JUDICIAL REVIEW OF ACTS OF THE SCOTTISH PARLIAMENT

The presumption of competence

In an effort to reduce the risk of conflict between the Parliament and the courts, **16–21** the Scotland Act 1998 ("the Scotland Act") requires the courts, in interpreting Acts of the Scottish Parliament, to choose the interpretation—assuming more than one interpretation is possible—that is compatible with the limits on the Parliament's competence. Where a provision "could be read in such a way as to be outside competence", s.101(2) of the Scotland Act requires it

> "to be read as narrowly as is required for it to be within competence, if such a reading is possible, and to have effect accordingly".

The underlying idea is that of judicial restraint in determining the validity of legislation; that unelected judges should be slow to intervene in the affairs of the elected branch of government.[50] The Parliament is thus presumed to have intended to legislate within the limits of its competence and it is only where a provision cannot be read in such a way as to be within its competence that it falls to be struck down as invalid.

Section 101(2) is the Scotland Act analogue of s.3(1) of the Human Rights Act **16–22** 1998, which, as we saw, requires legislation to be read and given effect, so far as it is possible to do so, in a way which is compatible with the Convention rights, the difference in the language of the two provisions reflecting the fact that the limits to the Scottish Parliament's legislative competence are not confined to the Convention rights but also include legislation relating to reserved matters as defined in Sch.5 and legislation that is in breach of the restrictions in Sch.4. The relationship between the two provisions was explained by Lord Hope in *DS v HM Advocate*[51] thus:

> "An attempt by the Scottish Parliament to widen the scope of its legislative competence as defined in those Schedules will be met by the [s.101(2)] requirement that any provision which could be read in such a way as to be outside competence must be read as narrowly as is required for it to be within competence."

But where the issue is incompatibility with the Convention rights, the

> "proper starting point is to construe the legislation as directed by section 3(1) of the Human Rights Act. If it passes this test, so far as the Convention rights are concerned it will be within competence".

The obligation to construe a provision in an Act of the Scottish Parliament so far as it is possible to do so in a way that is compatible with the Convention

---

[50] Peter W Hogg, *Constitutional Law of Canada*, 5th edn (Toronto: Thomson, 2007) para.15.5(i); JE Magnet, "The Presumption of Constitutionality" (1980) 18 Osgoode Hall L.J. 87.

[51] *DS v HM Advocate* [2007] UKPC D1; 2007 S.C. (P.C.) 1, [23]–[24]; see also *Salvesen v Riddell* [2013] UKSC 22 [46] (Lord Hope).

rights, Lord Hope added, is "a strong one. The court must prefer compatibility to incompatibility. This enables it to look closely at the legislation to see if it can be explained and operated in a way that is compatible and, if it is not, how it can be construed to make it so".[52]

> "But any section 3 interpretation must ... go with the grain of the legislation ... It is not for the court to go against the underlying thrust of what it provides for, as to do this would be to trespass on the province of the legislature."[53]

16-23 The s.101(2) presumption of competence was applied in *Henderson v HM Advocate*,[54] the High Court holding that s.201F of the Criminal Procedure (Scotland) Act 1995, which was inserted by s.1 of the Criminal Justice (Scotland) Act 2003, should be read and have effect as not extending the requirement to make an order for lifelong restriction to a situation in which the offender had been convicted of an offence under the (reserved) Firearms Act 1968, which prescribed a determinate number of years as the maximum penalty by way of imprisonment.

16-24 The presumption of competence applies only where a provision is open to more than one interpretation. It does not apply where no other interpretation is possible or, by implication, where the only other interpretation possible is one that goes against the grain of the legislation. In *Imperial Tobacco v Lord Advocate*,[55] Lord Reed rejected the submission that as "the authentic expression of the will of the people through their elected representatives" there was a legal presumption in favour of the validity of Acts of the Scottish Parliament.

> "In the context of the Scotland Act ... it is necessary to bear in mind that the Act of Parliament setting limits to devolved competence is itself 'the authentic expression of the will of the people', and that respect for their will as so expressed requires those limits to be enforced."[56]

The experience to date

16-25 The Parliament has passed upwards of 220 Acts in the first 16 years of its existence, 14 of which have been challenged before the courts, with some Acts being challenged more than once—the Protection of Wild Mammals (Scotland) Act 2002, the Tobacco and Primary Medical Services (Scotland) Act 2010, and the Criminal Justice and Licensing (Scotland) Act 2010—which is one measure of the degree of controversy attaching to the Parliament's legislation, or the importance of the commercial interests at stake. Most challenges have been on ECHR grounds with only two on reserved matters grounds.[57] There have also been two challenges on EU law grounds.[58]

---

[52] *DS v HM Advocate* [2007] UKPC D1; 2007 S.C. (P.C.) 1, [24].
[53] *Salvesen v Riddell* [2013] UKSC 22, [46]; pushing the boundaries to interpretation may nevertheless be seen as preferable to setting the legislation aside.
[54] *Henderson v HM Advocate* [2010] HCJAC 107; 2010 S.C.C.R. 909.
[55] *Imperial Tobacco v Lord Advocate* [2012] CSIH 9; 2012 S.C. 297.
[56] *Imperial Tobacco v Lord Advocate* [2012] CSIH 9; 2012 S.C. 297 [61]–[62].
[57] *Martin v Most* [2010] UKSC 10; 2010 S.C. (UKSC) 40; *Imperial Tobacco Ltd v Lord Advocate* [2011] UKSC 46; 2012 S.C. (UKSC) 122.
[58] *Sinclair Collis Ltd v Lord Advocate* [2012] CSIH 80; *Scotch Whisky Association v Lord Advocate* [2014] CSIH 38, currently under reference to the European Court of Justice.

Most challenges have been unsuccessful; in only two cases has a provision **16–26** been struck down as beyond the Parliament's competence. In *Salvesen v Riddell*,[59] the Supreme Court held that s.72(10) of the Agricultural Holdings (Scotland) Act 2003 was incompatible with art.1 of the First Protocol (the right to property), while in *Cameron v Cottam*,[60] the High Court held that s.58 of the Criminal Justice and Licensing (Scotland) Act 2010 was incompatible with art.5 ECHR (the right to liberty).[61] Where important (commercial) interests are at stake (tobacco advertising, alcohol minimum pricing), a challenge that is ultimately unsuccessful may nevertheless be regarded as having been worthwhile given the delay in the implementation of the legislation involved. In the case of tobacco advertising, there will have been a delay of more than five years before the legislation is fully brought into effect. With alcohol minimum pricing the implications are also EU-wide rather than being confined to Scotland.

Review at common law

The most important question to have arisen so far is whether Acts of the **16–27** Scottish Parliament are reviewable only on the grounds set out in s.29(2) of the Scotland Act or whether they are also reviewable at common law. In *Axa General Insurance Ltd v Lord Advocate*,[62] the Supreme Court held that the grounds of review were not limited to those set out in the Scotland Act. Section 29 of the Act, Lord Hope said, did not bear to be a "complete or comprehensive statement of limitations on the powers of the Parliament".[63] As there was no provision in the Scotland Act excluding the Court of Session's supervisory jurisdiction,

> "I think that it must follow that in principle Acts of the Scottish Parliament are amenable to the supervisory jurisdiction of the Court of Session at common law."[64]

The Court of Session's supervisory jurisdiction not having been excluded, the **16–28** "much more important question", in Lord Hope's view, was the grounds, if any, on which Acts of the Scottish Parliament were reviewable at common law. The fact that a challenge to primary legislation at common law was simply impossible while the only legislature was the sovereign Parliament of the UK at Westminster meant that the court was in uncharted territory. The issue had to be addressed therefore as one of principle.[65] The dominant characteristic of the Scottish Parliament was

> "its firm rooting in the traditions of a universal democracy. It draws its strength from the electorate. While the judges, who are not elected, are best placed to protect the rights of the individual, including those who are ignored or despised by the majority, the elected members of a legislature of this kind are best placed to judge what is in the country's best interests

---

[59] *Salvesen v Riddell* [2013] UKSC 22.
[60] *Cameron v Cottam* [2012] HCJAC 31.
[61] In both cases the court limited or suspended the effect of its judgment: in *Cameron*, the High Court limited the retroactive effect of its decision to "live" cases, i.e. cases that had not yet been concluded; in *Salvesen*, the Supreme Court suspended the effect of its judgment for 12 months to allow the incompatibility to be corrected.
[62] *Imperial Tobacco Ltd v Lord Advocate* [2011] UKSC 46; 2012 S.C. (UKSC) 122.
[63] *Imperial Tobacco Ltd v Lord Advocate* [2011] UKSC 46; 2012 S.C. (UKSC) 122, [45].
[64] *Imperial Tobacco Ltd v Lord Advocate* [2011] UKSC 46; 2012 S.C. (UKSC) 122, [47].
[65] *Imperial Tobacco Ltd v Lord Advocate* [2011] UKSC 46; 2012 S.C. (UKSC) 122, [48].

as a whole ... This suggests that the judges should intervene, if at all, only in the most exceptional circumstances".[66]

16–29   As to what these "most exceptional circumstances" might involve, Lord Hope said that it could not be assumed that Lord Hailsham's warning of "elective dictatorship",[67] which Lord Steyn had endorsed in *R (Jackson) v Attorney General*,[68] had no application to the Scottish Parliament:

> "I am not prepared to make that assumption. We now have in Scotland a government which enjoys a large majority in the Scottish Parliament. Its party dominates the only chamber in that Parliament and the committees by which bills that are in progress are scrutinised. It is not entirely unthinkable that a government which has that power may seek to use it to abolish judicial review or to diminish the role of the courts in protecting the interests of the individual. Whether this is likely to happen is not the point. It is enough that it might conceivably do so. The rule of law requires that the judges must retain the power to insist that legislation of that extreme kind is not law which the courts will recognise."[69]

16–30   Legislation of that extreme kind aside, however, Acts of the Scottish Parliament were *not* reviewable at common law on the grounds of irrationality, unreasonableness or arbitrariness. There was no need for such review given that they were reviewable on Convention rights grounds. It would also be "quite wrong" for the judges to substitute their views on the rationality or otherwise of Acts of the Scottish Parliament for the considered judgment of an elected legislature unless authorised to do so, as in the case of the Convention rights, by the constitutional framework laid down by the UK Parliament.[70]

16–31   Lord Reed agreed that the Scottish Parliament was subject to the Court of Session's supervisory jurisdiction. It could not be assumed, however, that the grounds upon which the lawfulness of Acts of the Scottish Parliament might be reviewed included all, or any, of the grounds upon which the Court of Session might exercise its supervisory jurisdiction in other contexts.[71] Law-making by a democratically elected legislature was "the paradigm of a political activity", and the reasonableness of the resultant decisions was inevitably a matter of political judgment.

> "In my opinion it would not be constitutionally appropriate for the courts to review such decisions on the ground of irrationality. Such review would fail to recognise that courts and legislatures each have their own particular role to play in our constitution, and that each must be careful to respect the sphere of action of the other."[72]

16–32   As to the possible grounds of review, Lord Reed said that the principle of legality meant

---

[66] *Imperial Tobacco Ltd v Lord Advocate* [2011] UKSC 46; 2012 S.C. (UKSC) 122, [49].

[67] Lord Hailsham, *The Dilemma of Democracy: Diagnosis and Prescription* (London: Collins, 1978) p.125.

[68] *R (Jackson) v Attorney General* [2005] UKHL 56; [2006] 1 A.C. 262, [71].

[69] *Imperial Tobacco Ltd v Lord Advocate* [2011] UKSC 46; 2012 S.C. (UKSC) 122, [51].

[70] *Imperial Tobacco Ltd v Lord Advocate* [2011] UKSC 46; 2012 S.C. (UKSC) 122, [52].

[71] *Imperial Tobacco Ltd v Lord Advocate* [2011] UKSC 46; 2012 S.C. (UKSC) 122, [140].

[72] *Imperial Tobacco Ltd v Lord Advocate* [2011] UKSC 46; 2012 S.C. (UKSC) 122, [148].

"not only that Parliament cannot itself override fundamental rights or the rule of law by general or ambiguous words, but also that it cannot confer on another body, by general or ambiguous words, the power to do so".[73]

The nature and purpose of the Scotland Act was consistent with the application of that principle. In *Robinson v Secretary of State for Northern Ireland*,[74] Lord Bingham of Cornhill said of the Northern Ireland Act 1998 that its provisions should be interpreted "bearing in mind the values which the constitutional provisions are intended to embody". That was equally true of the Scotland Act. The UK Parliament had not legislated in a vacuum but for "a liberal democracy founded on particular constitutional principles and traditions".

"That being so, Parliament cannot be taken to have intended to establish a body which was free to abrogate fundamental rights or to violate the rule of law."[75]

The Supreme Court was thus not prepared to exclude judicial review of Acts of **16–33** the Scottish Parliament on common law grounds. At the same time, it was unwilling to open the door to all the common law grounds of review, including in particular review on grounds of irrationality, which as mentioned has always been the most problematic of the common law grounds of review. By doing so, it avoided the otherwise very real risk of the Parliament being hamstrung by claims that it was acting irrationally whenever it did something to which objection was taken. As Lord Bingham of Cornhill said in *R (Countryside Alliance) v Attorney General*,[76] in a passage cited by Lord Hope, the democratic process is

"liable to be subverted if, on a question of political or moral judgment, opponents of an Act achieve through the courts what they could not achieve through Parliament".

PROSPECTS

The relationship between the Scottish Parliament and the courts has not so far **16–34** proved controversial. If anything, the relationship has proved less controversial than the relationship between the Westminster Parliament and the courts, notwithstanding the fact that the courts occupy a more powerful role in the devolved constitution than they occupy in the UK constitution. Judicial review of legislation in particular has not proved as controversial as some predicted; the fears expressed at the outset of "un gouvernement de juges" have not materialised.[77] The courts at both the UK and devolved levels of government have shown themselves acutely sensitive to the fact that they are dealing with the legislation of an elected body. Where controversy has arisen it has been between the Scottish Government and the UK Supreme Court, led by its Scottish members, rather than the Scottish Government and the Scottish courts, leading, as we have seen, to the restriction of the Supreme Court's recently acquired jurisdiction in Scottish criminal cases by the Scotland Act 2012.

[73] *Imperial Tobacco Ltd v Lord Advocate* [2011] UKSC 46; 2012 S.C. (UKSC) 122, [152].
[74] *Robinson v Secretary of State for Northern Ireland* [2002] UKHL 32; [2002] N.I. 390, [11].
[75] *Imperial Tobacco Ltd v Lord Advocate* [2011] UKSC 46; 2012 S.C. (UKSC) 122, [153].
[76] *R (Countryside Alliance) v Attorney General* [2007] UKHL 52; [2008] A.C. 719, [45].
[77] Aidan O'Neill, "The Scotland Act and the Government of Judges" 1999 S.L.T (News) 61.

16–35 Looking to the future, the more extensive the Scottish Parliament's powers the more important the question of checks, including judicial checks, on those powers becomes. In *R v Inland Revenue Commissioners, Ex p. National Federation of the Self-Employed and Small Businesses Ltd*,[78] Lord Diplock described the progress that had been made towards a "comprehensive system of administrative law" as "the greatest achievement of the English courts in my judicial lifetime". The reference to the "English courts" may not have been intentional, but the "rise and rise" of judicial review has been an English rather than Scottish phenomenon; despite starting with certain supposed advantages the Scots law of judicial review has lagged behind English law since the latter's emergence from the "great depression" in administrative law. If there is a concern about the constitutional future it is not that the Scottish judiciary will be "over active" or zealous in their defence of the rule of law, but that they will not be active enough; that conscious of the more exposed position in which they find themselves as a result of devolution, and possibly deprived of the backstop of the Supreme Court,[79] they will once again become—or remain— "stars which loss ther light ... quhen the sun shynes".[80] Were that to happen the prospects for limited government in Scotland would be bleak indeed.

---

[78] *R v Inland Revenue Commissioners, Ex p. National Federation of the Self-Employed and Small Business Ltd* [1982] A.C. 617 at 641.

[79] In its submission to the Smith Commission, the Scottish Government renewed its call for an end to the Supreme Court's jurisdiction in Scottish cases: *More Powers for the Scottish Parliament: Scottish Government Proposals* (October, 2014) p.29.

[80] Hope, *Major Practicks*, Vol.1, quoted in JR Philip, "Constitutional Law and History" in The Stair Society, *An Introductory Survey of the Sources and Literature of Scots Law* (Edinburgh: Robert Maclehose, 1936) p.364, a description, Philip commented, at least as picturesque as Bacon's "lions under the throne".

CHAPTER 17

THE SCOTTISH PUBLIC SERVICES OMBUDSMAN

"My ultimate commitment is to ensure justice for the people of Scotland."[1]

INTRODUCTION

The Scottish Public Services Ombudsman ("SPSO") was established by the **17–01** Scottish Public Services Ombudsman Act 2002 ("the 2002 Act") as a one-stop shop for the investigation of complaints about devolved public services.[2] The office was formed by the merger of three existing statutory ombudsmen—the Scottish Parliamentary Commissioner for Administration, the Health Service Commissioner for Scotland and the Commissioner for Local Administration in Scotland—and the non-statutory Housing Association Ombudsman for Scotland. The Scotland Act 1998 ("the Scotland Act") required the Parliament to make provision for the investigation of complaints of maladministration against the Scottish Administration, in place of the provision for the investigation of such complaints against the former Scottish Office under the Parliamentary Commissioner Act 1967.[3] It also gave the Parliament licence to go further if it wished, which it did by establishing the SPSO as a unified ombudsman service.[4] The Scottish Prisons Complaints Commission and the complaints function of Waterwatch Scotland were added to the SPSO's jurisdiction in 2010,[5] leaving the Police Complaints Commissioner for Scotland, now the Police Investigations and Review Commissioner, and the Scottish Information Commissioner, as the only single purpose ombudsmen. As well as investigating complaints of injustice or hardship sustained in consequence of maladministration or service failure, the SPSO is charged with simplifying and standardising complaints-handling procedures—and promoting best practice in complaints-handling—across the public sector.[6]

THE OMBUDSMAN

The Ombudsman is appointed by the Queen on the nomination of the Parliament **17–02** for a single non-renewable term of not more than eight years.[7] Under the

---

[1] Scottish Public Services Ombudsman, *Annual Report 2012–2013* (2013) p.9.
[2] Complaints about reserved services continue to be dealt with by the UK Parliamentary and Health Service Ombudsman.
[3] Scotland Act 1998 ("SA 1998") s.91(1); temporary arrangements were made by the Scotland Act 1998 (Transitory and Transitional Provisions) (Complaints of Maladministration) Order 1999 (SI 1999/1351).
[4] SA 1998 s.91(3).
[5] Public Services Reform (Scotland) Act 2010 ("PSR(S)A 2010") s.3(2); Scottish Parliamentary Commissions and Commissioners etc. Act 2010 Sch.3 para.20; universities and colleges were added by the Further and Higher Education (Scotland) Act 2005 s.27.
[6] PSR(S)A 2010 s.119.
[7] Scottish Public Services Ombudsman Act 2002 ("SPSOA 2002") s.1(1); the Act also made provision for the appointment of up to three deputy ombudsmen: s.1(3).

Scottish Public Services Ombudsman Act 2002, as originally enacted, the Ombudsman could be appointed for two terms of not more than five years each, with the possibility of reappointment for a third term,[8] but this was replaced by a standard single term of not more than eight years by the Scottish Parliamentary Commissions and Commissioners etc. Act 2010 in the interests of ensuring that the Ombudsman cannot be influenced by the prospect of not being re-appointed. In anticipation of the change the current Ombudsman was initially appointed for two years in May 2009 and then reappointed for a further six years in March 2011.

17–03 The Scottish Public Services Ombudsman Act includes a number of guarantees of the Ombudsman's independence. The Ombudsman may be removed from office, but only if the Scottish Parliamentary Corporate Body ("SPCB") is satisfied that there has been a breach of the Ombudsman's terms and conditions of office and the Parliament resolves that the Ombudsman should be removed from office for that breach, or the Parliament has lost confidence in the Ombudsman's willingness, suitability, or ability to perform the functions of Ombudsman, and, in either case, at least two-thirds of the total number of MSPs, i.e. 86 MSPs, vote in favour of removal.[9] The Ombudsman thus enjoys effective security of tenure. The Ombudsman is also not subject to the direction or control of any member of the Parliament, any member of the Scottish Government, or the SPCB in the exercise of the Ombudsman's functions.[10] And appointment for a single term, as mentioned, is meant to ensure that the Ombudsman cannot be influenced by the prospect of not being reappointed.

17–04 In common with the other parliamentary commissioners, including the Commissioner for Ethical Standards in Public Life in Scotland and the Scottish Information Commissioner, the Ombudsman is financed by and directly accountable to the Parliament in the shape of the SPCB. The commissioners' governance and accountability was the subject of a Finance Committee inquiry in 2006, which was prompted by concerns about "increasing costs, the perceived shortcomings of budgetary accountability, the lack of consistency in governance arrangements and other matters".[11] The Committee was highly critical of the existing arrangements:

> "It would appear to the Committee that, whilst protecting the independence of commissioners and ombudsman within established legislation, insufficient checks and balances have been put in place to reassure Parliament that commissioners and ombudsman represent value for money."[12]

The Committee rejected the argument that closer financial scrutiny was a threat to the commissioners' operational independence, and demanded that the SPCB tighten its scrutiny as a condition of retaining responsibility for sponsoring them.

---

[8] SPSOA 2002 Sch.1 para.4(2).

[9] SPSOA 2002 Sch.1 para.4(1)(d) and (2C), amplifying the original provision which simply provided for removal by a two thirds majority of all MSPs.

[10] SPSOA 2002 Sch.1 para.2.

[11] Finance Committee 7th Report, *Inquiry into Accountability and Governance* (Scottish Parliamentary Paper 631, 2006) para.4.

[12] Finance Committee 7th Report, *Inquiry into Accountability and Governance* (Scottish Parliamentary Paper 631, 2006) para.58.

The Scottish Parliamentary Commissions and Commissioners etc. Act 2010, a **17–05** Committee Bill promoted by the ad hoc Review of SPCB Supported Bodies ("RSSB") Committee, standardised the governance arrangements and terms and conditions of appointment of office holders and members of bodies supported by the SPCB. The SPCB's approval is now required for the SPSO's budget, the number and terms and conditions of staff, payments to advisers, and the acquisition and disposal of land.[13] The SPCB also has power to give the SPSO directions as to the location of its office, the sharing of premises, staff, services or other resources with other officeholders or public bodies, and the form and content of its annual report.[14] In addition, the SPSO is required to lay a four year strategic plan before the Parliament, setting out how it proposes to perform its functions during the four year period, and before doing so to provide a draft of the plan to, and invite comments from, the SPCB and such other persons as the SPSO thinks appropriate.[15]

The Ombudsman lays an annual report before the Parliament.[16] The report, **17–06** which may include general recommendations, must be made within seven months of the end of the reporting year and published.[17] The Ombudsman may also lay such other reports before the Parliament as the Ombudsman thinks fit.[18] The Finance Committee endorsed a proposal, from the SPCB, that committees take evidence more regularly from the commissioners and ombudsman, and that, in particular, they should take evidence on their annual reports.[19] The RSSB Committee expected the SPSO to be considered more frequently "given that one of the SPSO's roles is to let Parliament know how public services are working".[20] In common with the other commissioners, however, there has been little in the way of effective engagement between the Parliament and the Ombudsman.

THE SPSO'S JURISDICTION

The SPSO is charged with investigating "any matter consisting of action taken **17–07** by or on behalf of a person liable to investigation".[21] Three conditions must be satisfied in order for an investigation to be undertaken: the person must be liable to investigation; the matter must be one which the SPSO is entitled to investigate[22]; and it must be a matter in respect of which either a complaint has been made by a member of the public or a request for an investigation has been made by the person liable to investigation.[23]

---

[13] SPSOA 2002 Sch.1, paras 12D, 9, 10 and 12(3).
[14] SPSOA 2002 Sch.1 paras 12A, 12B and s.17(3).
[15] SPSOA 2002 s.17A.
[16] SPSOA 2002 s.17(1).
[17] SPSOA 2002 s.17(2A), (3A).
[18] SPSOA 2002 s.17(4).
[19] Finance Committee 7th Report, *Inquiry into Accountability and Governance* (Scottish Parliamentary Paper 631, 2006) paras 79–80.
[20] Review of SPCB Supported Bodies Committee First Report (Scottish Parliamentary Paper 266, 2009) para.131.
[21] SPSOA 2002 s.2(1)(a).
[22] SPSOA 2002 s.2(1)(b).
[23] SPSOA 2002 ss.2(1)(c), (2)(b) and 5(3); a "member of the public" does not include a local authority or a public body: SPSOA 2002 s.5(6). The SPSO does not therefore provide a means of resolving disputes between public authorities.

"Listed authorities"

17–08 The persons liable to investigation are listed in Sch.2 to the 2002 Act.[24] The schedule is in three parts:

(i) Part 1, which may be amended only by statute, covers the Scottish Administration, including members of the Scottish Government, local authorities, the health service, including family health service providers and independent providers of health services, and registered social landlords.

(ii) Part 2, which may be amended by order covers Scottish public authorities and cross-border public authorities.

(iii) Part 3, which may also be amended by order covers universities and colleges.

The power to investigate is a power to investigate action taken by or on behalf of a listed authority.[25] It thus covers action taken by arm's length external organisations such as local authority trusts as well as by listed authorities.

Matters subject to investigation

17–09 The matters that the SPSO is entitled to investigate are defined in one of the 2002 Act's less clearly drafted provisions. As defined in s.5, the matters the SPSO may investigate fall into five categories:

(i) action taken by or on behalf of listed authorities (other than health service bodies, independent providers, family health service providers and registered social landlords) in the exercise of their administrative functions[26];

(ii) action taken by or on behalf of health service bodies or independent providers, other than action consisting of a "service failure"[27];

(iii) "service failures" by listed authorities other than family health service providers and registered social landlords[28];

(iv) action taken by or on behalf of family health service providers in connection with the provision of family health services; and

(v) action taken by or on behalf of registered social landlords.[29]

17–10 At first glance, therefore, it would seem that the SPSO has no power to investigate service failures by family health service providers and registered social landlords.[30] The SPSO's advice, however, is that the concept of action taken, which includes failures to act,[31] is broad enough to cover a failure to provide a service as well as a failure in a service provided, and that, therefore, it has power to investigate complaints of service failure against *all* the bodies within its jurisdiction, including family health service providers and registered social landlords.[32] It would be simpler and preferable though if s.5 said that.

---

[24] SPSOA 2002 s.3(1).

[25] SPSOA 2002 s.2(1)(a).

[26] SPSOA 2002 s.5(1)(a).

[27] SPSOA 2002 s.5(1)(b).

[28] SPSOA 2002 s.5(1)(c); a service failure includes both a failure in a service provided and a failure to provide a service: SPSOA s.5(2).

[29] SPSOA 2002 s.5(1).

[30] SPSOA 2002 s.5(1)(c).

[31] SPSOA 2002 s.23(1).

[32] Review of SPCB Supported Bodies Committee First Report (Scottish Parliamentary Paper 266, 2009); *Supplementary Evidence to the Review of SPCB Supported Bodies Committee from the Scottish Public Services Ombudsman*, para.18.

A complaint or a request

Matters may be investigated only pursuant to a complaint from a member of **17–11** the public or a request from a listed authority. The SPSO has no power to undertake investigations on its own initiative. The SPSO sought "own initiative" powers of investigation in its submission to the RSSB Committee, but the Committee was not persuaded that the SPSO's role should be extended beyond the investigation and resolution of specific complaints.[33]

Matters may be investigated pursuant to a complaint from a member of the **17–12** public only if the member of the public claims to have sustained injustice or hardship in consequence of maladministration or service failure.[34] The concept of maladministration was intentionally left undefined.[35] The original "Crossman catalogue", after the Minister responsible for the Parliamentary Commissioner Act 1967, offered as examples: "bias, neglect, inattention, delay, incompetence, ineptitude, perversity, turpitude, arbitrariness and so on".[36] The "Reid supplement" after Sir William Reid, who was Parliamentary Commissioner for Administration between 1990 and 1996, added a long list of other examples, including "rudeness (though that is a matter of degree)"; "refusal to answer reasonable questions"; "knowingly offering no redress or manifestly disproportionate redress"; and "failure to mitigate the effects of rigid adherence to the letter of the law where that produces manifestly inequitable treatment".[37] As noted, a service failure includes a failure to provide a service as well as a failure in a service provided.[38]

Matters may be investigated pursuant to a request from a listed authority only **17–13** if the SPSO is satisfied that it has been alleged publicly that one or more members of the public have sustained injustice or hardship in consequence of maladministration or service failure *and* the authority has taken all reasonable steps to deal with the matter to which the allegation relates.[39] An authority cannot, therefore, request an investigation as an alternative to addressing allegations of injustice or hardship sustained in consequence of maladministration or service failure. There have been only a handful of requests from listed authorities, none of which has satisfied the requirements for investigation.

Restrictions

The Scottish Public Services Ombudsman Act imposes a number of restric- **17–14** tions on the matters the SPSO may investigate. The matters the SPSO may not investigate include:

(i) the merits of decisions taken without maladministration.[40] The SPSO does not provide a means of challenging decisions with which

[33] Review of SPCB Supported Bodies Committee First Report (Scottish Parliamentary Paper 266, 2009) para.310.
[34] SPSOA 2002 s.5(3); as drafted, s.5(3) is considerably more complex. The SPSO, however, first discusses the case with the complainant with a view to agreeing a statement of complaint which, were it to be upheld, it would regard as amounting to maladministration or service failure. If it emerges from that discussion that there is no claim of maladministration or service failure it will not take the complaint forward no matter how aggrieved or unhappy the complainant may be.
[35] Scottish Executive, *Modernising the complaints system* (October, 2000) para.3.4.
[36] House of Commons debate, October 18, 1966, Vol.734, col.51.
[37] Parliamentary Commissioner for Administration, *Annual Report for 1993* (HC 1993–1994, 290) para.7; see also the Parliamentary Commissioner for Administration and Health Service Commissioner's *Principles of Good Administration* (March, 2009).
[38] SPSOA 2002 s.5(2).
[39] SPSOA 2002 s.5(5).
[40] SPSOA 2002 s.7(1).

complainants disagree or are unhappy: maladministration must be alleged;

(ii) action taken by or on behalf of a member of the Scottish Government unless the action was taken in the exercise of functions conferred on the Scottish Ministers or on the First Minister alone.[41] The SPSO cannot therefore investigate action taken in the exercise of the Lord Advocate's "retained functions", i.e. the Lord Advocate's functions as head of the systems of criminal prosecution and investigation of death in Scotland;

(iii) action taken by or on behalf of a cross-border public authority unless the action taken concerned Scotland and did not relate to reserved matters. The SPSO can only investigate action taken in connection with devolved matters[42];

(iv) any matter in respect of which the person aggrieved has or had a right of appeal or a remedy by way of judicial proceedings, unless the SPSO is satisfied that it is not reasonable to expect the person aggrieved to resort or have resorted to the right or remedy.[43] This discretion is commonly exercised in complainants' favour. The SPSO does not normally expect a person to pursue a judicial remedy unless either there is a specific right of appeal that covers the matter in question, or the matter is one that only the courts can determine, for example, a question of statutory interpretation. Where litigation has already begun, the SPSO also considers it reasonable for it to continue; and

(v) a matter in respect of which a complaint can be made, or a review can be requested, under a procedure operated by an authority, unless the SPSO is satisfied either that the procedure has been invoked and exhausted, or that in the particular circumstances it is not reasonable to expect the procedure to be invoked or exhausted.[44] A complainant is thus expected to have exhausted the authority's own complaints procedure before turning to the SPSO (below).

Exclusions

17–15 The 2002 Act also excludes a number of matters from investigation. These include:

(i) action taken for the purposes of or in connection with the investigation or prevention of crime or the protection of the security of the state[45];

(ii) the commencement or conduct of civil or criminal proceedings, including in the case of civil proceedings inquiries under the Fatal Accidents and Sudden Deaths Inquiry (Scotland) Act 1976[46];

(iii) action taken in matters arising from concluded contractual or other commercial transactions of a listed authority.[47] The SPSO is not therefore prevented from investigating matters relating to the process leading up to the conclusion of a contract or commercial transaction; and

(iv) action taken in respect of personnel matters.[48]

---

[41] SPSOA 2002 s.7(3).
[42] SPSOA 2002 s.7(5).
[43] SPSOA 2002 s.7(8).
[44] SPSOA 2002 s.7(9), (10).
[45] SPSOA 2002 Sch.4 para.1.
[46] SPSOA 2002 Sch.4 para.2.
[47] SPSOA 2002 Sch.4 para.7.
[48] SPSOA 2002 Sch.4 para.8.

COMPLAINTS HANDLING

Complaints

Access to the SPSO is direct rather than through an elected representative; **17–16** there is no devolved equivalent of the "MP filter".[49] A complaint, which may be made to the SPSO by the person aggrieved or by a person authorised in writing by the person aggrieved,[50] must normally be made in writing or electronically unless the SPSO is satisfied that there are special circumstances that make it appropriate to consider a complaint made orally.[51] It must also normally be made within 12 months of the day on which the person aggrieved had notice of the matter complained of, subject to the proviso that a complaint made after the time limit has expired may be considered if the SPSO is satisfied that there are special circumstances which make it appropriate to do so.[52]

In 2013–2014, the SPSO received 363 enquiries and 4,456 complaints.[53] Local **17–17** government (39 per cent) and health (31 per cent) between them accounted for 70 per cent of all complaints, with the Scottish Government and devolved administration (12 per cent), water (6.5 per cent) and housing associations (8 per cent) accounting for the bulk of the remainder. Further and higher education accounted for 3 per cent.[54]

Advice and early resolution

The 2002 Act provides that the Ombudsman may take such action in connec- **17–18** tion with a complaint or request as may be thought helpful in deciding whether to initiate, continue or discontinue an investigation, including action with a view to achieving informal resolution of the complaint or request.[55]

The majority of complaints are dealt with by providing advice or guidance to **17–19** the complainant or authority concerned. In 2013–2014, out of a total of 4,408 complaints dealt with, 2,829 (64 per cent) were resolved by advice or guidance, compared with 2,476 out of 4,077 (61 per cent) the previous year.[56]

As well as providing advice and guidance, the SPSO's advice and early resolu- **17–20** tion team check whether complaints are "fit for SPSO", i.e. whether they are about an authority and a subject the SPSO can investigate and whether they have completed the authority's own complaints procedure. The most common reason for the rejection of complaints at this stage is prematurity—they have not been through the authority's complaints procedures. The percentage of premature complaints has fallen in recent years—from 51 per cent in 2009– 2010 to 34 per cent in 2013–2014.[57]

---

[49] Parliamentary Commissioner Act 1967 s.5(1).
[50] SPSOA 2002 s.9(1).
[51] SPSOA 2002 s.10(3).
[52] SPSOA 2002 s.10(1).
[53] Scottish Public Services Ombudsman, *Transforming Scotland's Complaints Culture: SPSO Annual Report 2013–2014* (2014) p.11.
[54] Scottish Public Services Ombudsman, *Transforming Scotland's Complaints Culture: SPSO Annual Report 2013–2014* (2014) p.11.
[55] SPSOA 2002 s.2(4) and (5).
[56] Scottish Public Services Ombudsman, *Transforming Scotland's Complaints Culture: SPSO Annual Report 2013–2014* (2014) p.13.
[57] Scottish Public Services Ombudsman, *Transforming Scotland's Complaints Culture: SPSO Annual Report 2013–2014* (2014) p.12.

17–21 Where the SPSO decides not to conduct an investigation pursuant to a complaint or request, a statement of the reasons must be sent to the complainant and the authority against which the complaint was made, or the authority which made the request, as the case may be.[58]

Investigations

17–22 Investigations are conducted at the SPSO's discretion.[59] The 2002 Act provides that investigations must be conducted in private, and that the authority, and any other person alleged to have taken the action complained of, must be given an opportunity to comment on the allegations contained in the complaint.[60] Otherwise it is for the SPSO to determine the procedure for conducting an investigation.[61] The SPSO has extensive information gathering powers, including the same powers as the Court of Session in respect of the attendance and examination of witnesses and the production of documents.[62] The Scottish Government is not entitled to the privileges in respect of the production of documents or the giving of evidence it would enjoy in legal proceedings.[63] Scottish Cabinet proceedings, however, including committee proceedings, are privileged.[64] A person cannot be compelled to give evidence or produce documents they could not be compelled to give or to produce in civil proceedings before the Court of Session.[65]

Decision letters and investigation reports

17–23 An investigation may be concluded by a decision letter (technically a "discontinued investigation") or an investigation report. Most investigations are concluded by a decision letter: in 2013–2014, the SPSO issued 850 decision letters, compared with 895 the previous year, and published 44 investigation reports, the same number as the year before. A decision letter is usually issued where the authority accepts there were failings, apologises and takes action to prevent the same thing happening again, or there is no evidence of maladministration or service failure (or insufficient evidence for the SPSO to reach a conclusion and the SPSO thinks it unlikely that further investigation will uncover more). A decision letter must be sent to the complainant and the authority against which the complaint is made.[66]

17–24 An investigation report involves an additional stage in which a draft report is prepared for comment and those comments are then considered before a decision is made. The Ombudsman approves all draft reports and also considers comments personally before a decision is made. The SPSO employs a set of public interest criteria in deciding whether an investigation report should be prepared. As well as precedent and test cases, the criteria, which were revised in 2010, provide for the reporting of cases involving "significant personal injustice" (defined as "an explicit administrative or service failure by a public body resulting in personal detriment of a severity and nature that requires wider acknowledgement and recognition"), systemic failures, and local complaints

---

[58] SPSOA 2002 s.11(1),(2) and (4).
[59] SPSOA 2002 s.2(3).
[60] SPSOA 2002 s.12(2).
[61] SPSOA 2002 s.12(3).
[62] SPSOA 2002 s.13(1) and (4).
[63] SPSOA 2002 s.13(6).
[64] SPSOA 2002 s.13(7).
[65] SPSOA 2002 s.13(9).
[66] SPSOA 2002 s.11(1) and (2).

procedure failures.[67] Since the criteria were revised the number of investigation reports has fallen—from 123 reports in 2009–2010 to 44 reports in both 2012–2013 and 2013–2014.

Investigation reports must be sent to the Scottish Ministers and laid before the **17–25** Parliament.[68] They are also normally made publicly available.[69] Decision letters are sent to the Scottish Ministers and laid before the Parliament at the SPSO's discretion. Decision letters were originally not made public, but the SPSO was given the power to send reports of discontinued investigations to the Scottish Ministers and to lay them before the Parliament by the Public Services Reform (Scotland) Act 2010.[70] The SPSO lays a report of decision letters before the Parliament each month. The report consists of a short digest of each complaint, with the SPSO's decision and recommendation. In 2012–2013, the first full year of publishing summaries of investigation decisions and recommendations, the SPSO published 806 out of a total of 895 decisions.[71] The complainant and the authority do not have the opportunity to comment on a draft of a decision letter before it is issued, but there is a six week period before decision letters are made public within which the complainant or the authority may request a review. Investigation reports once sent to the Scottish Ministers and laid before the Parliament are final. They may be challenged in judicial review proceedings, but such challenges are rare.[72]

REDRESS

The SPSO has no power to order redress, only a power to make recommenda- **17–26** tions. The Scottish Executive was concerned that authorities could be more reluctant to co-operate, or less open when providing information, if they knew that the SPSO was likely to take enforcement action against them.[73] The SPSO's general aim in making recommendations is to put the complainant as far as possible in the position they would have been in had the maladministration or service failure not occurred. It also aims to prevent the same thing happening to someone else. The SPSO made 1,197 recommendations for redress and improvements to public services in 2013–2014, an increase of 19 per cent on the previous year.[74] The most common recommendations are for specific action to put things right, including the reconsideration or alteration of decisions, changes in procedures and apologies. Financial redress may be recommended, usually where there has been a specific financial loss, e.g. the cost of private health care that should have been provided by the NHS. The SPSO does not deal with personal injury claims, however, which it considers are better dealt with through the courts, or seek to assess distress in financial terms. The SPSO is currently reviewing its policy on redress.

---

[67] Scottish Public Services Ombudsman, *Annual Report 2010–2011* (2011) p.8.
[68] SPSOA 2002 s.15(1).
[69] SPSOA 2002 s.15(4).
[70] PSR(S)A 2010 Sch.3 para.5, inserting SPSOA 2002 s.15(1A).
[71] Scottish Public Services Ombudsman, *Annual Report 2012–2013* (2013) p.22; the SPSO does not publish decisions if it considers there is a real risk of the complainant being identified.
[72] There has been one reported application for judicial review: *Argyll and Bute Council v Scottish Public Services Ombudsman* [2007] CSOH 168; [2008] S.C. 155.
[73] Scottish Executive, *Modernising the complaints system* (October, 2000) para.8.2.
[74] Scottish Public Services Ombudsman, *Transforming Scotland's Complaints Culture: SPSO Annual Report 2013–2014* (2014) p.24.

17–27 Recommendations are tracked to make sure that they are implemented. In 2013–2014, 74 per cent of 1,171 recommendations due for implementation were carried out within the agreed timescale, and 98 per cent within three months of the target date.[75] Where recommendations are not implemented, the SPSO may make a special report, which must be sent to the Scottish Ministers and laid before the Parliament.[76] The SPSO's reporting criteria envisage a special report being made where "persistent non-cooperation by an authority with SPSO recommendations (either through a decision or report) requires the non-compliance to be highlighted". The SPSO has not so far found it necessary to use this power.

17–28 The percentage of valid complaints fully or partly upheld has increased in recent years. In 2010–2011, 34 per cent of valid complaints (231 out of 673) were fully or partly upheld, a figure that the Ombudsman described as "unacceptable" given that these complaints had been through authorities' own complaints procedures.[77] In 2011–2012, that figure increased to 39 per cent:

> "This means that I am finding fault in well over a third of cases that have already been investigated by service providers and I find this worrying."[78]

In 2013–2014 it reached 50 per cent, "which tells me there is still work to do in supporting organisations in getting things right when people complain to them".[79]

IMPROVING COMPLAINTS-HANDLING

17–29 The first Ombudsman saw the diversity of listed authorities' complaints procedures as a source of confusion for people wishing to bring a complaint and recommended the introduction of a model complaints handling process for all public services in Scotland.[80] The subsequent Crerar Review of public sector scrutiny, which was asked to include complaints-handling as a distinct strand of external scrutiny, found the existing complaints arrangements difficult to navigate because of the number of complaints bodies, because providers had different ways of dealing with complaints, and because it was not always clear which body should be responsible for dealing with an issue.[81] The Review concluded that service users and the public would benefit from a less complex, faster and more easily accessed system, and recommended the introduction of a standardised complaints handling system for all service providers, which should be developed and overseen by the SPSO.[82] Its recommendation were

---

[75] Scottish Public Services Ombudsman, *Transforming Scotland's Complaints Culture: SPSO Annual Report 2013–2014* (2014) p.24.

[76] SPSOA 2002 s.16(2) and (3).

[77] Scottish Public Services Ombudsman, *Annual Report 2010–2011* (2011) p.4.

[78] Scottish Public Services Ombudsman, *Annual Report 2011–2012* (2012) p.5.

[79] Scottish Public Services Ombudsman, *Transforming Scotland's Complaints Culture: SPSO Annual Report 2013–2014* (2014) p.7.

[80] Scottish Public Services Ombudsman, *Annual Report 2004–2005*, pp.8–9.

[81] Crerar Review, *The Report of the Independent Review of Regulation, Audit, Inspection and Complaints Handling of Public Services in Scotland* (September, 2007) paras 11.4–11.5.

[82] Crerar Review, *The Report of the Independent Review of Regulation, Audit, Inspection and Complaints Handling of Public Services in Scotland* (September, 2007) para.11.14.

taken forward by a "Fit For Purpose Complaints System Action Group"[83] and given effect by the Public Services (Reform) Scotland Act 2010.[84]

As a first step towards simplifying and standardising complaints handling **17–30** procedures, the Act required the SPSO to publish a statement of complaints handling principles with which listed authorities' complaints handling procedures must comply.[85] The SPSO's *Statement of Complaints Handling Principles*, which was approved by the Parliament and published in January 2011, defines an effective complaints handling procedure as "user-focused, accessible, simple and timely, thorough, proportionate and consistent, and objective, impartial and fair"; it should also "seek early resolution" and "deliver improvement".

A statement of principles by itself would be unlikely to reduce the diversity of **17–31** complaints-handling procedures. The Act therefore also gave the SPSO power to publish model complaints-handling procedures ("CHPs") with which specified listed authorities must comply.[86] Where an authority's complaint-handling procedure does not comply with the relevant model CHP (or the *Statement of Principles* in the absence of specification or a model CHP), the SPSO may issue a declaration of non-compliance and specify the modifications required to allow the declaration to be withdrawn.[87] The SPSO has published model CHPs for local government (March, 2012), registered social landlords (April 2012), further and higher education (December, 2012) and the Scottish Government, Scottish Parliament and associated public authorities (March, 2013). The NHS operates a standardised process under the revised *Can I Help You?* guidance published by the Scottish Government in April 2012.

The SPSO is also responsible for monitoring and promoting best practice in **17–32** complaints-handling by listed authorities.[88]

THE SPSO AND ADMINISTRATIVE JUSTICE

The opportunity of devolution has thus been taken to rationalise ombudsman **17–33** functions and to lay the foundations of a two-tier public complaints system, with the first tier comprising front-line resolution and investigation by listed authorities and the second tier external review by the SPSO or equivalent. What has been missing is any consideration of where the SPSO and the emerging public complaints system fit into the wider landscape of administrative justice.[89] This may reflect the neglect of administrative justice more generally since devolution, with the exception of the Tribunals (Scotland) Act 2014, but the debates over the ombudsman have tended to be driven by individual dissatisfaction with individual decisions at the expense of any consideration of broader issues. Whether the Scottish Tribunals and Administrative Justice

---

[83] *Fit For Purpose Complaints System Action Group: Report to Ministers* (September, 2008).
[84] PSR(S)A 2010 s.119, inserting SPSOA 2002 ss.16A–16G.
[85] SPSOA 2002 s.16A(1) and (2); complaints handling procedures are defined as procedures for the examination of complaints or review of decisions in respect of action taken by a listed authority where the matter in question is one in respect of which a complaint to the SPSO can be made and investigated under the Act: s.16A(12).
[86] SPSOA 2002 ss.16B(1), 16C(2).
[87] SPSOA 2002 s.16D(1) and (2).
[88] SPSOA 2002 s.16G(1).
[89] On the four pillars of administrative justice, see Law Commission, *Administrative Redress: Public Bodies and the Citizen* (Law Commission CP No.187, 2008).

Advisory Committee, which was established by the Scottish Government in November 2013, following the abolition of the UK Administrative Justice and Tribunals Council and its Scottish Committee, to champion the needs of users across the administrative justice and tribunals system in Scotland, will repair that omission remains to be seen.

CHAPTER 18

FREEDOM OF INFORMATION

"Openness is central to a modern, mature democratic society. The Scottish Executive considers that a statutory right of access to official information is essential, and that it will make public authorities more accountable to the people they serve."[1]

INTRODUCTION

Information is vital to the business of holding government to account. New **18–01** Labour came to power in 1997 with a commitment to a Freedom of Information Act in place of the non-statutory Code of Practice on Access to Government Information which its Conservative predecessor had introduced as part of the Citizen's Charter in 1994. "The traditional culture of secrecy will only be broken down by giving people in the UK the legal right to know", the Prime Minister said in his preface to *Your Right to Know*, the White Paper that set out the UK Government's initial proposals.[2] In contrast to fundamental rights, which were dealt with on a UK-wide basis, by the Human Rights Act 1998, it was decided that it should be left to the Scottish Parliament

> "to determine the approach of the Scottish executive and other Scottish public bodies to openness and freedom of information within devolved areas in which it is competent to enact primary legislation".[3]

The Scotland Act 1998 ("the Scotland Act") accordingly excepts information held by the Scottish Parliament, any part of the Scottish Administration, the Scottish Parliamentary Corporate Body ("SPCB"), and any Scottish public authority with mixed functions or no reserved functions, from the reservation of public access to information held by public bodies or holders of public office.[4]

---

[1] Scottish Executive, *An Open Scotland. Freedom of Information: A Consultation* (November, 1999) para.2.1.

[2] Cabinet Office, *Your Right to Know. The Government's proposals for a Freedom of Information Act* (1997) Cm.3818; he later recanted, describing freedom of information as "utterly undermining of sensible government": Tony Blair, *A Journey* (London: Hutchinson, 2010) p.516.

[3] Cabinet Office, *Your Right to Know. The Government's proposals for a Freedom of Information Act* (1997) Cm.3818, para.2.1; Public Administration Committee, *Your Right to Know: the Government's Proposals for a Freedom of Information Act* (HC 1997–1998, 398–I) questions 391–394. As well as providing special protection for fundamental rights and freedoms within Scots law, the Scottish Constitutional Convention had expected the Scottish Parliament to pass a Freedom of Information Act: Scottish Constitutional Convention, *Scotland's Parliament, Scotland's Right* (1995) p.20.

[4] Scotland Act 1998 ("SA 1998") Sch.5 Pt II s.B13, inserted by the Scotland Act 1998 (Modification of Schedules 4 and 5) Order 1999 (SI 1999/1749) art.5; the exception does not extend to information supplied by a Minister of the Crown or UK government department and held in confidence. Scottish public authorities with mixed functions are defined by SA 1998 Sch.5 Pt III para.1.

18–02 The coalition agreement which the Labour and Liberal Democrat parties signed in May 1999 included a commitment to the early introduction of "an effective freedom of information regime".[5] There was initial speculation over whether an effective regime meant legislation, the UK Government's commitment to its proposals having begun to wane, but in a statement to the Parliament on June 23, 1999, the Deputy First Minister and Minister for Justice, Jim Wallace, made clear that it meant "a Scottish freedom of information bill that is introduced in this Parliament, scrutinised by this Parliament, and enacted at the hand of this Parliament".[6] A consultation paper was published in November 1999,[7] followed by consultation on a draft Freedom of Information (Scotland) Bill in March 2001,[8] which was closely modelled on the UK Freedom of Information Act 2000. The subsequent Freedom of Information (Scotland) Act 2002 ("the 2002 Act"), together with a separate regime for access to environmental information held by public authorities,[9] came into force on January 1, 2005, at the same time as the UK Freedom of Information Act enacted two years earlier.[10]

ACCESS TO INFORMATION

18–03 The Freedom of Information (Scotland) Act's most important provision is s.1, which provides that "a person who requests information from a Scottish public authority which holds it is entitled to be given it by the authority".[11] A request must be made in writing (or in some other form such as a recording capable of being used for future reference), state the name of the applicant and address for correspondence, and describe the information requested.[12] Where an authority requires further information in order to identify and locate the requested information, it is not obliged to give the requested information until it has the further information.[13] A request for information must be answered promptly and in any event within 20 working days following the date of receipt of the request or the further information.[14] Authorities are under a duty to provide advice and assistance to applicants and prospective applicants.[15] A fee may be charged for access to information.[16] Where an authority refuses to provide information on the grounds that it is exempt information (discussed further, below), it must

---

[5] Scottish Executive, *Partnership for Scotland: An Agreement for the First Scottish Parliament* (May 14, 1999).

[6] Scottish Parliament OR June 23, 1999 cols 655–657.

[7] Scottish Executive, *An Open Scotland. Freedom of Information: A Consultation* (November, 1999).

[8] Scottish Executive, *Freedom of Information: Consultation on Draft Legislation* (March, 2001).

[9] Environmental Information (Scotland) Regulations 2004 (SSI 2004/520).

[10] For the fullest treatment of the position under the Freedom of Information (Scotland) Act, see Kevin Dunion, *Freedom of Information in Scotland in Practice* (Dundee: Dundee University Press, 2011); for the UK-wide position, with some coverage of the position in Scotland, see Philip Coppel, *Information Rights Law and Practice*, 4th edn (Oxford: Hart Publishing, 2014) and John Macdonald, Ross Crail and Clive H Jones, *The Law of Freedom of Information*, 2nd edn (Oxford: OUP, 2009).

[11] Freedom of Information (Scotland) Act 2002 ("FOI(S)A 2002") s.1(1).

[12] FOI(S)A 2002 s.8(1); where a request is made on behalf of another person, the identity of the "true applicant" must be disclosed: *Glasgow City Council and Dundee City Council v Scottish Information Commissioner* [2009] CSIH 73; 2010 S.L.T. 9.

[13] FOI(S)A 2002 s.1(3).

[14] FOI(S)A 2002 s.10(1).

[15] FOI(S)A 2002 s.15(1).

[16] FOI(S)A 2002 s.9(1); Freedom of Information (Fees for Required Disclosure) (Scotland) Regulations 2004 (SSI 2004/467).

give the applicant a refusal notice specifying the exemption and stating, if not otherwise apparent, why the exemption applies.[17]

SCOTTISH PUBLIC AUTHORITIES

The right of access to information is a right to recorded information held by **18–04** Scottish public authorities, as defined by s.3 of the 2002 Act. They comprise the authorities listed in Sch.1 to the Act; authorities designated under s.5; and publicly-owned companies, as defined by s.6.

Listed authorities

The Scottish public authorities listed in Sch.1 include the Scottish Ministers, **18–05** the Scottish Parliament and the SPCB, non-ministerial office-holders in the Scottish Administration, local authorities, NHS bodies, further and higher education institutions, the police and a long list of other public bodies.

The Sch.1 list may be amended by order made under s.4(1) of the Act.[18] The **18–06** list has also been amended by primary legislation. The Scottish Courts and Tribunals Service and the Judicial Appointments Board for Scotland, for example, were added by the Judiciary and Courts (Scotland) Act 2008.

Designated authorities

New ways of delivering public services represent a continuing challenge for **18–07** freedom of information laws, with information rights at risk of being eroded as a result, for example, of the contracting out of services.[19] Section 5 of the Act makes provision for the designation as Scottish public authorities for the purposes of the Act of persons who either "appear to the Scottish Ministers to exercise functions of a public nature", or who "are providing, under a contract made with a Scottish public authority, any service whose provision is a function of that authority".[20] During the Stage 3 debate on the Bill, the Deputy First Minister assured the Parliament that the Executive intended to exercise this power,[21] an assurance which he later explained had been given in good faith and in the full expectation that it would happen sooner rather than later.[22] It was not until July 2010, however, that the Scottish Government formally consulted on the designation of public-private partnerships ("PPPs") involved

---

[17] FOI(S)A 2002 s.16(1).

[18] There have been three amending instruments: the Freedom of Information (Scotland) Act 2002 (Scottish Public Authorities) Amendment Order 2008 (SSI 2008/297); the Ethical Standards in Public Life etc. (Scotland) Act 2000 (Devolved Public Bodies and Stipulated Time Limit) and the Freedom of Information (Scotland) Act 2002 (Scottish Public Authorities) Amendment Order 2011 (SSI 2011/113); and the Freedom of Information (Scotland) Act 2002 (Scottish Public Authorities) Amendment Order 2013 (SSI 2013/126).

[19] Alasdair Roberts, "Structural Pluralism and the Right to Information" (2001) 51 U Toronto L.J. 262.

[20] FOI(S)A 2002 s.5(2).

[21] Scottish Parliament OR April 24, 2002 cols 8111–8112.

[22] Lord Wallace of Tankerness, "Scottish Freedom of Information: Hope and Experience", a public lecture delivered at the launch of the Centre for Freedom of Information, January 29, 2009. In the course of his lecture he said: "although I was careful in debate not to pre-empt a future consultation, I am free to say now that I did not think almost seven years after the legislation, the provisions of the Act would not have extended to the Glasgow Housing Association, or in another sphere of public sector activity, to Kilmarnock prison or the core public service activities of Reliance [the company contracted by the Scottish Prison Service to transport prisoners to/from courts and prisons]".

in the building and maintenance of schools, hospitals and roads; private companies managing prisons and providing prisoner escort services; Glasgow Housing Association; the Association of Chief Police Officers; and local authority leisure and recreation trusts.[23] In January 2011, however, the designation of additional bodies was deferred pending a review of the Act.[24] Following the enactment of the Freedom of Information (Amendment) (Scotland) Act 2013, the power was used for the first time in 2013 to designate local authority leisure, sports and cultural trusts.[25]

18–08 Against the background of successive Scottish Governments' apparent reluctance to exercise the power, the Freedom of Information (Amendment) (Scotland) Act 2013 imposes a duty on Scottish Ministers to lay a report before the Parliament at least every two years on their exercise or non-exercise of the power.[26]

Publicly owned companies

18–09 Section 6 of the 2002 Act defines a publicly owned company as a company which is wholly-owned by the Scottish Ministers or by any other Scottish public authority or authorities listed in Sch.1 to the Act. As a result, companies such as David MacBrayne Ltd and Scottish Water are subject to the Act.

EXEMPTIONS

18–10 The right to information held by Scottish public authorities is not an absolute right but is subject to a number of exemptions, which are listed in Pt 2 of the 2002 Act. There are two types of exemption: absolute exemptions and non-absolute or qualified exemptions.

Absolute exemptions

18–11 An individual has no right to information that is subject to an absolute exemption.[27] The following information is absolutely exempt[28]:

    (i)   information that an applicant can reasonably obtain other than by making an information request (s.25). Such information includes,

---

[23] Scottish Government, *Consultation on Extending the Coverage of the Freedom of Information (Scotland) Act 2002* (July, 2010); a discussion paper published in 2008 sought views on the possible designation of contractors providing public authority services, registered social landlords and local authority trusts or bodies set up by local authorities: *Discussion Paper—Coverage of the Freedom of Information (Scotland) Act 2002* (November, 2008).

[24] The Scottish Information Commissioner recorded it as "disappointing that the issue of designating additional bodies continues to be deferred with no indication of when it will be re-visited. The delivery of public functions is increasingly complex and we need a well thought out approach to designation. We cannot afford the risk that citizens' rights to information will be undermined because FOI legislation does not keep pace": *The 2011/2012 Annual Report of the Scottish Information Commissioner* (September, 2012) Foreword.

[25] The Freedom of Information (Scotland) Act (Designation of Persons as Scottish Public Authorities) Order 2013 (SSI 2013/278)

[26] FOI(S)A 2002 s.7A, inserted by the Freedom of Information (Amendment) (Scotland) Act 2013 s.1(2). The Scottish Information Commissioner has laid a special report before the Parliament in which she describes the power as having been "woefully underused": *FOI 10 years on: are the right organisations covered?* (January, 2015) Commissioner's introduction.

[27] FOI(S)A 2002 s.2(1)(a).

[28] FOI(S)A 2002 s.2(2).

but is not confined to, information available through a public authority's publication scheme (discussed further, below)[29];

(ii) information the disclosure of which is prohibited by statute,[30] is incompatible with an EU obligation, or would constitute, or be punishable as, a contempt of court (s.26)[31];

(iii) information obtained from another person the disclosure of which would constitute a breach of confidence (s.36(2)). Information held in confidence, having been supplied by a Minister of the Crown or by a department of the Government of the UK, is not held for the purposes of the 2002 Act and does not therefore require exemption[32];

(iv) court records (s.37); and

(v) personal information, including personal data the disclosure of which would breach the data protection principles set out in the Data Protection Act 1998, information contained in census records, and a deceased person's health records (s.38).[33]

Qualified exemptions

Qualified exemptions may be divided into content-based and class-based **18–12** exemptions. Content-based exemptions are subject to a substantial prejudice or harm test as well as a public interest test, class-based exemptions to the public interest test only.

The public interest test

All qualified exemptions are subject to a public interest test: is the public **18–13** interest in disclosing the information outweighed by the public interest in maintaining the exemption?[34] If it is not, or if the two interests are weighted equally, the information must be disclosed. The public interest in maintaining the exemption must therefore outweigh the public interest in disclosure before an authority is justified in refusing a request for information.

The harm test

Where information is covered by a content-based exemption, the information **18–14** may be withheld only if its disclosure would cause "substantial prejudice" to the interest protected by the exemption. The use of the substantial prejudice test ("would or would be likely to prejudice substantially"), rather than the simple prejudice test ("would or would be likely to prejudice") favoured in the UK Freedom of Information Act, is intended to make clear that information covered by a content exemption should be disclosed unless the prejudice caused would be "real, actual and of significant substance".[35]

---

[29] FOI(S)A 2002 s.25(3), as substituted by the Freedom of Information (Amendment) (Scotland) Act 2013 s.3.

[30] See *Dumfries & Galloway Council v Scottish Information Commissioner* [2008] CSIH 12; 2008 S.C. 327.

[31] The Freedom of Information (Relaxation of Statutory Prohibitions on Disclosure of Information) (Scotland) Order 2008 (SSI 2008/339) relaxes certain statutory bars on disclosure.

[32] FOI(S)A 2002 s.3(2)(a)(ii).

[33] On personal data, see *Common Services Agency v Scottish Information Commissioner* [2008] UKHL 47; 2008 S.C. (H.L.) 184, and *Craigdale Housing Association v Scottish Information Commissioner* [2010] CSIH 43; 2010 S.L.T. 655.

[34] FOI(S)A 2002 s.2(1)(b).

[35] Scottish Executive, *An Open Scotland. Freedom of Information: A Consultation* (November, 1999) para.4.11.

18–15 Substantial prejudice to the protected interest alone is not sufficient to justify withholding information covered by a content exemption. The public interest test must also be satisfied. It is only therefore where disclosure would cause substantial prejudice to the protected interest *and* the public interest in disclosure is outweighed by the public interest in maintaining the exemption that an authority is justified in refusing a request for information.

18–16 Where information is covered by a class-based exemption the harm test does not need to be satisfied in order to justify withholding the information.

> "In effect the information covered by a class-based exemption has already been deemed to have satisfied the harm test for withholding the information."[36]

Content-based exemptions

18–17 The following information is covered by content-based exemptions:

(i)   information obtained in the course of, or derived from, a continuing programme of research (s.27(2));

(ii)   information the disclosure of which would, or would be likely to, prejudice substantially relations between any administration in the UK and any other such administration, the administrations being the UK Government and the three devolved administrations (s.28);

(iii)   information the disclosure of which would, or would be likely to, prejudice substantially the maintenance of the convention of the collective responsibility of the Scottish Ministers; inhibit substantially the free and frank provision of advice or the free and frank exchange of views for the purposes of deliberation; or otherwise prejudice substantially the effective conduct of public affairs (s.30)[37];

(iv)   information the disclosure of which would, or would be likely to, prejudice substantially, the defence of the British Islands or of any colony, or the capability, effectiveness or security of any relevant forces (s.31(4));

(v)   information the disclosure of which would, or would be likely to, prejudice substantially relations between the UK and other states, international organisations or international courts, or the promotion or protection of the interests of the UK abroad (s.32(1)(a));

(vi)   information the disclosure of which would, or would be likely to, prejudice substantially commercial interests, the economic interests of the whole or part of the UK, or the financial interests of an administration in the UK (s.33(1)(b)(2));

(vii)   information the disclosure of which would, or would be likely to, prejudice substantially the business of law enforcement, including such matters as crime prevention or detection, the apprehension or prosecution of offenders, the administration of justice, the assessment or collection of tax, the operation of immigration controls, and the security of prisons (s.35);

---

[36] Scottish Executive, *An Open Scotland. Freedom of Information: A Consultation* (November, 1999) para.4.9.
[37] See *Scottish Ministers v Scottish Information Commissioner* [2007] CSIH 8; 2007 S.C. 330.

(viii) information the disclosure of which would, or would be likely to, endanger the physical or mental health or the safety of an individual (s.39(1)); and

(ix) information the disclosure of which would, or would be likely to, prejudice substantially the exercise of audit functions by any Scottish public authority or functions relating to the examination of the economy, efficiency and effectiveness with which Scottish public authorities use their resources (s.40).

Class-based exemptions

The following information is covered by class-based exemptions: **18–18**

(i) information intended for future publication (s.27(1));

(ii) information held by the Scottish Administration that relates to the formulation or development of government policy, ministerial communications, the provision (or request for the provision) of advice from any of the law officers, or the operation of any ministerial private office (s.29);

(iii) information the exemption of which is required for the purpose of safeguarding national security (s.31(1)); a certificate signed by a member of the Scottish Government is conclusive proof of the fact that exemption is required (s.31(2));

(iv) confidential information obtained from a State other than the UK or an international organisation or international court (s.32(1)(b));

(v) trade secrets (s.33(1)(a));

(vi) information held for the purposes of investigations or proceedings arising out of investigations (s.34);

(vii) information in respect of which a claim to confidentiality could be maintained in legal proceedings (s.36(1));

(viii) personal data the disclosure of which would contravene a notice under s.10 of the Data Protection Act 1998, or which the data subject would not have the right to access under the Data Protection Act (s.38(1)(b));

(ix) information obtainable under the Environmental Information (Scotland) Regulations 2004 (s.39(2))[38];

(x) information that relates to communications with Her Majesty, other members of the Royal Family or the Royal Household; or relates to the exercise by Her Majesty of Her prerogative of honour (s.41). The Constitutional Reform and Governance Act 2010 extended the types of Royal communication enjoying exemption under the UK Freedom of Information Act and granted them absolute exemption.[39] The Scottish Government proposed following suit in the Freedom of Information (Amendment) (Scotland) Act 2013 but, after reflection, the proposal was withdrawn at Stage 2.[40]

Discretionary disclosure

The 2002 Act provides that nothing in it is to be taken to limit the powers of a   **18–19** Scottish public authority to disclose information held by it.[41] A public authority is not obliged therefore to withhold information subject to an exemption unless

---

[38] Environmental Information (Scotland) Regulations 2004 (SSI 2004/520).

[39] Constitutional Reform and Governance Act 2010 Sch.7 paras 2, 3.

[40] Scottish Parliament OR December 15, 2012, cols 1938–1941.

[41] FOI(S)A 2002 s.66.

its disclosure is restricted for some other reason, e.g. because it would breach a statutory prohibition or constitute a breach of confidence. In *Kennedy v The Charity Commission*,[42] the Supreme Court emphasised that the UK Freedom of Information Act was not an exhaustive scheme governing the disclosure of information by public authorities. "[T]he idea that, as a general proposition, a public body needs particular authority to provide information about its activities to the public," Lord Toulson said, "is misconceived."[43]

THE SCOTTISH INFORMATION COMMISSIONER

18–20   The Scottish Information Commissioner ("SIC") is responsible for the promotion and enforcement of the 2002 Act. The Commissioner is appointed by the Queen on the nomination of the Parliament for a single non-renewable term of not more than eight years.[44] Under the Act as originally enacted, the Commissioner could be appointed for two terms of not more than five years each, with the possibility of reappointment for a third term if reappointment was desirable in the public interest,[45] but this was replaced by a single term of not more than eight years by the Scottish Parliamentary Commissions and Commissioners etc. Act 2010, which standardised the Commissioners' terms and conditions of appointment. The current Scottish Information Commissioner was appointed for six years in May 2012.

18–21   The Commissioner enjoys the same guarantees of independence as the Scottish Public Services Ombudsman ("SPSO") and the Commissioner for Ethical Standards in Public Life in Scotland.[46] The Commissioner may be removed from office but only if the SPCB is satisfied that the Commissioner has breached the terms and conditions of office and the Parliament resolves that the Commissioner should be removed from office for that breach, or the Parliament resolves that it has lost confidence in a Commissioner's willingness, suitability or ability to perform the functions of the Commissioner, and, in either case, at least two-thirds of the total number of MSPs, i.e. 86 MSPs, vote in favour of removal.[47] The Commissioner thus enjoys effective security of tenure. The Commissioner is also not subject to the direction or control of the SPCB or any member of the Scottish Government or of the Parliament in the exercise of the Commissioner's functions (except the function of preparing accounts).[48] And appointment for a single term is meant to ensure that the Commissioner cannot be influenced by the prospect of not being reappointed.

18–22   The SIC's governance arrangements follow those for the SPSO.[49] The SPCB's approval is required for the SIC's budget, the number and terms and conditions of staff, payments of fees to advisers, and the acquisition and disposal of land.[50] The SPCB also has power to give the SIC directions as to the location of the Commissioner's office, the sharing of premises, staff, services or other resources with other officeholders or public bodies, and the form and content

---

[42] *Kennedy v The Charity Commission* [2014] UKSC 20, [6].
[43] *Kennedy v The Charity Commission* [2014] UKSC 20, [107].
[44] FOI(S)A 2002 s.42(3), (5).
[45] FOI(S)A 2002 s.42(5).
[46] See paras 4–35 and 17–03.
[47] FOISA 2002 s.42(4A), amplifying the original provision which simply provided for removal by a two-thirds majority of all MSPs.
[48] FOI(S)A 2002 s.42(7).
[49] See para.17–05.
[50] FOI(S)A 2002 Sch.2 paras 3, 4A and 6, s.42(9C).

of the SIC's annual report.[51] The Commissioner is required to lay a four year strategic plan before the Parliament, setting out how the SIC proposes to perform its functions during the four year period, and before doing so to provide a draft of the plan to, and invite and consider comments from, the SPCB, the Keeper of the Records of Scotland, and such other persons as the Commissioner thinks appropriate.[52]

The Commissioner lays an annual report before the Parliament (which must **18–23** record the number of occasions, during the period covered by the report, on which the Commissioner failed to reach a decision on an appeal against the way a public authority has dealt with a request for information within the four month period specified by the 2002 Act).[53] The Commissioner may also lay such other reports before the Parliament as the Commissioner thinks fit.[54] As was noted in discussing the Scottish Public Services Ombudsman, the Finance Committee endorsed a proposal, from the SPCB, that committees take evidence more regularly from the commissioners and ombudsman, and that in particular they should take evidence on their annual reports,[55] but evidence has never been taken on the Information Commissioner's annual report.

REVIEW AND APPEAL

An applicant who is dissatisfied with the way in which a Scottish public **18–24** authority has dealt with a request for information may apply to the Commissioner for a decision whether the request has been dealt with in accordance with the Act.[56]

Before appealing to the Commissioner the applicant must first ask the authority **18–25** to review its handling of the request.[57] Internal review is intended to give the authority a chance to reconsider its initial decision, possibly in the light of arguments put forward by the applicant. It also gives the authority an opportunity to monitor the quality of its initial decisions, and to identify and correct problems or inconsistencies in its decision-making processes.[58] The Scottish Ministers' Code of Practice (discussed further, below) requires authorities to have in place "appropriate and accessible" procedures for handling reviews, which should, among other things, set out the process to be followed to ensure that reviews are "comprehensive and robust". The review procedure should be

---

[51] FOI(S)A 2002 Sch.2 paras 7 and 8, s.46(2A).

[52] FOI(S)A 2002 s.46A.

[53] FOI(S)A 2002 s.46(1), (2).

[54] FOI(S)A 2002 s.46(3); the first Commissioner laid a special report before the Parliament on demitting office: Scottish Information Commissioner, *Informing the Future—The State of Freedom of Information in Scotland* (January, 2012); the current Commissioner has laid two special reports before the Parliament—on the failure of public authorities to respond to requests for information or a review within the maximum of 20 working days permitted by the Act: *Failure to Respond to FOI Requests; extent, impact and remedy* (August, 2014); and on the lack of consistent progress on the extension of FOI: *FOI 10 years on: are the right organisations covered?* (January, 2015).

[55] See para.17–06.

[56] FOI(S)A 2002 s.47; no appeal lies against the handling of a request for information by the SIC, a procurator fiscal, or the Lord Advocate, to the extent that the information requested is held by the Lord Advocate as head of the systems of criminal prosecution and investigation of deaths in Scotland: FOI(S)A 2002 s.48.

[57] FOI(S)A 2002 s.20(1).

[58] Freedom of Information (Scotland) Bill Policy Memorandum, para.16.

"fair and impartial and allow decision makers to look at the request afresh. It should also enable different decisions to be taken".[59]

18–26 In common with an initial request for information, a review must be completed with 20 working days of a "requirement for review" being received.[60]

18–27 An appeal to the Commissioner must be made in writing (or in some other form such as a recording capable of being used for subsequent reference) and must normally be made within six months of the applicant being informed of the outcome of the review, or the failure by the authority to review its decision.[61]

18–28 Appeals are dealt with by an investigation rather than a hearing, in which respect the Commissioner is more akin to an ombudsman than an appellate body. The authority must be given notice of the application and its comments invited.[62] Otherwise it is for the Commissioner to determine the procedure for conducting an investigation.[63] Where an authority does not co-operate voluntarily with an investigation, the Commissioner may obtain information, other than information protected by legal professional privilege, by an information notice specifying the information required and the form in which it should be provided.[64]

18–29 The Commissioner is required to reach a decision within four months of receiving an application or such other period as is reasonable in the circumstances.[65] The Commissioner's annual report, as noted, must record the number of occasions, during the period covered by the report, on which the Commissioner failed to reach a decision within the four month period, underlining the importance attached by the Parliament to the expeditious determination of appeals.[66]

18–30 The Commissioner may endeavour to effect a settlement between the applicant and the authority.[67] A settlement usually involves the applicant receiving some of the information requested in return for withdrawing the application, which relieves the Commissioner of the obligation to reach a decision.[68] If no settlement is effected, the Commissioner must reach a decision, notice in writing of

---

[59] *Scottish Ministers' Code of Practice on the Discharge of Functions by Scottish Public Authorities under the Freedom of Information (Scotland) Act 2002 and the Environmental Information (Scotland) Regulations 2004* (December, 2014) Pt 2, paras 10.3.3–10.3.5.

[60] FOI(S)A 2002 s.21(1).

[61] FOI(S)A 2002 s.47(2), (4).

[62] FOI(S)A 2002 s.49(3)(a); the obligation to seek an authority's comments extends to any new material the SIC's inquiries elicit which is adverse to the authority's interests: *South Lanarkshire Council v Scottish Information Commissioner* [2013] UKSC 55; 2013 S.L.T. 799, [29]–[33] (Lady Hale).

[63] Scottish Information Commissioner, *The Scottish Information Commissioner's Investigations: A Guide for Scottish Public Authorities* (January, 2011) sets out the SIC's procedures.

[64] FOI(S)A 2002 s.50; on the shortcomings of the information notice procedure, see Scottish Information Commissioner, *Informing the Future—The State of Freedom of Information in Scotland* (January, 2012) p.14.

[65] FOI(S)A 2002 s.49(3)(b).

[66] FOI(S)A 2002 s.46(2); 78 per cent of appeals on average were closed within four months in the last three years.

[67] FOI(S)A 2002 s.49(4).

[68] Kevin Dunion, *Freedom of Information in Scotland in Practice* (Dundee: Dundee University Press, 2011) para.1.504; 52 per cent of cases (61 of 118 cases) closed during investigation in 2013–2014, were settled, compared with 44 per cent (67 of 152 cases) the previous year.

which must be given to the applicant and the authority.[69] Where the SIC finds that an authority has failed to comply with the Act, the decision specifies the steps that must be taken in order to comply and the time within which those steps must be taken.[70] Unlike the SPSO, who makes recommendations, the SIC makes decisions, which must be complied with unless successfully appealed against. A failure to comply with a decision notice is punishable by the Court of Session as a contempt of court, as is a failure to comply with an information notice.[71]

Appeals in practice

The Commissioner received 653 appeals, including appeals under the **18–31** Environmental Information (Scotland) Regulations, in 2005–2006, the first full year of operation of the 2002 Act. The number of appeals thereafter declined to 400 in 2008–2009, since when the number increased to 594 in 2012–2013, before dropping slightly to 578 in 2013–2014. The SIC has started collating statistics on the number of FOI requests received by authorities, which show that more than 60,000 (60,476) requests were recorded by Scottish public authorities between April 1, 2013 and March 31, 2014, less than 1 per cent of which resulted in appeals to the Commissioner. The number of appeals therefore represents a very small proportion of the total number of requests.[72]

An increasing number of appeals have arisen as a result of the failure by public **18–32** authorities to respond to requests for information or a review within the maximum of 20 working days permitted by the 2002 Act. The proportion of valid appeals accounted for by such "failure to respond" appeals reached 27 per cent in 2012–2013, causing the Commissioner to lay a special report before the Parliament exploring the issues and trends arising from failure to respond cases.[73] Five authorities, including the Scottish Government, with the largest proportion, and the Scottish Prison Service, accounted for 50 per cent of those appeals. The Commissioner's analysis suggested that the media and prisoners experience more failures to respond than the other requesters. There was a slight reduction in such appeals (2 per cent) in 2013–2014. Nevertheless, it "remains unacceptable that such cases still account for almost a quarter of our valid appeals".[74]

Local government accounts for the largest percentage of appeals: 41 per cent **18–33** in 2013–2014, compared with 43 per cent in 2012–2013. The Scottish Government and its agencies accounts for the next largest percentage: 25 per cent in 2013–2014, compared with 30 per cent in 2012–2013. Most appeals are by individuals: 62 per cent in 2013–2014 compared with 60 per cent in 2012–2013, with the media accounting for 14 per cent in 2013–2014 and 12 per cent in 2010–2013. Prisoners were shown for the first time in 2012–2013 (10 per cent), falling to 8 per cent in 2013–2014. Elected representatives (3 per cent) and the voluntary sector (3 per cent) account for only a small proportion of appeals.

---

[69] FOI(S)A 2002 s.49(3)(b), (5).
[70] FOI(S)A 2002 s.49(6).
[71] FOI(S)A 2002 s.53.
[72] Scottish Information Commissioner, *2013/2014 Annual Report, Taking FOI forward* (2014) p.20.
[73] *Failure to Respond to FOI Requests; extent, impact and remedy* (August, 2014).
[74] Scottish Information Commissioner, *2013/2014 Annual Report, Taking FOI forward* (2014) p.12.

18–34 Appeals may be closed as invalid, closed during investigation, or closed after investigation with a decision. The percentage of appeals closed before or during investigation increased from 51 per cent in 2011–2012 to 60 per cent in 2012–2013 before falling back to 50 per cent in 2013–2014. In roughly two-thirds of the appeals closed with a decision the SIC finds wholly or partially in favour of the applicant: 66 per cent in 2013–2014, compared with 63 per cent in 2012–2013.

Ministerial "override"

18–35 The Scottish Government retains the power to set aside a Commissioner's decision in certain limited circumstances. A Commissioner's decision may be overridden by a certificate issued by the First Minister within 30 days of notice of the decision being given, or an appeal against the decision being finally determined.[75] A certificate may only be issued in respect of a perceived failure to comply with s.1(1) of the 2002 Act in respect of requests for information covered by certain of the exemptions, namely the formulation of government policy (s.29), national security (s.31(1)), confidential information obtained from a state other than the UK or an international organisation or international court (s.32(1)(b)), information held for the purposes of investigations and proceedings arising out of such investigations (s.34), information in respect of which a claim to confidentiality could be maintained in legal proceedings (s.36(1)), and information that relates to the exercise by the Queen of her prerogative of honour (s.41(b)).

18–36 Before issuing the certificate, the First Minister must have consulted the other members of the Scottish Government; the certificate must also state that the First Minister has formed the opinion, after such consultation, that there was no failure to comply with s.1(1) *and* that the information requested is of "exceptional sensitivity".[76] Within 10 working days of issuing the certificate, a copy of it must be laid before the Parliament and a statement of the reasons for the First Minister's opinion must be given to the person who requested the information.[77] Unlike the corresponding power under the UK Freedom of Information Act, this power has not been exercised.[78]

Appeal to the Inner House

18–37 An appeal on a point of law lies against a decision of the Commissioner to the Inner House of the Court of Session.[79] In contrast to the UK Freedom of Information Act, there is no right of appeal to a tribunal.[80] The question of a right of appeal to a tribunal was the subject of consultation, but in the light of the "widely-held view that an Information Tribunal would add an unnecessary layer of bureaucracy and possibly undermine the Commissioner's powers", the

---

[75] FOI(S)A 2000 s.52.

[76] FOI(S)A 2002 s.52(2).

[77] FOI(S)A 2002 s.52(3).

[78] The power under s.53 of the UK Freedom of Information Act has been used seven times, including to prevent publication of minutes of Cabinet subcommittee meetings in 1997 relating to devolution.

[79] FOI(S)A 2002 s.56.

[80] The appeal under the UK Freedom of Information Act, which extends to the merits of decisions as well as points of law, lay originally to the Information Tribunal, and from there on a point of law to the High Court; it now lies to the First-tier Tribunal, and from there on a point of law to the Upper Tribunal: Transfer of Tribunal Functions Order 2010 (SI 2010/22) art.2(3)(a).

Scottish Executive did not consider the creation of an information tribunal either "necessary or appropriate".[81]

In its initial discussion of rights of appeal under the UK regime, the UK **18–38** Government also took the view that a right of appeal against the Commissioner's decisions would not be in the best interests of FOI applicants:

"Overseas experience shows that where appeals are allowed to the courts, a public authority which is reluctant to disclose information will often seek leave to appeal simply to delay implementation of a decision. The cost of making an appeal to the courts would also favour the public authority over the individual applicant."[82]

What appears to have prompted a change of mind was the decision to combine the functions of the Information Commissioner with those of the Data Protection Commissioner under the Data Protection Act 1998. The Data Protection Commissioner came complete with a Data Protection Tribunal, and the Commissioner and the tribunal were simply renamed the Information Commissioner and the Information Tribunal.

There have been 36 appeals to the Inner House against 2,246 decisions issued **18–39** since 2005. The principal repeat player has been the Scottish Government, which has brought seven appeals, four of which have been abandoned—the most recent an appeal against the Commissioner's decision requiring the Scottish Ministers to confirm whether they had taken legal advice on an independent Scotland's membership of the EU. There has also been one application for judicial review, which was abandoned.

In the absence of a right of appeal to a tribunal that can decide questions of **18–40** both fact and law, the Supreme Court has held that the Commissioner is under an "enhanced" duty to act fairly. Delivering the judgment of the Court in *South Lanarkshire Council v Scottish Information Commissioner*, Lady Hale said:

"I would add that the Commissioner is fulfilling more than an administrative function. He is adjudicating upon competing claims. And in Scotland, unlike England and Wales, there is no appeal to a tribunal which can decide questions of both fact and law. The Commissioner is the sole finder of facts, with a right of appeal to the Inner House on a point of law only. These factors clearly enhance his duty to be fair. If wrong findings of fact are made as a result of an unfair process, the Inner House will not be able to correct them."[83]

The disadvantage of any appeals arrangement, as the UK Government recog- **18–41** nised, is that it may be exploited by public authorities to delay the implementation of decisions. A public authority can delay complying with a decision by appealing on a point of law to the Court of Session, knowing that it will take 18 months or more to get a decision, by which time the information may well have lost much of its currency. The Scottish Government's use of the right of appeal to block access to its deliberations over local income tax or

[81] Freedom of Information (Scotland) Bill Policy Memorandum, paras 132–133.
[82] Cabinet Office, *Your Right to Know. The Government's proposals for a Freedom of Information Act* (1997) Cm.3818, para.5.16.
[83] *South Lanarkshire Council v Scottish Information Commissioner* [2013] UKSC 55; 2013 S.L.T. 799, [31].

(non-existent) legal advice on an independent Scotland's membership of the EU illustrates the risk. Against that must be set the interests of fairness and due process, and the contribution the courts can make to clarifying and developing the law.

PUBLICATION SCHEMES

18–42 The 2002 Act encourages the proactive disclosure of information by public authorities with a view to reducing the need for information to be formally requested. Public authorities are accordingly required to adopt and maintain a publication scheme specifying the information they will routinely publish.[84] Publication schemes require the SIC's approval.[85] The SIC also has the power to prepare and approve model publication schemes (or to approve such schemes prepared by other persons).[86] The SIC introduced a single model publication scheme in 2011, which was adopted by the Scottish Government, its agencies and non-ministerial office holders. The scheme is revised and reissued annually. All Scottish public authorities, including local government, the police, health and further and higher education bodies have now adopted the scheme.

PROMOTING GOOD PRACTICE

18–43 As well as determining appeals against the refusal of requests for information, the Commissioner is responsible for promoting the following of good practice by Scottish public authorities, with a view in particular to promoting observance of the 2002 Act and the codes of practice issued by the Scottish Ministers under the Act.[87] There are two codes of practice: the Scottish Ministers' Code of Practice on the Discharge of Functions by Scottish Public Authorities under the Freedom of Information (Scotland) Act 2002 and the Environmental Information (Scotland) Regulations 2004 ("the EIRs" December, 2014), issued under s.60 of the 2002 Act and reg.18 of the EIRs, and the Code of Practice on Records Management (December, 2011), issued under s.61 of the 2002 Act. The former, which was prepared in consultation with the SIC, provides guidance to Scottish public authorities on the practice which Scottish Ministers consider it desirable for authorities to follow in connection with the discharge of their functions under the Act and the EIRs. "Scottish public authorities are expected to adhere to the Code unless there are good reasons not to which are capable of being justified to the Commissioner."[88]

Intervention and enforcement

18–44 Where there is evidence that a public authority is not complying with its obligations under the Act, the EIRs or the codes of practice, the SIC may respond in a variety of ways, including by carrying out a formal assessment of whether the authority is following good practice.[89] The SIC's preference, in the initial stages at least, is to proceed by less formal means, typically involving the

---

[84] FOI(S)A 2002 s.23(1).
[85] FOI(S)A 2002 s.23(1).
[86] FOI(S)A 2002 s.24.
[87] FOI(S)A 2002 s.43(1).
[88] *Scottish Ministers' Code of Practice on the Discharge of Functions by Scottish Public Authorities under the Freedom of Information (Scotland) Act 2002 and the Environmental Information (Scotland) Regulations 2004* (December, 2014) Pt 1 para.4.
[89] FOI(S)A 2002 s.43(3).

provision of advice and support to authorities.[90] Where the SIC is not satisfied that the less formal approach will be effective, a formal "practice recommendation" may be issued,[91] which is not directly enforceable but which nevertheless carries "significant weight".[92] Were an authority to ignore a practice recommendation it could lead to an enforcement notice, breach of which is punishable by the Court of Session as a contempt of court in the same way as breach of a decision notice or an information notice.[93] Two such recommendations have been issued: to Scottish Borders Council and the University of the Highlands and Islands.

The SIC also has the power to issue enforcement notices. Where the SIC is **18–45** satisfied that an authority has failed to comply with a provision of Pt 1 of the 2002 Act, e.g. to maintain a publication scheme, or to review decisions, an enforcement notice may be served on the authority requiring it to take action to comply with the provision within a specified period.[94] An enforcement notice is enforceable in the same way as a decision notice or information notice.[95] No enforcement notices have been issued. A persistent failure by an authority to comply with its obligations may also be the subject of a special report to the Parliament (as described above).

---

[90] See e.g. Scottish Information Commissioner, *2013/2014 Annual Report, Taking FOI forward* (2014) p.13.
[91] FOISA 2002 s.44.
[92] *Failure to Respond to FOI Requests; extent, impact and remedy* (August, 2014) para.115.
[93] FOI(S)A 2002 ss.51, 53.
[94] FOI(S)A 2002 s.51(1).
[95] FOI(S)A 2002 s.53.

CHAPTER 19

THE UK DIMENSION

"We need to recall that devolution is not the whole story of Scottish governance."[1]

INTRODUCTION

One of the undoubted consequences of devolution has been to obscure the **19–01** UK dimension of the governance of Scotland—what used to be called the "second leg" of the government of Scotland.[2] The UK Government and the UK Parliament remain responsible, however, for many of the policy areas that affect those living in Scotland—foreign affairs, defence and national security, fiscal, economic and monetary policy, taxation, trade and industry, including employment, social security and pensions. The UK Parliament effectively determines the size of Scotland's annual block grant.[3] More than half the legislation enacted at Westminster extends to Scotland, excluding Westminster legislation in the devolved areas. And Scottish civil appeals continue to be taken to London, while UK or GB rather than Scottish tribunals account for the vast majority of tribunal decisions taken in Scotland. In this chapter we examine the continuing significance of the UK dimension of the governance of Scotland, as well as the various ways in which the relationship between Scotland and the rest of the UK has changed as a consequence of devolution. A recurring theme is the protection of Scottish interests in relation to matters decided at Westminster, which is no less a concern now than at the time of the Union.[4]

SCOTTISH REPRESENTATION AT WESTMINSTER

The Acts of Union gave Scotland 45 MPs and 16 representative peers in the **19–02** new Parliament of Great Britain (art.22). Scotland was initially less well represented in the House of Commons than England and Wales, the number of MPs having been fixed on the basis of its share of Britain's wealth with some

---

[1] Barry K Winetrobe, "Public Accountability in Scotland" in Aileen McHarg and Tom Mullen (eds), *Public Law in Scotland* (Edinburgh: Avizandum, 2006) p.148.
[2] The first leg being the Scottish Office: AW Bradley, "Devolution of Government in Britain—Some Scottish Aspects" in Harry Calvert (ed), *Devolution* (London: Professional Books, 1975) p.96. In his foreword to the Smith Commission Agreement, Lord Smith recommended that the Scottish Parliament's Presiding Officer and Speaker of the House of Commons meet "to agree on action to improve public understanding of Scotland's constitutional settlement": Smith Commission, *Report of the Smith Commission for further devolution of powers to the Scottish Parliament* (November 27, 2014).
[3] Commission on Scottish Devolution, *Serving Scotland Better: Scotland and the United Kingdom in the 21st Century* (June, 2009) para.4.197.
[4] See para.1–08.

allowance for population.[5] Parity of representation was eventually achieved in 1885 when the number of Scottish seats was increased to 72 (having been increased to 53 in 1832 and to 60 in 1867). When Ireland left the UK in 1922 Scotland became over-represented, both in terms of its share of the population and its share of the electorate,[6] but Scottish over-representation at Westminster was ended as part of the devolution settlement. The Scotland Act 1998 ("the Scotland Act") repealed the minimum guarantee of 71 Scottish seats at Westminster and provided that the number of Scottish seats should be determined on the basis of the same electoral quota as in England.[7] Following the fifth review of parliamentary constituency boundaries in Scotland, the number of Scottish seats was reduced from 72 to 59.[8]

19–03 A further reduction in the number of Scottish MPs at Westminster has sometimes been canvassed as a solution to the West Lothian question, which takes its name from the former MP for West Lothian, Tam Dalyell, who raised it during the devolution debates in the 1970s. The West Lothian question, or English question as it has also become known,[9] draws attention to the imbalance of representation caused by the fact that Scottish MPs continue to be able to vote on matters such as health or education in England when English MPs cannot vote on those matters in Scotland because they are devolved.[10] The question came to the fore immediately after the independence referendum when the Prime Minister said that

> "the question of English votes for English laws—the so-called West Lothian question—requires a decisive answer ... Just as the people of Scotland will have more power over their affairs, so it follows that the people of England, Wales and Northern Ireland must have a bigger say over theirs".[11]

In terms of possible answers, the McKay Commission on the Consequences of Devolution for the House of Commons had earlier rejected a reduction in the number of MPs in the devolved areas relative to England on the grounds that it

> "would be—and be seen to be—unfair and inimical to the link between representation and taxation falling on all UK citizens that is imposed at the UK level".[12]

---

[5] In 1801, the ratio of MPs to population was one to 17,800 in England and Wales, one to 36,000 in Scotland and one to 50,000 in Ireland: Julian Hoppit, "Introduction" in Hoppit (ed), *Parliaments, Nations and Identities in Britain and Ireland, 1660–1850* (Manchester: Manchester University Press, 2003) p.4.

[6] Iain McLean, "Are Scotland and Wales Over-Represented in the House of Commons?" (1995) 66 The Political Quarterly 250.

[7] Scotland Act 1998 ("SA 1998") s.86; the minimum guarantee was contained in Parliamentary Constituencies Act 1986 Sch.2 r.1(2).

[8] Parliamentary Constituencies (Scotland) Order 2005 (SI 2005/250); the reduction would have led to a reduction in the size of the Scottish Parliament had the size of the Parliament not been maintained by the Scottish Parliament (Constituencies) Act 2004: see para.4–10.

[9] Robert Hazell (ed), *The English Question* (Manchester: Manchester University Press, 2006).

[10] The inability applies equally to Scottish MPs, with consequences for their role in Scotland which tend to be overlooked. As Anthony King put it, "Scottish MPs are effectively eunuchs with regard to most matters that directly affect their own constituents while retaining their full virility with regard to matters that affect only other MPs' constituents": *The British Constitution* (Oxford: OUP, 2007) p.201.

[11] Cabinet Office, *The Implications of Devolution for England* (2014) Cm.8969, p.4.

[12] MacKay Commission, *Report of the Commission on the Consequences of Devolution for the House of Commons* (March, 2013) para.74.

This may not be the last word, but a reduction in Scottish representation at Westminster does not feature among the proposals to address the West Lothian question currently under discussion.[13]

The House of Lords

The House of Lords is not constituted on a territorial basis but it does not lack **19–04** Scottish members. The Royal Commission on the Reform of the House of Lords found that life peers from London, Scotland and the South East of England represented a significantly higher proportion of the membership than might be expected on the basis of regional populations alone,[14] confirming Lord Hope's observation in *Lord Gray's Motion* that there was no reason to think that the removal of the Scottish hereditary peers by the House of Lords Act 1999 would "deprive Scotland of a continuing and effective representation in this part of the legislature".[15]

THE UK GOVERNMENT

The UK Government is the government of Scotland in respect of reserved **19–05** matters. Its functions are carried out by departments, under the overall direction and control of the Cabinet, which before devolution included the Scottish Office and the other territorial departments. Devolution meant placing the bulk of the former Scottish Office under separate political control in Edinburgh (as the Scottish Executive—later renamed Scottish Government), with the residue becoming a smaller UK government department (the Scotland Office). The remaining UK government departments may be divided into those such as the Treasury or Work and Pensions whose functions were before devolution (and continue to be) mainly administered on a UK or GB-wide basis, and those such as Justice or Health whose functions were mainly undertaken in Scotland by the Scottish Office and whose functions post-devolution relate in most instances only to England. The former are of most significance in terms of the contemporary governance of Scotland, but departments in the latter group whose responsibilities have a strong EU dimension, such as Environment, Food and Rural Affairs ("DEFRA"), also have a continuing significance, since it is those departments that have the lead responsibility for relations between the whole of the UK and the European Union.[16]

The Secretary of State for Scotland

With devolution most of the Scottish Office's functions were placed under **19–06** separate political control in Edinburgh. The office of Secretary of State for Scotland, however, was retained, with the emphasis at first on the Secretary of

---

[13] Cabinet Office, *The Implications of Devolution for England* (2014) Cm.8969, pp.24–25 ("We are not in favour of proposals to address the West Lothian Question ... by reducing the number of Scottish MPs at Westminster.") When Northern Ireland had its own Parliament between 1922 and 1972 the number of Northern Ireland MPs at Westminster was reduced by roughly a third; were the Northern Ireland example to be followed, Scottish representation at Westminster would be reduced to about 40, which is five fewer than the 45 "guaranteed" by the Treaty of Union. In *Lord Gray's Motion*, 2000 S.C. (H.L.) 46, 54, Lord Nicholls observed that that there was room for argument that the Treaty of Union would be breached in respect of an implicit condition if Scotland ceased to have adequate representation in both Houses of Parliament.

[14] Royal Commission on the Reform of the House of Lords, *A House for the Future* (2000) Cm.4534, para.13.30.

[15] *Lord Gray's Motion*, 2000 S.C. (H.L.) 46, 64.

[16] Chapter 20.

State's traditional role as Scotland's "voice in the Cabinet", but with increasing emphasis on the Secretary of State's other role as the "Cabinet's voice in Scotland" once governments of the same or similar political complexion were no longer in power in Edinburgh and London. As well as ensuring that Scottish interests in non-devolved matters are properly represented and considered, the Scotland Office, which supports the Secretary of State, is responsible for the administration of the devolution settlement, including the making of Scotland Act orders and policing the boundary between reserved and devolved matters, with the latter responsibility being shared with the Scottish Government and the Scottish Parliament. The Scotland Office was incorporated into the Department of Constitutional Affairs (now the Ministry of Justice) in 2003 in what was widely interpreted as a preliminary to its eventual abolition, but with a referendum on independence in prospect it became a full department in its own right again in 2011. Notwithstanding its seemingly charmed life, the case for the merger of the three territorial departments—including the Scotland Office—to form a single department of intergovernmental or home affairs would seem overwhelming.[17]

The Advocate General for Scotland

19–07 Devolution did not remove the UK Government's need for advice on Scots law.[18] That need is met by the Advocate General for Scotland who replaced the Lord Advocate and the Solicitor General for Scotland as the UK Government's senior legal adviser on Scots law when the two Scottish law officers became members of the Scottish Executive in 1999.[19]

19–08 As well as advisory responsibilities, the Advocate General for Scotland has powers under the Scotland Act to intervene in judicial proceedings in which devolution issues or compatibility issues arise,[20] and (as do the Attorney General and the Lord Advocate) power to refer Bills of the Scottish Parliament to the Supreme Court where there are doubts about their legislative competence.[21]

INTERGOVERNMENTAL RELATIONS

19–09 Devolution did not mean an end to the need for co-operation and co-ordination between the former departments of what was once a single UK Government. What hitherto had been a need for cooperation and coordination between individual *departments* with a common political purpose and direction, however, became a need for co-operation and co-ordination between individual *governments* whose political direction might be different but which might nevertheless need to work together in order to achieve their objectives.[22] The need for some liaison machinery and "administrative conventions" of co-operation and joint working was recognised in the White Paper that preceded the Scotland

---

[17] JD Gallagher, *The Day After Judgment, Scotland and the UK After the Referendum* (September, 2014) section 4.
[18] Scottish Office, *Scotland's Parliament* (1997) Cm.3658, para.4.9.
[19] SA 1998 s.87.
[20] SA 1998 Sch.6; see paras 9–11 and 9–25.
[21] SA 1998 s.33(2); see para.13–41.
[22] The independence referendum is the prime example; had the Scottish Government tried to go it alone it would have faced a possibly lengthy legal challenge with no certainty about the eventual outcome.

Act,[23] and addressed in a series of multilateral and bilateral agreements, which are intended to foster communication and co-operation between the different governments within the UK.

The Memorandum of Understanding

The principal agreement is the Memorandum of Understanding, which sets out **19–10** the shared understanding of the UK Government and the devolved administrations of the principles, drawn from pre-devolution practice, on which relations between them are based.[24] The Memorandum of Understanding also provides for the establishment of a joint ministerial committee ("JMC"), which is the subject of a separate agreement. In addition to the JMC agreement, three separate overarching concordats apply broadly uniform arrangements to areas where a common approach was felt necessary: the handling of matters with an EU dimension, financial assistance to industry, and international relations touching on the responsibilities of the devolved administrations. There is also guidance on common working arrangements.[25]

The Memorandum of Understanding sets out three principles underlying rela- **19–11** tions between the administrations.

Communication and consultation

The first principle is good communication, which is sometimes referred to as **19–12** the principle of no surprises.

> "All four administrations are committed to the principle of good communication with each other, and especially where one administration's work may have some bearing upon the responsibilities of another administration. The primary aim is not to constrain the discretion of any administration, but to allow administrations to make representations to each other in sufficient time for those representations to be fully considered."[26]

They will therefore seek:

- to alert each other as soon as practicable to relevant developments within their area of responsibility, wherever possible, prior to publication;
- to give appropriate consideration to the views of the other administrations; and
- to establish where appropriate arrangements that allow for policies for which responsibility is shared to be drawn up and developed jointly between the administrations.[27]

---

[23] Scottish Office, *Scotland's Parliament* (1997) Cm.3658, paras 4.13–4.14.

[24] Cabinet Office, *Memorandum of Understanding and Supplementary Agreements between the United Kingdom Government, the Scottish Ministers, the Welsh Ministers and the Northern Ireland Executive Committee* (October, 2013).

[25] Cabinet Office, Devolution Guidance Note 1 *Common Working Arrangements*; for the origins of Devolution Guidance Note 1, see Johanne Poirier, "The Functions of Intergovernmental Agreements: Post-Devolution Concordats in a Comparative Perspective" [2001] P.L. 134, 147 fn 70.

[26] Cabinet Office, *Memorandum of Understanding and Supplementary Agreements between the United Kingdom Government, the Scottish Ministers, the Welsh Ministers and the Northern Ireland Executive Committee* (October, 2013) para.4.

[27] Cabinet Office, *Memorandum of Understanding and Supplementary Agreements between the United Kingdom Government, the Scottish Ministers, the Welsh Ministers and the Northern Ireland Executive Committee* (October, 2013) para.5.

Co-operation

19–13 The second principle, which is expressed in terms that fall some way short of an obligation, is co-operation.

> "All four administrations want to work together, where appropriate, on matters of mutual interest. The administrations recognise the importance of cooperation across a range of areas. They also recognise that it may be appropriate for them to undertake activities on each other's behalf, which may be covered in agency arrangements or other agreements."[28]

Confidentiality

19–14 The final principle is confidentiality.

> "Each administration will wish to ensure that the information it supplies to others is subject to appropriate safeguards to avoid prejudicing its interests. The four administrations accept that in certain circumstances a duty of confidence may arise and will between themselves respect legal requirements of confidentiality. Each administration can only expect to receive information if it treats such information with appropriate discretion."[29]

19–15 There is provision for the exchange of information, statistics and research; in order to enable each administration to operate effectively, the administrations

> "aim to provide each other with as full and open as possible access to scientific, technical and policy information including statistics and research and, where appropriate, representations from third parties".[30]

Bilateral concordats

19–16 Bilateral concordats between individual Whitehall departments and the Scottish Government set out more detailed provisions in relation to individual policy areas. Their aim and purpose is "to preserve existing good working relationships and ensure that the business of government is conducted smoothly and efficiently under devolution".[31] Good communication in both directions and the avoidance of surprises for either party are commonly identified as the key to an effective working relationship. In the concordat between the Department for Transport and the Scottish Executive, for example, the parties undertook

> "to keep each other informed ... of developments in policy and practice in respect of matters within or affecting their respective responsibilities,

[28] Cabinet Office, *Memorandum of Understanding and Supplementary Agreements between the United Kingdom Government, the Scottish Ministers, the Welsh Ministers and the Northern Ireland Executive Committee* (October, 2013) para.8.
[29] Cabinet Office, *Memorandum of Understanding and Supplementary Agreements between the United Kingdom Government, the Scottish Ministers, the Welsh Ministers and the Northern Ireland Executive Committee* (October, 2013) para.12; see also Freedom of Information Act 2000 s.28; Freedom of Information (Scotland) Act 2002 s.28.
[30] Cabinet Office, *Memorandum of Understanding and Supplementary Agreements between the United Kingdom Government, the Scottish Ministers, the Welsh Ministers and the Northern Ireland Executive Committee* (October, 2013) para.10.
[31] Cabinet Office, Devolution Guidance Note 1 *Common Working Arrangements*; Annex A.

including proposals for legislation and other initiatives, and other issues which may be relevant to each other".[32]

As well as concordats covering the whole range of a Whitehall department's activities, there are a number of subject specific concordats (e.g. on public procurement and related international obligations). The guidance on working practices recognises that concordats are not necessarily the only way to regulate relationships. Other, less formal, arrangements will be appropriate in many cases, and in others there will be no need for any standing arrangements at all.[33] With time many of these bilateral concordats have become out-of-date, with several remaining unchanged since they were first issued.[34]

A feature of all these agreements is that they are not intended to be legally **19–17** binding. The Memorandum of Understanding is

> "a statement of political intent, and should not be interpreted as a binding agreement. It does not create legal obligations between the parties".[35]

The overarching concordats are likewise "not intended to be legally binding, but to serve as working documents"[36]; while the purpose of bilateral concordats

> "is *not* to create legal obligations or restrictions on any party; rather, they will set the ground rules for administrative co-operation and exchange of information".[37]

The fact that they are not intended to be legally enforceable does not mean that **19–18** they may not ground a legitimate expectation of consultation. The Memorandum of Understanding expressly provides, however, that it does not create any statutory or other legal right to be consulted.[38] More recent bilateral concordats also make plain that they are not intended to create any right to consultation or prevent consultation beyond that required by statute, and that any failure to follow the terms of the concordat is not to be taken as invalidating decisions taken by the administrations.[39] Complete judge-proofing is doubtless

---

[32] *Concordat between the Department for Transport and the Scottish Executive*, 2nd edn (2007) para.14.

[33] Cabinet Office, Devolution Guidance Note 1 *Common Working Arrangements*; Annex A.

[34] The House of Lords Constitution Committee recommended that concordats should be for a fixed term only and periodically renegotiated: *Devolution: Inter-Institutional Relations in the United Kingdom* (HL 2002–2003, 28) para.43.

[35] Cabinet Office, *Memorandum of Understanding and Supplementary Agreements between the United Kingdom Government, the Scottish Ministers, the Welsh Ministers and the Northern Ireland Executive Committee* (October, 2013) para.2.

[36] Cabinet Office, *Memorandum of Understanding and Supplementary Agreements between the United Kingdom Government, the Scottish Ministers, the Welsh Ministers and the Northern Ireland Executive Committee* (October, 2013) para.3.

[37] Cabinet Office, Devolution Guidance Note 1 *Common Working Arrangements*; Annex A, original emphasis.

[38] Cabinet Office, *Memorandum of Understanding and Supplementary Agreements between the United Kingdom Government, the Scottish Ministers, the Welsh Ministers and the Northern Ireland Executive Committee* (October, 2013) para.7.

[39] See, e.g. the *Concordat between the Office of the Deputy Prime Minister and the Scottish Executive*, 2nd edn (2007) para.4.

impossible, but the language "clearly signals a strong aversion to judicial scrutiny of the workings of concordats, etc.".[40]

The Joint Ministerial Committee

19–19   The Memorandum of Understanding anticipated that most contact between the UK Government and the devolved administrations would be carried out on a bilateral or multilateral basis, between departments which dealt on a day-to-day basis with the issues at stake. Nonetheless, some central coordination of the overall relationship was felt necessary. The administrations therefore agreed to participate in a Joint Ministerial Committee consisting of UK Government, Scottish, Welsh and Northern Ireland Ministers. A supplementary agreement sets out the basis on which the Committee is intended to operate, pursuant to the Memorandum of Understanding.

19–20   The JMC's terms of reference are:

- to consider non-devolved matters which impinge on devolved responsibilities, and devolved matters which impinge on non-devolved responsibilities;
- where the UK Government and the devolved administrations so agree, to consider devolved matters if it is beneficial to discuss their respective treatment in the different parts of the UK;
- to keep the arrangements for liaison between the UK Government and the devolved administrations under review; and
- to consider disputes between the administrations.

19–21   The committee meets annually in plenary format (after six years between 2002 and 2008 in which it did not meet), and more regularly in domestic and European formats. There is also a Finance Ministers' Quadrilateral, which meets twice a year. In a limited concession to transparency, a brief annual report is published on the JMC's activities (including those of the Finance Ministers' Quadrilateral).[41]

The Calman Commission

19–22   For the Calman Commission, intergovernmental relations were "fundamentally important in a constitutional system with different levels of government".[42] The Commission regarded the arrangements that had been put in place as underdeveloped: the overarching machinery had not operated in "any systematic way", the systems in place for working-level discussions to clarify issues often "failed to do so before they escalated to more senior and political forums", and the regularity of JMC meetings was "insufficient and too ad hoc".[43] The Commission sought a

"much better developed and more robust framework ... to ensure that, where developed and reserved responsibilities overlap or impinge on one

---

[40] Richard Rawlings, *Delineating Wales: Constitutional, Legal and Administrative Aspects of National Devolution* (Cardiff: University of Wales Press, 2003) p.394.

[41] Rawlings described the JMC as a "black hole" at the heart of the emergent constitutional architecture of the union state: *Delineating Wales: Constitutional, Legal and Administrative Aspects of National Devolution* (2003) p.403.

[42] Commission on Scottish Devolution, *Serving Scotland Better: Scotland and the United Kingdom in the 21st Century* (June, 2009) para.4.116.

[43] Commission on Scottish Devolution, *Serving Scotland Better: Scotland and the United Kingdom in the 21st Century* (June, 2009) para.4.120.

another, proper coordination and joint working are more fully encouraged and supported, with appropriate scrutiny by the parliaments to which the governments are accountable".[44]

The primary purpose of intergovernmental mechanisms, in the Commission's view, should be

"to foster and support co-operation between the institutions, and their focus should be on achieving better results for the people of Scotland through closer working".[45]

The Commission recognised, however, that formal mechanisms and arrangements could only achieve so much: what was critical was the "willingness of those involved to work together constructively and with mutual respect".[46]

The Smith Commission

The Smith Commission saw increased powers for the Scottish Parliament as **19–23** demanding strengthened collaboration between the Scottish and UK Governments:

"The parties believe that the current inter-governmental machinery between Scottish and UK Governments, including the Joint Ministerial Committee (JMC) structures, must be reformed as a matter of urgency and scaled up significantly to reflect the scope of the agreement arrived at by the parties."[47]

Those reformed inter-governmental arrangements would include the development of a new and overarching Memorandum of Understanding between the UK Government and devolved administrations, and be underpinned by "much stronger and more transparent" parliamentary scrutiny.[48]

"In parallel, formal processes should be developed for the Scottish Parliament and UK Parliament to collaborate more regularly in areas of joint interest in holding respective Governments to account."[49]

In his foreword to the Agreement Lord Smith wrote: **19–24**

"Throughout the course of the Commission, the issue of weak inter-governmental working was repeatedly raised as a problem. That current

---

[44] Commission on Scottish Devolution, *Serving Scotland Better: Scotland and the United Kingdom in the 21st Century* (June, 2009) para.4.128.
[45] Commission on Scottish Devolution, *Serving Scotland Better: Scotland and the United Kingdom in the 21st Century* (June, 2009) para.4.136.
[46] Commission on Scottish Devolution, *Serving Scotland Better: Scotland and the United Kingdom in the 21st Century* (June, 2009) para.4.205; as recommended by the Commission (para.4.203), the revised version of the Civil Service Code, laid before Parliament in November 2010, defines the core civil service value of integrity as including "a particular recognition of the importance of cooperation and mutual respect between civil servants working for the UK Government and the devolved administrations and vice-versa".
[47] Smith Commission, *Report of the Smith Commission for further devolution of powers to the Scottish Parliament* (November 27, 2014) para.28.
[48] Smith Commission, *Report of the Smith Commission for further devolution of powers to the Scottish Parliament* (November 27, 2014) para.30(1), (2).
[49] Smith Commission, *Report of the Smith Commission for further devolution of powers to the Scottish Parliament* (November 27, 2014) para.29.

situation coupled with what will be a stronger Scottish Parliament and a more complex devolution settlement means the problem needs to be fixed. Both Governments need to work together to create a more productive, robust, visible and transparent relationship. There also needs to be greater respect between them."[50]

He recommended that the Prime Minister and First Minister meet shortly after January 25, 2015 to agree details of how this would be achieved. "I would encourage them to find solutions which will carry the confidence of the public and our civil institutions."[51]

19–25 At the plenary meeting of the JMC on December 15, 2014, Ministers agreed to commission work on a revised Memorandum of Understanding. They also discussed ways in which their respective Parliaments and Assemblies could be "kept informed" of the work of the JMC.

DISPUTE SETTLEMENT

19–26 The JMC's functions extend to the consideration of disputes between the administrations. The expectation from the outset was that disputes would be resolved bilaterally, or through the good offices of the Secretary of State, whose functions include the promotion of good relations between the UK Government and the devolved administrations. It is only where a dispute cannot be resolved bilaterally, or through the good offices of the Secretary of State, that resort is envisaged to the JMC.[52]

19–27 In dispute settlement mode the JMC is composed of "appropriate Ministers from the UK Government and the devolved administration concerned under the chairmanship of an appropriate senior UK Minister".[53] Where referral appears likely, the Memorandum of Understanding provides that the JMC Secretariat should be consulted at an early stage in order to ensure a consistent interpretation of the devolution settlements, and to provide advice on handling any differences of views.[54] The JMC has no power to make binding decisions. It is

> "a consultative body rather than an executive body, and so will reach agreements rather than decisions. It may not bind any of the participating administrations, which will be free to determine their own policies while taking account of JMC discussions. Nonetheless, the expectation is that participating administrations will support positions that the JMC has agreed".[55]

---

[50] Smith Commission, *Report of the Smith Commission for further devolution of powers to the Scottish Parliament* (November 27, 2014) Foreword.

[51] Smith Commission, *Report of the Smith Commission for further devolution of powers to the Scottish Parliament* (November 27, 2014) Foreword.

[52] Cabinet Office, *Memorandum of Understanding and Supplementary Agreements between the United Kingdom Government, the Scottish Ministers, the Welsh Ministers and the Northern Ireland Executive Committee* (October, 2013) paras 25–26, A1.7.

[53] Cabinet Office, *Memorandum of Understanding and Supplementary Agreements between the United Kingdom Government, the Scottish Ministers, the Welsh Ministers and the Northern Ireland Executive Committee* (October, 2013)) para.A1.5.

[54] Cabinet Office, *Memorandum of Understanding and Supplementary Agreements between the United Kingdom Government, the Scottish Ministers, the Welsh Ministers and the Northern Ireland Executive Committee* (October, 2013) para.A1.7.

[55] Cabinet Office, *Memorandum of Understanding and Supplementary Agreements between the United Kingdom Government, the Scottish Ministers, the Welsh Ministers and the Northern Ireland Executive Committee* (October, 2013) para.A1.10.

The dispute settlement procedures were revised in 2010 with the addition of a **19–28** protocol on dispute avoidance and resolution, which "builds on but does not replace" the procedures set out in the Memorandum of Understanding, the supplementary agreement on the JMC, and the UK Government's Statement of Funding Policy.[56] The protocol makes provision for an independent third party analysis of the issues relating to a disagreement,[57] but stops short of provision for the independent third party settlement of disputes that some of the devolved administrations apparently wanted.[58] In its 2002 report on inter-institutional relations, the House of Lords Constitution Committee recommended the referral of financial disputes to an independent body, such as Devolution Finance Commission,[59] but the UK Government rejected its recommendation: "Funding and fiscal policy are non-devolved matters and they are therefore matters for the Treasury and UK Government to decide."[60]

The protocol recognises that there may be circumstances, "particularly those **19–29** arising from differences in political outlook", where the UK Government and one or more of the devolved administrations are unlikely to be able to agree.

> "In those cases, the parties to this agreement recognise that the JMC machinery is unlikely to offer any prospect of resolution. They also recognise, consistently with the principle that the JMC is not a decision-making body, that the basis on which the procedures will operate is the facilitation of agreement between the parties in dispute, not the imposition of any solution."[61]

Under the Smith Commission Agreement, the reformed inter-governmental **19–30** arrangements will provide for

> "more effective and workable mechanisms to resolve inter-administration disputes in timely and constructive fashion with a provision for well-functioning arbitration processes as a last resort".[62]

Dispute settlement and the courts

The courts provide an independent third party mechanism for resolving **19–31** disputes. The Scotland Act enables the two governments to pursue legal proceedings against each other,[63] which the uncertain doctrine of the indivisibility of the Crown might otherwise have prevented, but the courts have not found favour as a means of settling disputes, governments as a rule preferring

---

[56] Cabinet Office, *Memorandum of Understanding and Supplementary Agreements between the United Kingdom Government, the Scottish Ministers, the Welsh Ministers and the Northern Ireland Executive Committee* (October, 2013) para.A3.1.

[57] Cabinet Office, *Memorandum of Understanding and Supplementary Agreements between the United Kingdom Government, the Scottish Ministers, the Welsh Ministers and the Northern Ireland Executive Committee* (October, 2013) paras A3.11a–c, A3.14a–c.

[58] Jim Gallagher, "Intergovernmental Relations in the UK: Co-operation, Competition and Constitutional Change" (2012) 14 British Journal of Politics and International Relations 206.

[59] House of Lords Constitution Committee, *Devolution: Inter-Institutional Relations in the United Kingdom* (HL 2002–2003, 28) para.102.

[60] The Government's Response to the Second Report of the Select Committee on the Constitution, Session 2002–2003 (HL 2002–2003, 28) Cm.5780, para.10.

[61] Cabinet Office, *Memorandum of Understanding and Supplementary Agreements between the United Kingdom Government, the Scottish Ministers, the Welsh Ministers and the Northern Ireland Executive Committee* (October, 2013) para.A3.4.

[62] Smith Commission, *Report of the Smith Commission for further devolution of powers to the Scottish Parliament* (November 27, 2014) para.30(3).

[63] SA 1998 s.99.

to work out differences by negotiation and agreement rather than litigation in the courts.[64] Where disputes arise over the interpretation of the devolution settlement, the protocol provides that the administrations will generally seek first to resolve them in line with the protocol.[65]

THE UK PARLIAMENT

Legislation

19–32 The UK Parliament is the legislature for Scotland in reserved matters. It also legislates in the devolved areas with the Scottish Parliament's consent. More than half the legislation enacted at Westminster is in the reserved areas; when Westminster legislation in the devolved areas is added, nearly all Westminster legislation extends to Scotland, in whole or in part.[66] Scottish legislation at Westminster now takes the form mainly of Scottish provisions in UK or GB Bills, rather than a combination of Scottish provisions in UK or GB Bills and Scotland-only Bills; there have been only two Scotland-only Bills since devolution.[67] With the decline in Scotland-only legislation the special procedures for Scottish legislation at Westminster involving the Scottish Grand Committee and Scottish standing committees have fallen into disuse. Concerns have been expressed about the sufficiency of the scrutiny of Scottish provisions in UK Bills or GB Bills, particularly where Westminster is legislating in the devolved areas.[68] The McKay Commission saw its proposed devolution committee of the House of Commons (below) as a means of ventilating concerns about the sufficiency of the scrutiny of provisions applicable outside England.[69]

Scrutiny

19–33 Devolution has not altered the formal power of Westminster to discuss Scottish matters, including those devolved to Edinburgh. In the words of the Memorandum of Understanding, Westminster retains "the absolute right to debate, enquire into or make representations about devolved matters".[70] For the

---

[64] Ronald L Watts, *Comparing Federal Systems*, 3rd edn (Quebec: McGill-Queen's University Press, 2008) pp.259–260; the Edinburgh Agreement, which paved the way for the independence referendum is, again, the prime example—one of its main purposes being to avoid the courts deciding whether the Scottish Parliament had competence to legislate for a referendum on independence.

[65] Cabinet Office, *Memorandum of Understanding and Supplementary Agreements between the United Kingdom Government, the Scottish Ministers, the Welsh Ministers and the Northern Ireland Executive Committee* (October, 2013) para.A3.5.

[66] Of the 11 Bills announced in the Queen's Speech in June 2014, nine apply in Scotland in whole or in part; the comparable figure for the Queen's Speech in May 2013 was 13 out of a total of 15 Bills.

[67] The Sunday Working (Scotland) Act 2003 and the Partnerships (Prosecution) (Scotland) Act 2013; as a constitutional enactment, the Scottish Parliament (Constituencies) Act 2004 applies throughout the UK.

[68] See, e.g. Barry K Winetrobe, "Public Accountability in Scotland" in Aileen McHarg and Tom Mullen (eds), *Public Law in Scotland* (Edinburgh: Avizandum, 2006) pp.149–150.

[69] MacKay Commission, *Report of the Commission on the Consequences of Devolution for the House of Commons* (March, 2013) para.278; the Calman Commission recommended that where Westminster legislated in the devolved areas on a matter of substance, consideration should be given to including one or more Scottish MPs on the public Bill committee considering the Bill: Commission on Scottish Devolution, *Serving Scotland Better: Scotland and the United Kingdom in the 21st Century* (June, 2009) para.4.156.

[70] Cabinet Office, *Memorandum of Understanding and Supplementary Agreements between the United Kingdom Government, the Scottish Ministers, the Welsh Ministers and the Northern Ireland Executive Committee* (October, 2013) para.15.

House of Commons Procedure Committee, however, it was essential that "parliamentary procedure or custom should not be called in aid" to undermine the decision that "certain powers and responsibilities should pass to the devolved legislatures".[71] While acknowledging that it was ultimately for Parliament to decide what use to make of its power, the UK Government undertook in the Memorandum of Understanding to

> "encourage the UK Parliament to bear in mind the primary responsibility of devolved legislatures and administrations in these fields and to recognise that it is a consequence of Parliament's decision to devolve certain matters that Parliament itself will in future be more restricted in its field of operation".[72]

This restriction is reflected in the scope for Scottish questions at Westminster. **19–34** In a "self-denying ordinance"[73] adopted in October 1999, the House of Commons resolved that questions may not be tabled on matters for which responsibility has been devolved to the Scottish Parliament or the National Assembly for Wales

> "unless the question:
>
> (a) seeks information which the UK Government is empowered to require of the devolved executive, or
> (b) relates to matters which:
>
> (i) are included in legislative proposals introduced or to be introduced in the UK Parliament,
> (ii) are concerned with the operation of a concordat or other instrument of liaison between the UK Government and the devolved executive, or
> (iii) UK Government ministers have taken an official interest in, or
>
> (c) presses for action by UK ministers in areas in which they retain administrative powers".[74]

Where questions relate to devolved matters, the guidance on common working **19–35** arrangements provides the UK Government will normally answer by making it clear that they should be addressed to the relevant devolved administration.[75] The guidance acknowledges, however, that in some cases a clear distinction between responsibilities may not be possible, for example where powers have been executively devolved to the Scottish Ministers but policy responsibility remains with the UK Government.[76]

---

[71] Procedure Committee, *The Procedural Consequences of Devolution* (HC 1998–1999, 185) para.5.

[72] Cabinet Office, *Memorandum of Understanding and Supplementary Agreements between the United Kingdom Government, the Scottish Ministers, the Welsh Ministers and the Northern Ireland Executive Committee* (October, 2013) para.14.

[73] Malcolm Jack (ed), *Erskine May's Treatise on the Law, Privileges, Proceedings and Usage of Parliament*, 24th edn (London: LexisNexis, 2011) p.190.

[74] House of Common debate October 25, 1999, Vol.336, col.774.

[75] Cabinet Office, Devolution Guidance Note 1, *Common Working Arrangements*, para.26.

[76] Cabinet Office, Devolution Guidance Note 1, *Common Working Arrangements*, para.27.

19–36 The Calman Commission suggested that Westminster had taken its self-denying ordinance too far in not debating devolved matters as they affect Scotland. It recommended that the House of Commons establish a regular "state of Scotland" debate.[77]

The Scottish Affairs Committee

19–37 The Scottish Affairs Committee is appointed to examine the expenditure, administration and policy of the Scotland Office (including: (i) relations with the Scottish Parliament; and (ii) administration and expenditure of the offices of the Advocate General for Scotland (but excluding individual cases and advice given within government by the Advocate General)). Among the roles the Committee envisaged after devolution was "a continuing role in carrying out inquiries into the implications for Scotland of UK policies in respect of non-devolved matters".[78] The Calman Commission also emphasised the importance of parliamentary scrutiny of the devolution settlement:

> "Scottish MPs should actively demonstrate appropriate oversight and stewardship of the constitution by way of regular scrutiny of the shape and operation of the devolution settlement."[79]

Not surprisingly, the referendum was a major focus of the Committee's work in the current Parliament with a series of combative reports on the "referendum on separation for Scotland". The Committee has also undertaken inquiries into zero hours contracts, the bedroom tax, land reform, blacklisting in employment and the Crown Estate.[80]

The Scottish Grand Committee

19–38 The Scottish Grand Committee, which consists of all MPs representing Scottish constituencies, provides a forum for questions and statements and debates on matters concerning Scotland, but the Committee has not met since 2003.

The McKay Commission

19–39 The McKay Commission on the Consequences of Devolution for the House of Commons saw the work of the territorial select committees as only a partial response to the challenges of devolution.

> "While the existing 'territorial' select committees—Northern Ireland and Scottish—take evidence from the appropriate Secretary of State on matters arising from the devolutionary process as it affects the relevant part of the UK, we think that there is a need to look across the process as

---

[77] Commission on Scottish Devolution, *Serving Scotland Better: Scotland and the United Kingdom in the 21st Century* (June, 2009) para.4.149.

[78] Scottish Affairs Committee, *The Operation of Multi-Layer Democracy* (HC 1997–1998, 460) para.86; the Committee thought there might even be two committees, one of which would scrutinise legislation for possible implications for Scotland.

[79] Commission on Scottish Devolution, *Serving Scotland Better: Scotland and the United Kingdom in the 21st Century* (June, 2009) para.4.200.

[80] The rules governing the composition of committees were "relaxed" in 2010 to allow an SNP MP to become a member of the Committee, but a row between that member and the chairman led to the former effectively vacating her place on the Committee, thus allowing the SNP to distance itself entirely from the Committee's reports.

a whole so far as it impacts on or concerns the responsibilities of the House of Commons for the whole UK, including England."[81]

It therefore recommended the appointment of a devolution committee of the House of Commons, as part of a more articulated Westminster response to the challenges of devolution, whose scrutiny work would include holding UK Ministers to their responsibilities in connection with devolution and their relations with the devolved administrations.[82]

THE SUPREME COURT

The Acts of Union were silent on the question of an appeal from the Scottish **19–40** courts to the new Parliament of Great Britain. The Claim of Right 1689 asserted

> "the right and privilege of the subjects to protest for remeed [remedy] of law to the King and Parliament against sentences pronounced by the Lords of Session, provided the same do not stop execution of these sentences",

but how "well and clearly established this remedy was by 1707 is questionable".[83] The conventional wisdom is that the omission was deliberate; had the Articles of Union made provision for an appeal to the new Parliament it might have provoked opposition to the Union. It was better therefore to leave the question open:

> "There must have seemed much good sense in leaving a curious point of constitutional law practically unsettled until by the lapse of twenty years or more every one should have become accustomed to the working of the Act of Union. For on the one hand it would probably be a benefit to Great Britain that it should possess one Court of Appeal to which important cases might be brought from every part of the British Kingdom for decision, whilst on the other hand it must have seemed highly imprudent, while the carrying of the Union was in doubt, to raise a most irritating, though somewhat speculative, question about appeals to the House of Lords."[84]

An alternative explanation is that the question was left open to avoid re-igniting **19–41** a controversy between the House of Lords and the House of Commons over

---

[81] MacKay Commission, *Report of the Commission on the Consequences of Devolution for the House of Commons* (March, 2013) para.275.

[82] MacKay Commission, *Report of the Commission on the Consequences of Devolution for the House of Commons* (March, 2013) paras 259–278.

[83] John W Cairns, "Historical Introduction" in Kenneth Reid and Reinhard Zimmermann (eds), *A History of Private Law in Scotland, Volume I: Introduction and Property* (Oxford: OUP, 2000) 123. "In 1674–1675, a substantial and influential element [of the Faculty of Advocates] were even prepared for a time to secede from the courts or accept banishment as a gesture of professional protest and solidarity when Charles II, at the request of the Scottish Judges, prohibited appeals from the Court of Session to the Scots' Parliament. Among the ultimate consequences of this action were the reassertion in the Claim of Right 1689 of the right of appeal to Parliament and the invocation of the jurisdiction of the British House of Lords after the Union": Nan Wilson "The Scottish Bar: The Evolution of the Faculty of Advocates in its Historical Setting" (1967–1968) 28 Louisiana L.R. 243. For the background, see Walter Ian Reid Fraser, *An Outline of Constitutional Law*, 2nd edn (London: William Hodge & Co, 1948) pp.221–223.

[84] Albert V Dicey and Robert S Rait, *Thoughts on the Union between England & Scotland* (London: Macmillan, 1920) p.193.

whether the House of Lords had jurisdiction to hear English appeals in equity, the Court of Session being a court of equity as well as of law.[85] The more likely explanation, however, is that the articles were silent by accident rather than design: having failed to agree among themselves, the Scottish Commissioners left the question to the Scottish Parliament, which in the event failed to come to a view.[86]

19–42 Following the Union, appeals were taken almost immediately to the House of Lords from the Court of Session. The first such appeal was *Earl of Rosebery v Inglis*.[87] In *Greenshields v Edinburgh Magistrates*,[88] the House of Lords' jurisdiction was challenged, but the challenge was unsuccessful. Appeals to London in fact became so common that the bulk of the House of Lords' appellate work during the eighteenth century was said to be Scottish.[89]

> "If this is something of an exaggeration, it is clear that Scottish cases at Westminster increased significantly from 8 per cent of appeals in 1708–09, to 22 per cent in 1740–41, 35 per cent in 1772–73 and 38 per cent in 1795–96, though the growth was not quite as steady as these figures suggest."[90]

It was not until the last quarter of the nineteenth century that the House of Lords became primarily an English court.[91]

19–43 Appeals were also taken to the House of Lords from the High Court of Justiciary,[92] but whereas the House of Lords' jurisdiction over the Court of Session "simply grew and was accepted",[93] its jurisdiction over the High Court of Justiciary never gained the same acceptance. What was in the end to prove decisive was the argument that the availability of an appeal would have a detrimental effect on the administration of criminal justice in Scotland.[94] The House of Lords eventually declined jurisdiction in *MacIntosh v Lord Advocate*,[95] and the matter was put beyond doubt by the Criminal Procedure (Scotland) Act 1887, which provided that "all interlocutors and sentences pronounced by the High Court of Justiciary ... shall be final and conclusive and not subject to review by any court whatsoever".[96]

19–44 By the time of devolution therefore an appeal lay to the House of Lords from the Court Session but not from the High Court of Justiciary, which

---

[85] AJ MacLean, "The 1707 Union: Scots Law and the House of Lords" (1983) 4 J. Legal History 50.

[86] John Ford, "The Legal Provisions in the Acts of Union" (2007) 66 C.L.J. 123–125.

[87] *Earl of Rosebery v Inglis* (1708) 18 H.L. Journals 464.

[88] *Greenshields v Edinburgh Magistrates* (1710–1711) Robert 12, HL.

[89] Robert Stevens, *Law and Politics: The House of Lords as a Judicial Body, 1800–1976* (Weidenfeld and Nicolson, 1979) p.7.

[90] Julian Hoppit, "Introduction" in Hoppit (ed), *Parliaments, Nations and Identities in Britain and Ireland, 1660–1850* (Manchester: Manchester University Press, 2003) p.8.

[91] Robert Stevens, *Law and Politics: The House of Lords as a Judicial Body, 1800–1976* (Weidenfeld and Nicolson, 1979) pp.69–70.

[92] *Magistrates of Elgin v Ministers of Elgin* (1713) Rob. 12.

[93] JDB Mitchell, *Constitutional Law*, 2nd edn (Edinburgh: W.Green, 1968) p.258.

[94] The story is told in AJ MacLean, "The House of Lords and Appeals from the High Court of Justiciary 1707–1887" 1985 J.R. 192.

[95] *MacIntosh v Lord Advocate* (1876) 3R (HL) 34.

[96] Criminal Procedure (Scotland) Act 1887 s.72; see now the Criminal Procedure (Scotland) Act 1995 s.124(2).

retained its status as "the court of last resort in all criminal matters in Scotland".[97]

Scottish representation

At around the same time as the House of Lords' jurisdiction in Scottish cases **19–45** was being worked out, Scottish judges came to be appointed to the House of Lords. The Lord President of the Court of Session, Duncan McNeill, was elevated to the peerage in 1867 to assist in the appellate business of the House[98]; and after the House of Lords' status as the UK's final court of appeal was confirmed by the Appellate Jurisdiction Act 1876, it became the practice to appoint at first one and then two Scottish law lords, whose primary role was to ensure that Scottish appeals were decided "according to the principles and practice of Scots law".[99] It also became the practice for Scottish appeals to be heard by a Committee including at least two Scottish law lords.[100]

The consequences of devolution

Devolution saw the Judicial Committee of the Privy Council acquire a jurisdic- **19–46** tion in Scottish criminal cases raising devolution issues, which the Supreme Court inherited when it replaced the House of Lords as the UK's final court of appeal.[101] In working out the Supreme Court's jurisdiction, no attempt was made to address the anomaly whereby appeals lay to the House of Lords from the Court of Session but not from the High Court of Justiciary. As regards criminal appeals, the UK Government's consultation paper simply stated that there was no evidence that the Scottish criminal appeal system required change; as regards civil appeals, it said that the Scottish Executive was "in principle content for civil appeals to the new Court to be on the same basis as currently operates in relation to the House of Lords", adding that there were

> "benefits to the Scottish [civil] justice system in having important cases reviewed by judges with a different background, and indeed advantages to the larger jurisdiction also in drawing on the resources of a different legal tradition at the highest level".[102]

What the Act did address were enduring sensitivities about the loss of the sepa- **19–47** rate identity of Scots law, which had been reawakened by the announcement that the time had come for the UK's highest court "to move out from the shadow of the legislature".[103] The issue was explained by Lord Hope in evidence to the House of Commons Constitutional Affairs Committee:

> "The problem is, I think, if you describe the court as a supreme court of the United Kingdom, it tends to suggest that there is a body of United Kingdom law. In a court which inevitably is filled with a majority of

---

[97] *McInnes v HM Advocate* [2010] UKSC 7; 2010 S.L.T. 266, [5] (Lord Hope).

[98] Lord Keith of Kinkel, "The House of Lords" *Stair Memorial Encyclopaedia* (1988) Vol.6, para.820.

[99] Lord Hope of Craighead, "Taking the Case to London—Is it All Over?" 1998 J.R. 135, 146.

[100] Lord Hope of Craighead, "Taking the Case to London—Is it All Over?" 1998 J.R. 135, 144.

[101] Constitutional Reform Act 2005 ("CRA 2005") s.40(4)(b), Sch.9.

[102] Department for Constitutional Affairs, *Constitutional Reform: A Supreme Court for the United Kingdom* (July, 2003) paras 26–27.

[103] Department for Constitutional Affairs, *Constitutional Reform: A Supreme Court for the United Kingdom* (July, 2003) para.5, echoing Bagehot's: "The supreme court of the English people ought to be a great conspicuous tribunal ... ought not to be hidden beneath the robes of a legislative assembly": Walter Bagehot, *The English Constitution* (Oxford: Fontana Press, 1993) p.149.

English judges there may be a temptation to say, 'Well we see differences between Scots law and English law on issues relating to property or other matters, what's the point of having a difference when we're sitting as a United Kingdom court?' The Scots may well feel that would introduce a drift away from their system of law into an English system, and there are signs in case law, even now, that there is a temptation along that line. I think Scots are anxious that anything that will tend to dilute the present system, which maintains a distinctive Scottish appellate structure, will give rise to the risk of losing the separate identity of Scots law."[104]

19–48 The Constitutional Reform Act 2005 ("the 2005 Act") therefore includes a guarantee of the separate identity of Scots law. Section 41 of the 2005 Act provides that nothing in Pt 3 of the Act, which established the Supreme Court, is "to affect the distinctions between the separate legal systems of the parts of the United Kingdom", while a decision of the Supreme Court on an appeal from any part of the UK, other than a decision on a devolution matter, "is to be regarded as the decision of a court of that part of the United Kingdom". A decision of the Supreme Court sitting as an English court thus continues to be of persuasive rather than binding effect in Scotland. Decisions on devolution matters, on the other hand, are binding on courts throughout the UK, other than the Supreme Court itself.[105]

19–49 The 2005 Act also includes a guarantee of continuing Scottish judicial representation on the Supreme Court bench. In selecting candidates to be recommended for appointment, a selection commission must ensure that "between them the judges will have knowledge of, and experience of practice in, the law of each part of the United Kingdom".[106] The inclusion of Scottish judges, as has been pointed out, is as much a matter of political as legal necessity; the Supreme Court would lack legitimacy in Scottish eyes if it lacked Scottish representation.[107] By convention two Scottish law lords and, more recently, two Scottish Justices of the Supreme Court have been appointed. The 2005 Act stops short of specifying the number of Scottish judges who must be appointed, but for the time being the convention continues to be observed.[108]

---

[104] House of Commons, *Judicial appointments and a Supreme Court (court of final appeal)* (HC 48–II, 2003–2004) question 96. Elsewhere he had written that "there is nothing more difficult to resist ... than a desire among the others on the Appellate Committee that the law on each side of the Border should be the same": Lord Hope of Craighead, "Taking the Case to London—Is it All Over?" 1998 J.R. 135, 146. While the point was not central to the argument, saying there is no such thing as UK law is rather like saying there is no such thing as EU law.

[105] CRA 2005 s.41(3).

[106] CRA 2005 s.27(8); the Lord President and the First Minister must be consulted as part of the selection process: s.27(2).

[107] Kate Malleson, "Selecting Judges" in Andrew Le Sueur (ed), *Building the UK's New Supreme Court: National and Comparative Perspectives* (Oxford: OUP, 2004) p.307.

[108] "Senior territorial judges", including members of the First and Second Divisions of the Inner House of the Court of Session, may also act as judges of the Court at the request of the President of the Supreme Court: CRA 2005 s.38(1), (8).

CHAPTER 20

THE EUROPEAN DIMENSION

INTRODUCTION

The European Union, it used to be said, was "blind" to Member States' consti- **20–01** tutional arrangements.[1] It is less blind than it used to be. Article 4(2) of the Treaty on European Union ("TEU") provides that the Union "shall respect the Member States' national identities inherent in their fundamental structures, political and constitutional, inclusive of regional and local self-government". "Constitutional regions" such as Scotland nevertheless occupy a very different position within the Union from that of the Member States.[2] Like the Member States, the exercise of their powers and responsibilities may be affected by decisions taken at the European level. In extreme cases they may even find themselves denied powers they are guaranteed under their domestic constitutional arrangements. And yet they have only limited access to the processes of policy formulation and judicial control at the European level. Despite attempts over the last 20 years or so to secure a greater role in law-making and judicial supervision for national regions, the European Union remains firmly a union of Member States.[3]

The Scotland Act 1998 ("the Scotland Act") reserves international relations, **20–02** including relations with the European Union.[4] The reservation does not extend, however, to observing and implementing international obligations, obligations under the ECHR and obligations under EU law, or to assisting UK Ministers in their conduct of international relations.[5] Acknowledging that EU policies and legislation would have a considerable effect on many of the matters for which the Parliament would be responsible, *Scotland's Parliament*, the White Paper that preceded the Scotland Act, said that the UK Government wished to involve the Scottish Executive

> "as directly and as fully as possible in the Government's decision making on EU matters. It is part of the Government's intention that Scottish Executive Ministers and officials should be fully involved in discussions within the UK Government about the formulation of the UK's policy position on all issues which touch on devolved matters".[6]

---

[1] Stephen Weatherill, "The Challenge of the Regional Dimension in the European Union" in Stephen Weatherill and Ulf Bernitz (eds), *The Role of Regions and Sub-National Actors in Europe* (Oxford: Hart Publishing, 2005).

[2] The description is Richard Rawlings: *Delineating Wales: Constitutional, Legal and Administrative Aspects of National Devolution* (Cardiff: University of Wales Press, 2003) p.435.

[3] Apart from TEU art.4(2), the principal achievements have been the inclusion in the Treaties of the principle of subsidiarity (TEU art.5(3)), the possibility that regions may represent their Member State in the Council (TEU art.16(2)); and the setting up of the Committee of the Regions as a forum for the representation of regional interests (TFEU art.300).

[4] Scotland Act 1998 ("SA 1998") Sch.5 Pt 1 para.7(1).

[5] SA 1998 Sch.5 Pt 1 para.7(2).

[6] Scottish Office, *Scotland's Parliament* (1997) Cm.3658, para.5.4.

The Scottish Executive would also be obliged to "ensure the implementation in Scotland of EU obligations which concern devolved matters", and "directly accountable through the Scottish courts to anyone affected by shortcomings in its implementation or enforcement of EU obligations".[7]

EU DECISION-MAKING

20-03 The Memorandum of Understanding and supplementary Concordat on Co-ordination of European Policy Issues, which govern relations between the UK Government and the devolved administrations in relation to EU matters, reiterate the UK Government's commitment to involving the devolved administrations as fully as possible in its decision-making on EU matters. In the Memorandum of Understanding, the UK Government "recognises that the devolved administrations will have an interest in international and European policy making in relation to devolved matters, notably where implementing action by the devolved administrations may be required", and that they "will have a particular interest in those many aspects of European Union business which affect devolved areas, and a significant role to play in them", before undertaking to involve them "as fully as possible in discussions about the formulation of the UK's policy position on all EU and international issues which touch on devolved matters".[8] In the concordat, it affirms its wish

> "to involve the Scottish Ministers as directly and as fully as possible in decision making on EU matters which touch on devolved areas (including non-devolved matters which impact on devolved areas and non-devolved matters which will have a distinctive impact of importance in Scotland)".[9]

20-04 In working out the arrangements for involving the devolved administrations in decision-making on EU matters, it was regarded as essential that the existing arrangements should not be weakened in any way

> "... those responsible for drafting the EU concordat (both within Whitehall and the devolved administrations) began from the premise that the prevailing administrative arrangements for handling EU business in the UK operated extremely well. In that sense the challenge facing officials was to ensure that any changes to the UK's European policy procedures did not weaken a tried and proven policy process".[10]

20-05 The three territorial departments had been involved in EU policy making and implementation since the UK's accession to the European Communities in 1973, the Scottish Office more so than the Welsh Office or the Northern Ireland Office because of its greater range of responsibilities. It was logical, therefore, that the existing arrangements for accommodating territorial concerns in EU policy-making should be adapted to the new conditions of devolved governance. "The old *intra*-government process for accommodating territorial

---

[7] Scottish Office, *Scotland's Parliament* (1997) Cm.3658, para.5.8.

[8] Cabinet Office, *Memorandum of Understanding and Supplementary Agreements between the United Kingdom Government, the Scottish Ministers, the Welsh Ministers and the Northern Ireland Executive Committee* (October, 2013) paras 18 and 20.

[9] Cabinet Office, *Concordat on Co-ordination of European Policy Issues* (October 2013) para. B1.5.

[10] Simon Bulmer et al, *British Devolution and European Policy-Making: Transforming Britain into Multi-Level Governance* (London: Palgrave Macmillan, 2002) p.39.

concerns therefore became a new *inter*-governmental process run on the basis of the same procedures."[11]

The procedures set out in the concordat have three main features. **20–06**

The "UK line"

First, they involve no departure from the "long-standing convention that all **20–07** parts of UK government adhered to an agreed line in EU policy negotiations".[12] The UK Government's commitment is thus to involve the Scottish Ministers in the formulation of the "UK line", which line, the concordat states, "will reflect the interests of the UK as a whole".[13]

Attendance at Council meetings

Second, participation in EU policy making extends to attendance at Council **20–08** meetings as a "necessary extension" of involvement in formulating the UK's initial policy position,[14] but attendance is at the lead UK Minister's discretion and conditional on adherence to the UK line.

> "One of the more controversial debates concerning the EU concordat was whether Ministers of the devolved administrations should have the right to attend meetings of the Council of Ministers where these were discussing matters in which they had a direct interest. This was successfully resisted by Whitehall on the basis that it would undermine the reserved status of European policy and could undermine the strengths of the UK bargaining in that Council. Instead, as set out in the EU concordat, it was for the lead UK minister to decide on the composition of the UK delegation attending Council meetings, and to respond to a request from a minister from a devolved administration to be a member of that delegation. However, where a minister from a devolved administration was invited to participate in a Council meeting, that minster would be required to represent the agreed UK position."[15]

More recent versions of the concordat stress the legitimate interest of Ministers **20–09** and officials of the devolved administrations in the preparation and presentation of the UK's EU policy where it touches on matters which fall within their responsibility.[16] "Requests by Ministers of Devolved Administrations to attend Council of Ministers should be welcomed unless there is a compelling reason not to do so and which the lead Minister should be willing to explain."[17] In its essential respects, however, the policy remains unchanged: attendance is at the lead UK Minister's discretion and conditional on adherence to the UK line.

---

[11] Charlie Jeffery, "Devolution and the European Union" in Alan Trench (ed), *The Dynamics of Devolution. The State of the Nations 2005* (Exeter: Imprint Academic, 2005) p.187.

[12] Simon Bulmer et al, *British Devolution and European Policy-Making: Transforming Britain into Multi-Level Governance* (London: Palgrave Macmillan, 2002) p.48.

[13] Cabinet Office, *Concordat on Co-ordination of European Policy Issues* (October, 2013) para. B1.6; hence the criticism that Scottish interests can be "lost or diluted" in the formation of the UK negotiating line: Scottish Government, *Europe and Foreign Affairs: Taking forward our National Conversation* (September, 2009) Executive summary.

[14] Scottish Office, *Scotland's Parliament* (1997) Cm.3658, para.5.6.

[15] Simon Bulmer et al, *British Devolution and European Policy-Making: Transforming Britain into Multi-Level Governance* (London: Palgrave Macmillan, 2002) p.48.

[16] Cabinet Office, *Concordat on Co-ordination of European Policy Issues* (October, 2013) para. B4.13.

[17] Cabinet Office, *Concordat on Co-ordination of European Policy Issues* (October, 2013) para. B4.14a.

20–10 Where Ministers and officials are involved in negotiations at the European level, their role is to

> "support and advance the single UK negotiating line which they will have played a part in developing. The emphasis in negotiations has to be on working as a UK team; and the UK lead Minister will retain overall responsibility for the negotiations and determine how each member of the team can best contribute to securing the agreed policy position".[18]

Confidentiality

20–11 Third, as was emphasised in the White Paper,[19] involvement is subject to mutual respect for the confidentiality of discussions, as well as adherence to the UK line, "without which it would be impossible to maintain such close working relationships".[20] "Complete confidentiality", the concordat explains, "is often essential in formulating a UK negotiating position in the EU and in developing tactical responses."[21] The effect, however, is to conceal intergovernmental relations behind a veil of secrecy, which may be inimical to effective parliamentary scrutiny (below).

20–12 In a common annex to the concordat, the UK Government undertakes to provide the devolved administrations with full and comprehensive information, as early as possible, on all business within the framework of the European Union that appears likely to be of interest to the devolved administrations, including notifications of relevant meetings within the EU.[22]

Overall

20–13 The virtue of these arrangements is that they grant the devolved administrations what regional governments in other Member States have had to fight for—a role in defining the position of the Member State.[23] Their weakness is their informal nature—the fact that they are "binding in honour only"[24]—which means that the devolved administrations lack any enforceable guarantees of their involvement in European policy-making in relation to devolved matters.

> "Whether through omission or commission, the experience of the last 10 years suggests that mechanisms which rely entirely on political or administrative goodwill will work imperfectly, and of course will only function as far as the limits set for them."[25]

---

[18] Cabinet Office, *Concordat on Co-ordination of European Policy Issues* (October, 2013) para. B4.15.

[19] Scottish Office, *Scotland's Parliament* (1997) Cm.3658, para.5.4.

[20] Cabinet Office, *Memorandum of Understanding and Supplementary Agreements between the United Kingdom Government, the Scottish Ministers, the Welsh Ministers and the Northern Ireland Executive Committee* (October, 2013) para.20; Concordat (n 9) B1.6

[21] Cabinet Office, *Concordat on Co-ordination of European Policy Issues* (October 2013) para. B4.2; see also Freedom of Information Act 2000 s.28; Freedom of Information (Scotland) Act 2002 s.28.

[22] Cabinet Office, *Concordat on Co-ordination of European Policy Issues* (October, 2013) para. B4.1.

[23] Charlie Jeffery and Roseanne Palmer, "The European Union, devolution and power" in Alan Trench (ed), *Devolution and Power* (Manchester: Manchester University Press, 2007) pp.223–224.

[24] Cabinet Office, *Concordat on Co-ordination of European Policy Issues* (October, 2013) para. B1.2.

[25] Scottish Government, *Europe and Foreign Affairs: Taking forward our National Conversation* (September, 2009) para.3.5.

Attempts to strengthen these arrangements from the point of view of the devolved administrations, however, have made little progress. One of the amendments the SNP Government sought but failed to secure to the Bill that become the Scotland Act 2012, in order to make it a Bill "worthy of the name", was a statutory right to be included in the UK delegation at formal and informal meetings of Ministers at which non-reserved matters affecting Scotland were to be considered.[26]

In its submission to the Smith Commission, the Scottish Government renewed **20–14** its call for "guaranteed rights to engage directly with EU institutions and EU decision-making processes in areas of devolved competence".[27] The Commission, however, said that the political parties recognised that foreign affairs would remain a reserved matter. They also recognised the need to reflect fully the views of the other devolved administrations when drawing up any revised governance arrangements in relation to Scottish Government representation of the UK to the EU. "In that context", the parties agreed that the implementation of the concordat should be "improved". This should be achieved by ensuring that Scottish Ministers were fully involved in agreeing the UK position in EU negotiations relating to devolved policy matters; ensuring that they were "consulted and their views taken into account" before final UK negotiating positions relating to devolved policy matters were agreed; and a presumption that a devolved administration Minister could "speak on behalf of the UK" at a meeting of the Council of Ministers according to an agreed UK negotiating line where the devolved administration Minister held the "predominant policy interest across the UK" and where the relevant lead UK Government Minister was "unable to attend all or part of a meeting".[28] Discussion of improved implementation of the concordat in the light of the Smith Commission recommendations is being pursued as part of the wider work on revising intergovernmental relations.[29]

THE "DIRECT" ROUTE

Scottish interests may also be pursued directly with the institutions of the EU **20–15** and interests within other Member States.[30] The Scottish Government European Union Office ("SGEUO") in Brussels is responsible for information gathering, helping to influence EU policy and raising Scotland's profile in the EU. Scottish Government guidance on handling EU obligations issued in 2009 emphasised that officials were responsible for ensuring that the Scottish Government's interests were clearly understood in London and Brussels. "We should not hesitate to explain the Scottish Government's position directly to the Commission if necessary."[31]

---

[26] Scottish Government, *Scotland Bill—EU Involvement* (August, 2012).

[27] Scottish Government, *More Powers for the Scottish Parliament: Scottish Government Proposals* (October, 2014) p.31.

[28] Smith Commission, *Report of the Smith Commission for further devolution of powers to the Scottish Parliament* (November 27, 2014) para.31.

[29] Scotland Office, *Scotland in the United Kingdom: An enduring settlement* (2015) Cm.8990, para.9.2.4.

[30] Cabinet Office, *Concordat on Co-ordination of European Policy Issues* (October, 2013) para.4.28.

[31] Scottish Government, *Handling EU Obligations: A guide for Scottish Government officials* (2009) p.21.

THE IMPLEMENTATION OF EU OBLIGATIONS

20–16 The functions transferred to the Scottish Ministers by s.53 of the Scotland Act include observing and implementing obligations under EU law in the areas not reserved to Westminster, for which purpose they have access to the wide subordinate law-making powers conferred by s.2(2) of the European Communities Act 1972.[32] In contrast to most other devolved subordinate law-making powers, the powers conferred by s.2(2) continue to be exercisable by UK Ministers concurrently with their Scottish counterparts.[33] This gives the Scottish Ministers the option of relying on GB or UK legislation where they judge it appropriate.

> "If the devolved administrations wish, it is open to them to ask the UK Government to extend UK legislation to cover their EU obligations."[34]

It also means that the UK Government, whose responsibility for complying with EU law is not affected by devolution,[35] can intervene to give effect to EU obligations should the Scottish Ministers fail to do so.

20–17 The Concordat on Co-ordination of European Policy Issues requires the lead Whitehall department formally to notify the devolved administrations at official level of any new EU obligation which concerns devolved matters and which it will be the responsibility of the devolved administrations to implement (although the arrangements for policy formulation and negotiation should ensure that the devolved administrations are already aware of any new obligations). It is then for the devolved administrations to consider, in bilateral consultation with the lead Whitehall department, and other departments and devolved administrations if appropriate, how the obligation should be implemented and administratively enforced (if appropriate) within the required timescale, including whether the devolved administrations should implement separately, or opt for GB or UK legislation.[36]

20–18 Devolution has created a presumption in favour of separate implementation.

> "The Scottish Government's presumption is that where the directive falls within a devolved area of responsibility, we will implement that directive through our domestic institutions."[37]

---

[32] The opening words of s.57(1) of the Scotland Act 1998 makes clear that the functions transferred include "functions in relation to observing and implementing obligations under EU law".

[33] SA 1998 s.57(1).

[34] Cabinet Office, *Memorandum of Understanding and Supplementary Agreements between the United Kingdom Government, the Scottish Ministers, the Welsh Ministers and the Northern Ireland Executive Committee* (October, 2013) para.21.

[35] "The Court has consistently held that a Member State cannot plead conditions existing within its own legal system in order to justify its failure to comply with obligations and time-limits resulting from Community directives. While each Member State may be free to allocate areas of internal legal competence as it sees fit, the fact still remains that it alone is responsible towards the Community under Article 169 for compliance with obligations arising under Community law": Case C-33/90 *Commission v Italy* [1991] E.C.R. 5987 [24].

[36] Cabinet Office, *Memorandum of Understanding and Supplementary Agreements between the United Kingdom Government, the Scottish Ministers, the Welsh Ministers and the Northern Ireland Executive Committee* (October, 2013) paras B4.17–B4.18.

[37] Scottish Government, *Influencing and Implementing EU Obligations: A guide for Scottish Government officials*, 3rd edn (2012) p.34; the presumption was there from the outset: Simon Bulmer et al, *British Devolution and European Policy-Making: Transforming Britain into Multi-Level Governance* (London: Palgrave Macmillan, 2002) p.66.

Where reliance on UK legislation is proposed, ministerial clearance must be obtained. Scottish Government guidance on influencing and implementing EU obligations warns officials to remember "the political sensitivities of allowing the UK to implement where the Scottish Parliament could reasonably be expected to do so".[38] The Minister is also expected to write to the convener of the relevant subject committee explaining the reasons for relying on UK legislation.[39] But whether because the Scottish Government does not wish to draw attention to the fact of continued reliance on UK legislation, or because the commitment has simply been forgotten about, Ministers have not written to committees explaining the reasons for relying on GB or UK legislation.[40]

Separate implementation by itself is of little consequence without the freedom **20–19** to implement differently. In *R (Horvath) v Secretary of State for the Environment, Food and Rural Affairs*,[41] the European Court held that the mere adoption by devolved administrations of different standards in the implementation of an EU obligation did not constitute discrimination contrary to EU law. Where therefore an obligation admits of discretion in its implementation, which is not always the case, the Scottish Ministers are not required to exercise that discretion in the same way as other implementing authorities within the UK. Most implementing measures, however, take a "similar or identical" policy approach to the rest of the UK.[42] Among the reasons for taking a similar approach is that the Scottish Government lacks the resources to explore alternatives. It is often simpler therefore to let Whitehall "take the strain".

> "It is likely that the lead UK Government Department (and possibly the other devolved administrations) will have drafted transposing legislation, and you may be able to transpose in Scotland more efficiently by drawing on such a draft as a template for a separate Scottish instrument. Always ask UK colleagues for a copy of any draft legislation they have available, although be careful to avoid unnecessary delay in taking forward transposition by waiting for the UK to act."[43]

---

[38] Scottish Government, *Influencing and Implementing EU Obligations: A guide for Scottish Government officials*, 3rd edn (2012) p.34.

[39] Scottish Government, *Influencing and Implementing EU Obligations: A guide for Scottish Government officials*, 3rd edn (2012) p.36.

[40] The Parliament's European and External Relations Committee receives regular (six monthly) reports on the transposition of EU obligations. The initial focus of these reports was on late transposition and the reasons for relying on UK legislation, but the focus is now solely on late transposition, with lack of resources being the most commonly cited reason for late transposition. Among the reasons commonly offered in the past for relying on UK legislation were the absence of specific Scottish interests, the difficulty of separating devolved from reserved matters—on which the Scottish Ministers would be unable to legislate—and the desirability of uniformity of treatment in matters concerning business.

[41] *R (Horvath) v Secretary of State for the Environment, Food and Rural Affairs* Case C-428/07; [2009] ECR I-6355, [58].

[42] Option 2 rather than option 3 in the Scottish Government's taxonomy of ways of implementing obligations: Scottish Government, *Influencing and Implementing EU Obligations: A guide for Scottish Government officials*, 3rd edn (2012) p.34.

[43] Scottish Government, *Influencing and Implementing EU Obligations: A guide for Scottish Government officials*, 3rd edn (2012) pp.35–36; see also in this regard, Edward C Page, *Governing by Numbers. Delegated Legislation and Everyday Policy-Making* (Oxford: Hart Publishing, 2001) pp.122–123.

20–20 Where the devolved administration opts to implement separately, it is required to consult the lead Whitehall department, and other departments as necessary, on its implementation proposals, to ensure that any differences of approach nonetheless produce consistency of effect and, where appropriate, of timing.[44]

PARLIAMENTARY SCRUTINY

20–21 *Scotland's Parliament* anticipated that the Scottish Parliament would be able to scrutinise EU legislative proposals to ensure that Scottish interests were "properly reflected" in those proposals.[45] The Parliament's approach to EU scrutiny developed in a fairly unsystematic way over the first three sessions, with the principal role being played by the European and External Relations Committee ("EERC"). Following a major inquiry by the Committee into the implications of the Treaty of Lisbon for Scotland, however, the Parliament adopted a "Parliament-wide" strategy for EU engagement and scrutiny in December 2010.[46] Perhaps somewhat optimistically, the Committee saw the Treaty of Lisbon as offering,

> "the very real prospect of improved democratic oversight of the EU decision-making process with potential for a substantially increased role for, and respect for, national parliaments, devolved parliaments with legislative powers and devolved governments including the Scottish Parliament and the Scottish Government".[47]

The Committee recommended that the Parliament develop a strategy for engagement and scrutiny that clearly defined the parliamentary objectives and priorities, set out the roles and responsibilities of committees, the relationships with external bodies, and the detailed processes and mechanisms for effective scrutiny.[48] The implementation of the strategy, in the Committee's view, would need to extend beyond the EERC to include the subject committees, the Parliament as a whole, the presiding officer and the Scottish Parliament's office in Brussels; the Committee considered that a "deeper engagement" with Europe by the subject committees in particular was vital in implementing a Parliament wide-strategy, particularly in monitoring and scrutiny.[49] Implementation of the strategy is therefore divided between the EERC and the subject committees, with the EERC responsible for overseeing and coordinating EU relations as a whole, and "horizon scanning" on behalf of the Parliament, and the scrutiny of

---

[44] Cabinet Office, *Concordat on Co-ordination of European Policy Issues* (October, 2013) para. B4.18.

[45] Scottish Office, *Scotland's Parliament* (1997) Cm.3658, para.5.7.

[46] European and External Relations Committee 4th Report, *Inquiry into the Impact of the Treaty of Lisbon on Scotland* (Scottish Parliamentary Paper 469, 2010).

[47] European and External Relations Committee 4th Report, *Inquiry into the Impact of the Treaty of Lisbon on Scotland* (Scottish Parliamentary Paper 469, 2010) para.338.

[48] European and External Relations Committee 4th Report, *Inquiry into the Impact of the Treaty of Lisbon on Scotland* (Scottish Parliamentary Paper 469, 2010) paras 345–346; also influential in the development of the Committee's thinking were its earlier inquiries into the scrutiny of European legislation and the transposition of EU directives: European and External Relations Committee 2nd Report, *Report on an inquiry into the scrutiny of European legislation* (Scottish Parliamentary Paper 783, 2007); 1st Report, *Report on an inquiry into the transposition of EU directives* (Scottish Parliamentary Paper 89, 2008).

[49] European and External Relations Committee 4th Report, *Inquiry into the Impact of the Treaty of Lisbon on Scotland* (Scottish Parliamentary Paper 469, 2010) para.347.

draft EU legislation and monitoring of transposition "mainstreamed" in subject committees.[50]

Scrutiny of government

The strategy defines the Parliament's main role as being "to scrutinise the **20–22** Scottish Government and its engagement in Europe". The European and External Relations Committee's earlier inquiries into the scrutiny of European legislation and the transposition of EU directives had highlighted the need for greater parliamentary scrutiny of the Scottish Government's role in ensuring that Scottish interests were "accounted for" in the UK Government's negotiating position, including the need for greater transparency in the Scottish Government's role throughout the EU legislative process including in the transposition of obligations.[51] The strategy envisaged evidence being taken from the Minister with responsibility for Europe before and after meetings of the Joint Ministerial Committee ("JMC") (Europe). Rather than evidence being taken, however, a "read out" is provided after meetings, which is hardly more informative than the JMC annual report. "Lack of openness to the public", Burrows suggested, "may be the price the devolved administrations have to pay if they are to be closely involved in European policy-making".[52] A price they may be only too willing to pay, it may be thought, especially if it conceals a failure to ensure that Scottish interests are reflected in the UK negotiating line.

Early engagement

The Parliament, in the Committee's view, also needed to develop its approach **20–23** to early engagement and the "upstream" setting of the agenda through scrutiny and intelligence gathering at the earliest stages of EU policy-making before legislative proposals emerged. The Committee's earlier inquiries into the scrutiny of European legislation and the transposition of EU directives had also highlighted the importance of "early engagement" in ensuring that Scottish interests were "accounted for" within the EU legislative process, and its direct correlation with effective implementation of obligations.[53] The Committee's focus in the first two sessions had been on the "downstream" implementation of EU obligations, by which stage the opportunity to influence the terms and scope of those obligations had passed.[54] "The earlier the engagement, the greater the potential influence", was the lesson the Committee took from those inquiries.[55] One of the EERC's key responsibilities is therefore for an early

---

[50] The strategy is set out in the European and External Relations Committee's 3rd Report, *Legacy Paper* (Scottish Parliamentary Paper 656, 2011) Annexe B. Committees currently report on both their engagement and scrutiny over the last year and their scrutiny priorities for the coming year: see European and External Relations Committee 1st Report, *EU Engagement and Scrutiny of the Committees of the Scottish Parliament on European Union policies 2014* (Scottish Parliamentary Paper 465, 2014).

[51] European and External Relations Committee 2nd Report, *Report on an inquiry into the scrutiny of European legislation* (Scottish Parliamentary Paper 783, 2007) para.66; 1st Report, *Report on an inquiry into the transposition of EU directives* (Scottish Parliamentary Paper 89, 2008) para.132.

[52] Noreen Burrows, "Scotland in Europe: Empowerment or Disempowerment?" in Aileen McHarg and Tom Mullen, *Public Law in Scotland* (Edinburgh: Avizandum, 2006) p.55.

[53] European and External Relations Committee 1st Report, *Report on an inquiry into the transposition of EU directives* (SPP 89, 2008) para.131.

[54] European and External Relations Committee 1st Report, *Report on an inquiry into the transposition of EU directives* (SPP 89, 2008) paras 5–8.

[55] European and External Relations Committee 2nd Report, *Report on an inquiry into the scrutiny of European legislation* (Scottish Parliamentary Paper 783, 2007) para.7.

warning system of horizon scanning to identify developments likely to be of interest to the Parliament and its committees.

Subsidiarity

20–24 The scrutiny of proposals by subject committees includes scrutiny for possible breaches of the principle of subsidiarity.

> "Under the principle of subsidiarity, in areas which do not fall within its exclusive competence, the Union shall act only if and in so far as the objectives of the proposed action cannot be sufficiently achieved by the Member States, either at central level or at regional or local level, but can rather, by reason of the scale or effects of the proposed action, be better achieved at Union level."[56]

The Treaties include "an early warning mechanism" in the form of a protocol on subsidiarity and proportionality under which *national* [i.e. Member State] parliaments are able to force the Commission to reconsider a proposal on the grounds that it violates the principle of subsidiarity.[57] The EERC saw the subsidiarity protocol as "offering a chance for the Parliament to challenge any incursion into areas of devolved interest", but recognised that to do so the Scottish Parliament would need to go through the UK Parliament.[58] Regional parliaments such as the Scottish Parliament have no formal role in this process, it being left to the national Parliament, or each chamber of the national Parliament, to consult, "where appropriate, regional parliaments with legislative powers".[59] The Scottish Parliament therefore depends on the UK Parliament as the national parliament to take up any concerns it may have. So far this has not been an issue, the Scottish Parliament's concerns having been shared by Westminster.[60] The difficulty the Parliament faces, rather, is that committees do not always receive proposals in sufficient time to enable them to come to a view within the short (eight week) period allowed for national parliaments to object to a proposal. The Parliament also relies on the Scottish Government, the UK Government and the UK Parliament to flag proposals with subsidiarity concerns. As it stands, therefore, the procedure provides not so much a means of challenging incursions into areas of devolved interest as an uncertain mechanism for adding the Parliament's voice to any concerns there may be about possible breaches of the principle of subsidiarity.

Scrutiny of implementation

20–25 The final element of the strategy comprises the "downstream" monitoring of the transposition and implementation of EU obligations through regular reports provided by the Scottish Government. Scrutiny of transposition has been a feature of the EERC's work from the outset, against the background that delays in transposition could lead to financial penalties (and UK Government intervention). Although infringement proceedings under arts 258 and 259

---

[56] TEU art.5(3).

[57] Protocol (No.2) on the Application of the Principles of Subsidiarity and Proportionality.

[58] European and External Relations Committee 4th Report, *Inquiry into the Impact of the Treaty of Lisbon on Scotland* (Scottish Parliamentary Paper 469, 2010) para.343.

[59] Protocol (No.2) on the Application of the Principles of Subsidiarity and Proportionality art.6.

[60] See e.g. European and External Relations Committee 6th Report, *The EU-related engagement of the Scottish Parliament's Committees 2011–2012* (Scottish Parliamentary Paper 213, 2012) Annex E.

TFEU may only be brought against Member States, the Memorandum of Understanding and concordat provide that the devolved administration is responsible for meeting any financial costs and penalties imposed on the UK as a result of failures of implementation or enforcement for which it is responsible.[61]

---

[61] Cabinet Office, *Memorandum of Understanding and Supplementary Agreements between the United Kingdom Government, the Scottish Ministers, the Welsh Ministers and the Northern Ireland Executive Committee* (October, 2013) para.21; Cabinet Office, *Concordat on Co-ordination of European Policy Issues* (October, 2013) para.B4.26.

INDEX

All references are to paragraph numbers.